Speech Science Primer

Physiology, Acoustics, and Perception of Speech

Third Edition

Speech Science Primer

Physiology, Acoustics, and Perception of Speech

Third Edition

Gloria J. Borden, Ph.D.
Emerita, Department of Speech, Temple University, Philadelphia, Pennsylvania, and
Haskins Laboratories, New Haven, Connecticut

Katherine S. Harris, Ph.D.
Department of Speech and Hearing Sciences, The Graduate School,
City University of New York, New York, New York, and
Haskins Laboratories, New Haven, Connecticut

Lawrence J. Raphael, Ph.D.
Department of Speech and Theatre, Herbert H. Lehman College,
City University of New York, Bronx, New York, and
Haskins Laboratories, New Haven, Connecticut

Williams & Wilkins
BALTIMORE • PHILADELPHIA • HONG KONG
LONDON • MUNICH • SYDNEY • TOKYO
A WAVERLY COMPANY

Editor: John P. Butler
Managing Editor: Linda S. Napora
Copy Editor: Jane Sellman
Designer: Wilma E. Rosenberger
Illustration Planner: Wayne Hubbel
Production Coordinator: Anne G. Seitz

428 East Preston Street
Baltimore, Maryland 21202, USA

Printed in the United States of America

First Edition 1980

Library of Congress Cataloging-in-Publication Data

Borden, Gloria J.
Speech science primer : physiology, acoustics, and perception of Speech / Gloria J. Borden, Katherine S. Harris, and Lawrence J. Raphael.—3rd ed.
p. cm.
Includes bibliographical references and index.
ISBN 0-683-00944-3
1. Speech. I. Harris, Katherine S. II. Raphael, Lawrence J. III. Title.
P95.B65 1994
612.7′8—dc20 93-7592
CIP

97
4 5 6 7 8 9 10

To our students,
past, present, and future

Preface

The reason for writing this text was to try to satisfy a need for a comprehensive but elementary book on speech science. The need was for a text that is easy to understand and that integrates material on the production, acoustics, and perception of speech.

Courses in speech science in the 1950s were often focused on speech production and hearing, the content being primarily anatomy and physiology. During the 1960s, the study of the acoustics of speech was added to many course curricula. Now, the most comprehensive courses also include speech perception, thus completing coverage of the communicative process from the speaker to the listener. In most college departments, a separate course treats the subjects of cognition, language, and memory, leaving the production and perception of the speech signal itself to speech science.

This text was the first to cover this expanded speech science curriculum in detail. The third edition brings the material up to date, and presents the most recent versions of the theories of speech motor control and speech perception. Among the more obvious changes is the division of Chapter 4 into two chapters. The first of these describes sources of energy and sound for the speech signal, and the second deals with the articulation and acoustics of speech sounds and with models of production. The chapter on research tools has been generally re-cast to reflect the many technological changes that have occurred during the past decade. We have tried to retain the style that faculty and students have found to be clear and easy to read. Some of the figures have been redrawn for clarity and uniformity, and several new figures have been added. We continue, however, to preserve many of the classic illustrations from the research literature in their original form, as we think their presence increases the value of the book.

The primary audience to which this text is addressed is the students of speech/language pathology and audiology. These students will find information about normal communication processes that will serve as a basis for comparison with the disorders that they will soon be treating in the clinic. The need for such information and the role of speech science in providing it will be made amply clear throughout the text. The book will also be of interest to students of medicine, psychology, education, and linguistics as each of these disciplines includes some aspects of the material that we have presented. Moreover, the text provides an opportunity for students to obtain a comprehensive view of speech science. Although this book is clearly introductory, it can also serve as a graduate text for students who never had a survey course in speech science as undergraduates.

It is only relatively recently that speech science has emerged as a unified discipline, although many of its components have been studied for centuries. Acoustics has long been an aspect of physics and engineering, speech physiology a part of biology, speech perception an outgrowth of both biology and sensory psychology, and speech in its relation to language in general has long been included in the study of phonetics and linguistcs. This book embraces each of these components and attempts to integrate them into a unified treatment.

When we undertake a course of study, we

are often led gently to the subject by some introductory readings and lectures, and, after the main body of the course, are again eased to the end of the term with some concluding remarks and provocative discussions. It is not unlike a traditional play in which the author sets the stage, unfolds the drama, and ends with the dénouement. The relative sizes of the sections of this text reflect some such organization. The first two chapters are the "stage-setters." The first chapter sets speech in the larger framework of language, and the second samples the history of speech science by discussing the work of a few pioneers in acoustics, phonetics, speech pathology, speech physiology, speech engineering, and speech perception. The scientists were selected by us to serve as examples of the diversity of approach used by workers in this field.

The middle four chapters, 3, 4, 5, and 6, which deal with acoustics, speech production, and speech perception, form the chief substance of the course, the equivalent of the major action of a play. The fact that speech is audible has mandated the study of sound as a prerequisite to the understanding of the production and perception of speech sounds. Thus, Chapter 3, our discussion of acoustics, lays the foundation upon which the structure of speech science is built. Chapters 4 and 5, which concern speech production, describe the dynamics of speech with an emphasis on physiology rather than on anatomy. We have made a serious attempt to integrate physiology and acoustics, as we have found that the physiology of speech production is better understood and remembered when the sound-producing mechanisms and processes are closely associated with the acoustic output.

Chapter 6, our account of speech perception, begins with a section on hearing that is followed by a discussion of the acoustic cues used by listeners and by some experimental results that hint at how the acoustic speech signal may be decoded by listeners.

Chapters 7 and 8 are the "dénouement" of the text. Chapter 7, on research tools, emphasizes the instruments and techniques that may be generally available to students in most college and university laboratories. We also describe the instrumentation and techniques that are found in larger speech science laboratories as well, so that students will be familiar with them when they study the research literature. Finally, a comprehensive text on speech could not omit consideration of its evolution. Theories on this subject in Chapter 8 are followed by descriptions of some relevant experimental evidence and by an attempt to reconstruct the evolutionary changes and prehistorical events that we can never directly verify, but which will continue to provoke thought and study. Chapter 8 serves particularly well as a final chapter because a consideration of speech evolution not only puts speech back into a larger framework, but demands some knowledge of neurophysiology and of the source-filter functions of the vocal tract, topics considered in Chapters 4, 5, and 6.

Since the book serves as an introduction to a large body of information, we do not presume to have covered every topic of importance nor to have dealt with the topics included in depth. A selected bibliography concludes each chapter, however, to encourage the student to pursue each subject further and to fill in the necessary gaps. In an undergraduate course, the text may be used as presented; in a graduate course many of the references might be added as required readings.

Gloria J. Borden
Katherine S. Harris
Lawrence J. Raphael

Acknowledgments

Most helpful in the original writing and revision of this book were comments made by the many students who have used it in class. In addition, several of our colleagues have critically read parts or all of the book. They include Fredericka Bell-Berti, Jane Collins, Franklin Cooper, Bonnie Engel, Carole Gelfer, Arlene Greenstein, Reinhardt Heuer, Gary Kuhn, Nancy McGarr, Gary Milsark, Mary Joseph Osberger, Claude Simon, and Michael Weiss. Their carefully considered comments and suggestions were gratefully received. We are also grateful for the advice and encouragement of Jean Lovrinic.

Most of the original figures for the book were drafted by Agnes McKeon to whom we are indebted. We want to thank Cully Miller for the photographs in Chapter 7, and Stephen Crump, president of Kay Elemetrics for producing most of the sound spectrograms in the text. Jolie Bookspan's efforts in compiling the glossary have enriched the text for future students, and the careful supervision of the typing of the many drafts of the manuscript provided by Dorothy Mewha has been invaluable. In addition to Dorothy Mewha's staff, we were aided in proofing the text by Jolie Bookspan, Elly Knight, and Abigail Peterson Reilly. We have been supported in our writing by our respective universities, Temple University and the City University of New York, both in the encouragement we have received and in the use of facilities. The chairmen of our respective departments have been particularly supportive: Murray Halfond and Ralph Towne, of the Department of Speech at Temple, Irving Hochberg of the Ph.D. Program in Speech and Hearing Sciences at the Graduate School of the City University of New York, and Albert Bermel, of the Department of Speech and Theatre at Herbert H. Lehman College of the City University of New York. We probably would not have written the text in its present form had we not had the common experience of working at Haskins Laboratories in New Haven, where research in speech production and speech perception are viewed as natural complements of one another.

We are grateful to our spouses and children for cheering us on: to John, Becky, Julie, Tom and Sam Borden, to George, Maud, and Louise Harris, and to Carolyn, Melissa and David Raphael. Finally, our many questions have been answered with patience by the editor for the first edition, Ruby Richardson, the editor for the second edition, William R. Hensyl, and the editor for the third edition, John P. Butler. The guidance, advice, and encouragement supplied for the third edition by our managing editor, Linda Napora, were of value beyond measure. We thank them all.

Gloria J. Borden
Katherine S. Harris
Lawrence J. Raphael

Contents

1
Speech, Language, and Thought

O chestnut tree, great rooted blossomer,
Are you the leaf, the blossom or the bole?
O body swayed to music, O brightening glance,
How can we know the dancer from the dance?
W. B. Yeats "Among School Children"—1928

This book is about speech. It is about spoken English in particular. It is not a book about language or thought. We do want to consider speech in its context, however, before we consider it separately and rather arbitrarily removed from it. If we were to study grapes used for wine without mentioning vineyards, it would be a little like the study of speech with no recognition of its cognitive origin. Also, speech is the manifestation of only one of many kinds of languages. A study of speech with no mention of language would be a little like a study of one particular grape with no acknowledgment of the many others used for winemaking.

First of all, speech is only one method of *communication*. A female ape assumes a sexually submissive and presumably inviting posture to communicate the fact that she will accept intercourse with a male. A dog with hackles raised growls at an intruder to communicate his determination to prevent further intrusion. The animal kingdom offers countless examples of signs that communicate various conditions within and across species. Human beings use many methods of communication. We signal to others by waving flags, by morse code, by television and radio transmission, by raising an eyebrow, by writing a newspaper column, by singing, by putting hands on hips, by swearing, by painting a picture, by sticking out tongues, by playing a musical instrument, by kissing, by blushing, by dancing, by throwing a plate through the air, and finally, by speaking. We speak in our homes, at work, at school, and at play. We speak to our babies, to our pets, and to ourselves. What is speech? How does it relate to language and to thought? If you have ever known an adult who has suffered brain damage sufficient to impair speech, you have probably observed that the speech impairment is accompanied by some effects upon language and upon some aspects of thought. Speech, language, and thought are closely related, but they can be considered separately, because they are qualitatively different.

SPEECH

If you have ever been to a foreign country and heard all those around you speaking a language that you do not understand, especially a language unrelated to your own, you are apt to have had two impressions. The first impression is that the spoken language seems like long spurts of a complex and constantly changing stream of sound without separations. You have no way of knowing the end of one word and the beginning of the next. The second general impression is that this strange tongue is extremely difficult. The speakers seem to talk much faster than speakers of your own language. Even small children do it with ease!

These impressions of a foreign tongue are more accurately a description of speech than are the impressions we have of our own speech. We take our own speech for granted. It seems simple, but the sounds change quickly, requiring complex articulatory gymnastics on the part of the speaker. It is no simple matter, yet children are quite good at it by 3 or 4 years of age. Although some children may have difficulties later in learning to read, all normal children learn to speak. They are natural language learners, and they develop language by hearing the speech of others. Speech is audible. It can be described in terms of its loudness, its pitch, and its duration. It is meaningful sound strung out in time. Speech is only one way in which we use language. We also write, read, and listen to others speak.

LANGUAGE

The reason, of course, that we fail to understand the strange speech of an unknown language is that, although we can hear the speech, we do not know the words, the sounds, the rules of the language. A particular *language* is a rule-governed communication system composed of meaningful elements, which can be combined in many ways to produce sentences, some of which are novel. Our knowledge of English permits us to say and understand something as prosaic as:

> It's hot as Hades this afternoon.

This sentence has undoubtedly been said many times because of laziness of mind, but our language also permits us to say and understand something completely new, something we have never heard said before, such as this quotation from a Tom Robbins novel:

> In any case, and whichever the ever, upon a sweaty but otherwise nondescript afternoon in early August 1960, an afternoon squeezed out of Mickey's mousy snout, an afternoon carved from mashed potatoes and lye, an afternoon scraped out of the dog dish of meteorology, an afternoon that could lull a monster to sleep, an afternoon that normally might have produced nothing more significant than diaper rash, Sissy Hankshaw stepped from a busted-jaw curbstone on Hull Street in South Richmond and attempted to hitchhike an ambulance.
>
> Tom Robbins, *Even Cowgirls Get the Blues*. Boston: Houghton Mifflin Co., 1976, p. 37.

We understand this sentence, although it is completely original with Robbins, because we share with the author the knowledge of the rules of a language. The rules of *semantics* enable us to associate words or phrases with meanings. We and the author have a common understanding of "diaper rash." The rules of *syntax* enable us to have common expectations of word order. As readers, we were kept waiting until the words "Sissy Hankshaw" for the subject of the sentence. When the verb "stepped" arrived, our mutual *morphological* rules dictated that it have an "-ed" ending to agree with the previous verbs in the past tense. Robbins and his readers know the same rules; they share a language. Users of language can be creative. They can create sentences never heard before.

Language, unlike speech, is intangible. It is knowledge of a creative communication system, and that knowledge is in the mind. How is language related to speech? Noam Chomsky of Massachusetts Institute of Technology writes about this knowledge of language as *linguistic competence* to distinguish it from the use of language, *linguistic performance*. Speech is the conversion of language into sound. However, there are other languages besides vocal ones. There are gestural languages, of which American Sign Language (Ameslan), used by the deaf, is an example.

The syntactic rules of Ameslan differ from English. Word order is often determined by the chronology of events or by stressed words. For example, in Ameslan one would sign "Sun this morning. I saw. Beautiful." rather than "It was a beautiful sun I saw this morning." If the word to be stressed in "I like the movies" is "movies," an Ameslan user would sign "Movies I like." The semantic rules are entirely different because the Ameslan user associates meanings with signs made by the hands, face, and arms. The shape of the sign, its movement or how it changes, and its position relative to the rest of the body are all meaningful. Again, the knowledge or competence one has in the system can be called language, in contrast to the use of it, which is called performance. As with speech, performance usually falls short of the user's competence. Signs are sometimes indicated quickly and incompletely. Mistakes are made, but the user's competence remains. In speaking, we often use fragments of sentences rather than sentences. We think of something else in mid-sentence, and start a new sentence before we have completed the first. Yet, when a teacher says, "Put your answer in a complete sentence," the student knows how to do it. He or she knows the language, even though that knowledge is rarely reflected fully in speech. How does this linguistic knowledge relate to thought?

THOUGHT

Thought may be defined as an internal representation of experiences. Jerome Bruner of Harvard suggests that the representation can be in the form of images, of action, or of language. We presumably use all available representations of our experiences, but some people report the use of some forms more than others. We may think via internal images, vaguely visual, when we are solving a problem, such as how many suitcases we think we can fit into the trunk of a car. Architects and artists often think in visual images. Thought also can be represented by internal action or muscle imagery. In solving the problem of the direction and force needed to place a tennis shot out of reach of an opponent, we think in terms of action. Choreographers, athletes, and some physicists think this way. Albert Einstein, in describing his understanding of how he thought, wrote:

> The words of the language, as they are written or spoken, do not seem to play any role in my mechanism of thought. The psychical entities which seem to serve as elements in thought are certain signs and more or less clear images which can be "voluntarily" reproduced and combined. . . . But taken from a psychological viewpoint, this combinatory play seems to be the essential feature in productive thought—before there is any connection with logical construction in words or other kinds of signs which can be communicated to others. The above mentioned elements are, in my case, of visual and some of muscular type.
>
> Quoted in Ghiselin, B., *The Creative Process.* New York: Mentor Books, 1955, p. 43.

Representation of thought in some language, whether it be verbal or mathematical, seems important in the mental activities of language users. Although it is apparent that we can think without knowledge of any formal language, it is equally apparent that those who do know a language use it to aid thinking. We shall first consider thought without language and then thought with language.

Thought without Language

We have all had the experience of having an idea that we find difficult to verbalize. Indeed, words often seem inadequate. Our ideas expressed seem but a rough sketch of our thinking. People with *aphasia*, language impairment caused by brain damage, demonstrate that thought is independent of language. Often an aphasic will seem to have an idea to express, but will lack the language to embody the thought.

Some deaf children, who have not been exposed to sign language, are quite delayed in learning the language of their community because of the difficulties they encounter in learning oral speech. Hans Furth has shown, however, that the cognitive abilities of these children develop almost normally. Helen Keller, the well-known author, who was blind and deaf from the age of 18 months, wrote that she did not understand the first important concept of language learning, the idea that symbols stand for elements of our experience, until she was 9 years old. When her teacher, Annie Sullivan, was communicating the word "water" by having the child feel her face with one hand as she said the word, and feel the water with the other hand, the child suddenly made the association. Helen quickly learned the "names" of everything soon after. Language learning had begun, yet Helen surely was not an unthinking child before that experience. Her thinking must have been represented in images.

The Swiss psychologist, Jean Piaget, concluded from his observations of normal children that cognition develops on its own. Language interacts with it and certainly reflects the child's thinking, but language does not determine the thinking. According to his view, it does no good to train a child in language in order to develop cognition. Rather, he held that stages of cognitive development are reflected in the child's use of language.

Lev Vygotsky, a Russian psychologist, also observed evidence of nonverbal thought in children. Infants demonstrate their understanding of relationships and their problem-solving abilities independently of their use of language, just as they also make speech-like babbling sounds that seem to lack intellectual content. Later in the child's development, speech and thought unite.

Thought and Language

Vygotsky's great contribution was his idea of "inner speech." Although he viewed early language as being essentially communicative, he maintained that some use of early language was egocentric; the child communicates with himself. From about 3 to 7 years of age, the vocal egocentric speech gradually becomes subvocal "inner speech," which is a way of internally talking to oneself. It is neither thought nor speech, but something in between. When we think in language, we think in linguistic fragments, in abbreviated phrases, the words fading quickly or only partly formed.

Piaget agreed with Vygotsky's description of inner speech, having observed its beginnings in the egocentric speech of the children in his studies. Preschool children echo words and phrases they hear around them (*echolalia*) and incorporate them into their own *monologues*. They talk about what they are doing, the toys they are playing with, the pictures they are painting. A whole room of kindergarten children can be talking, sometimes taking turns as in conversation, but each one is talking about his own experiences, in a *collective monologue*. The point that Piaget emphasized was that this use of language reflected a stage of thinking in which children seldom include the point of view of others. They see things primarily from their own viewpoint, hence the *egocentric speech*. Gradually, the frequency of the egocentric speech decreases as the frequency of socialized speech increases. If in some sense we "speak" to ourselves as well as speak to others, does this inner speech aid in thinking?

Language and Speech as a Carrier for Thought

Thoughts are not always sequential. Sometimes a thought is formed as an association internally "seen" as a whole. We necessarily distort it when we string it out on the time line of language and speech. Despite this distortion, there are many advantages in using language to represent thought. Language helps in making an idea or an experience available. By expressing the thought verbally or by a mathematical formula, it can be elicited more easily for further consideration. Language also aids thinking by providing a frame to hold information in memory. It enables us to express ideas about people, places, or things that are not present.

In all of this discussion, language has been viewed as a vessel for thought and as a reflection of thought, but not as something that determines thought. Linguistic determinism was advanced by the linguist Edward Sapir and even more strongly by his student, Benjamin Whorf. The *Whorfian hypothesis* in its strongest version—that language determines thinking—is not generally accepted today. It was based on comparative linguistic data that show that languages differ in the number of terms for such things as "color" or "snow." The reasoning was that people with many words for "snow" actually perceived distinctions that people with one word failed to perceive. Language determined their experiences and their thinking. A weak version of this idea is that it may be easier for an Eskimo to talk about snow than it is for a Guatemalan, but there is no significant difference between their abilities to perceive or to think about snow. The interests and needs of one language group may simply differ from those of another—hence the differences in vocabulary.

Instead of comparing languages, one can look at a particular language and observe differences based upon social group membership. Basil Bernstein, a sociolinguist, used cultural differences as an explanation of linguistic differences he observed between middle class and working class children in Great Britain. When children were asked to describe a picture, for example, the typical middle class child would be fairly explicit, using many nouns. One would not need to see the picture being described to imagine it. The typical working class child, in describing the same picture, would use far fewer nouns, substituting such words as "he," "it," or "they," so that it would be difficult to imagine the picture from the description alone. Bernstein attributed this difference to cultural differences: the working class family in England has a strong hierarchy so that children are not expected to express themselves creatively, but to listen to the head of the family, while the middle class family is less authoritarian and each member has a say. In addition, the working class family member usually talks about shared experiences, so the context is understood, whereas the middle class family member is more apt to talk about experiences of his own and does not assume so much knowledge on the part of the listener. Bernstein's choice of terms, *restricted code* (in the working class case) and *elaborated code* (in the middle class case) is unfortunate, as it connotes classist ideas, which Bernstein disavows. His studies, however, do point out the influence of cultural habits, if not differences in thinking, upon language.

Despite small differences in the use of language by different people who share a language, and despite the larger differences among the various languages of the world in their structure and vocabularies, there may be some universal features of all human languages. To the extent that this is true, one ought to be able to learn something about the human mind, as Chomsky suggests, by studying the rules of human language.

> There are any number of questions that might lead one to undertake a study of language. Personally, I am primarily intrigued by the possibility of learning something, from the study of language, that will bring to light inherent properties of the human mind.
> Chomsky, N., *Language and Mind* (enlarged edition). New York: Harcourt Brace Jovanovich, Inc., 1972, p. 103.

If language is conceived as a set of rules by which an infinite number of sentences can be generated, using a stock of words that constantly expands to cover all concepts one may choose to express, then humans are the only creatures yet known to have a command of language. Another factor that seems to be unique to human beings is that they can talk about their languages. Homo sapiens may well be the only creature on Earth who uses the brain in an attempt to understand brains and uses language in an attempt to understand languages. The interaction of thinking, language, and speech may seem clearer if we look further at language development in normal children.

DEVELOPMENT OF LANGUAGE AND SPEECH

Normal children have, at birth, the potential to walk and to talk, although as babies they can do neither. They are genetically endowed with the appropriate neurophysical systems, but time is needed for these systems to develop and mature. The brain is approximately 40 percent the size it will attain by adulthood; the more peripheral areas, the vocal tract and the legs, await the anatomical change and the development of motor-sensory associations appropriate to talking and walking. At 6 months, children sit up and *babble* in meaningless vocal play. By the arrival of the first birthday, they may have started to walk and to name things. By the second birthday, they may be putting two words together for rudimentary telegraphic sentences, and by the fourth, they will have mastered the essential rules of the language of their elders. The rapidity and apparent ease with which children learn language is a phenomenon of childhood and can never be repeated with such ease by adults. Many adults learn new languages, especially those who already know several languages, but the time most conducive to learning languages is before puberty. Wilder Penfield, the Canadian neurophysiologist, put the cut-off age at about 15 (somewhat after puberty, in most cases). Whatever the age, most researchers recognize the concept of a critical period for language acquisition. There is, however, considerable controversy about the seriousness of the limitations imposed upon the language learner who is beyond the critical period. Lenneberg and others who base their arguments on neuro-biological data suggest that natural language acquisition abilities cease to exist after the critical period. Others, including those who observed "Genie," a child who did not begin to acquire language until after puberty, argue that the native ability to learn language is never completely extinguished.

What children universally accomplish with spontaneity and speed, psychologists, linguists, and speech scientists have laboriously analyzed with only moderate success. The question they ask is: how do children acquire language? Theorists on this subject can be generally divided into two groups. One group of theorists analyzes language development in terms of learning principles. The other group analyzes language development in terms of an innate propensity for language. Perhaps the most currently popular view is that only the details or individual items of a particular language are learned, while the structural and creative underpinnings universal to all languages are inherited.

Learning Theory and Language

Learning in the classical sense is the formulation of a new bond or association between a stimulus and a response. The classic experiment, performed by Pavlov in Russia in the 1920s, resulted in an association or bond between the sound of a bell and a dog's salivation. This bond was new and therefore considered to be "learned," because before the experiment, the dog did not salivate at the sound of a bell. The learned behavior, or *conditioned response (CR)*, was produced by pairing an *unconditioned stimulus (UCS)*, in this case, meat powder, with the *conditioned stimulus (CS)*, the bell. Since meat powder reflexively causes increased salivation (an automatic physiological response to food), the contiguous presentation of meat powder and the bell sound produced a neural bond between the two, so that finally the bell alone would produce salivation.

1. UCS (meat powder) ⟶ UCR (salivation)
2. UCS (meat powder) + CS (bell) ⟶ UCR (salivation)
3. CS bell ⟶ CR (salivation)

In classical conditioning, the unconditioned response is involuntary (perspiration, heart rate change, salivation) and its cause is known (an object of fear, food). There is another model of learning in which the unconditioned response is under voluntary control (the subject pushes a lever or makes a sound) and the cause is not evident. In this case, the learning is effected, not by the pairing of stimuli, but by reinforcement or reward, a method called *operant conditioning*. If the operant response is rewarded with food, praise, or some other positive experience, the behavior is strengthened, but if it is punished with electric shock, criticism, or some negative experience, the behavior is weakened. The operant conditioning model was developed by B. F. Skinner whose theory of language learning is detailed in his book *Verbal Behavior*. Skinner believes that language is learned by selective reinforcement provided to the child as he uses language to operate upon his environment.

Another learning theorist, O. H. Mowrer, has suggested that the reinforcement or reward may not always produce an observable response but that responses may occur within the child. In the observable instance, the association of the utterance "mama" with the rewarding presence of the mother with food and comfort establishes "mama" as a learned response. In the case of an internal response, the child finds that just the word "mama" produces positive feelings, or rewards, even if the word is not said aloud. In what Mowrer has termed his *autistic theory*, children may subvocally rehearse new words they have heard that set up internal rewards sufficient for the words to become learned or conditioned behavior. This theory accounts for children suddenly using words that they have never before spoken.

Certainly, learning theories are consistent with facts about much of children's semantic acquisition, the learning of word meanings. They may even explain the initial stages of adopting the syntax or word order of the particular language. The shaping of the correct sounds of speech may also be dependent upon the reward of being understood and perhaps obeyed. If a child who has said /tuti/ "tootie" to no avail finds that /kuki/ "cookie" produces the desired delicacy, he or she is amply rewarded and will use "cookie" in the future.

Innateness Theory

There is much about language development, however, that learning theories cannot explain. Human language users are creative in their use of the system. They both understand and produce sentences they have never heard before and, therefore, could never have learned. Children, after hearing sufficient utterances of their language, pick up the rules and can use these stored rules to understand new sentences and to generate original sentences. They may learn an irregular verb form such as "ran" by conventional learning methods. However, once they have figured out the regular past tense rule, they are apt to cease using "ran" and to say "runned" instead, as their rule-seeking ability leads them to regularize language forms and to ignore the models that they have heard and initially learned. Many psycholinguists think that this ability to abstract the rules of the language is innate; some think that aspects of linguistic structure are innate.

Linguistic Competence

Noam Chomsky has written most persuasively on this subject. As we have seen, he is careful to distinguish between the competence one has in a language, the set of rules with which one produces language, and the performance, which consists of the speech, however fragmented, that we utter. One has only to contrast a skilled speaker with an inarticulate one to realize the differences that exist in performance. Nonetheless, basic linguistic competence seems to be accessible to all normal individuals, and it is this fundamental linguistic knowledge that linguists think humans have an inborn ability to acquire.

Eric Lenneberg, Phillip Lieberman and others have presented evidence that certain features of human anatomy and physiology have evolved in such a way that they are now specialized for the production of speech and language. It appears, then, that language potential is not only hereditary, but also species-specific, since Homo sapiens alone displays such anatomical and physiological adaptations.

Thinking provides a foundation for language; children can only talk about what they know, but they may know more than they can express with their incompletely developed language. Psycholinguists find that children are pattern-seekers. Based on the language they hear around them, they seem to form hypotheses about linguistic rules and apply them in their own way. The language of children appears not to be a poor imitation of adult language, but rather a different language with its own rules. The syntactic rule system, vocabulary, and phonology of child language are each comparatively undifferentiated. Children's syntactic rules for the negative may include the use of "no" with an affirmative sentence, such as "No go home," despite the fact that they have never heard adults produce a negative sentence in such form. In the vocabularies of children, "doggie" may, at first, refer to any four-legged animal; only later will they narrow the meaning of the term. Children's phonological systems may specify the use of stops, wherever stops, fricatives, or consonant clusters appear in adult speech. For example, they might pronounce "two," "Sue," and "stew" as /tu/ "two."

As they develop their language systems, they are enlarging their knowledge of *seman-*

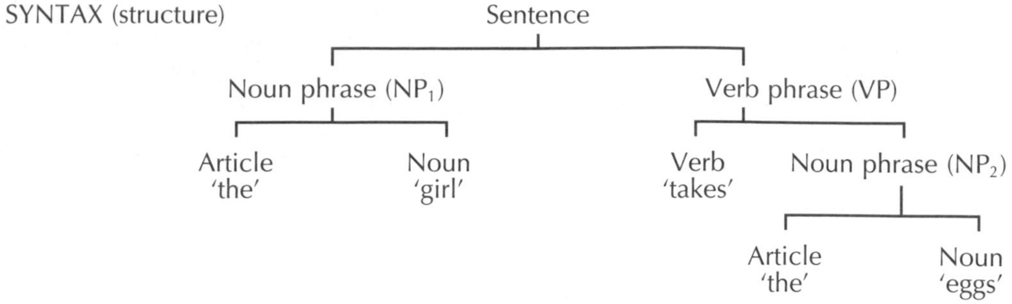

Transformation rule for changing active sentence to passive:

$T_{passive}$: NP_2 be + verb + en by NP_1

'The eggs are taken by the girl'

(NP_2) (be) (verb) (by) (NPO_1)

PHONOLOGY (sounds)

'eggs' = /ɛgz/

Progressive assimilation: the voiced /g/ changes the following /s/ to voiced /z/; /ɛgz/

Figure 1.1 Rules of syntax and phonology.

tics, the meanings associated with words and phrases and, at the same time, are discovering the rules by which their particular language is governed. The rules are of three sorts: *syntactic* rules, which account for the structure of sentences, including transformations of simple declarative sentences into questions or passives; *morphological* rules, which account for changes in meaning brought about by changing meaningful units of sound (cat, cats) or by intonation (Yes. Yes?); and *phonological* rules, thought to account for the sounds of the speech stream. Many linguists consider morphological rules to be redundant with syntactic rules on the one hand and phonological rules on the other.

A simple sentence may suffice as an example of how these rules are used in linguistic analysis: "The eggs are taken by the girl." (See Fig. 1.1.)

A *morpheme* is the smallest linguistic segment that means something. The word "cats," then, is composed of two morphemes "cat" and "-s" (which means "more than one.") There are two morphemes in "eggs" for the same reason. A *phoneme* is a family of sounds that functions in a language to signal a difference in meaning. The fact that "pat" and "bat" differ in meaning, demonstrates that /p/ and /b/ are phonemes in English. A phoneme, by itself, is meaningless. It cannot be described as a sound either, for a phoneme can be actualized as one of several different sounds. Thus, the sounds of /p/ in "*p*ie," "s*p*oon," and "to*p*" differ from one another: The first is produced with a burst of air, the second without the burst, and the third often with no lip opening at all. These variants of the phoneme are often called *allophones*, and the sounds themselves *phones*. The term "phoneme," then, is used when one wishes to refer to the function of a sound family in the language to signal differences in meaning, while the term "phone" is used when one wishes to refer to a particular sound. Slashed lines are used to indicate phonemes, /p/, while brackets indicate phones, [p]. Ordinary alphabetics will identify many sounds unambiguously, but for other sounds, we need a way of specifying them unambiguously. In our sample sentence, the word "girl" contains the phonemes /gɝl/. The word "curl" /kɝl/ differs from "girl" by only one phoneme /g-k/. The actual sound of a particular person saying "girl" might be transcribed [gɝl] or [gɝl] with the symbols in brackets. The most commonly used system for transcribing the sounds of speech, the International Phonetic Alphabet, appears in Appendix 1.

Spoken language arises from knowledge of meanings (semantics) formalized into structure (syntax, morphemes, phonemes) that is finally encoded into the sounds of speech. We conclude this chapter with a model of the interactions and conversions, as we view them, in going from thought to speech.

FROM THOUGHT TO SPEECH

Two young women in Philadelphia's Museum of Art pause before a painting by Henri Matisse entitled "Odalisque Jaune" (Fig. 1.2). One woman says to the second, "Look at this picture. There's something about the faces and the patterns that reminds me of some Japanese prints I saw in a museum in New York." We cannot presume to know how this utterance was derived from the young woman's linguistic knowledge and originally from her thought processes, but we must assume that some reference was made to stored visual experiences of Japanese prints and that associations were made between the highly patterned areas of the Japanese woodcuts (Fig. 1.3) and the juxtaposition of patterns in the Matisse painting. Entering into the process in some way must have been a sense of pleasure and a positive attitude toward the effects produced.

A model of thought, language, and speech conversions is presented in Figure 1.4. The circles overlap to suggest both the interrelationships involved and their simultaneity. The young woman's visual and aesthetic experiences, both in the present and the past, relate to ideas she has about their similarities and to her feelings about the pictures. The woman chose to represent her thought in language in order to communicate her response to the pictures to her companion.

There are a number of ways in which the woman could have framed her ideas and feelings, but based on certain semantic, syntactic, and morphophonological decisions, she expressed her thought in the utterance quoted above. She was constrained by the rules of her language and by the rules of her speech-pro-

Figure 1.2 Matisse painting: "Odalisque Jaune." Philadelphia Museum of Art: Samuel S. White, III and Vera White Collection.

Figure 1.3 Japanese woodcut. Kiyonaga: "Shigeyuki Executing Calligraphy," 1783. Philadelphia Museum of Art: Given by Mrs. John D. Rockefeller.

ducing mechanism. We shall make no attempt to suggest how the meaning is converted into a form ready for speaking. We recognize, too, that the delivery of the message could have been in writing or in some gestural language as well as in speech. Choosing speech, however, the young woman somehow readied for delivery the message that her friend eventually heard.

It seems probable that chunks of the message are briefly stored in a buffer (temporary storage) ready for output. The chunks are perhaps of sentence length or phrase length. Evidence for this storage comes from slips of the tongue. The fact that people make mistakes such as "He cut the knife with the salami," Victoria Fromkin's example, indicates the existence of such a buffer in order for the speaker to have substituted what should have been the last word for the fourth-to-the-last word.

Timing and *prosodic* aspects of the utterance are viewed in our model as superimposed upon the message as it is converted into speech. For example, the prosody, which includes the intonation pattern and the stress pattern of the phrase, remains constant despite slips of the tongue. Stress is placed upon the last word whether the speaker says "He cut the salami with the KNIFE" or "He cut the knife with the SALAMI," indicating separate instructions for word order and for prosody. Also, the utterance can be said at a variety of rates, from fast to slow, indicating somewhat separate timing commands. The timing within and across segments that distinguishes phonemes, however, is thought to be intrinsic to their specifications stored in the buffer. For example, the timing of laryngeal vibrations and lip movements that distinguishes /p/ from /b/ is stored as part of the schema or blueprint for the speech.

There may be a transformation on the speech level from a relatively abstract representation of the speech to the actual neuromotor activity that controls the muscle activity, cavity changes, and air pressure modifications heard as "speech." Alvin Liberman and Franklin Cooper have made a case for conversions in speech that are reminiscent of the deep to surface structure conversions suggested by Chomsky. In the language conversions, linguistic rules are used; in the speech conversions, neuromotor, myomotor, and articulatory rules are used, omitting for the sake of simplicity any mention of sensory control mechanisms. Figure 1.5 schematizes the conversions viewed as important in processing speech. The input to this model is an abstract representation of the phonemes the speaker intends to utter. These are stored in what we have called the buffer, perhaps in the form of such distinctive (phonological) features of speech production as manner and place of articulation and whether or not each sound is intended to be voiced or voiceless. Four conversions are shown in the figure: from the internal speech representation to nerve impulses, from nerve impulses to muscle contractions, from muscle contractions to vocal tract shape and air pressure changes, and from these changes to an acoustic waveform. These conversions result in an acoustic signal in which the phonetic realizations of phonolog-

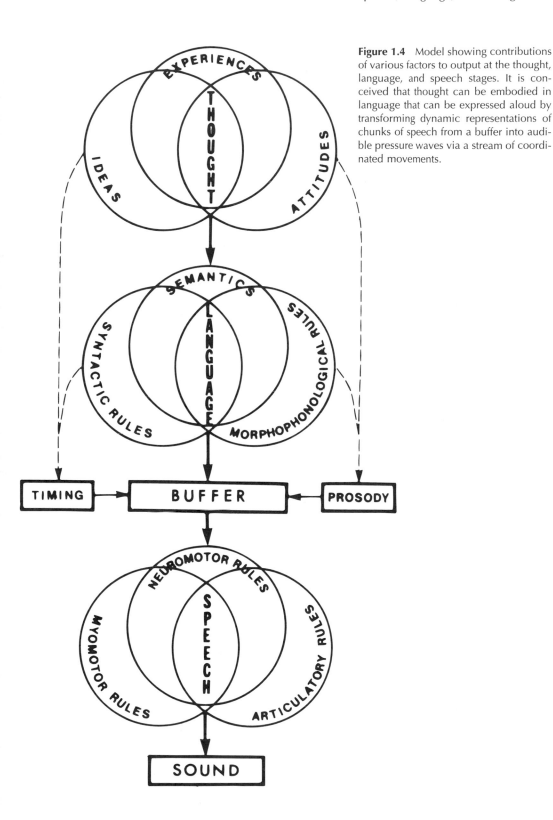

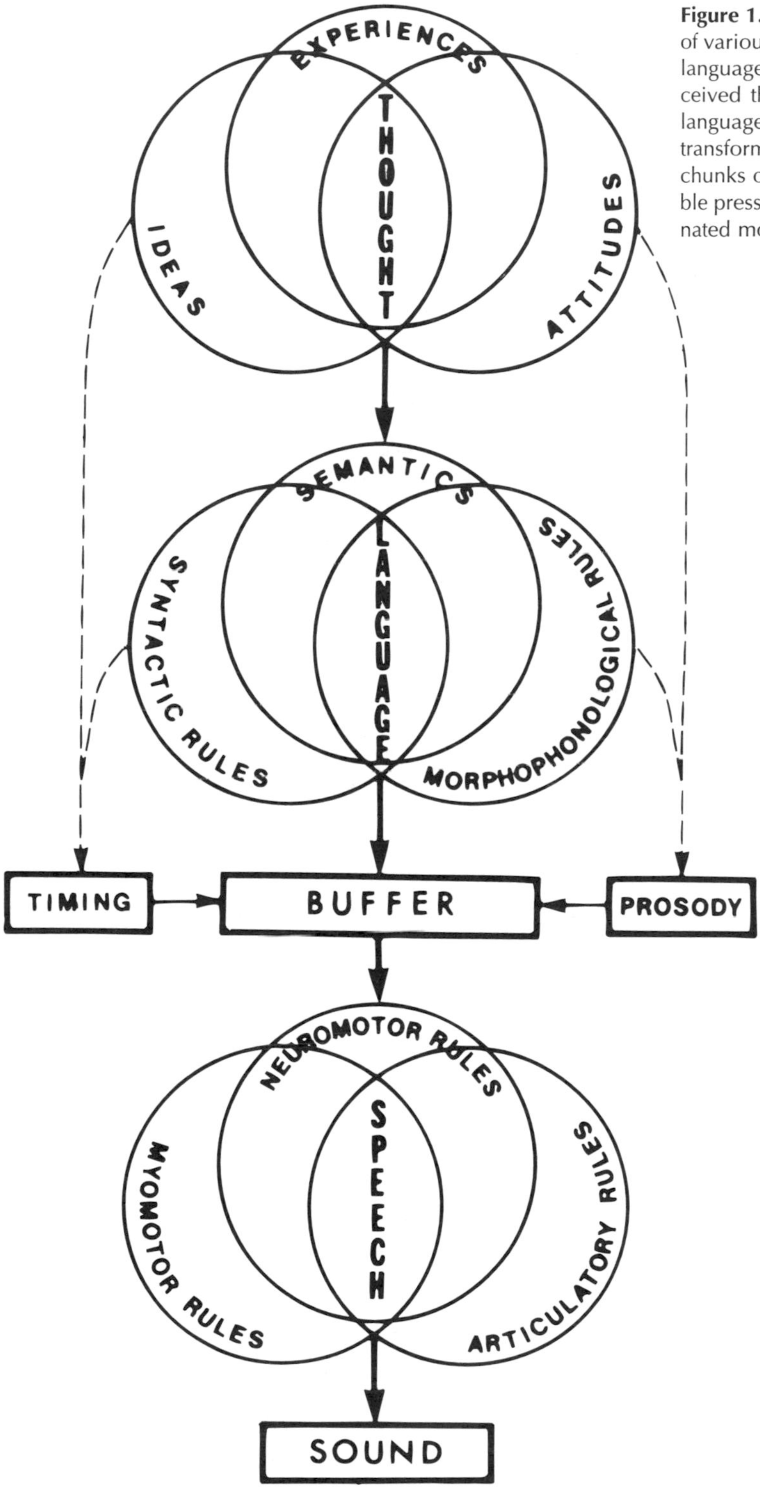

Figure 1.4 Model showing contributions of various factors to output at the thought, language, and speech stages. It is conceived that thought can be embodied in language that can be expressed aloud by transforming dynamic representations of chunks of speech from a buffer into audible pressure waves via a stream of coordinated movements.

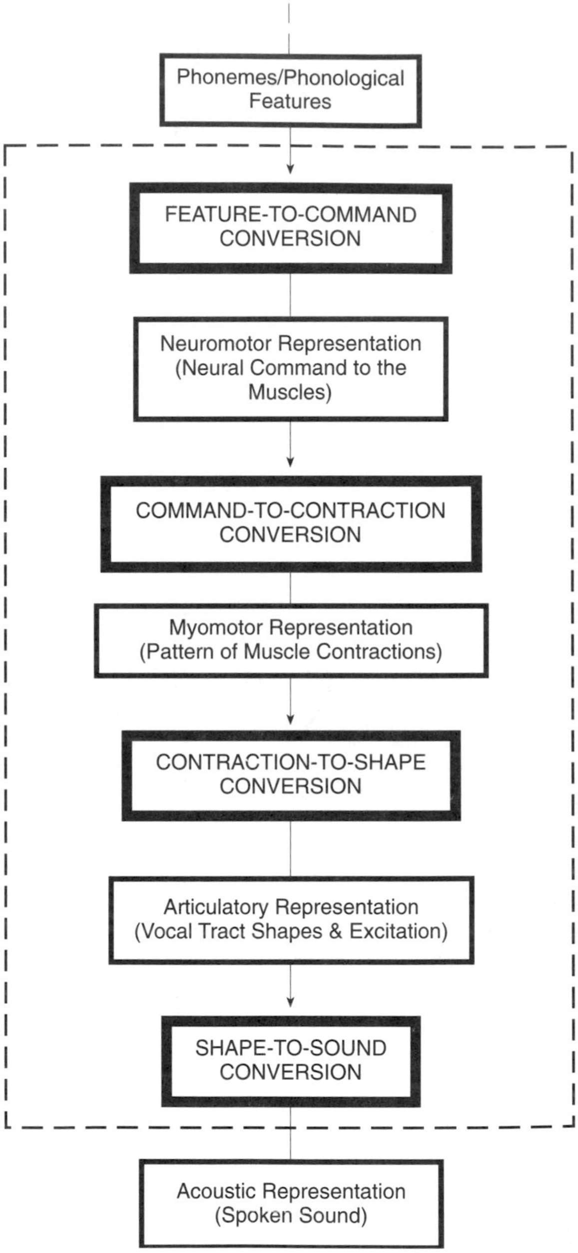

Figure 1.5 Model of the speech production process. It is assumed that each speech sound can be represented as a complex of abstract phonetic features. The features are actualized as neural commands to the articulatory muscles, which shape the vocal tract. The vocal tract shape determines the output speech acoustic signal. (Reprinted from F. S. Cooper: How Is Language Conveyed by Speech? In *Language by Ear and by Eye,* edited by J. F. Kavanagh and I. G. Mattingly, by permission of the M. I. T. Press, Cambridge, Mass. © 1972, p. 34.)

ical features overlap and in which the abstract phonemes no longer exist as discrete entities.

In our model (Fig. 1.4) the same speech rules are applied. They are seen to occur simultaneously and to relate to one another.

In the buffer, the utterance exists as an internal representation of the speaker's acoustic goal ("Models of Speech Production," in Chapter 5) and as an internal representation of the physiology of speech production in terms of its three-dimensional space coordinates (see the same chapter) and relative timing. The speaker knows the intended sounds and what has to be done to produce them. She unconsciously "knows" what cavity shapes and air pressure changes are required to go from the end of "Japanese" to the beginning of "prints" and from the /n/ to the /i/ in /dʒæpəniz/ "Japanese." Applying the rules of speech, a stream of sound is produced.

We are far from understanding how this works. Neither do we understand how a listener processes speech to arrive at the intent of the speaker. Speech science is the study of these issues: the production of speech, the acoustics of the signal, and the perception of speech by a listener. If the buffer is considered to hold the intended message, speech scientists concern themselves with everything downstream of that stage. The transformations from an intended phrase to its acoustic realization by a speaker, and the transformations from acoustics of speech to the decoding of the intended phrase by a listener, are within the province of investigation by the speech scientist.

REFERENCES

Bernstein, B., A Socio-linguistic Approach to Socialization: With Some Reference to Educability. In *Directions in Sociolinguistics*. J. J. Gumperz and D. Hymes (Eds.) New York: Holt, Rinehart & Winston, 1972, pp. 465–497.

Bruner, J. S., *Studies in Cognitive Growth*. New York: Wiley & Sons, 1966.

Carroll, J. B., *Language and Thought*. Englewood Cliffs, N.J.: Prentice-Hall, 1964.

Cherry, C., *On Human Communication*, 2nd Ed. Cambridge, MA.: M. I. T. Press, 1966.

Chomsky, N., *Language and Mind* (enlarged edition). New York: Harcourt Brace Jovanovich, Inc., 1972.

Cooper, F. S., How Is Language Conveyed by Speech? In *Language by Ear and by Eye*. J. F. Kavanagh and I. G. Mattingly (Eds.) Cambridge, MA: M. I. T. Press, 1972, pp. 25–45.

Cutting, J. E., and Kavanagh, J. F., On the Relationship of Speech to Language. *ASHA 17*, 1975, 500–506.

Dale, P. S., *Language Development: Structure and Function*, 2nd Ed. New York: Holt, Rinehart & Winston, 1976.

Fromkin, V., and Rodman, R., *An Introduction to Language*. (5th Ed.) New York: Harcourt Brace Jovanovich, 1993.

Furth, H., *Thinking Without Language: Psychological Implications of Deafness*. New York: The Free Press, 1966.

Krashen, S., The Critical Period for Language Acquisition and Its Possible Bases. *Annals of the New York Academy of Sciences. 263*, 1975, 211–224.

Lenneberg, E. H., *Biological Foundations of Language*. New York: Wiley & Sons, 1967.

Liberman, A. M., The Grammars of Speech and Language. *Cognitive Psychol. 1*, 1970, 301–323.

Lieberman, P., Crelin, E., and Klatt, D., Phonetic Ability and Related Anatomy of the Newborn and Adult Human, Neanderthal Man and the Chimpanzee. *American Anthropologist 74*, 1972, 287–307.

Mowrer, O. H., *Learning Theory and Personality Dynamics*. New York: Ronald Press, 1950.

Penfield, W., and Roberts, L., *Speech and Brain Mechanisms*. Princeton, NJ: Princeton University Press, 1959.

Piaget, J., *The Language and Thought of the Child*. Atlantic Highlands, NJ: Humanities Press, 1959. (Translation of *Le Langage et la Pensée chez L'Enfant*. Neuchâtel and Paris: Delachaux et Niestlé, 1923).

Skinner, B. F., *Verbal Behavior*. New York: Appleton-Century-Crofts, 1957.

Slobin, D. I., *Psycholinguistics*. Glenview, IL: Scott, Foresman & Co., 1971.

Vygotsky, L. S., *Thought and Language*. Cambridge, MA: M. I. T. Press, 1962.

Whorf, B. L., *Language, Thought, and Reality*. Cambridge, MA: M. I. T. Press and New York: Wiley & Sons, 1956.

2
Pioneers in Speech Science

History is the essence of innumerable biographies.
Thomas Carlyle, *On History*

So many people have been instrumental in the development of speech science that it would be more confusing than helpful to name them, even were we to limit ourselves to the most influential. Rather than attempt to outline a history of speech science, we have chosen to demonstrate the diversity of approach inherent in this discipline, by describing the contributions of a few of the pioneers in different aspects of the field. A pioneer, then, is not necessarily the most important person but is rather one of the first to use a given approach.

Speech science is the study of the articulation and physiology of speech production, the acoustical characteristics of speech, and the processes by which listeners perceive speech. The discipline has attracted the interest of phoneticians, linguists, psychologists, engineers, and speech pathologists. The interests of phoneticians and linguists have traditionally overlapped. Phoneticians concentrate on describing the normal production of phones (actual speech sounds, see Chapter 1) in terms of articulatory physiology and acoustics. Linguists tend to be more interested in describing sound systems (phonology) of languages, the rules under which those systems operate, and how those rules relate to the rules of syntax and semantics. The psychologists are primarily interested in psychoacoustics, the perceptual cues to speech, measurement of speech intelligibility, and the ways in which the human brain processes the speech signal. The engineers are primarily interested in the analysis of the sounds of speech, the transmission of speech in communication systems, the development of visual speech displays, and the development of speech synthesizers and machines that will recognize speech and individual speakers. The speech pathologists are primarily interested in speech production and its disorders, including its inception in the central nervous system, its control mechanisms, its muscle activity, movements, and the resulting changes in air pressure and sound. In practice, however, the phonetician, linguist, psychologist, engineer, and speech pathologist often share common interests and work together in one laboratory.

HERMANN VON HELMHOLTZ: ACOUSTICS OF SPEECH

The human ear has been a valuable instrument in the study of the acoustics of speech, long before the electronic age brought with it electrical frequency analyzers and computers. Hermann Ludwig Ferdinand von Helmholtz, born near Berlin in 1821 of English, German, and French ancestry, was to use his ears extensively in the study of the acoustics of the human voice and the resonances of the vocal tract cavities. A man of wide interests, living before the age of specialization, he studied mathematics, physics, and medicine and contributed to the fields of physiology, optics, acoustics, mathematics, mechanics, and electricity through his university teaching and research. His published papers and books numbered over 200. His father was a teacher of philology and philosophy. His mother was a descendent of William Penn on her father's side and of French ancestry on her mother's side. A sickly child, Helmholtz had trouble with grammar, history, and vocabulary and was confused in distinguishing left from right, but he read widely and showed an early curiosity and love of nature. After studying medicine at the University of Berlin and working as a surgeon in the army, he became a professor, first at Königsberg, then Bonn, and finally in Heidelberg and Berlin. Helmholtz always combined teaching with research. He thought it was important to experiment and to demonstrate to himself the principles to be taught in the lecture hall. He studied the sense of hearing, both in its physiology and in various aspects of sensation, pure tone sensation, and the hearing of combination tones. He worked out the mathematics of resonance. Noting that blowing across the open necks of bottles with more or less water in them produced different sounds, he found he could make one bottle sound like /u/ and two bottles, sounded simultaneously, resemble /o/.

Using hollow glass globes with two openings, later known as Helmholtz resonators (Fig. 2.1), he developed a technique to analyze the frequency components of complex tones. First, he would coat the smaller nipple-shaped end with sealing wax and obtain an airtight fit into his ear canal. Each globe was made to be tuned to a different tone. Stopping up his other ear with more sealing wax, he would listen to complex sounds. The resonator would dampen most sounds except those of its own natural frequency. Thus, he analyzed the fundamental frequency and harmonics of the human voice and the major resonances of the cavities above the larynx.

Wondering why a particular vowel has a distinctive quality whether said or sung, and whether said by men, women, or children, Helmholtz held tuning forks of different frequencies in front of his mouth and those of other people, with oral cavities shaped for a particular vowel. He found that different shapes had different resonant frequencies. Thus, Helmholtz determined what he thought were the absolute resonances of each vowel; later, however, the resonances were found to be relative for different size vocal tracts. In 1863, he

Figure 2.1. Helmholtz resonators. (Adapted from an illustration in *On the Sensations of Tone as a Physiological Basis for the Theory of Music*, 1863.)

published his great work on acoustics of speech and on harmonic theory: *On the Sensations of Tone as a Physiological Basis for the Theory of Music*.

Helmholtz is described as a calm, reserved scholar. He liked to go mountain climbing and claimed that thoughts often came to him when he was hiking. Married twice, he had two children by his first wife, who died when he lived in Heidelberg. His daughter married the son of Werner von Siemens, the founder of the Physico-Technical Institute near Berlin. Helmholtz was the first director of the institute. One of his students was Heinrich Hertz, who later demonstrated electromagnetic waves and was to have the unit for cycles per second (Hz) named after him. Besides his scholarly activities Helmholtz thought it was important to deliver popular lectures on scientific subjects to the public, which was unusual in Germany at that time. Helmholtz would undoubtedly be surprised to know that today he is being hailed here as a pioneer in speech science, as his interests were much more far ranging. For example, he invented the ophthalmoscope and provided mathematical proof of the conservation of energy. Nonetheless, Helmholtz helped us to understand some of the most important principles of the acoustics and physics of speech: that the puffs of air escaping through the vocal folds are the acoustic source of the voice, that the harmonics of the voice are resonated in the pharynx and oral cavities, and that vowels are recognized because of these distinctive resonances.

HENRY SWEET: DESCRIPTIVE PHONETICS

When Henry Sweet was born in England in 1845, Helmholtz was 24 years old and had already published his first paper on the connection between nerve cells and fibers. Sweet was to come to the study of speech by an entirely different route: an interest in languages and in phonetics. He was a teacher of English pronunciation and served as the model for George Bernard Shaw's Henry Higgins in the play *Pygmalion*, later to be adapted as Lerner and Loewe's musical *My Fair Lady*. Sweet graduated from Balliol College at Oxford, but partly because he obtained a low grade in "Greats," the examinations, he was never made a professor in philology and was more appreciated in Germany than in his own country. He was influenced by the German school of philology, by the impressive work in phonetics done in India, and by a phonetic transcription system called Visible Speech, which was developed by Alexander Melville Bell for educating the deaf. In 1877 Sweet wrote of his adaptation of Visible Speech (which he called "Broad Romic") as follows: ". . . I use. . . 'Broad Romic' as a kind of algebraic notation, each letter representing a group of similar sounds." The idea that a family of sounds, operating together in a language, may be distinguished from the individual sounds as spoken was new. Thus, he may be said to have been the first to hit upon the concept of the phoneme, although the word itself was not coined by him. Sweet's symbol system eventually led to the International Phonetic Alphabet (see Appendix 1). With the publication of his *Handbook of Phonetics* in 1877, he established England as the European birthplace of the science of phonetics. Despite his obvious preeminence in England in the field of phonetics, Sweet was not appointed in 1876 to the Chair of Comparative Philology at University College, London and was passed over again in 1885 as a candidate for Merton Professorship of English Language and Literature at Oxford. The final blow came in 1901 when he was denied the Professorship of Comparative Philology at Oxford. Linguistic scholars in Europe were astonished at the lack of academic recognition given Sweet in England. He was merely appointed a Reader in Phonetics at Oxford, a position that was, however, created especially for him.

Unlike the calm, reserved Helmholtz, Sweet was bitter and sarcastic. His scholarship and writings continued at full pace, despite his disappointments, and he published *A History of English Sounds* in 1874, revised in 1888, and *A Primer of Phonetics* with descriptions of each articulation in 1890. An early member of the Philological Society in London, the Society finally recognized his great contribution to the study of descriptive phonetics in the presidential address given by Christopher L. Wrenn in 1946, 34 years after Sweet's death.

ALEXANDER GRAHAM BELL: TEACHING THE DEAF

In 1847, only 2 years after the birth of Henry Sweet in England, Alexander Graham Bell was born in Edinburgh. Later to be world renowned as the inventor of the telephone, he always considered himself to be a scientist and inventor by avocation, but a teacher of the deaf by vocation. His father, Alexander Melville Bell, was a speech teacher and elocutionist who lectured at the University of Edinburgh and wrote pamphlets and books on elocution. Alexander Melville's greatest achievement was the development of Visible Speech (Fig. 2.2), originally a system of symbols representing the articulation underlying each speech sound. The tongue was represented by a horseshoe-shaped symbol, its position indicating the most active part of the tongue. With additional symbols for lip ac-

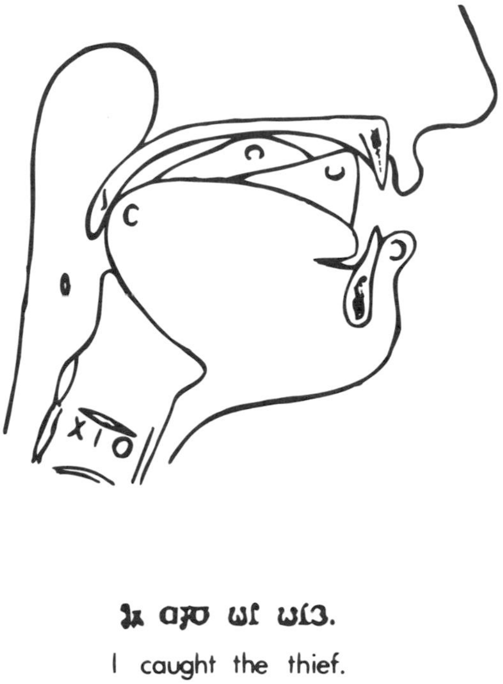

Figure 2.2 Simple utterance as represented in Bell's visible speech with a schematic drawing of the parts of the vocal tract involved in various sounds. Adapted from a figure in A. G. Bell's *English Visible Speech in Twelve Lessons*, 1895. Bell wrote this book to popularize his father's transcription system.

tivity and phonation, any speech sound could be represented visually. Alexander Graham Bell spent much of his life instructing teachers in the use of his father's system for describing speech production.

As a child, Alexander, then called Aleck, was extremely musical and curious about nature, but uninterested in formal studies. At 15, Aleck was called to London to live with his 70-year-old grandfather, also named Alexander, a teacher of public speaking, who instructed stutterers and those suffering with other impediments of speech. Under the guidance of his grandfather, Aleck learned how to apply himself to serious study, to be independent in the control of his own finances, to recite passages from Shakespeare's plays, and to dress "like a gentleman."

Back in Edinburgh a year later, he started his long career of teaching while he was still a student, first at Weston House at Elgin, then at Edinburgh University. Unaware that he was repeating the experiments of Helmholtz, Aleck discovered the resonances of the vocal tract cavities by snapping his finger against his throat and cheeks as he assumed various vocal tract positions. He also repeated the experiment of determining the frequencies of the resonators by vibrating tuning forks in front of his mouth as he assumed different vowel positions.

Having lost Aleck's two brothers to illness, the family emigrated to Canada for Alexander Melville's retirement when Aleck was 23. In Great Britain, Aleck had gained a reputation as an outstanding teacher of speech to the deaf, using his father's Visible Speech method. In America, he continued teaching the deaf and trained teachers in schools for the deaf to use the system. He came into contact with the scientific community in Boston, started work on his many ideas for inventions, and in 1876, shouted the famous sentence—"Mr. Watson, come here. I want to see you."—that his assistant, Thomas Watson, heard and understood through the receiver of the first telephone, installed between Bell's laboratory and his bedroom down the hall.

In 1877, Bell married Mabel Hubbard, the deaf daughter of Gardiner Hubbard, one of his partners in the newly established Bell Telephone Company. They returned briefly to England to promote the telephone and Visible Speech for the deaf, but the family, which eventually included two daughters, settled in Washington during the winters and at their large estate in Nova Scotia during the summers. Although Bell made many profitable inventions, he always considered his work for the deaf to be paramount. He established the Volta Bureau, a center of information about deafness, developed the audiometer for testing hearing, and continued to promote Visible Speech. Throughout his life, he was sleepless by night, preferring to sleep late into the morning. By working at night, he could be alone and more productive during his most active years. Basically a solitary man himself, Alexander Graham Bell helped other people to communicate with one another, even those who could not hear.

R. H. STETSON: SPEECH PHYSIOLOGY

Raymond Herbert Stetson provides an instructive example of a scientist whose current reputation is based more on his pioneering efforts in the development of methodology and instrumentation than on the acceptance of his research findings. Stetson was a broadly educated man whose knowledge spanned a number of sciences (psychology, zoology, chemistry) and the humanities. He received his undergraduate degree from Oberlin College in 1893 and his doctorate in 1901 from Harvard University. He returned to Oberlin in 1909 as the head of the psychology department and remained there until his death in 1950.

Stetson devoted much of his career to developing and refining objective methods for measuring the movements of the respiratory mechanism and the articulators in speech production. In the early 1920s he visited France where he worked and studied with L'Abbé Rousselot, who is often described as the father of modern experimental phonetics. Upon his return to the United States, Stetson did much to advance Rousselot's work with the kymograph, a device invented by Rousselot that was used to record air flow, air pressure, and articulatory movements. In later years he adapted the oscillograph for use in making physiological measurements of speech, and, in fact, named his workplace at Oberlin College the Oscillograph Laboratory.

Rousselot's influence can also be found in Stetson's refinement of palatography, a technique used to specify and measure the points of contact between the tongue and the roof of the mouth in the articulation of speech sounds. He studied the acoustic and physiological nature of vowels and consonants and the distinctions between them, and conducted a number of important experiments on the physiological basis underlying the distinction between voiced and voiceless consonants. His writings appeared in many of the important journals of his day, and ranged from studies of metrics and poetics to phonology.

Stetson's most well-known research concerned the nature of the syllable, both with regard to its production and its structure. In his *Motor Phonetics* (1928, rev., 1951) he posited the existence of a chest pulse as the basis for the production of syllables. Subsequent research has led to general rejection of his findings with regard to the chest pulse, and, as this was generally considered his most significant formulation with regard to speech production, has left Stetson with the label of "the brilliant scientist who was wrong."

It is a pity that so much emphasis has been placed on the failure of Stetson's theory, for it has surely directed attention away from a great deal of research and writing in which he made significant contributions to our knowledge of the production of speech and language. Virtually all of his research findings, right or wrong, were and are important because of the subsequent important studies and instrumental advances they engendered. It is for this reason that Stetson is still respected as a speech scientist and that he is remembered as the most important of the researchers who provided a modern scientific basis for the study of speech production in North America.

HOMER W. DUDLEY: ELECTRONIC SYNTHESIS OF CONTINUOUS SPEECH

The science of speech has benefited from the contribution of a psychophysicist in Helmholtz, a phonetician/linguist in Sweet, a speech pathologist in Bell, a physiological psychologist in Stetson, and an electrical engineer in the person of Homer Dudley. Dudley was a pioneer in speech synthesis, making machines that could produce speech-like sounds. In the 18th and 19th centuries, speech had been produced artificially by mechanical manipulation of artificial heads and mechanisms designed to simulate the lungs, larynx, and vocal tract of a speaker, but speech synthesis, as we know it, had to await the 20th century arrival of electronic circuits. It was Dudley's invention, called the Voder, built in 1937 and 1938 at Bell Telephone Laboratories, that first synthesized continuous speech by electric circuits.

Homer Dudley had started his career in Pennsylvania, where his family had moved from Virginia when he was a schoolboy. His father was a preacher and upon moving to Pennsylvania, his parents gave lessons to pupils who were interested in the classics, in other academic subjects, and in studying for the ministry. Dudley graduated from high school early. On his first teaching assignment, he taught the 5th, 6th, 7th and 8th grades in one room; his second position was that of a high school teacher. Finding it difficult to keep discipline in the classroom, Dudley abandoned his plans to teach and started working his way through Pennsylvania State University where electrical engineering courses were being introduced into the college curriculum. Dudley joined the technical staff of Bell Telephone Laboratories, the engineering laboratory of Western Electric, then located in New York City. He remained working there for over 40 years, much of that time in the telephone transmission division.

Later on, he worked with Robert Riesz and others on the development of the Vocoder. The purpose of the Vocoder was to filter speech into 10 bands in such a way that the information could be transmitted over narrower bandwidths than were previously possible. After transmission, the channel information, along with a noise circuit for consonant sounds and a buzz circuit for voicing, was used to synthesize speech that closely resembled the original, except for some loss in voice quality. The Vocoder was demonstrated at the tercentennial celebration at Harvard and led to the celebrated "talking machine," the Voder, a Voice Operation Demonstrator. The Voder synthesizer was shown at the 1939 and 1940 World's Fairs (Fig. 2.3). It made recognizable speech sounds, at least if listeners were cued to know the sort of utterances to expect. The operator pushed a pedal for the voice or hiss source and pressed 10 keys to control the resonances. Special keys simulated the stop consonants such as /p/ or /t/. In the demonstrations, a dialogue would be conducted between a person and the Voder operated by a woman. Over 20 telephone operators were extensively trained to operate the machine during the World's Fair demonstrations. Unlike previous synthesizers, the Voder was based more closely upon the acoustics of speech rather than its articulation. Just as radio transmission is accomplished by modulating a carrier tone by the signal of interest (in FM, the frequency is modulated; in AM, the amplitude is modulated), Dudley conceived of speech as a carrier tone or sound source that is modulated by the movements of the vocal tract.

Homer Dudley's contributions to speech science were that he made explicit the carrier nature of speech, and he applied the carrier idea to specific principles for speech analysis and synthesis. These ideas underlie modern conceptualizations of the speech process.

FRANKLIN COOPER, ALVIN LIBERMAN, AND PIERRE DELATTRE: SPEECH PERCEPTION AND THE PATTERN PLAYBACK

Our discussion, up to this point, has been limited to pioneers in the study of speech production and acoustics. Little systematic work in speech perception was possible until speech scientists knew enough about the acoustics of speech to control acoustic parameters one at a time in testing listeners. The development of the sound spectrograph in the 1940s at Bell Laboratories by Ralph Potter and his colleagues provided an instrument that allowed investigators to conveniently analyze the frequencies represented in speech across time, producing a visual display called a spectrogram. With it came a sudden increase in information about the acoustics of speech. Speech perception questions remained: what aspects of the complex sound pattern of speech are important in listening to speech, and what aspects are less important? In order to find out, an engineer, a psychologist, and a linguist combined their talents at Haskins Laboratories, then in New York, to investigate the perception of speech.

Potter had conceived of the reverse of the sound spectrograph as a machine that could convert a visual input to sound. Franklin Cooper at Haskins saw that the development of such a pattern playback would provide a powerful instrument for the study of speech perception. Cooper, born and educated in Illinois, had received his doctorate in physics from Massa-

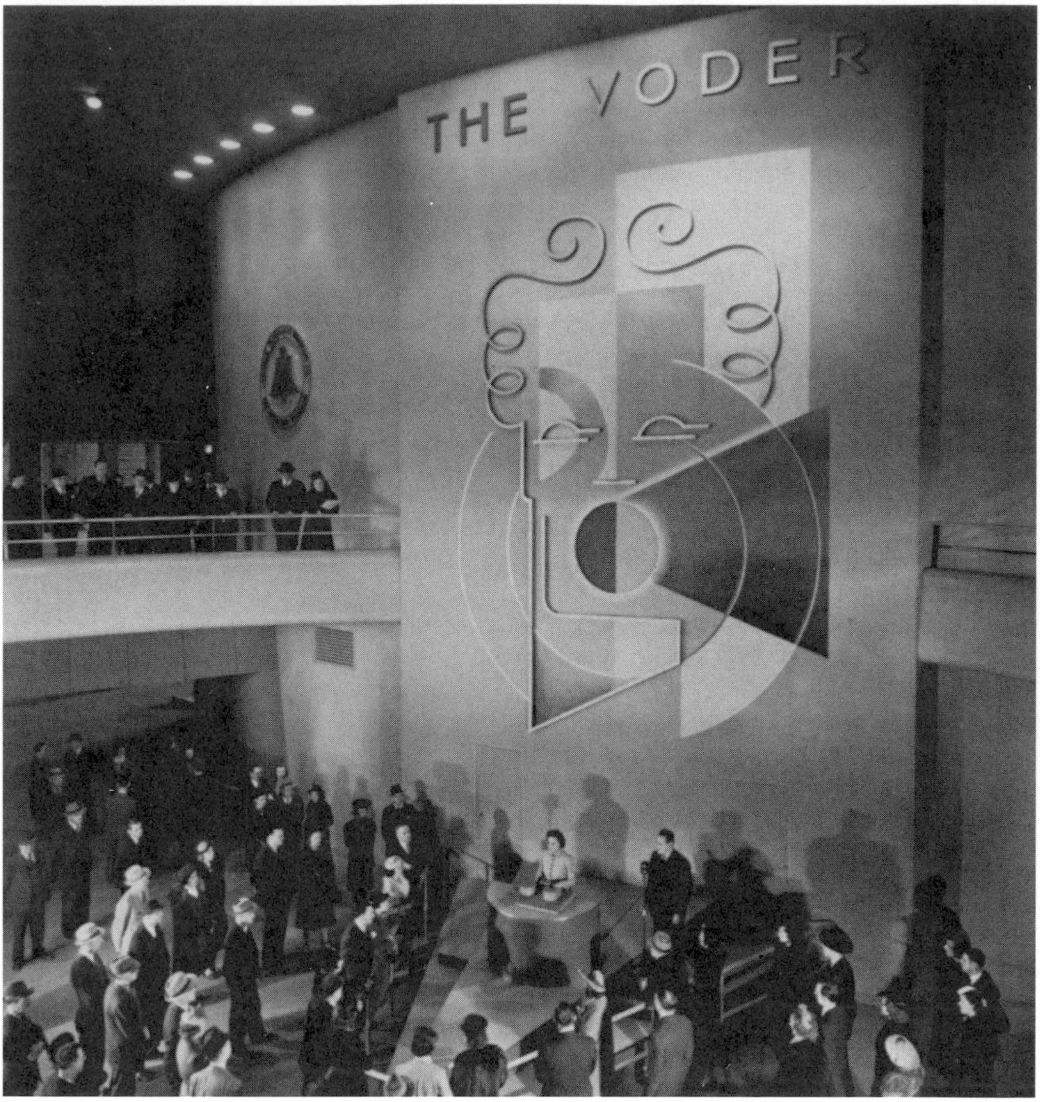

Figure 2.3 Bell Telephone demonstration of the Voder at the 1939 World's Fair. (Reproduced with permission of American Telephone and Telegraph Company.)

chusetts Institute of Technology in 1936. After a few years with General Electric Research Laboratories, in 1939, Cooper became Associate Research Director of Haskins Laboratories, where he remained as its president and director for 20 years. As part of his efforts to develop a reading machine for the blind, Cooper constructed a speech synthesizer called the Pattern Playback synthesizer (Fig. 2.4).

Alvin Liberman, a psychologist who received his bachelor and master of arts degrees at the University of Missouri and his doctorate at Yale, is a retired professor of psychology and linguistics at the University of Connecticut and at Yale. He joined Haskins Laboratories in 1944 and eventually succeeded Cooper as its president. Together with Cooper, he used the Pattern Playback to systematically vary the acoustic parameters of speech to determine the cues used in speech perception.

At the invitation of Cooper and Liberman, Pierre Delattre, a Frenchman by birth, joined the experimental work in speech perception conducted at Haskins during the 1950s. Delattre was an expert in French linguistics whose specialty was in teaching foreigners to master French phonetics. For 16 years he directed the French phonetics program held during summers at Middlebury College in Vermont. During much of this time, he was a member of the faculty at the University of Pennsylvania. He had a good eye for painting playback patterns and the patience to listen to their acoustic effects. He learned the rules for painting patterns for such sentences as "Oh, my aching back," and even composed a piece of synthesized music which he entitled "Scotch Plaid."

The collaboration of Cooper, Liberman, and Delattre lasted until Delattre's death and produced most of the early work in speech perception. The value of the Pattern Playback as an instrument for speech perception remained unsurpassed until computer-controlled synthesizers became available. The experimenter could see at a glance the whole acoustic pattern, could repeatedly hear how it sounded, and could easily modify it. Systematically varying an acoustic dimension thought to be important in perception, the investigators had listeners compare and label the synthesized stimuli. By such means, the Haskins group, which included many other investigators, demonstrated the role of linguistic experience upon speech

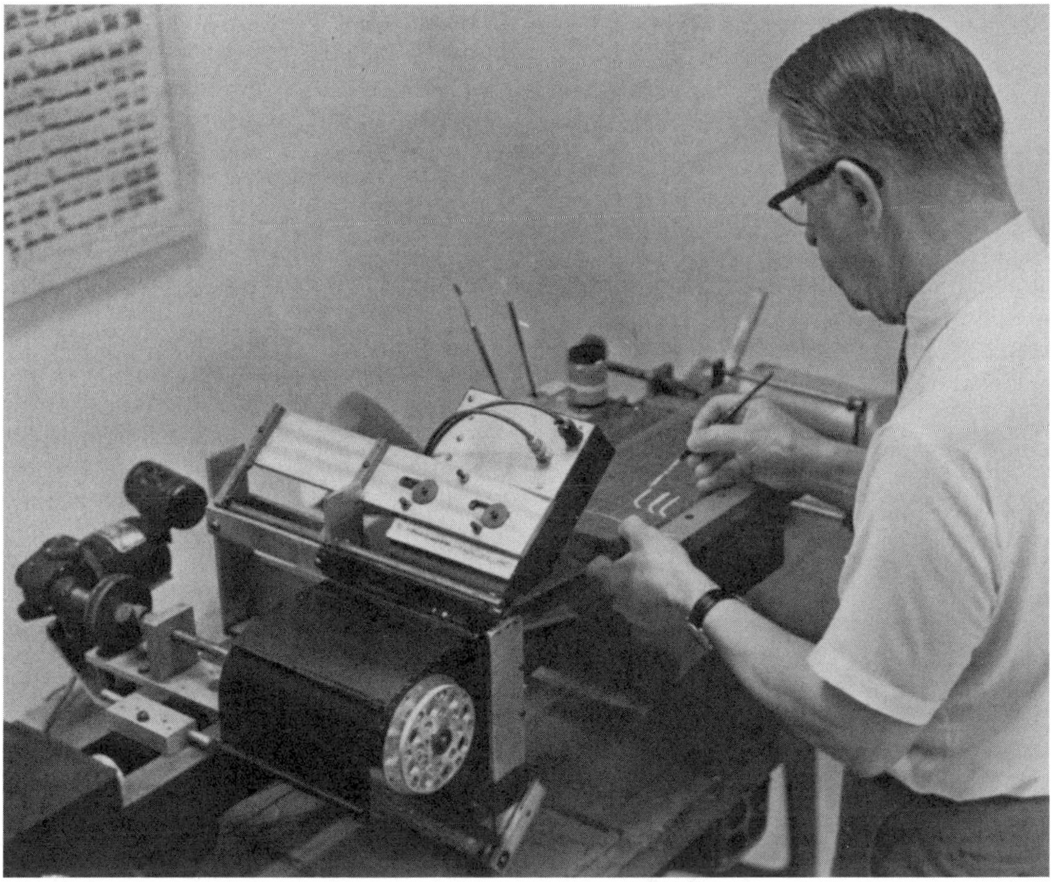

Figure 2.4 F. S. Cooper painting a syllable on the Pattern Playback synthesizer. Speech was synthesized by converting patterns painted on acetate film loops into acoustic signals by a photoelectric system (Haskins Laboratories).

perception and the role of context in the perception of individual phonemes. While Haskins Laboratories pioneered in the systematic study of speech perception, we cite it chiefly because it is a good example of the point we are trying to emphasize: that the roads to speech science are many and varied. At Haskins today, there are engineers, linguists, speech pathologists, and psychologists, all of them interested in experimental phonetics or speech science.

SINCE THEN

In general, the experimental study of the acoustics of speech is ahead of the study of speech physiology. Based upon spectrographic analysis, that is, the analysis of the speech signal according to the various sound frequencies in its composition and upon systematic synthesis of speech, we now know a substantial amount about the acoustics of speech. This knowledge has made synthetic speech or talking machines possible. We know less about speech physiology from experimental studies, but work in this area is increasing rapidly through the efforts of many speech scientists at universities and laboratories throughout the United States and abroad. Speech perception research is currently branching out in many directions: infant and animal perception, the role of the cerebral hemispheres in perception, the role of context and linguistic experience in perception, the role of memory and attention, and investigations of the stages of processing involved in the perception of speech.

There are two overlapping methods of sharing research information in speech. One method is to attend and participate in conventions organized by professional organizations. The largest common meeting ground is at the fall and spring meetings of the Acoustical Society of America (ASA). Research papers are presented at these meetings and ideas are exchanged. Another arena for professional exchange is at the annual convention of the American Speech-Language-Hearing Association (ASHA). Speech scientists belong to many other professional organizations, state, national, and international. A prominent international association is the International Congress of Phonetic Sciences, which meets in a different country every 4 years.

The second forum for exchange of ideas and research is in the journals published by ASHA and ASA, the above mentioned national associations. ASA publishes the *Journal of the Acoustical Society of America*, usually called *JASA*. ASHA publishes one basic research journal, the *Journal of Speech and Hearing Research*, and other journals of clinical research. Many other journals include research on speech production, acoustics of speech, and speech perception. The *Journal of Phonetics*; *Language and Speech*; *Brain and Language*; *Perception and Psychophysics*; *Phonetica*; *Clinical Linguistics and Phonetics*; and the *Journal of Voice* are names of but a few of these journals. Theoretical articles are sometimes published in *Psychological Review*, and a few innovative research studies appear in the journal of the American Association for the Advancement of Science, *Science*. Individual scientists often will send copies of their own articles on written request.

Speech laboratories exchange progress reports or working papers as another means of information dissemination. Widely read are the *Quarterly Progress Report* issued by the Research Laboratory of Electronics at Massachusetts Institute of Technology in Cambridge, Massachusetts, the *Speech Transmission Quarterly Progress and Status Report* issued by the Royal Institute of Technology (KTH) in Stockholm, Sweden; and the *Status Report on Speech Research* issued by Haskins Laboratories in New Haven, Connecticut. Many universities also distribute working papers in speech science written by faculty and students.

The future of speech science lies in work that will aim to show the ways in which speech production and speech perception may interact and in work that will lead to automatic speech recognition as well as synthesis. In the following four chapters, we shall survey some of what is now known about acoustics, speech production, and speech perception.

REFERENCES

Bell, A. G., *The Mechanism of Speech*. New York: Funk & Wagnalls Co., 1908.

Bell, A. G., *English Visible Speech in Twelve Lessons*. Washington, D.C.: Volta Bureau, 1895.

Bell, A. M., *Visible Speech: The Science of Universal Alphabetics; or Self-Interpreting Physiological Letters for the Printing and Writing of all Languages in one Alphabet; elucidated by Theoretical Explanations, Tables, Diagrams, and Examples*. London: Simpkin, Marshall, & Co., 1867.

Bronstein, A. J., Raphael, L. J., and Stevens, C. J. (Eds.), *Biographical Dictionary of the Phonetic Sciences*. New York: The Press of Lehman College, 1977.

Bruce, R.V., *Bell: Alexander Graham Bell and the Conquest of Solitude*. Boston: Little, Brown & Co., 1973.

Delattre, P. C., Liberman, A. M., and Cooper, F.S., Acoustic Loci and Transitional Cues for Consonants. *J. Acoust. Soc. Am. 27*, 1955, 769–773.

Dudley, H., The Carrier Nature of Speech. *Bell Syst. Tech. J. 19*, 1940, 495–515. Reprinted in *Speech Synthesis: Benchmark Papers in Acoustics*. J.L. Flanagan and L. R. Rabiner (Eds.) Stroudsburg, PA: Dowden, Hutchinson & Ross., Inc., 1973, pp. 22–42.

Dudley, H., Riesz, R. R., and Watkins, S. A., A Synthetic Speaker. *J. Franklin Inst. 227*, 1939, 739–764.

Helmholtz, H. L. F., *Die Lehre von den Tonempfindungen als physiologische Grundlage für die Theorie der Musik*. Braunschweig: F. Vieweg und sohn, 1863. Translated, *On the Sensations of Tone as a Physiological Basis for the Theory of Music*. 2nd English translation from the 4th German edition of 1877 by A. S. Ellis. New York: Dover Publications, 1954.

Koenig, W., Dunn, H. K., and Lacy, L. Y., The Sound Spectrograph. *J. Acoust. Soc. Am. 17*, 1946, 19–49.

Liberman, A. M., Cooper, F. S., Shankweiler, D. P., and Studdert-Kennedy, M., Perception of the Speech Code. *Psychol. Rev. 74*, 1967, 431–461. Also in *Human Communication: A Unified View*. E. E. David, Jr., and P. B. Denes (Eds.) New York: McGraw-Hill, 1972, pp. 13–50.

McKendrick, J. G., *Hermann Ludwig Ferdinand von Helmholtz*. New York: Longmans, Green & Co., 1899.

Stetson, R. H., *Motor Phonetics: A Study of Speech Movements in Action*. Amsterdam: North Holland, 1951. Revised by S. Kelso and K. Munhall, San Diego: Singular Publishing, 1988.

Sweet, H., *Handbook of Phonetics*. Oxford: Clarendon Press, 1877.

Sweet H., *History of English Sounds*. Oxford: Clarendon Press, 1874, revised 1888.

Sweet, H., *A Primer of Phonetics*. Oxford: Clarendon Press, 1890.

Wrenn, C. L., Henry Sweet: Presidential Address delivered to the Philological Society on Friday, 10th May, 1946. Reprinted in *Portraits of Linguists*. T. A. Sebeok (Ed.), Bloomington, IN: Indiana University Press, 1966, pp. 512–532.

3
Acoustics

"Holla your name to the reverberate hills,
And make the babbling gossip of the air
Cry out."
William Shakespeare, *Twelfth Night*

The study of sound is called acoustics. Since speech is a continuously changing stream of sound, it is necessary to have a clear understanding of the nature of sound in general, before one can fully understand either the production of speech sounds by speakers or the reception of speech sounds by listeners.

The first thing to understand about sound is that it has no substance; it is not a thing. It has no mass or weight, but it is rather a set of movements or a disturbance. A sound wave can exist as a disturbance in a gas such as air, in liquid such as water, or in a solid such as a pipe or railroad track. The medium of transmitting speech sounds is usually air; therefore, sound in air will be emphasized in this chapter.

One of the problems in the first attempt at understanding sound is the fact of its invisibility. Since the molecules of air are not visible to the human eye, the waves of disturbance moving through air cannot be seen. A second problem in understanding sound is the fact that most sounds are complex. This results in a complex pattern of air particle disturbance. To surmount these barriers of understanding, one must make visible the invisible, and one must start with the simplest of all sound patterns, the pure tone.

PURE TONE: AN EXAMPLE OF SIMPLE HARMONIC MOTION

One seldom hears a pure tone in the world of sounds. Most of the sounds we hear, the street noises, the sounds of speech, and even the sounds of music are complex in that they consist of many tones or frequencies heard simultaneously. A *pure tone* has only one frequency of vibration. It is the result of a vibration that repeats itself at a constant number of cycles per second. The number of cycles per second is termed its *frequency*. Some musical instruments are narrowly tuned and vibrate at few frequencies, but to achieve the effect of only one frequency, special metal tuning forks (Fig. 3.1) are forged that will vibrate mainly at a specified frequency. This vibration produces essentially a pure tone, the simplest of all sounds and therefore the easiest to describe.

The tuning fork, when struck and set into vibration, moves in *simple harmonic motion*. The tines, or prongs, of the fork move back and forth a fixed number of times per second no matter how hard it is struck to set it into motion. The initial impact will force both tines of the fork to move away from their rest position (Fig. 3.2). Because of the elasticity of the material, however, the tines will come back to their original rest positions. Elasticity is the restoring force that causes particles in an elastic medium to bounce back when displaced. Push your finger into the fatty part of your arm or leg and you will find that the tissue restores itself quickly. In simple harmonic motion, however, the movement does not stop with the elastic recoil of the tines. That is, the tines of the tuning fork will continue to move through their rest positions because of inertia. *Inertia* is the tendency for motion or lack of motion to continue. If something is not moving, it takes less energy for it to remain motionless than to start moving because of inertia. On the other hand, if something is moving, it is easier for it to keep moving than to stop, again because of inertia. When we continue to watch television after a program that interests us is finished, even though the following program is uninteresting, we are demonstrating a behavioral form of inertia. The tines of the tuning fork continue to move after their elastic recoil to their original rest positions, but they continue only so far, for the velocity gradually decreases because of the resistance of the elastic force. Then they return once more to the resting point, again because of elasticity, and the cycle repeats itself.

We should point out that the forces of elasticity and inertia are almost always simultaneously at work, although at any given moment one of them may be dominant. Elasticity causes the decrease in the velocity of movement of the tines as they approach their points of maximum displacement. The more the tines move away from their rest positions, the greater the elastic force becomes, until it overcomes the force of inertia and the tines come

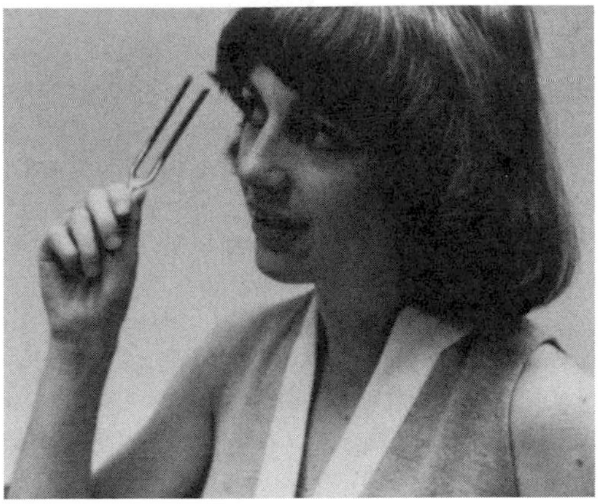

Figure 3.1. A tuning fork will produce a pure tone (Temple University).

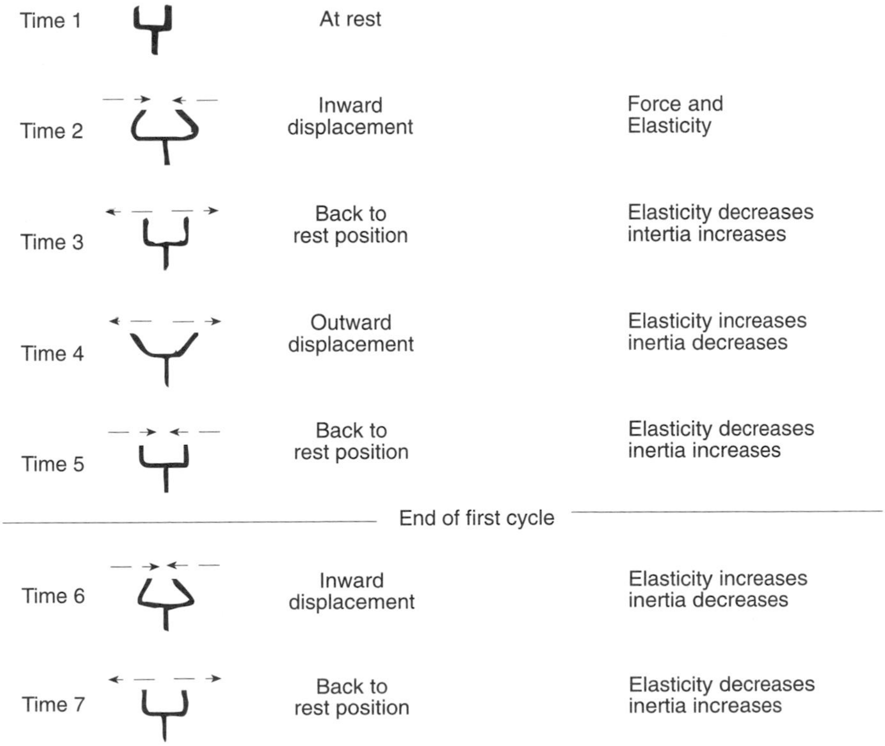

Figure 3.2. Tuning fork displacements in one and one-half cycles of vibration.

to their momentary rest. Then, as we have said, the elastic force begins to move the tines back toward their rest positions. This movement imparts an inertial force to the tines, which increases as they move away from each other and which causes them to overshoot their rest positions. The overshoot re-introduces the elastic force (which was neutralized at the rest position) that continues to increase again as the tines move toward each other. The repeated cycles of movement are thus generated by a simultaneous interplay of the two forces and not by their alternation.

We have described one cycle of vibration in simple harmonic motion, but it needs to be illustrated further for clarity. Figure 3.2 illustrates the motion and positions of the tines of a tuning fork during its first one and one-half cycles of vibration.

The Swing Analogy: Example of Velocity Gradation in Simple Harmonic Motion

Consider the *simple harmonic motion* (*SHM*) of a swing hanging from the branch of a tree. When you displace the swing from its resting position by pulling it back, it not only returns to its original position but goes past it. This back and forth movement, although different in some respects, is analogous to the movement of a tuning fork and to the movement of air particles that are set into vibration during the transmission of a sound. The example of the swing illustrates an important property of simple harmonic motion, which is the continuous manner in which the displaced object changes velocity. *Velocity* is the speed, in a certain direction, of an object; in this case, the swing. In Figure 3.3, the spot on the ground over which the swing hangs when at rest is labeled *2*. Consider that a given force will displace the swing to *3*; then it will swing back and forth between *1* and *3* until its motion dies down. While swinging, the velocity changes, gradually diminishing as it approaches *1* and *3*, where it drops for an instant to *0* before changing direction. Maximum velocity is reached each time the swing passes over the resting place. Since the swing comes to a momentary standstill at each end of the excursion, the maximum *acceleration*, which is the rate of change in velocity, is at these extreme points where the swing changes direction.

If the movement of the swing were graphed as it changes position in time, it would look like Figure 3.4.

The velocity is graded, with zero velocity and maximum acceleration at *B, D, F, H, J,* and *L* and maximum velocity at the zero crossings *C, E, G, I,* and *K*. Notice, too, that the motion is dying down gradually because of the loss of energy from friction. That is, the points of maximum displacement are closer together—less

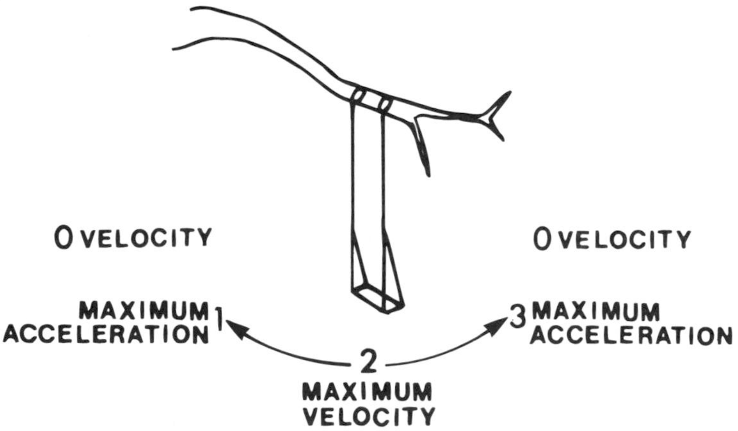

Figure 3.3. Simple harmonic motion (SHM) of a swing period. The swing is at zero (*0*) velocity at the extremes of its excursion, as it changes direction, and at maximum velocity at *2*, the middle of the excursion.

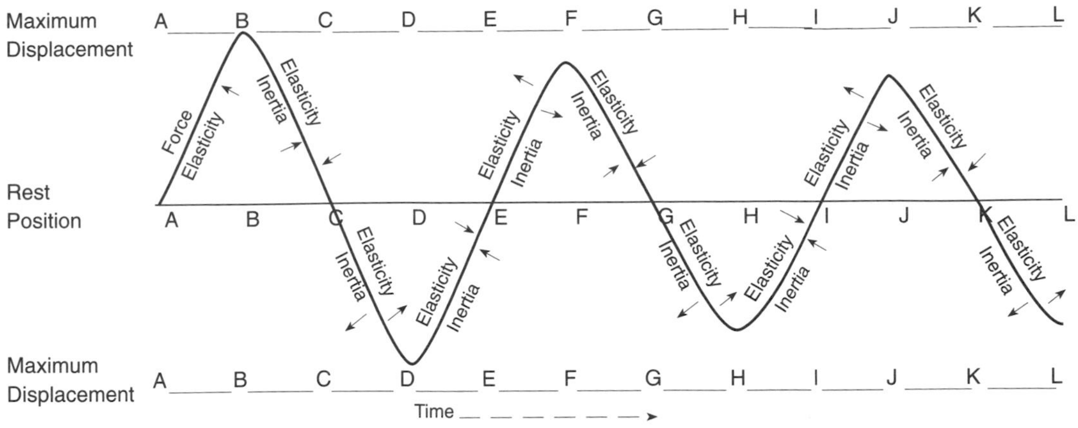

Figure 3.4. Waveform produced by graphing SHM of a swing.

distant from the rest point—on each successive cycle. This decrease in the amplitude of displacement over time is called *damping*. Although the excursion of the swing is dying down, the frequency remains constant. Frequency is the number of cycles per second, and as shown in Figure 3.4, the time it takes for the swing to go back and forth one complete cycle (*A* to *E*) is equal to the time it takes to complete the second cycle (*E* to *I*). The time taken for each cycle is termed the *period*. If the frequency were 20 Hz, then the period would be 1/20 of a second or 50 ms. The graph of a simple harmonic motion is the same as a graph of a *sine wave*. The pattern is simple because there is only one frequency of vibration. It repeats itself (until it damps out) and is therefore periodic.

Particle Movement in Sound

In the sound of a pure tone, the individual air particles move in SHM in response to the movement of the pure tone vibrator in SHM. They do not, however, move along an arc as a pendulum or swing does. Air particles moving in response to a pure tone vibrator move in SHM but in the direction of the wave propagation, as we shall illustrate further on in the chapter.

Practice moving in SHM. Place your pencil or finger on the middle dot marked *B* in Figure 3.5 *a*. Move it to *C*, then *A*, then *C*, and continue at a fixed, relatively slow frequency without stopping. Try moving your finger at the same frequency but with a larger excursion from the resting place using Figure 3.5 *b* to set the range.

The movements you make with your pencil or finger could be displayed as an amplitude-by-time graph called a *waveform* (Fig. 3.6).

Return to Figure 3.5 and practice SHM at a constant frequency for both *a* and *b*, but this time make the movements at a relatively high frequency (an increased number of cycles per second). The waveforms would then look more like those in Figure 3.7.

These movements back and forth over the resting place are magnified versions of the movement of a single air particle when a pure tone is sounded. If a tuning fork specified to vibrate at 440 Hz (the A above middle C on the piano) were sounded in the middle of the room, every molecule of air in the room would soon move in place. Each particle would initially move away from the tuning fork (because of the force exerted against it by a neighboring particle), then back to the resting place (because of elasticity), then further toward the fork (because of inertia), then back to the resting place (elasticity), and so on as long as the vibration lasted. Each particle would complete 440 of these cycles during each second.

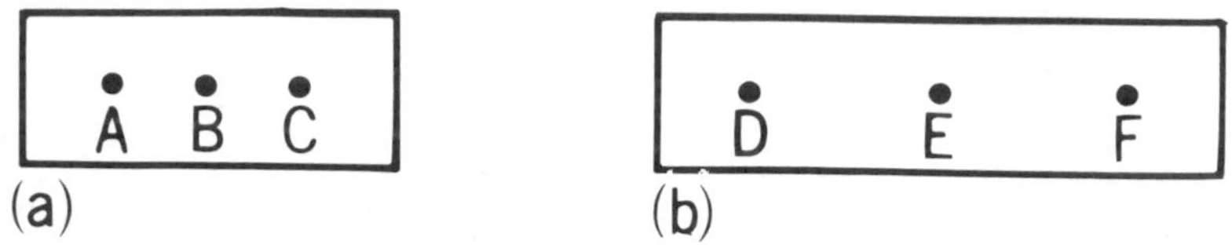

Figure 3.5. Simulate SHM by moving finger rhythmically from *B* to *C* to *A* to *C*, oscillating with gradually and continuously changing velocity. Repeat with *EFDF* at same frequency.

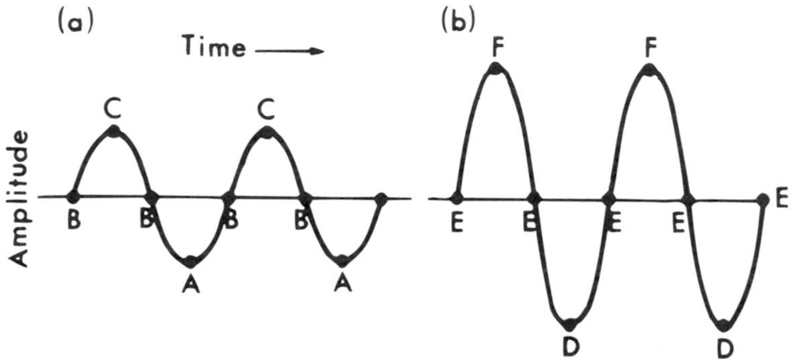

Figure 3.6. Waveform of SHM traced in Fig 3.5; *a* and *b* differ in amplitude but are equal in frequency.

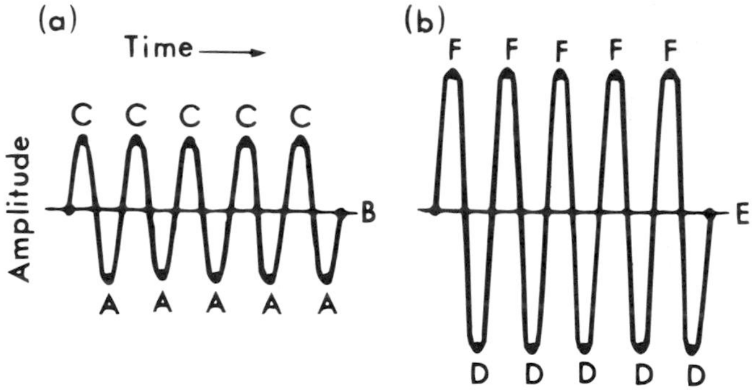

Figure 3.7. Waveforms of a higher frequency than represented in Fig 3.6; *a* and *b* differ in amplitude but are equal in frequency.

Pressure Wave Movement in Sound

We have been analyzing the movement of individual particles during a pure tone stimulus. If each particle is moving in place, how does the disturbance move from one location to another? Particles surrounding the vibrator start moving before particles further away from the sound source. The molecules of air oscillating in SHM disturb adjacent molecules and thus the disturbance is transmitted away from the source. This disturbance takes the form of a pressure wave radiating outward, much as the ripples seen emanating from a point in still water after a pebble has been tossed. Since the pure tone is periodic, the pressure wave is repeated and is followed by evenly spaced pressure waves. Figure 3.8 is a schematic representation of 10 individual air molecules. At Time 1, before the pure tone vibrator is set into motion, the particles are at rest, equidistant from one another. At Time 2, the outward movement of one of the tines of the tuning fork has forced Particle A to move away from the fork approaching Particle B. At Time 3, Particle A has bounced back to its resting place because air is an elastic medium, but Particle B has been

```
     A B C D E F G H I J
  1  •  x  ⊡  ★  o  ◻  •  x  ⊡  ★
  2  •x  ⊡  ★  o  ◻  •  x  ⊡  ★
  3  •  x⊡  ★  o  ◻  •  x  ⊡  ★
  4 •  x   ⊡★ o  ◻  •  x  ⊡  ★
  5  •x  ⊡   ★o ◻  •  x  ⊡  ★
  6  •x⊡   ★  o◻  •  x  ⊡  ★
  7  •  x⊡★  o    ◻•  x  ⊡  ★
  8 •  x  ⊡★o  ◻   •x  ⊡  ★
  9  •x  ⊡   ★o◻  •  •   x⊡  ★
 10  •x⊡   ★  o◻•  x    ⊡★
 11  •  x⊡★  o   ◻•x  ⊡   ★
 12•  x  ⊡★o  ◻   •x⊡   ★
 13  •x  ⊡   ★o◻  •   x⊡★
 14  •x⊡   ★  o◻•  x    ⊡★
```

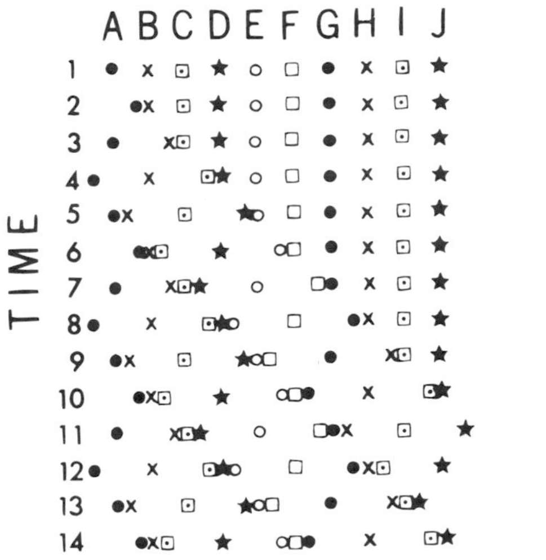

Figure 3.8. Schematic drawing of 10 air particles in SHM at 14 moments in time. The sound source is conceived to be to the *left*. Pressure waves move to the *right*. Time runs from *top* to *bottom*. Notice that although the pressure wave, indicated by a clustering of three adjacent particles, moves from *left* to *right*, each individual particle moves relatively little around a rest position.

displaced by the influence (during Time 2) of the impinging Particle A. Notice that as time proceeds, areas of *compression*, in which molecules are closer together, alternate with areas of *rarefaction*, in which molecules are further apart. For example, in Time 7 a high pressure area formed by the juxtaposition of Particles B, C, and D, is surrounded by relatively low pressure areas. By Time 10, the first pressure wave has moved further away from the sound source and now consists of Particles E, F, and G. At the same time, a second pressure wave is emanating from the vibrator and consists of Particles A, B, and C.

It is helpful to visualize compression waves moving through a medium by a simple demonstration using coiled wire. A toy called a Slinky serves well. Spreading the coil along a table top between your hands, hold one hand steady and move the other back and forth in SHM until waves can be seen to flow through the coil. Observe that the waves move in the same direction as the hand movement. This type of wave, in which particle movement is in the same direction as wave movement, is called

a *longitudinal wave*. Sound waves are longitudinal whether in air or in liquid. Waves seen radiating from tossing a stone or dipping a finger into water are called *transverse waves* because although the waves move out from the source of the disturbance, the water particles move at right angles to the wave: up and down, as any cork-watching fisherman will attest.

If all the air molecules in a room were colored green, a tuning fork vibrating in the center of the room would be surrounded by a globe of relatively dark green (an area of compression of air particles) that would move away from the vibrator. Although each particle moves back and forth in place, the disturbance moves throughout the room. Each compression area is followed by a pale green area (rarefaction area), which in turn is followed by another compression area (see Fig. 3.9). The alternating areas of compression and rarefaction constitute a pressure wave that moves away from the tuning fork in all directions and that can be represented as a sine wave in the same way as the motion of individual particles (see Fig 3.10).

Waveforms are common representations

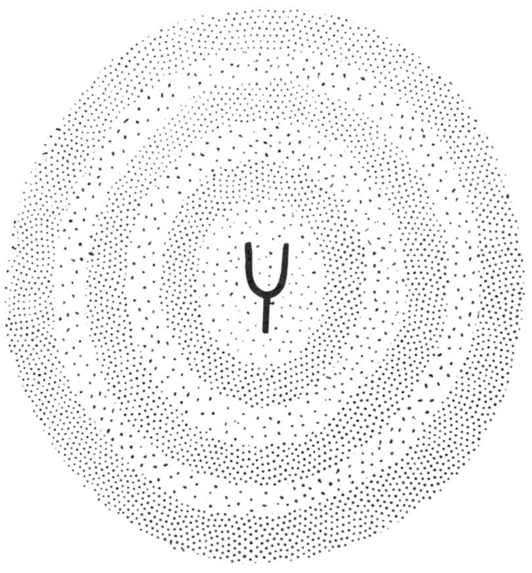

Figure 3.9. Pressure wave emanating from a sound source. (The areas of compression should encircle the vibrator as a globe, a representation not indicated in this two-dimensional figure.)

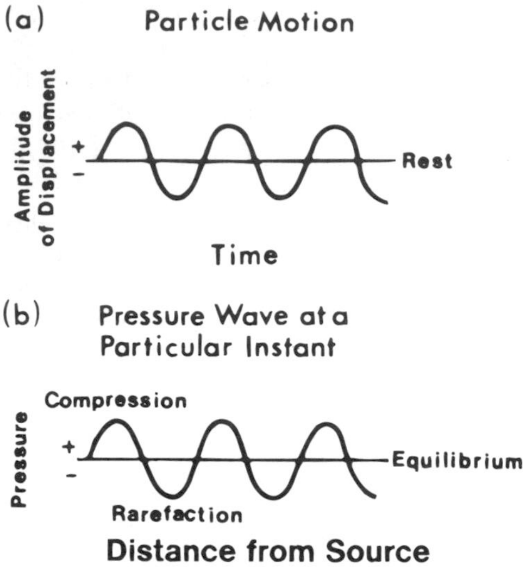

Figure 3.10. Waveform of a pure tone *(a)* and a graph of pressure variations as a function of distance from the source *(b)*. The waveforms look alike although they have different coordinates.

of sound signals. A waveform is a display of how amplitude varies over time and therefore represents particle motion as in Figure 3.10a, but it is understood that it also represents the pressure variation in the medium as a whole as in Figure 3.10b.

A cathode ray oscilloscope is an instrument that can display any sound as a waveform. Remember that the movement of any particular particle, were it visible, would not look like that waveform. Rather, the waveform is an abstract representation of the displacement from rest that the particle undergoes during a certain time span. The *amplitude* of displacement indicates the intensity or power of the sound, and by convention, the *ordinate* (Y or vertical axis) of a waveform often indicates units of intensity. Time is represented along the *abscissa* (X or horizontal axis) again by convention.

Essential Constituents of Sound

Are these periodic pressure waves sound? It is the old "tree in the forest" question. If a tree falls in a forest with no one about to hear it, is there a sound? We know that the prerequisites for sound include an energy source, a vibrating source that produces a disturbance, and a medium through which the disturbance travels. To complete the definition of sound, the disturbance must be potentially audible. It must be capable of producing corresponding vibrations in some receiving ear, but the ears of different creatures are tuned to different sounds. Bats hear sounds of extremely high frequency that are inaudible to the human ear. Although some dictionaries limit the definition of sound to those vibratory disturbances audible to man, this seems unnecessarily restrictive. Yet there are some vibrations that are inaudible to any creature on Earth because of their extremely low intensity. Can the disturbances that result from these vibrations be called sound? That seems too extreme.

Let us arbitrarily define *sound,* then, as an audible disturbance of a medium produced by a source. The source could be a guitar string energized by the pluck of a finger or human vocal folds energized by air from the lungs. The medium could be gas, liquid, or solid; any elastic medium can carry an acoustic signal. The disturbance must be such that it could cause corresponding vibrations in a receiver. The receiver could be the auditory system of any creature to whom the signal is audible. According to our definition, then, the falling tree can create an audible disturbance, which, even if it is not heard, could be called a sound.

Interference Patterns

It is remarkable that the air can be filled with many sounds, all of which can be transmitted simultaneously. Because air molecules vibrate in place, they can be responsive to many signals at once. It does happen, however, that signals of the same frequency can interfere with one another. This occurs when the frequency is generated from two sources or, more often, when the signal is reflected from a barrier such as a wall to compete, in a sense, with itself.

The waveforms of two signals having a common frequency sum in a straightforward way. The resulting summed waveform depends upon the phase relationship between the signals. In order to understand phase relation-

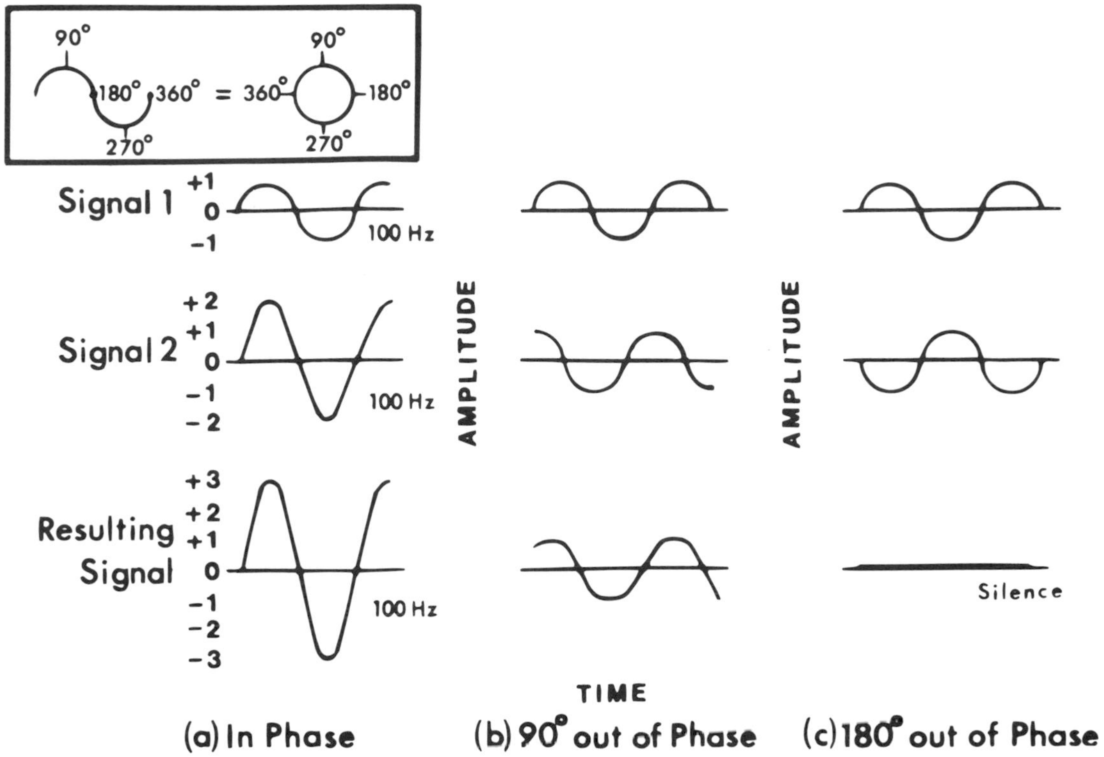

Figure 3.11. Results of adding two pure tones (*Signal 1* and *Signal 2*) differing in phase and amplitude, but of the same frequency. In all cases, the *Resulting Signal* will be a pure tone of the same frequency, but phase and amplitude will vary. The addition of two pure tones of the same frequency and amplitude but 180° out of phase will produce silence, as shown in *Column c.*

ships, it helps to conceive of a cycle of vibration as a circle. Every circle has a total of 360° (degrees), so that one-half of a cycle would be 180°, one-fourth of a cycle would be 90°, and three-fourths 270°. Although sine waves are not actually made up of semi-circles, we have depicted them as circles twisted open in the middle at the top of Figure 3.11 in order to illustrate the concept of phase.

If two signals of the same frequency are *in phase,* their pressure waves crest and trough at the same time, and, if their amplitudes are identical, the sum of the signals will have twice the amplitude of each component signal. Figure 3.11 illustrates pure tone signals that are in phase, 90° out of phase, and 180° out of phase. When signals are 90° out of phase, one signal is one-fourth of a cycle ahead of the other. At each instant, the amplitudes of the two waveforms are simply added. When two acoustic signals having the same frequency and amplitude of vibration are 180° out of phase, the result is silence, for each particle receives two equal forces in opposite directions. Each particle then remains at rest.

The problem of interference patterns is especially acute in the design of concert halls, requiring the services of people trained in architectural acoustics. Unless halls are designed with acoustic considerations, sounds produced in them may reflect from the hard walls in such a way that they will *reverberate* excessively, which means the sound is overly prolonged as it bounces back and forth. This prevents listeners from adequately hearing the next sound. Also, because of the interference patterns, sounds will be louder in some places and softer in others. The presence of a large audience dressed in sound-absorbing clothes helps the situation, as do absorbent materials used as wall and ceiling coverings, floor coverings, and chair upholstery. On the other hand, too much absorption dulls the power of the sounds by causing insufficient reverberation. The right balance is difficult to achieve, yet none of us wants to have the misfortune of sitting in an acoustically dead spot in an auditorium where interference patterns caused by reflected sound and sound absorption create partial sound cancellation.

COMPLEX TONES

Most sound sources, unlike the tuning fork, produce vibrations that are complex. Rather than vibrating in SHM, they move in a complex manner that generates more than one frequency. When these movements are graphed, a more complex waveform replaces the sine wave of the pure tone. To understand the derivation of a *complex tone,* simply add two sine waves of different frequencies. It is important to remember that many sounds of the same frequency and in phase may be added (as in Fig. 3.11), but the result will always be a sine wave: a representation of a pure tone. If two or more pure tones of different frequencies are added, however, the result will be a complex tone. Figure 3.12 shows an instance of the addition of pure tones to form a complex tone. There are two kinds of complex sound waves:

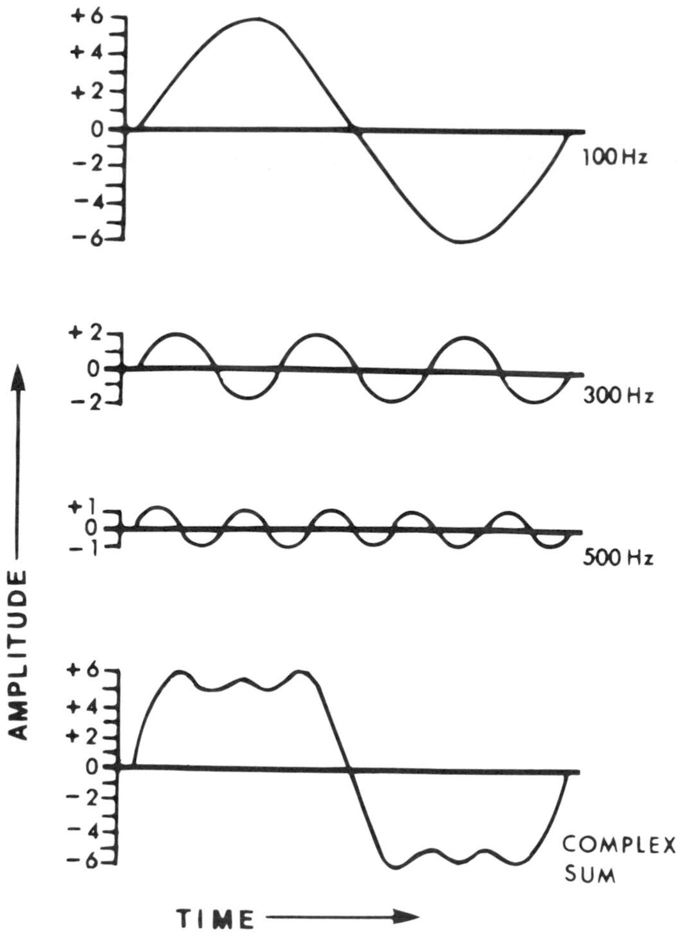

Figure 3.12. Waveform of a complex tone derived from three pure tones of differing frequency.

Periodic sound waves are those in which the pattern of vibration, however complex, repeats itself. *Aperiodic* sound waves are those in which the vibration is random and has no repeatable pattern.

Play a note on the piano or sing "ah" and the resulting sounds will be complex but periodic in their waveforms. Drop a book on the floor or hiss through your teeth and the resulting sounds will be complex (having more than one frequency) but aperiodic (having no repeatable pattern) in their waveforms.

Harmonics: Characteristics of Periodic Complex Tones

Periodic complex vibrations produce signals in which the component frequencies are integral multiples of the lowest frequency of pattern repetition, or *fundamental frequency*. This fundamental frequency derives from the rate at which the sound source produces its vibratory cycle. As an example, let's consider a vibrating source such as a string on a guitar or a violin. When the string is plucked or bowed it will vibrate along its entire length at a given rate, say 100 Hz. This is the fundamental frequency of vibration of the string. If the string were vibrating in SHM, 100 Hz would be the only frequency generated and the resulting sound would be a pure tone. But strings, as well as reeds, vocal folds and most other sound sources, do not vibrate in SHM: At the same time that the whole string is vibrating at a rate of 100 Hz, both halves of the string are vibrating at a rate of 200 Hz—twice the rate of the string's fundamental frequency. The string will therefore be generating frequencies of both 100 and 200 Hz simultaneously. But the complexity of the string's vibration goes well beyond what we have just described, for just as the entire string and each of its halves are vibrating at rates of 100 and 200 Hz, each third of the string is vibrating at a rate of 300 Hz, each quarter at a rate of 400 Hz, each fifth at a rate of 500 Hz and so on in ever-decreasing fractions of the string's length and ever-increasing frequencies of vibration. Each of the tones generated by this complex vibration is called a *harmonic*, and the full set of harmonics is referred to as a *harmonic series*.

As you have probably noticed, the frequency of each harmonic is a whole number multiple of the fundamental frequency (which is also called the first harmonic). In our example, then, the harmonic series consists of the following:

Harmonic	Frequency
First	100 Hz (100 × 1)
Second	200 Hz (100 × 2)
Third	300 Hz (100 × 3)
Fourth	400 Hz (100 × 4)
Fifth	500 Hz (100 × 5)
.	.
.	.
.	.

There is a tendency for the harmonics in a harmonic series to decrease in amplitude as their frequency increases. Therefore, although there is no theoretical limit to the number of harmonics a vibrating source can produce, the effect of very high frequency harmonics on the overall quality of a sound is considered to be negligible for most common sources of sound, including the human voice.

This whole-number-multiple relationship between the frequency of the fundamental and frequencies of the higher harmonics holds for all complex periodic waves. So, if the fundamental frequency of a complex periodic wave were 200 Hz, the second, third, fourth, and fifth harmonics would have frequencies of 400, 600, 800 and 1000 Hz, respectively. At the bottom of Figure 3.13, we have depicted the waveform of just such a wave. It is actually the waveform generated by a female speaker saying the vowel [a]. If we compare this waveform with the 200 Hz pure tone at the top of the figure, we can see that both patterns repeat themselves at the same frequency.

Notice that waveforms supply us with a fair amount of information about the sound signal: We can determine the fundamental frequency of the sound the waveform represents by counting the number of times its pattern is repeated each second; Once we have determined the fundamental frequency, we will be able to calculate the frequencies of the individual harmonics. We cannot, however, directly discover the amplitudes of the individual harmonics (although variations in the overall amplitude of the signal over time are apparent in the waveform).

In order to depict harmonic amplitude we must turn to a different sort of display: The line (or amplitude) *spectrum* (plural, *spectra*). In a line spectrum the ordinate (the vertical axis) represents amplitude (as in a waveform), but the abscissa (the horizontal axis) represents frequency. It is thus possible, using a spectral display, to indicate the frequency and amplitude of each harmonic in a complex periodic wave. Figure 3.14 pairs several of the waveforms previously presented with their corresponding spectra. Notice that a line spectrum does not depict the dimension of time. The information it presents is thus valid only for a particular instant in time. If we want to see how harmonic amplitude varies over time, we will have to make a sequential series of line spectra or resort to alternative types of displays, some of which are described in later chapters.

We can conclude our discussion of periodic complex signals by pointing out that the sort of analytic process that produces a line spectrum reverses the synthetic process of adding sine waves to each other (see Fig. 3.12). In the synthetic process of addition, as long as the simple waves being added are harmonically related, the summed wave will be periodic (and, of course, complex). Applying the analytic process to a periodic wave allows us to discover the frequencies and amplitudes of the simple waves—the harmonic components—of which it is composed. This process, called Fourier Analysis, was first devised by J. B. Fourier, a French mathematician, during the first quarter of the 19th century. Originally a long and rather complex mathematical procedure, Fourier analysis is today performed directly and rapidly by a number of commercially available analytic devices.

Aperiodic Complex Signals

The sounds of a book dropped on a table or a hiss made between the teeth are complex as they consist of more than one frequency, but the frequencies are not harmonically related as they are for periodic sounds. In both cases, the air is set into random excitation with a broad band of frequencies of vibration as a result. The waveforms are *aperiodic* as there is no repetition of a displacement pattern. The sound of the book hitting the table top is, however, *tran-*

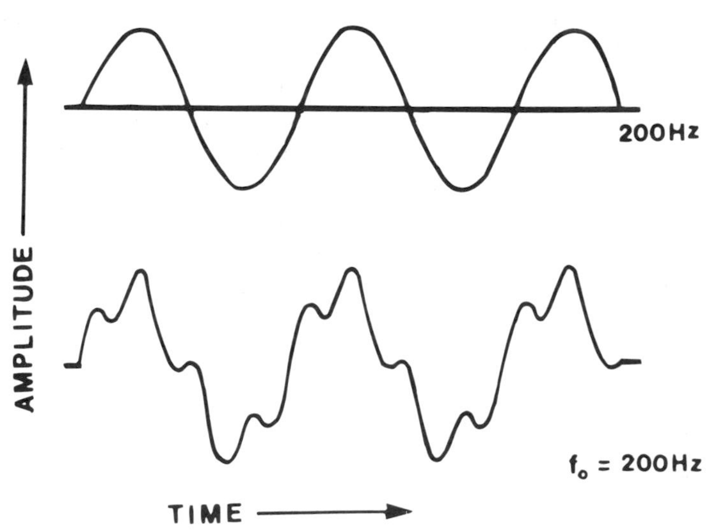

Figure 3.13. Waveforms of a pure tone and a complex tone, each with a frequency of 200 Hz.

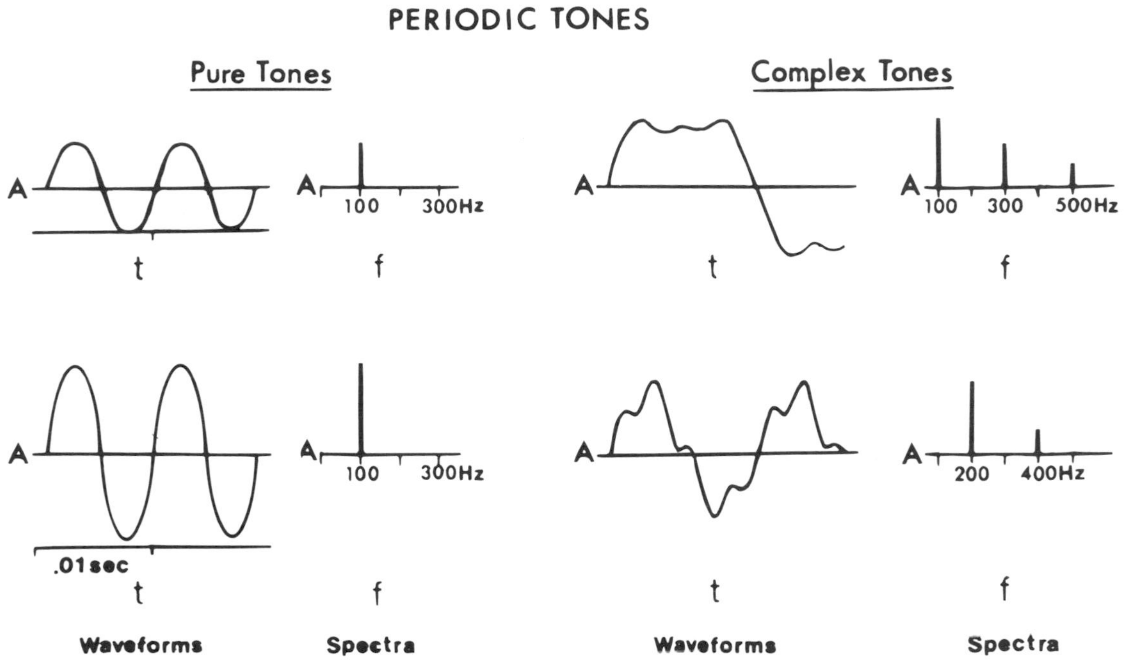

Figure 3.14. Waveforms (shown as a function of amplitude and time) and corresponding spectra (shown as a function of amplitude and frequency). The two signals on the *left* are vibrations at a single frequency (pure tones) while the two signals on the *right* represent different complex vibrations, analyzed as a fundamental frequency and higher harmonics.

sient, producing a burst of noise of short duration, while the hiss is continuous for as long as the airstream is set into turbulence by passing through a narrow constriction. Amplitude spectra can be made for aperiodic as well as periodic signals. Figure 3.15 shows the waveforms and spectra of typical aperiodic sound signals.

FREQUENCY AND PITCH

We have stated that frequency is the number of vibratory cycles per second. The notations 100 cps, 100 ~, and 100 Hz (Hertz) all mean the same thing: 100 cycles per second. The abbreviation Hz is preferred in the speech and hearing literature. People differ in the frequency range to which their ears are tuned, but in general, young, healthy, human ears can detect vibrations as low as 20 Hz and as high as 20,000 Hz. Vibrations too low in frequency to be audible are called subsonic, those too high, ultrasonic. We may not hear extremely low frequencies as sound, but we can often feel them. The frequencies important to the speech signal are within the 100- to 5000-Hz range. Contrasting this frequency range with that used by bats, which emit sound between 20,000 and 100,000 Hz, one sees that sound can be used for different purposes. Human beings use sound to communicate thoughts and feelings, while bats use sound to locate insects for food. Whether sound emission is used for localization or for communication, however, it is important that the frequency response of the auditory system be matched to the frequency characteristics of the sound-producing mechanism. Human vocal folds normally vibrate between 80 Hz and about 500 Hz during speaking situations, but some of the speech noises made in the mouth contain frequencies that extend to several thousand cycles per second. The human auditory system then is responsive to the appropriate range of frequencies of vibration.

Frequency relates directly to *pitch*. Pitch is a sensation. In general, when frequency of

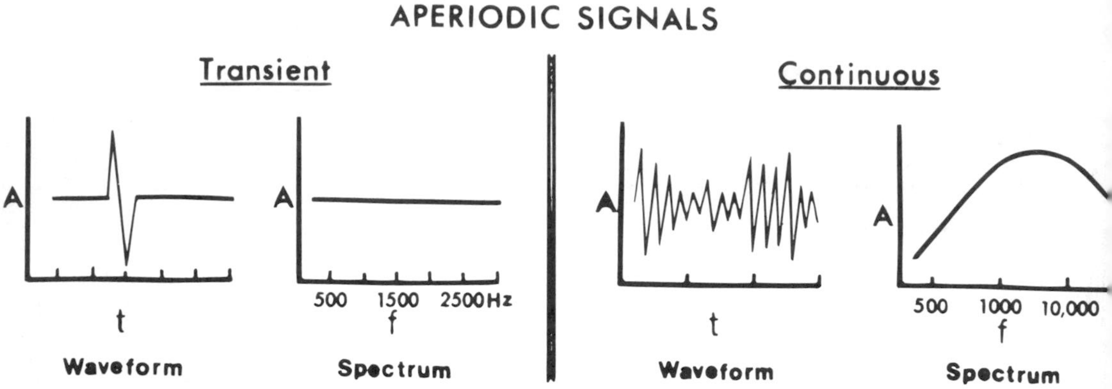

Figure 3.15. Noise signals. The graphs to the *left* are the waveform and spectrum of a sound similar to a book hitting a table top. The graphs to the *right* are the waveform and the spectrum of a hissing noise. The envelope of the amplitude as a function of frequency is indicated. Since there are many frequency components that are not harmonically related, the amplitudes are indicated by continuous lines.

vibration is increased, we hear a rise in pitch, and when frequency is decreased, we hear a lowering of pitch. The relationship is not linear, however. A constant interval of frequency increase does not result in a constant change in pitch. Frequency is a fact of physics, an event that can be measured by instruments: the number of cycles in a specified time. Pitch, in contrast, is a psychological phenomenon. It is the way in which frequency changes and differences are perceived by the listener. It can be measured only by asking listeners to make judgments.

The human auditory system is more responsive to some frequency changes than to others. In the frequencies below 1000 Hz perceived pitch is fairly linear in its relationship to frequency, but as the frequencies get higher, it takes a larger change in frequency to effect a change in the sensation of pitch. The relationship between the physical property of frequency and the psychological sensation of pitch is illustrated in Figure 3.16. The units of frequency are cycles per second; the units of pitch are *mels*. Testing listeners at various frequencies, the pitch of a 1000 Hz tone is used as a reference and is arbitrarily called 1000 mels. Whatever frequency is judged to be half that pitch is called 500 mels, twice that pitch is called 2000 mels. The mel curve shown by the *solid line* in Figure 3.16 is the result of this scaling procedure.

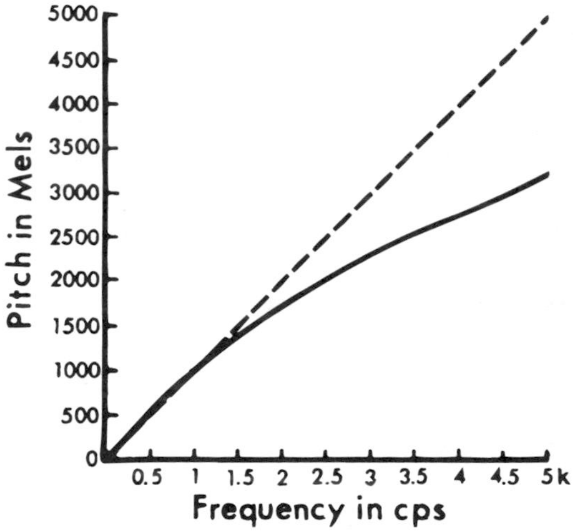

Figure 3.16. Replotting of the Stevens and Volkmann mel scale. The *solid line* indicates the way in which pitch (measured in mels) increases with frequency in cycles per second (Hz). The *dashed line* shows the relationship if correlation were perfect. (Adapted from S. S. Stevens et al.: *J. Acoust. Soc. Am.* 8, 1937.)

It can be seen that the word "frequency" refers to cycles per second and the word "pitch" is reserved for the perception of frequency. The mel scale was plotted by having listeners judge the pitch of pure tones. What about complex tones? How do listeners judge the pitch of a sound containing more than one frequency? The pitch of a complex periodic tone is judged by listeners to correspond to the fundamental frequency of the harmonic series. Surprisingly, even if the fundamental frequency of a harmonic series is not present, the auditory system compensates for the loss of the lower harmonics and "hears" the f_0. For example, a complex tone composed of the frequencies 600, 900, and 1200 Hz is judged to have the pitch of a 300 Hz tone, because 300 Hz, the largest divisor, is the rate at which the basic pattern of the complex wave repeats itself. Judgments of pitch for aperiodic sounds are more generally influenced by the center of the frequency band or the frequency at which the amplitude is highest.

THE DECIBEL: A MEASURE OF RELATIVE INTENSITY

We have referred to the fact that the amplitude of vibration, the extent of particle displacement, is an indication of the intensity or power of the sound. In order to describe the relative intensity of two sounds, we use a unit of measurement called a *decibel* (dB), literally one-tenth of a Bel (a unit named in honor of Alexander Graham Bell, 1847-1922, the American inventor of the telephone and educator of the deaf. See Chapter 2.) The decibel scale of intensity is an example of a logarithmic scale. In a *linear scale,* such as a measuring stick, there is a zero, and each increment is equal to the next, so you can sum units by addition. A *logarithmic scale,* as you can see on the chart below, is based on "exponents" of a given number called the base. For decibels, the base is 10, and the scale is constructed with increments that are not equal but represent increasingly large numerical differences.

Linear scale	
1,000	
	>diff. = 1,000
2,000	
	>diff. = 1,000
3,000	
	>diff. = 1,000
4,000	

Logarithmic scale	
10^2 = 100	
	>diff. = 900
10^3 = 1,000	
	>diff. = 9,000
10^4 = 10,000	
	>diff. = 90,000
10^5 = 100,000	

10 = base; 2, 3, 4, and 5 are logarithms

Why use a logarithmic scale for sound intensity? There are two reasons: The first reason is that the human ear is sensitive to a large intensity range, as many as 10^{13} (10,000,000,000,000 or 10 trillion) units of intensity in a linear scale. That would be too many numbers to handle, but on a condensed logarithmic scale, the number is reduced to 130 decibels.

The second reason is that the logarithmic scale more nearly approximates the way human ears judge loudness. It has been known since the 19th century writings of German scientists Ernst Weber (1834) and Gustav Fechner (1860) that equal increases in sensation (in this case loudness) are obtained by multiplying the stimulus by a constant factor. This principle does not work for all the intensities of sound to which the ear is sensitive, but is accurate enough to be practical. Each step in the decibel scale, then, corresponds roughly to an equal growth in loudness, even though the sound power differences are large.

The power of a sound is proportional to the square of the pressure, or to put it in reverse, the pressure is the square root of the power. Just as an inch or a centimeter is a unit of measurement used for length, the units of measurement used in acoustics are *watts* (for power) and *dynes* (for pressure). In physics, *intensity level* refers to the power of the signal as measured in watts per square centimeter. In the acoustics of speech and hearing, *sound pressure level* has customarily been used as the measure, and the pressure unit is dynes per square centimeter. Either power or pressure units can be converted to decibels.

You may have heard that a certain airplane takes off with a sound level of 100 dB *SPL* (sound pressure level), or that the average intensity of conversational speech is about 60 dB *IL* (intensity level). The first measure uses pressure as the reference; the sound pressure of the airplane noise is 10^5 more than a barely audible sound (100,000 : 1 ratio). Were it to be measured by using a power reference, it would still be 100 dB, but the intensity ratio would be 10^{10} to 1 (10,000,000,000 : 1), since the power increments are the square of the pressure increments. The second measure, the speech intensity, used a power reference. This relationship between power and pressure makes it necessary to use separate formulas to compute the decibel, one when using a power reference (watts) and the other for use with a pressure reference (dynes).

The important thing to remember about measuring the intensity of a sound is that there is always a standard. The decibel is a unit of intensity that is really a ratio, a comparison of the sound in question with a reference sound. The power reference is 10^{-16} watts/cm², and the pressure reference is 0.0002 dynes/cm², both signals at the threshold of human audibility. The formula for decibels using an intensity (power) reference is:

$$\text{dB IL} = 10 \left(\log_{10} \frac{W_o}{W_r}\right)$$

where IL = intensity level (reference is 10^{-16} watts/cm²), W_o = output power in watts (power of signal to be measured), W_r = reference power in watts (power of the reference signal 10^{-16} watts/cm²), and $\log_{10}$ = logarithm of the ratio W_o/W_r. The base is 10. The log is the exponent. For example, if the ratio were 100 : 1, the log would be 2 because $10^2 = 100$, and the exponent is 2.

The formula used to compute decibels using a sound pressure level reference for comparison is:

$$\text{dB SPL} = 20 \left(\log_{10} \frac{P_o}{P_r}\right)$$

In this formula, P_o represents the pressure you wish to measure (output) and P_r the pressure you use for comparison (reference). For example, if the sound to be measured were to have a pressure level of 20 dynes/cm², that sound would be 100,000 times the reference pressure.

$$\frac{20 \text{ dynes/cm}^2}{0.0002 \text{ dynes/cm}^2} = \frac{100{,}000}{1}$$

Since the ratio is 100,000 : 1, the logarithm to the base 10 of the ratio is 5. (Simply count the zeros.) The formula instructs us to multiply the log of the ratio by 20. Since 20 × 5 = 100, the answer is 100 dB SPL.

Remember that the $\boxed{\log_{10} \frac{P_o}{P_r}}$ is one small number, the exponent, in this case, 5.

To take another example, if a sound with 10 times as much pressure as a barely audible sound were to be measured, how many decibels SPL would it be? The log of 10 is 1 (only one zero) and 20 × 1 = 20; therefore, it would be 20 dB SPL.

You should also be able to compute the ratio or the pressure in dynes when given the decibels. A 60 dB SPL conversation, as an instance, is how much more sound pressure than what is barely audible?

$$60 \text{ dB SPL} = 20x$$

$$\left(x = \log_{10} \frac{P_o}{P_r}\right)$$

$$x = 3$$

Since the log is 3, the ratio must be 1,000 : 1 (3 zeros).

So the sound of an average conversation is 1,000 times more sound pressure than barely audible sound pressure, or to be exact, 0.2 dynes/cm².

$$\begin{array}{r} 0.0002 \text{ dynes/cm}^2 \\ \times 1{,}000 \\ \hline 0.2000 \text{ dynes/cm}^2 \end{array}$$

What does 0 dB mean? If a sound is measured to have an intensity of 0 dB, does it mean that there is no sound? Not at all.

$$\text{dB} = 20 \text{ (log of the ratio)}$$
$$0 \text{ dB} = 20 \times 0$$

The log is zero. Since there are no zeros in the ratio, the ratio is equal to 1, which means that the output is equal to the reference pressure.

Ratio	Log	dB (20 × log of ratio)
1,000:1	3	60 dB SPL
100:1	2	40 dB SPL
10:1	1	20 dB SPL
1:1	0	0 dB SPL

Thus, it can be seen that 0 dB means the sound in question is equal to the reference sound rather than silence.

The sound pressure levels of certain familiar sounds are approximated below:

All sound within a few feet of the listener:	
0 dB	Threshold of hearing
20 dB	Rustling of leaves
30 dB	Whisper (3 feet)
35 dB	Residential area at night
45 dB	Typewriter
60 dB	Conversation
75 dB	Shouting, singing (3 feet)
100 dB	Approaching subway train, for people on waiting platform
120 dB	Jet airplane, for man on runway Amplified rock music (6 feet)
130 dB	Painfully loud sound

INTENSITY AND LOUDNESS

Intensity or sound pressure, like frequency, is a physical property of the acoustic signal that can be measured by an instrument called a sound level meter. The loudness of a signal is directly related to its intensity. As intensity is increased, the sound is judged by listeners to be louder. *Loudness* is the subjective, psychological sensation of judged intensity. Like frequency and pitch, intensity and loudness are not linearly related. Again, the human auditory system acts on the signal, so that sensations of equal loudness for different frequencies require very different intensities.

A *phon* is a unit of equal loudness. Figure 3.17 is a plot of equal loudness levels at different frequencies. The *heavy line* is the important *absolute threshold of audibility*, the intensities at each frequency that are just audible by young, healthy ears. It is clear that the human auditory system is designed to receive the middle frequencies (1000 to 6000 Hz) with much less intensity than is needed for the extremely low and high frequencies. This information is used in the specifications for manufacturing audiometers: instruments used to test hearing, to compare a person's threshold with that of young healthy ears. The zero setting on an audiometer is simply the *heavy line* in Figure 3.17 that is straightened out on the graph paper used to chart the test, the audiogram.

The *lighter lines* are the phon curves of equal loudness. The 20-phon line is equally loud at all frequencies to a 1000-Hz tone at 20 dB, while a 70-phon line is equal in loudness at all frequencies to a 1000-Hz tone at 70 dB. At low loudness levels, there is a large difference between the middle and the extreme frequencies in the amount of intensity needed to effect equal loudness judgments, but at higher loudness levels, the large intensity differences disappear.

When listeners are asked to judge relative loudness (half as loud, twice as loud) in a scaling procedure similar to that used to obtain the mel scale for pitch, the unit of loudness is called a *sone*, with *1 sone* equal in loudness to a 1000-Hz tone at 40 dB. By this method, it can be determined that the sensation of loudness increases more slowly than the actual increase in intensity.

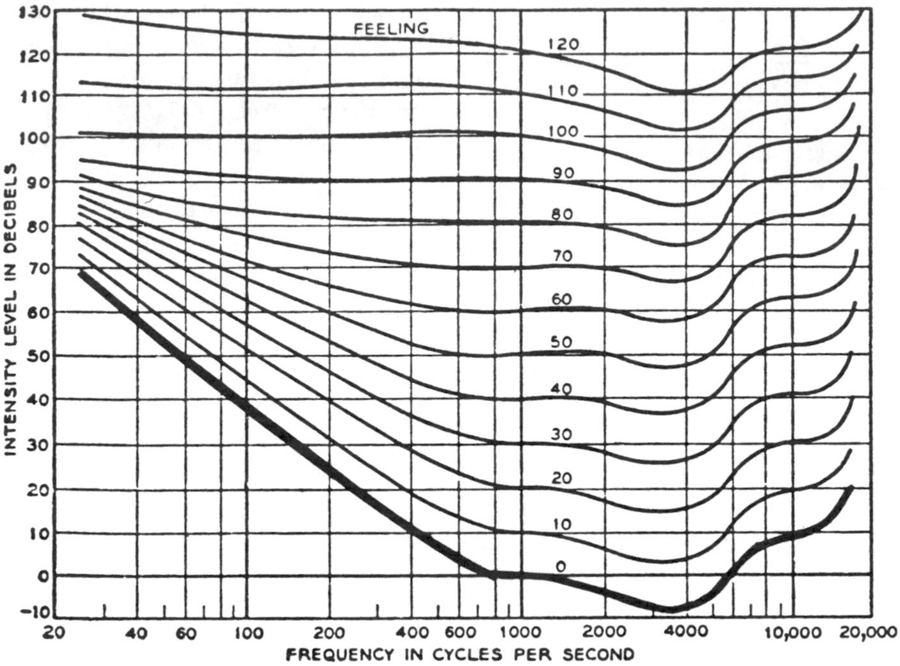

Figure 3.17. Loudness level contours derived by Fletcher and Munson. Each *curve* sounds equally loud at all frequencies. The loudness in phons is indicated on each curve. (Adapted from H. Fletcher and W. A. Munson: *J. Acoust. Soc. Am.* 5, 1933.)

Physical Properties		Psychological Properties	
Name and Units		Name and Units	
Frequency:	Hz	Pitch:	Mel (Scaling)
Intensity:	dB	Loudness:	Sone (Scaling) Phon (Equal)

VELOCITY OF SOUND THROUGH SPACE

Velocity is simply speed in a certain direction. Light travels faster than sound or has greater velocity as we know from our experience with lightning and thunder. We see the flash before we hear the crash. At normal atmospheric conditions, sound travels through air at about:

344 meters per second
or
1130 feet per second
or
758 miles per hour

It travels much faster through liquids and the fastest along solids because the elasticity and density of the medium affect the velocity of conduction. Velocity is independent of pressure as long as the temperature remains the same. A faint sound will travel just as fast as a loud sound. The soft sound will not travel as far because of the *Inverse Square Law* (intensity varies inversely as the square of the distance from the source), but it will travel as fast as a loud sound. Temperature does make a difference, however, and sounds will travel faster on a hot summer day than on a wintry day.

Velocity of particle movement must not be confused with velocity of sound wave propagation. Particles vibrating in SHM constantly change velocity, moving with maximum velocity over their resting places. The velocity of the sound wave moving through space, that is, the speed with which the disturbance moves from one spot to another, is, by contrast, a constant (refer back to Fig. 3.8).

WAVELENGTH

The length of a sound wave is the distance in space that one cycle occupies. One can measure from any point in one cycle to the corresponding point in the next cycle. The symbol used to denote *wavelength* is the Greek letter lambda (λ). Figure 3.18 illustrates the wavelength of complex and pure tone signals.

Wavelength depends upon two factors, the frequency of the vibration and the velocity of sound wave propagation in the medium.

Observe wavelength changes by taking a small pan of water and dipping your finger into the water repeatedly, first at a slow frequency then at a higher frequency. Notice that the distance between the crests of the ripples in the lower frequency condition is greater than in the higher frequency condition. High frequency sounds occupy less space per cycle, have a shorter wavelength, than do low frequency sounds.

We can further illustrate the factor of frequency-conditioned wavelength using a speech sound. Imagine a man and a woman each saying the vowel [a]. The woman is likely to produce the sound with a fundamental frequency of around 200 Hz, and the man with a fundamental frequency of about 100 Hz. Given that wavelength (λ) equals the velocity of sound (c) divided by the frequency (f):

$$\lambda = \frac{c}{f}$$

The wavelength of the man's voice would be more than 3 meters, while the woman's voice

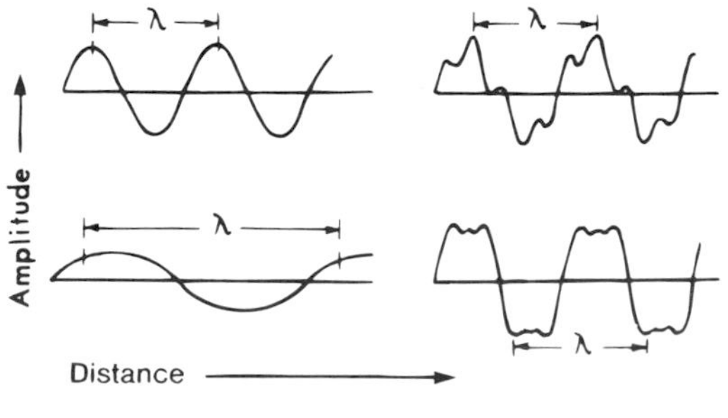

Figure 3.18. Wavelength (λ) is the distance occupied by one complete cycle of vibration.

would have a wavelength of almost 2 meters (each meter corresponding to some 3 inches more than a yard):

$$\lambda = \frac{c}{f}$$

$$\lambda = \frac{\text{344 meters per second}}{\text{200 Hz}} = \text{about 1.75 meters or 67 inches (5'7")}$$

$$\lambda = \frac{\text{344 meters per second}}{\text{100 Hz}} = \text{3.4 meters or 11'3"}$$

The second factor, that of the medium through which the sound travels, is also important. We have seen that sound waves are conducted through solids at a higher velocity than through liquids, and through liquids at a higher velocity than through gases. Given the formula for the wavelength:

$$\frac{\lambda}{f} = c$$

a sound of a certain frequency would have a longer wavelength in water, for example, than in air, because the higher velocity increases the numerator of the fraction, c.

When saying an aperiodic sound such as /⟨sh⟩/, in order to quiet someone, the high energy frequencies are closer to 2500 Hz, which would make a wavelength as short as 14 cm (between 5 and 6 inches).

$$\lambda = \frac{\text{34,400 cm per sec}}{\text{2,500 Hz}} = \sim\text{14 cm}$$

Sounds of high frequency and short wavelengths are more directional than low frequency sounds. Longer wavelengths radiate more and go around corners more easily.

This is why the high frequency (ultrasonic) sounds emitted by bats are useful in helping them to locate the small flying insects upon which they prey. The sound from the bat reflects from any object in its path with more intensity than from neighboring objects, thereby localizing the prey for the kill. Only a signal with a short wavelength and little radiation could localize such a small target. Bats, even if blind, can analyze the reflected sound for information on size and distance of either obstacles or food.

Variation in wavelength also explains why we often hear voices in an adjoining room quite clearly but fail to understand what they are saying. Speech contains both high and low frequency components. The low frequency sounds with longer wavelengths diffract around the wall and enter through the door. The higher frequency components of speech having shorter, more directional wavelengths, radiate less widely and are largely unheard. Receiving only part of the signal, we listeners cannot understand what is being said.

RESONANCE

If you have ever pushed a child in a swing, you know that you must time each push to coincide with the harmonic motion of the swing. If you were to run forward and push the swing at some central point in its swing toward you, instead of waiting for it to reach the maximum distance in its excursion, you would simply shorten its arc. It is also possible that you would be knocked to the ground. The frequency with which the swing completes a cycle during one second is the *natural resonant frequency* of the swing. This frequency is independent of amplitude. Push a child with less force, then with more force; the arcs will vary in amplitude, but the frequency will be the same. What if the swing broke and a piece of weak rope were removed from each side, making the swing shorter? Would the natural resonant frequency of the shorter-roped swing be the same as the swing with longer ropes? We know by experience that this new swing would have a higher natural frequency (more cycles per second) than the previous swing. In general, smaller things vibrate at higher frequencies than larger versions of the same thing.

Everything that vibrates has a natural frequency, or in many cases, has frequencies of vibration when left to vibrate freely (*free vibration*). A machine could be attached to the swing forcing it to vibrate at any frequency (*forced vibration*), but even under these circumstances, the swing would vibrate at maximum amplitude only if forced to vibrate at its own natural resonant frequency. The *resonance* of a vibrator depends upon its physical characteristics as we know from the design of tuning forks.

Everything vibrates and can therefore resonate, whether at audible frequencies or not. A *resonator* is something that is set into forced vibration by another vibration. Resonators do not initiate the sound energy. A sound is created elsewhere and the resonator will vibrate in sympathy with it if the sound from the source is at or near the resonant frequencies of the resonator.

Take the damper off a piano string by pressing the key gently down so there is no sound, then loudly sing the note that corresponds with the depressed key, and you will demonstrate sympathetic resonance for yourself as the string vibrates in response to your singing. The piano string, the swing, and the tuning fork are examples of mechanical resonators. An *acoustic resonator* is something that contains air. A body of air will resonate in response to sound containing frequencies that match the natural resonant frequencies of the volume of air. We can understand this principle by thinking about the construction of musical instruments. It is not enough to have strings of various lengths and thicknesses mounted on a board to achieve the various qualities of sound associated with a violin, cello, or guitar. Although the energy for the sound is provided by a bow or a pluck, and the source of the sound is in the vibration of the strings, the air-filled boxes behind the strings also serve to resonate certain frequencies that make the instruments distinctive. The small volume of air in the box of a violin will naturally vibrate at higher frequencies than the large volume of air in the box of a cello.

As you add water to a bottle, the sound increases in frequency as the air space gets smaller. If the resonant frequency of the air volume at the top of the bottle were matched, by the addition of water, to the frequency of a tuning fork, one could tilt the bottle, altering the shape of the air space, without changing the resonant frequency of the air. The shape of the air cavity is not as important as the volume in determining the frequencies to which it will resonate.

An acoustic resonator that relates to speech because it is analogous to the resonance of the vocal tract and the ear canal is an air-filled tube that is open at one end and closed at the other end. The air within the tube vibrates at certain frequencies depending on the length of the tube. The wavelength of the fundamental resonance in such a tube is 4 times the length of the tube. To put it another way, only ¼ of the wave can fit into the tube at any one pass. Figure 3.19 contrasts the resonator length with the waveform of the resonant frequencies. Quarter wave resonators vibrate only at odd multiples of the fundamental frequency because of the closure at one end. These resonators will be discussed more fully in later chapters.

Resonators vary with respect to the range of frequencies to which they will respond. We can divide them roughly into two types: Sharply- (or narrowly-) tuned resonators that respond to a very limited number of frequencies; and broadly-tuned resonators that respond to a relatively great number of frequencies. Another difference correlates with the sharply-tuned versus broadly-tuned distinction. Sharply-tuned resonators are slow to reach maximum amplitude and, analogously, slow to cease vibrating once they are no longer being driven by a sound source. Broadly-tuned resonators, in contrast, reach maximum amplitude quickly and stop vibrating very soon after the sound to which they are responding has ceased.

A tuning fork is a good example of a sharply-tuned resonator: Ideally, it will vibrate only in response to one particular frequency; it will respond very slowly when resonating (as opposed to when it is struck); it will take a long time for its vibrations to die out. A telephone

¼ WAVE RESONATOR

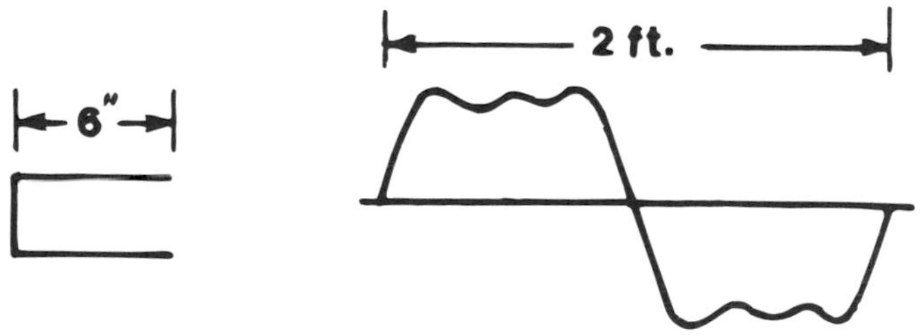

Given tube 6" long
open at one end

$$f = \frac{c \text{ (constant velocity)}}{4 \cdot 1 \text{ (length of tube)}}$$

$$f = \frac{1130 \text{ ft}}{4 \cdot 1/2 \text{ ft}} = \frac{1130}{2} = 565 \text{ Hz}$$

$$3f = 1695 \text{ Hz}$$
$$5f = 2825 \text{ Hz}$$

Figure 3.19. A tube open at one end, closed at the other, will resonate at odd multiples of its lowest resonant frequency. Lowest frequency has a wavelength that is 4 times the length of the tube.

earpiece provides a good example of a broadly-tuned resonator: It will respond to much of the broad range of frequencies found in the human voice; it will respond almost immediately to the electrical current that drives it; it will cease vibrating almost immediately once that electrical current ceases. Since the electrical current is controlled, ultimately, by a human voice, we are able to hear a person speak from the very beginning of his or her utterance and are not troubled by the persistence of vibrations after the person has stopped talking. You will, of course, realize that the air molecules in a room, as well as the mechanical components of the hearing mechanism, constitute broadly-tuned resonating systems.

ACOUSTICS AND SPEECH

This chapter will serve as a foundation for much of the rest of the book. The marvel of speech is the way in which the distinctive sounds that can be produced by the human vocal folds and vocal tract are varied and combined with one another to serve as a code for communication. In the next chapter, the general way in which humans make these significant sounds will be outlined.

REFERENCES

Textbook Treatments of Acoustics

Benade, A. H., *Horns, Strings, and Harmony*. Garden City, NY: Doubleday (Anchor Books), 1960.

Denes, P., and Pinson, E., *The Speech Chain*. New York: Doubleday, 1973.

Fry, D. B., *The Physics of Speech*. Cambridge, England: Cambridge University Press, 1979.

Kent, R. D., and Read, C., *The Acoustic Analysis of Speech*. San Diego: Singular Publishing Group, 1992.

Ladefoged, P., *Elements of Acoustic Phonetics*. Chicago: University of Chicago Press, 1962.

Pierce, J. R., and David, E. E., Jr., *Man's World of Sound*. Garden City, NY: Doubleday, 1958.

Stephens, R. W. B., and Bate, A. E., *Acoustics and Vibrational Physics*. New York: St. Martin's Press, 1966.

Van Bergeijk, W. A., Pierce, J. R., and David E. E., Jr., *Waves and the Ear*. Garden City, NY: Doubleday (Anchor Books), 1960.

Wood, A. *Acoustics*. New York: Dover Publications, 1966.

Classic References

Fletcher, H., and Munson, W. A., Loudness, Its Definition, Measurement, and Calculation. *J. Acoust. Soc. Am.* 5, 1933, 82–108.

Fourier, J. B. J., *Théorie Analytique de la Chaleur*. Paris: F. Didot, 1822.

Rayleigh, J. W. S., *Theory of Sound*. New York: Dover Publications, 1960. First published by Macmillan in London, 1878.

Stevens, S. S., Volkmann, J., and Newman, E. B., A Scale for the Measurement of the Psychological Magnitude Pitch. *J. Acoust. Soc. Am.* 8, 1937, 185–190.

4

Speech Production: The Raw Materials—Neurology, Respiration, and Phonation

"Breath's a ware that will not keep."
A. E. Housman "A Shropshire Lad"

Under ordinary circumstances, a speaker is conscious of the meaning of his message, of his search for appropriate words to express that meaning, and perhaps of his feelings about the topic or listener. Only under circumstances of change or novelty, such as attempting new words, or speaking with a new dental appliance, does the speaker become conscious of the processes involved in sound production. Beginning students of phonetics are surprised at their inability to describe what they are doing when they produce certain speech sounds. The fact that skilled speakers can effortlessly produce such a complex and rapidly changing acoustic stream beguiles some students into the assumption that the study of phonetics must be equally effortless. If speech is so easy, should not the study of speech be equally easy?

We do, in fact, know a substantial amount about the sounds that emerge from the mouth of a speaker and, from acoustic analyses, we have derived information on production. We know something about the movements of parts of the speaker's articulators, and we are currently learning about the muscle activity accompanying some of these movements. We can infer from information on muscle activity something about the nerve impulses that fire the muscles. We know little, however, about the organization and coordination of these impulses in the brain and even less about how these impulse patterns are derived from stored linguistic knowledge and ultimately from thought.

We will not attempt to explore the mysterious realms of decision-making, conceptualization, memory, nor the many linguistic choices that are made either by volition or by habit as a speaker prepares to say something: choices in semantics, syntax, and phonology. Yet, even though we are considering the act of speech as a more-or-less isolated phenomenon, we have a wealth of topics to consider: the neurophysiology of speech production, the physics of respiration for speech, the dynamics of phonation, the articulation of speech sounds, the resonance of the vocal tract, the feedback mechanisms used to monitor speech, and some of the theories of how the speech production mechanisms work. In all sections of this chapter, the emphasis will be on physiology, the dynamics of speech production. Our discussion of anatomy will be kept to a minimum; only the most important nerves, muscles, cartilages, and bones will be mentioned.

The goal in producing speech is to make certain meaningful sound combinations. It is an acoustic goal. To effect that goal, the speaker uses air to make a number of sounds (in English, some 40 different sounds), which vary when they are produced in context with one another. The sounds are produced by regulat-

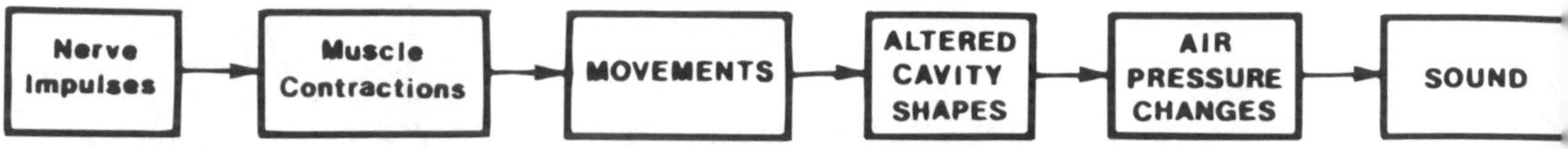

Figure 4.1. Chain of events leading to speech sound production.

ing the airstream as it passes from the lungs to the atmosphere. This regulation is brought about by movements of jaw, lips, tongue, soft palate, walls of the pharynx, and vocal folds to alter the shape of the vocal tract. The movements are mainly the result of muscle contractions, which are caused by nerve impulses, and of course the whole process is controlled in the nervous system. Figure 4.1 shows the flow of motor activity for speech in its several states.

NEUROPHYSIOLOGY OF SPEECH

The brain and the nerve fibers that extend from the brain are constantly active. As long as there is life, nerve impulses are fired throughout the system. Unlike a computer, it is always turned on. When a signal, such as a sound, is received by the brain, the activity in certain areas sharply increases. There is increased activity, too, as a person prepares to do something. The nervous system is a network of specialized cells called *neurons*. The neurons are supported by other protective and nourishing cells and are oxygenated by a generous blood supply.

The nervous system can be divided into the central nervous system (*CNS*), consisting of the brain and the spinal cord, and the peripheral nervous system (*PNS*), consisting of the nerves that emerge from the base of the brain (*cranial nerves*) to serve the head region and from the spinal cord (*spinal nerves*) to serve the rest of the body (see Fig. 4.2). Some neurons are motor or *efferent,* which means that they carry impulses from the central nervous system to the periphery. Other neurons are sensory or *afferent,* which means they carry information from the peripheral sense organs to the CNS. For example, when a person decides to close his lips, efferent neurons (*motor* nerve fibers) carry the impulses to the lip muscles, which contract. When the lips close, touch receptors near the surface of the skin are stimulated carrying *sensory* information that the lips have touched along afferent neurons to the brain. The courses of nerve fibers through the spinal cord and throughout the body are unidirectional and can therefore be classified as afferent or efferent. However, the nerve fibers that make up the higher centers of the brain itself are interconnected in a compact, three-dimensional mesh and are not easily classified as either afferent or efferent. We will discuss the respective roles of the CNS and the PNS in the control of speech production after a brief review of the brain and the activity of the neurons that make up both systems.

The Brain

The brain is formed by a central *brainstem* on top of the spinal cord with the *cerebellum* positioned behind it and two *cerebral hemispheres*, which partly obscure the brainstem, on top. The higher brainstem includes the *thalamus* and the *basal ganglia*. The lower brainstem includes the *pons* and *medulla oblongata*. The medulla narrows into the spinal cord. Figure 4.3 is a lateral view of one hemisphere, showing the position of the brainstem underneath the cover of the cerebrum. The human brain weights approximately 1.5 kg (kilograms) or about 3 pounds. The surface of the cerebrum called the *cortex* is made up of billions of cell bodies of individual nerve cells. It is the general function of nerve cells, or neurons, to which we now turn our attention.

The Neuron

Neurons assume many shapes and lengths, but they always have a cell body and extensions that receive and transmit impulses. Each neuron leads its own independent biological life and upon adequate stimulation, gener-

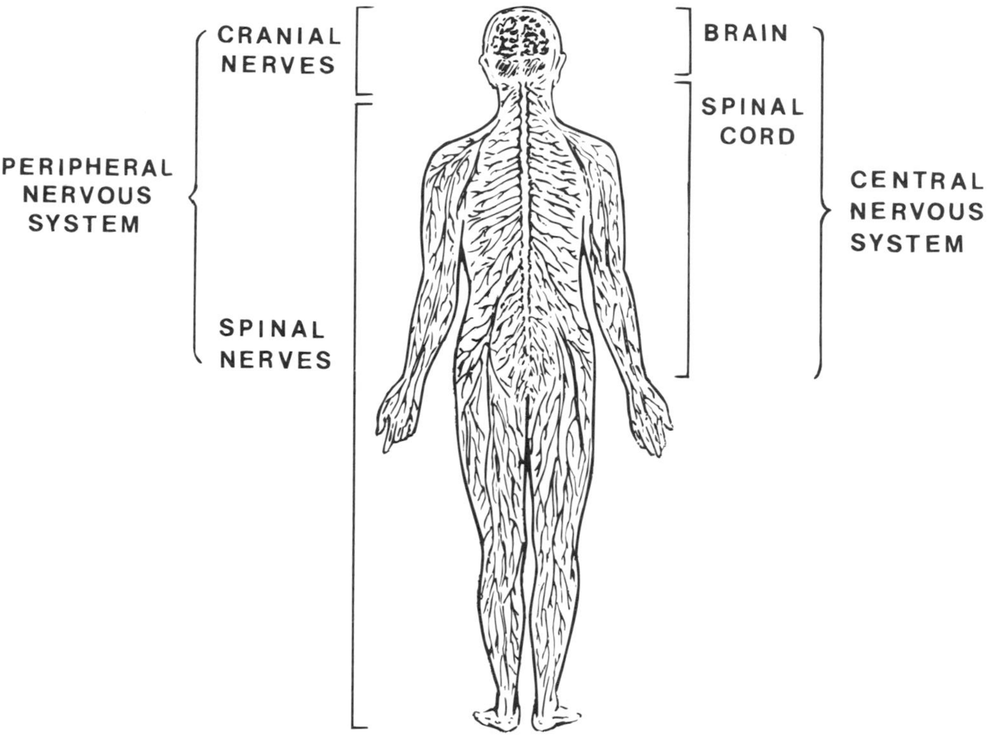

Figure 4.2. Divisions of the nervous system, posterior view.

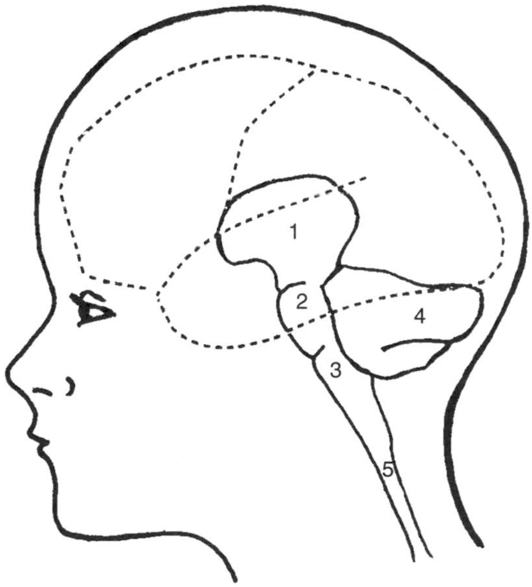

Figure 4.3. Brain in lateral view. Two cerebral hemispheres are shown as *dotted structures* lying over the higher brainstem (*1*), pons (*2*), cerebellum (*4*), and medulla (*3*). The medulla narrows into the spinal cord (*5*).

ates its own electrical activity. A type of neuron is illustrated in Figure 4.4. Nervous activity approaches the cell body of the neuron via *dendrites*. The impulse leaves the cell body by way of the *axon*. The nervous system works under an *all-or-none principle* of firing. In order for an impulse to be conducted along an axon, the first part of the axon beyond the cell body must be stimulated to its threshold. If the stimulation falls below the particular threshold for that neuron, the axon does not fire at all. If it reaches its threshold, however, the axon fires at full capacity no matter how high the stimulation (see Fig. 4.5). A strong group of impulses arriving at the cell body can increase frequency of impulses but not the amplitude of each impulse. Within the nervous system, intensity is coded in terms of frequency.

If a neuron fires, what actually happens? The excitation is conducted along the axon leading from the cell body. The critical change that takes place at the point of excitation is an increased permeability of the membrane that

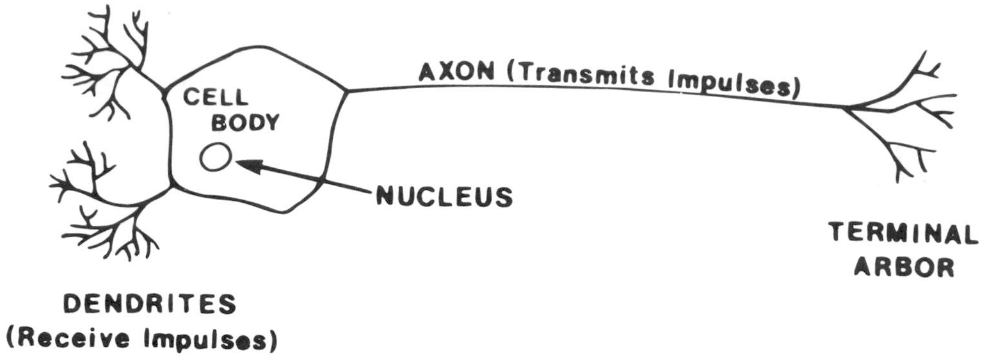

Figure 4.4. Single neuron. Impulses travel from *left* to *right*.

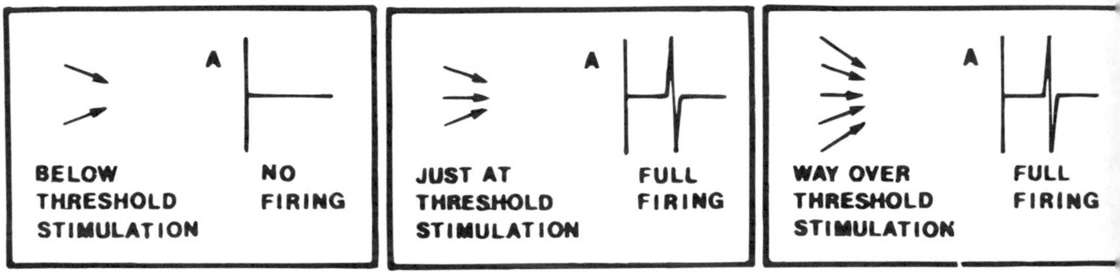

Figure 4.5. All-or-none principle. Three panels show stimulation of a nerve below threshold, at threshold, and above threshold levels. If the neuron fires, it fires with a fixed amplitude (A).

encases the axon or nerve fiber. At the point of stimulation, a momentary increase in permeability of the membrane allows an exchange of ions that depolarizes the nerve fiber for an instant.

Imagine a cross-section of an axon. The interior of the nerve fiber is filled with a jelly-like substance rich in potassium ions (K^+). Outside the membrane that sheaths the axon is a seawater-like fluid rich in sodium ions (Na^+). Most of the sodium ions are excluded from the axon by the nature of the membrane itself and by complex metabolic interactions. Potassium ions, however, are free to cross the membrane.

At rest, the interior of the nerve fiber is negative by some 50–80 millivolts (mV; thousandths of a volt) relative to the electrical charge outside the neuron.

When a stimulation that reaches the threshold for that neuron arrives, the membrane surrounding the axon becomes more permeable allowing the sodium ions (Na^+) to enter. Potassium ions (K^+) then start to leave the neuron, and for that instant, about 0.5 ms, the interior of the axon is more positively charged than the exterior by about 30–50 mV. Immediately after the moment of firing, the chemistry of the neuron is restored to that of the resting state until another nerve impulse comes along. Figure 4.6 schematizes this electrochemical event.

A particular point along the axon is depolarized, which stimulates the next point and the next. Once fired, the neuron is self-stimulating. It is interesting to note that although the nervous impulse travels along the nerve fiber longitudinally, the actual movement of particles is across the membrane and therefore is perpendicular to the nerve fiber (Fig. 4.7).

The velocity with which each impulse travels along the nerve fibers depends upon the diameter of the nerve fiber and upon its myelinization. Conduction velocity in mammals is proportional to about 6 times the diameter of the neuron. For example a small neuron of 10-μ (microns) diameter will conduct an impulse approximately 60 meters per second, while a 20-μ neuron, the largest in the human body, will conduct at a velocity of about 120 meters per second. The rate of nerve impulse conduction also depends on the presence or absence of *myelin* encasing most human nerve fibers. Its fatty whitish appearance accounts for the term *white matter* for parts of the nervous system. The myelin coats each axon, with interruptions spaced along the neuron exposing the axon. The nervous impulse skips along from one exposed area to the next at high velocities. The cell bodies, by contrast, are not coated with a myelin sheath and are therefore referred to as *gray matter*.

Conduction from one neuron to another involves the release of chemicals at the *synapse*, the juncture of the neurons. The chemicals act to bridge the small space between nerve fibers. There are approximately 1,000 billion such synapses in the human brain (Fig. 4.8).

Some chemicals facilitate the firing of the next cell, while other chemicals inhibit the firing of the next cell. Many neurons can converge to fire a single neuron, and conversely a single neuron can stimulate many other neurons simultaneously. This arrangement of convergences and divergences of neurons combines with the chemical variations that can inhibit or facilitate synaptic transmission to account for the enormous flexibility of the nervous system. A myriad of different three-dimensional patterns of nerve fiber networks can be established in both the central nervous system and the peripheral nervous system.

A bundle of neuron fibers is called a

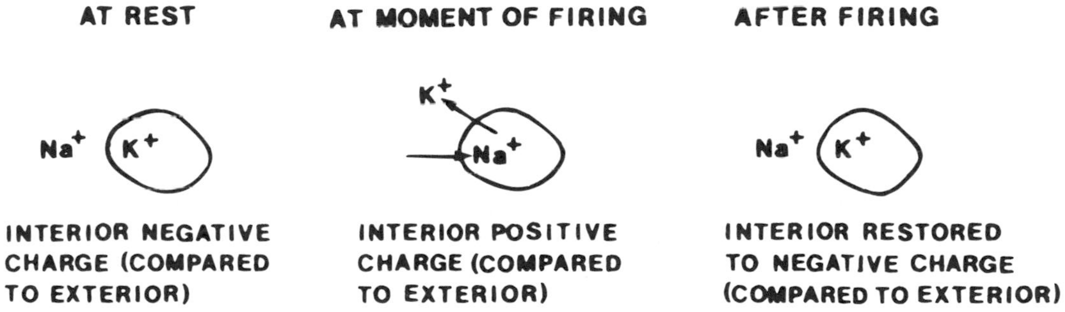

Figure 4.6. Electrochemical events at the cell membrane before, during, and after a nerve cell fires.

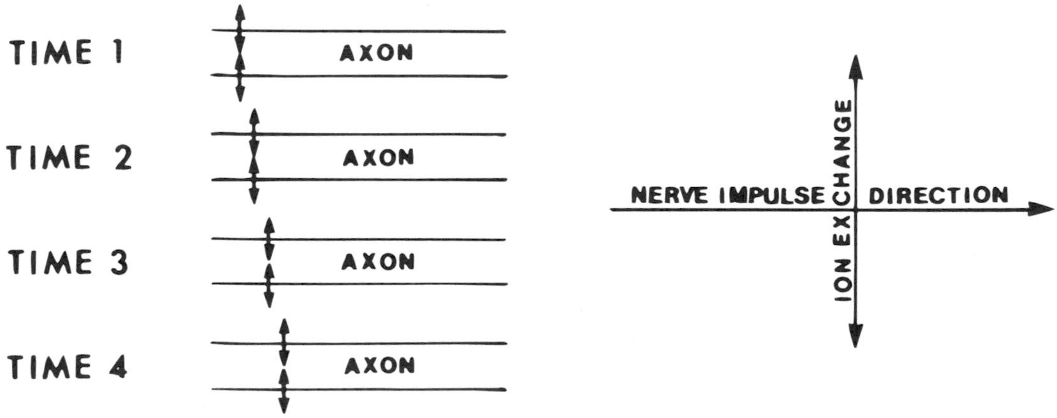

Figure 4.7. Transmission of an impulse along an axon. On the *left,* the position of ion exchange is shown at successive moments in time. The nerve impulse travels in a direction perpendicular to the direction of ion exchange, as shown on the *right.*

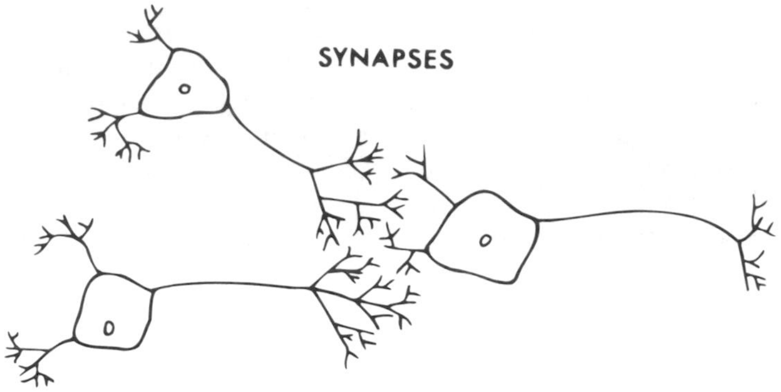

Figure 4.8. Schematic drawing of three neurons. The two at the *left* synapse with the one at the *right*. Impulses travel from *left* to *right*.

nerve. Each neuron fires independently, but a nerve often serves a particular area of the body. The auditory nerve, as an instance, is a bundle of some 30,000 fibers, most of them sensory, carrying information from the inner ear to the brain.

Frequency of neuronal firing is limited by the fact that an axon must restore itself after each firing to its state of rest before it can fire again. Some neurons can fire about 200 times a second, or as in some highly specialized nerve cells, over 1,000 times a second.

With this basic review of nerve fiber function as a background, let us consider what is known about how the central nervous system controls spoken language.

Central Nervous System Control of Speaking

Although we are far from understanding the nerve networks that may govern speech, we have obtained information about certain general areas of the brain that are related to the production of speech. It has long been known that when a gunshot wound or other trauma is inflicted on the brain, or when a person suffers a stroke—damage to the cells of the brain caused by a ruptured blood vessel or a blood clot (*cerebral vascular accident* or *CVA*)—language disturbances often result. The language impairment, termed *aphasia*, can take many forms: disabilities in forming utterances, in comprehension, in articulation, in writing, in reading, in naming things, or multiple combinations of these disabilities in varying degrees of severity.

Long known, too, is the fact that the left cerebral hemisphere of the brain controls movement and sensation on the right side of the body, while the right cerebral hemisphere controls movement and sensation on the left side of the body. Thus, a victim of a CVA or stroke in the right hemisphere might be partially or completely paralyzed on his left side depending upon the location and extent of the brain damage.

It was as recently as 1861, however, that the Parisian neurosurgeon and anthropologist, Paul Broca, discovered by autopsy of a formerly aphasic patient that speech production was controlled in the third convolution of the *frontal lobe* of the left cerebral hemisphere (see Fig. 4.9). Not long after, in 1874, Carl Wernicke localized the understanding of speech in the first convolution of the left *temporal lobe*. Such strict localization of function has given way in recent times to a view of the brain as more flexible in its assignment of function. Neurologists agree, however, that the left hemisphere is dominant for the control of speech in almost all right-handed people and the majority of left-handed people. They also agree that the critical area of the cerebrum for language in general is the area around the temporal-parietal juncture, and that, although the exact site known as Broca's area can, in some cases, be removed without affecting speech, the production of the motor impulses for speech muscles involves some portion of the posterior inferior area of the left frontal lobe.

Broca and Wernicke performed autopsies on a few patients to develop and substantiate their theories, but their theories have been confirmed in part and the important areas of the cerebral cortex for speech have been further delineated by Wilder Penfield, a neurosurgeon in Montreal, using an entirely different approach. While treating epilepsy by surgical methods, Penfield and Lamar Roberts, Penfield's colleague and former student, stimulated the exposed areas of the brains of over 70 patients, in order to map the cortex before surgery. The stimulations were used to locate the areas contributing to the epileptic seizures, but as a by-product, the surgeons learned a great deal about brain function.

Since the brain contains no pain receptors, electrical stimulation can be conducted without general anesthesia, permitting patients to be fully conscious and to speak during the procedure. A small current was applied via a fine wire touching the exposed cortical cells at many locations. The patient would respond by a muscle contraction at one location, by reporting a tingling sensation at another location, by vocalizing, by reexperiencing auditory and visual events of the past, or by a sudden inability to speak. Locations for each response were numbered by dropping tiny pieces of paper on the site and the numbered cortex was photographed. Figure 4.10A shows a photograph of a mapped cortex with the positive responses to each stimulation numbered. The schematic drawing *below* (Fig. 4.10B) indicates the area in relation to the entire side of the cerebrum.

A glance at Figure 4.9 or 4.10B shows the *Fissure of Rolando* creating a vertical division between the *frontal* and *parietal lobes*. Stimulations in front of this fissure, when applied to the posterior portion of the frontal lobe, usually resulted in motor responses: muscle contractions and movements. This area is referred to as the motor strip, although a few of the responses were sensory. Behind the Rolandic fissure, almost all of the responses to stimulation were sensory. In both motor and sensory strips of the cortex, the body is represented upside down as illustrated in a cross-section of the motor strip in the right hemisphere (Fig. 4.11). Notice the way in which the motor responses of the toes and lower limbs are represented at the top of the cortex, while the motor responses of the head are represented on the inferior surface of the frontal lobe. Remarkable is the extent of cortical representation assigned to the lips, tongue, jaw, and laryngeal mechanism in both the motor and sensory areas of the cerebrum. Along with the hand, the body parts implicated in speech have the highest representation of associated gray matter along the motor and

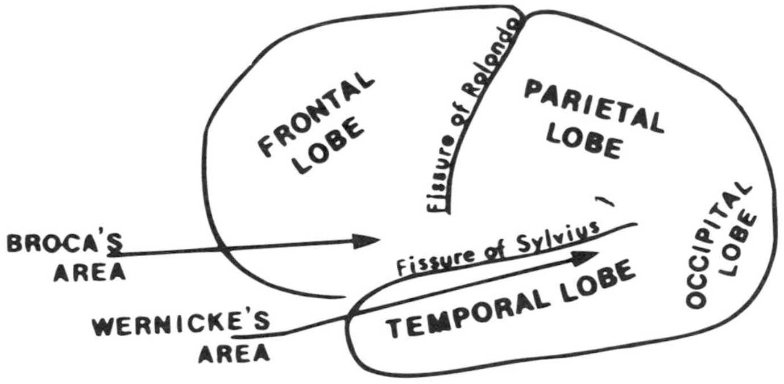

Figure 4.9. Lateral view of the cerebral cortex with the major divisions marked. Lateral surface of the cortex is divided into four lobes: frontal, parietal, temporal, and occipital. The Fissure of Rolando divides the frontal lobe from the parietal, while the Fissure of Sylvius separates the temporal lobe from the parietal and frontal lobes. Areas believed by Broca and Wernicke to be implicated in speech production and speech understanding are indicated.

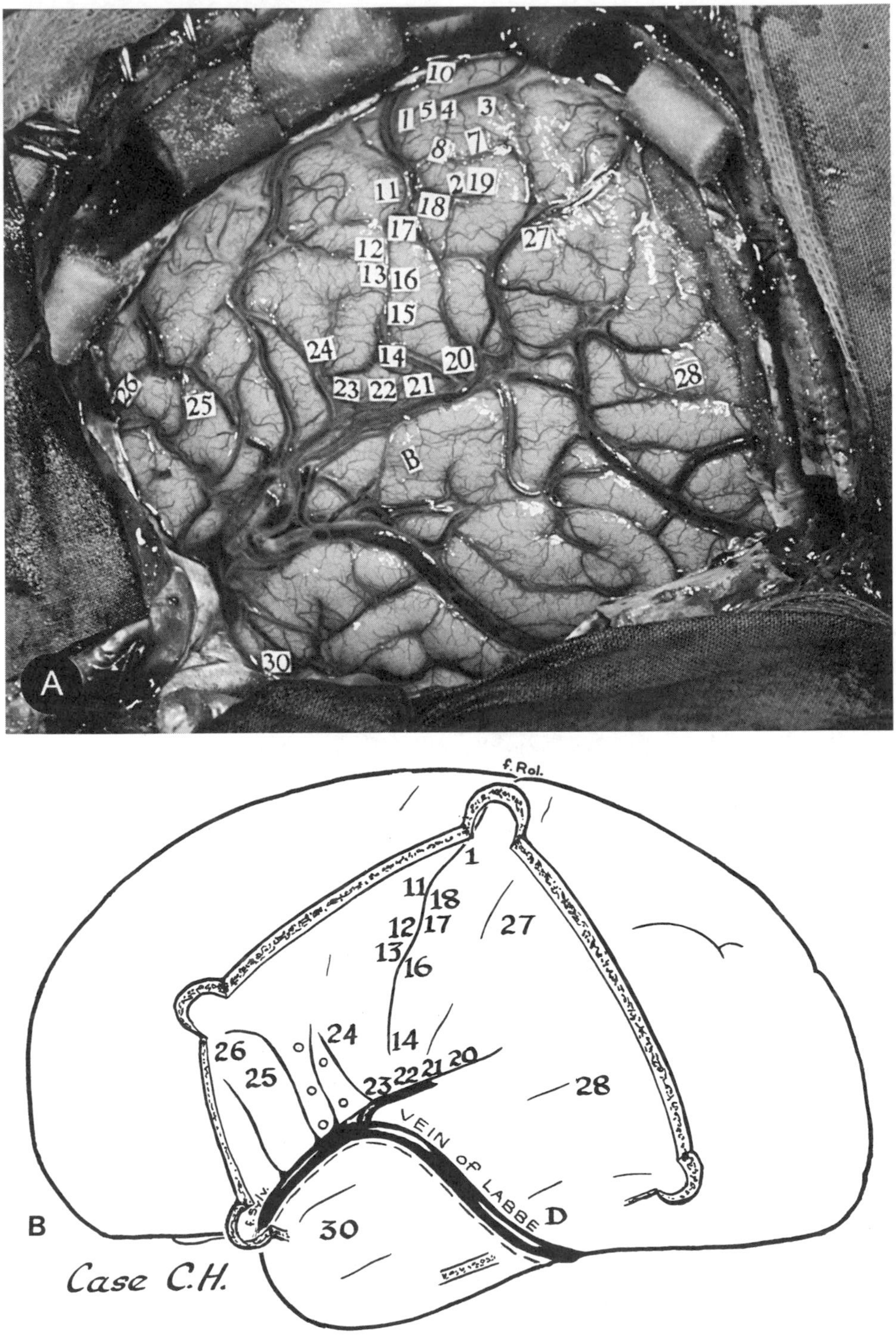

Figure 4.10. (*A*) Left cortical surface of Case CH after speech mapping. *Numbers* indicate points stimulated. (*B*) Penfield's drawing of Case CH on a standard chart. Aphasia (aphasic arrest) was produced by the stimulating electrode placed at *Points 26, 27* and *28*. Anarthria (motor speech arrest) was produced at *Points 23* and *24*. (From Wilder Penfield and Lamar Roberts: *Speech and Brain-Mechanisms*, © 1959 by Princeton University Press. Reprinted by permission of Princeton University Press.)

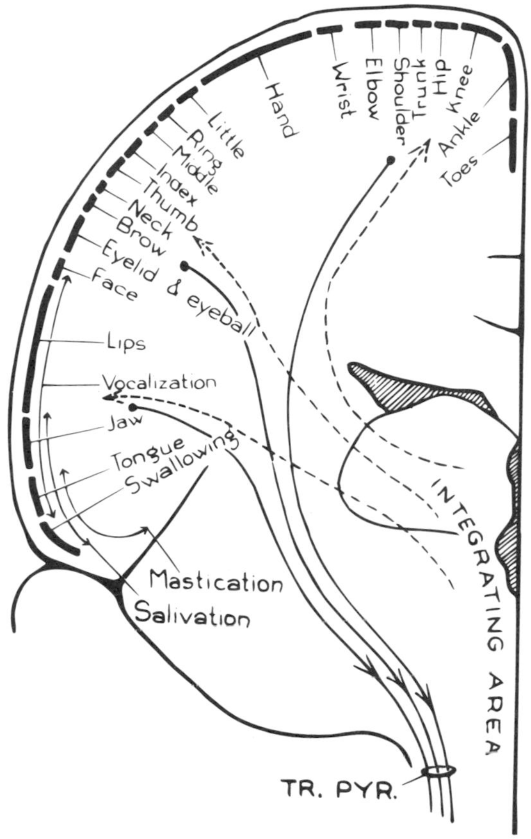

Figure 4.11. Frontal cross-section through the motor strip of the right hemisphere, showing the location of response to electrical stimulation. *TR. PYR.* refers to the pyramidal tract. (From Wilder Penfield and Lamar Roberts: *Speech and Brain-Mechanisms,* © 1959 Princeton University Press. Reprinted by permission of Princeton University Press.)

sensory strips of both cerebral hemispheres. It is as if most of the rest of the body were meant to nourish and transport the head and hands, which act upon and receive information from the environment.

Although some of the strictly motor and sensory aspects of speech production mechanisms seem to be controlled from both hemispheres, the overall control of organized spoken language resides in one hemisphere, usually the left. When Penfield stimulated certain regions of the cortex, patients were unable to name pictures or answer questions. At other sites they spoke but with slurred articulation. It was possible, upon a single stimulation in the temporal-parietal region, to elicit a sequential auditory and visual experience. One patient reported that she was in her kitchen and could hear the sounds of the neighborhood outside. It was more than a memory of an event. The subject relived and reheard the event while simultaneously being conscious of being in Montreal with Dr. Penfield. These experiences could, on occasion, be elicited several times by consecutive stimulation. Another stimulation in the temporal-parietal region interrupted the naming of pictures. When a picture of a butterfly was shown to the subject, he could not elicit its name. After the stimulation stopped, the patient reported that he had also tried unsuccessfully to recall the word "moth." Figure 4.12 summarizes the areas found by Penfield and Roberts to be important for speech, based upon stimulation evidence. The anterior area in the lower frontal lobe coincides with Broca's area, and stimulation here most often resulted in slurred speech or temporary *dysarthria*. The posterior area is large—including part of the temporal lobe, an extension of the area known as Wernicke's area, and part of the parietal lobe. Penfield considers this region to be most critical for language and speech. Stimulations in this region not only produced sequential experiences of past events but would interrupt the ability to use language. The patient sometimes could not say what he wanted to say or failed to understand what was spoken to him, thus simulating aphasia. The superior speech cortex was considered to be least important but supplemental to the motor area.

Twenty years later, Lassen and his Scandinavian colleagues suggested, on the basis of blood flow studies, that the supplementary motor area is involved in the planning of sequential motor tasks. It seems that the planning and execution of speech may be physiologically separate as well as behaviorally separate. Behavioral evidence of the separation of planning from execution lies in the symptoms of certain forms of brain damage. Speech motor planning problems (apraxia) and speech motor execution problems (dysarthria) have long been seen as different from one another by speech and language pathologists working on

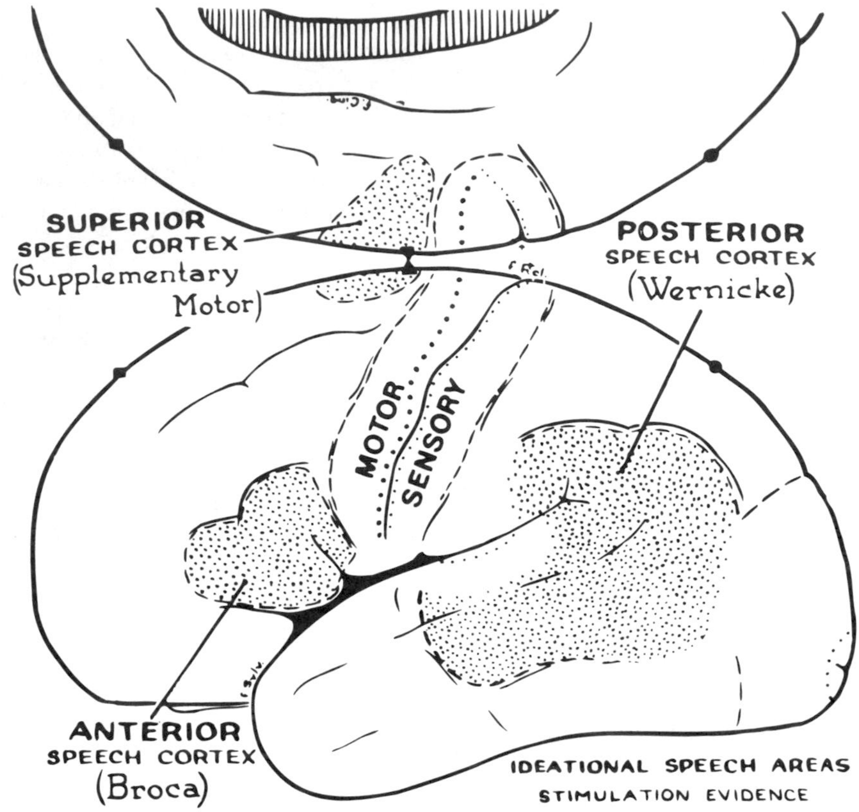

Figure 4.12. Summary map of the areas of the surface of the left cerebral hemisphere found by Penfield to be important for speech. The *lower drawing* shows the lateral surface, while the *upper drawing* shows the continuation of the areas on the medial cortical surface. (From Wilder Penfield and Lamar Roberts: *Speech and Brain-Mechanisms,* © 1959 by Princeton University Press. Reprinted by permission of Princeton University Press.)

the communication difficulties associated with aphasia. The work of Lassen and others on the role of the supplementary motor cortex has revived interest among speech scientists in this area of the brain, largely neglected since the work of Penfield. It should be noted that although three general areas of the cortex were cited by Penfield and Roberts as important to speech, the functions of the areas were not found to be as discrete as they had expected. They attribute the overlaps to subcortical connections among the areas. They were careful to point out that an electrical stimulus would disrupt whole systems and networks, implicating nerve cells far from the site of the stimulating electrode.

The Penfield and Roberts evidence is rich in implications about the central nervous system control of speech, of language, of sequential memory, and even of thought. It is worth our attention that the simple responses of vocalization or movement of speech muscles were bilaterally induced in their studies, while the more complex responses of recounting experiences or aphasic interruptions of speech were lateralized to one side of the brain. No stimulation resulted in a spoken word. At no point did a stimulation result in the patient involuntarily saying something like "chair." Speech involves simultaneous action in many parts of the brain and is apparently too complex to be elicited by a single stimulus, although its production can be interrupted by stimulation.

With the knowledge that one hemisphere of the cerebrum is dominant for speech, the Montreal group developed what is known as the

Wada Test to establish which side is dominant for a particular person. Physicians are reluctant to operate on the brain unless they know which areas control language. Medical decisions on the extent of the operation depend on assessing the relative importance of tumor removal and disrupting the patient's ability to communicate. A physician can remove more extensive tissue on the side of the cerebrum that is not dominant for speech.

To obtain this information, sodium amytal is injected into the carotid artery on one side of the neck at a time. The *carotid artery* conducts the blood supply to the brain, and the sodium amytal will produce a temporary effect upon the side in which it is injected. Normal function returns quickly, so there is little time for elaborate testing. The patient often lies upon a table with his arms extended toward the ceiling and his knees flexed. The effect of the injection is immediate and dramatic. The leg and the arm on the side opposite the affected cerebral hemisphere collapse. The patient is asked to count, to name pictures, and to answer questions. The whole procedure is then repeated on the other side. Usually, sodium amytal injection has a much more disruptive effect on speech and language for one side of the brain than for the other. Brenda Milner of McGill University in Montreal found that among 140 right-handed and 122 left-handed people, 96% of the right-handers had speech represented on the left side of the brain, and 70% of the left handers also had left hemisphere dominance. When speech was represented bilaterally, as it was in a few subjects, naming was stronger on one side and the ability to order words on the other. All of the evidence for lateralization of speech production, whether from the autopsies performed by Broca or Wernicke, from the electrical stimulation work by Penfield and Roberts, or from the sodium amytal test as described by Wada and Rasmussen, is taken from the cerebral hemispheres. Many neurophysiologists view the cerebrum as the source of voluntary motor activity. Penfield, in contrast, views the motor cortex as merely a platform at which voluntary motor impulses arrive, having originated in the higher brainstem. From the motor cortex, in any case, they course down the *pyramidal* (cortico-spinal) *tract* to the muscles.

Damage or dysfunction at the cortical level can result in *spasticity*, often observed among victims of *cerebral palsy*. Muscles contract but fail to relax. Damage in the higher brainstem can result in uncontrolled addition of movement to voluntary acts (*athetosis*), another common symptom of cerebral palsy, or in the hypokinesis or rigidity common in Parkinson's disease. Overall damage or oxygen deprivation can result in *mental retardation*, which decreases the level of language ability, among other things, according to the degree of the damage. More discrete CNS disorders can produce a variety of learning disabilities, such as the inability to attend to something, problems in reading (*dyslexia*), inability to attach meaning to the sound patterns of speech (*auditory agnosia*), various and complex disorders in language (*developmental aphasia*) or problems not only with language but with communication and human relationships in general (*autism*).

When there is a lack of coordination and integration of movement, the disorder may reside in the cerebellum. The cerebellum, posterior to and below the cerebrum, has long been known to coordinate the timing and regulation of complex skilled movements. John Eccles has made the study of the cerebellum a chief concern and proposes that the cerebellum has been programmed to execute automatically the most complex skilled tasks. He gives as an example the command to "write your name." The command originates, according to Eccles, in the cerebrum, while the cerebellum automatically controls the timing, intensity, and interaction of the multitude of muscle commands from the cerebrum. The muscles contract and relax in a set pattern without the need for the person's voluntary control over each segment of the signature. Motor impulses from the cerebrum are simultaneously relayed to the opposite lobe of the cerebellum. Within a few hundredths of a second, the cerebellum is thought to be directing the complex flow of impulses from the motor cortex, which it continues to do during the action. The cerebellum receives position and movement information from muscles and joints and has many connections with the spinal cord as well as the cerebrum. While Wilder Penfield would say that the command to write or speak originates in the higher brainstem rather than the cerebrum, as in Eccles' account, neurologists agree that the cerebrum, cerebellum, and *basal ganglia* interact in any skilled voluntary activity such as speaking, albeit in ways not yet understood.

Spoonerisms: Evidence for Preplanning

William A. Spooner, an English clergyman and dean of New College at Oxford at the turn of the century, is less famous for his lectures than for his amusing speech reversals. Instead of saying "You've missed my history lectures," he would say "You've *h*issed my *my*stery lectures," a confusion now known as a "spoonerism." "Work is the curse of the *d*rinking class," he is reputed to have said. Word reversals and phoneme reversals do suggest that speakers hold a complete phrase in some stage of readiness for speech. Otherwise, the transposition of a word or sound from the end of the intended phrase to the beginning would not occur. Speech errors, and there are other kinds of error in addition to spoonerisms, reveal something about speech production. The chart in Table 4.1 lists examples of speech sound errors collected by Victoria Fromkin of UCLA. Notice that consonants and vowels are never interchanged, that the errors are always consistent with the rules of English (optimal is *m*optimal, never *ng*optimal, because /ŋ/ in English never initiates a syllable), and that most errors involve the first syllable, often the first sound, of a word. Interesting, too, is the observation that the stress and intonation of the phrase or sentence remain constant in the face of word changes. In Fromkin's example "Seymour sliced the knife with the salami," the pitch rise and increased intensity that would have been vested in "knife" in the intended sentence, were incorporated in the production of "salami." These errors serve to hint at neurophysiological mechanisms in speech production in the planning stages prior to the transmission of motor impulses to muscles. It is clear that speakers do not normally call forth and speak a sentence one word at a time.

Table 4.1. Segmental Errors in Speech[a]

Errors	Examples	
Consonant errors		
Anticipation	A reading list	A leading list
	It's a real mystery	It's a meal mystery
Perseveration	Pulled a tantrum	Pulled a pantrum
	At the beginning of the turn	At the beginning of the burn
Reversals (Spoonerisms)	Left hemisphere	Heft lemisphere
	A two-pen set	A two-sen pet
Vowel errors		
Reversals	Feet moving	Fute meeving
	Fill the pool	Fool the pill
Other errors		
Addition	The optimal number	The moptimal number
Movement	Ice cream	Kise ream
Deletion	Chrysanthemum plants	Chrysanthemum p ants
Consonant clusters split or moved	Speech production	Peach sedduction
	Damage claim	Clammage dame

[a] Segmental errors in speech can involve vowels as well as consonants. Some typical types of substitution of sounds are shown. Such errors provide evidence that the discrete phonetic segments posited by linguistic theory exist in the mental grammar of the speaker. Taken from V. A. Fromkin, Slips of the tongue. *Scientific American 229,* 1973, 114.

Peripheral Nervous System Control of Speaking

More is known about the activity of the cranial and spinal nerves that form the peripheral nervous system than is known about the more complex activity of the brain. The circuitry of the PNS has been mapped. We know that certain motor neurons activate certain muscles, and that particular sensory neurons conduct information from certain kinds of sense receptors. The interactions, coordination, and use of this circuitry, however, are not well known. The coordination of various motoneurons for a particular act, for example, is not completely understood, nor is the role of sensory information in movement control. We understand that someone intends to do something, and we understand the more peripheral actions that result (nerve activity, muscle contractions, movements), but we fail as yet to understand how one gets from intention to action, that is, the method of coordination and control, especially of complicated actions such as speaking or playing a sport. These actions require rapid adjustments to constantly changing conditions from within the performer and from without. We return to this question later in the section on Models of Speech Production.

What do we know about the role of the peripheral nervous system in the control of speech? Cranial nerves emerge from the base of the brain, and many of them activate groups of muscles important in speech. The muscles innervated by cranial nerves lie in the head and neck area. Also within the head and neck area are receptors (for hearing, touch, and sense of position and movement) that are presumed to be used in learning to speak. Information is carried from these receptors along sensory fibers among the cranial nerves. These systems are considered in more detail in the section on Feedback Mechanisms.

Spinal nerves are also active in speech. Those that emerge from the ventral (front) side of the vertebral column activate muscles used in the control of respiration for speech. These nerves come primarily from the cervical (neck), thoracic (chest), and abdominal sections of the vertebral column and serve the muscles of inhalation and exhalation. Similarly, receptors sensitive to muscle activity in these areas are served by sensory fibers that enter the dorsal (back) side of the vertebral column. That is why you might temporarily lose your sense of feeling or touch in your hand if you were to carry an unduly heavy backpack pressing on a dorsal root of sensory fibers serving that hand. Among the spinal nerves the sensory fibers are closer to the surface, emerging as they do from the dorsal aspect of the spinal cord. See Appendix 2 for a list of the most important peripheral nerves implicated in speech. These will be detailed when the muscles and receptors that they serve are introduced.

The Motor Unit

The interface between the nervous system and the muscular system is the assembly known as the *motor unit*. Striated muscles, which form the voluntary motor systems used for activities such as speech, are innervated by motoneurons in such a way that each nerve fiber or neuron typically activates several muscle fibers. A single motoneuron, along with the muscle fibers that it serves are considered to be one motor unit. When the neuron stimulates the muscle fibers, a mechanical twitch is produced by a small electrical signal called an *action potential*. This signal can be amplified and recorded using a technique known as *electromyography* (*EMG*). (See Chapter 7). When we say that we are contracting a particular muscle, we are really firing many motor units simultaneously. The action potentials from motor units produced at low levels of muscle contraction are small in amplitude compared with the higher amplitude of the motor units recruited later at higher levels of contraction. The electrical signal given off when a muscle contracts is an interference pattern that is the sum of the activity from the individual motor units involved, just as an acoustic interference pattern is the sum of the particular frequencies and phase differences of its component tones. Figure 4.13 illustrates the summation of many

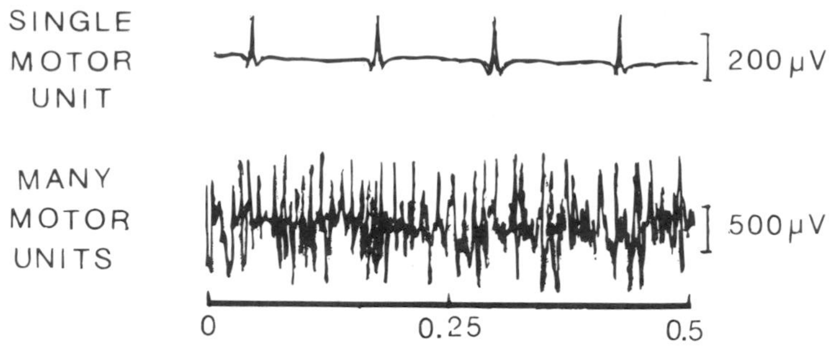

Figure 4.13. The interference pattern represented in the lower part of the figure reflects the summed activity of many motor units. Both single motor units and complex muscle activity may be recorded by electromyography.

motor units to form an interference pattern recorded by the technique of electromyography.

The firing of motor units produces muscle activity but not necessarily movement. You can tense the muscles of your index finger, both the flexor and the extensor, producing an EMG signal from both, but the finger does not move because agonist-antagonist activity is balanced. The movements that are involved in speech, however, are the result of the coordination of many muscles whose activity is the result of the firing of many motor units.

In summary, the nervous system activates many groups of muscles that are coordinated in such a way that they produce movements of the abdomen, chest, larynx, vocal tract, and lips, resulting in air pressure changes that are audible. To power the whole system, then, we need air.

RESPIRATION

Modification of Airstream for Speech Sounds

The production of all speech sounds is the result of modulation of the air flow from the lungs. The speaker must produce a stream of exhaled air and then modulate it in ways that make it audible to a listener.

The number of ways that humans have to do this in order to produce the multitude of sounds found in the languages of the world is impressively large, the more so since the speech mechanism comprises a limited set of component parts and a limited set of processes for modifying the airstream. A speaker has only a few movable parts with which to create sounds: the vocal folds, tongue, jaw, lips, and soft palate. There are only a few cavities to use as resonators: the mouth, pharynx, and nasal cavities being the primary ones. Yet speakers of the world produce speech sounds in a multitude of ways. They phonate during the production of some sounds, but not others. They create a large variety of vocal tract shapes to vary resonance. They generate aperiodic sounds of various durations such as hisses, clicks, and small explosions of air. They grunt, murmur, and vary loudness. A few sounds are produced on air intake rather than outflow, and in some languages, sounds that are otherwise identical are made distinctive by a change in relative pitch.

In English, there are approximately 40 phonemes. They are listed in Appendix 1. They are all created by making exhaled air audible. The two primary methods used for making the airflow audible are phonation and the creation of consonant noises. Phonation is the creation of a nearly periodic sound wave by the rapid opening and closing of the vocal folds. The continuous flow of air from the lungs is thus chopped into a discontinuous series of tiny puffs of air that are audible. Consonant noise is created by the positioning of parts of the speech mechanism in such a way that they form occlusions or constrictions. As the flow of air is released from the occlusions or channeled through the constrictions, aperiodic sounds are created in the vocal tract, mostly in the mouth or *oral cavity*. Some English phonemes require both periodic and aperiodic sources of sound. Both the sounds of phonation and the sounds of consonant noise are resonated in the *vocal tract*.

Say "ah" (ɑ). That is an example of a voiced sound. All English vowels are classified as voiced sounds. The vocal folds are set into vibration producing the source of the sound, which gets its characteristic ɑ quality (as opposed to "ee" ([i]), also voiced) by the acoustic resonance provided in this case by a large oral cavity and a relatively small pharyngeal cavity. Try the sounds of [s] and [k]. These sounds are examples of two different kinds of consonant noise. The source of these sounds is not at the vocal folds but in the oral cavity. The [s] noise is produced by forcing the airstream through a narrow constriction. The air is stopped completely for [k] so that it can be released suddenly to produce a transient burst of sound as the air is channeled through the broken occlusion.

Finally, these two methods can be combined for speech sounds that are really a combination of periodic and aperiodic sound. Try prolonging [s] and then continue the noise but start phonating at the same time. Another speech sound is produced, [z], using yet another means of modulating the airstream.

The speech production mechanisms can be likened to a peculiar musical instrument with a variable resonator, capable of producing sounds that are at one moment based on oscillation and, at the next, on turbulence. Figure 4.14 diagrams the process.

Negative Pressure Breathing

Preparatory to exhaling air for the production of speech sounds, sufficient air must be inhaled. Under normal circumstances, air is taken into the lungs in much the same way it is taken into an accordion or bellows (Fig. 4.15) Press the keys as hard as you will on an accordion, and no sound will emerge unless you have first increased the volume of its air reservoir by pulling the ends of the accordion away from each other. This enlargement reduces the pressure inside the air reservoir, relative to the external air pressure, in accordance with Boyle's Law. Robert Boyle, a 17th century British physicist, discovered that volume and pressure are inversely related. Therefore, increasing the volume of an enclosed space will decrease the air pressure within it. The air reservoir of an accordion, however, is not a completely enclosed space because it has an inlet for outside air. Because unequal pressures will always equalize themselves if given the chance, air will be drawn into the accordion through the inlet. In order to produce musical tones you must, of course, reverse the process just described by pushing the ends of the accordion toward each other, thus decreasing the volume of the air reservoir. Once again the inverse relationship between volume and pressure described by Boyle's Law comes into play. In this case, the decrease in volume momentarily increases the internal air pressure, which will again equalize as air rushes out of the instrument, setting its reeds into vibration and producing musical tones.

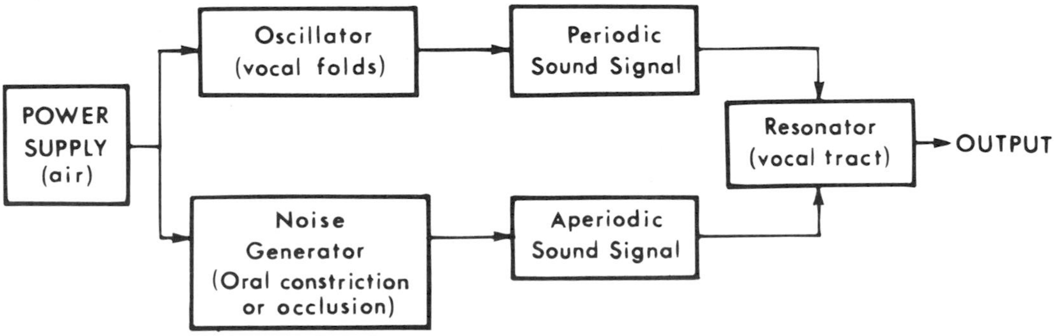

Figure 4.14. Block diagram of the speech production process. Air is converted into a periodic or an aperiodic acoustic signal, which is modified by the vocal tract.

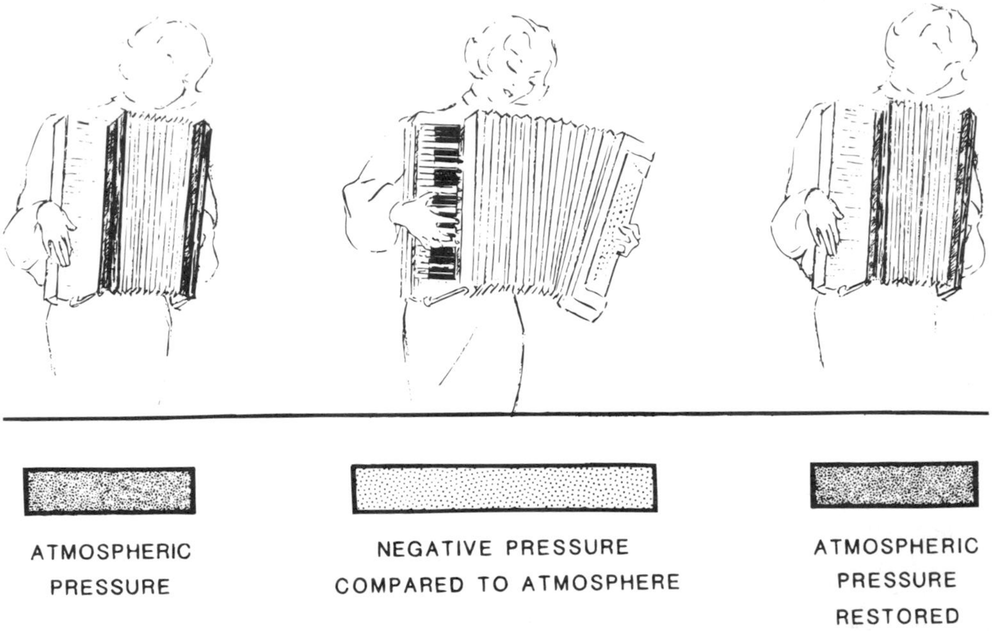

Figure 4.15. Air pressure-volume relations in an accordion. When the player enlarges the accordion, pressure falls. Air then enters through an inlet valve, to equalize pressure.

The flow of air into and out of the air reservoir of an accordion is analogous to what occurs in the lungs as we breathe: we expand our chest and lungs causing air to flow in to equalize the negative pressure or partial vacuum created, then we contract our chest and lungs causing air to flow out to equalize the positive pressure created by the contraction. It is by changing the volume that we change the pressure.

Thus, air is brought into the lungs via the larynx, trachea, bronchi, bronchioles, the passageways increasingly branching until they reach the small air sacs (alveoli) that compose the major part of the lungs. It is there that the exchange of oxygen for carbon dioxide from the blood takes place, an exchange which is essential for life.

The Respiratory Mechanism

A surplus of carbon dioxide and a need for oxygen is automatically signaled in the *medulla oblongata*, the reflex seat for respiration in the brainstem. The medulla, in turn, initiates nerve impulses from the brain and spinal cord to various muscles in the thorax or chest. The thorax (Fig. 4.16) is bounded by the *vertebrae* in the back and the *sternum* or breast bone in the front. Completing the cylinder are 12 sets of *ribs*, which form a skeletal framework from the front to the vertebrae in the back. The ribs are *osseous* (bony) except for the section of each rib contiguous with the sternum. These sections are made of cartilage. The lower ribs share cartilaginous attachments to the sternum, and the lowest two ribs are only attached at the back to the vertebral column.

This barrel-shaped cavity, the thorax, has as its floor a dome-shaped muscle sheet called the *diaphragm*, which simultaneously serves as the ceiling for the abdominal cavity. The lungs rest on the diaphragm and since they are spongy, elastic masses of air cells and lack muscles, they change shape by assuming the form of their container. When the diaphragm lowers or elevates, the lungs go along for the ride. In a similar manner, when the thorax expands or contracts by rib elevation and depression, the lungs also expand and contract because they are linked to the ribs. The rib cage is lined with a membrane called the *costal* (rib) *pleura* or alternatively, the *parietal pleura*. The lungs are covered by another membrane called the *pulmonary pleura* or sometimes the *visceral pleura*. These two membranes, the costal and pulmonary pleurae, adhere to one another and, at the same time, can slide across one another without friction, because of the presence of a viscous fluid between them. (Similarly, liquid between two thin plates of glass enables the plates to move across each other, while the surface tension of the fluid holds the plates of glass together.) This pleural linkage between the lungs and ribs enables the lungs to expand and contract as the thoracic cage changes volume (Fig. 4.17). Even without movement, the pleural linkage helps to keep the lungs expanded and the ribs compressed.

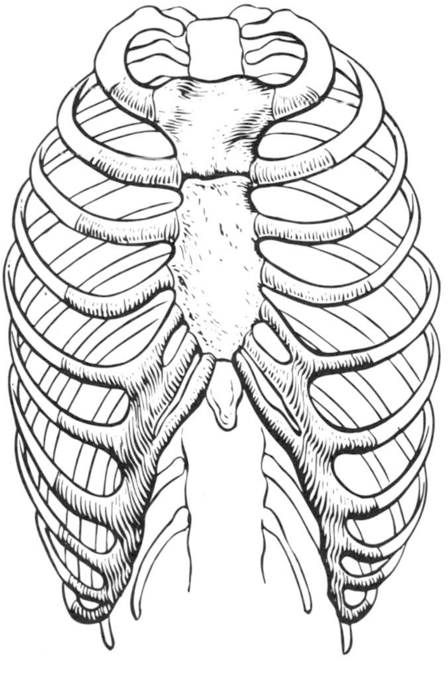

Figure 4.16. The thoracic cage. (Adapted from J. V. Basmajian: *Primary Anatomy*, 6th Ed., Williams & Wilkins © 1970).

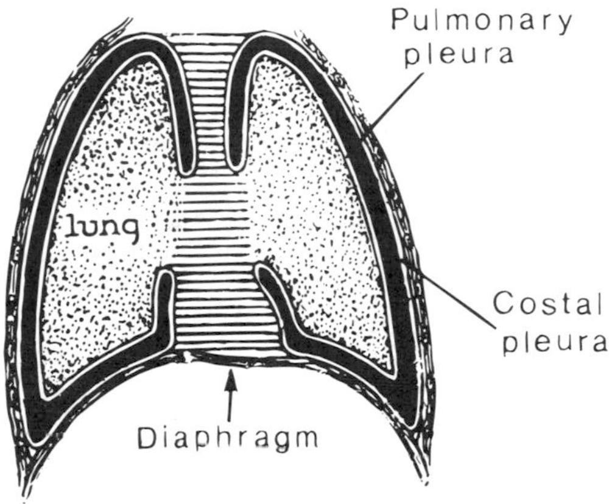

Figure 4.17. Schematic coronal section of thorax, showing costal and pulmonary pleurae.

Inspiration

For Quiet Breathing. For quiet inspiration (or inhalation), the medulla automatically sends neuronal impulses via the spinal cord to the pertinent thoracic muscles. Several nerves emerge from the spinal cord at the level of the neck (*cervical nerves*) and join to form a nerve bundle known as the *phrenic nerve*. The phrenic nerve innervates the diaphragm, the convex sheet of muscle fibers that separates the thoracic and abdominal cavities. When nervous stimulation is sufficient to cause a contraction of the diaphragm, the muscle fibers shorten, pulling the central part downward toward the edges, which are attached to the lower ribs. The effect is to lower and flatten the diaphragm to some extent. As the diaphragm forms the floor of the thoracic cavity, thoracic volume is increased vertically as the floor is lowered (Fig. 4.18). One can often observe the abdomen protruding upon inspiration, because of the downward pressure of the diaphragm upon the abdominal contents.

At the same time that the diaphragm is lowering, nerve impulses are transmitted via nerves emerging from the spinal cord at the level of the chest (*thoracic nerves*) to innervate muscles that run between the ribs (intercostal muscles: inter = between; costal = ribs). There are 12 ribs on each side of the thorax, allowing for 11 sets of intercostal muscles to connect them. Furthermore, there are two layers of in-

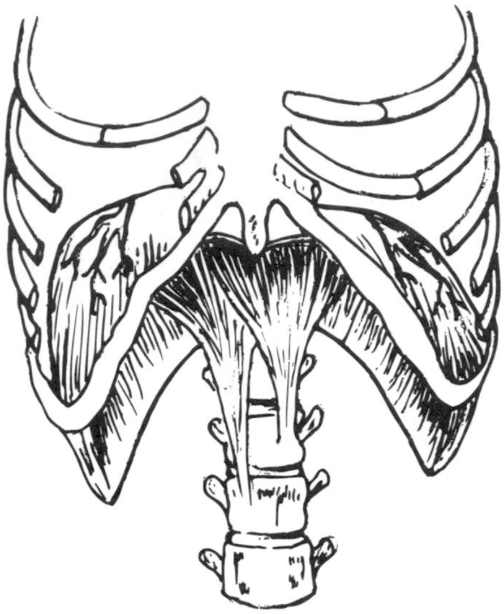

Figure 4.18. Anterior view of the diaphragm, innervated by the phrenic nerve.

tercostal muscles, one layer superficial to the other. The *external intercostal muscles* connect the osseous portion of the ribs but do not connect the cartilage sections near the sternum. They lie superficial to the *internal intercostal muscles,* which connect the cartilage and osseous portions of the ribs starting at the front, but not at the rear where the ribs are attached to the vertebrae (Fig. 4.19). The muscle fibers of the external and internal intercostal muscles course in opposite directions. The external fibers course obliquely from the vertebrae down and out as they extend toward the sternum, while the internal fibers course obliquely in the opposite direction from the sternum down and out, as they extend toward the vertebrae. On a legal size piece of paper, draw a schematic representation of the intercostals as shown in Figure 4.19, which you can wrap around one side of your rib cage.

During inspiration, the external intercostal muscles and the section of the internal intercostals that lies between the cartilaginous portions of the ribs (the *interchondral part*) contract to elevate the ribs. Observe from the muscle representation that you have wrapped around your side that the vertebrae act as the fulcrum for the external intercostals, supplying leverage so that when the muscles shorten, the main effect is to lift the rib below. The same effect can be imagined in the front, where the internal intercostal muscles join the interchondral portions of the ribs. The muscle fibers course down and away from the sternum, which gives support to the upper part of each muscle, again supplying the leverage necessary to lift the rib below. This action is aided by the twisting of the cartilages. Elevation of the ribs is thus produced by the joint efforts of the external intercostal muscles and the interchondral parts of the internal intercostal muscles, aided by a slight rotation of the cartilages. The result of these actions is an expansion of the thoracic cavity in both the anterior to posterior dimension and the lateral dimension (Fig. 4.20).

As the volume within the thorax increases with corresponding lung volume increase insured by the pleural linkage, air pressure inside the lungs decreases relative to atmospheric pressure outside. Consequently, air from the outside moves to the area of less density or lower pressure, within the lungs.

The upper airways serve as the conduit for the inhaled air (Fig. 4.21). Air normally enters the nasal cavities, where it is warmed, moistened, and filtered before it proceeds down the pharynx, passes as previously described through the larynx, down the trachea or windpipe, and then enters into increasingly branched tubes (bronchi, bronchioles) until the final multitudinous subdivisions ending at the alveolar sacs of the lungs. Mouth breathing is also possible, but tends to dry out the throat.

For Speech Breathing. There are several differences between inspiration during quiet breathing and inspiration for speech breathing. The first one we will mention is that the volume of air inspired for speech sounds is generally greater than that inspired during quiet breathing, especially if the speaker knows that he is going to generate an utterance that is long and loud (or both). To accomplish the inspiration of a greater volume of air, the diaphragm and intercostal muscles can be augmented by any of several muscles capable of sternum and rib elevation: the *sternocleido-*

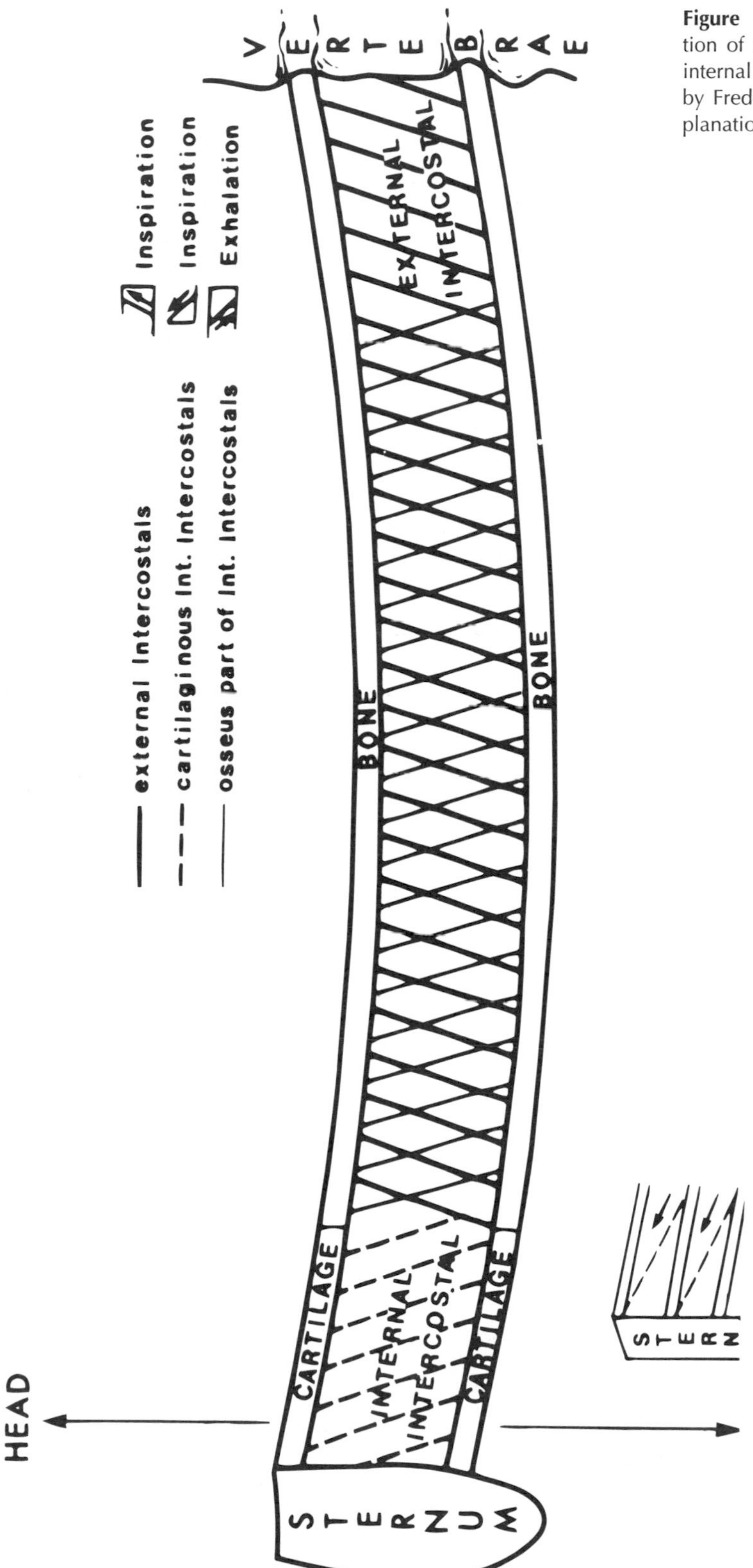

Figure 4.19. Wrap-around representation of the functions of the external and internal intercostal muscles as suggested by Fredericka Bell-Berti. (See text for explanation.)

mastoid, the *scalenus*, the *subclavius*, and the *pectoralis major* and *minor* muscles in front, the *serratus anterior* muscle at the sides, and the *levatores costarum* muscles, *serratus posterior superior* muscle and *latissimus dorsi* muscle at the back.

A second difference is in the degree of automaticity. We breathe in and out, day and night, conscious and unconscious, and the process is under reflexive control, with the rate and depth of volume change dependent upon need. However, we can assume more voluntary control over our breathing. When we are reading a poem or singing a song, we are often conscious of making a larger volume change on inspiration in order to have enough air pressure to complete a long phrase without interruption.

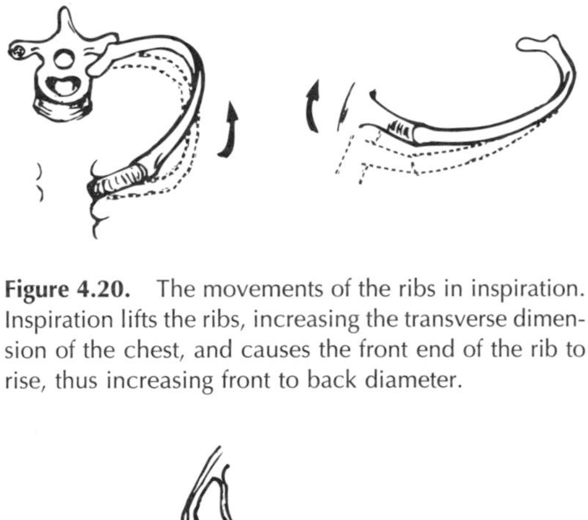

Figure 4.20. The movements of the ribs in inspiration. Inspiration lifts the ribs, increasing the transverse dimension of the chest, and causes the front end of the rib to rise, thus increasing front to back diameter.

Thirdly, inspiration for speech comprises less of the total respiratory cycle than during quiet breathing. Time your breaths during rest and during the reading of a paragraph; you may not find a significant difference in breaths per minute, which may range from 12 to 20 a minute, but the ratio between inspiration and expiration will differ markedly. During quiet breathing the ratio is roughly 40% inspiration and 60% expiration while for speech it is about 10% inspiration and 90% expiration (Fig. 4.22), although the ratio varies somewhat according to context.

People who are speaking usually tense the abdominal muscles slightly during inhalation as well as during exhalation. This is thought by Hixon, Mead, and Goldman to keep the diaphragm elevated to some extent and "tuned," ready for its rapid contraction and descent necessary to provide such quick inspira-

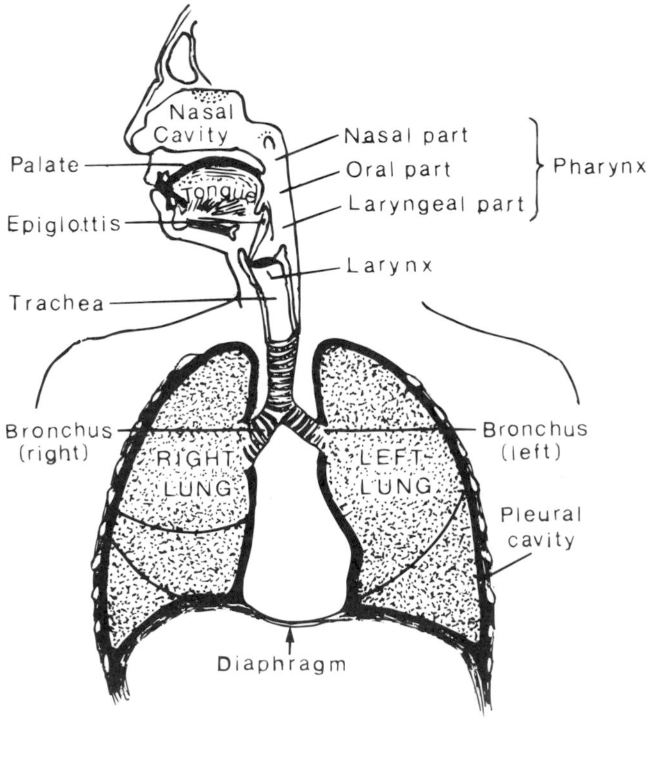

Figure 4.21. The airways of the respiratory system.

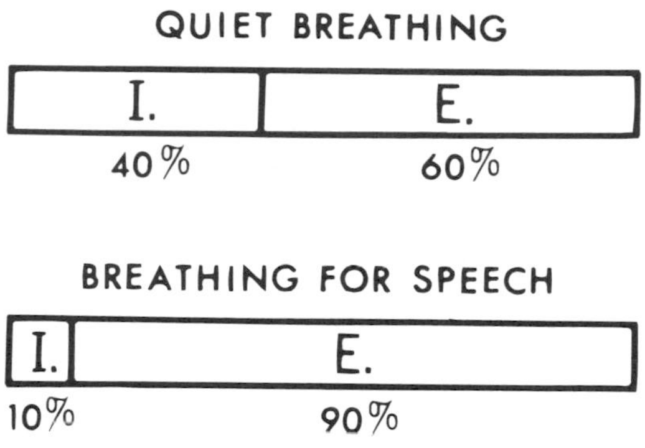

Figure 4.22. Comparison of the inspiratory (*I*) and expiratory (*E*) proportions of the respiratory cycle for quiet breathing and speech.

tions. Interruptions to ongoing speech can be limited in frequency because of the rapid and relatively deep inhalations that are employed.

Expiration

When the glottis is open for inspiration, air from the outside enters the lungs; when the inspiratory muscle effort is complete (depending upon the pressure needs of the task ahead), there is a moment of equalized pressure. The pressure in the lungs is equal to the atmospheric pressure. At a relatively high thoracic volume, however, a large inspiratory force is required to maintain the volume. If one were to relax the inspiratory muscles, the air would suddenly rush out because of the lung-rib recoil. Try it yourself. Inhale deeply by enlarging your rib cage and lung volume. Then, while holding the volume constant, hold your breath but open the *glottis*. If the glottis is open, pressure above and below must be equal. If you let the inspiratory muscles relax, the air will rush out because of three passive forces: the *elastic recoil* of the lungs and rib cage (the expanded elastic tissues of the lungs contracting to their natural shape), *torque*, the force of the untwisting of the cartilages next to the sternum, and *gravity*, which may aid in lowering the rib cage. These three passive forces suffice to decrease the volume of the rib cage and lungs. According to Boyle's law, the decrease in volume increases the pressure within, causing air to flow out. In Figure 4.23 we can see how the pressure-volume relationships for inspiration and expiration contrast with each other. For inspiration an increase in thoracic volume effects a decrease in pressure. For expiration, a decrease in thoracic volume causes an increase in pressure.

In quiet expiration, the exchange of air is small (approximately 0.5 liter). With deeper breaths like those that accompany exercise, the volume of air exchanged increases. The amount of air exchanged during ins and outs of quiet respiration is called *tidal volume*. At rest, people take from 12 to 20 breaths per minute and the inspiration phase is only somewhat shorter in duration than the expiration phase. If one were to make a maximum inspiration, followed by a maximum expiration, the volume of air inhaled or exhaled would be one's *vital capacity* (*VC*). The vital capacity of a person is related to sex, size, and breathing habits. As an average, human vital capacity is approximately 5 liters (somewhat more than 5 quarts), but large male mountain climbers would surely have larger vital capacities than many people. The half a liter exchanged during quiet breathing is only 10% of the exchange one is capable of, and since there is an additional 2 liters of residual air that one is unable to expel, the tidal volume of 0.5 liter is only about 7% of total lung volume. Lung volumes and some of the standardized terminology are given in Figure 4.24.

For Sustained Phonation. The passive expiratory forces of elasticity, torque, and gravity are not sufficient by themselves to support singing or speaking. Expiration during phonation then differs from that during quiet breathing, and expiration during speech differs from both.

In order to maintain a constant pressure to produce a note sung at a constant intensity, the passive recoil force of the rib cage-lung coupling is used as a background force that is supplemented by active muscle contractions, first of the inspiratory muscles, then of the expiratory muscles. If a singer permitted expiratory forces to act unaided, the lungs would collapse suddenly and the note could not be sustained. The purpose of the active inspiratory

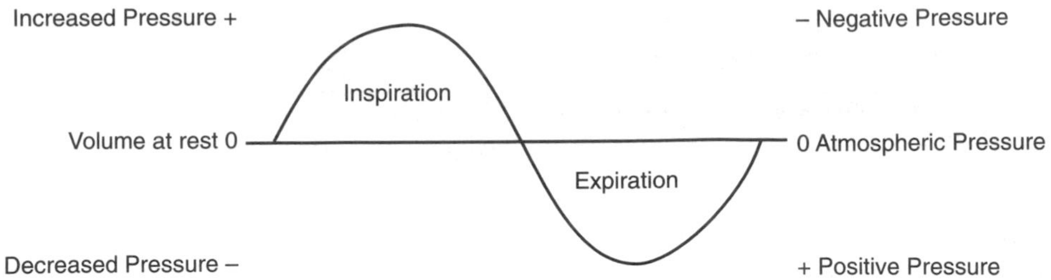

Figure 4.23. Changes of lung volume and pressure during inspiration and expiration.

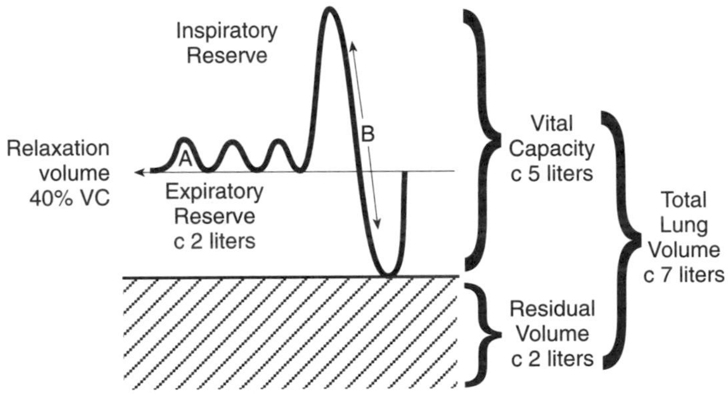

Figure 4.24. Inspiration and expiration during quiet, or tidal breathing (*A*) and in a maximum exhalation and inhalation (*B*). Standard terminology for various parts of the total lung capacity is indicated.

forces (muscle contractions) is to slow down the outflow. The expiratory muscle forces are recruited later to further decrease thoracic size below the limits set by elastic recoil.

A pressure-volume diagram of the human chest showing the spring-like action of the respiratory system was first presented by Rahn *et al.* (1946). It shows how pressures vary at different lung volumes (Fig. 4.25). Lung volumes are plotted on the ordinate axis in terms of the percentage of vital capacity. The relaxation pressure curve (R) is plotted by asking people to adjust to a certain lung volume and then open the glottis and relax. At high lung volumes, people exhale upon relaxation, while at low lung volumes, they inhale. Pulmonary pressure (on the abscissa) is measured and recorded for each lung volume. At high lung

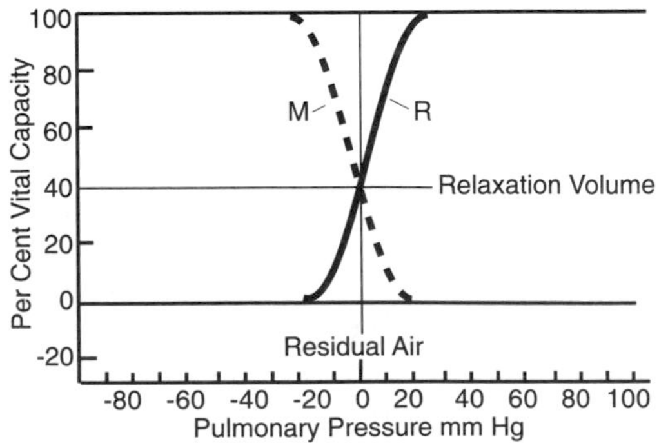

Figure 4.25. A simplified version of Rahn's pressure-volume diagram. In the figure, *R* represents the pressure generated when you relax at different lung volumes. Relaxation volume occurs at about 40% vital capacity; here the elastic forces of the ribs and lungs are balanced. *M* represents the muscle forces needed at various lung volumes to balance the pressure supplied by passive forces.

volumes, a positive pressure is recorded upon relaxation; at low lung volumes, a negative pressure. The S-shaped curve that results is an index of average pressures supplied by the *passive* (non-muscular) inspiration and expiration forces.

Take a quiet breath. At the end of the expiration, one reaches a relaxed state in which the tension between the rib cage (which tends to expand) and the lungs (which tend to collapse) are balanced. This happens at about 40% of vital capacity, the *relaxation volume*. At high volumes, as we know from our trial, there is a force created, mostly from the elasticity of the lungs, which is expiratory. Conversely, at low lung volumes, the relaxation pressure of the lungs and rib cage recoil forces is inspiratory. For example, if you exhale all the air that you can and open your glottis, you will have created a large force to assist in inspiration. Let go and you'll see. This relaxation pressure curve then represents a background force of lung elasticity and rib cage elasticity including torque and gravity that we can use in respiration to assist our muscles in changing lung volume.

The pressure-volume relationships are altered somewhat when a person is lying down, since the abdominal contents press upon the diaphragm and increase lung pressure.

Mead, Bouhuys, and Proctor depict the modifications made to this background of recoil force when singers attempt to sustain a tone of low but constant intensity. Maintaining a subglottal pressure of 7 cm of H_2O (air pressure is traditionally measured by how far a column of water or mercury would be moved), the vocalist adds active muscle force of the inspiratory muscles (during expiration) for the first half of the tone in order to check the recoil force, and then starts to contract the expiratory muscles with increasingly greater force (Fig. 4.26). For the first part of the tone, the vocalist continues to activate the external intercostal muscles and the interchondral part of the internal intercostal muscles, only gradually reducing the contractions so that the rib cage and lungs will decrease in volume smoothly. These muscles serve to brake the recoil forces. Thus, inspiratory muscles are used during expiration. As lung volume approaches the state in which the natural output pressure is 7 cm of H_2O, the expiratory muscles prepare to increase activity in order to maintain that pressure at decreasing lung volumes. Mead makes the point that muscle activity must constantly change in order to

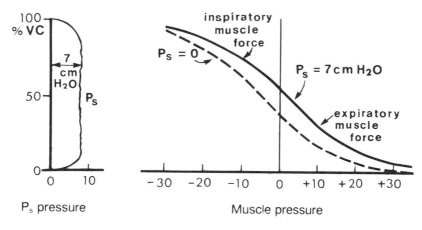

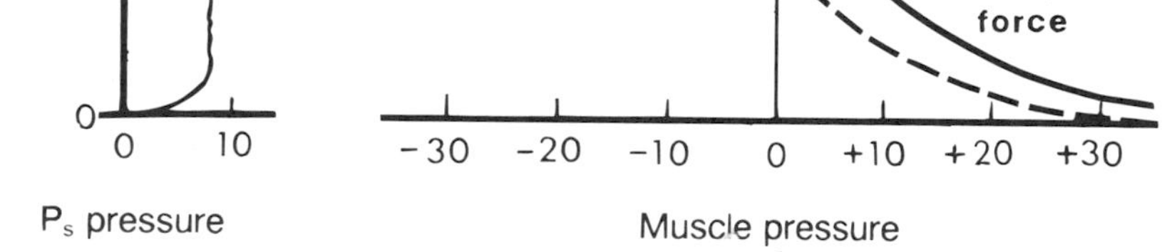

Figure 4.26. Forces required to maintain a constant subglottal pressure (P_s) for a sustained tone, at varying lung volumes. The *dashed line* indicates the inspiratory and expiratory muscle forces needed to balance the recoil forces for zero subglottal pressure. By convention, inspiratory muscle forces are given a minus sign and expiratory muscle forces a plus sign. The *solid line* indicates the inspiratory or expiratory muscle forces required to produce a constant subglottal pressure of 7 cm of water.

sustain a constant subglottal pressure at different lung volumes.

For Speech. The continued action of the inspiratory muscles to check the rate of expiration seen in sustaining a tone is also evident during expiration for speech.

The process of respiration is summed up in Table 4.2 by outlining the chain of events from neural impulses to the results in air pressure and air movement.

The expiratory muscles are innervated by spinal nerves. The thoracic nerves (T_1–T_{11}) innervate the internal intercostal muscles, the interosseus portions of which contract to shorten the distance between the ribs by depressing them, thereby reducing thoracic volume. The abdominal muscles are active in extended expiration as their contraction presses in upon the abdominal contents forcing the diaphragm up. The chief abdominal muscles used in expiration are the *rectus abdominis*, the *external* and *internal obliques*, and the *transversus abdominis* (Fig. 4.27).

Draper, Ladefoged, and Whitteridge recorded muscle activity from inspiratory muscles (external intercostals and diaphragm) and expiratory muscles (internal intercostals and abdominal muscles) while subjects spoke. In Figure 4.28, air pressure and muscle activity are indicated as measured in a subject counting from 1 to 32 at conversational loudness. The technique of electromyography is explained in Chapter 7. Note that the lung volume drops gradually. The muscles of inspiration continue to contract, gradually decreasing activity. Aided by the force of the relaxation pressure, or elasticity of the respiratory system, the expiratory muscles are gradually activated to further reduce lung volume, extending the exhalation. More recent evidence based on abdominal movements indicates that the abdominal wall is stiffened for both inspiration and expiration during running speech.

Expiration for speech differs from expiration for a sustained tone, however, because of the addition of several factors. During speech, intensity is constantly changing because certain sentences, phrases, words, and syllables are given emphasis. In order to increase the intensity of the speech sound, the speaker must increase subglottal pressure. For example, during one expiration a speaker might say "The *quality of mercy* is not *strained* but *droppeth* as the *gentle rain* from *heaven* upon the *place beneath*," and would stress the italicized words or syllables. Stetson was the first phonetician who emphasized the contribution of the respiratory muscles to speaking. He believed that although the larger muscles of the chest and abdomen contributed to exhalation, it was the smaller internal intercostal muscles that would produce the small pulses overlaid on the breath

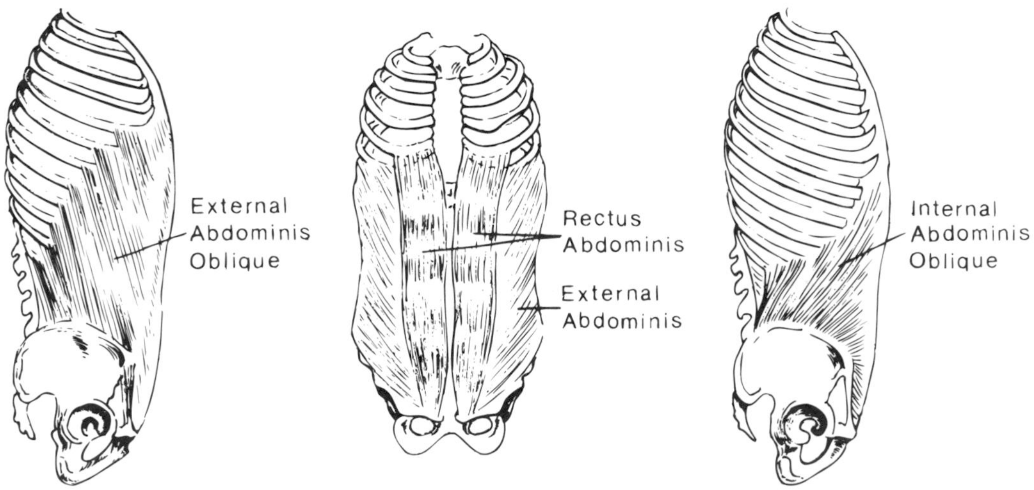

Figure 4.27. Two lateral views and one frontal view of the abdominal muscles used in respiration for speech.

Table 4.2. Summary Chart of Events during Respiration[a]

Brain	Peripheral nerves	Muscles	Movements	Air pressure changes	Air movement
Medulla and higher centers (INSPIRATION)	Spinal nerves: Phrenic n. C_3–C_5	Inspiratory: Diaphragm	Lowered, increasing vertical thorax	Air pressure within lungs negative relative to atmospheric pressure	Air inhaled into lungs through respiratory tract to equalize pressure
	Thoracic n. T_1–T_{11}	External intercostal muscles	Ribs lifted up and out, and		
		Interchondral internal intercostal muscles	Ribs twisted increasing ant.-post. lateral thorax		
(EXPIRATION)			Thorax compressed by elastic, recoil, gravity and torque	Air pressure within lungs increased relative to atmospheric pressure	Air exhaled from lungs through tract to equalize pressure
	Thoracic n. T_1–T_{11}	Expiratory: Internal intercostal muscles	Ribs lowered		
	Thoracic n. T_7–T_{12}	Abdominal muscles	Abdominal contents press against diaphragm elevating it. Decreasing thoracic volume		

[a] This chart represents the basic motor (efferent) events for respiration. There is also sensory (afferent) information sent back to the central nervous system. There are automatic feedback mechanisms which signal the need for more oxygen to the medulla. There are also specialized muscle fibers in the respiratory muscles which are responsive to muscle stretch. These along with the sensation of air movement through the respiratory tract enable the breather to consciously or unconsciously control respiration.

stream. Stetson related the pulses to individual syllables, but if we modify that concept and relate the added internal intercostal contractions to stress, we would find agreement with him. The activity of the abdominal muscles increases in order to supply the added expiratory force needed for utterances that are heavily stressed or long in duration.

Increases in syllable duration, fundamental frequency and intensity may each accompany the production of stressed syllables. The intensity of the voice is primarily controlled by subglottal pressure, and it increases as a function of between the 3rd and 4th power of the subglottal air pressure.

$$I = P_S^3 \text{ or } P_S^4$$

As the formula above indicates, a small change in pressure generates a large change in intensity. If you double the subglottal pressure, the intensity will increase between 8 and 16 times ($2^3 = 8$, $2^4 = 16$), a 9- to 12-dB increase in sound intensity. It seems likely that momentary increases in intensity, generated by pulses of activity in the internal intercostals and the abdominal muscles, are associated with stressed syllables. Distinctions among consonants, at any rate, do not seem to be attributable to differences in subglottal pressure, as Ladefoged and Netsell have shown. Their experimental evidence indicates that, if stress differences are ignored or neutralized, subglottal pressure is constant or tends to decrease during an utterance. This means that air pressure differences (measured at the mouth), which distinguish speech sounds from each other, are caused by the closing and opening of constrictions at the glottis and in the upper vocal tract.

Another difference between expiration for speech and for either sustained phonation or for quiet breathing is that phrase groups determine the duration of the expiration. In

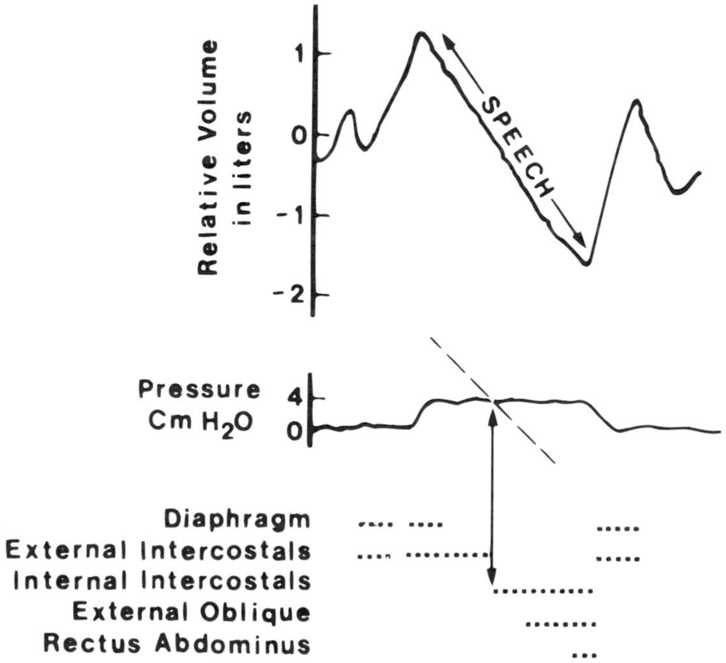

Figure 4.28. Relative lung volume, estimated air pressure, and muscle activity during speaking. Muscle activity changes from inspiratory to expiratory as lung volume decreases, to maintain subglottal pressure. Active muscles are indicated below figure. (Adapted from P. Ladefoged: *Three Areas in Experimental Phonetics,* Oxford University Press, © 1967.) More recent findings show the abdominal muscles are often active during inspiration as well as during expiration.

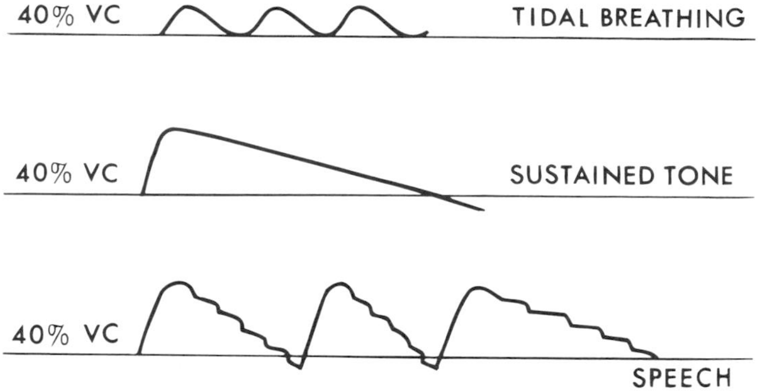

Figure 4.29. Lung volume as a function of time for various respiratory conditions.

saying: "I'm nobody. Who are you? Are you nobody too?," a speaker might use one expiration or perhaps two. The break for a breath is partially determined by the text, however, as Emily Dickinson would surely not have wanted us to interrupt her phrase by taking a breath after "Who." Variations in expiratory duration depend upon what is spoken (Fig. 4.29). It results in relatively long durations of the expiratory part of the respiratory cycle. A speaker who wants to finish a long phrase without interruption often contracts expiratory muscles, using some of his expiratory reserve volume, even at the expense of his comfort.

A final difference between quiet breathing and breathing for speech is the volume of air expended. During normal relaxed breathing, we use only 10% of our vital capacity. For example, we may inhale up to 50% of VC and then exhale to 40%. Hixon reports that in conversational speech, we typically inspire up to roughly the 60% VC level and do not take another breath until we have reached an appropriate stopping place near a resting expiratory level of about 30 to 40% VC. Therefore, we use only about 25% of our vital capacity for conversational speech. During loud speech, we use 40% of vital capacity, the expiratory phase going from perhaps 80% to 40% VC (Fig. 4.30). It would seem that, barring some respiratory ailment, the problems of respiration common to some speech pathologies are not a matter of needing more air energy, since only the middle ¼ of vital capacity is usually used at conversational levels, but more likely are problems in control and modification of the airstream.

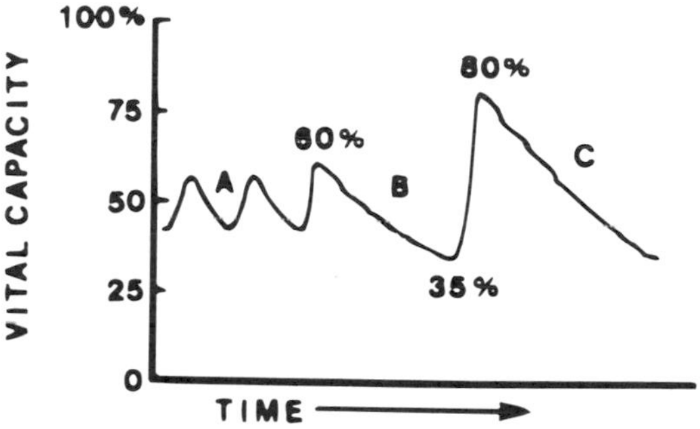

Figure 4.30. Lung volume changes during tidal breathing (*A*), conversational speech (*B*), and loud speech (*C*). (Adapted from Thomas J. Hixon: Respiratory Function in Speech. In *Normal Aspects of Speech, Hearing, and Language*, F. D. Minifie, T. J. Hixon, and F. Williams (Eds.), © 1973, p. 115. Reprinted by permission of Prentice-Hall, Inc., Englewood Cliffs, NJ.)

In voice disorders, the airstream is often wasted through inefficient use of the energy, rather than lack of air. The irregularities seen in the respiratory patterns of speakers with severe hearing loss are related to anomalies of vocal fold and vocal tract modifications of the airstream as well as to respiratory control itself. Respiratory irregularities are often seen, too, in the patterns produced by speakers with motor disorders (for example, cerebral palsy). Irregularities also appear as a lack of coordination between abdominal and thoracic respiratory systems, evidenced during the dysfluent utterances of some speakers who stutter. Again, it is less a problem of inability to change lung volumes sufficiently to produce appropriate pressure than a problem in affording proper resistance to the airstream at the vocal folds or in the upper vocal tract. Sometimes, a speaker with a motor dysfunction will contract all of the internal intercostal muscles concurrently with the external intercostal muscles as he inhales, a seemingly contradictory maneuver, even though the external intercostals win the battle (the speaker actually inhales). Often, one can observe in less efficient breathers a tendency to expend a great deal of muscular energy lifting the sternum and upper rib cage, a process sometimes called clavicular breathing, when with the same energy applied to different muscles, a speaker could lift the lower ribs and produce a greater thoracic expansion. People with normal speech, however, seem to vary a great deal in whether they move the abdomen-diaphragm region more or the upper chest, and may engage in contradictory respiratory maneuvers, as people with speech disorders do.

PHONATION

Conversion of Air Pressure into Sound

The power supply for speech is the expired air from the lungs, but it falls to the actions of the upper airways to convert this air supply into audible vibrations for speech. As mentioned before, speakers use two methods of transforming the air into sounds for speech. The first method involves using the air pressure to set the elastic vocal folds in the larynx into vibration, producing a periodic sound wave (one with a repeated pattern). The second method involves allowing air to pass through the larynx into the upper vocal tract (the passages between the vocal folds and the outside air), where various modifications of the airstream result in noises: bursts, hisses, or combinations of these aperiodic sound waves (with no repeated pattern of vibration). The first method is termed *phonation*, and it is this vocal mode and its variation that we now consider.

Myoelastic Aerodynamic Theory of Phonation

The vocal folds are shelf-like elastic protuberances of tendon, muscles, and mucous membrane that lie behind the "Adams's apple" or thyroid cartilage and run in an anterior-posterior direction. Their tension and elasticity can be varied; they can be made thicker or thinner, shorter or longer; they can be opened wide, closed together, or put into intermediate positions, and they can be elevated or depressed in their vertical relationship to the cavities above. In running speech, all these adjustments occur at very rapid rates. These dynamic variations of vocal fold position and shape are the result of an evolutionary change from a simple sphincter or valve-like mechanism in lower forms of life to the human larynx, in which the muscles controlling the folds are divided into several groups with specific functions, allowing a wide range of adjustments.

When the vocal folds are together and vibrating, they are in the phonatory mode. Before considering the laryngeal structures and their functions in phonation, you can gain an immediate understanding of vocal fold physiology by producing that vibration of the lips known in the United States as the "Bronx cheer" and in Great Britain as a "raspberry." Insure your privacy and then put your lips together in such a way that air pressure from behind sets them into an audible vibration. The sound is that of air escaping in rapid bursts, not the sound of the lips moving. It is apparent that it is the air pressure producing the lip movements, not the lip muscles, and yet the lips have to be put together and with just the right amount of pressure for it to work. Try it with lips slightly apart, or tightly pursed and you will meet with failure. Although the "Bronx cheer" is quite easily observed, there was not general agreement until relatively recently that the vocal folds worked in somewhat the same way.

In the middle of the 18th century, it was generally thought that vocal folds vibrated like strings, thus directly producing vibrations in air. Even as late as 1950, Husson, with the neurochronaxic theory, proposed that the vocal folds vibrated as a consequence of individual nerve impulses, at the fundamental frequency rate, to the vocalis muscle rather than as a consequence of the action of expired air on the vocal folds. The currently accepted theory of phonation, however, is essentially that proposed by both Helmholtz and Müller in the 19th century and amplified by van den Berg in a series of papers in the 1950s, the *myoelastic aerodynamic theory* of phonation. The key word is aerodynamic. The vocal folds are activated by the airstream from the lungs rather than by nerve impulses. "Myoelastic" refers to the ways in which the muscles (myo-) change their elasticity and tension to effect changes in frequency of vibration.

The number of times the vocal folds open and close per second is the frequency of vocal fold vibration. The frequency of vocal fold vibration directly determines the lowest frequency (fundamental frequency) of the sound that is produced. Men have voices that have an average fundamental frequency (f_0) of approximately 125 Hz. Women are more apt to phonate with a f_0 over 200 Hz, and children, over 300 Hz. Size of the vocal folds is one determinant of fundamental frequency. The larger the vibrating mass of the vocal folds, the lower the frequency. Typically men have larger vocal folds than women. They have vocal fold lengths approximating 17 to 24 mm, while women's vocal folds are more apt to range between 13 and 17 mm. Given a pair of vocal folds of a particular length and weight, however, a person can increase the frequency of vibration appreciably by lengthening and tensing the folds, thus decreasing the effective mass. Usually, the vocal folds may be stretched by 3 or 4 mm. Singers are trained to have a range of 2 octaves (each octave is a doubling of frequency). A bass voice can go as low as about 80 Hz and a lyric soprano higher than 1 kHz. Muscular action is thus important in the control of voicing. Muscles act to bring the folds together so that they can vibrate, and muscles regulate their thickness and tension to alter the fundamental frequency.

The essential point of the myoelastic theory, however, is that the determinants of the vibratory cycle are aerodynamic. Air pressure from the lungs opens the glottis during each vibration. The folds come together again during each vibration because of their inherent elasticity and the sudden pressure drop between the folds (Bernoulli principle) as the air streams through the open glottis.

More recent theorizing about vocal fold vibration has led to the development of the Cover-Body Theory (also called the Two-Mass Model) of vocal fold vibration. This theory attempts to account for the wide range of frequencies, amplitudes, and vocal qualities that a human can produce while phonating in terms of the unique structure of the vocal folds. That structure, described in great detail by Hirano and others, consists of a relatively pliable "cover," formed partly of mucous membrane, which overlies a relatively stiff "body," composed mainly of muscle fibers. The vibration of the cover ranges from being very similar to being very dissimilar to that of the body. The degree of similarity or difference, which determines many of the acoustic characteristics of phonation, depends on the activity of the intrinsic laryngeal muscles.

Whatever the theory, an explanation of the details of phonation requires anatomical knowledge of the larynx. Only the anatomy essential to a basic understanding of vocal fold function for speech will be presented in this text.

Framework of the Larynx

In addition to its use for speech, the larynx is used to control the flow of air into and out of the lungs, providing oxygen to the body and eliminating carbon dioxide, to prevent food, water, or other substances from entering the lungs, to aid in swallowing, and to enable a build-up of pressure within the thorax for such functions as coughing, vomiting, defecating, and lifting heavy objects.

The larynx is suspended from the *hyoid bone* and sits on top of the *trachea* (Fig. 4.31). The trachea, formed by a series of horseshoe-shaped cartilages with the open part at the back, can be located at the base of the neck, while the hyoid bone is floating under the jaw and can best be felt by tilting the head back slightly. A small horseshoe-shaped bone, it can be distinguished from the cartilages by its rigidity. The laryngeal framework lies anterior to

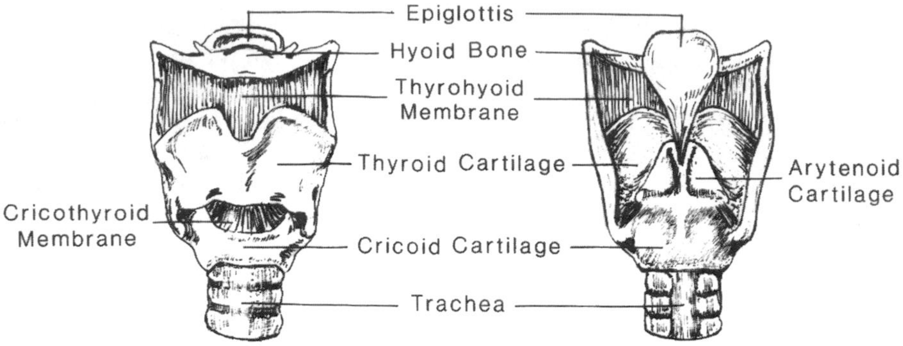

Figure 4.31. Anterior and posterior views of the larynx.

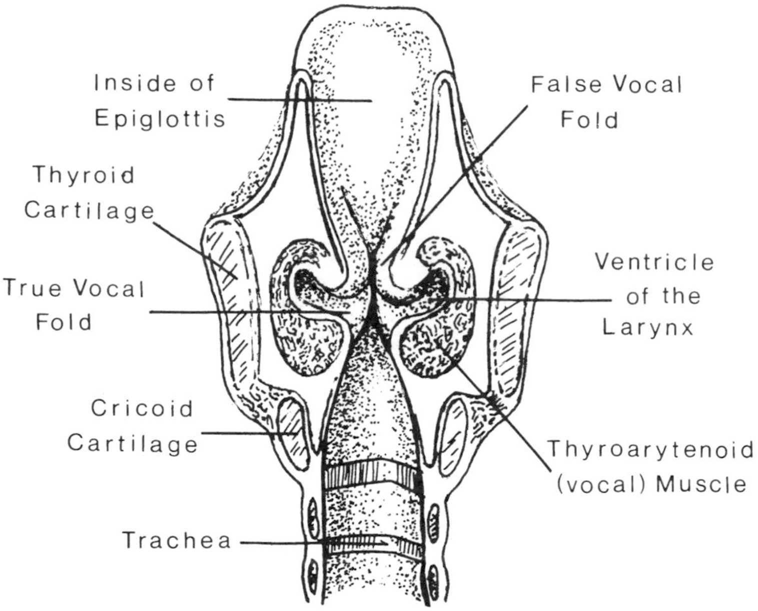

Figure 4.32. Frontal section of the larynx. Notice the constrictions formed by the ventricular folds and the "true vocal folds" below.

the lower pharynx, which leads to the esophagus and on to the stomach. Therefore, food and liquids must pass over the entrance to the lungs to gain access to the entrance to the stomach, a seemingly inefficient arrangement, which is the price paid for the evolutionary adaptation of the larynx as a sound source for speech. During swallowing, a leaf-shaped cartilage, the *epiglottis,* covers the entrance to the larynx. In other animals, the larynx is positioned high in the throat and can be coupled to the nasal airways, in which case food and liquids pass from the mouth around the sides of the larynx and straight into the esophagus, with no danger of entering the windpipe.

The larynx is a tube composed of cartilages connected by ligaments and connecting membranes and covered by mucous membrane. The enclosed area forms an hourglass space (Fig. 4.32) with a vestibule above two sets of folds, the *ventricular folds* or "false vocal folds," and the "true vocal folds" used for phonation. The ventricular folds form a second constriction, just above the true vocal folds. The vertical space between the two sets of folds is called the *laryngeal ventricle,* and the horizontal space between the true vocal folds is called the *glottis*. Below the vocal folds the space widens again within the cartilaginous framework.

The cartilages that serve to maintain the laryngeal space and to support the muscles that regulate its changes are the *thyroid, cricoid,* and *arytenoid cartilages*. The cricoid cartilage, so named because it is shaped like a signet ring (Greek, krikos = ring, oid = like), can be considered to be an overgrown tracheal ring. It is the top ring of the trachea, and is distinctive because of the large plate (lamina) that forms its posterior surface, in contrast to the other tracheal rings, which are open at the back. The narrow front and sides of the cartilage form the arch, and the broad lamina at the back forms the signet-like part of the ring, which faces posteriorly (Fig. 4.33).

Although the vocal folds are not attached to the cricoid cartilage, the cricoid articulates with three cartilages that do support the vocal folds: the thyroid cartilage and two arytenoid cartilages. The arytenoid cartilages are roughly pyramidal in shape and articulate with the cricoid cartilage at oval depressions on their inferior surfaces that correspond with convex facets on the top sides of the cricoid lamina. When the arytenoids are in place, a small projection at the base of each cartilage (the vocal process) points anteriorly and is the point of attachment for the vocal ligament with its associated folds. The vocal ligament and the *thyroarytenoid muscle* lying along it are stretched between the vocal process of the arytenoid cartilages in the back and the deep angle of the thyroid cartilage in the front (Fig. 4.34).

These structures (the vocal process of the arytenoid cartilage, the vocal ligament, the thyroarytenoid muscle, and the mucous membrane lining the inner surface on both sides) form the true vocal folds. The cartilage projects into the posterior one-third of the folds, the cartilaginous portion, leaving the anterior two-thirds as the membranous portion. As might be expected, the cartilaginous part often differs from the membranous part in its pattern of vibration.

The larger extension at the base of each arytenoid cartilage is called the muscular pro-

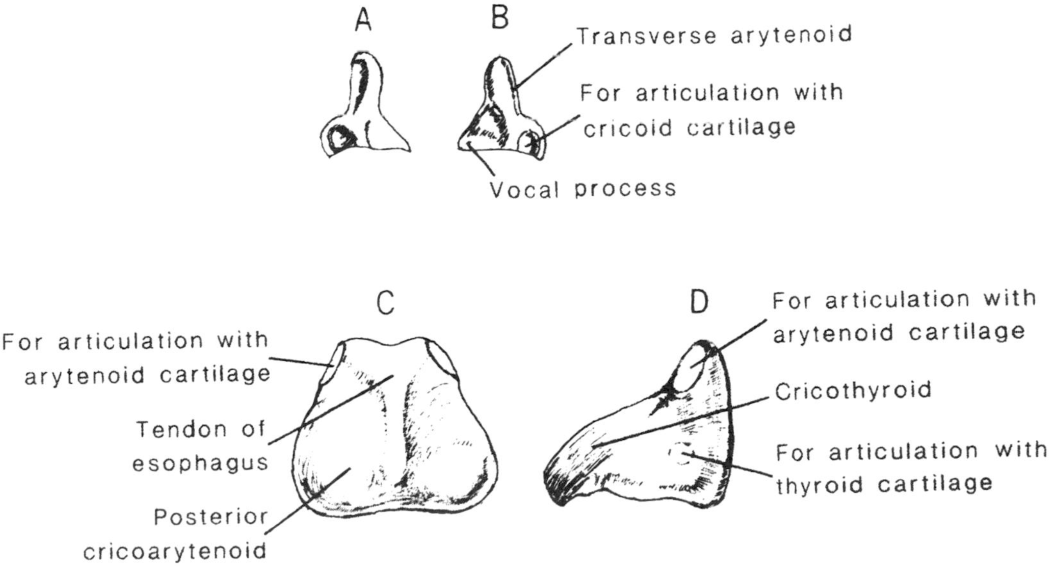

Figure 4.33. The arytenoid and cricoid cartilages. (*A*) The left arytenoid cartilage, medial aspect. (*B*) The right arytenoid cartilage, medial aspect. (*C*) The cricoid cartilage, posterior aspect. (*D*) The cricoid cartilage, left lateral aspect.

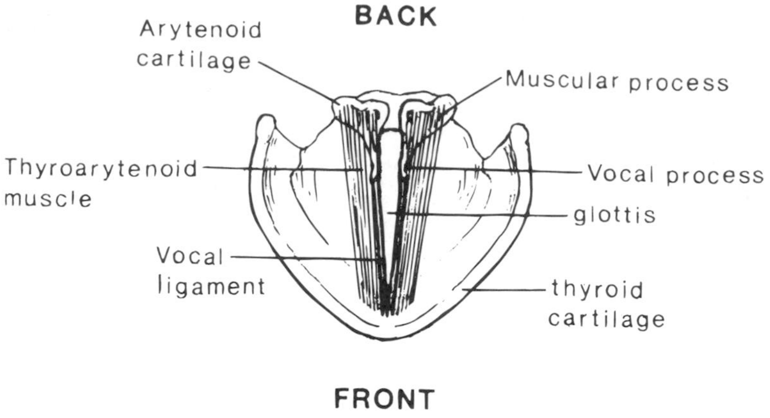

Figure 4.34. The larynx from a superior view, showing the relationships among the thyroid, cricoid, and arytenoid cartilages, and the thyroarytenoid muscle.

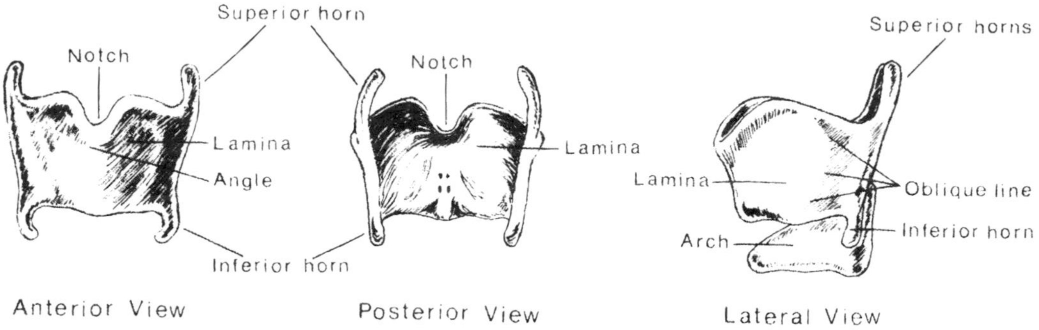

Figure 4.35. Anterior, posterior, and lateral views of the thyroid cartilage. Lateral view includes the cricoid cartilage.

cess because three muscles important for the positioning of the vocal folds are attached to it. The muscular process extends posteriorly and somewhat laterally.

The largest cartilage, the thyroid cartilage, so named because it is like a shield (Greek, thyreos = large shield), is positioned anterior to the arytenoid cartilages, which its sides enclose, and superior to the cricoid cartilage, the top laminal crest of which it also encloses. It forms an angle in the front that is more acute in men (~90°) than in women (~120°), hence the common term "Adam's apple" instead of "Eve's apple." There is a notch (Fig. 4.35) where the laminae separate above the angle that can usually be located by feeling along the midline of your neck with your index finger. The plates are widely separated in the back and extend into two superior horns that project toward the cornua (horns) of the hyoid bone above. The two smaller inferior horns articulate with the cricoid cartilage below by fitting into a round facet on each side of the cricoid lamina. The cartilages of the larynx can move in relation to one another to a limited degree. The thyroid and cricoid cartilages can rock back and forth upon each other. We will describe these motions later in reference to pitch change. The arytenoids can rotate and rock on the cricoid cartilage and can slide a bit toward one another. The muscles attached to the muscular process of the arytenoids control these movements, as we shall see in the following discussion of vocal fold adjustments.

Vocal Fold Adjustments during Speech

The vocal folds at rest are apart (*abducted*), creating a V-shaped glottal space with its apex behind the thyroid cartilage and its widest separation at the back, where the folds attach to the vocal process of the arytenoid cartilages. During running speech, the vocal folds are separated for voiceless speech sounds, such as the consonants /s/ or /t/, are brought together (*adducted*) for voiced sounds, such as the vowels and diphthongs /u/, /i/, and /aɪ/ in the words "two" /tu/, "tea" /ti/, and "tie" /taɪ/. They are less firmly brought together for voiced consonants such as /z/ and /v/ where phonation is needed in addition to large air pressures in the oral cavity (Fig. 4.36).

Voiceless Consonants. The simplest adjustment of the vocal folds for speech is the one made for voiceless consonants. The folds abduct in order to allow the passage of sufficient air from the lungs to create noises in the oral cavity. As speech proceeds, voiceless consonants are interspersed in the speech stream singly or in clusters, demanding rapid glottal opening to interrupt phonation. The job is done by a pair of large triangular muscles attached by tendons to the top of the muscular process of each arytenoid cartilage; the muscle fibers fan out as they course back and down to attach to the dorsal plates of the cricoid cartilage (Fig. 4.37). Named for their position and attachments, the *posterior cricoarytenoid muscles* (PCA) upon contraction rotate the arytenoid cartilages by pulling the muscular processes down and medially, thereby moving the vocal processes apart. Innervation to these and almost all of the other intrinsic muscles of the larynx is supplied by the *recurrent nerve*, a branch of the Xth cranial nerve, the vagus nerve.

Voiced Speech Sounds. Widely separated vocal folds cannot be set into vibration, so in order to produce the voiced sounds of speech, the normally separated folds must be adducted or nearly so. To approximate the vocal folds, the arytenoid cartilages must be brought closer together with their vocal processes rocked inward toward one another. A strong band of muscular fibers runs horizontally across the posterior surfaces of the arytenoid

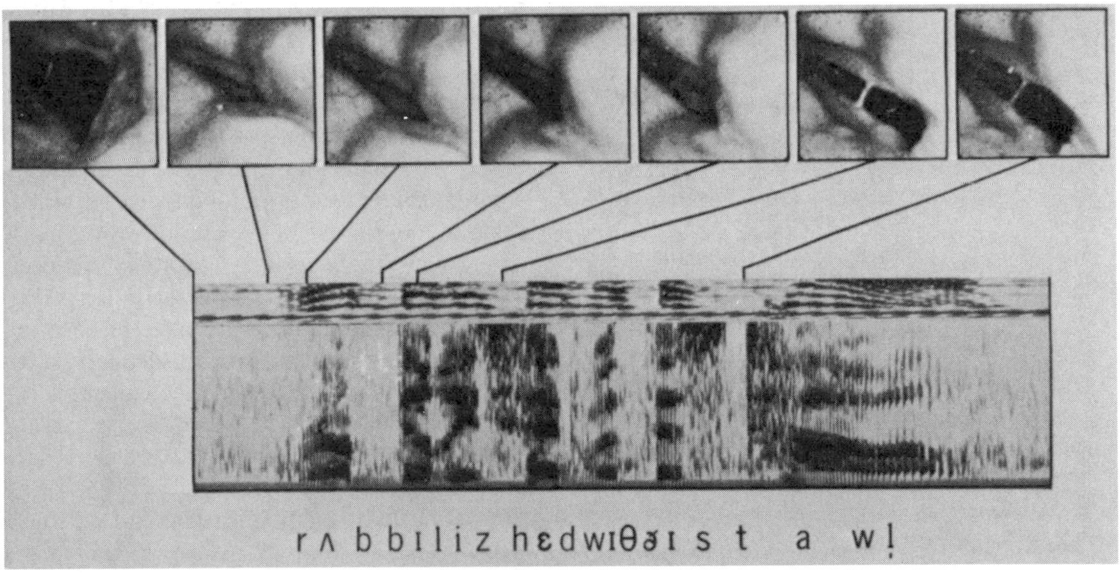

Figure 4.36. The glottis, viewed from above with a fiber bundle, at various times in the production of a sentence. The posterior part of the glottal chink is at the *lower right* in each view. Note the open glottis in the first frame for inspiration, the relatively closed glottis in the third frame for a vowel, and the relatively open glottis in the sixth frame for a voiced consonant. (The structure apparently connecting the folds in the *rightmost views* is a bead of mucus.) (Reprinted with permission from M. Sawashima *et al.*: © 1970.)

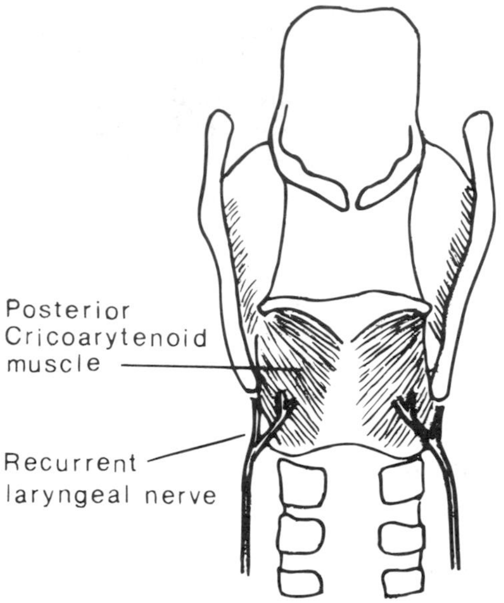

Figure 4.37. Posterior view of the posterior cricoarytenoid muscle. Innervation is via the recurrent branch of the vagus (Xth cranial) nerve.

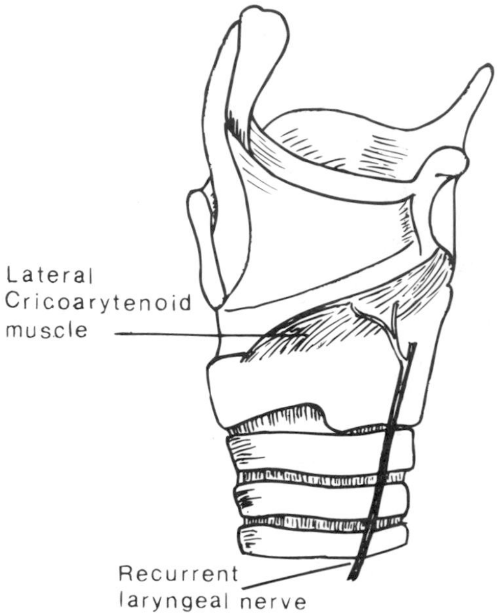

Figure 4.39. Lateral view of the lateral cricoarytenoid muscle with the left side of the thyroid cartilage removed.

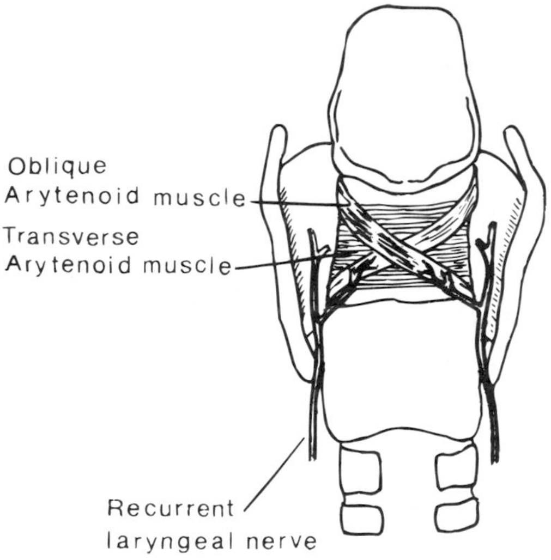

Figure 4.38. Posterior view of the transverse and oblique arytenoid muscles. Together, these muscles are referred to as the interarytenoid muscle.

cartilages. This muscle, the *transverse arytenoid muscle*, is overlaid by some muscular fibers in the shape of an X called the *oblique arytenoid muscles* (Fig. 4.38). Together, termed the *interarytenoid muscle* (*IA*), they adduct the arytenoid cartilages and thereby, the vocal folds. The interarytenoid muscle is thought to be the primary adductor of the vocal folds. The *lateral cricoarytenoid muscles* (*LCA*) also aid in adduction of the vocal folds, by rocking the muscular process of the arytenoids forward and down, thereby pressing the vocal processes together (Fig. 4.39). For stronger adduction of the folds, as in vowel production, both the IA and LCA are usually used. For speech sounds requiring phonation and also a continuous flow of air for a sound source above the glottis, the vocal folds are often less closely completely adducted. Hirose and Gay (Fig. 4.40) have differentiated the functions of laryngeal muscles by measuring the electrical activity generated as these muscles contract. The recording method (electromyography or EMG) is explained in Chapter 7.

The vocal folds themselves are composed of (1) the vocal ligaments, which are the thickened edges of the *conus elasticus* membrane rising from the cricoid cartilage, (2) the muscles that are attached to the ligaments, the internal part of the *thyroarytenoid muscles* commonly called the *vocalis muscles*, and (3) the mucous membrane that covers them. The vocal

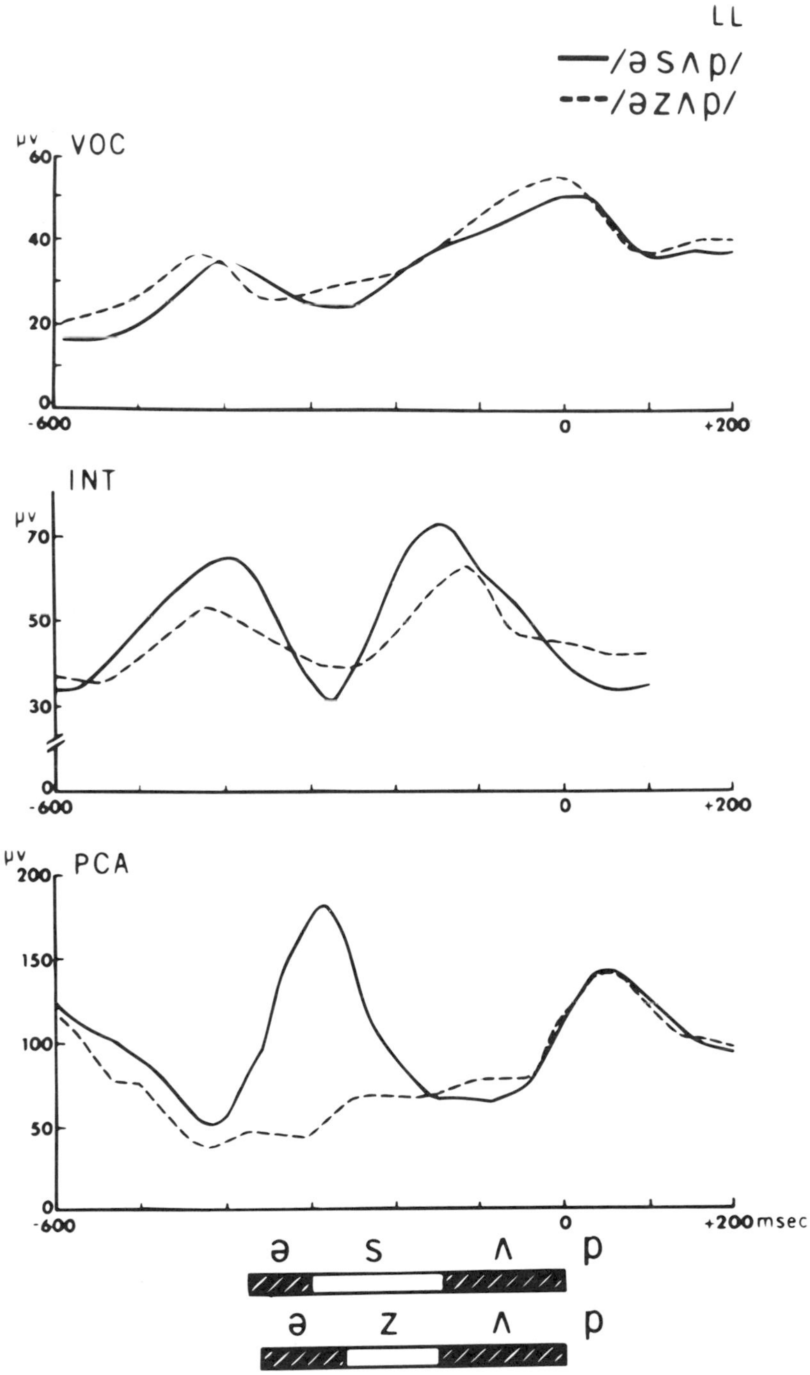

Figure 4.40. Superimposed EMG curves for voiced (z; *dashed line*) and voiceless (s; *solid line*) fricatives in nonsense syllables. Although vocalis muscle (*VOC*) activity is similar for both, for /s/, interarytenoid (*INT*) activity is reduced during the time that posterior cricoarytenoid activity (*PCA*) is greatly increased. (Reprinted with permission from H. Hirose and T. Gay: *Phonetica, 25,* S. Karger AG, Basel, © 1972.)

ligaments and the vocalis muscles, which form the body of the vocal folds, emerge from the projection of the arytenoid cartilage known as the vocal process. The posterior portions of the vocal folds are thus stiffer, because of the presence of the arytenoid cartilage, and become increasingly flexible in their anterior portions. When relaxed, the vocal folds are relatively thick, and open and close in an undulating manner, the mucous membrane moving somewhat independently like flabby skin on a waving arm. The lateral fibers of the thyroarytenoid muscle extend to the muscular process of the arytenoid cartilage, some of them wrapping around the arytenoid where they commingle with the interarytenoid muscles. More research is needed to differentiate the role of the medial (vocalis) and lateral fibers of the thyroarytenoid muscles in phonation, but in general they are thought to tense the folds.

The muscle activity needed to adduct and tense the vocal folds simply readies them for vibration but does not cause the vibration itself. For the "Bronx cheer," you had to put your lips together, and that required muscular effort, but the sound itself was produced by aerodynamic forces acting upon the elastic bodies of your lips. The two aerodynamic forces that produce vibration of the vocal folds are the *subglottal air pressure* (P_s) applied to the lower part of the folds, forcing them apart, and the negative pressure that occurs as air passes between the folds (the *Bernoulli effect*). These positive and negative pressures set the vocal folds into vibration because of the elasticity of the folds.

Subglottal Air Pressure

Consider first the subglottal air pressure that parts the vocal folds. During each opening, a tiny puff of air escapes, cut off sharply by the abruptly closing glottis. Since the folds vibrate rapidly (usually over 100 times per second), one puff follows another in rapid succession. This chain of air puffs sets up a pressure wave at the glottis that is audible. A necessary condition for phonation is that the air pressure below the folds must exceed the pressure above the folds. If the pressure above the folds builds up so that the pressure drop across the glottis necessary for phonation is lost, then phonation ceases. You can test this by trying to prolong a voiced stop consonant such as a [b]. You can phonate during the [b] closure only for a short time because the labial and velopharyngeal closures for the [b] cause the supraglottal air pressure to increase until it equals the subglottal air pressure. Since there is no longer more pressure below the folds than above them, phonation is not possible. For speech at conversational level, a subglottal air pressure in the range of 7–10 cm of H_2O (centimeters of water pressure) is sufficient to produce phonation at approximately 60 dB intensity.

The effect of subglottal air pressure sufficient to separate a pair of vocal folds can be seen in Figure 4.41, schematic diagrams made from a movie of a vibrating larynx. The vocal folds open at the bottom first and then the opening proceeds up to the top of the folds. As the top part of the vocal folds opens, the bottom part can be seen to be closing. Thus, there is a vertical phase difference, creating a wave-like motion of the folds, the normal movement during vibration for chest voice. If the speaker speaks or sings in a high falsetto voice, however, the vertical phase difference is lost and each of the taut folds moves as a unit. The closing phase of each cycle is the result of the tendency of the elastic folds to move into their rest positions and of the second aerodynamic phenomenon important to voicing, the pressure drop ascribed to the Bernoulli effect.

The Bernoulli Effect

Daniel Bernoulli, an 18th century Swiss mathematician and physician, developed the kinetic theory of gases and liquids, part of which is known as the Bernoulli effect or principle. The Bernoulli effect is based upon the observation that when a gas or liquid current runs through a constricted passage, the velocity (speed in a given direction) increases. Simply stated, the Bernoulli principle is that such an increase in velocity results in a drop in the

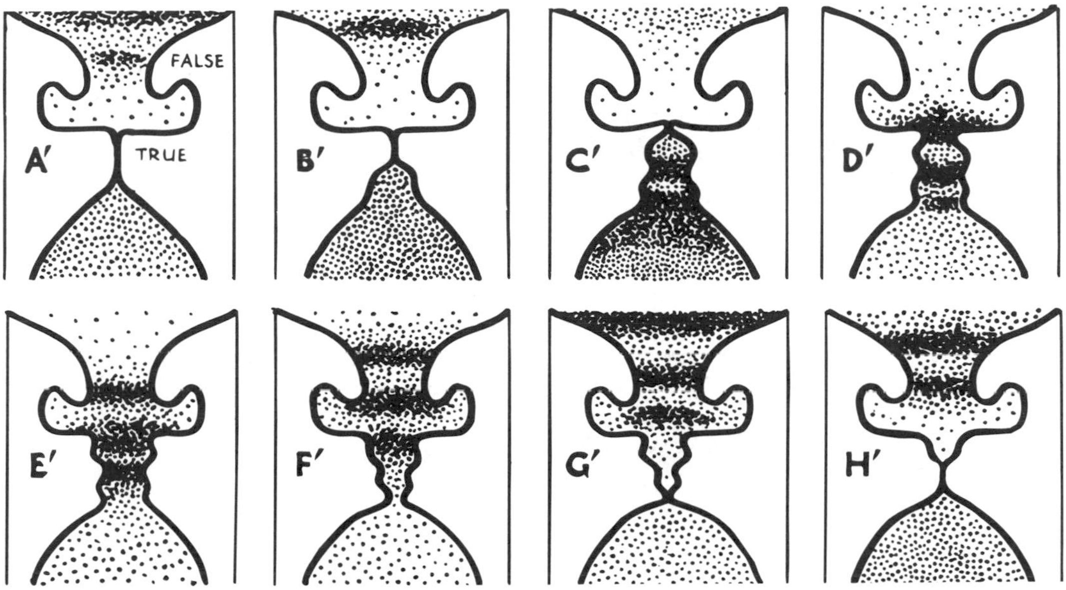

Figure 4.41. Schematic cross sections of the vocal folds during vibration. It can be seen that the folds open and close from *bottom* to *top*. (From *Singing: the Mechanism and the Technic,* 4th Ed., by William Vennard, © 1967 by Carl Fischer, Inc. All rights reserved. Reprinted by permission of the publisher.)

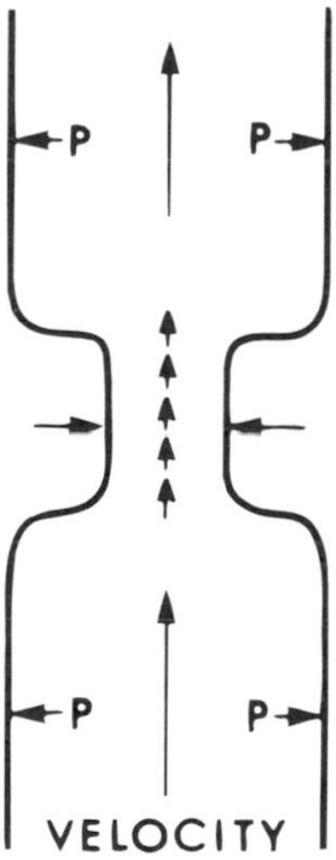

Figure 4.42. Schematic diagram of flow through a constricted passage. In the constriction, velocity is greater, but pressure on the inner sides of the constriction is correspondingly reduced.

pressure exerted by the molecules of moving gas or liquid, the pressure drop being perpendicular to the direction of the flow. Figure 4.42 illustrates the increase in velocity within a narrow portion of a passage and the resulting decrease in pressure against the lateral walls.

The conventional airplane wing is designed to take advantage of the Bernoulli effect to elevate the aircraft. The wing is streamlined on the top surface (Fig. 4.43), permitting a higher velocity of air current than that passing underneath. The higher velocity results in a drop in pressure against the top surface, which creates a difference between the pressures under and over the wings, thereby elevating the plane. You can elevate a piece of paper, using the same principle, by holding one end of it under your lips and blowing air across the top (Fig. 4.44).

We experience the Bernoulli phenomenon constantly. When a draft of air flows through a narrow corridor, the doors opening into rooms off the hall slam shut, because the pressure on the hall side of the doors is lower than that on the room side. If you have ever been in a lightweight car cruising alongside a heavy truck on a highway and felt your car being sucked alarmingly close to the truck, it is because the faster airstream created between your car and the truck has lowered the pressure against the truck side of your car relative to the other side.

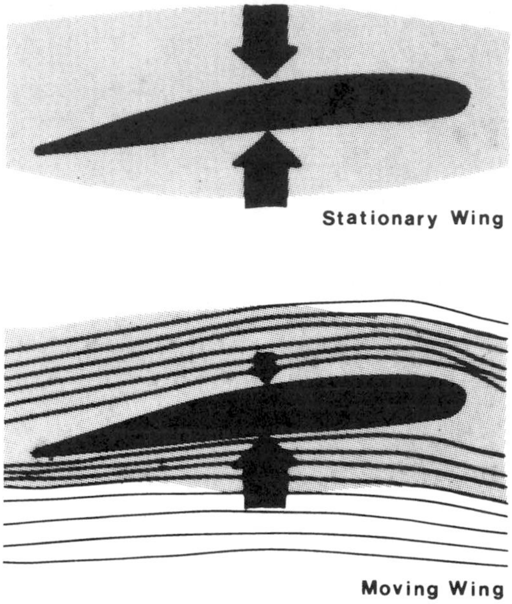

Figure 4.43. Aerodynamic forces on an airplane wing. (See text for discussion.)

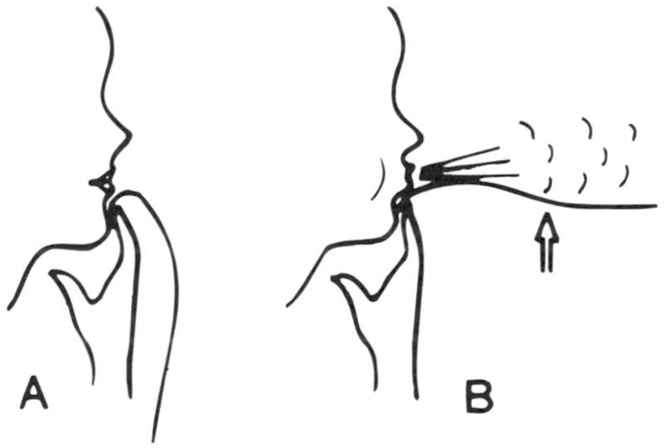

Figure 4.44. Illustration of the Bernoulli principle. When airflow is increased on the top side of the paper by blowing, pressure is lower on the top side than on the bottom side, causing the sheet to rise.

Vocal Fold Vibration

During phonation, each cycle of vocal fold vibration is caused both by the subglottal air pressure that has built up sufficiently to separate the folds and to the Bernoulli effect which, as the air rushes through the glottis at an increased velocity, accounts for a sudden drop in pressure against the inner sides of each fold and sucks them together again. The whole process is made possible by the fact that the folds themselves are elastic. Their elasticity not only permits them to be blown open for each cycle, but the elastic recoil force (the force that restores any elastic body to its resting place) works along with the Bernoulli effect to close the folds for each cycle of vibration.

The vocal folds move in a fairly periodic way. During sustained vowels, for example, the folds open and close in a certain pattern of movement that repeats itself. This action produces a barrage of air bursts that sets up an audible pressure wave (sound) at the glottis. The pressure wave of sound is also periodic; the pattern repeats itself. Like all sound sources that vibrate in a complex periodic fashion, the vocal folds generate a harmonic series (see Chapter 3), consisting of a fundamental frequency and many whole-number multiples of that fundamental frequency. The fundamental frequency is the number of glottal openings per second.

The human voice is a low frequency sound compared to most of the sounds of the world, including the other sounds that humans make above the larynx. Since it contains many harmonics, the voice is also a complex sound. We never hear the unmodified sound of vocal fold vibration, however, because by the time it has reached the lips of the speaker, it has been changed by the vocal tract. If we were to lower a microphone down to the vocal folds, we would record a sound that has a spectrum resembling Figure 4.45. The lowest frequency, the frequency of the vibration itself, sets up a 2nd harmonic (2 times the f_0), a 3rd harmonic (3 times the f_0), and so forth. Notice that it is characteristic of the human voice that the higher harmonics have less intensity than the lower harmonics, so that although the voice contains many high frequency components, the emphasis is on the low frequencies. The intensity falls off at about 12 dB per octave (each doubling of the frequency).

Low pitched and high pitched voices sound different in part because the spacing of their harmonics is different. Figure 4.45 shows the difference. Notice the closer spacing of the harmonics in the adult male's voice, which has

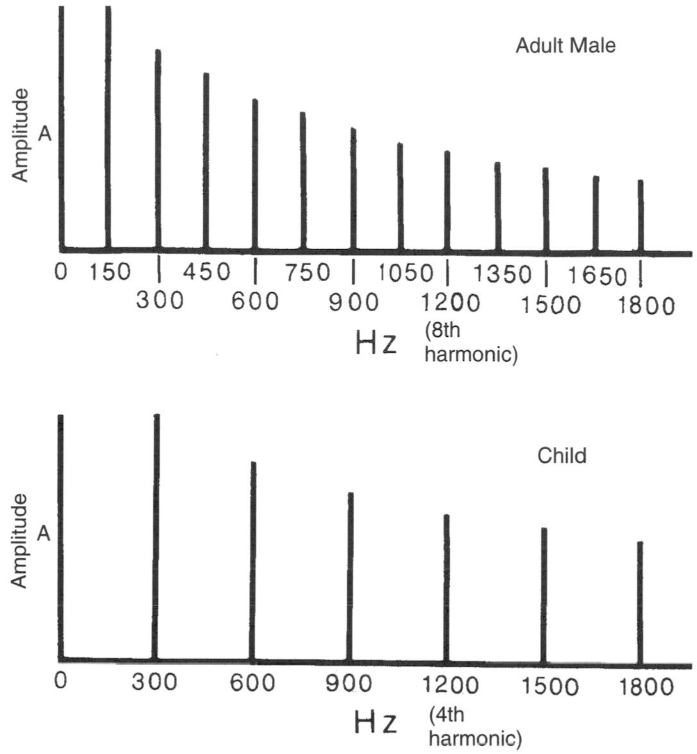

Figure 4.45. Schematic spectra of sounds resulting from vocal fold vibration. The spectra represent two different frequencies of phonation, thus the harmonic spacing is different.

a lower fundamental frequency. A child with a f_0 of 300 Hz would have a 2nd harmonic at 600 Hz, a 3rd at 900 Hz, and a 4th at 1200 Hz. In contrast, a man with a f_0 of 150 Hz would have a 2nd harmonic at 300 Hz, and the 8th harmonic in the adult voice would correspond with the child's 4th harmonic. In the same way, a single person adjusting the frequency of his voice also changes the harmonic spacing. Notice, in the figure, that the shape and slope of the spectrum remain similar for man and child.

Fundamental Frequency

The human voice is composed of many frequencies; it is a complex tone. The human listener perceives the lowest frequency, the fundamental frequency, as the speaker's pitch. The fundamental frequency is constantly changing, as we know when we listen for the *intonation* patterns of sentences. "Are you sure?" has a rising intonation pattern, while "I'm sure" has a falling intonation pattern. The speaker produces these different patterns by altering the fundamental frequency of vocal fold vibration.

According to the myoelastic aerodynamic theory of phonation, frequency of vocal fold vibration is determined by the elasticity, tension, and mass of the vocal folds. More massive folds (longer and thicker) vibrate at naturally lower frequencies than shorter and thinner folds. Vocal folds vibrate faster when they are tense than when they are slack. The primary way to make a given set of vocal folds more tense is to stretch them.

You may have noted that longer folds contribute to increased mass and lower f_0 in one condition and to increased tension and higher f_0 in another condition. This is because a longer pair of vocal folds (compared to other speakers) will be more massive and produce a lower frequency voice; men's voices are lower than children's voices. Yet a lengthening of

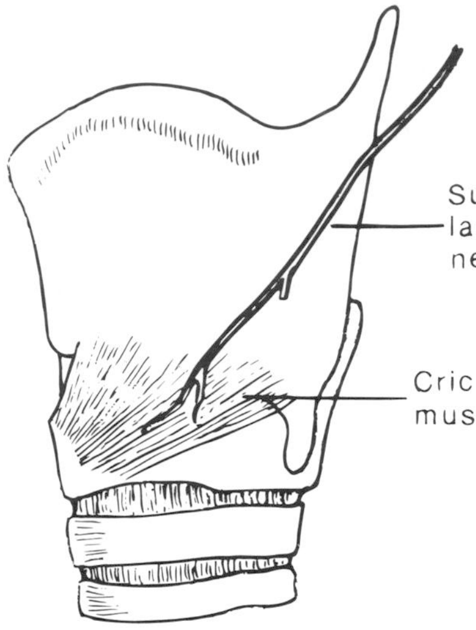

Figure 4.46. Lateral view of the cricothyroid muscle, innervated by the superior laryngeal branch of the vagus (Xth cranial) nerve.

vocal folds (within the same speaker) will stretch and thin the effective vibrating portion of the vocal folds, adding tension and thereby producing a higher fundamental frequency. The pair of muscles responsible for stretching the vocal folds and thereby controlling f_0 change are the *cricothyroid muscles*.

Since the vocal folds lie between the thyroid cartilage and the two arytenoid cartilages, the way to stretch the folds would be to increase the distance between these cartilages. The cricothyroid muscles can do just that. Since they are attached to the side of the cricoid ring and rise (part straight up and the other part at an oblique angle) to the thyroid cartilage, their contraction pulls the two cartilages toward one another by lifting the anterior arch of the cricoid cartilage toward the thyroid cartilage. The closing of the space between the cricoid arch and the front of the thyroid has been likened to the closing of the visor on a suit of armour. Figure 4.46 shows the location of one of the cricothyroid muscles on the left side of the larynx. The effect that their contraction has in elevating the front of the cricoid cartilage, is to tip the posterior plate of the cricoid backward. The arytenoid cartilages ride on the cricoid cartilage and the vocal folds are stretched. Van den Berg refers to this effect of cricothyroid muscle action as longitudinal tension. The innervation of the cricothyroid muscle is from the superior laryngeal nerve (vagus, Xth cranial nerve) unlike all the other intrinsic muscles of the larynx, which are innervated by the recurrent nerve (another branch of the vagus nerve).

The addition of longitudinal tension to the vocal folds increases the fundamental frequency at which they vibrate, at least for much of the frequency range used in speech. For extreme frequencies, other mechanisms are thought to be instrumental in pitch control. At high frequencies, such as for falsetto voice, the cricothyroid is used to further increase tension although no further lengthening is possible. The vocal folds are pulled extremely taut and forego their usual wave-like motion. The vocal ligaments vibrate more like strings.

At extremely low frequencies, the strap muscles of the neck (particularly the *sternohyoid muscle*, Fig. 4.47) assume more responsibility for lowering f_0. You may have noticed the larynx move up slightly in the vertical plane for high frequencies or, more noticeably, move down in the neck for low frequencies. The muscles above the hyoid bone (*suprahyoid mus-*

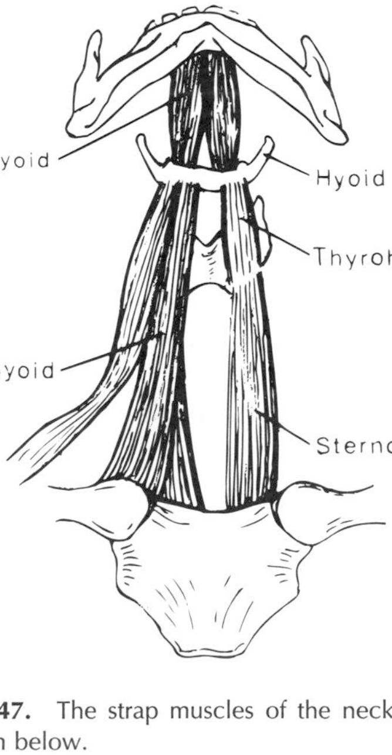

Figure 4.47. The strap muscles of the neck, anterior view from below.

cles) elevate the larynx. These movements are thought by some to add vertical tension to the membranes that serve as a lining for the larynx, and for the trachea below. Increased vertical tension in the conus elasticus during laryngeal elevation and decreased vertical tension in the case of laryngeal lowering would affect the vocal folds. The conus elasticus membrane emerges from the cricoid cartilage and rises in a medial direction to the vocal folds where its thickened border becomes the vocal ligament.

A further source of tension in the vocal folds is the internal tension possible with the contraction of the thyroarytenoid muscles themselves, especially the vibrating portions known as the vocalis muscles. The vocalis muscles are antagonistic to the cricothyroid muscles, since they shorten rather than lengthen the folds, but both sets of muscles can increase tension in the folds to raise f_0. Perhaps the vocalis muscles serve to tune the vocal folds to make the cricothyroid lengthening more effective. Research is needed to clarify the interaction of muscular and non-muscular contributions to frequency change. Atkinson suggests that the relative contributions of various muscular and non-muscular forces may vary in different parts of an individual's pitch range.

It seems that fundamental frequency is primarily affected by applying more or less longitudinal tension to the vocal folds via the cricothyroid muscles. Secondary affects result from (1) applying more or less vertical tension to the folds by elevating or depressing the larynx, and from (2) varying subglottal pressure.

Voice Quality

Much of what distinguishes one voice from another results from the effects of the resonating cavities and structures above the larynx, but part of what is called voice quality or timbre is due to the way in which the vocal folds themselves vibrate. One obvious difference among voices is fundamental frequency, which listeners perceive as pitch. Other differences have to do with how closely the folds are approximated or with irregularities along the edges of the folds. If one or both of the folds are paralyzed, compensations must be made to set up a vibration if possible. Sometimes one vocal fold can be trained to move more than halfway to meet the paralyzed one. If part or all of the larynx has been surgically removed because of cancer, the speaker must learn to vibrate other tissues and muscle masses such as scar tissue or the cricopharyngeus muscle. Some alaryngeal speakers (people whose larynges have been removed) have to resort to an artificial sound source which they hold to the outside of the neck. This produces a "voice" with an artificial, mechanical quality.

Quality differences depend upon various modes of vocal fold vibration. A breathy voice, popular with some movie stars and celebrities in the 1950s, is achieved by failing to adduct the vocal folds sufficiently for full voicing, particularly in the cartilaginous portions. They are close enough to be vibrated, but the sound of continuously released air accompanies the sound wave set up by the air pressure volleys. A hoarse voice is caused by irregularities in the folds. When the vocal folds are irritated or swollen, as they may be during a cold with laryngitis, the voice becomes hoarse. Hoarseness can also be indicative of vocal abuse, either from focusing too much tension in the larynx, causing *contact ulcers*, lesions produced by the arytenoid cartilages banging against one another, or from overusing the voice as happens commonly to women and occasionally to men who develop nodules along the edges of the vocal folds. *Vocal fry* or *creaky* voice (Ladefoged's term) consists of extremely low frequency phonation. About the only practical value of vocal fry is that (because of its low frequency) it provides an audible example of the individual puffs of air that are released in each vibratory cycle of the vocal folds.

One characteristic of voice quality is related to the way in which some speakers initiate the vibrations. Efficient use of the voice requires phonation to be initiated from lightly adducted or approximated folds. Some speakers initiate phonation with what is called a *glottal attack* (or sometimes harsh glottal attack) for which the vocal folds are tightly adducted prior to vibration. This causes their eventual separa-

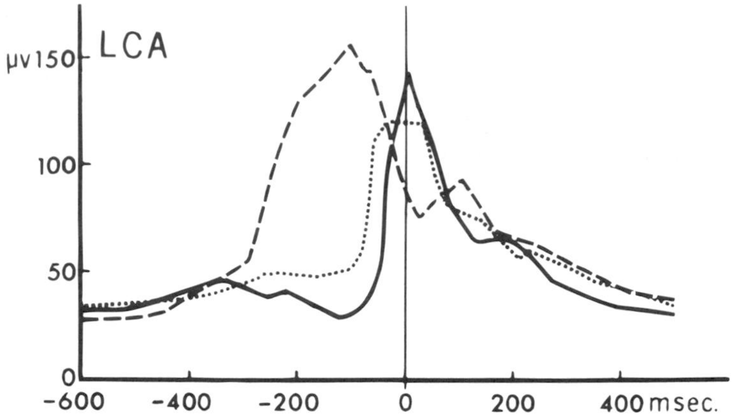

Figure 4.48. Contrasting muscle activity patterns in the lateral cricoarytenoid muscle (*LCA*) for various forms of vocal attack. The onset of the vowel is marked as *O*. Activity is earliest for glottal attack (*dashed line*) later for normal voiced attack (*dotted line*) and latest for voiceless aspirate attack (*solid line*). The measure of muscle activity is obtained by smoothing muscle interference patterns. (See Fig. 4.13 and the discussion of Fig. 7.24). (Reprinted with permission from H. Hirose and T. Gay: *Folia Phoniatrica (Basel). 25,* S. Karger AG, Basel, 1973.)

tion to release the air burst of a stop consonant, similar to those of /p/ or /t/ but produced at the glottis rather than at the lips or the alveolar ridge. Hirose and Gay have shown that glottal attack is accompanied by an early onset of activity in the lateral cricoarytenoid muscles (Fig. 4.48) which compress the center of the vocal folds. This early compression provides the time needed for the pressure build-up required for the stop-like release burst mentioned above.

The symbol for this glottal stop is [ʔ]. Thus, we transcribe a vowel or diphthong initiated by a glottal stop as [ʔaɪ] or [ʔa], rather than with the simple symbols usually associated with them. Harry Belafonte, a popular singer in the United States, made repeated visits to the hospital during the height of his career to have vocal nodules removed from his vocal folds, nodules caused by glottal attack. This is an affliction suffered by many singers, teachers, and others who make heavy use of their voices at high intensity levels.

Relationship between Frequency and Intensity

We have seen that by increasing the subglottal air pressure, keeping other things constant, we can increase vocal intensity. However, if subglottal pressure is increased without muscular adjustments of the vocal folds, the fundamental frequency as well as the intensity will increase. If someone is phonating a steady tone and is (gently) punched in the stomach, the tone not only gets louder but increases in pitch. The pitch rise may be caused by reflexive tensing of the vocal folds or be due to the fact that the increased subglottal air pressure causes the vocal fold closure to occur more quickly because of the Bernoulli effect. In contrast, when one is speaking, at the end of a breath, the f_0 drops naturally along with the intensity by about 2–7 Hz per cm of H_2O decrease. A singer or a speaker can reverse this affinity, however. If a singer wants to increase intensity but maintain the f_0, he must lower the resistance to the airflow at the vocal folds, either by relaxing the cricothyroid a bit or by lowering the internal tension by relaxing the thyroarytenoid muscle. Similarly, when asking "Are you sure?," in order to signal the question with a rising fundamental frequency, the speaker must work against the natural fall in frequency at the end of a breath group by increasing cricothyroid activity, stretching the folds, and at the same time, increasing internal intercostal muscle activity to give added stress to the word "sure."

Increased vocal intensity is due to greater resistance (afforded by the vocal folds) against

Table 4.3. Summary Chart of Events during Phonation*

Peripheral nerves	Muscles	Movements	Air pressure	Air movement
Xth cranial n. (vagus) Recurrent branch	PCA	Open vocal folds before thorax enlargement →		Air enters via larynx to lungs
→	IA →	Adduction of vocal folds		
→	LCA →	Medial compression of vocal folds	P_s builds; Pressure drops across glottis, $P_{sub} > P_{supra}$	
→	Voc. →	Intrinsic tension		
Xth cranial n. (vagus) Ext. branch of sup. laryngeal n. →	CT →	Longitudinal tension	Resistance offered to P_s by vocal fold tension	
		Vocal folds blown open →	Subglottal air pressure overcomes vocal fold resistance	→ Released puff of air
		Folds sucked together ←	Negative pressure *vs.* lateral edges of folds as velocity of air increases (Bernoulli effect)	→ Airstream cut off
		Vocal folds part ←	P_{sub} builds again	→ Another puff of air released

[a] The abbreviations used in the table are: PCA, posterior cricoarytenoid muscle; IA, interarytenoid muscle; LCA, lateral cricoarytenoid muscle; Voc., vocalis muscle; CT, cricothyroid muscle.

the increased airflow. The vocal folds are blown wider apart, releasing a larger puff of air that sets up a sound pressure wave of greater amplitude. The vocal folds not only move farther apart for each vibratory cycle of increased intensity, but they stay adducted for a larger part of each cycle. In Figure 4.49, the changes in the vocal fold movement are schematized and presented with the resulting change in waveform.

Summary

We have seen that phonation is a dynamic process, varying as it does during running speech in intensity, frequency, and quality. The output is a rapidly varying acoustic stream made up of segments of silence, periodic sounds, and noises. The alternation between sequences of phonated and unphonated segments is particularly complex. As a result, normal speakers frequently simplify such sequences to eliminate the alternation. For example, we say "cats" [kæts] with a voiceless (unphonated) [s], but after a voiced stop, it is easier to continue phonating and change the [s] to a [z] as in "dogs" [dɔgz]. Indeed, such alterations are so general in English that they are usually considered to be rule-governed: The word-final morpheme {-s}, whether a plural, a verb ending, or a possessive marker, is usually pronounced [s] after most voiceless sounds and [z] after voiced sounds. Contrast the final [s]'s in "mops," "loafs," "Kit's" and "pecks" with the final [z]'s in "mobs," "loaves," "kid's" and "pegs." For

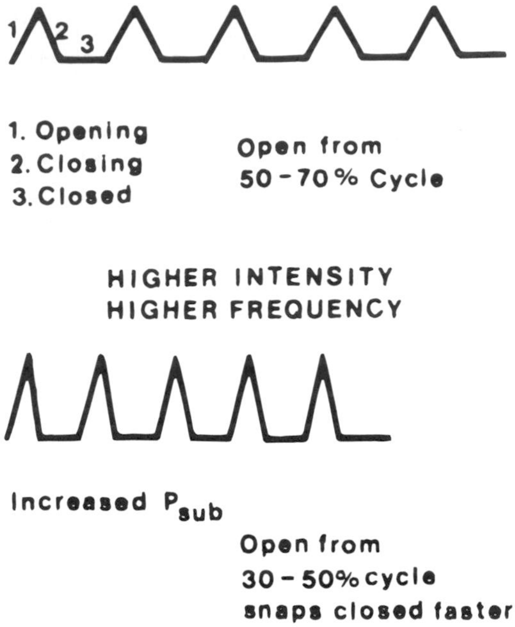

Figure 4.49. Schematic of the movement of the vocal folds during phonation. At higher subglottal pressure, the folds remain closed for a greater proportion of the vibratory cycle, and close more rapidly. Frequency tends to increase, as well as intensity.

those with certain speech disorders, it is particularly difficult to coordinate shifts back and forth between phonated and unphonated sound production. A person who stutters, for example, attempting to say his name, "Sam," might prolong the first sound, [s:æm], or repeat it [s-s-s-s-sæm], but he is not really stuttering the [s]. Rather, he produces the [s] very well, but fails to make a smooth transition to the voiced [æ].

Phonation must be coordinated with respiration. The motor commands to the larynx must be related to those of the respiratory system. To take a breath for speech, the glottis opens quickly before the thorax expands, and when the vocal folds adduct for voicing, the action is simultaneous with expiration. Table 4.3 summarizes the chain of events in vocal fold vibration from neural impulses to the results in air pressure and movements. For muscular adjustments the arrows move from left to right, while for aerodynamic forces the arrows move from right to left.

REFERENCES

General Works on Speech Production

Daniloff, R., Schuckers, G., and Feth, L., *The Physiology of Speech and Hearing*. Englewood Cliffs, NJ: Prentice-Hall Inc. 1980.

Dickson, D. R., and Maue-Dickson, W., *Anatomical and Physiological Bases of Speech*. Boston: Little, Brown and Co. 1982.

Kahane, D. R., and Folkins, J. F. *Atlas of Speech and Hearing Anatomy*. Columbus, OH: Charles E. Merrill, 1984.

Harris, K. S., Physiological Aspects of Articulatory Behavior. In *Current Trends in Linguistics*, Vol. 12, No. 4, T. A. Sebeok (Ed.) The Hague: Mouton, 1974, pp. 2281–2302.

Kent, R. D., Atal, B. S., and Miller, J. L. (Eds.), *Papers in Speech Communication: Speech Production*. Woodbury, NY: Acoustical Society of America, 1991.

Lieberman, P., *Speech Physiology and Acoustic Phonetics: An Introduction*. New York: Macmillan, 1977.

Minifie, F., Hixon, T. J., and Williams, F. (Eds.), *Normal Aspects of Speech, Hearing, and Language*. Englewood Cliffs, NJ: Prentice-Hall, Inc., 1972.

Perkell, J. S., *Physiology of Speech Production: Results and Implications of a Quantitative Cineradiographic Study*. Cambridge, MA: M. I. T. Press, 1969.

Van Riper, C., and Irwin, J. V., *Voice and Articulation*. Englewood Cliffs, NJ: Prentice-Hall Inc., 1958.

Zemlin, W. R., *Speech and Hearing Science: Anatomy and Physiology*, Ed. 2. Englewood Cliffs, NJ: Prentice-Hall Inc., 1981.

Neurophysiology References

Broca, P., Remarques sur la siege de la faculté du langage articule, suivies d'une observation d'aphémie (perte de la parole). *Bull. Soc. Anatom. Paris. VI: 36*, 1861, 330-357.

Eccles, J. C., *The Understanding of the Brain*. New York: McGraw-Hill, 1973.

Fromkin, V. A., Slips of the Tongue. *Sci. Am. 229*, 1973, 110–116.

Lassen, A. R., Ingvar, D. H., and Skinhoj, E., Brain Function and Blood Flow. *Sci. Am. 239*, 1978, 62–71.

MacKay, D. G., Spoonerisms: The Structure of Errors in the Serial Order of Speech. *Neuropsychologia 8*, 1970, 323–350.

Milner, B., Branch, C., and Rasmussen, T., Observations on Cerebral Dominance. In *Psychology Readings: Language*. R. C. Oldfield and J. C. Marshall (Eds.) Baltimore: Penguin Books, 1968, pp. 366–378 (Later figures given in present text from oral presentation by Milner at ASHA meeting, Las Vegas, 1974.)

Penfield, W., and Roberts, L., *Speech and Brain-Mechanisms*. Princeton, NJ: Princeton University Press, 1959.

Pribram, K. H., *Languages of the Brain*. Englewood Cliffs, NJ: Prentice-Hall, Inc., 1971.

Wada, J., and Rasmussen, T., Intracarotid Injection of Sodium Amytal for the Lateralization of Cerebral Speech Dominance: Experiments and Clinical Observations. *J. Neurosurg. 17*, 1960, 266–282.

Wernicke, C., *Der Aphasische Symptomencomplex*. Breslau: Max Cohn and Weigert, 1874.

Respiration References

Campbell, E., The Respiratory Muscles. *Ann. N. Y. Acad. Sci. 155*, 1968, 135–140.

Draper, M. H., Ladefoged, P., and Whitteridge, D., Respiratory Muscles in Speech. *J. Speech Hear. Res. 2*, 1959, 16–27. Reprinted in Kent *et al.*, 1991, 3–14.

Fenn, W. O., Mechanics of Respiration. *Am. J. Med. 10*, 1951, 77–91.

Hixon, T. J., Respiratory Function in Speech. In *Normal Aspects of Speech, Hearing, and Language*. F. D. Minifie, T. J. Hixon, and F. Williams (Eds.) Englewood Cliffs, NJ: Prentice-Hall, Inc., 1973.

Hixon, T. J., Mead, J., and Goldman, M. D., Dynamics of the Chest Wall during Speech Production: Function of the Thorax, Rib Cage, Diaphragm, and Abdomen. *J. Speech Hear. Res. 19*, 1976, 297–356. Reprinted in Hixon, T. J. *Respiratory Function in Speech and Song*. San Diego, CA: Singular Publishing Group, 1991, 135–197. Also reprinted in Kent *et al.*, 1991 (q.v.), 297–356.

Lofqvist, A., Aerodynamic Measurements for Vocal Function. In *Neurological Disorders of the Larynx*. A. Bletzer, C. Sasaki, S. Falin, M. Brill, and K. S. Harris. (Eds.), New York: Thieme, 1992.

Mead, J., Bouhuys, A., and Proctor, D. F., Mechanisms Generating Subglottic Pressure. *Ann. N. Y. Acad. Sci. 155*, 1968, 177–181.

Netsell, R., Subglottal and Intraoral Air Pressures during the Intervocalic Contrast of /t/ and /d/. *Phonetica 20*, 1969, 68–73.

Rahn, H., Otis, A. B., Chadwick, L. E., and Fenn, W. O., The Pressure-Volume Diagram of the Thorax and Lung. *Am. J. Physiol. 146*, 1946, 161–178.

Stetson, R., *Motor Phonetics*. Amsterdam: North-Holland, 1951.

van den Berg, J., Direct and Indirect Determination of the Mean Subglottic Pressure. *Folio Phoniatr. (Basel). 8*, 1956, 1–24.

Phonation References

Atkinson, J. E., Correlation Analysis of the Physiological Factors Controlling Fundamental Voice Frequency. *J. Acoust. Soc. Am. 63*, 1978, 211–222.

Faaborg-Andersen, K., Electromyographic Investigation of Intrinsic Laryngeal Muscles in Humans. *Acta. Physiol. Scand. 41*, Suppl. 140, 1957, 1–148.

Hirose, H., and Gay, T.. The Activity of the Intrinsic Laryngeal Muscles in Voicing Control. *Phonetica. 25*, 1972, 140–164.

Husson, R., *Étude des Phénomenes Physiologiques et Acoustiques Fondamentaux de la Voix Chantée*. Thesis, University of Paris, 1950.

Ishizaka, K., and Flanagan, J. L., Synthesis of Voiced Sounds from a Two-Mass Model of the Vocal Cords. *Bell System Technical Journal. 51*, 1233–1268. Reprinted in Kent *et al.*, 1991 (q.v.), 183–218.

Ludlow, C. L., and Hart, M. O. (Eds.), *Proceedings of the Conference on the Assessment of Vocal Pathology, ASHA Reports*, 1981.

Müller, J., *The Physiology of the Senses, Voice, and Muscular Motion with the Mental Faculties*. Translated by W. Baly. London: Walton and Maberly, 1848.

Negus, V. E., *The Comparative Anatomy and Physiology of the Larynx*. New York: Hafner Publishing Co., 1962. (A rewriting of V. E. Negus, *The Mechanism of the Larynx*. London: William Heinemann Medical Books, Ltd., 1928.)

Shipp, T., Vertical Laryngeal Position during Continuous and Discrete Vocal Frequency Change. *J. Speech Hear. Res. 18*, 1975, 707–718.

Sundberg, J. *The Science of the Singing Voice*. De Kalb, IL: Northern Illinois Press, 1987.

Titze, I. R., On the Mechanics of Vocal-Fold Vibration. *J. Acoust. Soc. Am. 60*, 1976, 1366–1380.

van den Berg, I., Myoelastic-Aerodynamic Theory of Voice Production. *J. Speech Hear. Res.* 1, 1958, 227–244.

Von Helmholtz, H., *Die Lehre der Tonempfindungen als physiologische Grundlage für die Theorie der Musik*. Braunschweig: F. Vieweg und sohn, 1863.

5

Speech Production: The Finished Products—The Articulation and Acoustics of Speech Sounds

"Take care of the sense, and the sounds will take care of themselves."
—The Duchess in *Alice's Adventures in Wonderland* Chap. IX. by Lewis Carroll (Charles Ludwidge Dodgson)

ARTICULATION AND RESONANCE

In the last chapter we saw that air from the lungs can either be exhaled through the open larynx to provide energy for sound production above the larynx, as for the sound /s/, or can be chopped into bits at the vibrating larynx, setting up the periodic sound of phonation. In either case, whether the sound source is at the glottis or in the mouth, the sounds are further modified by the resonances of the vocal tract. In speech production terminology, *articulation* refers to movements of the tongue, pharynx, palate, lips, and jaw to make speech sounds. Resonance, in this context, refers to the acoustic response of air molecules within the oral, nasal, and pharyngeal cavities to some source of sound; the air can be set into vibration in response to a sound from the larynx or a sound created in the oral cavity. It will be seen that movements of the articulators are necessary both for producing sounds in the vocal tract itself and for altering the acoustic resonance characteristics of the tract.

The Vocal Tract: Variable Resonator and Sound Source

The vocal tract includes all of the air passages above the larynx from the glottis to the lips (Fig. 5.1). The large resonating cavities are the pharyngeal cavity, the oral cavity, and when the velopharyngeal port is open, the nasal cavity. The air spaces between the lips, between the teeth and the cheeks (*buccal* cavities), and within the larynx and trachea are also resonators. You recall from Chapter 3 that an air-filled tube resonates at certain frequencies depending upon whether it is open at one or both ends, upon its length, its shape, and upon the size of its openings. We know that musical instruments have resonators to amplify and filter sound. Stringed instruments are designed with resonating boxes graded in size to impart different qualities to the music. The large resonating cavity of the bass viol emphasizes the low frequencies of a complex sound, while the smaller resonating cavity of a violin emphasizes the high frequencies.

The remarkable characteristic of the human vocal resonators, compared to those of musical instruments, is that their shape and areas can be varied. It is, of course, the movements of the articulators that are responsible for the variations in shape and area. Tongue elevation and fronting creates a smaller area in the oral cavity but enlarges the area of the pharyngeal cavity. Conversely, tongue depression and backing enlarge the area in the oral cavity while reducing the pharyngeal area. Lip

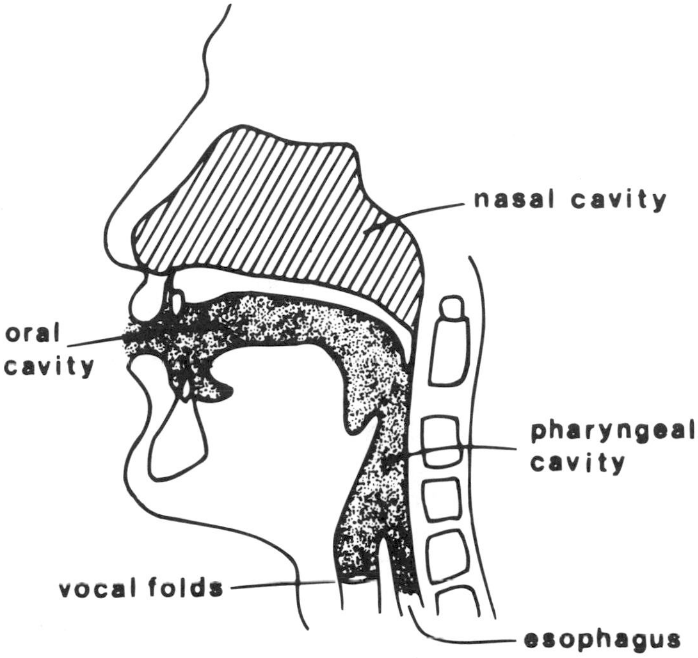

Figure 5.1. A section of the head showing the major cavities of the vocal tract.

protrusion lengthens the vocal tract creating lower resonant frequencies.

Types of Sound Sources. The speech sounds that we know as vowels, diphthongs, semivowels, and nasals are usually the result of filtering the periodic wave produced at the glottis through the vocal tract, which varies its configuration and thereby the resonant frequencies for each sound. The characteristic cavity configurations and resulting resonances for each sound are what make them distinct from one another. The sounds that emerge at the lips are periodic when the source of sound is the repeated vibrations of the vocal folds.

But the vocal folds can also be used to generate an aperiodic source of sound to be resonated in the cavities of the vocal tract. This is accomplished by partially adducting the folds, bringing them close enough to each other to make the breath stream turbulent as it flows through the glottis, but not so close as to induce vibrations of the folds themselves. The generation of a noise source at the glottis is the basis for whispered speech.

Aperiodic sources of sound can also be generated at various locations within the supraglottal vocal tract. One way to do this is to block the flow of air completely for a brief period of time and then to release the built up air pressure suddenly, as in the *stop* consonant /t/. The term plosive is also used for this kind of sound, in recognition of the explosive nature of the air burst.

A second way to produce an aperiodic source of sound is to force the air stream through a constriction formed by the articulators for a relatively extended period of time. As in the case of the partially closed glottis, this will cause the air stream to become turbulent and will result in a continuous source of noise that lasts longer than the transient noise bursts of the stops. The *fricative* /ʃ/, as in "shoe," is an example of a sound that uses a continuous noise source.

Combined Sound Sources. Speech sound sources can be combined in a variety of ways. The periodic source produced by the vibrating vocal folds and the continuous noise source produced by channeling the air flow through a constriction are frequently heard si-

Table 5.1. Speech Sound Sources

Source	Resonator	Sound	Manner	Examples
Vocal folds	Vocal tract	Periodic	Vowels	/i/ /u/
			Diphthongs	/ai/ /ou/
			Semivowels	/w/ /y/
			Nasals	/m/ /ŋ/
Vocal tract	Vocal tract	Aperiodic	Stops	/p/ /k/
			Fricatives	/s/ /f/
			Affricate	/tʃ/
Vocal folds and vocal tract	Vocal tract	Mixed periodic and aperiodic	Voiced stops	/b/ /g/
			Voiced fricatives	/z/ /v/
			Voiced affricate	/dʒ/

multaneously during the productions of voiced fricatives such as /vðzʒ/ and at the end of the voiced affricate /dʒ/. Similarly, in certain contexts, the periodic source may be simultaneously combined with the transient aperiodic source in the production of the voiced stops /bdg/ and at the start of the voiced affricate /dʒ/. Finally, although not combinations in the same sense, sequences of the transient and continuous aperiodic noise sources are required to produce both affricates, /tʃ/ and /dʒ/. In all of these instances of sounds produced in the vocal tract, the cavities of the tract also serve to resonate the sounds. Therefore, the vocal tract is always a resonator and often a source of speech sounds as well (Table 5.1).

Following a description of the vocal tract, we shall consider the sounds of English, starting with the most resonant, open tract sounds (the vowels, diphthongs, and semivowels), and proceeding to the less resonant sounds produced with a more constricted vocal tract (the nasals, fricatives, stops and affricates). For each class of speech sounds, we shall discuss the physiology of its production and the acoustic result.

Landmarks of the Tract

The posterior part of the vocal tract is formed by a tube of muscles known as the *pharynx*. The muscles are divided into three groups according to their position (Fig. 5.2). The *inferior constrictor muscles* are at the level of the larynx, the *middle constrictor muscles* start high in the back and course down to the level of the hyoid bone, and the *superior constrictor muscles* form the back of the pharynx from the level of the palate to the mandible. Contraction of the constrictor muscles narrows the pharyngeal cavity, and relaxation of the muscles widens it. The nasal, oral and laryngeal cavities open into the pharyngeal cavity. The parts of the pharynx adjacent to each cavity are called the nasopharynx, oropharynx, and laryngopharynx, respectively. (See Fig. 5.1)

Oral Cavity. The oral cavity is bounded in front and along the sides by the teeth set into the *alveolar processes* of the upper jaw or *maxillary bone* (Fig. 5.3) and the lower jaw or *mandible* (Fig. 5.4). The most important teeth for speech are the *incisors*, the flat-edged biting teeth in the front of the mouth. There are two central incisors and two lateral incisors in each jaw. They are used with the lower lip, with the tongue, and with each other to create a constriction for such sounds as /f/, /θ/, and /s/. The roof of the oral cavity consists of the *hard palate* (Fig. 5.5) and the soft palate or *velum*. The anterior ⅔ of the hard palate is formed by the palatine process of the maxillary bone, and the other ⅓ is formed by part of the palatine bone. An important landmark on the hard palate is called the superior alveolar ridge. You can feel the alveolar ridge as the ridged shelf behind the upper teeth. In the region of the alveolar ridge behind the front teeth, you can feel a series of irregular ridges called *rugae*. Many speech sounds are either generated or resonated as a result of actions of the tongue in relation to the rugae along the alveolar ridge.

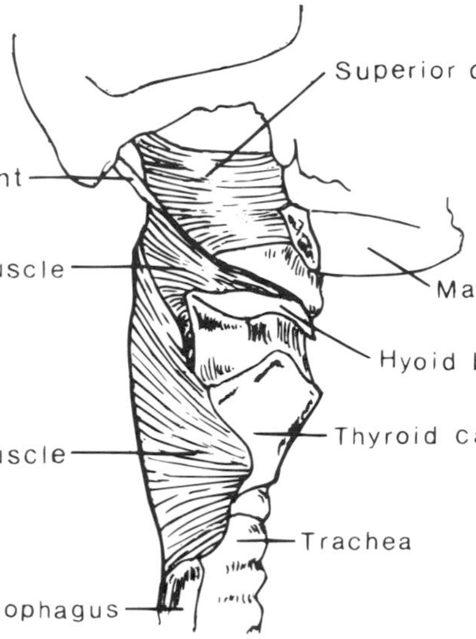

Figure 5.2. Lateral view of the pharyngeal constrictor muscles.

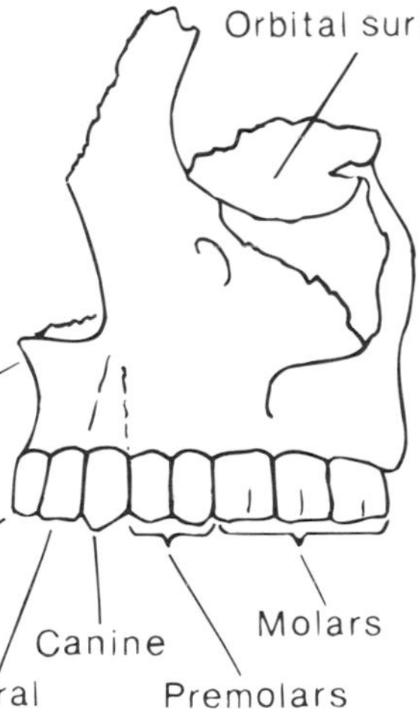

Figure 5.3. The maxilla, with teeth indicated.

The Velum. The velum or soft palate has one muscle intrinsic to it called the uvular muscle. You can see the *uvula* hanging down in the back of your mouth when you look in a mirror. The greater part of the soft palate, however, consists of a broad muscle entering the sides of the velum from the temporal bones behind and above on each side. These muscles, the *levator palatini* muscles, are appropriately named because their function is to elevate the soft palate, thus closing the entrance to the nasal cavities above. (Look ahead to Fig. 5.34) When the levator palatini muscles contract, the soft palate is lifted up and back toward the posterior wall of the pharynx. This action (*velopharyngeal closure*) occurs to some degree for all of the speech sounds in English, except the three nasal consonants, /m/, /n/, and /ŋ/, which require nasal resonance. For these exceptions, the port to the nasal cavities is left open by relaxing the levator palatini muscles.

The Tongue: Extrinsic Musculature. The floor of the oral cavity is largely formed by the three-dimensional muscle mass, the tongue. The tongue can be moved as a mass in three directions; up and back, down and back, and up and forward. The extrinsic muscles of the tongue are capable of moving the tongue body in the oral and pharyngeal spaces because of their attachments outside of the tongue (Fig. 5.6).

The *styloglossus* muscles are attached to the styloid process of each temporal bone. The muscle fibers run down and forward inserting into the sides of the tongue. Contraction of the styloglossus muscles pulls the tongue back and up. This movement is important for sounds such as /u/ as in "Sue."

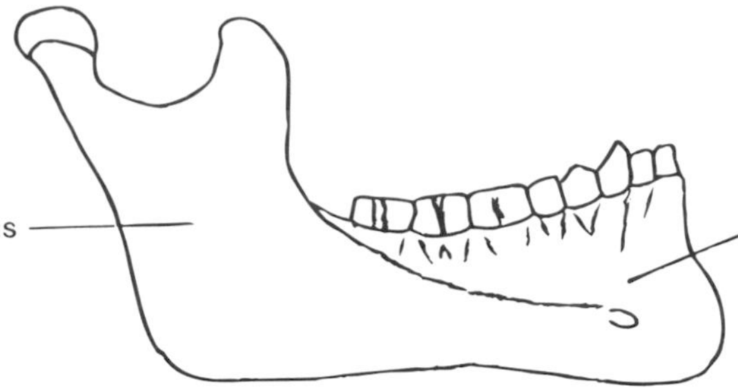

Figure 5.4. The mandible. The two major sections, the ramus and corpus of the mandible, are indicated.

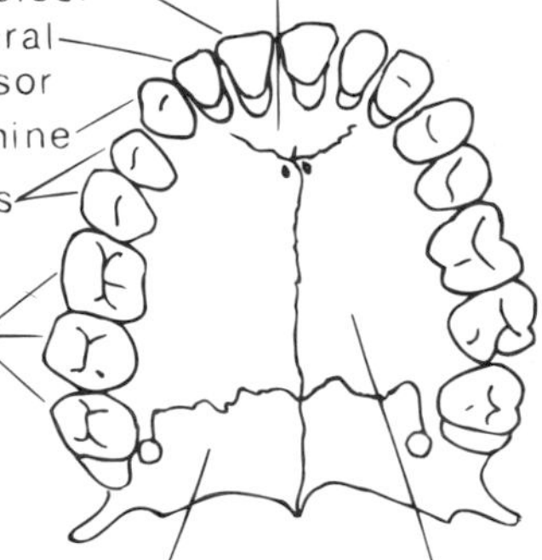

Figure 5.5. The hard palate, consisting of the premaxilla and palatine processes of the maxillary bone and the palatine bone. The bones are fused along the lines indicated. The irregular ridges along the anterior portion of the premaxilla are called rugae and serve as the locus of maximum constriction for many speech sounds.

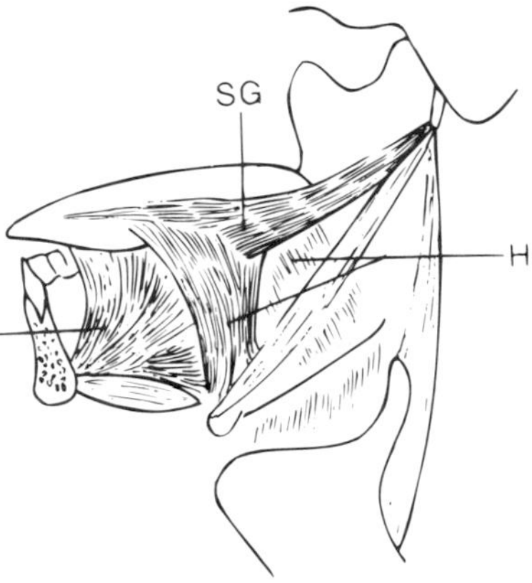

Figure 5.6. A schematic diagram of the extrinsic tongue musculature in lateral view. The styloglossus muscle (SG) elevates and backs the tongue, the hyoglossus muscle (HG) depresses the tongue, and the genioglossus muscle (GG) fronts and elevates the tongue.

The *hyoglossus* muscles are attached to the hyoid bone, and the fibers run in a thin sheet up into the lateral base of the tongue. Hyoglossus contraction results in tongue depression and backing. The sounds /ɑ/ and /a/ have low tongue positions. The *genioglossus* muscles are attached to the inside of the mandible at the superior mental spine. The muscle fibers radiate up and back to insert throughout the length of the tongue down to and including the hyoid bone. Contraction of the genioglossus muscle draws the hyoid bone and tongue root forward. High forward tongue placement is important for /i/, as in "see."

The fourth and last of the extrinsic muscles of the tongue, the *palatoglossus* muscles, will be described below in our discussion of the velopharyngeal mechanism.

The Tongue: Intrinsic Musculature. While the extrinsic muscles determine the gross position of the tongue body, the intrinsic muscles of the tongue determine the shape of its surface. (Fig. 5.7).

The *superior longitudinal* muscle consists of many muscle fibers coursing from the back of the tongue to the tip. Contraction of the superior longitudinal muscle curls the tongue tip up.

The *inferior longitudinal* muscles, also running from the root to the tip of the tongue,

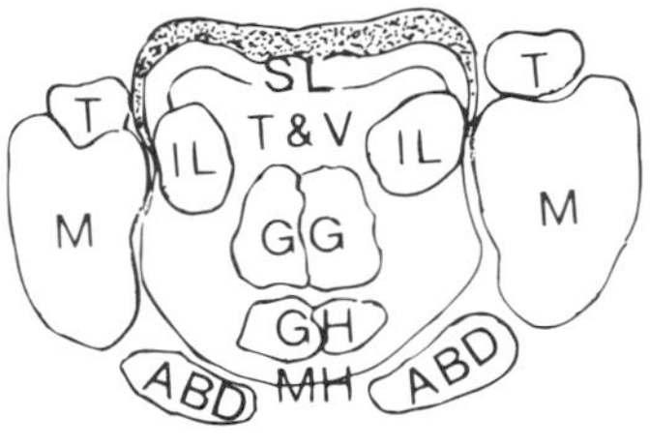

Figure 5.7. The tongue in frontal section. Intrinsic muscles indicated by * in the following list. **SL,* the superior longitudinal muscles; **T & V,* transverse and vertical muscles; **IL,* inferior longitudinal muscles; *GG,* genioglossus muscles; *GH,* geniohyoid muscles; *MH,* mylohyoid muscles; *ABD,* anterior belly of the digastric muscles; *T,* teeth; *M,* mandible.

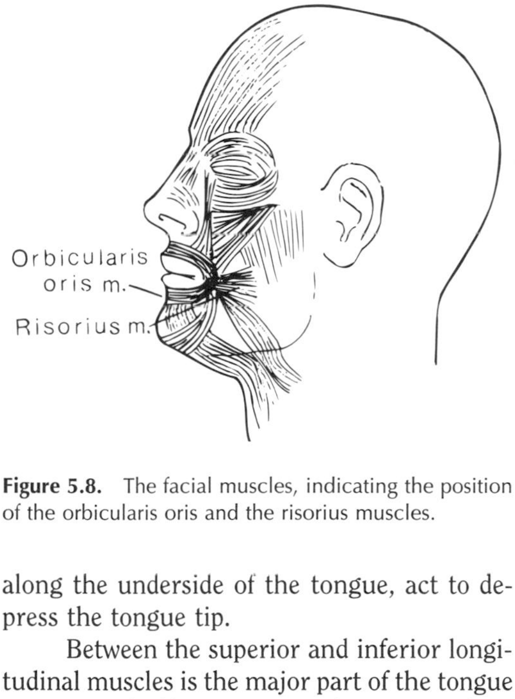

Figure 5.8. The facial muscles, indicating the position of the orbicularis oris and the risorius muscles.

along the underside of the tongue, act to depress the tongue tip.

Between the superior and inferior longitudinal muscles is the major part of the tongue mass. Muscle fibers coursing from top to bottom of the mass (*vertical muscles*) interweave with muscle fibers coursing from the middle of the tongue out to the sides (*transverse muscles*). Together the intrinsic muscles shape the tongue, especially its tip, into a variety of configurations.

The Lips. Many facial muscles intermingle with the fibers of the major lip muscle, the *orbicularis oris,* which encircles the lips (Fig. 5.8). To close the lips for bilabial sounds, /p/, /b/ or /m/, or to protrude the lips for /u/ or /w/, contraction of the orbicularis oris muscle is necessary.

Other facial muscles, such as the *risorius,* are active in adjusting the corners of the mouth to aid in the sort of lip spreading that many speakers employ when articulating vowels such as /i/ in the word "we." The fibers of the facial muscles vary considerably in the way they are distributed from one individual to another.

Acoustic Theory of Vowel Production

In 1941, Chiba and Kajiyama wrote a classic monograph on the acoustic derivation of the vowel. Based upon earlier work by von Helmholtz and others, Crandall at Bell Telephone Laboratories had calculated the resonances of the vocal tract for different vowels, by applying acoustic laws of double resonators from equations stated in 1896 by Rayleigh. Chiba and Kajiyama measured the vocal tract from x-ray photographs and, using Crandall's formulas, calculated the resonant frequencies for single and double resonators of comparable size. When the frequencies as computed coincided with the frequencies of real vowels, the Tokyo group considered that they had gained information on that resonator. The resonances of the vowel /i/ matched those of a single resonator, while those of /u/ and /ɑ/ corresponded with those of double resonators. Gunnar Fant of Sweden presented a comprehensive study of the acoustics of vowels based upon measurements of the vocal tract taken from x-ray photographs of a Russian speaker during vowel production. His *Acoustic Theory of Speech Production* was published in 1960. It relates a source-filter account of vowel production to the resonances as shown on a sound spectrograph. Fant found the Helmholtz resonator model to be appropriate for only a few vowels. He used a three-parameter model developed by Stevens and House, determining the location of the main tongue constriction, the amount of lip protrusion, and vocal tract cross-sectional area.

Resonance of Tube Open at One End. During vowel production, the vocal tract approximates a tube closed at one end and open at the other because the vocal folds are essentially closed during phonation, and the speaker's lips are open. The lowest natural frequency at which such a tube resonates will have a wavelength (λ) 4 times the length of the tube. A male vocal tract, for example, may be approximately 17 cm long. The wavelength of the lowest resonant frequency at which the air within such a tube would naturally vibrate, would be 4 × 17 cm or 68 cm. To determine the frequency of vibration (f = velocity/wavelength), one must also consider the velocity of sound in air, 344 meters/sec. We must, however, express this in centimeters (34,400 cm/sec), because the length of the tube was calculated in centimeters. If the length of the tube had been measured in feet, the velocity of sound in air in feet (1130 ft/sec) would have been used in the formula.

$$f = \frac{c}{\lambda} = \frac{34{,}400 \text{ cm}}{68 \text{ cm}} = \text{about } 506 \text{ Hz}$$

where c is used for constant, since in a given medium and at a given temperature, sound travels at a constant velocity. The lowest reso-

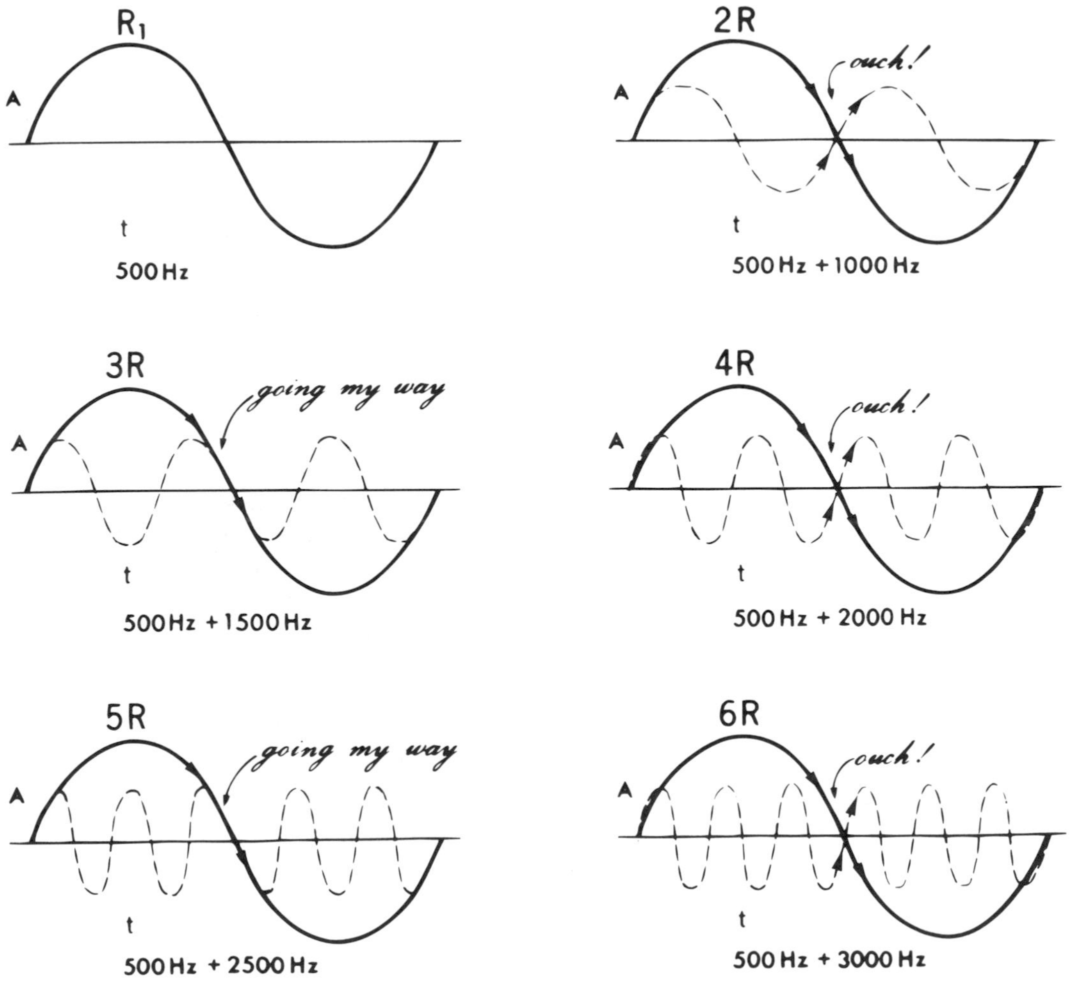

Figure 5.9. The resonant frequencies of a tube open at one end and closed at the other. The even harmonics are not effective resonant frequencies because they are canceled at the entrance to the tube ("ouch!"), while the odd harmonics are compatible ("going my way").

nant frequency of such a tube is, thus, about 500 Hz, and it also resonates at odd multiples of that frequency. Why odd multiples? The even multiples are not effective resonant frequencies. Figure 5.9 illustrates the compatibility of the odd multiples with the 500-Hz resonance of the tube. The compression waves and rarefaction waves coincide in direction at the zero crossing, while the frequencies that are even multiples of the principle resonant frequency affect the air particles with opposing forces neutralizing one another.

Resonance of Male Vocal Tract. Tubes, then, resonate naturally at certain frequencies when energized, frequencies that depend upon the configuration and the length of the tube. A human vocal tract is similar to the sort of acoustic resonator we have been describing. There are some differences: Unlike the rigid tube, the vocal tract has soft, absorbent walls. Further, unlike the tube, it is never of absolutely constant cross-sectional area. Nonetheless, the approximation is close enough for our discussion.

Chiba and Kajiyama illustrated the resonances of a tube open at one end, and they related these resonances to those occurring in a vocal tract that is fairly uniform in cross-section (Fig. 5.10). The first resonance of such a tube or tract as schematized at the top of the figure, is a frequency that has a wavelength 4 times the length of the tube. Therefore only $\frac{1}{4}$ of the pressure wave can energize the air within the tube at any one time. The first pressure wave will reach maximum velocity (V) at the opening of the tube, or in the case of the human resonator, at the lips. The second frequency at which such resonators vibrate, shown in the middle of the figure (3R), is 3 times the lowest resonant frequency, because $\frac{3}{4}$ of the wave fits into the length of the tube. This sets up two points of maximum velocity and one point of maximum pressure within the vocal tract. The third resonance (5R) is a frequency with a wavelength shorter than the tube or vocal tract. It is 5 times the lowest resonance, so $\frac{5}{4}$ of the wave fits into the length of the tube. Velocity is maximum at three places, and there are two

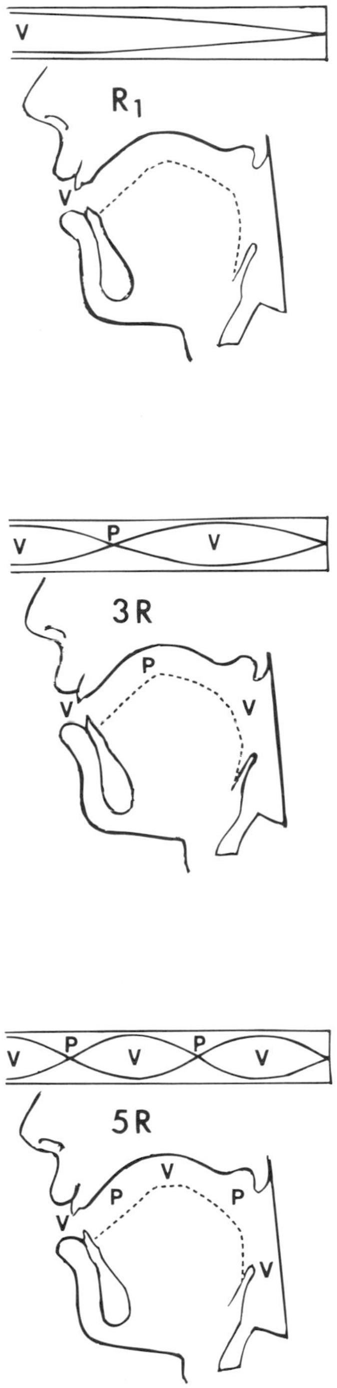

Figure 5.10. The resonances of the vocal tract. (See text for explanation.) *V,* points of maximum velocity; *P,* points of maximum pressure; *R,* resonances. (Adapted from T. Chiba and M. Kajiyama: *The Vowel: Its Nature and Structure,* Kaiseikan, Tokyo, 1941.)

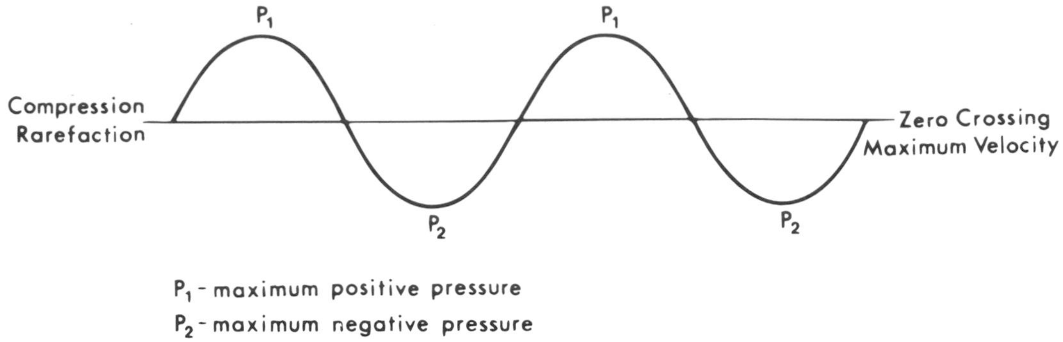

Figure 5.11. The inverse relationship between pressure and velocity for a sine wave. Pressure is greatest at points P_1 and P_2 for positive and negative values. Velocity is greatest at zero crossings, and at a minimum at P_1 and P_2.

locations of maximum pressure in the oral cavity.

The points of maximum velocity and pressure are important, because resonances change in frequency if the tract is constricted near a point of maximum velocity or a point of maximum pressure. Remember that points of maximum pressure correspond to points of minimum velocity and vice versa (see Chapter 3 for a discussion of simple harmonic motion). Figure 5.11 may serve to illustrate the inverse relationship between pressure and velocity. In general, constrictions at points of maximum velocity lower the resonant frequency, while constrictions at points of maximum pressure raise the frequency of the resonances.

Vocal tract resonances are called *formants*. The first formant (R1) is most responsive to changes in mouth opening. Speech sounds requiring small mouth openings have low frequency first formants. Conversely, open mouth sounds are characterized by relatively high frequency first formants. (The first formant at its highest frequency value is still the lowest resonance of the tract.) The second formant (3R) is most responsive to changes within the oral cavity. Tongue backing or lip activity might lower the frequency of this formant, as these constrictions would occur in areas of high velocity, but any tongue or jaw activity that would narrow the region in the oral cavity where the pressure is relatively high would result in raising the frequency of the second formant. The third formant (5R) is responsive to front versus back constriction.

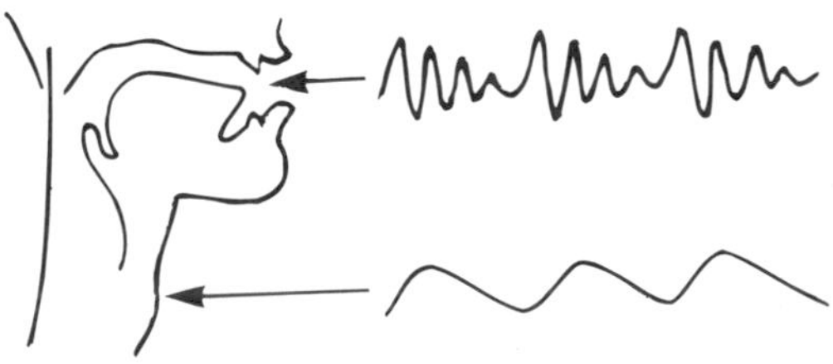

Figure 5.12. A sound wave at the lips and at the glottis. Notice that the waveform is changed by passage through the vocal tract. The tract has acted as a filter.

Let us return to our consideration of an unconstricted vocal tract. Imagine a sound produced at the vocal folds passing through the air-filled cavities of a tract that resonates at frequencies of 500, 1500, and 2500 Hz, about the same resonant frequencies as the 17-cm tube that we discussed in the previous section. Stevens and House as well as Fant have presented simplified versions of how a sound produced by vibrations of the vocal folds is changed by the resonant response of the vocal tract. The changes that occur can best be understood by comparing the sound at its source at the glottis with the final output at the lips. Whatever acoustic changes might occur can be attributed to the effects of transmission through the vocal tract.

Figure 5.12 contrasts the waveforms of a vowel sound at its source and at the lips. The source waveform must be inferred, as one would have to lower a microphone into the larynx to record it directly. At first glance, it looks as if the vowel has more high frequency energy than the glottal waveform. The exact nature of the changes undergone in transfer can better be appreciated by contrasting the Fourier spectra. A Fourier analysis, as you recall from Chapter 3, is a process of analyzing a complex wave into its component frequencies.

The spectrum of the sound source (the sound produced at the vocal folds) can be seen to consist of a fundamental frequency (corresponding to the frequency of vocal fold vibration) and many multiples, or harmonics, of the fundamental (Fig. 5.13). These harmonics diminish in intensity as they increase in frequency. If we could hear it, the sound of phonation would sound like a buzz. The middle spectrum is a plot of the resonant frequencies of a neutral vocal tract, which we have computed to be 500, 1500, and 2500 Hz. These are the frequencies at which the air in a tract of that shape and length would vibrate maximally in response to another complex sound. When the sound represented by the first spectrum is transmitted through a vocal tract that resonates at the frequencies indicated in the second spectrum, the resulting sound will be a product of the two. Specifically, the glottal source with its many harmonics (termed the *source function*) is filtered according to the frequency response of the vocal tract (termed the *transfer function*). The harmonics of the glottal sound wave which are at or near the spectral peaks of the transfer function of the vocal tract are resonated, and those distant from the resonant frequencies of the tract lose energy and are thus greatly attenuated. The sound that emerges at the end of the tract (the lips) has the same harmonics as the sound at the source (the glottis), but the amplitudes of the harmonics have been modified, altering the quality of the sound.

The frequencies that we have described as appropriate for a neutral male tract would not be the resonant frequencies for the same vocal tract if it were longer, shorter, or different in its configuration. A speaker can move his lips, tongue, and jaw creating many different vocal tract sizes and shapes. Any change of vocal tract configuration alters the frequencies at which the cavities resonate. Unlike the neutral tube-like configuration of the vocal tract when a speaker says "uh" [ʌ] or the [ə] in "sofa," most of the vocal tract shapes assumed for speech sounds are much more constricted in certain parts of the tube than in other parts. This alters the cavity sizes, which then resonate at different frequencies. The odd multiples of the lowest resonance that occurred for the neutral tubular tract are lowered or raised in frequency because of the locations of the constrictions and volume changes of the cavities. The resonances thus no longer have a simple mathematical relationship to one another.

The vocal tract is thus a variable resonator, and, as its shape varies, the resonances or formants change in frequency, producing a variety of sounds. A convincing demonstration of the effect of the vocal tract as a variable resonator is to phonate at a constant pitch while articulating a continuous sequence of vowels. The sound source produced by the vocal folds remains constant; the only changes are in the shapes of the resonator. You will discover that simply by changing vocal tract shape, you can make all the vowel sounds.

Vowels: /i/, /ɑ/, and /u/. To better understand the production of the vowels we hear, let us follow the sounds /i/, /ɑ/, and /u/, which represent articulatory extremes, from their source at the vocal folds as they are transferred through the vocal tract (which amplifies certain harmonics and attenuates others) until they emerge at the lips.

The sound that emerges from the lips is a product of the sound of vocal fold vibration (the source function) and the resonances of a particular vocal tract shape and length (the transfer function) plus an effect of sound radiation at the lips. The source function is largely independent of the transfer function. For example, you can assume a fixed vocal tract shape and produce the same vowel sound repeatedly with widely different fundamental frequencies. Singing the vowel [i] up the scale, you are conscious of maintaining the appropriate resona-

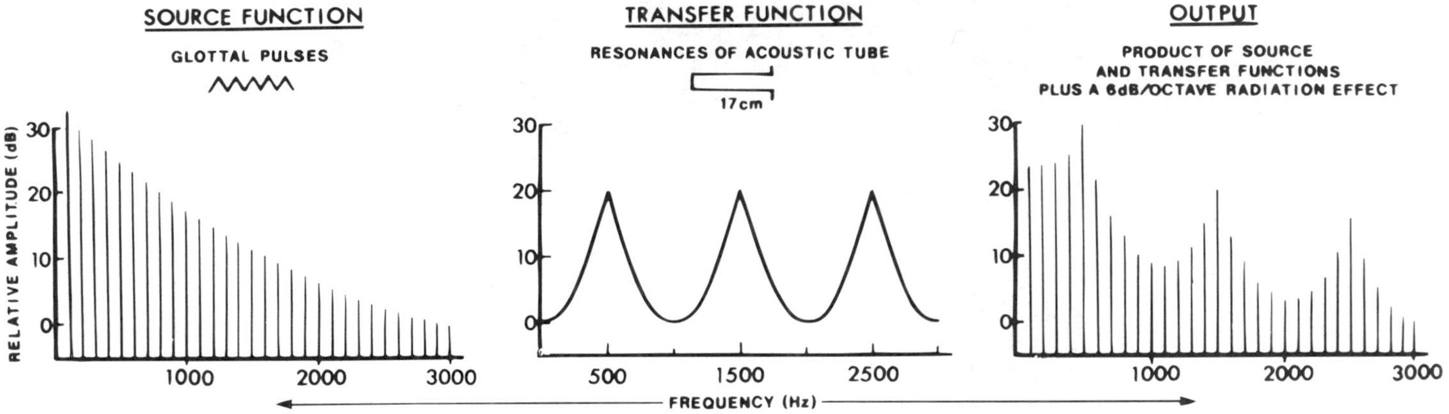

Figure 5.13. The panel at the *left* shows the spectrum of the glottal source. The panel at the *right* shows the spectrum of the source after filtering by a transfer function corresponding to a neutral vocal tract, with a radiation effect added. The transfer function is indicated in the *middle panel*.

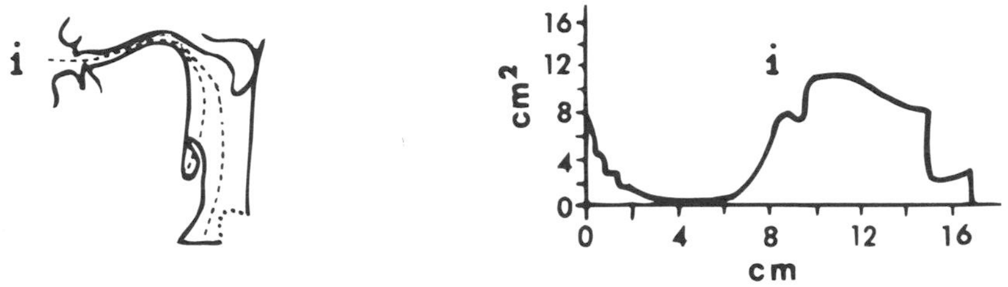

Figure 5.14. On the *left* is shown a lateral view of the tongue for the vowel [i]. The *right panel* shows the cross-sectional area of the vocal tract for [i]. The *abscissa* indicates distance from the lips. (Adapted from G. Fant: *Acoustic Theory of Speech Production,* Mouton, The Hague © 1970.)

tor for [i] for each note, while the source of the sound is changing. When the source changes, there are two differences: the fundamental frequency is different, and the spacing between the harmonics is different, as we discussed previously in connection with phonation (see Fig. 4.45). Despite these differences, the resonances of the vocal tract remain the same.

High, Front, Unrounded Vowel. The sound /i/ in the word "key" is distinctive because of the high frequency energy from the resonances in the oral cavity. In order to resonate at such high frequencies, the oral cavity must be made small. That is why the speaker fronts and elevates the tongue toward the alveolar ridge. In a tracing from an x-ray picture of the vocal tract of a speaker saying [i], it can be seen that the tongue mass fills most of the oral cavity, leaving a small volume of air to vibrate (Fig. 5.14). The pharynx, however, enlarges because the posterior part of the tongue, which normally occupies pharyngeal space, moves up and forward.

The right side of Figure 5.14 shows Fant's measurements of the cross-sectional area in square centimeters at various distances from the lips. These calculations were made by using lateral x-ray measures to estimate three-dimensional cross sections of the vocal tract. The vocal tract is narrowly constricted at 4 and 6 cm back from the lips and widens considerably at 10 and 12 cm back from the lips. The muscle that is the primary agent for this adjustment of tongue fronting and elevation is the genioglossus muscle, innervated by the hypoglossal

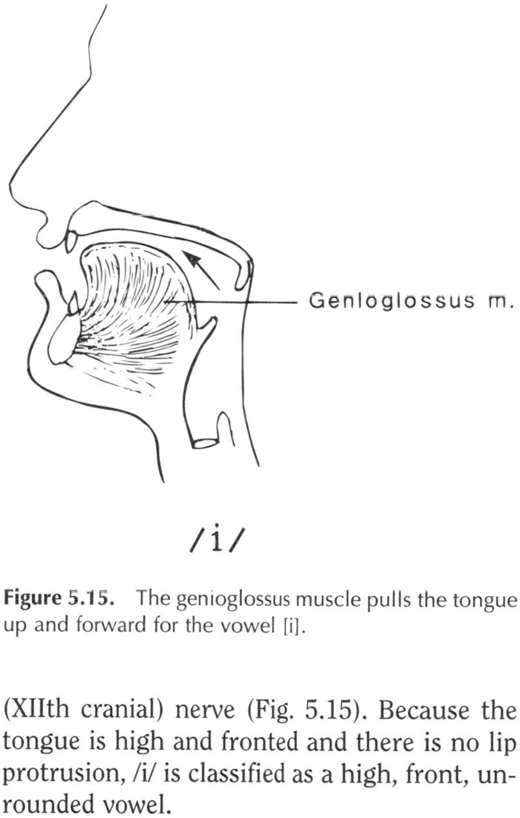

Figure 5.15. The genioglossus muscle pulls the tongue up and forward for the vowel [i].

(XIIth cranial) nerve (Fig. 5.15). Because the tongue is high and fronted and there is no lip protrusion, /i/ is classified as a high, front, unrounded vowel.

The left side of Figure 5.16 shows a possible output spectrum for the articulation of /i/, which we have been discussing. Note that the fundamental frequency of the source is 150 Hz. The transfer function of the vocal tract configuration for /i/ is superimposed on the spectrum. Suppose that we had used this transfer function with a sound source having a fundamental frequency of 300 Hz. The harmonic structure of the vowel would be different, since every other harmonic in the figure would be absent. But because the articulation, and therefore, the transfer function, remain the same, the resonant (formant) frequencies would remain unchanged. Figure 5.17 demonstrates this principle for three sources with fundamental frequencies of 100, 150 and 250 Hz. When each source serves as the input to a vocal tract that is shaped to produce the vowel /i/, the output spectra have peaks of resonance at the same frequencies. A different speaker, of course, with a different size vocal tract and slightly different articulatory habits would produce different formant frequencies, but the pattern of one very low formant (F_1), and two relatively high formants (F_2, F_3) would be the same, as long as the articulation conformed to the pattern for /i/ which we have described. A typical formant pattern for this vowel is: F_1 = 270 Hz, F_2 = 2290 Hz, F_3 = 3010 Hz (see Table 5.2).

If we compare the output spectrum in Figure 5.16 with the spectrum for the neutral vowel (Figure 5.13), we can see that for /i/ F_1 is lower (the high velocity area between the lips is narrowed), while F_2 and F_3 are both higher in frequency (the narrowed oral cavity resonates at higher frequencies).

We can see, then, that the output of the vocal tract is primarily determined by the transfer function of the resonating cavities and, thus, ultimately, by the articulators that shape those cavities. In the output (the sound that emerges at the lips) the harmonics closest to the resonances of the tract have been resonated, and those furthest from the resonances have lost energy in transmission. The schematic rendering of a *sound spectrogram* of [i] on the right side of Fig. 5.16 depicts the formants of the vocal tract as broad bands of energy. Formants are traditionally numbered from low to high frequency. The formant around 300 Hz is F_1, at 2500 Hz is F_2, and at 3000 Hz is F_3.

The frequency of a formant is measured at the center of the band of energy. This frequency may or may not correspond to the frequency of one of the harmonics. In the example given in Figure 5.16, the formant frequency is 2500 Hz, but the harmonic with the greatest amplitude in this formant is 2550 Hz for the voice with a 150 Hz fundamental frequency, and would be 2400 Hz for a voice with a fundamental frequency of 300 Hz.

As we have mentioned, an alternative method of displaying vowel formants is shown at the right of Figure 5.16. This is a schematic rendering of a wideband spectrogram. It differs from the output spectrum at the left of the figure in several ways, most importantly in that time is a parameter of the display: The output

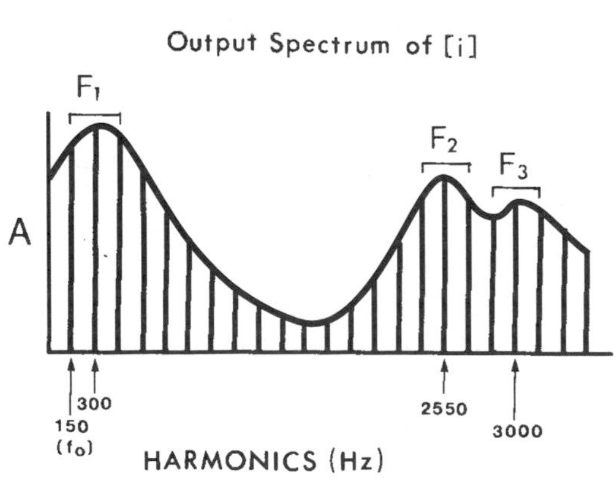

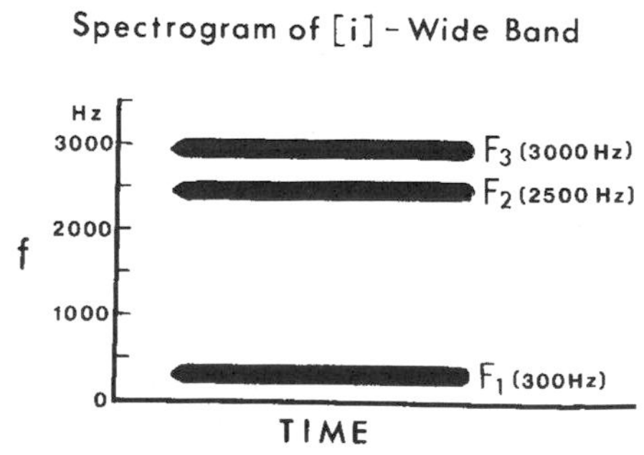

Figure 5.16. On the *right* is a schematic spectrogram of the vowel [i] as in the word "beat." On the *left* is shown a spectrum of the same sound. F_1, F_2, and F_3 represent the vocal tract resonances. The spectrogram shows frequency (*f*) changes in time. The spectrum shows the amplitude (*A*) of the component frequencies or harmonics. Notice that the center frequency of the formants does not always match the frequency of an individual harmonic.

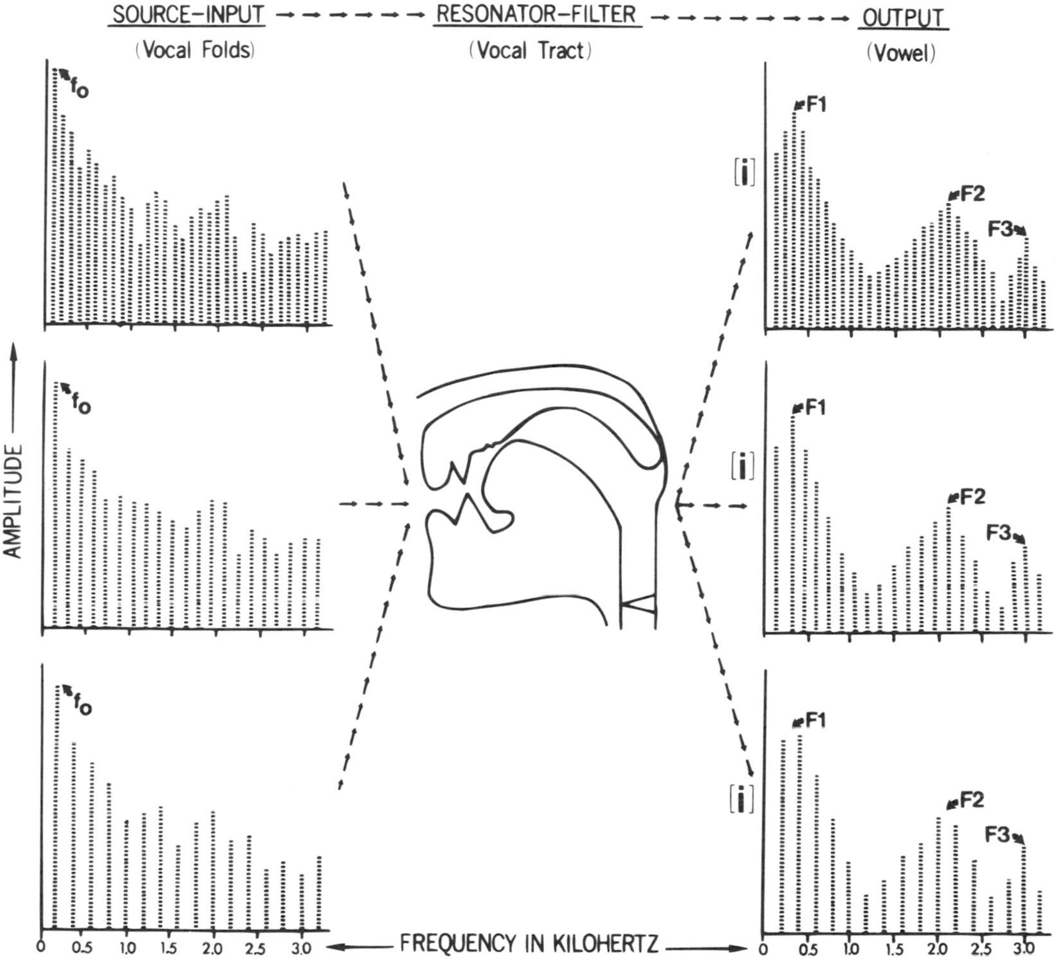

Figure 5.17. Input/output spectra for a single resonator/filter: the vocal tract shaped to produce to vowel /i/. Note that the frequencies of the resonance peaks of the output spectra are identical.

spectrum is an instantaneous representation of the resonant characteristics of the vowel, while the spectrogram depicts the peaks of resonance as they change over time. Since we are assuming a static vocal tract shape, the formants in this spectrogram do not, of course, change in frequency. In normal speech, however, the articulators are in virtually continuous motion, and so the cavity shapes and the formants are continuously changing. Thus it is much easier to display those changes in a wideband spectrographic representation than it would be if we had to refer to a sequence of many output spectra made at different times during the production of an utterance. Descriptions of devices that produce spectrograms may be found in Chapter 7.

Another way in which the wideband spectrogram differs from the output spectrum is that it provides no specific information about the frequencies of the individual harmonics that compose the resonance peaks of the vocal tract. You cannot tell, from looking at the schematic wideband spectrogram in Figure 5.16, which harmonic frequencies make up the formants or, for that matter, how many harmonics fall within the bandwidth of each formant. Such information, however, is irrelevant if it is the center frequencies of the formants (resonance peaks) that are of interest, since they are

Table 5.2. Averages of Fundamental and Formant Frequencies of Vowels by 76 Speakers*

		i	ɪ	ɛ	æ	ɑ	ɔ	ʊ	u	ʌ	ɝ
Fundamental frequencies (cps)	M	136	135	130	127	124	129	137	141	130	133
	W	235	232	223	210	212	216	232	231	221	218
	Ch	272	269	260	251	256	263	276	274	261	261
Formant frequencies (cps)											
F_1	M	270	390	530	660	730	570	440	300	640	490
	W	310	430	610	860	850	590	470	370	760	500
	Ch	370	530	690	1010	1030	680	560	430	850	560
F_2	M	2290	1990	1840	1720	1090	840	1020	870	1190	1350
	W	2790	2480	2330	2050	1220	920	1160	950	1400	1640
	Ch	3200	2730	2610	2320	1370	1060	1410	1170	1590	1820
F_3	M	3010	2550	2480	2410	2440	2410	2240	2240	2390	1690
	W	3310	3070	2990	2850	2810	2710	2680	2670	2780	1960
	Ch	3730	3600	3570	3320	3170	3180	3310	3260	3360	2160

* Abbreviations: M, man; W, woman; Ch, child. Taken from G. E. Peterson and H. L. Barney, Control methods used in a study of the identification of vowels. *Journal of the Acoustical Society of America 24*, 1954, 183.

determined by the articulation of the vowel and will remain essentially unchanged if the frequencies of the fundamental and harmonics were higher or lower, or even if they changed during the articulation of the vowel. In fact, for the same articulatory/vocal tract configuration, the center formant frequencies will be the same even when the vocal tract is resonating to an aperiodic source, containing no harmonics, as in the whispered vowels we mentioned earlier.

Low, Back Vowel. The oral cavity is larger, and the pharyngeal cavity smaller for the vowel /ɑ/ than for /i/. The size of the oral cavity may be increased in two ways: lowering the tongue passively by lowering the jaw, or by actively depressing the tongue. It is also possible to combine these two strategies.

Jaw lowering is partially controlled by the anterior belly of the digastric muscle (ABD). This paired muscle originates near the posterior surface of the mandibular symphysis and attaches to the body of the hyoid bone near the minor horn. Figures 5.18 and 5.42 show lateral and midline views, respectively, of the ABD. The muscle is innervated by motor fibers from the trigeminal (Vth cranial) nerve.

Enlargement of the oral cavity by active lowering of the tongue can be achieved by contraction of the hyoglossus muscle. As you can see in Figure 5.18, the fibers of this muscle course down from the tongue and insert into the body and major horn of the hyoid bone. It is innervated by the hypoglossal (XIIth cranial) nerve. See if you can alternate the sounds [i] and /ɑ/, first enlarging the oral cavity by jaw lowering and then by active tongue depression.

Active or passive lowering of the tongue for /ɑ/ provides the large oral cavity and small pharyngeal cavity volumes that characterize this vowel (Fig. 5.19). As we would expect, the small pharyngeal cavity resonates to higher frequency harmonics in the source, generating a relatively high frequency first formant, while the large oral cavity resonates to low frequency harmonics in the source and thus generates a relatively low frequency second formant. Typical frequencies for the first three formants of /ɑ/ are F_1: 730 Hz, F_2: 1090 Hz, F_3: 2440 Hz (see Table 5.2). Thus the articulatory differences between /i/ and /ɑ/ are reflected in the acoustic differences (Remember that /i/ has a large pharyngeal cavity/low frequency F_1 and a small oral cavity/high frequency F_2).

High, Back, Rounded Vowel. The third articulatory extreme in vowel production is /u/. This vowel is articulated with the dorsum of

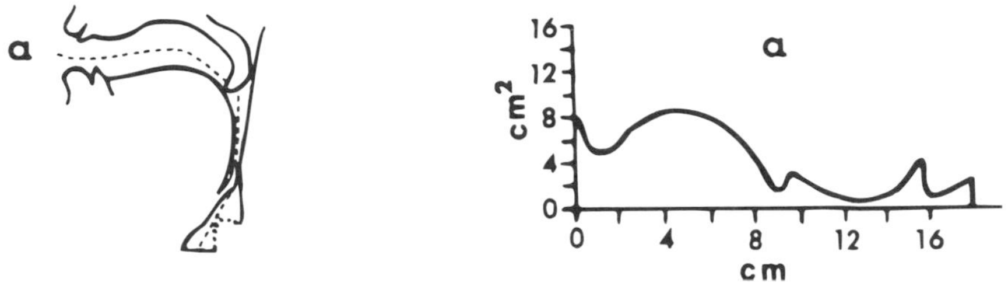

Figure 5.18. Lateral view of the vocal tract and vocal tract area function for /ɑ/. (Adapted from G. Fant: *Acoustic Theory of Speech Production,* Mouton, The Hague © 1970.)

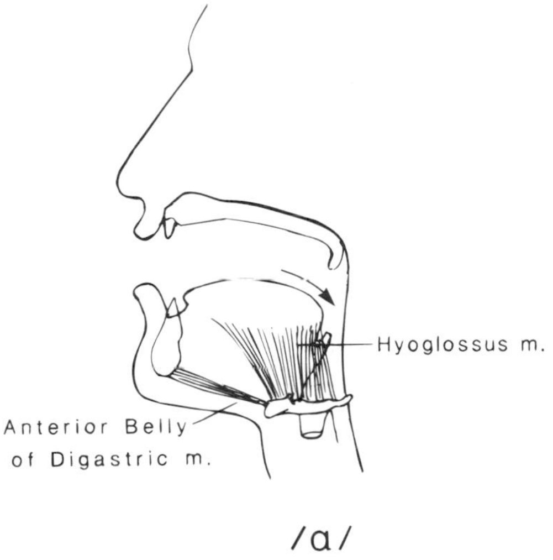

Figure 5.19. For [a], the anterior belly of the digastric muscle is active in jaw opening and/or the hyoglossus muscle is active in depressing the tongue.

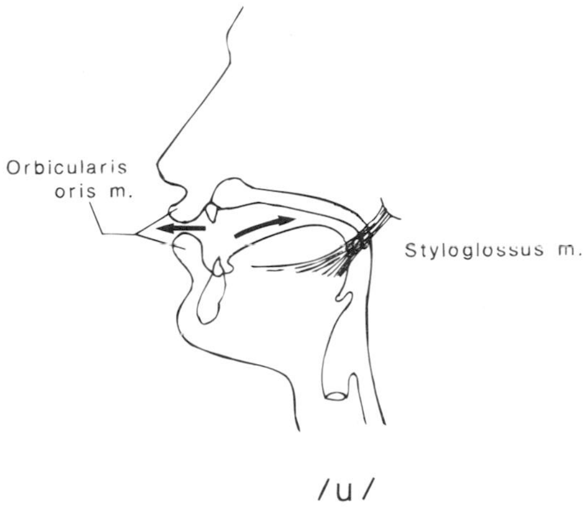

Figure 5.20. The activity of the orbicularis oris muscle protrudes the lips, while the styloglossus muscle elevates the back of the tongue for [u].

the tongue raised toward the roof of the mouth in the area of the juncture between the hard palate and the velum. This is accomplished by contracting the styloglossus muscle (Figs. 5.20 and 5.6), which is innervated by the hypoglossal (XIIth cranial) nerve. In many instances speakers will also round and protrude the lips by contracting the orbicularis oris muscle (Fig. 5.20), which is innervated by the facial (VIIth cranial) nerve.

The acoustic effect of this positioning of the lips and tongue is threefold: First, the protrusion of the lips increases the overall length of the vocal tract and thus lowers the frequencies of all the formants. Second, the raising of the tongue dorsum pulls the bulk of the tongue out of the pharyngeal cavity, enlarging it and allowing it to resonate to the low frequency harmonics composing the first formant of this vowel. Third, the posterior constriction formed by the raised tongue dorsum and the protrusion of the lips lengthens the oral cavity, allowing it to resonate to the relatively low frequency harmonics that make up the second formant of /u/ (Fig. 5.21). Typical frequencies for the first three formants of /u/ are F_1: 300 Hz, F_2: 870 Hz, F_3: 2240 Hz (see Table 5.2).

We should note that at normal rates of speech /u/ is frequently produced with little or no lip protrusion. In order to achieve the appropriate elongation of both the oral cavity and the vocal tract as a whole, speakers must therefore resort to alternative articulatory strategies. These include a greater degree of tongue retraction than would be used if the lips were protruded (which specifically lengthens the oral cavity and contributes to the lowering of the frequency of the second formant) and lowering the larynx (which increases the length of the entire vocal tract and so lowers the frequencies of all the formants). Thus, the desired acoustic effect can be achieved by more than one articulatory configuration. We shall see that this one-to-many relationship between acoustics and articulation is typical of many speech sounds.

Let us make one final observation before going on to discuss other vowels: The formant frequencies that we have provided above for /i/, /ɑ/, and /u/ have been purposely labeled as "typical." Absolute frequencies cannot be given because the resonance characteristics of each vocal tract differ to some extent from those of every other. This variability is a function of three kinds of differences among speakers. First, as we noted earlier, the overall size of vocal tracts differs among speakers. Second, the relative size of parts of the vocal tract may differ. For example, the size of the pharynx is generally smaller relative to the oral cavity in women compared to men. And third, a particular sound may be articulated differently by individual speakers because of their dialect or idiolect. The differences account, in part, for our ability to recognize individual speakers on the basis of differences between the qualities of equivalent sounds, aside from the differences between voice (source) characteristics. We shall see, in the following chapter, that these differences raise interesting and difficult questions about how to explain the fact that listeners can perceive different acoustic signals as linguistically equivalent entities.

The Relationship Between Acoustics and Articulation. The sounds that we have been discussing, /i/, /ɑ/, and /u/, occupy a special place in traditional, articulatory-based descriptions of most languages. The earliest of these articulatory descriptions, now well over 100 years old, were based almost entirely on the impressionistic, introspective evidence of phoneticians who viewed vowel articulation primarily as functions of tongue shape and tongue position within the oral cavity. Lip posture, since it was so easily observable, also formed one of the bases for description.

With the introduction of more objective techniques for describing articulation, the importance of the tongue root and jaw position became known, and the development of acoustic analysis led investigators to explore the relationships among articulation, the dimensions of the resonating cavities, and the acoustic features of speech, especially with regard to formant frequencies. Research into these relationships has led to general agreement that the frequencies of formants cannot be attributed solely to a particular resonating cavity within the vocal tract. That is, the formants are under-

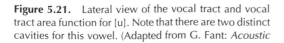

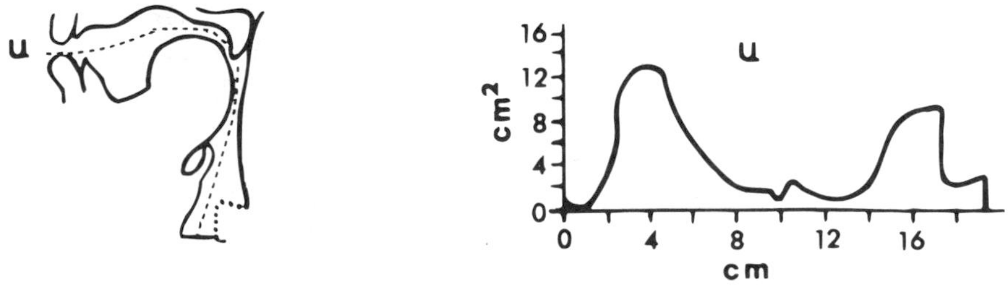

Figure 5.21. Lateral view of the vocal tract and vocal tract area function for [u]. Note that there are two distinct cavities for this vowel. (Adapted from G. Fant: *Acoustic Theory of Speech Production,* Mouton, The Hague © 1970.)

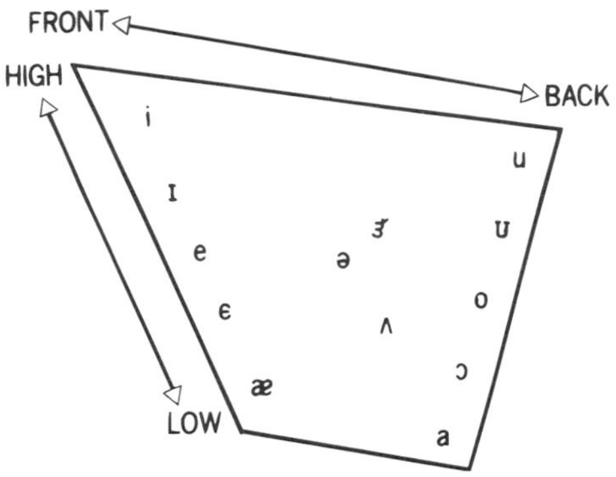

Figure 5.22. The traditional vowel quadrilateral. The location of each phonetic symbol represents the position of the high point of the tongue within the part of the oral cavity in which vowel constrictions are formed.

stood as the acoustic response of the vocal tract as a whole to the components of the source.

Nonetheless, in practice, speech scientists have found it impossible to ignore the well-established correlations (which we have implied above in our discussion of /i/, /ɑ/, and /u/) among (1) the frequencies of the first two formants, (2) the dimensions of the oral and pharyngeal cavities, and (3) the traditional description of tongue, jaw, and lip position in vowel articulation. Let us now be explicit about the basis of these correlations.

Figure 5.22 depicts the traditional vowel quadrilateral (sometimes called the vowel triangle, despite the fact that it has four sides!). The basic parameters of this quadrilateral are tongue height (high-to-low) and tongue advancement (front-to-back). The quadrilateral is thus a schematic representation of that portion of the oral cavity within which the high point of the tongue moves while forming constrictions during vowel articulation. The relative position of any phonetic symbol in the quadrilateral is taken to represent the position of the highest point on the superior surface of the tongue in the articulation of the vowel it represents. Despite the existence of some discrepancies between the locations of these symbols and the high point of the tongue as viewed in x-ray studies, the description given in the vowel quadrilateral generally conforms to the known facts and, as we shall see, it is particularly relevant to the measured frequencies of vowel formants.

The correlation between the articulatory parameters of the vowel quadrilateral and the acoustic output of the vocal tract will be obvious if we inspect Figure 5.23, a plot of the average first and second formant frequencies of 33 adult males taken from Table 5.2. The basic similarity between this formant frequency plot and the arrangement of the vowel symbols in the vowel quadrilateral is clear, and it is not merely a coincidence.

To fully explain the basis of the similarity, we must describe how the positioning of the articulators affects the size and shape of the oral and the pharyngeal resonating cavities. In Figure 5.24 the articulatory, resonance cavity, and acoustic data are combined. We can see that the frequency of F_1 is closely correlated with (1) the area of the back or pharyngeal cavity and (2) the degree of mouth opening at the

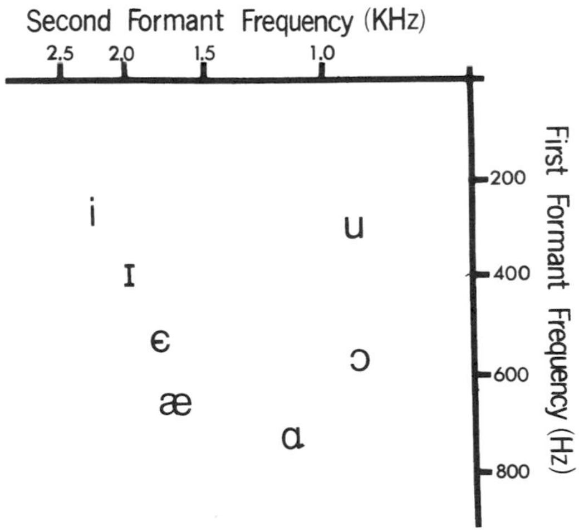

Figure 5.23. Average formant frequencies of 33 adult male speakers of English. The data are taken from the study by G. E. Peterson and H. L. Barney: Control methods used in a study of the vowels. *Journal of the Acoustical Society of America 24,* 1954,183.

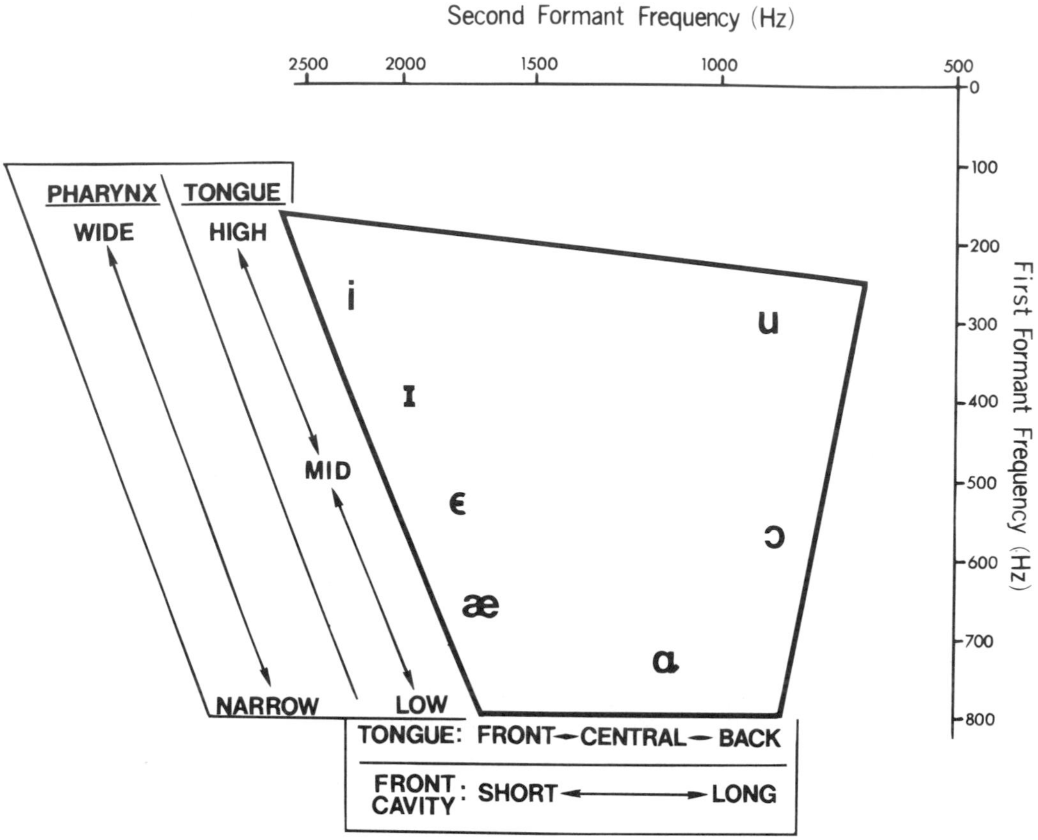

Figure 5.24. The relationships among tongue position, cavity size, and formant frequency for some English vowels.

lips. The frequency of F_2 is correlated with the length of the front (oral) cavity.

Let us consider the first formant. As the tongue moves from a high to a low position, the pharyngeal cavity decreases in volume (see Fig. 5.28). The basic reason for the decrease in volume is the noncompressibility of the tongue: As it descends into the smaller area within the mandible, the tongue root is forced back into the pharyngeal cavity. Conversely, as the tongue body rises, the tongue root is pulled out of the pharyngeal cavity. This means that vowels with higher tongue positions have larger pharyngeal cavities that will resonate to lower frequencies in the source. Vowels with lower tongue positions will have smaller pharyngeal cavities that will resonate to higher frequencies in the source. The correlation between lip opening and F_1 frequency can be inferred from the articulation, as the higher vowels are characterized by raised jaw positions and smaller lip apertures, while the lower vowels display low jaw positions and larger lip apertures.

The second formant frequencies of the vowels correlate in a straightforward way with the length of the oral resonating cavity. Note that in the front vowel series in the traditional vowel quadrilateral (see Figs. 5.22 and 5.28) each vowel has a slightly more retracted tongue position than the one above it. For the back series, each vowel has a slightly more retracted tongue position than the one below it. If we assume that the location of the vowels within the quadrilateral is correct, then as we articulate the vowels on the perimeter of the quadrilateral from /i/ down to /æ/, across the bottom to /ɑ/ and then up to /u/, we are constantly retracting the high point of the tongue. Since it is the high point of the tongue that marks the posterior limit of the oral cavity, that cavity grows longer throughout this series of vowels. Lip rounding will supplement the retraction of the tongue by elongating the oral cavity in the anterior dimension for most of the back vowels. Thus the shorter oral cavity associated with the advanced tongue positions of the more front vowels such as /i/ and /I/ resonates to higher frequencies in the source. The longer the oral cavity becomes as the tongue is retracted (and the lips protruded), the lower the frequencies in the source that will be resonated.

Notice that, acoustically, the critical dimension is front cavity length and not tongue position or lip protrusion. We remarked earlier that back, "lip-rounded" vowels are not always articulated with maximum rounding (protrusion). We can see now that reduced degrees of lip-rounding can be compensated for by increased degrees of tongue retraction to yield a front resonating cavity of the appropriate length for a given vowel.

The effect of these articulatory/acoustic relationships on the formant frequencies of the vowels on the perimeter of the vowel quadrilateral can be seen in Figures 5.25, 5.26, and 5.27: (1) A generally consistent lowering of F_2 as the front resonating cavity is enlarged because of tongue retraction (and lip protrusion), and (2) a general raising of F_1 from /i/ through /ɑ/ as pharyngeal cavity size is decreased (because of tongue lowering) and lip aperture is increased (because of jaw lowering), and a lowering of F_1 from /ɑ/ through /u/ as pharyngeal cavity size is increased (as the tongue rises) and lip aperture diminished (as the jaw rises) (Fig. 5.28).

At this point it would be wise to recall that these explanations are only a first approximation to causality, and that the response of the vocal tract as a whole, rather than of the individual resonating cavities, must be considered to account fully for formant frequencies. This is obvious if we consider the articulation of the vowel /ɑ/, in which the highest point of the tongue is so depressed that it can scarcely be said to divide the vocal tract into front (oral) and back (pharyngeal) cavities. Nonetheless, as we have said, speech scientists generally rely on the causal component of the correlations we have presented here, and often make such assumptions as "the fronting of the tongue will result in a rise in the frequency of F_2," or "a rise in the frequency of F_1 indicates that the tongue and jaw have been raised." The perva-

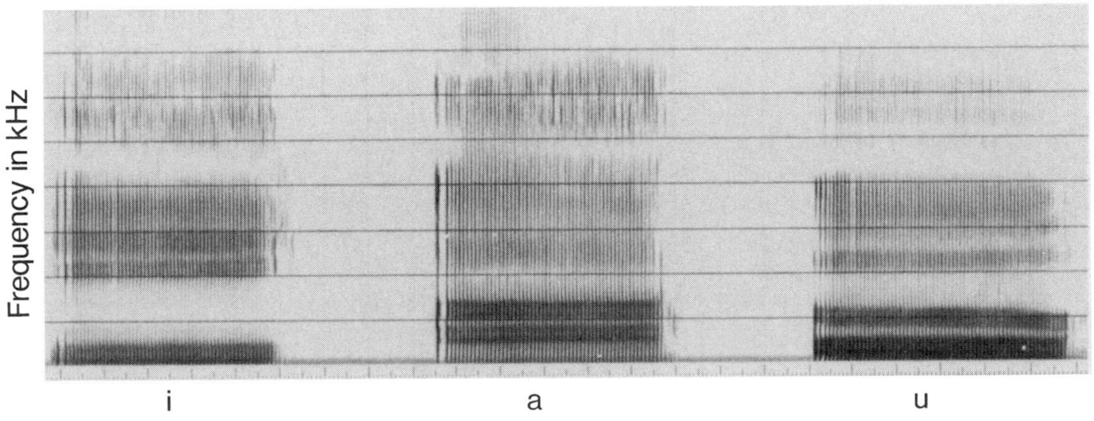

Figure 5.25. Spectrogram of steady state productions of the vowels [i], /ɑ /, and [u]. A 1 kHz calibration tone is indicated. (Spectrogram courtesy of Kay Elemetrics.)

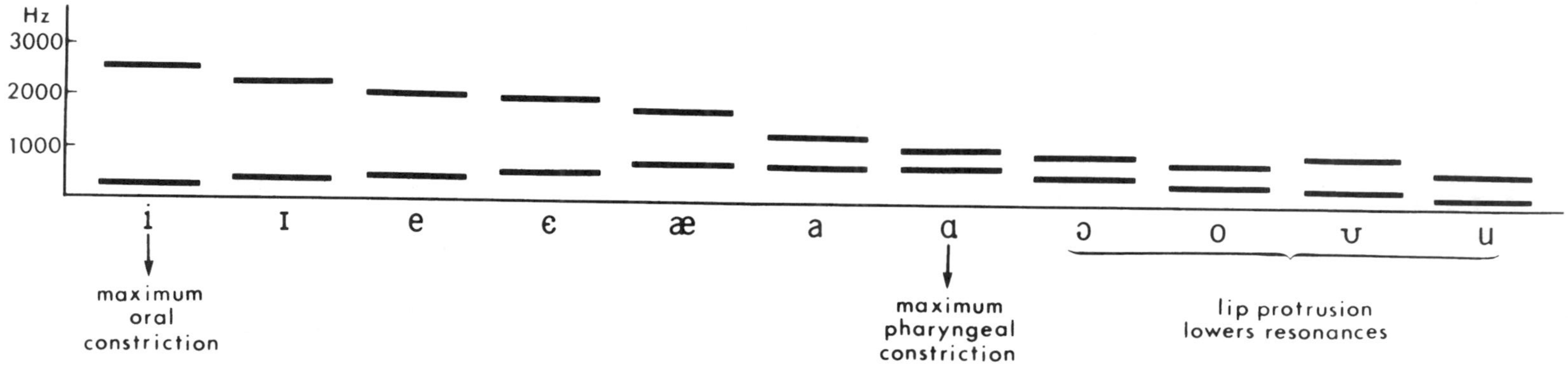

Figure 5.26. Two-formant vowels, synthesized on the Pattern Playback. The *symbols* indicate the identification of each pattern by listeners. The *lettering* indicates the vocal tract characteristics of the corresponding vowels.

	i	ɑ	u
F_1	300	800	300
F_2	2500	1000	900
F_3	3000	2500	2500

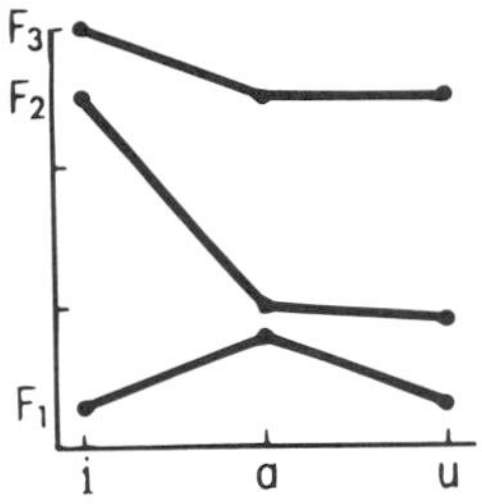

Figure 5.27. Relationships among F_1, F_2, and F_3 for /i/, /ɑ/, and /u/.

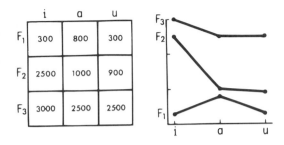

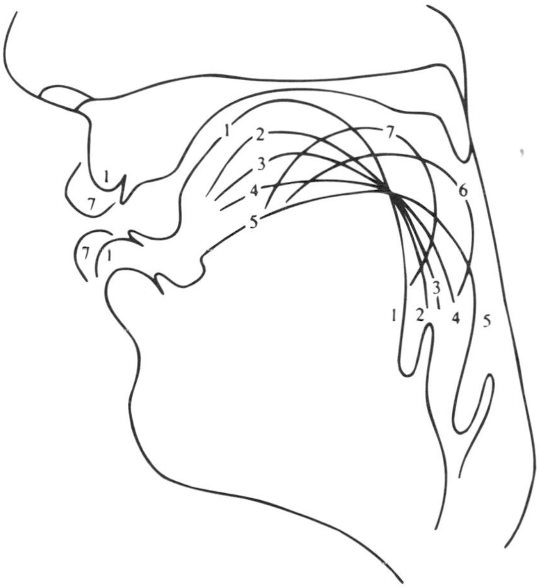

Figure 5.28. The vocal tract shape, for the vowels in the words (*1*) "heed," (*2*) "hid," (*3*) "head," (*4*) "had," (*5*) "father," (*6*) "good," (*7*) "food." (Reprinted from Peter Ladefoged: *A Course in Phonetics* © 1975 by Harcourt Brace Jovanovich, Inc. By permission of the publisher.)

siveness and usefulness of such assumptions suggest that they are, for the most part, warranted.

In point of fact, the correlations between articulation and acoustics can be more satisfactorily represented in a number of ways. Ladefoged, for example, achieves a closer match between formant frequencies and actual tongue positions and shapes (as depicted in x-rays) by plotting F_1 against the difference between F_2 and F_1 (rather than simply plotting F_1 directly against F_2.) This results in a more physiologically accurate placement of the back vowels (Fig. 5.29) by showing [ɔ] and [ɑ] to be further back than [u] and [U].

It may well be that phoneticians have been unconsciously charting the vowels according to their acoustic reality rather than their articulatory reality. It seems clear that the vowel quadrilateral data are more nearly a direct reflection of the acoustic, rather than the articulatory data. As Ladefoged points out, the impressions of vowel height are "more closely determined by the first formant frequency than by the [actual] height of the tongue." Similarly, impressions of tongue advancement are "more simply expressed by reference to the difference between the first and second formant frequencies that to any measurement of the actual [horizontal] position of the tongue." In addition, Fant has observed that the highest point of the tongue is not as important as the maximum constriction and the length of the tract from the glottis to this point. For example, the highest point of the tongue for /ɑ/ is in the oral cavity, but the point of maximum constriction is in the pharyngeal cavity, closer to the glottis.

The Relationship Between Acoustics and Vocal Tract Size. We have already mentioned that there is no set of absolute formant frequency values for any of the vowels. This is because vocal tracts of different size will resonate to different frequencies. In an early (1952) study, Peterson and Barney measured the formant frequencies of 76 speakers (33 men, 28 women, and 15 children). The subjects were recorded as they produced English vowels in a /hVd/ context. The average formant frequencies for the three groups of speakers are shown in Table 5.2. We can see that there are marked differences among the groups for the first three formant frequencies for each vowel. Nonetheless, the relative positions of the vowels in an F_1 by F_2 formant plot (Fig. 5.30) are remarkably similar. In general, as we would expect, the larger vocal tracts generate lower resonant frequencies than the smaller ones. Thus the lowest formant frequencies are those of the adult males, and the highest are those of the children, while those of the adult females display intermediate values. The frequency differences, however, are not related simply to the differences in overall vocal tract dimensions because the adult males have a relatively larger ratio of pharyngeal area to oral cavity area compared to the adult females or children.

Tense-lax Vowels. Some of the vowels (and diphthongs) in English are of intrinsically greater duration than others. These vowels are usually characterized by tongue movements that deviate more from the so-called "neutral position" for schwa than do the vowels of intrinsically shorter duration. However, the vowels with the more extreme tongue positions and greater duration are termed *tense* vowels, more because of evidence about their distribution in words than because of their method of production. Tense vowels can appear in open syllables, such as "see, say, so, sue, saw, sigh, cow, and soy." The vowels with less extreme tongue positions and shorter duration are called *lax* vowels. Most lax vowels appear only in closed syllables (syllables that end in consonants) and not in open syllables. In English, examples of lax vowels are found in the words in "sit, set, sat, and soot."

The tense vowels can be divided into two subclasses according to whether the vocal tract is held relatively constant throughout the vowel, or whether there is a distinct change in

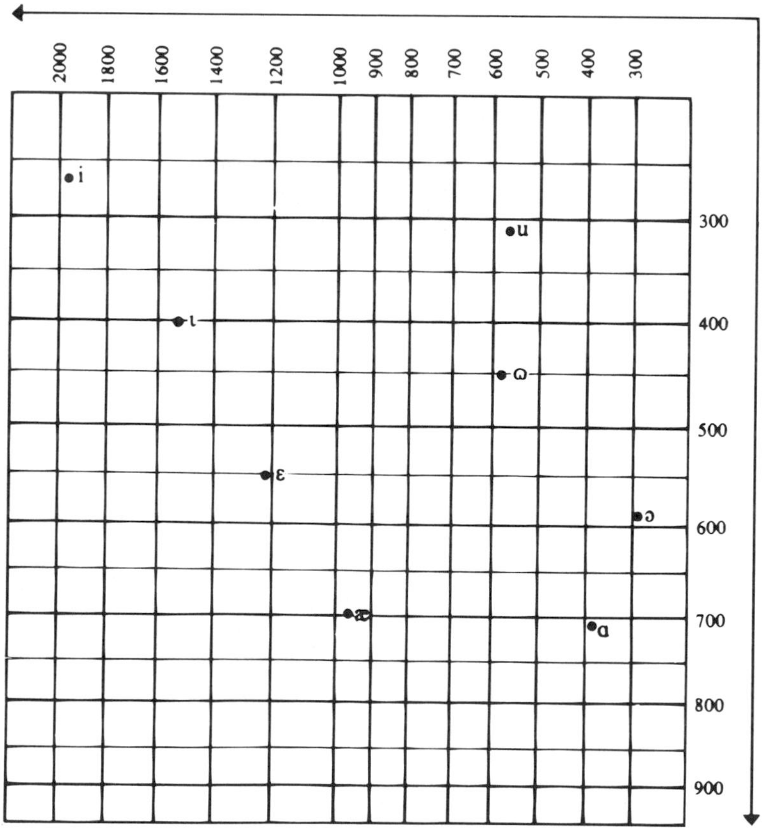

Figure 5.29. A formant chart showing the frequency of the first formant on the *ordinate* (the vertical axis) plotted against the difference in frequency of the first and second formants on the *abscissa* (the horizontal axis) for eight American English vowels. The symbol "ʊ" is equivalent to "U." (Reprinted from Peter Ladefoged: *A Course in Phonetics* © 1975 by Harcourt Brace Jovanovich, Inc. By permission of the publisher.)

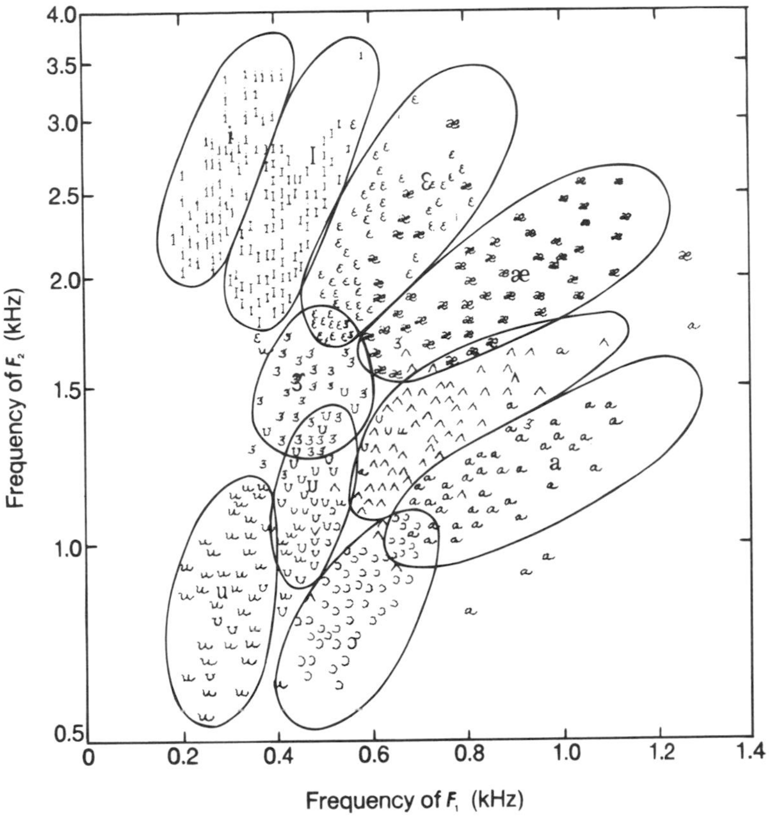

Figure 5.30. Average formant frequencies for some English vowels spoken by adult males, adult females and children. The data are taken from the study by G. E. Peterson and H. L. Barney: Control methods used in a study of the vowels. *Journal of the Acoustical Society of America 24,* 1954,183.

vocal tract shape during production. Virtually all of the "simple" tense vowels are diphthongized to a greater or lesser extent. Vowels such as those in the words "say" and "so" are marked by more extreme diphthongization than those in the words "see" and "sue." Try saying the words above to see if you can distinguish between (1) the changes in vocal tract shape and differences in duration that differentiate the more diphthongized tense vowels from those that are less diphthongized, and (2) the tense from the lax vowels in general.

Diphthong Production

A diphthong is a vowel of changing resonance. Common diphthongs are the vocalic portions of the words in the following sentences:

How Joe likes toy trains!
/aU/ /oU/ /aI/ /ɔI/ /eI/
I don't play cowboy.
/aI/ /oU/ /eI/ /aU/ /ɔI/

Those "tense" vowels that you found to require a changing vocal tract shape are considered to be diphthongs. Notice that the diphthongs ending with vocal tract cavities appropriate for [I] ([eI], [aI], and [ɔI]) entail tongue movement forward and up from the [e], [a], and [ɔ] positions, and that the diphthongs ending with vocal tract cavities appropriate for [U] ([oU] and [aU]) entail tongue movement back and up, concurrent with lip protrusion. As we suggested above, the sounds [Ii] and [Uu] as in "see" and "sue" are often diphthongized too, but the vocal tract and resonance changes are less extensive than in the other diphthongs.

Acoustic studies of formant changes in diphthongs have shown F_1 and F_2 formant shifts characteristic of each diphthong. Holbrook and Fairbanks measured formant frequencies of diphthongs from spectrograms of 20 male speakers saying "My name is John ____," with Hay, High, Hoy, Hoe, Howe, and Hugh as last names. F_1 by F_2 plots show acoustic overlaps, but when the samples are limited to those closest to the median, patterns are more discrete. Figure 5.31 shows that the longer diphthongs with more extensive changes ([aI], [aU], and [ɔI]) undershoot the final goals [I] and [U] more than the shorter diphthongs ([eI], and [oU]). The authors noted that [eI] extends from [aI] in an almost continuous fashion, as does [oU] from [aU]. Together, they form the trough of an inverted triangle.

Muscle use for diphthongs is similar to that for vowels, although contractions sometimes shift gradually from one muscle group to another. For example, to produce [aI], the tongue lowering muscles are gradually replaced by tongue fronting and elevating muscles, such as the genioglossus and geniohyoid muscles.

Peterson and Lehiste measured the durations of diphthongs, along with other *syllabic nuclei*, and found that the shorter diphthongs (which they called tense monophthongs) [eI], [oU], and [ɝ] change slowly and continuously, whereas the longer diphthongs [aI], [aU], and [ɔI] evidenced a steady state at the beginning, followed by a longer transition, and ended with a shorter off-glide near the terminal target.

Vowels and diphthongs, which constitute the nuclei of almost all syllables, are not perceived or produced well by people with hearing loss. Without acoustic/auditory input, the subtle differences and changes in the shape of the relatively open vocal tract are difficult to identify. In production, they typically tend to articulate vowels with limited movement of the tongue away from the neutral (schwa) position and with much greater than normal variability.

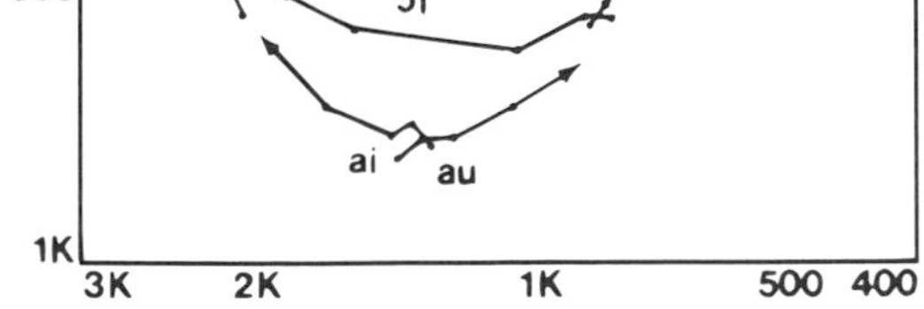

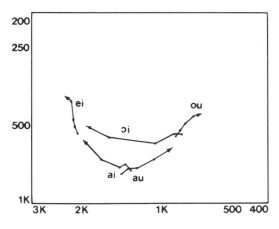

Figure 5.31. First and second formants for the diphthongs. The first formant frequencies are plotted on the ordinate and the second formant frequencies on the abscissa. The direction of formant movement is shown by the *arrows*. (Replotted with permission from data in A. Holbrook and G. Fairbanks: *Journal of Speech and Hearing Research. 5,* 1962.)

Consonant Production

Resonant Consonants I: The Semivowels. The sounds /w/, /j/, /r/, and /l/ as in "we," "you," "right," and "light" are often called semivowels because their formant structures are like those for vowels and diphthongs. The /r/ and /l/ sounds, when produced in syllable final position, can be prolonged as in "car" or "full" and sound much like vowels. If you pronounce /w/ or /j/ slowly enough, as in "we" and "you," the diphthongs [ui] and [iu] can be heard.

Although the vocal tract is relatively open for the semivowels, as it is for vowels and diphthongs, and although the semivowels are characterized acoustically by formants, yet they are considered to be consonants, not vowels. The reason for this is that the semivowels occur on the periphery of syllables, as do other consonants, and not in the nuclei of syllables, as do the vowels and diphthongs. For example, "win" /wɪn/, "yoke" /jok/, "rat" /ræt/ and "leap" /lip/ are possible in English but /twn/, /pjk/, /drt/ and /plp/ are not, because the latter syllables lack appropriate nuclei formed by vowels and diphthongs articulated with an open vocal tract. The semivowels, being nearly as open and resonant as the vowels, are always positioned next to the vocalic nuclei, both individually (as in the examples above) and in contexts containing consonant clusters: In "spring," " splash," "twin," and "cute," the semivowels are all adjacent to the vowels or diphthongs: /spriŋ/, /splaeʃ/, /twɪn/, and /kjut/.

Occasionally, though, some of the semivowels do serve as nuclei of syllables. They share this opportunity with their highly resonant neighbors, the nasals. For example, the word "table" has two nuclei, the diphthong [eI] of the first syllable and the [l̩] of the second syllable. When a consonant pinch hits as a vowel, a dot is put under the phonetic symbol to indicate a *syllabic consonant*. Examples are "bottle" [badl̩], "cotton" [kɑtn̩], and "up or down" [ʌpr̩daʊn], which can be used to express a preference in the cooking of fried eggs.

Semivowels are often subclassified as *glides* (/j/ and /w/) and *liquids* (/l/ and /r/). Glides are well named, for both the articulators and the formants are characterized by movement. Spectrograms of the glides show their formants gliding up or down depending upon context (Fig. 5.32).

The /j/ is a palatal glide. The tongue blade approximates the palate (more anteriorly for [ji] than for [jɑ]) at a position that is not far from that for a high front vowel, and which thus requires genioglossus muscle activity. During [ɑjɑ], the high first formant frequency for [ɑ] swings down as the mouth constricts, while the second formant swings up, reflecting the resonance of the narrowed front cavity. Production of glides requires movement of the tongue and lips to change vocal tract shape from the starting position (high front tongue at start of /j/, high back tongue and protruded lips at start of /w/) to the next vowel position. It is the sound of "getting there" that is the sound of the glide. Glides are similar to diphthongs but with faster transitions.

Notice that /w/ has two places of articulation: the bilabial protrusion effected by the orbicularis oris and other lip muscles and the lingua-palatal approximation effected by such muscles as the styloglossus to elevate and back the tongue when needed.

The liquids, /r/ and /l/, are produced in syllable initial position by raising the tongue toward the alveolar ridge. Differences in tongue tip configuration and position create the distinctions between the two sounds. For /l/, the tip is resting lightly against the alveolar ridge, dividing the pressure waves into two streams that emerge at each side (hence it is often termed a *lateral*). For /r/, the tongue is grooved and does not touch the alveolar ridge, so some of the acoustic energy emerges centrally. Lips are often rounded. Many speakers *retroflex* the /r/, which means the tongue tip is pulled back further and tensed.

Since tongue tip position is crucial for the liquids, we find the superior longitudinal muscle to be particularly active in their production. The antagonist muscle, the inferior longitudinal muscle, may act more for /r/ than for /l/, especially if the /r/ is retroflexed. The shaping of the tongue dorsum is probably achieved by the interaction of the vertical muscle and the transverse muscle.

The acoustic results of these tongue tip adjustments (Fig. 5.33) are reflected somewhat in the second formant but are particularly obvious in third formant changes. For /r/, F_3 plunges below the F_3 frequencies typical of the neighboring vowels, while for /l/, it does not depart from them significantly.

There are some noticeable differences between the liquids when they occur in final, as opposed to initial position. Syllable-initial /l/, as in the words "leave" and "lip," is articulated with the dorsum of the tongue very low in the mouth. In contrast, syllable-final /l/, as in the words "full" and "cool," is articulated with the dorsum of the tongue raised somewhat toward the velum. This type of /l/ is associated with high back vowels, as well as with syllable-final position. It is sometimes referred to as "dark /l/," in distinction to the "light /l/" found in syllable- initial position (which is also associated with front vowels).

Similarly, syllable-final /r/ differs from its counterpart in initial position. It often loses its consonantal quality and simply colors whatever vowel it follows. Speakers of some dialects omit the articulatory constriction for [r] at the end of "car," "hear," or "sure" and replace it with vowel lengthening or movement toward a neutral tract shape ([ə]): "hear" becomes /hɪə/ or [hɪː]. Speakers who do produce "r" coloring when they articulate syllable-final /r/ do so by elevating the tongue dorsum toward the palate. This produces the lowered F_3 of the preceding vowel which, as we have seen, is characteristic of other allophones of /r/.

The fact that /r/ and /l/ are so consistently confused in English by native speakers of several Oriental languages demonstrates their acoustic similarity. Children with developmental speech substitutions often produce the more easily articulated /w/ for the liquids, or

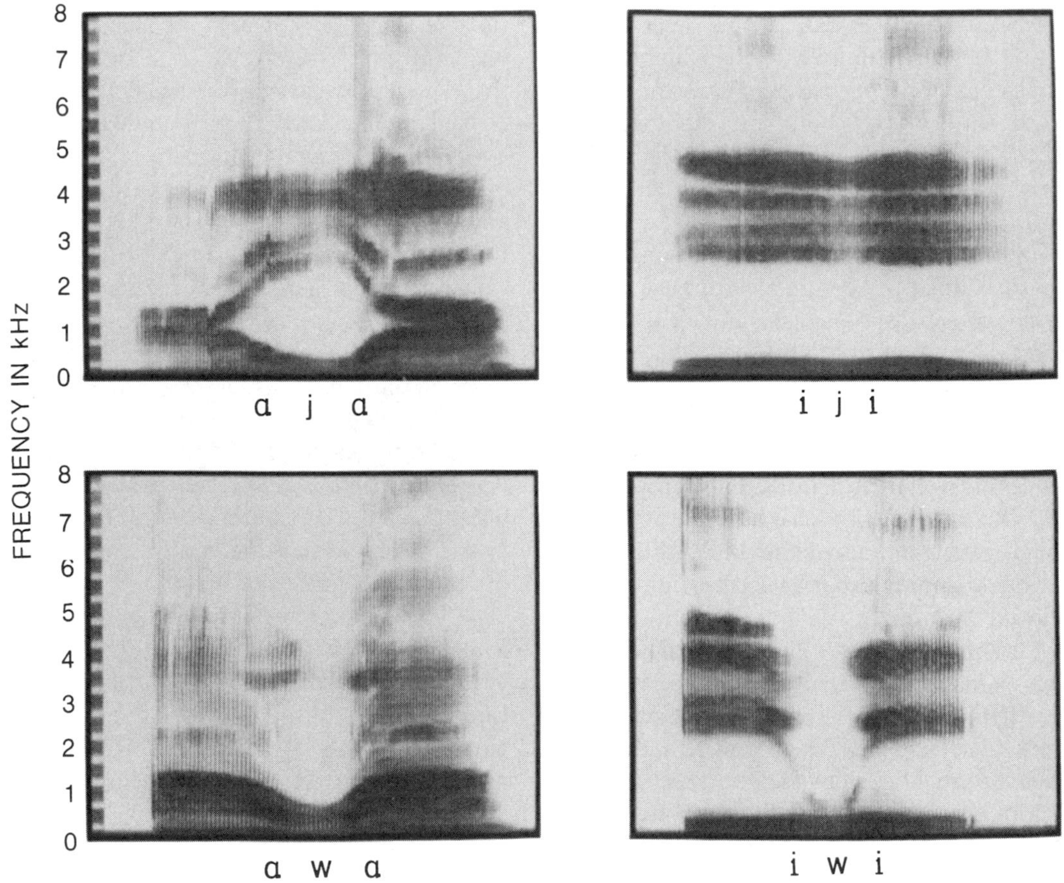

Figure 5.32. Spectrograms of /ɑjɑɑ/, /iji/, /ɑwɑ/, and /iwi/. Notice that F_2 movement is larger for /ɑjɑ/ than for /iji/, while F_2 movement is smaller for /ɑwɑ/ than for /iwi/.

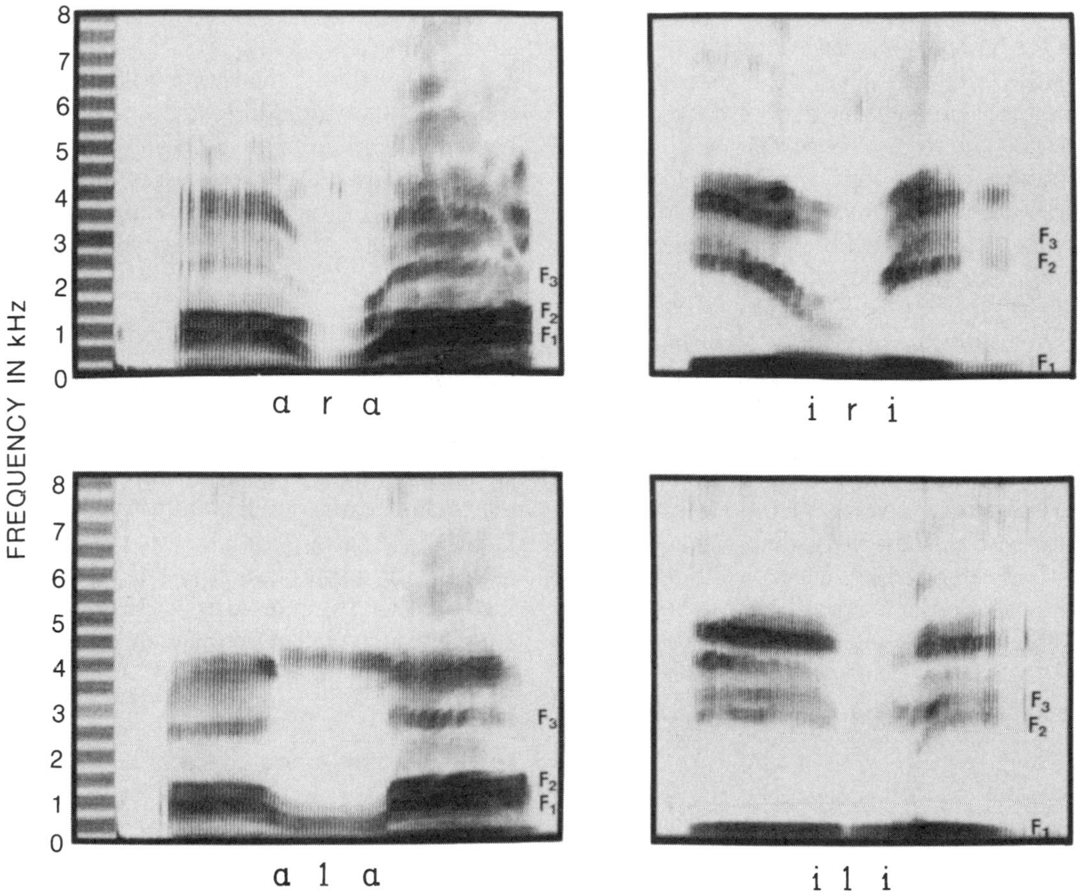

Figure 5.33. Spectrograms of /ɑrɑ/, /iri/, /ɑlɑ/, and /ili/. Notice that F_3 lowers close to F_2 for /r/, while it remains high for /l/.

sometimes use /j/ for /l/, and /w/ for /r/. "The little rabbit likes carrots" might be rendered as [dəjɪtəwæbəjaɪkskæwəts].

Resonant Consonants II: The Nasals

Velopharyngeal Port: Vocal Tract Modifier. Most of the speech sounds in the English language are resonated in a two-part tract consisting of the pharyngeal and oral cavities, extending from the vocal folds to the lips. There are three exceptions, sounds that require added resonance in the nasal cavities: the /m/, /n/, and /ŋ/ as in "mining." During continuous speech, the entrance to the chambers of the nose must be closed off most of the time because almost all speech sounds are *oral sounds*. It must be open for the three *nasal sounds*. The entrance to the large nasal chambers from the pharyngeal and oral cavities is called the *velopharyngeal port* because it lies between the velum and the walls of the pharynx. It can be closed by elevating and backing the velum until it approximates the posterior pharyngeal wall.

The levator palatini is the muscle primarily responsible for closing the velopharyngeal port. This paired muscle arises from the petrous portion of the temporal bone and from the lower part of the eustachian tube cartilage. It courses down and forward, curving medially from each side to enter the soft palate, anterior to the uvula. The fibers from each side intermingle and form the middle of the soft palate (Fig. 5.34). The muscle fibers are positioned like a sling coming from the upper back part of the nasopharynx down and forward to make up the soft palate. The angle of insertion of the levator palatini enables it, upon contraction, to elevate and retract the soft palate, closing the entrance to the nasal cavities. Electromyographic investigations conducted by Lubker, by Fritzell, and by Bell-Berti have demonstrated the importance of levator palatini activity as the prime agent for velopharyngeal closure. Cinefluorographic studies by Moll and others, along with fiberoptic studies by Bell-Berti and her colleagues, have provided movement information to relate to the information on muscle activity. (See Chapter 6 for descriptions of research techniques involved in electromyography, cinefluorography, and fiberoptic viewing.)

Pharyngeal wall movement normally accompanies velopharyngeal closure, but it is not clear whether the movement is a consequence of levator activity or contraction of the constrictor muscles.

Innervation of the levator palatini muscles is by the *pharyngeal plexus*, a group of neurons formed from the accessory (XIth cranial) nerve (which supplies most of the motor innervation), the vagus (Xth cranial) nerve, and sensory fibers from the glossopharyngeal (IXth cranial) nerve.

The velum or soft palate is coupled to the tongue by a muscle confusingly termed the *palatoglossus* muscle in some references and the glossopalatine muscle in others. The *anterior faucial pillars*, which one can observe in an open mouth (see Fig. 5.35), are made up of the palatoglossus muscles. Since the palatoglossus muscle arises from the transverse muscle fibers within the back of the tongue, ascending to the soft palate on each side to form each anterior faucial pillar, contraction can either

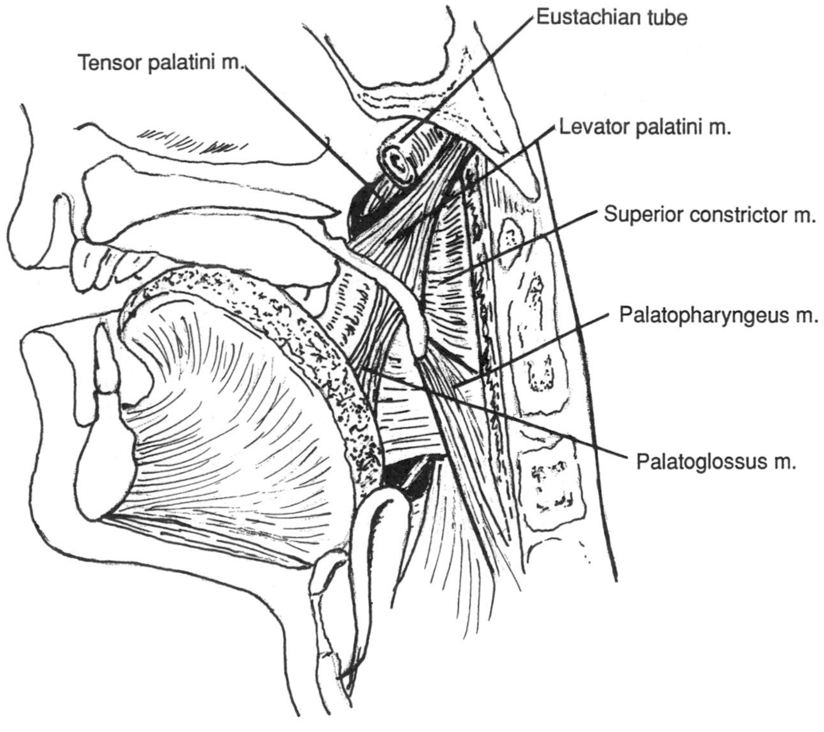

Figure 5.34. Mid-sagittal section of the head, showing the muscles of the pharyngeal port. The palatopharyngeus muscle is not discussed in the text, but it forms the bulk of the posterior faucial pillar. It is active in reducing pharyngeal size for low vowels, and in assisting in velopharyngeal closure.

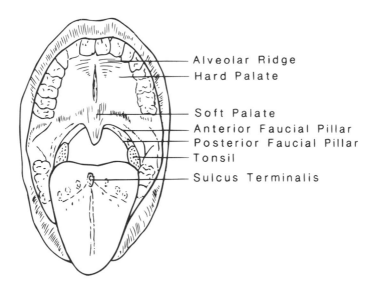

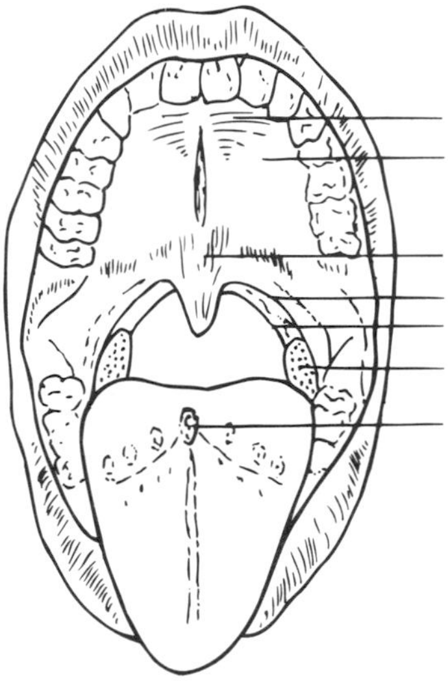

Figure 5.35. Schematic diagram of the structures of the oral cavity. The uvula can be seen at the rear of the soft palate.

lower the palate or elevate the sides and back of the tongue. It is active for some speakers for tongue elevation involved in the production of velar consonants /k,g/ and perhaps for lowering the soft palate for /m,n,ŋ/.

The uvula possesses its own musculature (the *uvular* muscle) and may add thickness to the velum in closure. The *tensor palatini* muscle does not contribute to velopharyngeal closure, but is active in opening the eustachian tube leading to the middle ear.

The degree of constriction or closure of the velopharyngeal mechanism varies according to phonetic context, from the low position typical for nasals, to the intermediate positions typical for low vowels, to the more nearly closed positions typical for high vowels, to the highest positions typical for oral consonants. The high vowels, /i/ and /u/, as in "see" and "Sue," are accompanied by a higher velum than are the low vowels, /ɑ/ and /æ/ as in "hot" and "hat." Maximum velar elevation and backing, needed to achieve the tightest seal, occur during the articulation of oral consonants, especially stops, which require a complete cessation of airflow through the mouth and nose, and fricatives, which require substantial intraoral air pressure (air pressure within the oral cavity). Leakage of air into the nasal cavities could, depending on its degree, render acceptable production of these sounds difficult or impossible.

In general, then, the levator palatini is least active for nasal consonants and most active when going from a nasal consonant to an oral consonant demanding high intraoral pressure. A general rule is that when the velum comes within 2 mm of the pharynx (producing an open area of about 20 mm^2) there is no apparent nasality. A wider opening produces nasal resonance, and speech is definitely perceived as nasal if the velopharyngeal port attains an area of 5 mm (50 mm^2).

Velar height also plays an important role in adjusting the volume, and thereby the pressure, within the cavities above the larynx. This adjustment is used to facilitate the voiced-voiceless distinction in consonant production. You will recall that in order to maintain vocal fold vibration, pressure below the vocal folds (subglottal pressure) must exceed pressure above the vocal folds (supraglottal pressure). This pressure drop across the glottis is difficult to maintain during voiced stops, for the very act of stopping the airstream creates a sudden build up of supraglottal air pressure, which will eventually eliminate the pressure difference across the vocal folds. A brief enlargement of the supraglottal volume during the stop reduces the supraglottal pressure and permits phonation to continue.

Bell-Berti reports electromyographic findings indicating that speakers vary in their method of enlarging the supraglottal space. Some speakers rely more on elevating the velum, others on relaxing the constrictor muscles or lowering the larynx. The role of the velum in enlarging the supraglottal space will be discussed further, when we consider the production of stop consonants later in this chapter.

Two disorders may result from failure to make perceptually acceptable adjustments of the velopharyngeal mechanism: *hypernasality* and *hyponasality*, with too much nasal resonance in the first instance and too little nasal resonance for /m,n,ŋ/ in the second instance. The problem of hypernasality is most apparent in speakers who are born with a *cleft palate*, a condition in which part or all of the palate has failed to fuse. Even after surgery to close the palate, the velum may be too small or lack the muscle force to adequately close off the nasal cavities. This condition not only results in too much nasal resonance for the vowels but also prevents the speaker from building up sufficient pressure in the oral cavity for stops and fricatives because of the unchecked escape of air through the nose. Persons with degenerative disorders of the nervous system may also produce inappropriate degrees of nasal resonance for a different reason: muscle weakness in the levator palatini.

Too little nasal resonance often occurs when speakers suffer from nasal congestion caused by colds. In some cases, hypernasality and hyponasality occur in the same speaker because both velar contraction and relaxation are mistimed. People with cerebral palsy sometimes evidence this disorder.

The Production of Nasal Consonants. Nasal resonance is mandatory for the production of /m,n,ŋ/ in English, so the velum is low, leaving the entrance to the nasal cavities open. Simultaneously, the oral cavity is occluded in one of three ways. For /m/, the lips are closed by the orbicularis oris muscles, innervated by the facial (VIIth cranial) nerve. The sound from the vocal folds is thus resonated not only in the pharyngeal cavity and in the cul-de-sac created by the closed oral cavity, but in the spacious chambers of the nasal cavities as well. The alveolar nasal /n/ and the palatal/velar nasal /ŋ/ are produced in much the same way as the bilabial nasal /m/, except the place of oral cavity occlusion differs. For /n/, the blade or tip of the tongue touches the upper alveolar ridge of the hard palate, with the back sides of the tongue touching the upper molars. For /ŋ/, the tongue dorsum touches the posterior part of the hard palate or the soft palate, allowing much less of the oral cavity to resonate as a side branch of the vocal tract. Produce the nasal consonants /m/, /n/, and /ŋ/, one after another to feel the place of occlusion move back in the mouth. You can verify the presence of nasal resonance by placing your fingers lightly against the side of your nose as the sounds are produced.

The addition of the nasal branches to the vocal tract creates a larger, longer resonator. We know that the longer the resonator, the lower the frequencies to which it naturally responds. Fujimura describes the acoustic result of closing the oral cavity while keeping the velum low to give nasal resonance to the phonated sounds /m,n,ŋ/ as the addition of a characteristic nasal "murmur," within the 200–300 Hz range for a male tract. This resonance, or formant, is a bit lower in frequency for [m] than for [n], and lower for [n] than for [ŋ] because of the progressively decreased volume of the oral cavity as the closure moves back in the mouth.

Acoustically, nasal consonants are relatively weak sounds for several reasons. First of all, their articulation creates *antiresonances* within the vocal tract. Antiresonances are, as the term implies, frequency regions in which the amplitudes of the source components are severely attenuated. Although vowels and diphthongs also display antiresonances (as troughs between resonance peaks in spectra—see Figs. 5.13, 5.16, and 5.17), their effects are generally much more marked in consonants. This is so because consonants are articulated with more

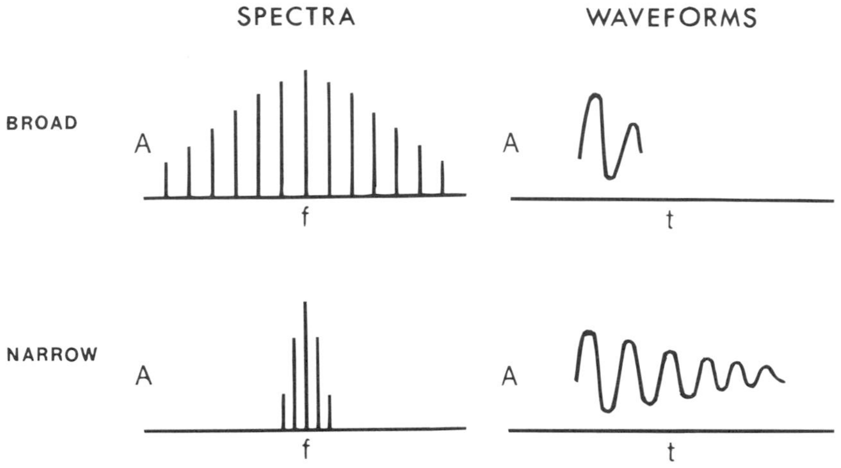

Figure 5.36. Waveforms and spectra of broadly and narrowly tuned resonators. Notice that damping occurs more rapidly for a broadly than for a narrowly tuned resonator.

els. Since all the nasal consonants are produced with a complete occlusion of the oral cavity, we are not surprised to find antiresonances in their spectra. We should note that resonances and antiresonances can affect each other in a number of ways. For example, if they are close enough in frequency, they can cancel each other. Sometimes a narrow antiresonance occurring in the midst of a broad resonance will have the effect of making one resonance appear to be two.

The elongation of the vocal tract caused by the opening of the velopharyngeal port is another cause of relatively weak intensity of the nasal sounds. The elongated tract results in a broader band of frequency response, and, as you will recall, broadly tuned resonators are more highly damped than narrowly tuned resonators (Fig. 5.36). The principal effect, in the case of the nasals, is the creation of antiresonances which cause attenuation of their higher formants relative to those of neighboring vowels.

Antiresonances can also be attributed to the anatomy of the nasal resonator, as well as to the articulation of the nasal consonants. For example, nasals suffer a loss in intensity because sound is absorbed by the soft walls and convolutions within the nasal cavities. The mucous membrane-covered conchae soak in sound energy like acoustic tiles in a sound-treated room. In addition, because the oral cavity is completely occluded, all of the airflow must be emitted through the nostrils, which do not radiate sound efficiently because of their relatively small apertures. Even the presence of hair within the nostrils accounts for a measure of sound attenuation.

The frequency ranges for the antiresonances associated with [m], [n], and [ŋ] vary with place of articulation (and thus with the size of the oral cavity, which acts like an acoustic cul-de-sac). The labial nasal consonant [m] is characterized by an antiresonance which is lower (in the 500–1500 Hz range) than that for [n] (around 2,000–3,000 Hz) or for [ŋ] (above 3,000 Hz). A second antiresonance in the area of 600 Hz for a male tract seems to be consistent regardless of place of articulation. Figure 5.37 shows the usual formants for [i] which fade for the nasals. Note the added nasal murmur for [m] and [n]. The engineering terms used to describe resonances and antiresonances are *poles* and *zeros*, respectively.

Nonresonant Consonants I: The Fricatives The sounds we have been considering thus far, the semivowels and the nasals, are characterized in their articulations by a relatively free flow of air. Acoustically, they are characterized by formant structure, which is, of course, why they are called resonant conso-

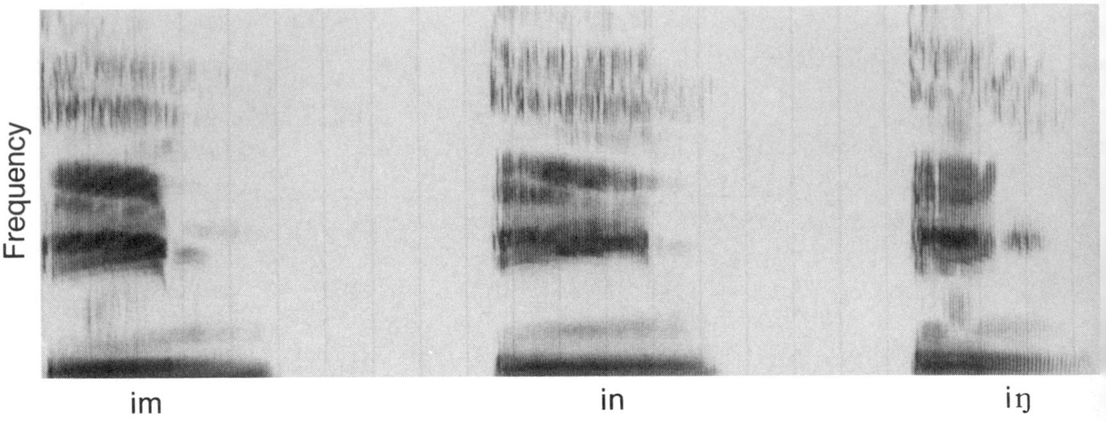

Figure 5.37. Spectrogram of [im], [in], and [iŋ]. Note that formants lose intensity during the nasal. (Digital spectrogram courtesy of Kay Elemetrics.)

nants. We shall turn our attention now to the nonresonant consonants: the fricatives, stops, and affricates. These sounds are characterized in articulation by a restricted airflow. Acoustically, they display little (or nothing) like the sort of formant structure we have observed in the vowels and resonant consonants.

The obstructions of the airflow in the nonresonant consonants are caused by the articulators forming constrictions and occlusions within the vocal tract which generate aperiodicity (noise) as the airflow passes through them. This aperiodic source of sound is resonated in the tract in much the same way as the periodic source produced by phonation. The most effective resonators for noise sources are those immediately anterior to the constrictions and occlusions that produce them.

The presence of audible noise in the nonresonant consonants accounts for another difference between them and the resonant consonants (and the vowels). In English, and in most other languages, resonant consonants and vowels are classified as voiced sounds. There are exceptions, of course, but phonologically voiceless vowels, semivowels, and nasals are the exception, rather than the rule in most languages. There is a practical reason for this: without a periodic source, many of the resonant sounds would be inaudible at any appreciable distance from a speaker. You can test this by whispering any of the nasals. A voiceless /m/, for instance, is nothing more than an exhalation through the nose.

In the case of the nonresonant consonants, however, the presence of audible noise in the speech signal makes it possible for the sounds to be heard whether or not phonation accompanies their articulation. This creates the possibility of using a single articulation to produce two distinctive speech sounds, one phonated (voiced) and the other unphonated (voiceless): If you articulate the sounds /f/ and /v/ in isolation, you will notice that they are identical, except for the phonation that accompanies the production of /v/.

The aperiodic source that marks fricatives is created in the vocal tract by sending the breath stream (either phonated or unphonated) through constrictions formed in the tract. The airflow must be strong enough and the constriction must be narrow enough to make the airflow turbulent, creating frication (noisy random vibrations). The fricative sounds of speech thus depend upon compressing a continuous flow of air through a constriction formed by closely approximating two articulators.

In English, these constrictions are formed at four primary places of articulation: labiodental, linguadental, alveolar, and palatal. Figure 5.38 schematizes the four constriction sites. If the glottis is open, the airstream is made audible only at the point of constriction, but if the glottis is closed with the vocal folds

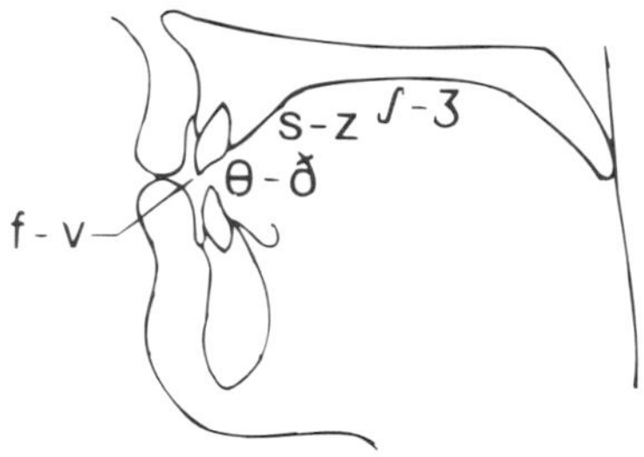

Figure 5.38. Place of articulation for the fricatives of American English; labiodental; linguadental, alveolar, and palatal.

vibrating, the result is two sound sources, the periodic sound of phonation and the aperiodic sound of the airstream passing through the constriction.

To develop enough air pressure in the oral cavity to produce a noise, the levator palatini muscle must contract, closing the velopharyngeal port sufficiently to avoid leakage. This is an essential aspect of the articulation of all the nonresonant consonants.

The labiodental fricatives, /f/ (voiceless) and /v/ (voiced), as in "fan" and "van," are formed by bringing the lower lip close to the inferior edges of the upper central incisors. This requires contraction of several muscles in the lower part of the face, (especially the inferior orbicularis oris) which are innervated by the facial (VIIth cranial) nerve. The linguadental fricatives /θ/ (voiceless) and /ð/ (voiced), as in "*th*igh" and "*th*y" are formed by approximation of the tip of the tongue with the upper incisors. This strategy is not very different from that used for the labiodentals, but the motor activity is centered in the tongue muscle group, with the superior longitudinal muscle, innervated by the hypoglossal (XIIth cranial) nerve, playing a primary role. Because the labiodental and linguadental fricatives are similar in production, they are also similar in their acoustic properties, as we shall see shortly.

The alveolar /s,z/ and palatal /ʃ,ʒ/ fricatives are produced a bit differently, and their distinctive, hissing, shushing quality has earned them a subtitle among fricatives, the *sibilants*. Let us first analyze the production of [s] (voiceless) and [z] (voiced) as in "Sue" and "zoo." The constriction is formed between the alveolar ridge and the tongue, but speakers vary in which part of the tongue is elevated. Many speakers form the constriction between the tip of the tongue and the ridge (a *high-point* /s/), while others tuck the tip down behind the lower incisors while bunching up the dorsum of the tongue, so that the constriction is formed between the blade of the tongue and the alveolar ridge (a *low-point* /s/).

For [s] and [z], a groove is often formed along the tongue midline to channel the airstream. This is accomplished by raising the lateral edges of the tongue to the medial edges of the upper teeth while depressing the center of the tongue. The seal between the edges of the tongue and the teeth is, in any case, essential in order to prevent the airstream from passing over the sides of the tongue, which would produce what is often called a lateral lisp. A second constriction is important to the production of the alveolar fricatives; the opening between the upper and lower incisors must be narrow so that the air stream is directed over the edge of the teeth, creating a turbulent airflow behind the tooth edge. The difficulties in producing /s/ and /z/ for someone with an open bite or missing front teeth demonstrate the importance of this second constriction.

The muscle groups implicated in these maneuvers are those of the jaw and of the tongue. Depending, of course, upon the jaw and tongue positions at the onset of motor activity for /s/ or /z/, the jaw closers (principally the *medial pterygoid* muscle, Fig. 5.39), innervated by the mandibular branch of the trigeminal (Vth cranial) nerve and tongue elevators (genioglossus m. and geniohyoid m.), are more or less active. The pattern of muscle activity within the intrinsic muscles of the tongue also varies with the individual methods of forming the alveolar constriction. Speakers who produce a high-point /s/ or /z/ evidence more activity in the superior longitudinal muscle, while those producing low-point sounds show active contraction of the inferior longitudinal muscle.

The palatal /ʃ/ (voiceless) and /ʒ/ (voiced), as in "shoe" and "azure" are similar in several

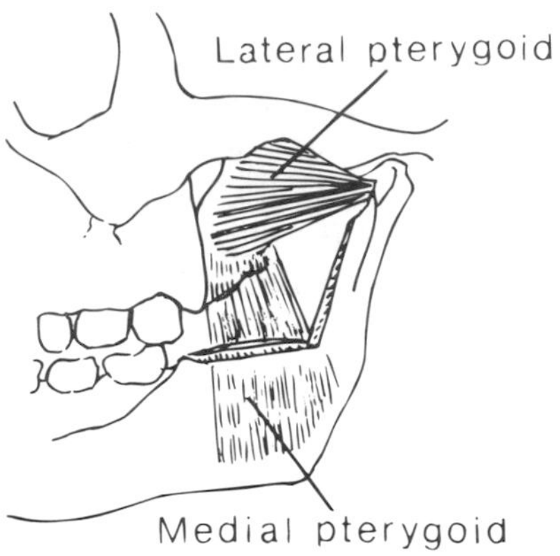

Figure 5.39. The lateral and media pterygoid muscles in lateral view. The medial pterygoid acts to raise the jaw in speech. The lateral pterygoid has two portions, each with a different function: the superior part acts to elevate the jaw, while the inferior part acts to lower the jaw, according to Tuller, Harris, and Gross.

respects to /s/ and /z/. The constriction is made a bit further back, in the post-alveolar area, and the midline groove is slightly wider than for /s/ and /z/. In addition, the lips may be somewhat rounded and protruded. Lip-rounding may also accompany the production of /s/ and /z/, but is far more common for /ʃ/ and /ʒ/. You can gauge the degree of similarity between the two sets of sibilants by producing a lip-rounded [s] and slowly retracting your tongue until you hear [ʃ]. Because of the similarity in articulation, speakers may substitute the alveolar and post-alveolar fricatives for each other. The alveolar constriction for /s/ averages about 1 mm and the incisor constriction about 2–3 mm, according to x-ray studies by Subtelny. The length of the alveolar constriction (~2.5 cm) may be more important than the width. A wide range of openings beyond those for /s/ result in /ʃ/-type sounds; therefore, it is not surprising that the prevailing misarticulation is /ʃ/ in place of /s/ and not the other way around.

There is another fricative that fits less neatly into the scheme of articulatory phonetics. The *aspirate*, /h/, is a fricative with the constriction located in the larynx, at the glottis. It is usually voiceless as in "hat" but can be voiced when embedded between voiced segments, as in "ahead." The only required movement is the approximation of the vocal folds, controlled by the laryngeal adductors and abductors. The vocal tract takes the shape of whatever vowel is to follow. During the production of the [h] in "heat" and "hot," the vocal tract takes the shape of [i] and [ɑ], respectively.

Fricatives are *continuants*. Unlike stops, they can be prolonged. In common with all speech sounds, fricatives are the product of a sound source (sometimes two sources) modified by transfer through a resonator and further modified by the effect of the sound radiating at the output. The source of the fricative noise is at the constriction. Heinz and Stevens have shown that the spectrum of the sound at the lips is determined largely by the resonant characteristics of the constriction and the vocal tract anterior to the noise source. Figure 5.40 shows sound spectrograms of the fricatives. Although the noise bands in these spectrograms have been enhanced to make them visible, typically the fricative energy is very low for /f/, /v/, /θ/, and /ð/, mainly because there is no appreciable resonating cavity anterior to the point of constriction. Despite the low energy, the frequency band is broad. A narrower band of high frequency, high energy noise characterizes the alveolar fricatives /s/ and /z/. Most of the sound energy for /s/ is above 4 kHz, while for /ʃ/ it is around 2000 Hz and above for a male speaker. Because the point of articulation for /ʃ/ is further back in the mouth than that for /s/, the resonating cavity anterior to it is longer than that for /s/, resulting in its lower frequencies. The lip-rounding and protrusion that is more usually associated with /ʃ/ will also lengthen the resonating cavity and contribute to its lower frequency. This acoustic effect of lip posture is much the same as that which we discussed with regard to the back vowels.

As an example of the source-filter account of consonant production, let us detail the acoustic production of /s/, much as we did with /i/, /ɑ/, and /u/ for the vowels. The poles, or resonances, for /s/ are derived from the natural resonant frequency of the constriction and the natural resonant frequency of the cavity in

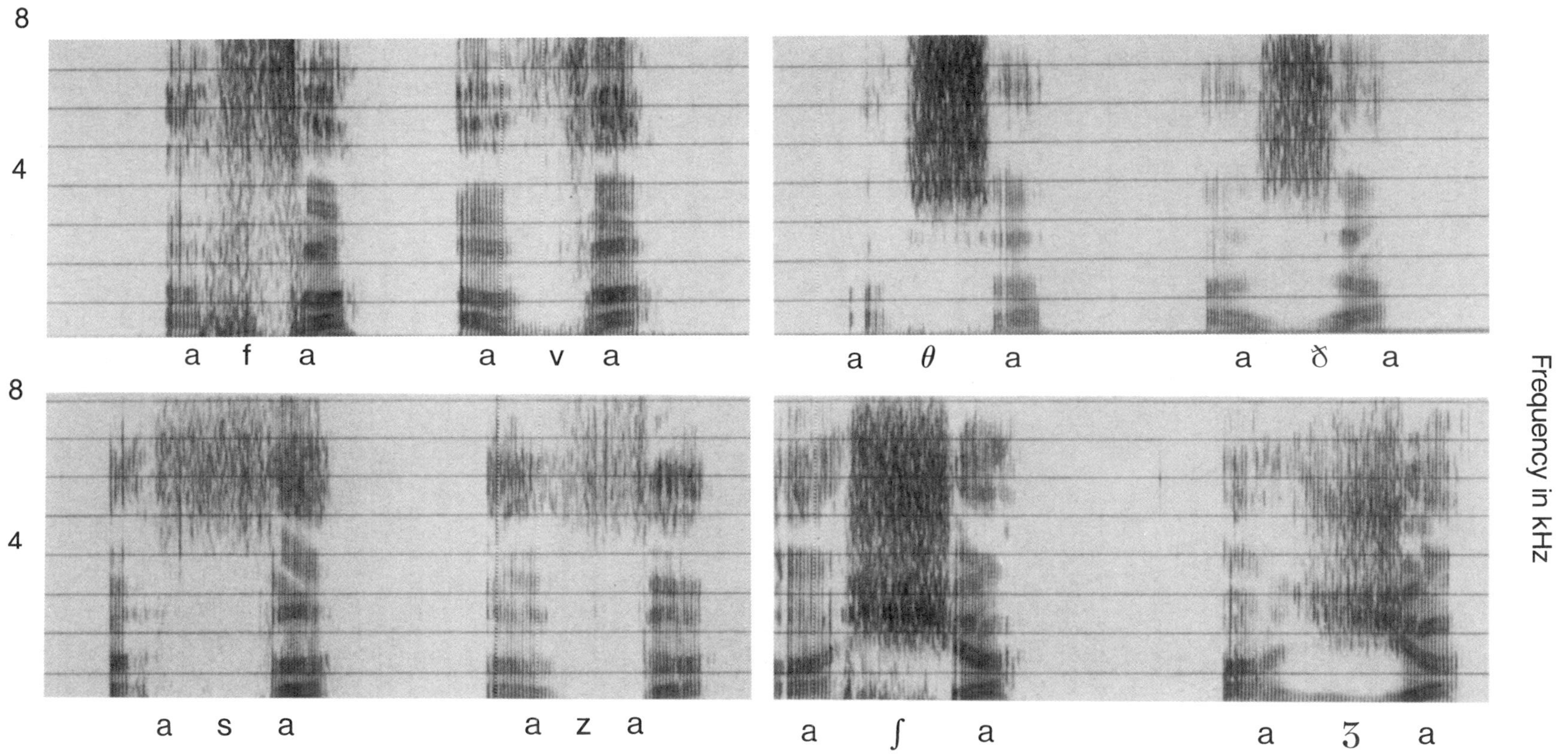

Figure 5.40. Sound spectrograms of the fricatives. (Digital spectrograms courtesy of Kay Elemetrics.)

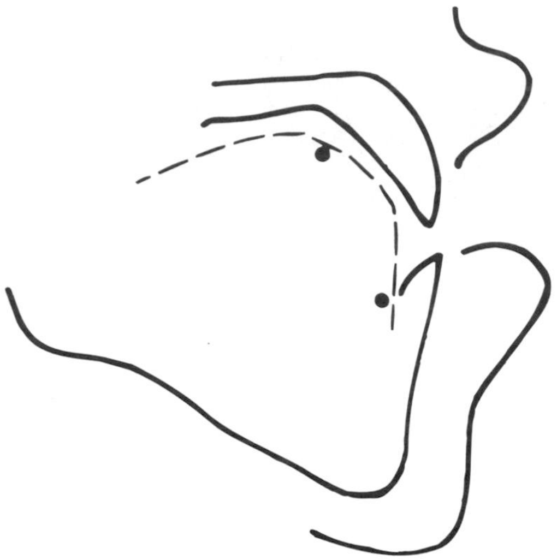

Figure 5.41. Tracing made from a lateral view x-ray film of the vocal tract in position for [s] production. The *black dots* represent lead pellets. Movements of the tongue were analyzed by following the movements of the pellets from frame to frame.

front of the constriction. Figure 5.41 shows a vocal tract configuration appropriate for /s/ production. The narrow constriction can be considered to resonate like any tube open at both ends; the lowest resonant frequency has a wavelength (λ) 2 times the length of the tube. To use Subtelny's measurements, this would be 2 × 2.5 cm or 5 cm. The natural resonant frequency for such a tube is thus about 6800 Hz.

$$f = \frac{\text{velocity of sound}}{\lambda \text{ (wavelength)}}$$

$$= \frac{34{,}000 \text{ cm}}{5 \text{ cm}} = 6{,}800 \text{ Hz}$$

The source of the fricative noise is at the anterior edge of the constriction. The air-filled cavity in front of the noise source can be likened to a tube closed at one end, because the constriction is extremely narrow at the source. Tubes closed at one end and open at the other are ¼ wave resonators rather than ½ wave resonators, as you may recall from our earlier discussion, so that the resonance for the anterior cavity approximates 8600 Hz.

$$f = \frac{\text{Velocity}}{\lambda} = \frac{34{,}000 \text{ cm}}{4 \text{ (1 cm)}}$$

$$= \frac{34{,}400 \text{ cm}}{4 \text{ cm}} = 8{,}600$$

Because of the narrowness of the constriction, the back cavity resonances are not heard. Thus, there is little energy below 4000 Hz. The resonances that would have been produced below 4 kHz are canceled by the back cavity antiresonances. We have seen that most of the energy for /s/ lies above 4000 Hz. For /ʃ/ the energy is above 2000 Hz.

Uldall reported that when /s/ is next to a stop, the lower border of the fricative noise changes, reflecting vocal tract adjustments being made during the fricative. The border lowers in frequency as the tract approaches labial closure, increases in frequency during the approach to alveolar stops, and remains stable for the palatal-velar stops.

Nonresonant Consonants II: The Stops. We turn now to the class of sounds articulated with the greatest degree of obstruction to the breath stream: the stop consonants, /ptk/ (voiceless) and /bdg/ (voiced). The term "stop" is an apt designation because the single distinguishing characteristic of these sounds is the momentary cessation of airflow caused by the complete occlusion of the vocal tract.

The articulators form the occlusion during what is usually called the "closing phase" of stop formation. There are, in fact, two simultaneous occlusions that are essential for each of the six stop consonant phonemes. One is the velopharyngeal closure that seals off the nasal cavities from the rest of the vocal tract and the other is an occlusion formed by the lips or tongue within the oral cavity. The locations of the oral occlusions are identical to those made for the nasals: bilabial for /p/ and /b/; lingua-alveolar for /t/ and /d/, and linguapalatal/velar for /k/ and /g/.

The occlusions are maintained throughout the second phase in stop articulation, the "hold" or "closure" phase, during which they induce the cessation of airflow and the increase in intraoral pressure that are needed to produce the stop consonants.

The final phase in most stop articulations is the "release." In this phase one of the two occlusions, almost always the oral occlusion, is broken, releasing the pent-up air pressure and allowing the resumption of airflow. It is also possible to release a stop by lowering the velum. This strategy, called nasal release, is normally employed when a stop is followed by a *homorganic* nasal (one with the same place of articulation as the stop). The most obvious occurrence of nasal release is when the nasal is syllabic, as in a word such as "hidden" ([hɪdn̩]). If you say this word slowly, consciously maintaining the alveolar contact for the /d/ until you hear the /n/, you should be able to sense the movement of the velum that releases the stop.

When stops are released, there is an audible burst of noise caused by the outward rush of the air that was blocked by the occlusion. This burst of noise, which is part of the release phase, is another example of an aperiodic sound source produced in the supraglottal vocal tract. It is analogous to the frication generated in the production of fricatives, but differs from frication in that it is transient, rather than being prolongable. Stops, then, differ from all of the sounds we have discussed thus far in that they are not continuants.

Because stop articulation most usually ends with the release of a transient burst of noise, the term *plosive* is sometimes used as a label for the class of sounds. We have avoided using this label because the release phase of articulation is occasionally omitted in certain phonetic contexts. Release will not usually occur, for instance, when two homorganic stop sounds occur in sequence, as in the word "hotdog." In this context, the /t/ closure is maintained unbroken and serves for the /d/ closure as well. It is thus the /d/, and not the /t/, that is released. Many phoneticians have noted that stops in absolute final position are often unreleased in English, although some recent research has questioned the validity of this observation. It is certainly possible to maintain the closure for the final bilabial and alveolar stops in sentences such as "He worked in his lab" and "She wore a hat." It is less likely, however, that the final velar stop in "They ate some cake" will be unreleased.

The muscular activity underlying the articulation of stops must, obviously, vary considerably from one place of articulation to another, with the exception of that for the velopharyngeal closure that accompanies each of the sounds. Activity of the orbicularis oris and other facial muscles contributes to labial closure for /p/ and /b/. The alveolar stop /t/ and its voiced cognate /d/ are produced by moving the tip or blade of the tongue forward and up to contact the alveolar ridge of the hard palate. The superior longitudinal muscle, fibers of which course along the dorsum of the tongue from front to back, aids in producing this closure of the oral cavity. It, like the other tongue muscles, is innervated by the hypoglossal (XIIth cranial) nerve. Closure for /k/ and /g/, like /ŋ/, results from elevation of the back of the tongue, along the dorsum, to contact the hard or soft palate. The place of articulation often depends upon the context. For example, the place of articulation for /k/ preceding the front vowel /i/ in "keep" is further forward than for /k/ preceding the back vowel /u/ in "coop." Thus, although /k,g,ŋ/ are often classified as velar consonants, palatal-velar is sometimes a more correct description. The styloglossus and palatoglossus muscles are in positions to be instrumental in the tongue backing and elevation necessary for this closure. The mylohyoid muscle (Fig. 5.42), a flat trough-like muscle that is attached to each inner side of the mandible, serves as the floor of the oral cavity. This muscle, like the anterior belly of the digastric muscles below it, is innervated by the motor component of the mylohyoid branch of the trigeminal (Vth cranial) nerve, which is normally considered to be a sensory nerve serving the facial area. Contraction of the mylohyoid fibers elevates the floor of the oral cavity, assisting in raising the heavy back of the tongue for /k,g,ŋ/. Figure 5.43 contrasts the places of articulation for the labial, alveolar, and palatal-velar stops.

Before going on to discuss the acoustic

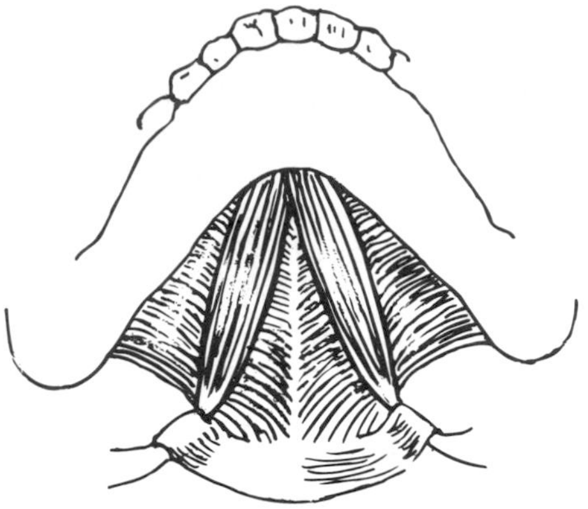

Figure 5.42. The mylohyoid muscles form the floor of the mouth and contract to help elevate the tongue. The paired muscles lying below the mylohyoids are the anterior bellies of the digastric muscle, which act in lowering the jaw.

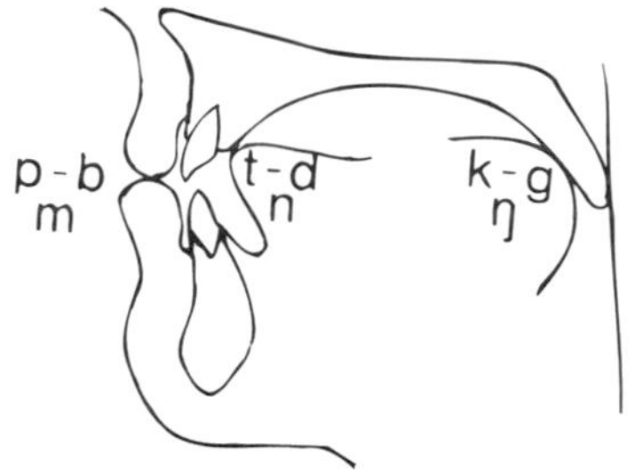

Figure 5.43. The place of articulation for bilabial, alveolar, and palatal-velar stops and nasals.

features of stop production, we should mention that there is a seventh stop, called the glottal stop ([ʔ]), that occurs with some frequency in English. Unlike the other stop sounds, the glottal stop is not classified as a phoneme of English. In American English, the glottal stop is sometimes used to initiate vowels, as we mentioned earlier in our discussion of glottal attack in the section on phonation. The sound also has currency as an allophone of /t/ or /d/ in certain dialects. For instance, it is the sound some New Yorkers have been heard to substitute for the /t/ in "bottle," [baʔl̩], or for the /d/ in [kUʔn̩t]. Speakers of British dialects, such as Cockney, commonly employ the glottal stop as a substitute for all of the stop consonants.

The glottal stop, as its name indicates, is articulated at the glottis by tightly approximating the vocal folds. Although the folds are the articulators for this sound, they do not vibrate during its production, and so it is classified as voiceless. The folds behave analogously to the lips and tongue in the production of the oral stops, forming an occlusion, holding it, and then releasing the airstream when they are abducted. Since the occlusion is below the level of the velopharyngeal port, velopharyngeal closure is irrelevant to its production, although it normally occurs as it does in the articulation of the oral stops.

We shall now turn our attention to the acoustic features that characterize stop production. Let us first consider those features that are a function of stop manner of articulation. These are four in number. The first, and the most pervasive, is the presence of what is usually termed a "silent gap." This period of silence is a result of the "hold" period in articulation, during which there is no flow of air out of the vocal tract. In point of fact, the silent gap is not always literally silent. In the cases of the voiced stops, /bdg/, a low intensity harmonic, the fundamental frequency, may run through all or part of the duration of the stop closure. Nonetheless, the term "silent gap" is often employed to describe the closure for all the stop consonants. In any case, the gap is always devoid of any appreciable degrees of formants or noise. In Figure 5.44 we can see examples of the silent gaps, both those which are truly silent, and those in which a fundamental frequency is evident (at the baselines of the spectrograms of /bdg/).

The second acoustic feature associated with stop production is the presence of a noise burst at the moment of release. This burst appears in spectrograms (Fig. 5.44) as a vertical spike following the silent gap, and is somewhat more intense, and thus more conspicuous for the voiceless than for the voiced stops. Release bursts are very brief in duration (10–35 ms), but often cover a broad range of frequencies with varying intensity. The frequencies at which the bursts are most intense are relevant to place of articulation and will be considered below.

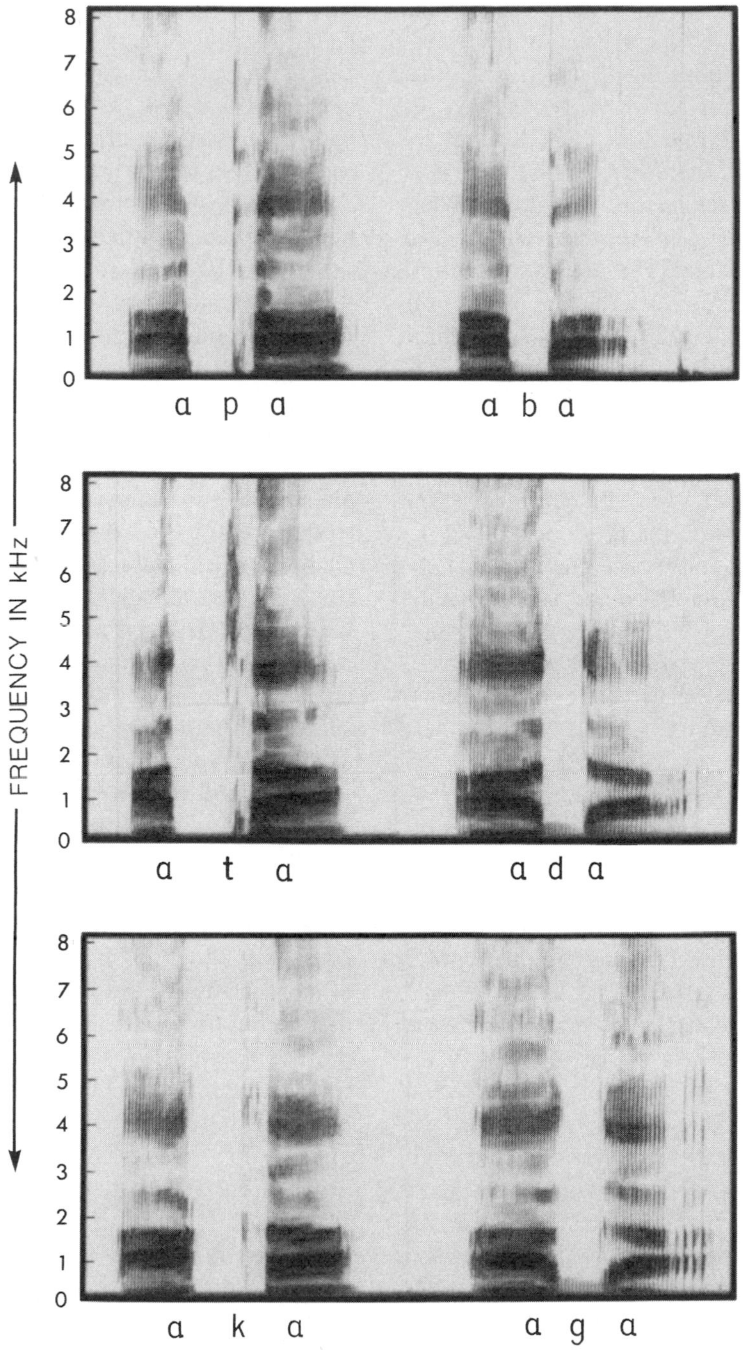

Figure 5.44. Wideband spectrograms of vowel-stop-vowel disyllables. Note the truly silent gap in the closure for /ptK/ and the voicing (phonation) during the closure for /bdg/. Each closure is followed by a characteristic burst of transient noise as the tongue releases the air trapped behind the closure at the alveolar ridge.

A third identifying acoustic feature is the speed with which the acoustic signal attains maximum intensity (for syllable-initial stops) or falls to minimum intensity (for syllable-final stops). These are referred to, respectively, as *rise time* and *fall time*. Rise and fall times are both very rapid for stops, compared to other consonants. The reason for this is the relatively rapid opening and closing gestures associated with stop articulation. The increased air pressure behind the point of occlusion, when it is released, also contributes to the rapid rise time of stops in initial position. Rise time may be indicated on spectrograms by the inclusion of an amplitude display (see Fig. 7.7).

The final identifying acoustic feature of stop manner that we shall consider is the change in the first formant frequency that occurs as the vocal tract shape changes after the release of syllable-initial stops and before the occlusion is completed for syllable-final stops. The first formant rises rapidly following the initial stops and falls rapidly before the final stops. As in the case of all the acoustic features, there is an articulatory basis that explains this feature. You will recall that the frequency of the first formant is positively correlated with the size of mouth opening. This means that F_1 frequency should be minimal during stop articulation, as the oral cavity is completely occluded. Opening the tract will raise the frequency of F_1 in the case of initial stops, and closing the tract will force the frequency down in the case of final stops. The degree of rise or fall will vary considerably, depending on the F_1 frequency of the neighboring sounds. For example, we will find a much greater increase/decrease in F_1 when a stop precedes/follows a vowel such as /ɑ/, which has a high frequency first formant, than when it precedes/follows a vowel with a low frequency first formant such as /i/.

There are two acoustic features associated with the place of articulation of stop consonants. We have already mentioned that the most intense frequency of the transient burst of noise associated with stop release is a function of the point in the oral cavity where the occlusion is made. The bursts of labial stops, /p/ and /b/, generally exhibit a peak in their spectra at low frequencies (around 600 Hz and below). The high frequencies (around 3000 Hz) are characteristically most intense in the bursts of the alveolar stops, /t/ and /d/. The velars, /k/ and /g/, present a more variable picture, with spectral peaks for the bursts being linked to the F_2 frequency of the vowel following the stop: For the velars, the intense portion of the burst usually extends upward for a few hundred Hz from the frequency of the second formant.

A second acoustic feature associated with place of articulation is the direction of frequency change of the second formant of the vowel following or preceding a stop. During the formation (closing phase) of a stop occlusion and just after an occlusion is released, the rapid movements of the articulators cause sudden changes in the resonance peaks of the vocal tract. We have already discussed such changes in connection with the feature of F_1 change associated with stop manner. Because these changes occur during the transition from one speech sound to another, they are referred to as *formant transitions*.

You will recall that in our discussion of vowels, we indicated that the frequency of F_2 was correlated with the length of the front cavity. In general, this correlation holds for the stops, and so F_2 will be a reflection of the movement of the tongue or lips from or to a place of stop occlusion. Unfortunately, because the destination (for prevocalic stops) or origin (for postvocalic stops) of F_2 varies, depending on the neighboring vowel, there is no simple way of associating a particular direction or degree of transition change with a particular place of articulation. We shall consider these transitions more fully in our discussion of speech perception in Chapter 6.

There remains the topic of the acoustic features that are associated with the voicing classes of stop consonants. Recall that the stops of English can be grouped into cognate pairs by place of articulation (/p-b/, /t-d/, /k-g/), with one member of each pair being classified as voiceless (/ptk/) and the other as voiced (/bdg/). In many contexts, such as the intervocalic context shown in Figure 5.44, this simply means that phonation continues throughout the period of articulatory closure for /bdg/, and ceases during the closure for /ptk/—a classic example of the voiced-voiceless difference.

In other contexts, however, the difference between the members of the cognate pairs is not as straightforward. In initial, prevocalic position, for instance, speakers of English do not normally phonate during the closures of either /ptk/ or /bdg/. In this context the opposition between the two sets of stops is maintained by a difference in the timing of the onset of phonation relative to the release burst of the stop: Phonation for /bdg/ begins very shortly after stop release, while there is a delay of at least 50 ms before phonation begins following the release of /ptk/. This relative timing of stop release and phonation has been termed *voice onset time (VOT)* by Lisker and Abramson. On wideband spectrograms VOT is measured in milliseconds as the duration between the vertical spike marking the transient burst of stop release and the first vocal pulse that can be observed at the baseline. When the onset of voicing follows stop release, VOT values are positive; when voicing onset precedes stop release, negative values are assigned to VOT.

Voice onset time, then, can be understood as an acoustic measurement, but, as always, one that is the result of a coordinated articulatory strategy. Let us inspect that strategy. In Figure 5.45 we can see both the labial and glottal adjustments employed to produce

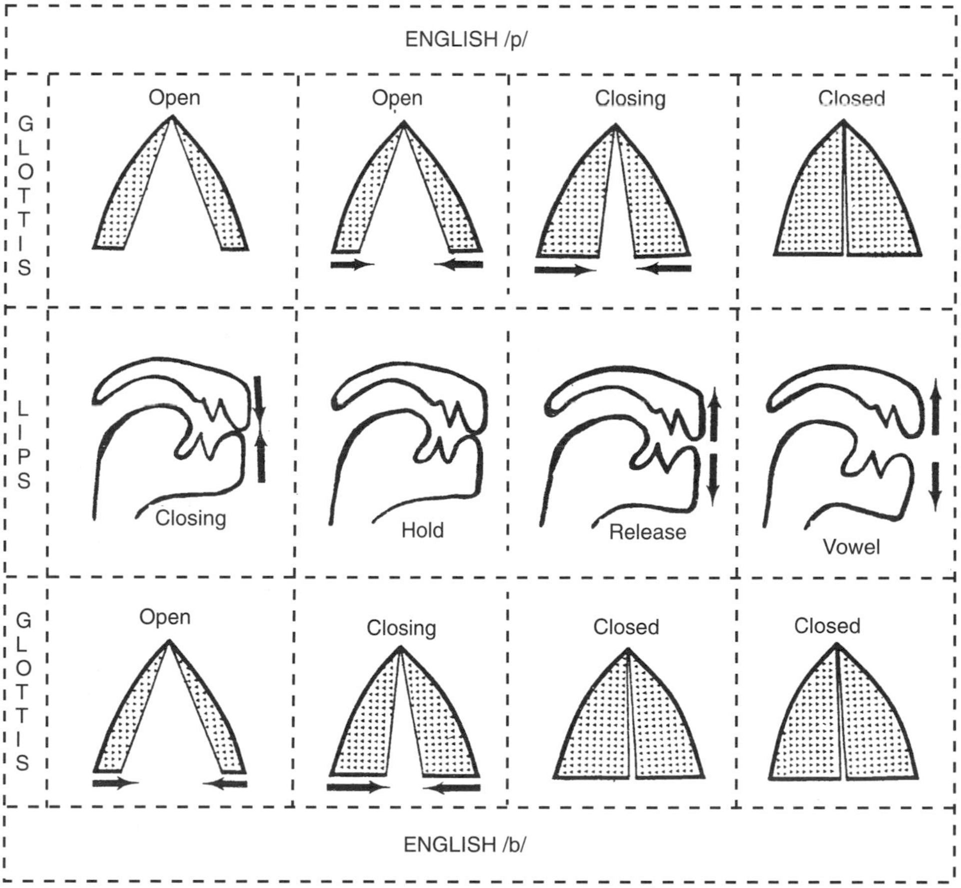

Figure 5.45. The relationships between glottal states and labial articulation for prevocalic /p/ and /b/ in English.

initial, prevocalic /p/ and /b/ in English. Notice that at the moment of labial occlusion the vocal folds have begun to adduct for /b/. Adduction continues during the hold period, so that by the time the /b/ is released, the folds are in phonatory position, ready to vibrate. This accounts for the low, positive VOT values (between zero and +10 ms) that characterize /b/.

In contrast, the folds do not begin to adduct for /p/ until sometime during the hold period, so that at the moment of stop release the glottis is still open. Adduction is not attained until sometime after the release of the stop, during the articulation of the following vowel. This accounts for the long, positive VOT values (about +60 to +70 ms) that characterize /p/. It also accounts for the presence of another acoustic feature that differentiates the voiced from the voiceless stops: aspiration.

Aspiration, a period of voicelessness following stop release, is associated only with /ptk/ in English. It is present following those stops because the open glottis at the moment of stop release allows the breath stream to flow freely into the upper vocal tract without generating phonation. The reverse is true for /bdg/: The closed glottis at the moment of stop release forces the breath stream to set the vocal folds into vibration and to carry the periodic phonated vibrations into the upper vocal tract. Phonation and aspiration are, therefore, complementary phenomena in English. The VOT differences between /ptk/ and /bdg/, and the presence versus absence of aspiration in those stops are clearly visible in Figure 5.44.

We should note that other languages employ different timing contrasts to distinguish between voicing classes of stop consonants. Spanish, Italian and French /bdg/, for example, display negative values of VOT. That is, phonation commences during the hold period for the stops because vocal fold adduction begins during the closing phase of stop articulation. This insures that the folds will be in phonatory position during the hold period, so that phonation can commence. In contrast, the VOT values for /ptk/ in these languages are much like the values for /bdg/ in English. In fact, speakers of Spanish, Italian and French often appear to English-speaking listeners to produce only voiced stops: none of the stops in these languages is aspirated because the glottis is always closed at the moment of stop release and does not allow the free flow of a voiceless breath stream.

It should be clear from our discussion of VOT that differentiating between voiced and voiceless stops requires complex and highly coordinated motor activity. The timing of the activity of the abductor and adductor muscles of the larynx must be precise, not only with respect to each other, but also with respect to the muscles controlling the articulators of the supraglottal vocal tract. This implies that speakers who have poor control over the timing of motor activities are likely to produce VOT values that deviate from the expected norms. Clinical researchers have, in fact, seized upon this implication, and have investigated VOT in a great number of speech disorders that involve poor motor control. Many studies of VOT in stuttering, apraxia, Parkinson's disease and other disorders have appeared in recent years and continue to appear in the literature with great regularity.

Nonresonant Consonants III: The Affricates. There are only two affricates in English, [tʃ] (voiceless) and [dʒ] (voiced), as in "chair" and "jar." An affricate is simply a stop with a fricative release. An alveolar closure is made for the [t] or [d], and when the speaker releases the closure, the tongue is retracted to the post-alveolar region of the palate and shaped appropriately for the production of sounds which are essentially identical to the fricatives [ʃ] and [ʒ]. The lips are usually rounded slightly during the articulation of the fricative portions of the affricates. Acoustically, as you would expect, the affricates present a combination of stop and fricative features. In Figure 5.46 we can see the "silent" gaps of stop closures (both with and without voicing striations at the baseline of the spectrogram for /dʒ/ and /tʃ/, respectively), as well as the bursts of noise marking stop release and the extended durations of aperiodicity (frication) that are characteristic of fricatives.

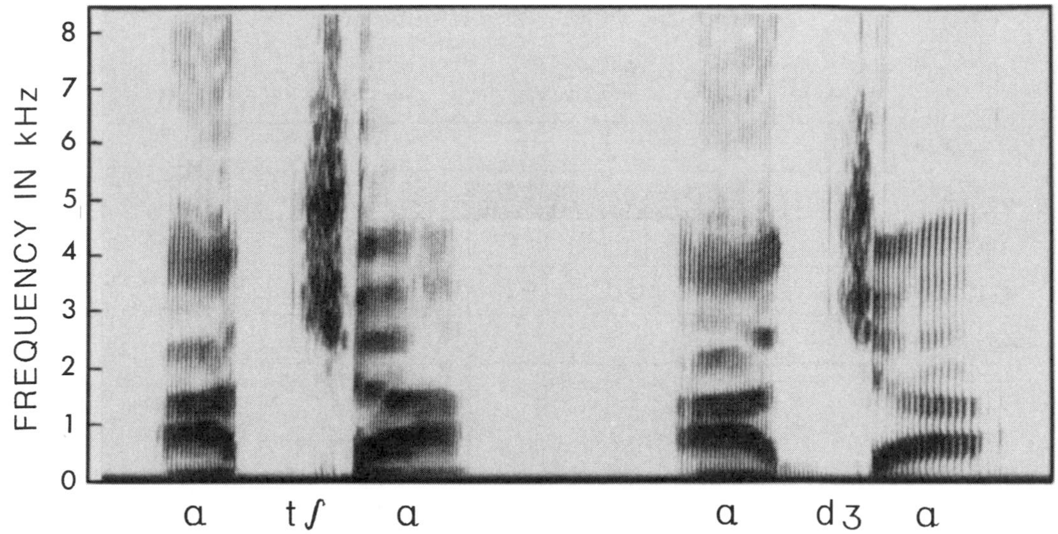

Figure 5.46. Spectrograms of [ɑtʃɑ] and [ɑdʒɑ].

	Both Lips (bilabial)	Lip-Teeth (labio-dental)	Tongue-Teeth (lingua-dental)	Tongue-Ridge (alveolar)	Tongue-Hard Palate (post-alveolar)	Tongue-Blade Palate (palatal)	Tongue-Velum (velar)	Glottis (glottal)
Stops	p b			t d		(k) (g)	k g	ʔ
Fricatives		f v	θ ϑ	s z	ʃ ʒ			h
Affricates					tʃ dʒ			
Nasals	m			n			ŋ	
Semivowels	w			ɩ	r	j	(w, r)	

Figure 5.47. Classification of the American English consonants. Voiceless consonants appear to the *left* in each column, voiced consonants to the *right*. Secondary forms of the same sound are shown in *parentheses*.

Summary

Having surveyed the consonant sounds of English, it may be helpful to show how they how they are related to each other as a function of the parameters of production. A traditional way of doing this is to chart the consonants according to place and manner of articulation (Fig. 5.47). The various places of articulation are conventionally displayed across the top of the chart, with the most anterior articulations (labial) at the left, and the most posterior articulations (velar, glottal) at the right. The manners of articulation are listed vertically at the left, arranged either in increasing or in decreasing order of degree of constriction. Figure 5.47 uses the latter arrangement, beginning at the top with the stops and proceeding to the semivowels.

This type of chart, which can be found in most phonetics or linguistics texts, has been adapted in an interesting way by Peterson and Shoup so that it is a less abstract analog of the vocal tract. In adapting the chart, they included the places of constriction of the vowels in order to show how consonants and vowels, normally charted separately (see Fig. 5.22), are related to each other in their articulation. Figure 5.48 is an adaptation of their chart, from which all but the English sounds have been omitted. The vertical axis represents complete vocal tract

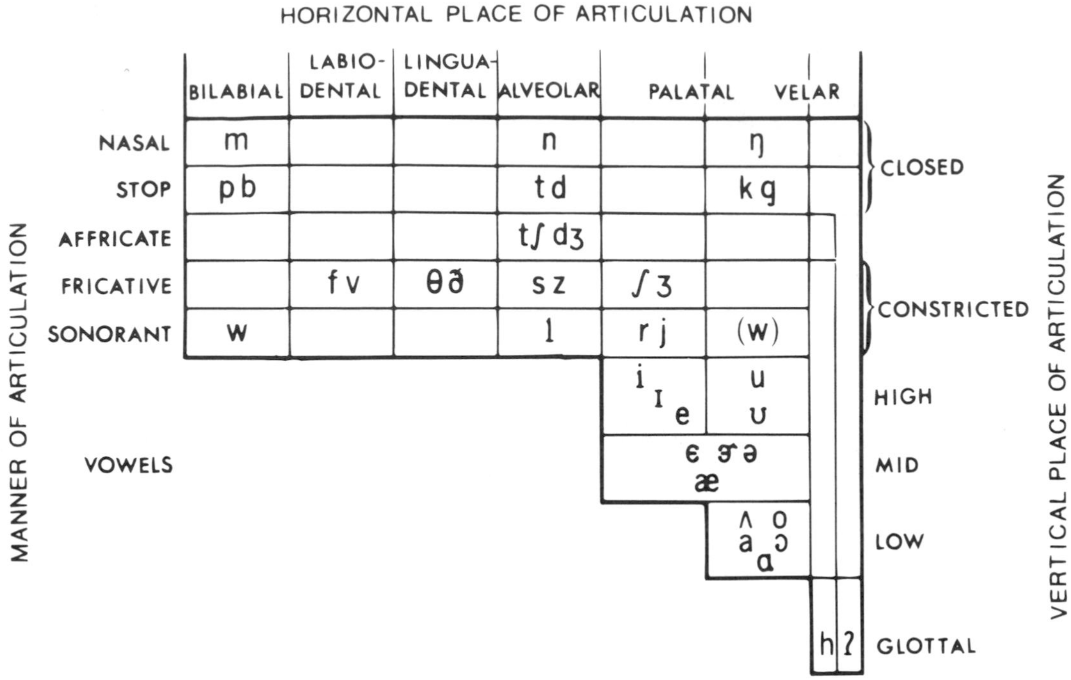

Figure 5.48. Peterson and Shoup's chart for the sounds of American English. (See text for further discussion.) (Adapted from G. E. Peterson and J. E. Shoup: *Journal of Speech and Hearing Research. 9,* 1966.)

closure at the top and proceeds to an open tract at the bottom, with sounds having a common manner of articulation connected. For example, following the level for stops across the chart and around the corner, one ends at the glottal stop. Place of articulation is represented as it was in Figure 5.47. "Vertical Place of Articulation" unites the tongue height and manner of articulation descriptions of vowels and consonants.

Charts of this sort serve several useful purposes. For instance, they remind us that all segmental speech sounds, both consonants and vowels, are produced by a single articulatory system and a single vocal tract. In addition, the systematic relationships among various sounds are easy to discern: the relationship of one sound's place of articulation to those of others, or the similar pattern of distribution of stops and nasals. Moreover, the inclusion of the vowels reveals that the place of articulation of the "front" vowels is well posterior to the position of the front-articulated consonants and reminds us of the similarities between the high front vowels /i/ and /u/ and the initiation of the glides /j/ and /w/.

The Effects of Context on the Production of Speech Sounds

Up to this point, we have discussed most speech sounds as if they were produced one at a time, independently of each other. This is not, of course, the case. The sounds of speech occur in context and are affected and altered by neighboring sounds. An understanding of the nature of the alterations caused by context is critical to the understanding of speech, because the effects of context influence every aspect of production—muscular activity, articulatory movement, and the acoustic signal.

We shall identify two basic types of context effects in this section. The two types will be differentiated from each other on the basis of the number of articulators involved in the effect and the timing of their movements.

Assimilation

The most basic type of sound change involves an alteration in the movement of a single articulator. In a sense, the articulator takes a shortcut. Let us consider an example. You intend to say "Eat the cake." Normally, you articulate /t/ with your tongue tip on your alveolar ridge, and /ð/ with your tongue tip against your upper incisors. In the context of this sentence it would thus be necessary for you to move the tip of your tongue from one place of articulation to the other, hence the shortcut: You place your tongue tip directly on your incisors for the /t/, forming a linguadental occlusion, and leave it there, where it has to be for the following /ð/. What you have done, of course, is what most speakers do in this context: You have produced a dentalized /t/.

Let us be clear about what has occurred. The fricative sound has influenced its neighbor, /t/, so that the /t/ becomes more like /ð/ in its articulation. We say that the /t/ has been *assimilated* to the place of articulation of the /ð/. Notice that in this example the change is phonetic: from one allophone of the phoneme /t/ (alveolar) to another allophone (dental) of the *same* phoneme. We call this type of assimilation *partial*, as there is no phonemic change.

X-ray studies have provided very specific evidence of the effect of articulatory position upon articulator movement in partial assimilation: Tongue-palate contact for the [k] in preceding the front vowel in "key" is often further forward than for the [k] preceding the back vowel in "caught," as the consonant is assimilated to the vowel. MacNeilage has given a different sort of example: speaking with a pipe clenched between the teeth. Tongue elevation for an alveolar stop would have to assimilate to this high mandible position compared with the movement required were the mouth open and the jaw lowered for /ɑ/. In either case, we would expect that the intended phoneme would be produced, and that the assimilation would thus be partial.

Assimilation can, however, involve a change from an allophone of one phoneme to an allophone of a *different* phoneme. We call this type of change *complete* assimilation. Consider the utterance "ten cards." In most cases, the alveolar /n/ in "ten" will be articulated with the dorsum of the tongue on the velum, in anticipation of the lingua-velar /k/. But this, of course, will produce the lingua-velar nasal /ŋ/, a different phoneme from the /n/ we normally expect to occur at the end of "ten." The complete assimilation of /n/ to the place of articulation of a following velar stop is one that has occurred many times in the history of English. Words such as "think," "bank," and "anger," although they are all spelled with the letter "n," are and have been pronounced with the nasal /ŋ/ for hundreds of years.

Assimilations, both complete and partial, can be subclassified in many ways. When a sound is influenced by a following sound, as in the examples we have just considered, *anticipatory* (also called right-to-left) assimilation is the result. When a sound is influenced by a preceding sound, *carryover* (left-to-right) assimilation will occur. Carryover assimilation is exemplified by the voicing class of the plural morpheme following nouns ending in voiced consonants: the /s/ in "cats" remains an [s], but the /s/ in "dogs" has become [z]. The voicing in the /g/ is carried over to the /s/, producing [z].

Assimilations can also be categorized according to the way in which articulation is affected. We have already seen examples of assimilations of place of articulation ("eat the cake," "ten cards") and voicing ("dogs"). Assimilations of manner of articulation, though less frequent than the other types, do occasionally occur. The word "educate," originally pronounced with a sequence of stop plus glide --/dj/-- ([ɛdjuket]), a pronunciation still favored by some educators, is now pronounced almost universally with an affricate ([ɛdʒuket]). This manner change has occurred because of what was originally an assimilation of place of articulation: the assimilation of the /d/ to the palatal place of articulation of the /j/. The movement of the tongue back toward the palate as the stop was released generated a fricative release and thus resulted in the affricate that we usually hear in this word. This type of assimilation is called *palatalization.*

So far, we have described assimilation only in terms of articulatory movement. Let us turn now to muscular activity and acoustics and see how they cause and reflect the effects of assimilation.

On the level of muscle activity, electromyographic recordings associated with a given speech sound vary with phonetic context. MacNeilage and De Clerk found pervasive influences of adjacent vowels or consonants upon the EMG signal associated with a particular phone. An example of partial assimilation, drawn from the work of Bell-Berti and Harris, is the activity of the genioglossus muscle, which, you will recall, fronts and elevates the mass of the tongue. Genioglossus muscle activity (see Fig. 5.50) was found to be larger for [u] after the low vowel [ɑ] plus a consonant than it was after an already elevated vowel, [i] plus the same consonant. The tongue had farther to go in its travels from the low, back [ɑ] position to the high [u] position. In contrast, when the tongue was already high, for [i], it had less of a journey to the [u] position. Thus, articulatory positions at a given time affect the muscle activity necessary to produce forthcoming movements.

An acoustic effect of partial assimilation can be seen in Figure 5.49. To produce the [t] closure at the end of "eat," a relatively small change in oral cavity shape is made, resulting in a small F_2 transition, while the same closure after [ɔ] requires a shortening of the vocal tract (which had been lengthened for [ɔ]) and a more extensive tongue elevation, reflected in a large positive F_2 transition. Thus, the method of producing each /t/ has been assimilated to its vowel environment.

Acoustic evidence also exists for the assimilation of vowels that results from a change in rate of speaking. Faster speaking rates cause the tongue to fall short of its target positions. Lindblom has provided spectrographic analyses showing that increased speaking rate neutralizes the formant patterns of vowels, making them more like those of adjacent sounds. Usually, the neutralization is rather subtle, but you can hear the difference between the non-neutralized and neutralized versions of a vowel if you compare the /æ/ in the protest "But you have!" with a quickly delivered "You have seen it," with primary stress on "seen."

Coarticulation. Another kind of phonetic influence evident in speech production is called coarticulation. A strict definition of *coarticulation* is that two articulators are moving at the same time for different phonemes. This differs from assimilation (one articulator modifying its movements because of context), although these two types of context effect are obviously related.

An example of coarticulation is when a speaker, saying "two" [tu], rounds the lips for [u] while the tongue is active for [t]. A simple trial will verify that it is possible to say "two" with a great deal of lip-rounding or with little or no lip rounding during the [t].

Coarticulation has been observed in acoustic, movement, and EMG studies. Kozhevnikov and Chistovich found that lip rounding for [u] can start at the beginning of a CCV (consonant-consonant-vowel) syllable, if none of the intervening sounds requires a movement that is antagonistic to it. Öhman, of Sweden, postulated, from spectrographic evidence, that the tongue moves from vowel shape to vowel shape with the consonantal gestures superimposed. Coarticulation results because of the temporal overlap between the articulatory gestures for the vowels and the consonants.

X-ray investigations also present evidence of coarticulation. Perkell cites examples, one of which is the coarticulation of the mandible and the tongue for nasal plus vowel utterances, as in "not" [nɑt]. When the initial sound is a nasal, such as /n/, that employs tongue movement, the mandible is free to lower for the /ɑ/ at the same time as the tongue. In contrast, if the initial sound is a stop, such as /t/, the mandible does not begin to lower until the alveolar closure is made. The reason for this is that stops require high intraoral pressure behind the point of closure that nasals, as you know, do not. Premature jaw lowering would threaten the loss of that pressure.

If an articulator is free to move, it often

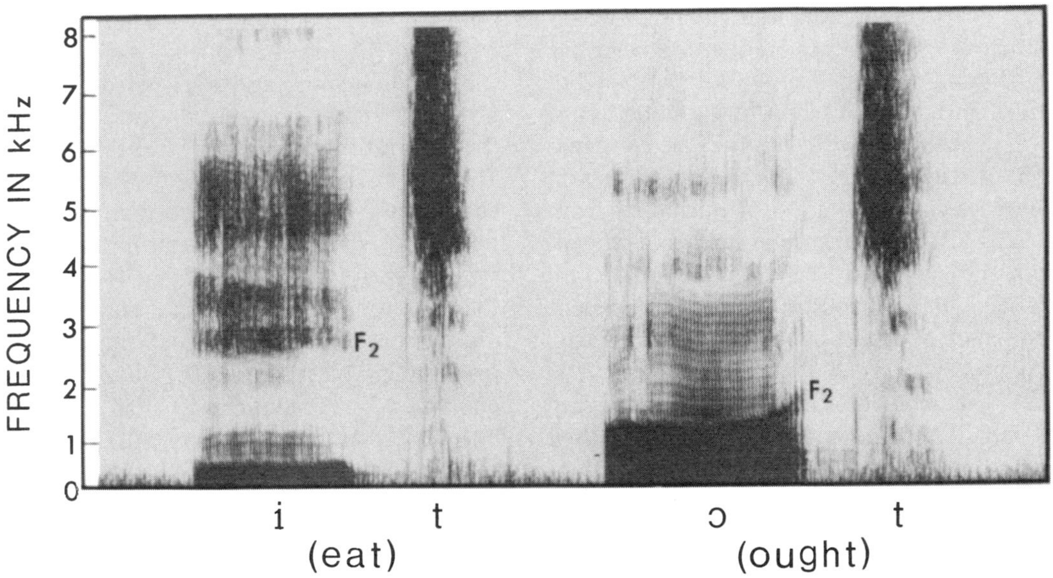

Figure 5.49. Acoustic partial assimilation. The F_2 transition for [t] in "eat" is very small relative to the F_2 transition for [t] in "ought."

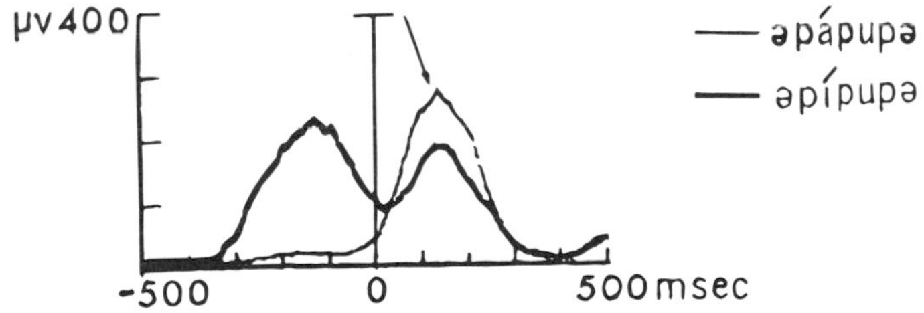

Figure 5.50. Genioglossus muscle activity for [u] after [ɑ] and [i]. The amount of activity is greater after [ɑ] because the tongue must move a greater distance. *Arrow* indicates peak activity for [u]. (From F. Bell-Berti and K. S. Harris: *Some Aspects of Coarticulation,* 8th International Congress of Phonetic Sciences, Leeds, England, Aug. 1975).

does. Daniloff and Moll found that the lips move for /u/-rounding several phones before the vowel. Bell-Berti and Harris, who reported orbicularis oris muscle activity for the /u/, found it to occur at a relatively fixed time before the vowel sound, coarticulating with the activity for the consonant or consonant cluster preceding it, but unaffected by the number of consonants there.

Öhman noted from his observations of spectrograms that the tongue might act as three somewhat independent articulators with the tip, blade, and dorsum coarticulating. Borden and Gay, in a cinefluorographic study, verified this theory with movement data. That part of the tongue free to lower for /ɑ/ during stop production, proceeded to lower. If the tip of the tongue were elevated for /t/, the back of the tongue lowered simultaneously for the /ɑ/. If the dorsum was involved with /k/ closure, the front of the tongue got a head start in lowering. Stone has presented ultrasound and x-ray microbeam data showing that portions of the tongue move independently of each other. The available evidence thus indicates quite strongly that it is possible for the tongue to coarticulate with itself. There are, however, individual differences between the patterns of coarticulation.

Coarticulation and assimilation of one articulatory movement to another are pervasive in running speech. It is what Liberman has called, in both perception and production of speech, *parallel processing*. It is the combination of assimilation and coarticulation that makes speech transmission rapid and efficient. As we shall see in the chapter on speech perception, the extent to which speech sounds are encoded in the acoustic signal is dependent upon such processes as assimilation and coarticulation.

The segmental modifications necessary for rapid transmission should not be confused with the different, but interesting, kinds of sound changes and differences associated with dialects and idiolects. These include deletions such as [laɪbɛrɪ] for [laɪbrɛrɪ] in "library," additions such as [aɪdiɝːv] for [aɪdiəːv] in "idea of," and *metathesis* (reversals in the sequencing of sounds), such as [æks] for "ask" or [larnɪks] for "larynx." All sound influences, however, demonstrate that speech is not produced as beads are put on a string, one phone after another.

It is important to remember this, because in a great deal of our introductory discussion it was necessary to treat phonemes as if they were isolated segments of speech. This mistaken notion is further reinforced when we write or read phonetic transcriptions, which record speech sounds as isolable and permutable segments. Yet we know that phonemes exist as independent units only in our minds (and, perhaps, as symbolic representations on paper in transcriptions). It is our mental ability to segment the unbroken stream of speech that leads us to identify individual speech sounds, assign them to families (phoneme classes) and refer to them as *segmental* phonemes.

When we know a language, we know which families of sounds act contrastively. If we are speakers of English, for example, we understand that the family of /p/ sounds contrasts with the family of /t/ sounds, in utterances such as "pie" and "tie." In running speech, however, these segments rarely exist independently. Sometimes, we use a speech sound alone, as when we exclaim "Oh!" or when we quiet someone with "sh." In utterances such as "pie," however, the production is never accomplished by saying [p] and then quickly saying [aɪ]. If the sounds are produced independently of each other, no matter how quickly the [aɪ] follows the [p], the utterance will not be heard as [paɪ]. The reason, as we know now, is that speakers coarticulate, producing more than one phoneme at the same time: while the lips are closed for the [p] in [pai], the tongue is lowering for the beginning of the [aɪ], and while the lips are opening to release the burst, the tongue is fronting and elevating for the off-glide of the diphthong. The sounds thus overlap and merge into one continuously changing stream of sound, further bonded by slowly changing modifications overlaid upon it. These overlaid changes are the prosody, the rhythm and music of speech.

Suprasegmentals

The *suprasegmental,* or prosodic, features of speech usually occur simultaneously with two or more segmental phonemes. They are overlaid upon syllables, words, phrases, and sentences. The suprasegmental features that we shall consider are stress, intonation, duration, and juncture.

Stress. The coarticulation of consonants and vowels is what binds sounds together into syllables, and it the *syllable* that is the unit of stress. Utterances may be organized as monosyllables, such as "bat," "eat," and "tea," as disyllables, such as "beyond," "hidden," and "table," and as polysyllables containing more than two syllables, such as "unicorn," "immediate," and "unsophisticated." Listeners can usually count the number of highly resonant centers of each syllable, the syllabic nuclei, in order to determine the number of syllables in an utterance, even though they are not aware of the basis of this determination. Each nucleus will be counted, regardless of the degree of stress it has received. The following passage contains 13 syllables, but only four of them receive the highest level of stress, called *primary stress*. Read the passage aloud and see if you can count the number of syllables and identify the four bearing primary stress.

"What 'wisdom can you 'find that is 'greater than 'kindness?" Jean Jacques Rousseau
Emile; On Education (1762).

In English, as in other languages, stress functions as a "pointer," by indicating which information in an utterance is most important. Let's see how this pointing function works in sentences, clauses, and phrases. Here is a series of questions and statements:

1. WHICH one of those green books is yours?
2. That's NOT your green book!
3. That's MY green book.
4. Is that your RED book?
5. WHAT is that?

Respond to each of the questions and statements by repeating the following sentence, in its entirety:

THIS IS MY GREEN BOOK.

In each succeeding repetition you will find that the heaviest stress moves from one word to the next, starting with "THIS" and ending with "BOOK," in response to the information that is requested or provided by each of the five sentences above.

Native speakers are usually able to place stress accurately in sentences without any conscious effort. Moreover, they are quite sensitive to stress that is misplaced. For instance,

"This is my green *BOOK*."

as a response to

"*WHICH* one of those green books is yours?"

will sound peculiar to them.

Stress also functions on the word level to point to the most important syllable(s). There are several reasons for doing this. One is that nouns and verbs are often differentiated mainly by stress placement in English. For example the word "'PERmit," with the first syllable stressed, is a noun meaning "a document of authorization," but "per'MIT," with the second syllable stressed, is a verb meaning "to allow." "Permit" is a rather unusual word in this regard because the vowel in its lesser stressed syllable is often produced without being changed. More typical examples, which do evidence vowel change, are pairs such as "EXtract" (n.), vs. "exTRACT" (v.); "DIgest, (n.)" vs. "diGEST" (v.); and "INcrease," (n.) vs. "inCREASE" (v.). In words of more than two syllables, there is a tendency to retain a second stress for verbs [ˈɛstəˈmendɪt] as "to EStiMATE," but to lose the secondary stress for the noun, [ˈɛstəmət] as "an EStimate."

There are instances, in English, of syllables that are normally only weakly stressed becoming important because of the contrasts they provide. Thus,

"I told you to REceive the guests, not to DEceive them."

requires that the first syllables of "receive" and "deceive" be heavily stressed, because these are the syllables that differentiate the two words. This use of stress is called *contrastive*, probably because the contrast is made explicit by speakers.

But all the uses of stress rely on contrasts, even if they are only implied. In some instances the implied contrast will be with something that was not said. When you stressed "green" in "This is my GREEN book," you implied the contrast with the name of any other color that might have been said (but was not), as well as the contrast with any other syllable in the sentence that might have been stressed (but, again, was not). The contrast between strongly and weakly stressed syllables in English is what makes the pointing function of stress possible. In a sense, the more weakly stressed syllables are as important as the strongly stressed syllables, since without them, there would be no contrast possible between the more important and the less important information.

The alternation between heavily and weakly stressed syllables in English gives the subjective impression that the stressed syllables occur at fairly regular intervals, a phenomenon called *isochrony* (iso = equal; chrons =

time) or *stress-timing*. Recent research, however, has cast doubt on the physical reality of isochrony, particularly on the acoustic level of analysis.

How does a speaker use his vocal mechanism to generate the different degrees of stress required? The general answer is that the more stress a speaker wishes to place on a syllable, the more effort he will expend in producing the syllable, and the less stress, the less effort. This answer, however, needs to be made more specific in terms of the use of respiratory, phonatory and articulatory behaviors. Interestingly, these behaviors were first inferred from acoustic analyses.

There are three acoustic characteristics associated with heavily stressed syllables. They (1) have a higher fundamental frequency, (2) they are of greater duration, and (3) they are of greater intensity than weakly stressed syllables. Let us see how each of these characteristics arises from the use of the vocal mechanism.

The higher fundamental frequency associated with stressed syllables is, of course, a function of increased tension on the vocal folds. This extra effort within the larynx on the part of the cricothyroid muscle may be supplemented by increased respiratory effort, which will raise subglottal pressure and so assist in raising fundamental frequency. It will also drive the folds further from their rest position, causing the more intense signal associated with stressed syllables.

The greater duration of stressed syllables indicates that more muscular effort must be used generally, most particularly within the articulatory system. The increased amount of time used to articulate highly stressed syllables allows the articulators to reach target positions for the vowels of the stressed syllables. This is reflected in the formant frequencies of stressed vowels as compared to those of lesser-stressed syllables that display the effects of articulatory undershoot.

Intonation. The suprasegmental features are capable of revealing the attitudes and feelings of the speaker in ways the segmental information alone can never do. Stress, for example, when used for emphasis, can express disdain for children in general, "not that 'child!" or dislike of a particular child, "not 'that child!" The use of changing f_0, perceived as the pitch pattern or *intonation* contour of a phrase or sentence, is particularly effective in expressing differences in attitude. For instance, in the example given above, the stressed words ("child" or "that") would be marked by a sharp rise in f_0.

Intonation can also signal differences in meaning. "Today is Tuesday" said with a rising intonation contour (the pitch increasing during "Tuesday"), turns a statement into a question. We see that it is possible for the prosodic information that is transmitted along with the segmental information to override the literal meaning of the words being spoken. The sentence "That's a pretty picture!" can be said in such a way that it conveys genuine admiration of the picture or a sarcastic and negative evaluation of its artistic worth. It is even possible to use intonation to convert a grammatically constructed question into a statement. Try saying "Am I a good tennis player" in such a way as to let your listeners know that you could make them forget Steffi Graf in a minute.

Intonation patterns (perceived changes in fundamental frequency) can be imposed on a sentence, a phrase, or even a word. American English sentences are often characterized by a rise-fall intonation curve. The pitch rises during the first part of an utterance and falls at the end. This is generally true of declarative sentences and of questions that are impossible to answer with yes or no.

Declarative sentence:
He left an hour ago.
[hilɛftən ʔauɚ əgou]

Question impossible to answer with yes/no:
How do you like it here?
[haʊdəju laɪk ɪth ɚ]

Special emphasis:
Wow!
[wa ʊ]

Another intonation contour common in English is the end-of-utterance pitch rise. Pitch rise indicates a question to be answered with yes or no. It may also indicate that a sentence is incomplete.

Yes/no question:

Is it ready?
[ɪzit /rɛdɪ]

Incomplete sentence:

As I think about it . . .
[æzaɪθ /ɪŋk \ əbaʊt /ɪt]

Because it signals incompletion, a pitch rise can be used by speakers to "hold the floor" during a discussion. If a speaker pauses to think in the midst of a phrase, with the pitch rising, a polite discussant will be less likely to interrupt than if the pause occurred at a fall in intonation.

Rising intonation results chiefly from increased cricothyroid muscle activity, which tenses the vocal folds, causing them to vibrate faster. Falling intonation can result from decreased cricothyroid activity. It can be caused by the decrease in subglottal pressure that is typically found at the end of what Lieberman calls the *breath group*. The end of a declarative sentence, for example, will be marked by a decrease in f_0 and a decrease in intensity. The falling subglottal pressure contributes to the decrement in both of these acoustic features.

This falling pattern of f_0 and intensity in simple declarative sentences is what Lieberman calls an *unmarked breath group*. There is disagreement about the relative contributions of subglottal air pressure and decrease in cricothyroid muscle activity to the f_0 decline. The rise in f_0 that occurs in what is called a *marked breath group* is most probably caused by cricothyroid contraction.

If one measures the natural *declination* of fundamental frequency for each of many unmarked breath groups, one finds that, although the f_0 may vary considerably in its higher starting points, it falls at the end of each breath group to about the same frequency. Cooper and Sorensen regard this as evidence of some degree of preplanning. We saw the same phenomenon in our study of respiration. There was a tendency for each breath group to end at about 35–40% vital capacity despite a large variation in starting volumes.

It seems that the decrease in subglottal pressure at the end of a phrase is a the most important factor in the overall declination of f_0, but that the elevation of f_0 for each stressed syllable is the combined result of cricothyroid muscle and internal intercostal muscle activity, elevating both the fundamental frequency and the intensity of the voice.

You can demonstrate the natural declination of f_0 by producing an audible sigh. Notice that the pitch falls intonation as lung volume decreases. Now add the alternating stressed and unstressed syllables typical of English:

Jack and Jill went up the hill
To fetch a pail of water.
Jack fell down and broke his crown,
And Jill came tumbling after.

You will observe that each stressed syllable is higher in f_0 and intensity than its neighboring unstressed syllables, but that each succeeding stressed syllable in a phrase is a bit lower in f_0 than its predecessor. Although a case may be made that a pattern of falling intonation is one that is natural to the speech system, it is obvious that we can override the system for linguistic reasons. We could choose to emphasize that Jack broke his crown instead of his leg or to turn "Jill came tumbling after" into a question. Intonation thus functions to mark syntactic contrasts (phrase endings, interrogation *versus* declaration), to change meaning, and to signal attitudes and feelings. Excitement, including some kinds of anger and states of enthusiasm, is often accompanied by large shifts in intonation, while calm, subdued states, including some forms of grief, anger, peacefulness, and boredom are characterized by a narrow range of intonation variation. We know how a person feels as often by how he says his message as by the message itself.

Duration and Juncture. Segmental duration has been mentioned, in the discussion of vowels. Speech sounds vary in intrinsic duration. In general, the diphthongs and tense vowels (which are diphthongal in nature) are described as intrinsically "long" sounds. The lax vowels, in contrast, are described as intrinsically "short" sounds. The continuant consonants (fricatives, nasals, and semivowels) are, of course, longer than the bursts of stops.

In addition to possessing intrinsic durations, sounds may vary durationally because of the effects of context. For example, vowels in English are of greater duration when they occur before voiced consonants, as in "leave," than when they occur before voiceless consonants, as in "leaf." They are also longer before continuants as in "leave," than before stops, as in "leap." While this pattern of durational differences is found across languages, suggesting that it is basically conditioned by physiology, English shows very large differences in vowel duration before voiced and voiceless consonants, suggesting a learned overlay. In English, it is not unusual to find that vowels preceding voiced consonants are half again as long as those preceding voiceless consonants. Even greater durational differences can be found. This is in marked contrast with differences found in some other languages. In Spanish, for instance, research has shown a small average difference (18 ms) between vowels preceding voiced and voiceless consonants.

A final suprasegmental feature, related to duration, is *juncture*. As its name implies, juncture has to do with the way sounds are joined to (or separated from) each other. For example, consider the following sequence of sounds:

[əneɪm]

If the sequence is articulated so that the [n] is more closely linked to the preceding schwa than to the following [eɪ], then "an aim" will be produced. On the other hand, "a name" will be heard if the [n] is joined to the [ei] and disjoined from the schwa. In this example, the affiliation of the [n] is determined by differences in duration combined with other sound changes. In "an aim" the [n] will be of greater duration than in "a name." In addition, speakers often insert a glottal stop before the [eɪ] of "an aim," which inhibits coarticulation between the nasal and the following vowel. A great many durational, intonational, assimilative and coarticulatory effects are used to establish the junctural differences between the members of such pairs as "nitrate" vs. "night rate," "it sprays" vs. "its praise," and "why choose" vs. "white shoes," in which the sequence of segmental sounds is essentially identical. Junctural distinctions are being studied in an effort to produce more natural synthetic speech and to better understand speech production rules.

FEEDBACK MECHANISMS IN SPEECH

Speech scientists are interested in how a speaker controls the production of speech. To what degree does the speaker monitor his actions, and to what degree and under what situations might he produce speech with little or no information on how he is proceeding?

To answer this question, we must consider the science of self-regulating machines, called *cybernetics*. The term, coined by Norbert Wiener, from the Greek word meaning "steersman," refers to the study of systems that control themselves on the basis of their actual performance rather than being controlled by an external operator who compares the system's performance with the performance expected of it. A thermostat that turns off the furnace when the temperature actually reaches the set temperature is an example of a *servomechanism*, the engineering term for a self-regulating machine. If a device controlling the temperature in your home was not a servomechanism, you would have to consult a thermometer periodically and make the required adjustments according to your preference.

Servomechanisms have been developed to perform a wide variety of functions. During the Second World War, the United States government was interested in developing anti-aircraft artillery that could track airplanes by predicting their future position based upon information on changes in position fed back to the machine. Today we are familiar with com-

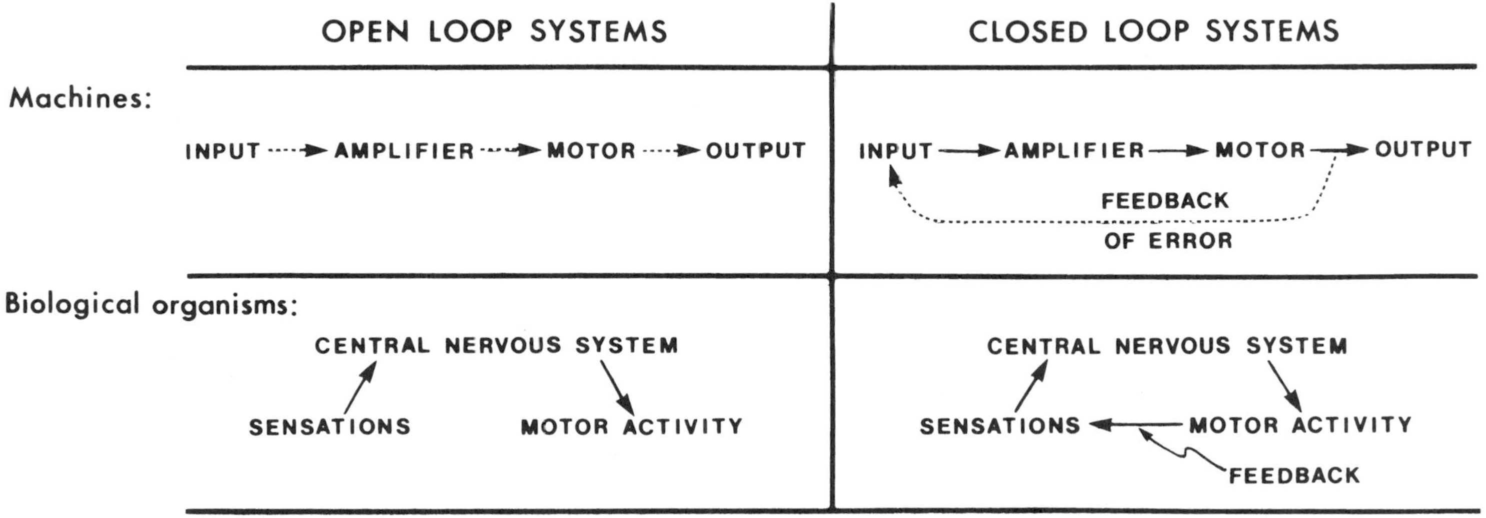

Figure 5.51. Schematic diagram comparing open and closed loop control, for machines and biological systems.

puters that are programmed to perform certain computations based upon the results of previous computations.

In servomechanisms, the output of the machine is fed back to some point in the assembly, where the feedback information controls the ensuing output. When the information that is fed back indicates that performance is within the prescribed limits and should be continued unchanged, we call the feedback *positive*. If the information indicates that performance is outside the prescribed limits (i.e., that an error has been made) and that a change in performance is required, we call the feedback *negative*. Systems operating under feedback control are described as *closed loop* systems. Figure 5.51 contrasts *open loop* and closed loop systems in machines and in biological organisms. The difference between them is that in open loop systems, the output is preprogrammed and does not require feedback, while in closed loop systems, the performance of the system is fed back to be matched with the program. If there is a discrepancy between the program and the performance, adjustments are made to correct the error.

The production of speech requires the simultaneous and coordinated use of respiratory, phonatory, and articulatory mechanisms, an activity which is so complex that some method of feedback control seems likely. There are at least four kinds of information available to a speaker that could be used in feedback control: auditory, tactile, proprioceptive, and central neural feedback.

Auditory Feedback

Simply put, auditory feedback is what occurs when we hear our own speech. Unlike the solely air-conducted acoustic signal that our listeners hear, auditory feedback is both air- and bone-conducted. Because a great deal of our own speech is conducted to our hearing mechanism by way of the bones in the skull, which emphasizes low frequencies, we do not sound to ourselves the way we sound to others. This is why speakers are often surprised at what they hear when a tape recording of their speech is played back to them.

Interest in the role of feedback mechanisms in the control of speech was aroused by an accidental discovery made by a New Jersey engineer, Bernard Lee, in 1950. While he was recording himself on a tape recorder, he noticed that under some circumstances, the auditory feedback from his own speech could make him dysfluent. In a tape recorder, the record head ordinarily precedes the playback head, as diagrammed in Figure 5.52. If a speaker listens to his own previously recorded speech through a headset plugged into the playback head, which provides a slight time delay, fluent speech often becomes dysfluent, syllables are repeated, or inappropriately prolonged.

This *delayed auditory feedback* (DAF) effect provoked much excitement and a flurry of studies in the 1950s. The DAF effect was interpreted by many as proof that speech acts like a servomechanism, with auditory feedback as the chief control channel. This theory has been challenged by some, who note that some speakers can continue to speak fluently under DAF by attending to the printed page and ignoring the acoustic signal, that the duration of the error corrections, when they occur, in the form of stalls, are not linearly related to the amount of delay time, and that DAF is disruptive only at high intensity. An alternate interpretation of the DAF effect is that it is a result of forcing attention upon auditory feedback information that conflicts with information received from articulatory movements. It is a case of your muscles telling you "Yes," you have said something, but your ears telling you "No." In any case, it is important to remember that DAF is a very abnormal feedback condition, and that forcing a speaker to function under abnormal conditions of feedback is not the same as depriving him of the sort of feedback he normally receives. In other words, DAF does not reveal how a speaker might perform if he simply could not hear himself.

There are ways of interfering with auditory feedback other than delaying it. In general, the speaker will normalize any distortion. If the air-conducted sound is amplified, speakers de-

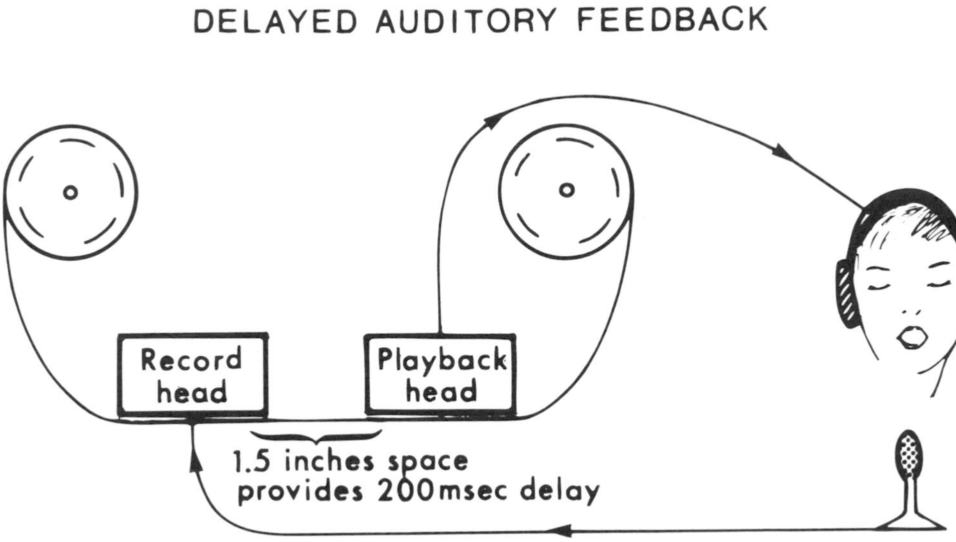

Figure 5.52. The delayed auditory feedback effect. A speaker records his own voice, while listening to the recording at a time delay, by monitoring the playback head of the tape recorder. A 1.5-inch space provides a 200-msec delay at a tape speed of 7.5 inches per sec. This delay leads to maximum speech interference in adults.

crease vocal intensity; if it is attenuated, they increase vocal intensity. If they cannot hear themselves at all, they increase intensity (the *Lombard effect*) and prolong voicing, as you know if you have ever tried to talk to someone sitting under a hair dryer. Even filtering out frequency regions of the speech that is fed back causes speakers to make articulatory adjustments in order to modify some of the resonance characteristics of the speech they produce. Garber has found that if speakers hear their own speech through a low pass filter, they will respond by decreasing the low frequency nasal resonance, raising fundamental frequency, and increasing intelligibility. The explanation is that speakers are presumably attempting to restore the missing high frequency information.

These effects demonstrate that audition does operate as a feedback system for speech control, but they fail to settle the question of whether auditory feedback is essential for a skilled speaker. If so, is it used continuously or only in difficult speaking conditions? Adventitiously deafened speakers suffer little immediate effect upon the intelligibility of their speech; after a period of deafness, certain sounds deteriorate, notably /s/, and the suprasegmental structure of speech suffers. Despite evidence that speakers attempt to compensate for distortions in auditory feedback, audition may not serve effectively as a feedback mechanism to monitor ongoing, skilled articulation, because the information it provides to the speaker arrives too late; he has already spoken and can only make corrections after the fact. Speakers do use audition, however, to sharpen their speech sound targets, and, if they are attending to themselves, to catch errors.

Tactile Feedback

Tactile feedback is the information you receive from your sense of touch. The act of speaking can generate perceptions of touch in many ways. The articulators, for instance, are continually coming into contact with one another, the lower lip touching the upper lip, the tip or blade of the tongue touching the alveolar ridge, the dorsum of the tongue touching the roof of the mouth, or the velum touching the pharyngeal walls. Even air pressure differences caused by valving the breath stream at the glottis or in the supraglottal cavities will impinge on the walls of the vocal tract and induce sensations of touch.

Tactile sensations include the perception of light touch, mediated by free nerve endings of sensory fibers lying near the surface of articulators, and the perception of deeper pressure, mediated by more complex nerve bodies further from the surface. When touch receptors are stimulated, the responsiveness of surrounding cells is inhibited, which aids in localizing and sharpening sensations. The lips, alveolar ridge, and anterior tongue are highly endowed with surface receptors responsive to light touch. The tongue dorsum contains more sensory fibers than any other part of the human body. In addition to touch, some of these receptors are responsive to taste, temperature, and pain.

A method of measuring tactile sensation is to explore *two-point discrimination* with an instrument called an esthesiometer. A subject can feel two separate points on the tip of the tongue when the points are only 1–2 mm apart, but further back on the tongue or on its lateral margins, the points must be nearly 1 cm apart to be differentiated. There are more touch receptors on the superior surface of the tongue than on the inferior surface and more in the alveolar ridge area of the hard palate than on the posterior part of the palate. Tactile sensation from the anterior ⅔ of the tongue is transmitted by sensory fibers in the lingual branch of the trigeminal (Vth cranial) nerve. The trigeminal nerve also transmits impulses from touch receptors of the lips and palate. The glossopharyngeal (IXth cranial) nerve carries sensory information from the posterior ⅓ of the tongue. It is thought that some of the sensory fibers of the lingual nerve may course with the motor nerve to the tongue, the hypoglossal (XIIth cranial) nerve.

A second method of evaluating tactile sensation in the mouth is to test *oral stereognosis* by putting shapes into the mouth of a subject for either identification or discrimination. The ability to identify (name) the shapes by feeling them with the tongue and palate and then pointing to the appropriate pictures was found to have little or no relationship to speech proficiency. On the other hand, the ability to discriminate two shapes (i.e., to tell if they are the same or different) was found by Ringel to bear some relation to the ability to articulate speech sounds with normal proficiency.

There have been attempts to determine the importance of taction to speech by interfering with normal tactile feedback and looking for the effects of the interference upon speech. Using the same techniques that dentists use to block the conduction of nerve impulses from the oral area, speech scientists have anesthetized various branches of the trigeminal nerve, thus depriving the speaker of tactile feedback. Such nerve block conditions often result in distorted articulation of speech, especially the consonant /s/, but in general, speech remains highly intelligible. Even when the ability to perform oral stereognosis and two-point discrimination tasks is markedly impaired or absent, subjects can move the tongue in all directions and feel its points of contact with other articulators. When auditory masking is added to the nerve block, no significant increase in articulation errors occurs.

Several theories have been advanced to account for the speech distortions that result from the application of sensory anesthesia. They range from the peripheral sensory theory (sensory feedback is needed for accuracy of articulation), to the central sensory theory (a more general reorganization of motor activity occurs as a result of sensory loss), to the peripheral motor theory (based upon evidence that the anesthesia affects motor as well as sensory neurons), and, finally, to the central motor theory (the anesthesia enters the blood stream and produces a small motor effect similar to drunk speech). These theories have not been adequately tested because of the difficulty in controlling variables inherent in the nerve block technique.

Audition and taction are called *external feedback* systems, because the information they provide is delivered to external receptors. The flow and pressure exerted by the air stream and the points of contact between articulators stimulate the tactile receptors in the vocal tract. These receptors are located on the surfaces of the organs in the tract. Analogously, the sound waves produced by the speech mechanism are first delivered to and processed by the peripheral organs of hearing.

Although auditory and tactile information are both generated by muscle activity, they do not contain feedback about the muscle activity itself. Such feedback, which is available to the speech production mechanism, is our next topic of discussion.

Proprioceptive Feedback

Direct feedback from muscles, a type of *response feedback*, is delivered more quickly than external feedback, and is part of the sense of movement and position called proprioception.

In the early part of the 19th century, Charles Bell differentiated touch from the muscle sense that he called *kinesthesis*. Later in the same century, Bastian enlarged the definition of kinesthesis to include a complex sense of movement derived from receptors in the joints, tendons, and muscles. In 1900, Sherrington proposed the term exteroceptors for the receptors of taction, and proprioceptors for the receptors stimulated by the action of the body itself, which provide the sensations of movement and position of limbs, joints and organs.

Proprioceptive information is provided by sensors in joints, which transmit information about bone angles, and by receptors along tendons, which respond to any contractions in the muscle to which they are attached and that are therefore able to transmit data about both muscle stretching and shortening. These data translate, on a functional level, to your ability to perform a task such as touching your forefinger to the tip of your nose while your eyes are closed.

Of special interest to speech physiologists are the receptors embedded in striated muscles. These receptors are called *muscle spindles* because they are often shaped like the slender fiber holders from which thread is twisted in spinning. Muscle spindles are more complex in their innervation than tendon and joint receptors. They have efferent as well as afferent neurons. The spindles (Fig. 5.53) are encapsulated muscle fibers (intrafusal fibers) lying parallel to the main muscle fibers (extrafusal fibers). When the efferent neurons stimulate the main muscle, the smaller efferent neurons that supply the muscle spindles are activated simultaneously. In effect, the intrafusal fibers of the muscle spindle mimic the activity of the main muscle fibers. The motoneurons to the main muscle are larger (8–20 μm in diameter) and are therefore called *alpha* (α) motoneurons, in contrast to the smaller motoneurons (2–8 μm

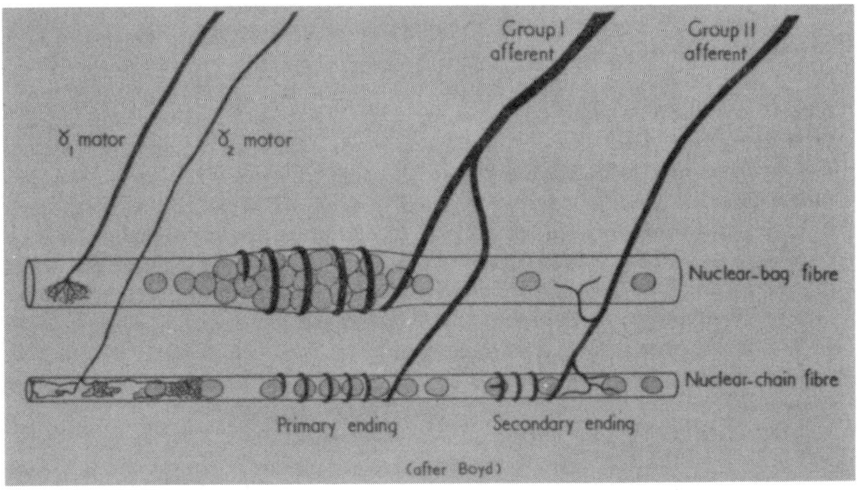

Figure 5.53. Simplified diagram of the central region of two types of muscle spindles. (Reprinted with permission from P. B. C. Matthews: *Physiological Review*. 44, 1964.)

in diameter), called *gamma* (γ) motoneurons, which innervate the spindle fibers at each end. Primary (Ia) and secondary (IIa) afferents are stimulated by, and provide information about, the lengthening of the intrafusal fibers and by the rate at which length of the fibers changes. This information is then fed back to the central nervous system.

The primary afferents from spindles are among the largest of human neurons, ranging from 12 to 20 μm in diameter, conducting impulses up to 120 meters/sec. The velocity with which the spindles convey the feedback information makes them attractive as possible mechanisms for ongoing control of rapid motor activities, including speech. Muscle spindles are found in the intercostal muscles, all of the laryngeal muscles, the genioglossus muscle, the intrinsic muscles of the tongue and, sparsely, in the facial muscles. Thus, muscles involved in speech production seem well supplied with spindles which can be tuned to feed back information on muscle length changes.

While the neural pathways for spindle information from some muscle systems are known, the route is not clear for the tongue. Spindle afferents from the tongue are currently believed to course along the otherwise motor hypoglossal (XIIth cranial) nerve and to enter the brain stem by way of the dorsal cervical nerves C_1–C_3.

The proprioceptive feedback system may operate on both reflex and voluntary levels. Some pathways go to the spinal cord, but others go to the cerebral cortex and the cerebellum. Although the sensation of muscle activity is usually unconscious, it can be made conscious, but only under carefully designed and controlled experimental conditions. Goodwin, McCloskey, and Matthews stimulated the spindles of a man's arm with a vibrator. The blindfolded man was instructed to flex his other arm to match the position of the arm under stimulation. The subject misjudged the position, thinking the muscles in his vibrated arm were more extended than they actually were. The investigators then paralyzed the joint and cutaneous afferents in the index finger of a subject to see if spindles alone were consciously perceived without information from joint receptors. As one of the investigators manipulated the finger, the subject could sense the movement and the direction of the movement; hence, the spindle output could be consciously perceived.

Proprioception for speech is difficult to investigate directly. Indirectly, proprioceptive feedback has been investigated by mechanically interfering with normal positional relationships to study compensatory adaptations. Subjects try to speak with bite blocks interfering with normal jaw raising; with metal plates unexpectedly opening between the lips, interfering with labial closure; or with palatal prostheses placed in the mouth, altering the width of the alveolar ridge. There is much to be learned about the nature of speaker compensations made in response to these mechanical alterations. What does seem to be true is that speakers compensate immediately in response to such experimental perturbations of the speech production mechanism. They continue to speak intelligibly and at a normal rate, with no need to pause or rehearse new or alternative strategies of articulation. At this time, it is not clear what feedback information, auditory, tactile, proprioceptive, or some combination of these, is instrumental in directing the compensations observed.

Two interesting attempts have been made to block γ motoneurons from speech muscles directly. Critchlow and von Euler paralyzed the γ fibers to the external intercostal muscles. The Ia fibers stopped firing during inspiration, firing during expiration only because of passive stretch of the inspiratory muscles. This had no effect upon speech but indicated that the γ and α motoneurons are activated together, since the spindle afferents are normally active from the inspiratory muscles during inspiration. Had the experiment involved paralysis of the less accessible expiratory intercostals, any effect there might have been upon speech would have become apparent.

In another study, Abbs attempted to selectively block the γ motoneurons to the mandibular muscles by anesthetizing the mandibular branch of the trigeminal nerve bilaterally, thus blocking both the large fibers (α motoneurons to main muscle fibers and afferents from tactile and proprioceptive receptors) and small fibers (γ motoneurons and afferents for pain and temperature). Since large fibers recover before smaller fibers, it was assumed that when muscle force and touch returned to normal but pain and temperature senses were still blocked, the motor supply to the spindles would be blocked. Under this condition, subjects moved the jaw with less velocity and acceleration when jaw lowering was required. There were, however, no perceptually obvious effects on speech.

Direct studies of proprioception are possible on animals. Investigations of monkeys deafferented bilaterally from muscles of the limbs or from jaw muscles, suggest that purposeful movements can be performed without either vision or somatic sensation from the muscles involved. Further study is needed to establish whether control of fine motor adjustments is perfect despite the deafferentation. Well-learned motor patterns are maintained, at least grossly, but the ability to adjust to unexpected change needs further exploration, as does the ability to learn new motor patterns.

Thus, normal adult speakers compensate immediately (with no trial and error) for any perturbation such as an unexpected load on an articulator or the insertion of a bite block; monkeys can perform learned movements without proprioceptive (stretch reflex) information. Apparently, learned motor performance can proceed without proprioceptive feedback. Polit and Bizzi suggest, furthermore, that when a monkey is blocked from pointing to a target as it has been taught to do, the limb can store the energy needed, in the form of some equilibrium point previously set, so that when the limb is released, it simply springs forward to the target without a reprogramming of the gesture.

The idea that speech, too, may be controlled automatically at the level of the coordinating muscle groups is inherent in a mass-spring model of motor behavior known as *action theory*, developed by Fowler, Turvey, Kelso, and others. According to this theory, the system acts like a series of functionally coupled oscillators, so that if one of the vibrators is constrained, one or more of the others will automatically compensate. We have already seen a potential example of this type of compensation in our discussion of front cavity length for the back vowels. Let us assume that you are the subject in an experiment and have been asked to produce the vowel [u]. Your intention is to lengthen the front cavity to produce an appropriately low F_2 by using the muscle group that rounds and protrudes the lips. The experimenters, however, foil your plan by placing a metal plate in front of your lips just as you begin to protrude them. Your response will be to resort to the use of another muscle group, either the lingual muscles that can retract the tongue or the strap muscles of the neck that can lower the larynx. Whichever alternate plan you adopt to enlarge the resonating cavities and lower F_2, the compensation is virtually immediate, and well below the level of consciousness.

Internal Feedback

Internal feedback is the conveyance of information, within the brain, about motor commands prior to the motor response itself. Feedback of this type is possible because, in addition to information fed back from the periphery, the nervous system can convey information in loops that are central, entirely within the brain.

In light of the many neural connections among the motor areas of the cerebral cortex, the cerebellum, and the thalamus, neurophysiologists have suggested that the control of the type of skilled patterns of movement found in piano-playing or speech, may operate under a feedback system housed in the central nervous system. Learned patterns under cerebellar control might be activated by the midbrain in association with the motor strip of the cerebrum. Accordingly, information could then be returned to the cerebellum from the motor cortex about whether the neural messages were dispatched as intended. This information would be received and processed well before the muscle response.

There is as yet no direct evidence for in-

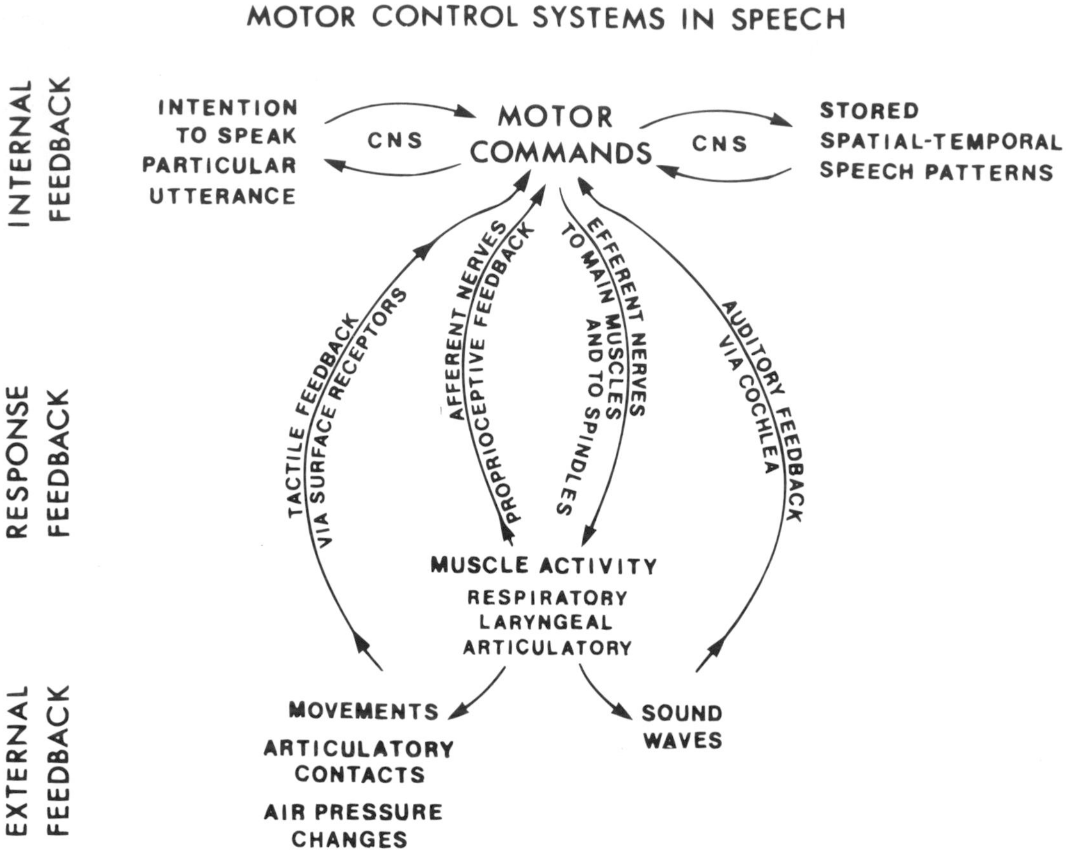

Figure 5.54. A conceptualization of the feedback systems available to a speaker.

ternal feedback. Although it is known that the cerebellum and thalamus are active about 100 msec prior to movement, this discharge cannot be related directly to a specific feedback loop with present techniques.

In summary, there are several kinds of feedback available to the speaker (Fig. 5.54). These include the theoretically rapid, central internal feedback systems in the central nervous system, capable of feedforward (prediction) and high-level feedback of initiated motor commands; the relatively fast, proprioceptive response feedback systems of the peripheral nervous system, capable of movement and positional feedback for the fine control needed in skilled motor acts; and the slower, external feedback of the results of motor acts, including, for speech, the acoustic signal, the air pressure variations, and the articulators touching one another. The more central the system, the earlier it can feed back information and the more effective it can be for ongoing control of rapid and complex motor patterns. The more peripheral systems, operating after the motor response, can be effective for comparing result with intention and may, therefore, be important for learning a new motor pattern.

Developmental Research on Feedback Mechanisms

As we have seen, most of the experimental evidence provided by normally skilled speakers seems to indicate that feedback is not essential for the maintenance of speech production. But we ought to consider the possibility that the degree of dependence upon control systems of adolescents and adults may be quite different from the degree to which infants and young children use these feedback systems when they are learning to speak.

No one who is aware of the difficulty encountered by children with profound hearing loss in learning speech can doubt the importance to the developing speaker of comparing his own auditory output to the speech of the community in which he lives. People deafened later in life, however, suffer relatively minor consequences in speech intelligibility. Moreover, among the hearing population, children are more adept than adults in acquiring the stress and intonation patterns of a new language. This suggests a more adaptable auditory-motor linkage in young speakers than among older people. Siegel and his colleagues have found that normal 5-year-olds are more affected by delayed auditory feedback (DAF) than older (8-year-old) children. Adults were found to be least affected. Under DAF, the 5-year-olds displayed the greatest reduction in the number of syllables produced per second and the greatest increase in the number of nonfluencies per sentence. This indicates that children may monitor their speech more closely than adults and so are less able to ignore the delay in feedback. An investigation by MacKay showed younger children to be maximally affected by a different delay than adults—500 msec for the 4 to 6-year-olds and 375 msec for the 7 to 9-year-olds, rather than the 200 msec delay that maximally affects adults. It seems that children are more affected than adults only when there is a mismatch between auditory and proprioceptive information. When feedback information is simply diminished, there is no marked difference between groups. When speaking in the presence of noise, children increase their vocal intensity as adults do, and interference with the sense of taction by the nerve block technique shows the same minor effect upon the speech of 4-year-olds as it does for adults.

The essential combination for learning coordinated speech gestures is perhaps proprioception and audition. Proprioceptive information is available during muscle length changes and the child need not wait for the result of the movement to get the feel of the gestural pattern. Also, because the primary afferents from the spindles are larger than the afferents from the tactile receptors, they feed back the information more quickly. The sense of movement can then be associated with its acoustic and tactile results, and the whole sensation can be compared to the intended sound pattern. Thus, a child trying to perfect his production of the word "ball," makes a stab at it based on what he has learned from previous trials, senses the movements and positions of his articulators, which he quickly associates with their tactile and acoustic results, and compares this output with the adult sound of "ball," a sound pattern he has stored. It is difficult to test the importance of proprioception. Auditory or tactile masking alone are insufficient to disrupt speech when testing linguistic items that the child already knows. Future studies should focus on the effects of interference with feedback channels while subjects, both children and adults, are learning new speech patterns.

MODELS OF SPEECH PRODUCTION

When we partially understand a system, such as the speech production mechanism, we sometimes make a model of it. A model is a simplification of a system, or part a system. By testing the model under various conditions, to see if it behaves like the system or the part of it that we seek to understand, we may learn something about the system.

Many different types of models may be fashioned. Perhaps the most obvious type is the mechanical model, a physical version of the system to be tested. Békésy, for example, constructed a mechanical model of the cochlea, in which the basilar membrane was represented by a sheet of rubber of varying thickness. The model looked like a tank of water with a flexible shelf in it. No attempt was made to have it look like the cochlea. Yet it served as the model of von Békésy's traveling wave theory of hearing. At high frequencies of vibration, the waves set up in the tank produced maximum vibrations in the thin part of the flexible shelf, and at low frequencies of vibration, the displacement of the membrane was greatest for the thicker portion at the far end of the tank.

If von Békésy were constructing his model today, he most likely would have used a computer to create a representation of his mechanical "cochlea." This type of model can be generated by feeding a physical description of the system into a computer along with the rules by which the system is presumed to operate. The rapid calculating and graphics capabilities of the computer can then be used to determine the changes in the system under various conditions and to display them visually for inspection. An example of this type of computer modelling is Flanagan's work at Bell Laboratories on a two-mass model of the vocal folds (in which the upper and lower parts reflect the vertical phase differences that we have described in Chapter 4). Computers are also used today for purely mathematical modeling. This type of computer modelling is, of course, a much faster and more complex extension of the sort of work that was once done with pencil and paper, slide rules, and mechanical calculating machines.

We should note that the validity of all modelling depends to a great extent on the accurate description of the system. If von Békésy's understanding of the structure of the basilar membrane had been faulty, the vibratory pattern of his rubber sheet might have been very different from that found within the human cochlea. The same would be true for the vibratory patterns that Flanagan found for the vocal folds if either his description of the folds or the rules he projected for their response had been incorrect.

Although mechanical and computer modelling have been used in connection with speech, most speech production models are expressed in natural language. They consist of verbal descriptions, with charts, definitions, and rules. We shall discuss several models of this type, including those with a strong linguistic basis and emphasis, those which view the goal of speech production as the attainment of targets of one sort or another, those which focus on the role of timing and those which take a stand on the role of feedback in speech production.

Linguistically Oriented Models

Linguistic and phonetic analysis has long been concerned with the structure of the sound systems of languages. Indeed, one of the outcomes of such an analysis, the International Phonetic Alphabet (IPA), can be understood as an implied model of speech production because the symbols it employs are tacit representations of the parameters of articulation (e.g, manner and place of articulation, voicing for consonants, and tongue, lip and jaw position for vowels).

In 1966, Gordon Peterson and June Shoup, taking the IPA as a starting point, attempted to describe all the sounds of spoken language, using physiological and acoustic data from experimental phonetics, as their basis. The physiological component of their model is built from 19 preliminary definitions, 22 axioms, and 77 definitions, followed by 2 phonetic charts, the first representing 8 manners of articulation in 13 horizontal and 13 vertical places of articulation, and the second chart representing 12 secondary phonetic parameters. In addition, they also described 3 parameters of prosody. The acoustic component of their model comprises verbal and mathematical descriptions of 6 types of speech waves, 6 types of acoustic phonetic parameters, and 3 acoustic parameters of prosody. Finally, the authors relate acoustic phonetics to physiological phonetics by discussing the transformations possible between the physiological and acoustic characteristics of speech.

Another linguistically based model is based on a distinctive feature analysis of speech sounds. Early work on this type of model was done by Roman Jakobson, Gunnar Fant, and Morris Halle. They presented a model which attempted to account for the phonetic features of all known languages. An account of the model, "Preliminaries to Speech Analysis," appeared in a Massachusetts Institute of Technology Acoustics Laboratory Report in 1952 and was later published. The model employed was based upon a binary system of description, in which each sound was specified in terms of one member of a pair of opposing production features. These features were largely derived from the inspection of sound spectrograms, which were then being systematically explored for the first time. The model posits a set of 12 features, including fundamental and secondary acoustic source features and features of resonance.

In 1968, with the publication of *The Sound Pattern of English*, Noah Chomsky and Morris Halle redesigned the binary distinctive feature system in articulatory rather than in acoustic terms. For example, instead of the Jakobson, Fant, and Halle opposition of "grave" versus "acute," in which the "grave" feature refers to sounds which occupy the lower frequency regions of the spectrum, and the "acute" feature refers to the high frequency regions of the spectrum, Chomsky and Halle reformulated the distinctive features in terms of such articulatory features as ± "rounded," ± "high tongue body," and ± "back tongue body." They posited a total of 27 feature pairs, divided among the categories of major class features, cavity features, manner of articulation features, and source features.

Because each sound in a sequence is described by a (unique) set of distinctive features, this model is essentially static. It cannot account for the dynamic nature of speech without a supplementary set of rules to account for the acoustic results of the articulatory features, including the assimilative and coarticulatory effects of context. To be fair, the authors are more interested in the phonological competence of speakers than in the realization of their phonetic output, and even though they do not specify the role of timing and the effects of context, the Chomsky and Halle features are more useful to a speech production model than a purely acoustic set of features.

Students should be aware that there is no one set of distinctive features that is universally accepted for use in speech analysis or in modelling speech production. Individual linguists and phoneticians propose different feature inventories, often to meet different requirements. Clearly, someone interested in phonology will make different decisions about the number and types of features that are important, as opposed to someone interested in specifying the physiological, articulatory or acoustic output of the speech mechanism. There is even a disparity of opinion concerning the binary nature of the features. Ladefoged, for instance, proposes a system in which each occurrence of a feature is specified by a percentage, indicating the extent to which it is employed. This strategy permits both a phonological characterization of each sound and a characterization of each sound as it varies in context.

The final linguistically oriented model of speech production that we shall consider stems from work on speech perception. It was first presented in a paper by Liberman, Cooper, Shankweiler, and Studdert-Kennedy written in 1967. As we shall see in the next chapter, this paper presented a theory that linked speech perception to speech production. The authors maintained that speech sounds are encoded in the acoustic signal because of the way in which they are produced by the speech mechanism. They therefore found it necessary to project a model of speech production which explained the process by which the speech sounds become encoded. The model depicts the encoding process as a series of transformations, from the phonemes (or the sets of features which they comprise) to the acoustic signal which transmits them in their encoded forms to the listener. This model rejects the notion that there is a simple and direct conversion from phoneme to sound. It holds, rather, that there is acoustic "smearing" of the phonemes, resulting from parallel processing of more than one phoneme simultaneously (Fig. 5.55).

According to this model, the appropriate neuromotor rules govern the simultaneous transmission of neural signals to many muscles. The articulatory gestures produced when these muscles contract cause variations in vocal tract shape which conform to a set of articulatory rules. The time-varying changes in cavity shape are then converted into what we hear as speech by a set of acoustic rules. The

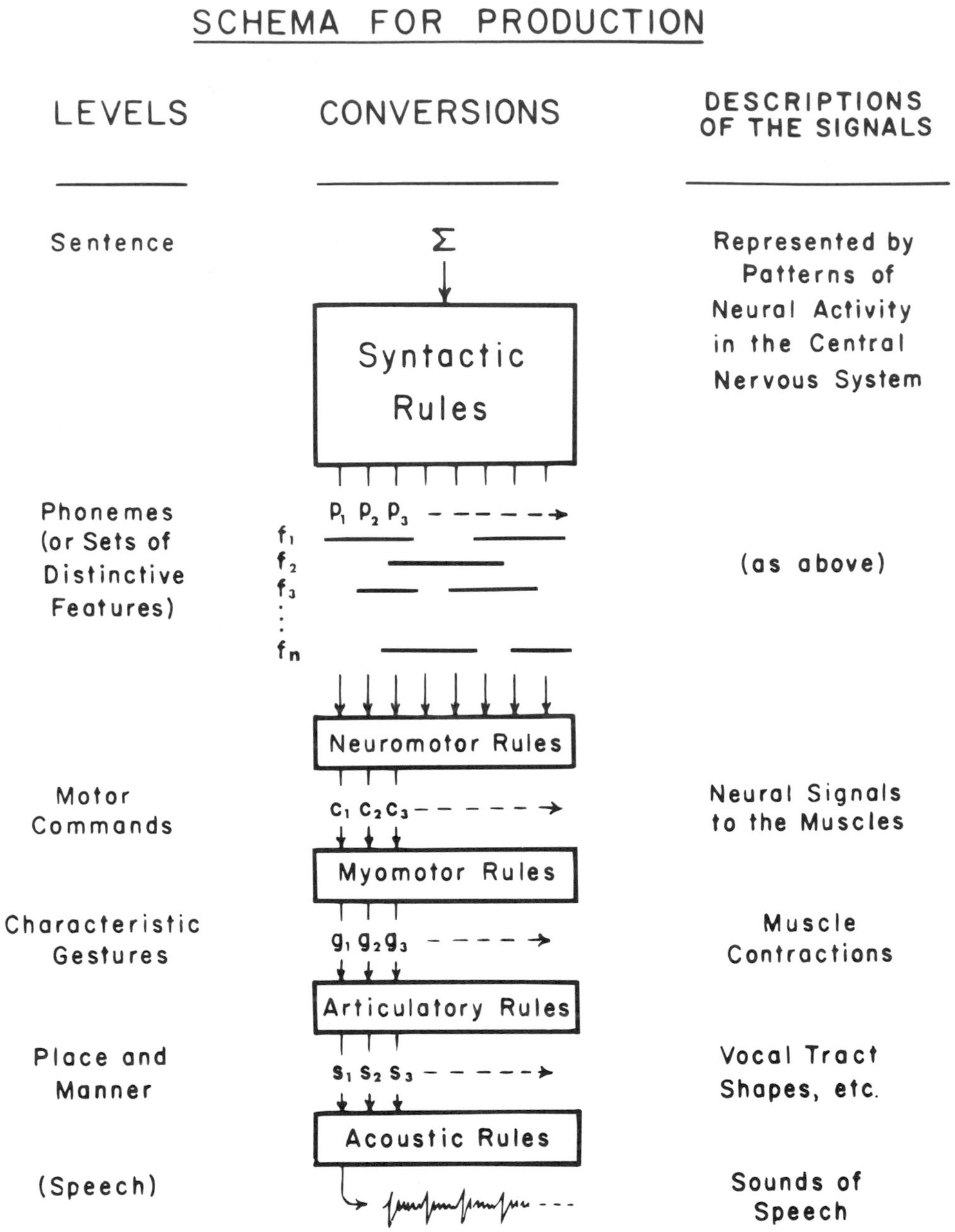

Figure 5.55. A diagram of the speech production process, as conceptualized by Liberman. Perception is conceived as the reverse of the process diagrammed here. (Reprinted with permission from A. M. Liberman *et al.*: Psychological Review. 74, © 1967, American Psychological Association.)

point is, that in these multiple conversions, the phoneme as a static entity is modified by its context, because more than one phoneme is being transmitted by the motor system of the speaker at one time. The acoustic signal must therefore reflect the overlap in muscle activity and articulatory movements. We will describe this model further in the context of speech perception in the next chapter. The models discussed above are strongly influenced by linguistic considerations. Other models of speech production emphasize neurophysiological considerations more strongly.

Target Models

It is not difficult to think of speech production as a process in which a speaker attempts to attain a sequence of targets corresponding to the speech sounds he is attempting to produce. Theorists have used this concept to construct models of speech production, although there is some disagreement over whether the targets are spatial, auditory/acoustic, or somewhat more abstract.

Let us first consider models that propose spatial targets as the basis of speech production. Peter MacNeilage, in a 1970 paper "Motor Control of Serial Ordering of Speech," has presented a speech production model compatible with Hebb's idea of motor equivalence and the then current work on γ loop control in motor systems. An example of motor equivalence is the fact that if you can write the letter B with your right hand, you will be able to write it with your left hand, or by holding the pencil between your toes. Even though the muscles used are different and you may be clumsier in some versions than others, your production will retain some aspects of your individual style. A specific example of motor equivalence in speech, given by MacNeilage, is the ability of any speaker to produce "pipe speech," even though the jaw, tongue, and lip movements and underlying muscle activity must be altered. You can sense the differences in muscular behavior by saying "hot" first while your jaw is lowered and your mouth open, and then again with your teeth immobilized by holding a pencil or pipe between your teeth. MacNeilage argues that this sort of motor equivalence provides an example of the fact that speakers do not issue an invariant set of motor commands for each speech segment, because speakers must approach the vocal tract shapes for a particular segment from many different starting positions. Rather, the goal of the speaker is a spatial target. In the brain, there is an internalized spatial representation of the areas of the vocal tract within which the articulators move. To reach a desired spatial target, the speaker must adapt his articulatory movements to the target position in relation to the particular starting position of the articulators at a given time. The theory posits speech production essentially as an open loop system, with a series of targets specified in advance, although it is likely that the γ loop feedback mechanism facilitates the articulatory adjustments required in varying contexts by monitoring muscle behavior.

Acoustic/auditory targets (as opposed to spatial targets) have also been used as a basis for modeling speech production. The concept of acoustic/auditory targets was implied above in our account of Björn Lindblom's observations on vowel reduction. These targets are presumably specified in terms of invariant vowel formant frequencies for which the speaker aims with varying degrees of success: As we have seen, weakly stressed vowels are reduced, becoming more schwa-like as the result of articulatory undershoot. Nonetheless, listeners are able to compensate perceptually for the reduction and so recover the identity of the vowel as if the targets had, in fact, been attained. Hence the target is idealized psychologically by the listener, and is not a function of motor equivalence in the articulation of the speaker.

It is also possible to construct models that employ both spatial and acoustic auditory targets. Sibout Nooteboom concurs with MacNeilage's target theory, finding an internalized spatial coordinate system more efficient than stored motor patterns for each possible action, but he proposes that MacNeilage did not go far enough in his model. MacNeilage proposes spatial targets as the goals with γ loop control of muscle activity to facilitate the articulatory adjustments that are conditioned by context and required to achieve motor equivalence. Nooteboom, referring to the work of Lindblom, cautions that the goal of the speaker is to be understood, and is, therefore, primarily a perceptual one. Even spatial targets sometimes vary, and so motor equivalence is not always required for the speaker to a produce a given sound in a variety of phonetic contexts. Nooteboom offers the example of speakers producing [u] with and without lip rounding. If lip protrusion is not used to lengthen the tract for the lowering of formants, then depression of the larynx may be substituted to achieve the desired acoustic result. The spatial targets thus differ from one production strategy to the other, but both generate the same phoneme, /u/. Nooteboom's speech production model would include an internal representation of an auditory perceptual space. Accessing both the auditory and the spatial representations, the brain of the speaker uses rules relating these representations to calculate the motor commands necessary to attain a target starting from any current articulatory state.

Ladefoged has also suggested an acoustic/auditory theory of speech production, at least for vowels. He implies that there may be a difference in production control for consonants and for vowels.

Targets of a more abstract nature than articulatory-spatial configurations or formant frequencies have been proposed by action theorists such as Fowler. They posit a model of speech production that directly transforms phonological targets into sound without multiple conversions. A target in this view is a relatively unspecified vocal tract adjustment. Self-regulated functional units of muscle groups and articulators control both the active and passive forces required to attain the target. There is an ecological emphasis in this theory that takes into account both the inherent mechanical properties of the speech production system (the momentary tension, elasticity, and inertia acting on the muscle groups involved) and the external mechanical influences on the system (a child places his hand on a speaker's chin).

Timing Models

The search for the invariant correlate of the phoneme is not the only concern of the experimental phonetician. The fact that speech is ordered in time has led to several speech production models which emphasize timing. Karl Lashley's classic paper, published in 1951, succeeded in discrediting associate chain theories of speech production in the minds of most theorists who have followed him. An associate chain theory holds that each movement serves as the stimulus for the movement which follows it. In contrast, Lashley theorized that speech production incorporates several interacting but independent systems corresponding to the speaker's intention, the store of images and words, the motor organization, and a temporal ordering mechanism. The important point here is that the temporal ordering is not inherent in the idea, the word, or the motor organization, but it can control their ordering. The temporal ordering device is a syntax, an integrating schema, which orders the words and the motor activity of speech production. Lashley's is an open loop model, comprising continually interactive systems.

Sven Öhman, has constructed a mathematical model of the articulation of VCV (vowel-consonant-vowel) utterances in which the vocal tract is sectioned by 50 radial planes. Using the highest point of the palate and the beginning of the curved oral cavity as coordinates, the model mathematically summarizes the coarticulation that Öhman described from spectrograms. The model includes static properties of phonemes and dynamic rules which blend the phonemes into running speech. Öhman views the temporal ordering of motor activity as the result of the speaker superimposing consonant articulations on what is essentially a string of vowel-to-vowel articulations. This assumption accounts for the coarticulatory effects he observed in the VCV syllables and also implies separate control mechanisms for vowels and consonants.

William Henke has developed a computer model based on articulatory data. The timing component of the model is a scan ahead mechanism for motor control. Motor commands may be initiated simultaneously for a sequence of segments, as long as no intervening segment in the sequence requires a contradictory command. For example, according to this sort of model, the scan ahead mechanism, operating on the intended production of the word "strew' (/stru/), would permit lip-rounding for the [u] to begin with the articulation of the [s], since none of the sounds before the /u/ requires some other lip posture. The model thus generates a string of phonemes with coarticulation resulting from the spread of features from one phone to other, adjacent phones. Research by Bell-Berti and Harris suggests that the features for a target phone simply begin at a fixed time before that phone and so do not actually migrate. This finding explains why a feature does not occur in an unlimited number of neighboring segments.

Rhythm is another temporal aspect of speech that has provided the basis for a model. James Martin has proposed a model of speech rhythm in which the timing of the more highly stressed syllables in a phrase is planned first and given primary articulatory emphasis by the speaker, while the timing and articulation of the lesser stressed syllables receive secondary consideration in planning and articulation. The production mechanism is under CNS control. Although some languages (English is one) appear to be more obviously stress-timed than others, Martin considers such relative timing patterns, or rhythms, to be universal. Stress timing (isochrony) is the tendency for primary stresses to occur at equal intervals in an utterance. Listeners seem to sense the rhythm of speech and use it to help predict the rest of a message.

However, when one sets out to measure the rhythm of speech in the laboratory, isochrony turns out to be as elusive as the phoneme. It may be that it exists in the mind of the speaker but is temporally blurred as it is transformed into the acoustic stream of speech, much as the features of segmental phonemes are smeared by coarticulation. The listener, however, according to Martin, is capable of perceptually reconstructing the intended isochronous timing (perhaps in a process analogous to the one in which the identities of reduced vowels are recovered), despite the irregularities in the speaker's rate or in other factors that contribute to the perception of rhythm.

Closed-Loop and Open-Loop Models

The status of feedback in the production of speech has motivated a number of models. As we saw above, in our discussion of feedback, that status has recently been questioned. A number of years ago, however, it was more or less generally assumed that feedback is an essential component of speech production, and the models of that period reflected that assumption. A classic (and the first) example of a closed-loop model was developed by Grant Fairbanks and published in 1954. Fairbanks depicted the speech mechanism as a servomechanism in which auditory, tactile and proprioceptive feedback played prominent roles.

The model is depicted graphically in Figure 5.56. The storage buffer holds in memory the utterance that is to be produced. The comparison unit performs two tasks: It relates the intended signal to the feedback of the actual output for correction, and it employs a predicting device so that the speech production process need not be delayed until the error signal disappears. When a discrepancy between the intended and the obtained signal appears in the comparison unit, it is sent to the mixer, so that the motor production control unit can be adjusted.

Among the first models to depict speech production as an open loop process was the one published in 1965 by the husband and wife research team of Kozhevnikov and Chistovich of the Pavlov Institute in Leningrad. It stimulated thought on speech organization by presenting a model of speech timing and of syllable control. By measuring the duration of phrases (*syntagma*) separated by pauses (the syntagma is sometimes one syllable, but averages seven), the investigators showed the pauses to be much more variable than the intervals within the syntagma. They concluded that time can only be measured meaningfully within a syntagma. When the rate of speech is changed within a syntagma, they found that the relative durations of the syllables and words remained constant; only by measuring the durational changes in consonants and vowels within each syllable did they find a significant difference in relative time. The duration of the consonant of the syllable changes little at faster or slower rates, but the duration of the vowel changes considerably. Kozhevnikov and Chistovich con-

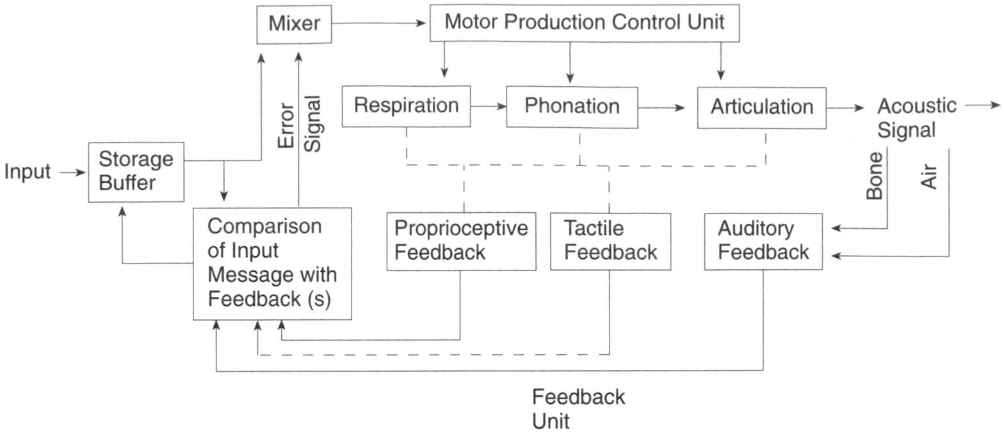

Figure 5.56. Fairbanks' model of the speech production process. (See text for explanation.) (Adapted from G. Fairbanks: *Journal of Speech and Hearing Disorders, 19,* 1954.)

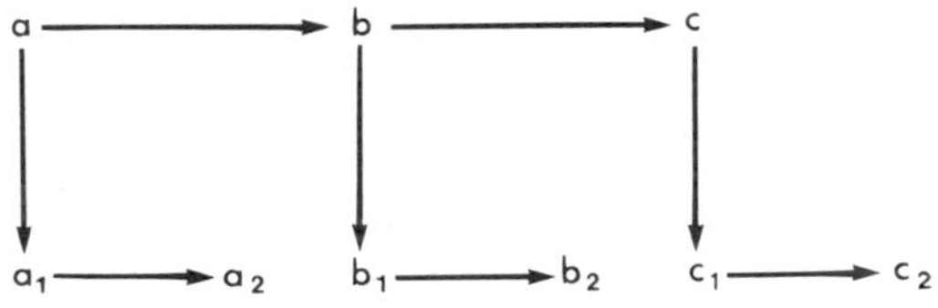

Figure 5.57. Commands for syllables *a, b,* and *c.* The syllable commands include consonant commands (a^1, b^1 *and* c^1) and vowel commands (a^2, b^2, *and* c^2). Commands for consonants and vowels may be issued simultaneously though they are realized sequentially. (Adapted from V. A. Kozhevnikov and L. A. Chistovich: *Speech: Articulation and Perception,* United States Department of Commerce © 1966.)

cluded that the organization of articulatory timing was contained in motor commands specifying complete syllables. The commands for syllable "a" (Fig. 5.57) include instructions for both the consonant "a_1," and the vowel "a_2." Further, as Henke's model predicted (see above) movements required by different segments within the syllable may be initiated simultaneously unless they are contradictory.

The control of the syllable commands was hypothesized to be open loop on the basis of a comparison of predictions from an open loop and a closed loop model. Figures 5.58 and 5.59 contrast the alternate hypotheses. In the first hypothesis, the command to begin each syllable awaits afferent feedback indicating that the preceding syllable command was issued. This is a form of closed loop control. The second hypothesis is that syllable commands are issued without afferent return from the muscle response. Testing these two hypotheses by measuring the inevitable durational changes obtained when a phrase is repeated about 150–200 times, Kozhevnikov and Chistovich tentatively concluded the first hypothesis of closed loop control to be less probable. The phrase was "Tonya topila banyu," which means "Tonya heated the bath." The investigators reasoned that if syllable duration varied more than the variability for the whole phrase, and if adjacent syllables were negatively correlated, it would support an open loop model. Finding the variance of the syllables to be considerably greater than the variance of the whole phrase, and a negative correlation between adjacent syllables, they concluded that syllables are articulatory events independent of adjacent syllables, in the sense that each syllable command is automatically initiated under the guidance of an unspecified rhythm generator in the nervous system.

At this point, it seems likely that speech operates on a system (see Figs. 5.54 and 5.61) in which the more general speech goal (the kind of sound stream the speaker intends to produce) is roughly planned by a feed-forward predictive flow of information within the brain (internal feedback) based on the speaker's

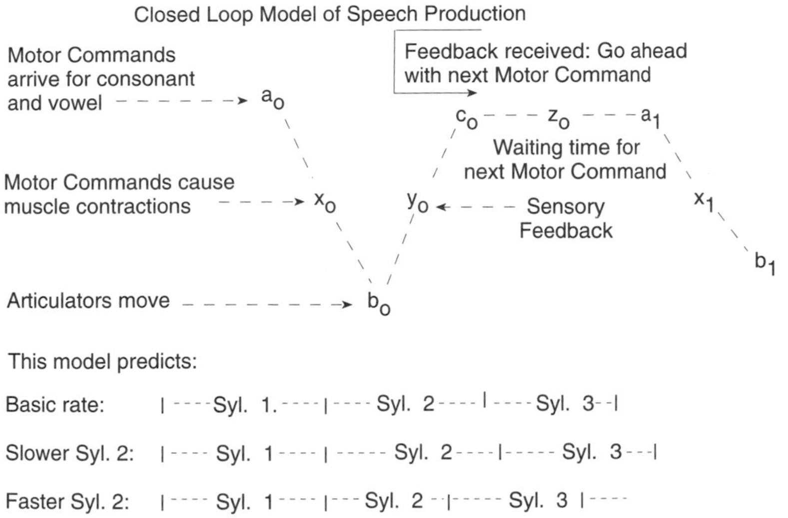

Figure 5.58. Hypothesis of closed loop control. The command to begin the next syllable is issued in response to an afferent impulse indicating the beginning of the preceding syllable. a_0, and a_1 are the moments of arrival of the syllable commands; b_0, and b_1 are the moments of the beginning of the corresponding movements; and c_0, and c_1 are the moments of entry into the nervous system of the afferent impulsation indicating the beginning of the movement. (x and y indicate time for motor and sensory transfer, z, the interval between movement and the next command.) (Adapted from V. A. Kozhevnikov and L. A. Chistovich: *Speech: Articulation and Perception,* United States Department of Commerce © 1966.)

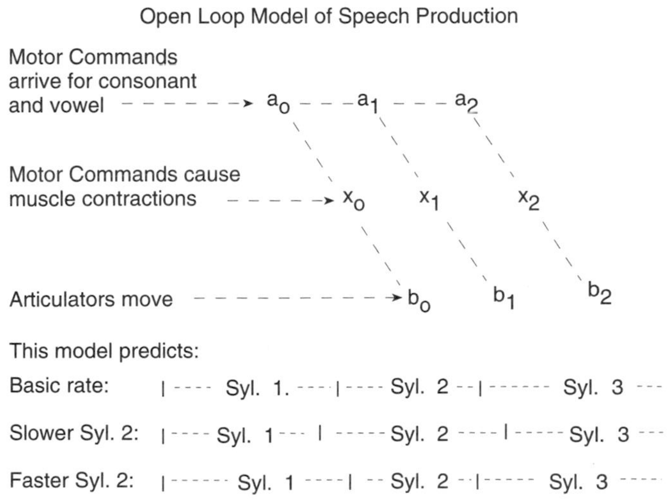

Figure 5.59. Hypothesis of open loop control. Commands for successive syllables are centrally issued. Afferent impulses do not affect the onset of successive syllables. *Symbols* as in Figure 4102 (Adapted from V. A. Kozhevnikov and L. A. Chistovich: *Speech: Articulation and Perception,* United States Department of Commerce © 1966.)

knowledge of acoustics of speech coupled with knowledge of his or her own speech production system. The details of muscle activity and coarticulation are the natural result of muscle groups cooperating to perform a unified function. The flow of proprioceptive information among these groups of muscles is normally available and is important to the establishment of speech patterns in children but may be largely redundant for those who have learned to speak. Much of the tactile and auditory feedback (external feedback) available to the speaker is not thought to be used for ongoing control, but rather is reserved for catching and correcting errors, and for maintaining an internal schema. This model does not support the notion that the speech production mechanism of the established speaker acts like a servomechanism.

Questions of the role of closed and open loop control systems for speech remain unresolved today. So, too, do the fundamental principles governing motor programming, as they are revealed in speech rhythm and coarticulation. As our knowledge increases, the models, the feature systems, and even the definitions will continue to be modified. There is no better way to realize both how much and how little we know and how complex speech production is, than to describe just the peripheral events that occur in the production of a short utterance. The last section of this chapter is such a description.

PRODUCTION OF A SENTENCE

We beat you in soccer:
[ˈwiˈbiˈtjuənˈsɑkɝ] or [ˈwiˈbiˈtʃunˈsɑkɝ]

Having been soundly defeated by a rival college football team, a member of the defeated team retorted to a comment by one of the victors with "We may have lost in football, but we beat you in soccer." If we were inside the brain of that speaker pushing buttons to produce "we beat you in soccer," what might be the order and integration of the commands to the speech production mechanism? The phrase is appealing because it contains stops, fricatives, a nasal, semivowels, and our favorite vowels [i], [ɑ], and [u]. Also, when said with the [ju] unassimilated with the [t] as in the first alternative pronunciation, there is a pleasing symmetry in having [wi] and [ju], which are not only opposites in that they refer to the rival teams, but are also spectrographic mirror images of one another, [wi] starting at an acoustic [u] and gliding to [i], while [ju] starts at an acoustic [i] and glides to [u] (Fig. 5.60).

Whatever intentions the speaker may have had of retribution, of a desire to inform, or merely of offering a friendly but slightly barbed joke, we shall not attempt to determine. Nor shall we trace the interactions of syntactic and semantic recall and decision. Presuming that "we beat you in soccer" was put momentarily in a buffer for output, and that the timing and prosodic control was imposed upon it as it was fed out into motor commands, we shall indicate some of the motor events peripheral to the more general motor goals, whatever they may have been. The logical way to indicate the motor events is in terms of nerves, muscles, movements and resulting cavity changes, air pressure changes, and acoustic results. Omissions outnumber inclusions. Not included are all the constantly effective passive forces of elasticity, gravity, mass, and inertia. Only some of the obvious active muscle forces are included. Auxiliary muscle activity and agonist-antagonist relationships are not described. Also omitted are the many possible transmissions of sensory information from changes in muscle length, from contact between articulators, and from acoustic/auditory signals, which provide the speaker with information about his performance. We have made some specific assumptions, however, about the particular way (out of many possibilities) in which the speaker has articulated the sentence in order to make the description concrete. Despite the omissions, the exercise is worth doing, if only to demonstrate the interrelationships among the processes of respiration, laryngeal activity, and articulation (activities which are usually described separately) and to remind ourselves of the complexity of speech.

The speaker, let us say, needs a quick inhalation for the phrase to begin (see Table 5.3).

Table 5.3. Production of a Sentence (See footnote at end of table for explanation of abbreviations used.)

Innervation	Muscles	Movements	Pressure changes	Result
Phrenic n. →	Diaphragm →	Lowering thoracic floor →	Thoracic vertical volume increase, pressure decrease →	Inhalation
Thoracic n. (T_1-T_{11}) →	EIm and interchondral IIm →	Ribs elevated and expanded →	Lateral and anterior-posterior thoracic volume increase, pressure decrease →	Inhalation (~65% VC)
XII n. →	GGm →	Tongue elevated to 'ready' position		
VII n. →	OOm →	Lip protrustion for [w]		
XI n. →	LPm →	Velum raised and backed to block nasal resonance during [wibitju]		
XII n. →	SGm →	Tongue dorsum elevated to [u] position for [w] →	Lower the resonance characteristics by elongated vocal tract	
X n. →	IAm →	Adduction of vocal folds for [wibi]		
X n. →	LCAm →	Aids in adduction of vocal folds		

(continued)

Table 5.3.–*continued*

Innervation	Muscles	Movements	Pressure changes	Result
	Diaphragm relaxes gradually →	Thorax and lungs slowly restored by elasticity, gravity, and torque →	Decrease in vertical thoracic volume; pressure increase →	Exhalation of about 7 cm H_2O P_s during utterance
		Folds part as high velocity air flows ←	P_s opens glottis ←	
		between them →	Bernoulli effect (negative	
		Adducts folds ←	pressure between vocal folds)	
		→	P_s builds and opens glottis again →	Repetition of this cycle releases a rapid train of air pulses which excite air (voicing) in broad band of
			Source sound ← amplified and filtered by resonance of vocal tract set for	freq. (f_0 and harmonics) during [wibi]
			[u] →	Onset of [w]; low freq. periodic sound
XII n. →	GGm contracts as SGm relaxes →	Tongue moves from high back to high front for [wi] and remains for [bit] →	Phonated sound pressure resonated in changing tract [u] → [i] →	F_2 glides up from low resonances of [u] tract to high resonances of [i] tract producing [wi]
VII n. →	Rm contracts as OOm relaxes →	Lips move from rounded to spread for [wi] → (to Pressure changes)		

X n. →	IAm continues to contract but LCAm relaxes →	Glottis more open continues to vibrate →	More P_s air released into tract for stop	
VII n. →	OOm →	Lips close →	Pressure builds behind closure →	Vocal tract resonances damped
	OOm relaxes →	Lips forced open for [b] (← from Pressure builds behind closure)	Sharp air pulse released without aspiration →	Transient aperiodic burst added to phonation for [b]
T_1–T_{11} →	IIm →	Depresses ribs →	Adds pressure to P_S →	Increases intensity for stressed [i]
XII n. →	GGm remains contracted →	Tongue blade high in oral cavity; pharyngeal cavity larger, oral smaller than neutral →	Pressure wave from glottis amplified by resonances of vocal tract →	Low F_1; high F_2 and F_3 due to small oral cavity [i]
X n. →	PCAm →	Abduct vocal folds; vibration stops →	Increased airflow into oral cavity for stop/affricate	
XII n. →	SLm added to GGm →	Tongue tip and blade up for alveolar contact →	Intraoral pressure builds behind occlusion →	Silence during closure

(continued)

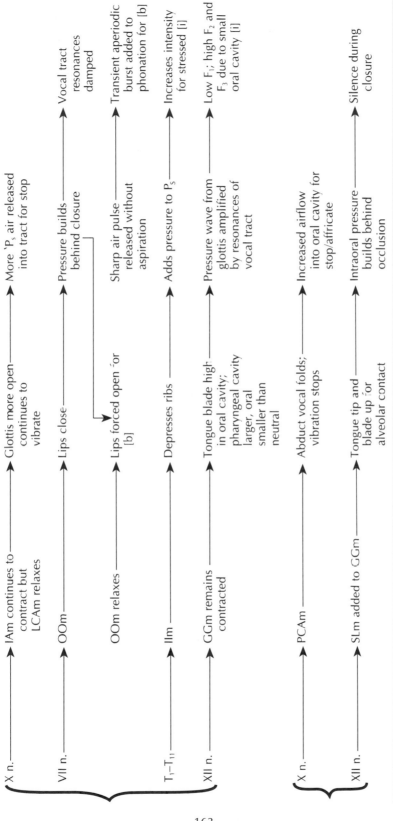

Table 5.3.–*continued*

Innervation	Muscles	Movements	Pressure changes	Result
XII n. →	SLm relaxes →	Contract released →	Sharp air pulse released with aspiration →	Transient aperiodic high freq. burst [t]
X n. →	IAm and LCAm →	Adduct vocal folds to resume phonation →	Sudden reduction in intraoral pressure →	f_o and [i] resonance
XII n. →	GGm still active giving way to SGm contraction →	Tongue remains high for [i] shape at onset of [i] and shifts to high back [u] shape →	Resonances change from [i] to [u] →	F_1 stays low; F_2 goes from high to low freq. [ju]
VII n. →	OOm →	Lips protrude (→ Resonances change from [i] to [u])		
Or alternate pronunciation: [tʃən]				
		Slow release of blade, into palatal constriction →	Higher velocity airflow through constriction →	[ʃ] turbulence at release of stop: [tʃ] affricate
XII n. →	GGm still active giving way to SGm contraction →	Tongue backing and elevating to [u] position →	Lower resonances →	Lower formants
X n. →	IAm and LCAm →	Adducts vocal folds; resumes phonation for [uən] →	Reduced intraoral pressure →	f_o and [u] resonances
VII n. →	OOm →	Lip protrusion →	Lengthen tract, lowering resonances →	Lower formants

XII n. inactive →		Tongue returns to neutral →	Neutral resonances of [ə] →	Evenly spaced formants
XII n. active →	SLm →	Blade raised to alveolar ridge →	Small pressure increase within oral cavity →	F_2 rising
XI n. decreases activity →	LPm relaxes →	Velum lowers; opening to nasal cavities →	Pressure drop as tract volume increases →	Low freq. nasal resonance added; also antiresonances [n]

Or alternate: /n̩/

(Same as above but timing is different, with first alternative [ən] having oral to nasal resonance transition and second alternative [n̩]having faster velar lowering.

XII n. →	SLm →	Blade up to alveolar ridge →	Intraoral pressure increase →	F_2 rising
XI n. →	PGm →	Lowers velum →	Sudden pressure drop; nasal resonance →	Low freq. nasal resonance; upper formant antiresonances

(continued)

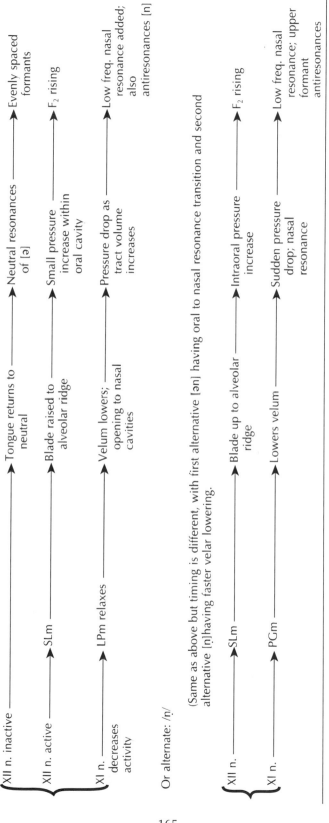

Table 5.3.—*continued*

Innervation	Muscles	Movements	Pressure changes	Result
XI n.	LPm	Abrupt high elevation and backing of velum, especially for [s] but maintained for rest of utterance		
X n.	PCAm	Abduction of vocal folds to stop phonation	Airflow increased for high pressure fricative	
XII n.	GGm with SLm (or ILm if tip down)	Blade to palate constriction	High pressure flow through constriction; turbulence	Aperiodic noise 4 kHz and higher [s]
XII n.	SLm (or ILm) remains active	Blade remains high for [s] as		
	HGm contracts	Dorsum starts to lower for [a]	Pressure reduced as oral cavity enlarges	
V n.	ABDm	Opens jaw		
X n.	IAm and LCAm	Adducts vocal folds resume phonation	Sound pressure from glottis	
T_1–T_{11}	IIm	Ribs depressed	P_s increased; vocal fold increases opening amplitude	Increased intensity for stressed [ɑ]
X n.	CTm	Lengthens vocal folds	Increased tension of folds; faster vibration	Raise f_o for [sɑ] prominence
XII n.	Maintains HGm activity, as GGm and tip muscles relax	Ant. tongue lowers, occupying space in pharyngeal cavity	Increased volume in oral cavity; open tract increases SPL at output	High F_1; low F_2 for [ɑ] resonance

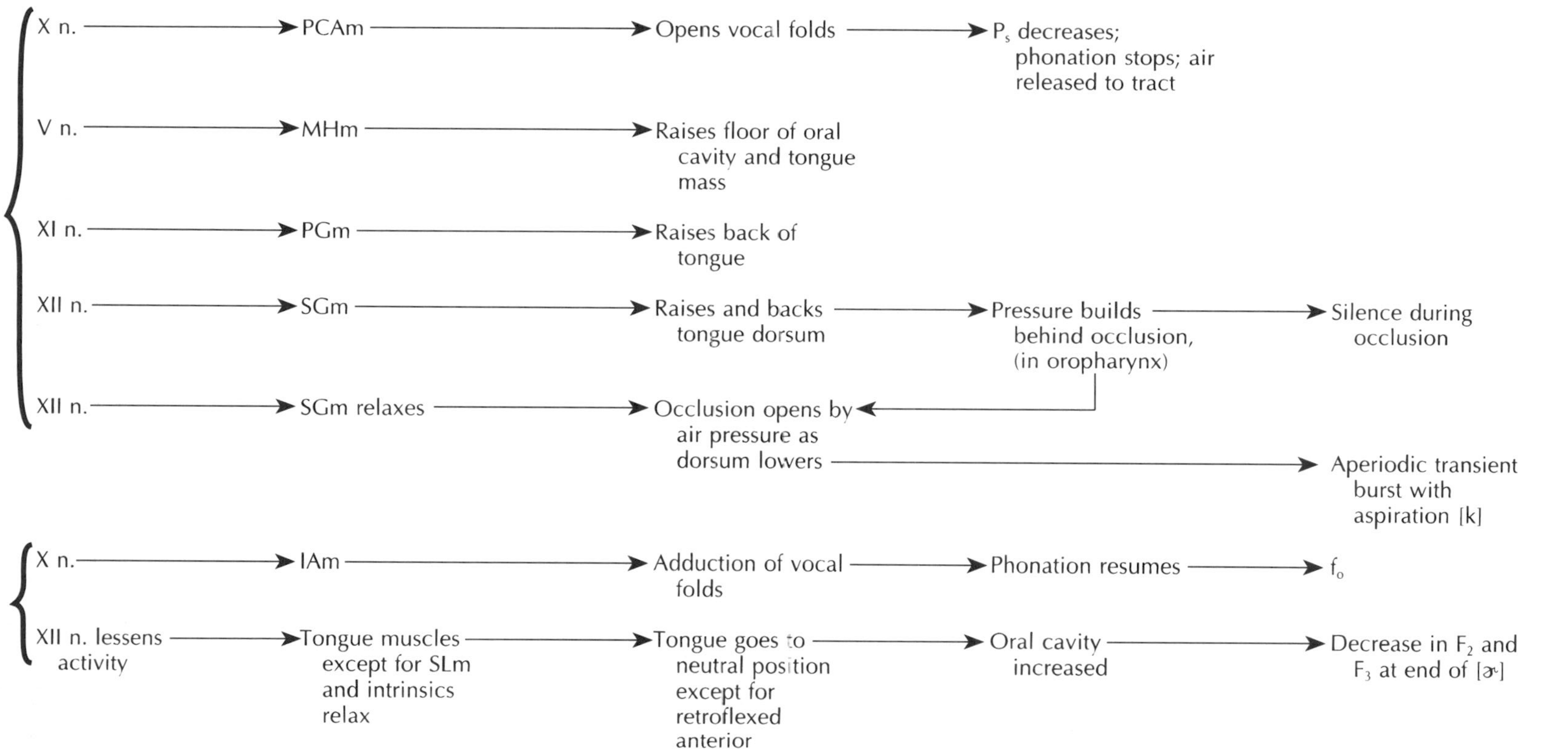

The abbreviations used for the muscles in the chart are: EIm, external intercostal; IIm, internal intercostal; GGm, genioglossus; OOm, orbicularis oris; LPm, levator palatini; SGm, styloglossus; IAm, interarytenoid; LCAm, lateral cricoarytenoid; Rm, risorius; PCAm, posterior cricoarytenoid; SLm, superior longitudinal; PGm, palatoglossus; ILm, inferior longitudinal; HGm, hyoglossus; ABDm, anterior belly of diagastric; CTm, cricothyroid; and MHm, mylohyoid muscle. Other abbreviations include SPL, sound pressure level; VC, vital capacity; P_s, subglottal pressure; f_o, fundamental frequency; F_1, F_2, F_3, first second and third formants; and freq., frequency.

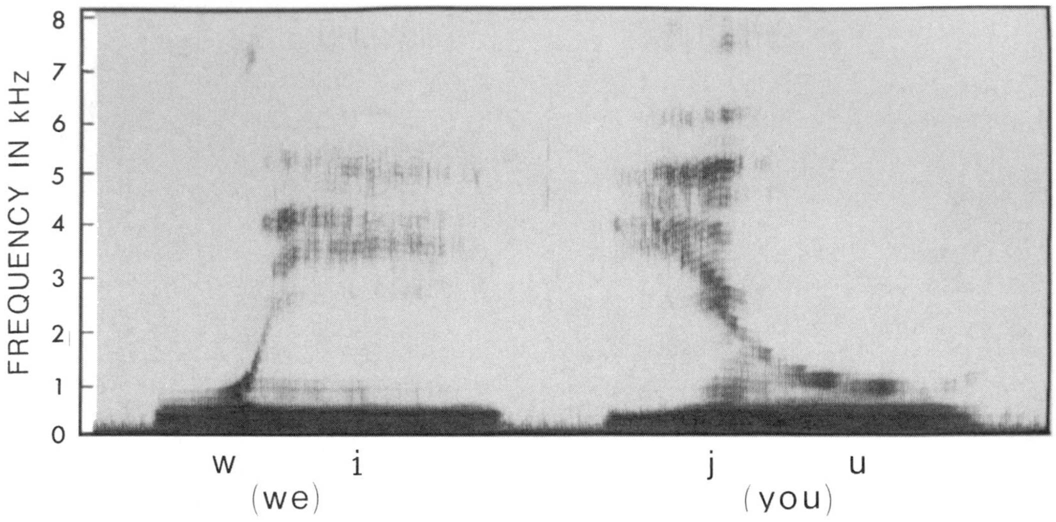

Figure 5.60. Spectrograms of [wi] and [ju].

Lest this attempt to interweave the respiratory, phonatory, and articulatory events of speech give anyone the mistaken notions that speech is the result of parallel but separate nerve to air pressure transformations or that there are direct phoneme to sound conversions, permit us to frame the process another way with a model that may better represent the coordination among muscle groups involved in speech. Figure 5.61 shows the initial speech goal to be an auditory perceptual representation of "we beat you in soccer." We know the general sound of the phrase that we plan to say. At this prespeech stage, there may be an internal loop of neural activity among the basal ganglia, cerebrum, and cerebellum of the brain, readying the system for speech output. The motor schema for producing the phrase may be in a rather abstract and flexible state, allowing for variations in the actual production. Rough specifications for changes in the speech mechanisms might form the schema. The general changes of the vocal tract for the utterance may be elicited from storage through cerebellar control of the motor areas of the cerebrum, and this representation may be fed forward in chunks of at least syllable size. The organization of particular muscle groups, such as the muscles that cooperate to regulate f_0, may be self-regulating via the response feedback of muscle spindles. We indicate how two chunks might overlap as the schema for [tʃuən] activates the muscle groups.

The muscle groups organized for a particular function not only are coordinated among themselves but also are coordinated with other muscle groups organized for a different function. This larger coordination may be made possible largely by feeding forward well-practiced interactions of specifications. The movements of articulators and the changes in cavity shapes are continuous, blurring phoneme and syllable boundaries as we define them. Variations in movement caused by context or by differences in initial position are the rule and are automatically produced as a result of the intimate coordination within each muscle group. Air pressure variations and the resultant acoustic stream are likewise dynamic in the ways they change across time. External feedback of the tactile and auditory feedback sensations may be too late to influence the peripheral motor patterns of muscle group activity, but they do influence the more general schema so that any mistake may be corrected on the next attempt.

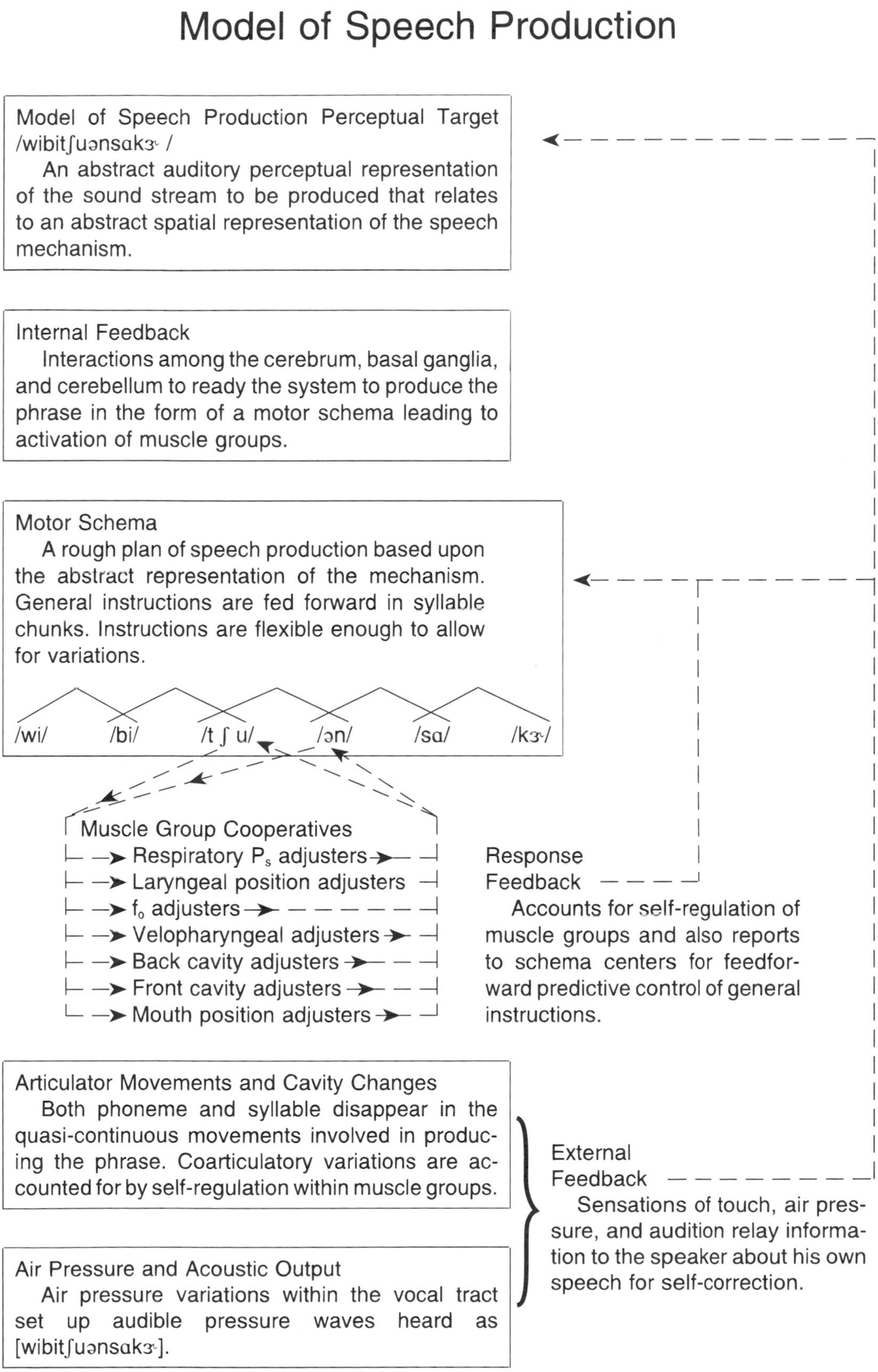
Model of Speech Production
Model of Speech Production Perceptual Target /wibitʃuənsɑkɝ /
An abstract auditory perceptual representation of the sound stream to be produced that relates to an abstract spatial representation of the speech mechanism.
Internal Feedback
Interactions among the cerebrum, basal ganglia, and cerebellum to ready the system to produce the phrase in the form of a motor schema leading to activation of muscle groups.
Motor Schema
A rough plan of speech production based upon the abstract representation of the mechanism. General instructions are fed forward in syllable chunks. Instructions are flexible enough to allow for variations.
/wi/ /bi/ /t ʃ u/ /ən/ /sɑ/ /kɝ/
Muscle Group Cooperatives
Respiratory P_s adjusters
Laryngeal position adjusters
f_0 adjusters
Velopharyngeal adjusters
Back cavity adjusters
Front cavity adjusters
Mouth position adjusters
Response Feedback
Accounts for self-regulation of muscle groups and also reports to schema centers for feedforward predictive control of general instructions.
Articulator Movements and Cavity Changes
Both phoneme and syllable disappear in the quasi-continuous movements involved in producing the phrase. Coarticulatory variations are accounted for by self-regulation within muscle groups.
Air Pressure and Acoustic Output
Air pressure variations within the vocal tract set up audible pressure waves heard as [wibitʃuənsɑkɝ].
External Feedback
Sensations of touch, air pressure, and audition relay information to the speaker about his own speech for self-correction.

Figure 5.61. Model of speech production. (See text for discussion.)

The goal of the speaker, then, is to produce sounds that fit an auditory perceptual target, in order to be understood by the perceptual system of a listener. Let us turn in the next chapter to a consideration of that perceptual system and of the processes that may be involved in listening.

REFERENCES

General Works on Speech Production

Harris, K. S., Physiological Aspects of Articulatory Behavior. In *Current Trends in Linguistics*, Vol. 12, No. 4, T. A. Sebeok (Ed.) The Hague: Mouton, 1974, pp. 2281–2302.

Kent, R. D., Atal, B. S., and Miller, J. L. (Eds.) *Papers in Speech Communication: Speech Production*. Woodbury, NY: Acoustical Society of America, 1991.

Lieberman, P., *Speech Physiology and Acoustic Phonetics: An Introduction*. New York: Macmillan, 1977.

Minifie, F., Hixon, T. J., and Williams, F. (Eds.), *Normal Aspects of Speech, Hearing, and Language*. Englewood Cliffs, NJ: Prentice-Hall, Inc., 1972.

Perkell, J. S., *Physiology of Speech Production: Results and Implications of a Quantitative Cineradiographic Study*. Cambridge, MA: M. I. T. Press, 1969.

Van Riper, C., and Irwin, J. V., *Voice and Articulation*. Englewood Cliffs, NJ: Prentice-Hall Inc., 1958.

General References in Acoustics of Speech

Denes, P. B., and Pinson, E. N., *The Speech Chain*. 2nd ed. New York: W.H. Freeman and Co., 1993.

Fant, G., *Acoustic Theory of Speech Production*. The Hague: Mouton, 1970.

Flanagan, J. L., *Speech Analysis, Synthesis, and Perception*. Berlin: Springer-Verlag, 1965.

Fry, D. B. (Ed.), *Acoustic Phonetics: A Course of Basic Readings*. New York: Cambridge University, 1976.

Kent, R. D. and Read, C., *The Acoustic Analysis of Speech*. San Diego: Singular Publishing Group, 1992.

Lehiste, I. (Ed.), *Readings in Acoustic Phonetics*. Cambridge, MA: M. I. T. Press, 1967.

Pickett, J. M., *The Sounds of Speech Communication*. Baltimore: University Park Press, 1980.

Potter, R. K., Kopp, G. A., and Green, H. C., *Visible Speech*. New York: D. Van Nostrand Co., Inc., 1947.

Articulation and Resonance References

Bell-Berti, F., The Velopharyngeal Mechanism: An Electromyographic Study. *Haskins Laboratories Status Report (Suppl.)*. New Haven, Connecticut: Haskins Laboratories, 1973.

Bell-Berti, F., Control of Pharyngeal Cavity Size for English Voiced and Voiceless Stops. *J. Acoust. Soc. Am. 57*, 1975, 456–461.

Bell-Berti, F., and Hirose, N., Palatal Activity in Voicing Distinctions: A Simultaneous Fiberoptic and Electromyographic Study. *J. Phonetics 3*, 1975, 69–74.

Chiba, T., and Kajiyama, M., *The Vowel: Its Nature and Structure*. Tokyo: Kaiseikan, 1941.

Crandall, I. B., Sounds of Speech. *Bell Syst. Tech. J. 4*, 1925, 586–626.

Fritzell, B., The Velopharyngeal Muscles in Speech: An Electromyographic and Cinefluorographic Study. *Acta Otolaryngolog. (Stockh.) Suppl. 250*, 1969.

Fujimura, O., Analysis of Nasal Consonants. *J. Acoust. Soc. Am. 34*, 1962, 1865–1875. Reprinted in Kent, R. D. *et al.* (q.v.), 301–311.

Heinz, J. M., and Stevens, K. N., On the Properties of Voiceless Fricative Consonants. *J. Acoust. Soc. Am. 33*, 1961, 589–596.

Holbrook, A., and Fairbanks, G., Diphthong Formants and their Movements. *J. Speech Hear. Res. 5*, 1962, 38–58.

Joos, M., Acoustic Phonetics. *Language*. Monograph 23 (Suppl. to Vol. 24), 1948.

Kuehn, D. P., and Dalston, R. M. Cleft Palate Studies Related to Velopharyngeal Function. In *Human Communication and Its Disorders*. H. Winitz (Ed.) Norwood, NJ: Ablex, 1988.

Kuhn, G. M., On the Front Cavity Resonance and its Possible Role in Speech Perception. *J. Acoust. Soc. Am. 58*, 1975, 428–433.

Ladefoged, P., *A Course in Phonetics*. 3rd Edition. New York: Harcourt Brace Javanovich, Inc., 1993.

Lisker, L., and Abramson, A. S., A Cross-Language Study of Voicing in Initial Stops: Acoustical Measurements. *Word 20*, 1964, 384–422.

Lubker, J. F., An Electromyographic-Cinefluorographic Investigation of Velar Function during Normal Speech Production. *Cleft Palate J. 5*, 1968, 1–18.

Moll, K., and Daniloff, R. G.. Investigation of the Timing of Velar Movements during Speech. *J. Acoust. Soc. Am. 50*, 1971, 678–684.

Netsell, R., Subglottal and Intraoral Air Pressures during the Intervocalic Contrast of /t/ and /d/. *Phonetica 20*, 1969, 68–73.

Peterson, G. E., and Barney, H. L., Control Methods Used in a Study of the Vowels. *J. Acoust. Soc. Am. 24*, 1952, 175–184.

Peterson, G. E., and Lehiste, I., Duration of Syllable Nuclei in English. *J. Acoust. Soc. Am. 32*, 1960, 693–703.

Peterson, G. E., and Lehiste, I., Transitions, Glides, and Diphthongs. *J. Acoust. Soc. Am. 33*, 1961, 268–277.

Raphael, L. J., and Bell-Berti, F. Tongue Musculature and the Feature of Tension in English Vowels. *Phonetica 32*, 1975, 61–73.

Rayleigh, J. W. S., *Theory of Sound*. London: Macmillan, 1878.

Shadle, C. H. Articulatory-Acoustic Relations in Fricative Consonants. In *Speech Production and Speech Modelling*. W. H. Hardcastle and A. Marchal (Eds.) Boston: 1990, 197–209.

Stevens, K. N., and House, A. S., An Acoustical Theory of Vowel Production and Some of its Implications. *J. Speech Hear. Res. 4*, 1961, 303–320.
Stevens, K. N., and House, A. S., Development of a Quantitative Description of Vowel Articulation. *J. Acoust. Soc. Am. 27*, 1955, 484–493. Reprinted in Kent, R. D., *et al.* (q.v.), 401–410.
Subtelny, J. D., Oya, N., and Subtelny, J. D., Cineradiographic Study of Sibilants. *Folio Phoniatr. (Basel) 24*, 1972, 30–50.
Tuller, B., Harris, K. S., and Gross, B. Electromyographic Study of the Jaw Muscles during Speech. *J. Phonetics 9*, 1981, 175–188.
Uldall, E., Transitions in Fricative Noise. *Lang. Speech. 7*, 1964, 13–15.

English Speech Sounds

Sound Influence References

Bell-Berti, F., and Harris, K. S., Some Aspects of Coarticulation. Paper presented at the International Congress of Phonetic Sciences, Leeds, England, Aug. 1975.
Bell-Berti, F., and Harris, K. S. Temporal Patterns of Coarticulation: Lip Rounding. *J. Acoust. Soc. Am. 71*, 1982, 449–454. Reprinted in Kent, R. D., *et al.* (q.v.), 599–604.
Borden, G. J., and Gay, T., Temporal Aspects of Articulatory Movements for /s/-Stop Clusters. *Phonetica. 36*, 1979., 21–31.
Daniloff, R. G., and Hammarberg, R. E., On Defining Coarticulation. *J. Phonetics. 1*, 1973, 239–248.
Daniloff, R. G., and Moll, K., Coarticulation of Liprounding. *J. Speech Hear. Res. 11*, 1968, 707–721.
Kent, R. D., and Minifie, F. D., Coarticulation in Recent Speech Production Models. *J. Phonetics. 5*, 1977, 115–135. Reprinted in Kent, R. D., *et al.* (q.v.), 651–669.
Kozhevnikov, V. A., and Chistovich, L. A., Rech artikulyatsya i vaspriyatie. Moscow-Leningrad, 1965. Translated as *Speech: Articulation and Perception*. Springfield, VA: Joint Publications Research Service. United States Department of Commerce, 1966.
Liberman, A. M., Cooper, F. S., Shankweiler. D. P., and Studdert-Kennedy, M., Perception of the Speech Code. *Psychol. Rev. 74*, 1967, 431–461.
Lindblom, B. E. F., Spectrographic Study of Vowel Reduction. *J. Acoust. Soc. Am. 35*, 1963, 1773–1781. Reprinted in Kent, R. D., *et al.* (q.v.), 517–525.
MacNeilage, P. F., Motor Control of Serial Ordering of Speech. *Psychol. Rev. 77*, 1970, 182–196. Reprinted in Kent, R. D., *et al.* (q.v.), 701–715.
MacNeilage, P. F., and De Clerk, J. L., On the Motor Control of Coarticulation in CVC Monosyllables. *J. Acoust. Soc. Am. 45*, 1969, 1217–1233.
Öhman, S. E. G., Coarticulation in VCV Utterances: Spectrographic Measurements. *J. Acoust. Soc. Am. 39*, 1966, 151–168. Reprinted in Kent, R. D., *et al.* (q.v.), 567–584.
Perkell, J. S., *Physiology of Speech Production: Results and Implications of a Quantitative Cineradiographic Study*. Cambridge, MA: M. I. T. Press, 1969.
Peterson, C. E.. and Shoup, J. E., A Physiological Theory of Phonetics. *J. Speech Hear. Res. 9*, 1966, 5–67.

Suprasegmentals References

Cooper, W. E., and Sorensen, J. M., *Fundamental Frequency in Sentence Production*. New York: Springer-Verlag, 1981.
Fry, D. B., Prosodic Phenomena. In *Manual of Phonetics*. B. Malmberg (Ed.) Amsterdam: North-Holland, 1970.
Lehiste, I. *Suprasegmentals*. Cambridge, MA: M. I. T. Press, 1970.
Lieberman, P., *Intonation, Perception and Language*. Cambridge, MA: M. I. T. Press, 1967.

Feedback References

General

Borden, G. J., An Interpretation of Research on Feedback Interruption. *Brain Lang. 7*, 1979, 307–319.
Ringel, R. L., Oral Sensation and Perception: A Selective Review. *ASHA Rep. 5*, 1970, 188–206.
Wiener, N., Cybernetics, *Sci. Am. 179*, 1948, 14–19.
Wiener, N., *The Human Use of Human Beings*. 2nd Ed. Rev. Garden City, NY: Doubleday, 1954.

Auditory Feedback

Black, J. W., The Effect of Delayed Side-Tone upon Vocal Rate and Intensity. *J. Speech Hear. Disord. 16*, 1951, 56–60.
Borden, G. J., Dorman, M. F., Freeman, F. J., and Raphael, L. J., Electromyographic Changes with Delayed Auditory Feedback of Speech. *J. Phonetics 5*, 1977, 1–8.
Fairbanks, G., and Guttman, N., Effects of Delayed Auditory Feedback upon Articulation. *J. Speech Hear. Res. 1*, 1958, 12–22.
Cooper, W. E., and Sorensen, J. M., *Fundamental Frequency in Sentence Production*. New York: Springer-Verlag, 1981.
Fairbanks, G., Selective Vocal Effects of Delayed Auditory Feedback. *J. Speech Hear. Disord. 20*, 1955, 333–346.
Garber, S. F., The Effects of Feedback Filtering on Nasality. Paper presented at ASHA convention, Houston, Nov., 1976.
Lane, H. L., Catania, A. C., and Stevens, S. S., Voice Level: Autophonic Scale, Perceived Loudness, and Effects of Side Tone. *J. Acoust. Soc. Am. 33*, 1961, 160–167.
Lane, H. L., and Tranel, B., The Lombard Sign and the Role of Hearing in Speech. *J. Speech Hear. Res. 14*, 1971, 677–709.
Lee, B. S., Effects of Delayed Speech Feedback. *J. Acoust. Soc. Am. 22*, 1950, 824–826.
Peters, R. W., The Effect of Changes in Side-Tone Delay and Level upon Rate of Oral Reading of Normal Speakers. *J. Speech Hear. Disord. 19*, 1954, 483–490.
Siegel, G. M.. and Pick, H. L., Jr., Auditory Feedback in the Regulation of Voice. *J. Acoust. Soc. Am. 56*, 1974, 1618–1624.

Stromstra, C., Delays Associated with Certain Sidetone Pathways. *J. Acoust. Soc. Am. 34,* 1962, 392–396.

Von Békésy, G., The Structure of the Middle Ear and the Hearing of One's Own Voice by Bone Conduction. *J. Acoust. Soc. Am. 21,* 1949, 217–232.

Webster, R. L., and Dorman, M. F., Changes in Reliance on Auditory Feedback Cues as a Function of Oral Practice. *J. Speech Hear. Res. 14,* 1971, 307–311.

Yates, A. J., Delayed Auditory Feedback. *Psychol. Bull. 60,* 1963, 213–232.

Tactile Feedback

Borden, G. J., Harris, K. S.. and Catena, L., Oral Feedback II. An Electromyographic Study of Speech under Nerve-Block Anesthesia. *J. Phonetics 1,* 1973, 297-308.

Borden, G. J., Harris, K. S., and Oliver, W., Oral Feedback I. Variability of the Effect of Nerve-Block Anesthesia upon Speech. *J. Phonetics 1,* 1973, 289–295.

Gammon, S. A., Smith, P. J., Daniloff, R. G., and Kim, C. W., Articulation and Stress/Juncture Production under Oral Anesthetization and Masking. *J. Speech Hear. Res. 14,* 1971, 271–282.

Hardcastle, W. J., Some Aspects of Speech Production under Controlled Conditions of Oral Anesthesia and Auditory Masking. *J. Phonetics 3,* 1975, 197–214.

Horii, Y., House, A. S., Li, K.-P, and Ringel, R. L., Acoustic Characteristics of Speech Produced without Oral Sensation. *J. Speech Hear. Res. 16,* 1973, 67–77.

Hutchinson, J. M., and Putnam, A. H. B., Aerodynamic Aspects of Sensory Deprived Speech. *J. Acoust. Soc. Am. 56,* 1974, 1612–1617.

Leanderson, R., and Persson, A., The Effect of Trigeminal Nerve Block on the Articulatory EMG Activity of Facial Muscles. *Acta Otolaryngol. (Stockh.) 74,* 1972, 271–278.

Locke, J. L., A Methodological Consideration in Kinesthetic Feedback Research. *J. Speech Hear. Res. 11,* 1968, 668–669.

Prosek, R. A., and House, A.S., Intraoral Air Pressure as a Feedback Cue in Consonant Production. *J. Speech Hear. Res. 18,* 1975, 133–147.

Putnam, A. H. B., and Ringel, R., A Cineradiographic Study of Articulation in Two Talkers with Temporarily Induced Oral Sensory Deprivation. *J. Speech Hear. Res. 19,* 1976, 247–266.

Putnam, A. H. B., and Ringel, R., Some Observations of Articulation during Labial Sensory Deprivation. *J. Speech Hear. Res. 15,* 1972, 529–542.

Scott, C. M., and Ringel, R. L.. Articulation without Oral Sensory Control. *J. Speech Hear. Res. 14,* 1971, 804–818.

Proprioceptive Feedback References

Abbs, J., The Influence of the Gamma Motor System on Jaw Movements during Speech: A Theoretical Framework and Some Preliminary Observations. *J. Speech and Hear. Res. 16,* 1973, 175–200.

Bowman, J. P.. *Muscle Spindles and Neural Control of the Tongue: Implications for Speech.* Springfield, IL: Charles C Thomas. 1971.

Cooper, S., Muscle Spindles and Other Muscle Receptors. In *The Structure and Function of Muscle,* Vol. I. G. H. Bourne (Ed.) New York: Academic Press. 1960, pp. 381–420.

Critchlow, V., and von Euler, C., Intercostal Muscle Spindle Activity and its Motor Control. *J. Physiol. 168,* 1963, 820–847.

Fitzgerald, M. J. T., and Law, M. E., The Peripheral Connexions between the Lingual and Hypoglossal Nerves. *J. Anat. 92,* 1958, 178–188.

Folkins, J. W., and Abbs, J. H., Lip and Jaw Motor Control during Speech: Responses to Resistive Loading of the Jaw. *J. Speech Hear. Res. 18,* 1975, 207–220. Reprinted in Kent, R. D., *et al.* (q.v.), 605–618.

Fowler, C. A., Rubin, P., Remez, R. E., and Turvey, M. T., Implications for Speech Production of a General Theory of Action. In *Language Production: Volume I Speech and Talk* B. Butterworth (Ed.) New York: Academic Press, 1980.

Goodwin, G. M., and Luschei, E. S., Effects of Destroying the Spindle Afferents from the Jaw Muscles upon Mastication in Monkeys. *J. Neurophysiol. 37,* 1974, 967–981.

Goodwin, G. M., McCloskey, D. I., and Matthews, P. B.C., The Contribution of Muscle Afferents to Kinaesthesia Shown by Vibration Induced Illusions of Movement and by the Effects of Paralyzing Joint Afferents. *Brain 95,* 1972, 705–748.

Hamlet, S. L., Speech Adaptation to Dental Appliances: Theoretical Considerations. *J. Baltimore Coll. Dent. Surg. 28,* 1973, 52–63.

Higgins, J. R., and Angel, R. W., Correction of Tracking Errors without Sensory Feedback. *J. Exper. Psychol. 84,* 1970, 412–416.

Kelso, J. A. S., Tuller, B., and Harris K. S., A 'Dynamic Pattern' Perspective on the Control and Coordination of Movement. In *The Production of Speech*. P. MacNeilage (Ed.) New York: Springer-Verlag, 1983.

Ladefoged, P., and Fromkin, V. A., Experiments on Competence, and Performance. *IEEE Trans. Audio Electroacoust.* March 1968, 130–136.

Matthews, P. B. C., Muscle Spindles and their Motor Control. *Physiol. Rev. 44,* 1964, 219–288.

Mott, F. M., and Sherrington. C. S., Experiments upon the Influence of Sensory Nerves upon Movement and Nutrition of the Limbs. *Proc. Roy. Soc. Lond. Biol. 57,* 1875, 481–488.

Polit, A., and Bizzi, E., Processes Controlling Arm Movement in Monkeys. *Science 201.* 1978, 1235–1237.

Smith, T. S., and Lee, C. Y., Peripheral Feedback Mechanisms in Speech Production Models? In *Proceedings of 7th International Congress of Phonetic Sciences*. A. Rigault and R. Charbonneau (Eds.) The Hague: Mouton, 1972, 1199–1202.

Taub, E., Ellman, S. J., and Berman, A. J., Deafferentation in Monkeys: Effect on Conditioned Grasp Response. *Science. 151,* 1966, 593–594.

Vallbo, Å. B., Muscle Spindle Response at the Onset of Isometric Voluntary Contractions in Man: Time Difference between Fusimotor and Skeletomotor Effects. *J. Physiol. (Lond.) 318,* 1971, 405–431.

Internal Feedback

Eccles. J. C., *The Understanding of the Brain*. New York: McGraw-Hill, 1973.

Evarts. E. V., Central Control of Movement. *Neurosci. Res. Program Bull. 9,* 1971.

Stelmach, G. E. (Ed.), *Motor Control*. The Hague: Mouton, 1976.

Developmental Feedback

Borden, G. J., Use of Feedback in Established and Developing Speech. In *Speech and Language: Advances in Basic Research and Practice Vol. 3*. N. Lass (Ed.) New York: Academic Press, 1980.

MacKay, D. G., Metamorphosis of a Critical Interval: Age-linked Changes in the Delay in Auditory Feedback that Produces Maximal Disruption of Speech. *J. Acoust. Soc. Am. 43,* 1968, 811–821.

Siegel, G. M., Fehst, C. A., Garber, S. R., and Pick, H. L. Jr., Delayed Auditory Feedback with Children. *J. Speech Hear. Res. 23,* 1980, 802–813.

Siegel, G. M., Pick, H. L. Jr., Olsen, M. G., and Sawin, L., Auditory Feedback in the Regulation of Vocal Intensity of Pre-School Children. *Dev. Psychol. 12,* 1976, 255–261.

Models of Speech Production

Chomsky, N., and Halle, M., *The Sound Pattern of English*. New York: Harper & Row, 1968.

Fairbanks, C., A Theory of the Speech Mechanism as a Servosystem. *J. Speech Hear. Disord. 19,* 1954, 133–139.

Fant, G., Auditory Patterns of Speech. In *Models for the Perception of Speech and Visual Form*. W. Wathen-Dunn (Ed.) Cambridge, MA: M. I. T. Press, 1967.

Fowler, C. A., Rubin, P., Remez, R. E., and Turvey, M. T., Implications for Speech Production of a General Theory of Action. In *Language Production: Volume I Speech and Talk*. B. Butterworth (Ed.) New York: Academic Press, 1980.

Hebb, D. O., *The Organization of Behavior*. New York: Wiley, 1949.

Henke, W., Dynamic Articulatory Model of Speech Production Using Computer Simulation. Ph.D. thesis, Massachusetts Institute of Technology, Cambridge, Mass., 1966.

Jakobson, R., Fant, C. G. M., and Halle, M., *Preliminaries to Speech Analysis*. Cambridge, MA: M. I. T., Press, 1963. (Originally published in 1952 as *Technical Report No. 13,* Acoustics Laboratory, Massachusetts Institute of Technology).

Kozhevnikov, V. A., and Chistovich, L. A., *Rech: Artikulyatisiya i Vospriyatiye*, Moscow-Leningrad, 1965. Translated as *Speech: Articulation and Perception*. Springfield, Va.: United States Department of Commerce, Joint Publications Research Service Vol. 30, 1966.

Ladefoged, P., De Clerk, J., Lindau, M., and Papçun, G., An Auditory-Motor Theory of Speech Production. *UCLA Working Papers in Phonetics* Vol. 22, Los Angeles: UCLA, 1972, pp. 48–75.

Lashley, K. S., The Problem of Serial Order in Behavior. In *Cerebral Mechanisms in Behavior*. L. A. Jeffress (Ed.) New York: Wiley, 1951.

Liberman, A. M., Cooper, F. S., Shankweiler, D. P., and Studdert-Kennedy, M., Perception of the Speech Code. *Psychol. Rev. 74,* 1967, 431–461.

MacNeilage, P., Motor Control of Serial Ordering of Speech. *Psychol. Rev. 77,* 1970, 182–196. Reprinted in Kent, R. D., *et al.* (q.v.), 701–715.

6
Speech Perception

The intellect pierces the form, overleaps the wall, detects intrinsic likeness between remote things and reduces all things into a few principles.
—Ralph Waldo Emerson, *Intellect*, 1841

The only reason that we understand one another at all, and there are those who may argue that we do a poor job of it, is that the human mind has developed into a remarkable seeker of patterns. It receives the seemingly chaotic variety of sights, sounds, and textures, searches for common properties among them, makes associations, and sorts them into groups. In this sense, then, we all perceive in the same way. In speaking to one another, we seem to extract the essences of sound and meaning from utterances diverse in dialect, vocabulary, and voice quality.

There is a duality, however, in our perception of other speakers; although we seek common denominators, we also impose ourselves upon what we perceive. Like the legend of the blind men describing an elephant, each having touched a different part of the animal, each person perceives the world a bit differently, depending upon individual experiences and expectations. In perceiving the speech communications of others, we tend to impose our own points of view upon the messages. We often think we hear what we expect to hear. If part of a word is missing, our minds supply it and we fail to notice its absence. Even the sounds of speech are heard within the framework of our particular language, so that if we hear a less familiar language being spoken, we try to fit the less familiar sounds into the categories of speech sounds we have in our own language. Adults trying to imitate a new language, for this reason, speak with an obvious "accent," retaining the sound categories of their first language. In trying to say "tu" in French, an English speaker might say /tu/ instead of /ty/ and not even perceive the difference in the vowels of a French person saying "tu" /ty/ and "vous" /vu/.

Yet, we normally do perceive an elephant with enough of a common ground of shared experiences that we agree that it is an elephant. In speech communication, despite the fact that we retain our individual and language-based perspectives, we receive the same acoustic signal, and our ears act upon this signal in similar ways. Thus, we have learned the acoustic patterns that correspond to the distinctive speech sounds in our language. We seem to learn these despite the fact that the acoustic cues for individual speech sounds overlap in time. In this chapter, we shall discuss speech perception in terms of how we English- speaking listeners act in common upon the sounds of English, bearing in mind that we differ from speakers of other languages, and to some extent, from one another.

THE LISTENER

Communication by speech is the transmission of thoughts or feelings from the mind of a speaker to the mind of a listener. The concepts and attitudes that the speaker intends to express are embodied within a linguistic frame and rendered audible by the physiological processes that we considered in the last two chapters. This chapter continues the discussion of what Denes and Pinson have called the "speech chain," the chain of events from speaker to listener. The listener hears the speech signal and interprets its meaning. These events are obviously interrelated, but we shall consider them separately. Audition, the process of registering the sounds in the brain of the hearer, will be considered first, and speech perception, the process of decoding a message from the stream of sounds coming from the speaker, will form the main consideration of the chapter.

We can appreciate the difference between speech audition and speech perception when we compare the effects of deafness with those of developmental aphasia. When a child is born deaf or hard-of-hearing, the difficulty in learning language is based on dysfunction of the peripheral hearing mechanism. If the child could hear speech, he or she could learn to interpret it. When a child is born with brain damage that specifically interferes with speech perception, the child has normal hearing but is unable to interpret the sounds in any linguistically useful way. Although there are several different syndromes called by such terms as developmental aphasia or *auditory agnosia*, a common difficulty seems to lie in the processes leading to the discrimination and identification of speech sounds rather than in the auditory processes themselves.

Listeners use more than acoustic information when they receive a spoken message. They use their knowledge of the speaking situation and their knowledge of the speaker, as well as visual cues obtained by watching the face and gestures of the speaker. These non-acoustic cues used in speech perception are important, but they fall outside the range of study usually ascribed to speech science as we have defined it. In this chapter, we shall limit ourselves to a discussion of what is known and conjectured about the perception of speech as it involves extracting the sounds of speech from acoustic information. This limitation means that we shall largely ignore other important areas of investigation: the processes by which listeners arrive at meaning through semantic and syntactic analyses of the message.

Usually, listeners are only aware of the meaning of speech and remain quite unconscious of the components of the message. As a person who sees a dog run by is conscious of perceiving a dog, not a changing pattern of light, so a person perceiving speech is aware of the meaning of the message, not the individual sounds or sound patterns that form it. Linguistic information seems to be stored by meaning or by imagery. For example, Bartlett found that people tested repeatedly on folk stories that they had read, often used entirely different words to relate the tale than the words used in the original, but the story outline and prominent images were remembered.

As strongly as listeners seem to seek meanings, they must be extracting these meanings from the sound patterns of speech. We shall focus upon the acoustic, phonetic, and phonemic analyses that presumably form the basis for further linguistic decisions. It does seem unlikely, however, that a listener would take the auditory information and proceed "up the ladder" to make phonetic then phonemic, then morphemic, and finally syntactic decisions, to arrive at the meaning of the message. More likely, operating on certain expectations of what the speaker may be saying, the listener hears some of the message, makes a rough analysis, and leaps to synthesize it into something meaningful, simultaneously verifying it at all the levels mentioned.

No matter how a listener analyzes a message, the data upon which he/she operates are the acoustic patterns of speech. The essential step is, then, that the listener hear the speech. Since the nature of the hearing mechanism *per se* is somewhat removed from the main concerns of this book, we will merely say a few words about the peripheral reception of speech, as the auditory system itself imposes certain changes upon speech sounds.

HEARING

The human auditory mechanism analyzes sound according to changes in frequency and intensity over time. As a receptor, the ear falls short of the eye in sensitivity, but seems to be remarkably responsive to sounds that hu-

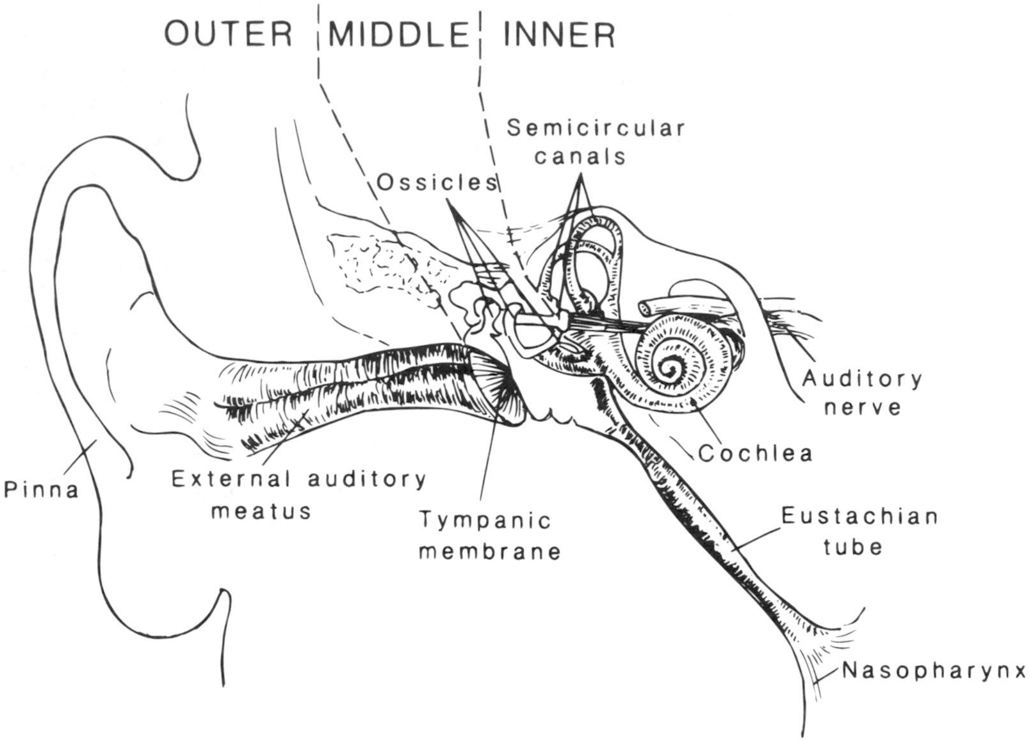

Figure 6.1. Drawing of the outer, middle, and inner ear based on a frontal section of the head.

mans produce, the sounds of speech. These sounds change not only in amplitude but in their mode of transmission as they travel through the outer ear, middle ear, cochlea, and auditory nerve to the brain. Figure 6.1 differentiates these parts of the mechanism. As we know from Chapter 3, the pressure waves of speech are usually disturbances in air and thus they continue in the outer ear. In the middle ear, however, they are converted from pressure waves to mechanical vibrations by a series of small bones leading to the cochlea of the inner ear. In the *cochlea*, a snail-shaped cavity within the temporal bone of the skull, the vibrations are again transformed. This time the transformation is from mechanical vibrations to vibrations in fluid, since the cochlea is filled with fluid. Finally, the nerve endings in the cochlea act to transform the hydraulic vibrations into electrochemical changes that are sent to the brain in the form of nerve impulses.

The Outer Ear

The outer ear is composed of two parts: the external part you can readily see, called the *auricle* or *pinna*, and the ear canal, named the *external auditory meatus*, leading from the pinna to the eardrum. Meatus means "channel," and the channel of the outer ear is specified by the term "external," distinguishing it from the internal auditory meatus that runs from the inner ear out of the temporal bone to the brain. The pinna funnels the sound somewhat, being a little more receptive to sounds in front of the head than behind. The pinna also serves to protect the entrance to the canal, especially the small projection of the pinna, situated over the opening to the canal, called the *tragus*. One way to reduce the intensity of a loud sound is to press the tragus into the entrance to the auditory meatus with your finger.

The external auditory meatus protects

the more delicate parts of the ear from trauma and from the intrusion of foreign objects. A waxy substance called *cerumen* is secreted into the canal, and aided by the hairs lining the canal, *cilia*, filters out dust and any flying insects that may have intruded into the canal. Some people constantly clean out the cerumen, but they are depriving themselves of their natural protection. If the cerumen should harden or an object become lodged in the meatus, it should be removed by an otolaryngologist.

In addition to offering protection to the more critical parts of the ear, the external auditory meatus functions to boost the high frequencies of the sounds it receives. The canal is an air-filled cavity, open at one end, and therefore acts as a quarter wave resonator. The lowest resonance has a wavelength 4 times the length of the tube, and the higher resonances are its odd multiples. Thus, the first resonance of a canal 2.5 cm long is about 3440 Hz.

$$f = \frac{\text{velocity of sound}}{4 \text{ (length)}} = \frac{34{,}400}{10} = 3{,}440 \text{ Hz}$$

A female or child's ear canal would probably be shorter than 2.5 cm and would resonate at even higher frequencies. High frequency emphasis provided by the outer ear is useful for speech perception, because much of the sound energy that distinguishes fricatives from each other is in the frequency range above 2000 Hz.

Before leaving the outer ear, consider why we have ears on both sides of our heads. To reverse the question, what happens when there is a loss of hearing in one ear because of something like a case of mumps in adulthood? The good ear hears perfectly well, so there is little loss of acuity in a quiet environment, but large group conversations become difficult for the person to follow. Localization of the sound is impaired. Normally, having an ear on each side of the head aids in localizing the source of the sound. In a meeting room with voices coming from all directions, the unilaterally deaf person seeking to locate the speaker may look in the wrong direction.

The Middle Ear

The outer ear is separated from the air-filled *middle ear* cavity by the eardrum, properly called the *tympanic membrane* (Fig. 6.2). The tympanic membrane is slightly concave as seen from the outer ear and is responsive to small pressure variations across a wide range of frequencies. The tension of the eardrum can be altered by a muscle, the *tensor tympani,* which pulls on the *manubrium* or handle of a small bone attached to the inside of the drum. The bone is called the *malleus*. At low frequencies, the tympanic membrane vibrates as a whole, but at high frequencies, different areas of the membrane are responsive to different frequency ranges. On the internal side of the tympanic membrane is the *ossicular chain,* three tiny bones connected to one another, called the *ossicles*. The aforementioned malleus (hammer) is attached to the tympanic membrane, the *incus* (anvil) acts as a fulcrum between the other two bones, and the *stapes* (stirrup) inserts into the membranous *oval window* leading to the inner ear. Thus, the ossicular chain bridges the space between the tympanic membrane and the cochlea. The chain is suspended in the air-filled cavity of the middle ear by ligaments and is held in such a delicate balance that no matter what position the body takes,

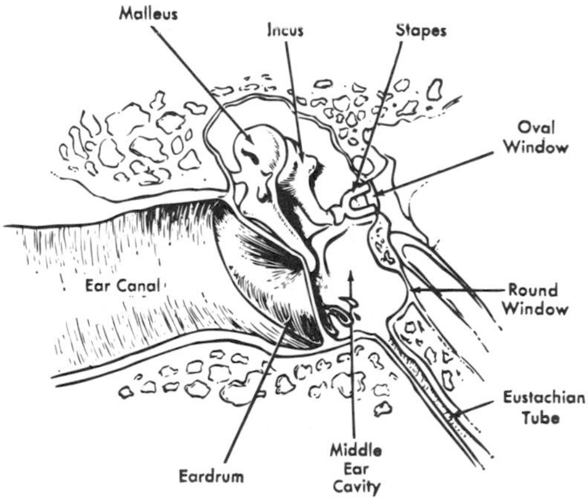

Figure 6.2. Cross-sectional diagram of the middle ear and ossicles. (Reprinted with permission of Doubleday & Co., Inc. from P. B. Denes and E. N. Pinson: *The Speech Chain,* Doubleday © 1963.)

the tiny bones are held in suspension, free to vibrate in response to sound. The vibrations in the outer ear take the form of disturbances of air molecules, but in the middle ear, they take the form of mechanical vibrations of the bony ossicles. The tympanic membrane and the ossicular chain taken together are especially responsive to the frequencies of the acoustic signal that are important for speech.

Why have a middle ear at all? Why not have the fluid-filled cochlea on the other side of the tympanic membrane? The problem is a mismatch in *impedance*. Impedance is a force determined by the characteristics of a medium itself (gas, liquid, or solid) and is a measure of the resistance to transmission of signals. Liquid offers a higher impedance or resistance to the sound pressure than does gas. When sound pressure waves traveling through air (a gas) suddenly come to a fluid, most of the sound energy is reflected back, with very little admitted into the liquid. The cochlea is filled with fluid. In order to overcome the difference in impedance between air and fluid, a transformer is needed to increase the sound pressure so that more of it will be admitted into the liquid. The transformer function is performed by the middle ear.

The middle ear increases sound pressure by approximately 30 dB. The ossicles by themselves are not able to effect such a large amplification of the signal, although they do act like a lever to increase the sound pressure by about 5 dB (Fig. 6.3). Leverage is the force long used by farmers to remove a heavy rock from a field. If the rock is too heavy for the farmer to lift, leverage can be used by placing a pole over a fulcrum, with the shorter part of the pole under the heavy object, and the longer part on the other side of the fulcrum. The farmer puts pressure on the long end of the pole. The fulcrum works with the farmer, resulting in an increased pressure under the rock to be moved. Thus, a given pressure applied by the farmer results in a much larger pressure under the rock. In somewhat the same way, the pressures applied to the relatively long malleus are transmitted by the incus, which acts something like a fulcrum to the much smaller stapes. The result is an increase of a few decibels in transmission because of the increase in the pressure exerted on the oval window.

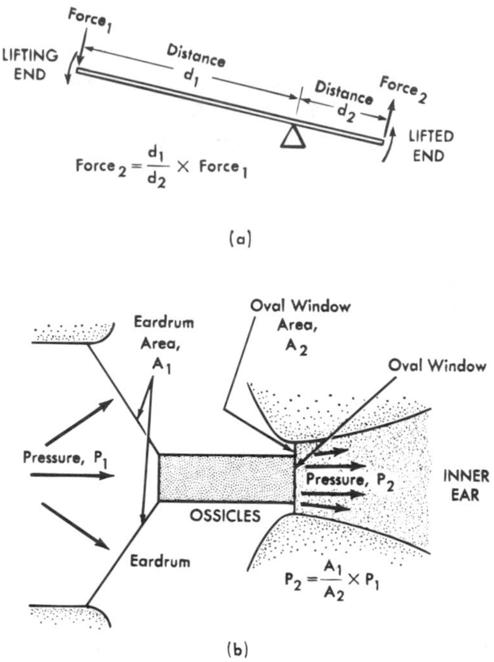

Figure 6.3. The *a* portion shows the lever principle of the ossicles. The *b* portion shows the effect of the area difference between the tympanic membrane and the oval window. (Reprinted with permission of Doubleday & Co., Inc. from P. B. Denes and E. N. Pinson: *The Speech Chain,* Doubleday © 1963.)

The leverage applied along the ossicles helps to overcome some of the impedance mismatch, but the larger part of the increase in pressure comes from the design of the tympanic membrane relative to the oval window. The area of the tympanic membrane is about 0.85 cm^2 (although only about 0.55 cm^2 of that area is active in vibration), while the area of the oval window is 0.03 cm^2. When a given force (F) is applied to a smaller area (A), the pressure (p) will be greater than if it is applied to a larger area. This is expressed by the formula $p = F/A$. Thus, as area (A) increases the absolute value of the fraction F/A, which is the pressure, decreases.

Consider the following example: If your friend were to fall through the ice, you would be well-advised to spread your weight over a large area in attempting to reach the victim. By lying flat, or better, by distributing your weight over an even larger area, by crawling along on a ladder, you are in much less danger of falling through the ice yourself. The pressure on any point is much less than if you were to attempt to walk to your friend on the ice, focusing all the pressure at the points on the ice beneath your feet. In an analogous manner, the sound vibrations occurring over the larger vibrating area of the tympanic membrane are focused by the stapes to the smaller area of the oval window, resulting in an increase in pressure of approximately 25 dB. Thus, the impedance matching function of the middle ear is accomplished by the area difference between the tympanic membrane and the oval window, and by the leverage afforded by the ossicular design, which adds a few more decibels.

Besides the important function of impedance matching between the air and the cochlear fluid, the middle ear mechanism serves two other functions. First, it attenuates loud sounds, by action of the *acoustic reflex*. Second, by the action of the eustachian tube, it works to maintain relatively equal air pressure on either side of the eardrum despite any changes in atmospheric pressure.

The acoustic reflex is elicited when a sound having a pressure level of 85 or 90 dB reaches the middle ear. This causes a contraction of the smallest muscle in the body, the *stapedius muscle*, which is attached to the neck of the smallest bone in the body, the stapes. There are two theories to account for the function of this acoustic reflex. The first theory, that it protects the inner ear from loud sounds, posits that the contraction of the stapedius muscle pulls the stapes to one side, changing the angle of its coupling to the oval window and reducing the pressure it applies. The second theory is that the stapedius muscle, along with the tensor tympani muscle, acts to stiffen the ossicular chain, thereby regulating intensity changes, much as the eye adjusts to changes in light. In either case, the stapedius muscle takes a few milliseconds to act, allowing sounds with sudden onset to penetrate the inner ear before the reflex has occurred. Also, like any muscle, it eventually fatigues, so that in a noisy environment, the reflexive attenuation of the sound will gradually lessen, allowing the full impact of the sound pressure to impinge again upon the inner ear. The stapedius muscle is innervated by the facial (VIIth cranial) nerve, but is somehow associated with the innervation of the larynx (vagus; Xth cranial nerve) because phonation activates the acoustic reflex. It is interesting to note that the acoustic reflex attenuates frequencies below 1 kHz by about 10-dB and that the spectral energy of the human voice is also largely below 1 kHz. The acoustic reflex may keep us from hearing ourselves too loudly, for we hear our own voices not only by the air-conducted sound coming through our outer ears, but also by bone-conducted sound, as our facial and skull bones vibrate in response to our own voices.

The middle ear also functions to equalize differences between internal and external air pressures. This is accomplished by the *eustachian tube*, leading from the middle ear to the nasopharynx. The eardrum will not vibrate properly if the air pressure within the middle ear is different from the air pressure in the external auditory meatus. Relatively high pressure within the middle ear pushes out on the tympanic membrane, causes discomfort, and attenuates outside sounds. A sudden change in pressure, as when one drives up into the mountains or descends in an airplane, can create this pressure difference if the eustachian tube, normally closed, fails to open. The outside air pressure is suddenly lower while the air pressure in the middle ear cavity (containing the same air as when one was at sea level) is relatively higher. Swallowing, yawning, and chewing facilitate the opening of the tube, which is why airline attendants sometimes offer chewing gum to passengers on landing.

The Inner Ear

Within the temporal bone of the skull, there are several coil-shaped tunnels filled with fluid called *perilymph*. The fluid is like seawater in many of its properties. Floating in the fluid are coiled tubes made of membrane and filled with a more viscous fluid called *endo-*

lymph. Figure 6.4 depicts the membranous labyrinth. The snail-shaped coil is the *cochlear duct*, containing the sensory receptor for hearing, and the system of three coils is the *vestibular system*, consisting of the *semicircular canals*, which, along with the *vestibule* (utricle and saccule) connecting them, contain organs that sense changes in body position and movement.

We shall limit our description to the cochlea, for audition is the first step in speech perception. As the footplate of the stapes vibrates in the oval window, the vibrations set up disturbances in the perilymph of the cochlea. These pressure waves in the perilymph surrounding the snail-shaped cochlear duct, set up vibrations in the duct itself. Especially important are the resulting vibrations of the "floor" of the duct, which is called the *basilar membrane*.

The cochlea in humans is a cavity within bone that coils around a bony core almost three times. The membranous duct (or cochlear duct) within is attached to the bony core on the inside and by a ligament to the bony wall on the outside. It is perhaps easier to visualize if we imagine the cochlear chambers uncoiled as in Figure 6.5. Pressure variations applied by the stapes rocking in the oval window are translated into pressure variations within the fluids of the cochlea, which in turn lead to displacements of the basilar membrane. The beauty of the system is that different parts of the basilar membrane respond to different frequencies. The membrane is narrow and stiff at the base, gradually getting wider and less stiff at the apex (the opposite of what one might expect). As a result, low frequency sounds produce traveling waves in the fluid that stimulate the basilar membrane to vibrate with the largest ampli-

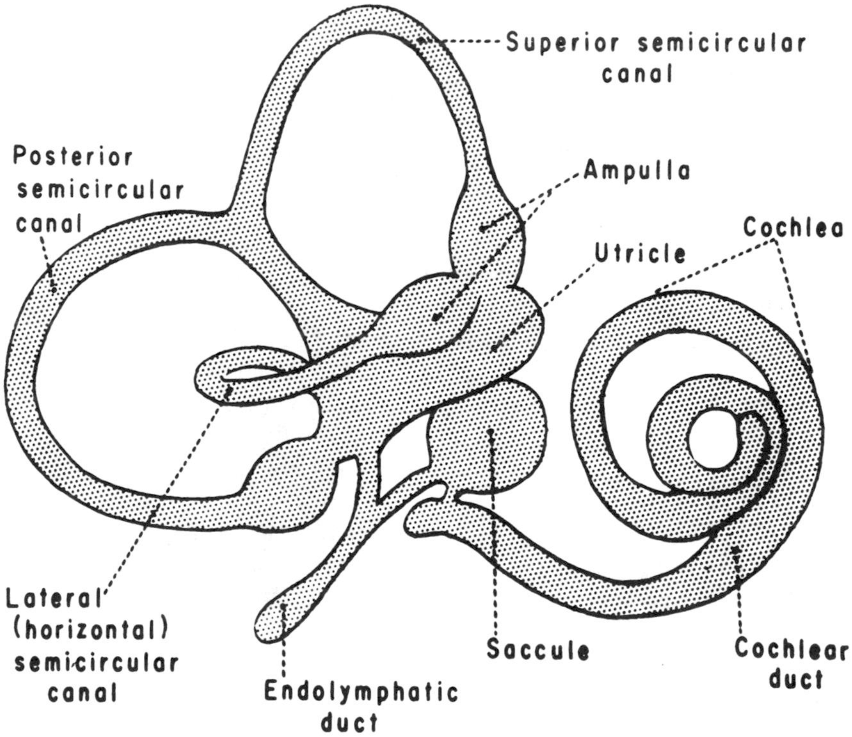

Figure 6.4. Schematic drawing representing the parts of the membranous labyrinth. The three semicircular canals, the ampulla, utricle, and saccule make up the vestibular organs which are responsible for sensing body position and movement. The cochlea contains the organ of hearing. (Reprinted from J. D. Durrant and J. H. Lovrinic: *Bases of Hearing Science*, Williams & Wilkins, Baltimore, © 1977. From D. D. DeWeese and W. H. Saunders: *Textbook of Otolaryngology*, Ed. 3, C. V. Mosby Co., St. Louis © 1968.)

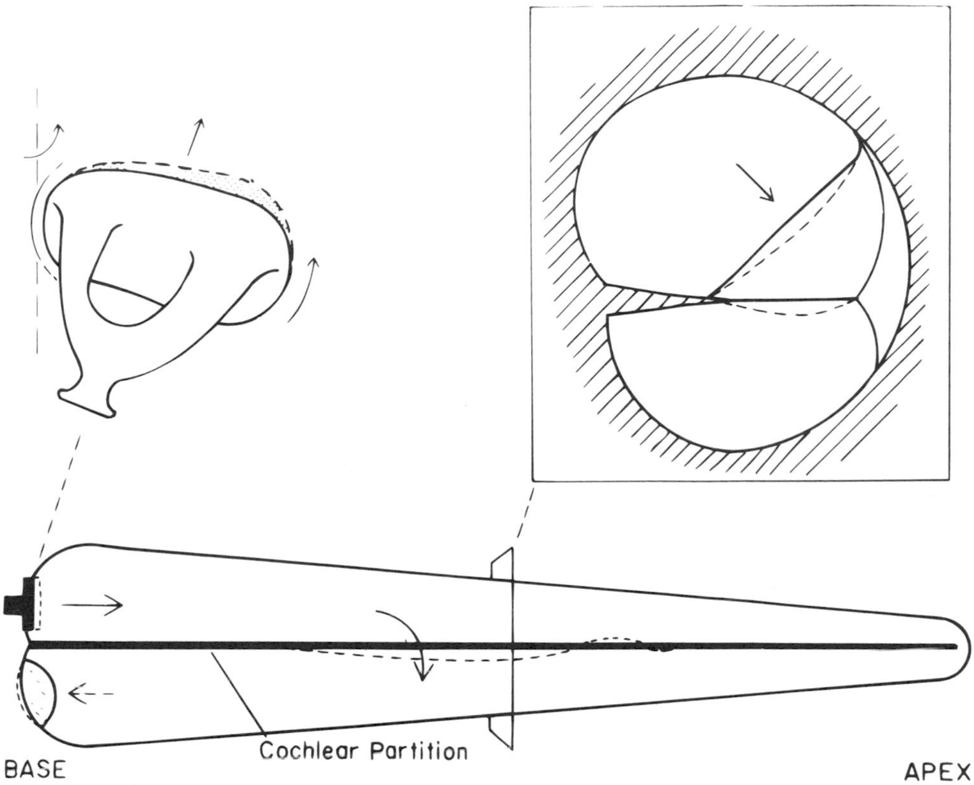

Figure 6.5. The *lower section* shows the uncoiled cochlea, while the *upper right section* shows a cross-section. The stapes, shown in the *upper left,* rocks in the oval window, leading to displacement of the cochlear partition, and the basilar membrane in particular. (Reprinted from J. D. Durrant and J. H. Lovrinic: *Bases of Hearing Science,* Williams & Wilkins, Baltimore, © 1977. Adapted from G. von Békésy: *Experiments in Hearing,* translated and edited by E. G. Wever, McGraw-Hill © 1960.))

tude of displacement at the wider, more flaccid tip. On the other hand, high frequency sounds create pressure waves with the largest displacement of the basilar membrane at the thinner, stiffer base (Fig. 6.6).

The basilar membrane is not the sense organ of hearing, however. The *Organ of Corti,* lying on the basilar membrane for the length of the cochlear duct, is the auditory receptor. It consists of rows of hair cells, along with other cells for support. Above the rows of thousands of hair cells is a gelatinous mass called the *tectorial membrane.* The basilar membrane and the tectorial membrane are attached to the cochlear duct at different points and therefore move somewhat independently. Figure 6.7 shows a cross-section of the cochlea. The scala vestibuli and scala tympani containing perilymph lie on either side of the cochlear duct. Pressure waves in the perilymph set up traveling waves within the cochlear duct. In some way imperfectly understood, the undulating motions of the basilar membrane cause the hair cells to be stimulated. The tectorial membrane above the hairs shears across the hairy endings of the cells, and the result is an electrochemical excitation of the nerve fibers serving the critical hair cells.

The cochlea performs a Fourier analysis of complex sounds into their component frequencies. The sound of [i] as in "see" would result in many traveling waves moving along the basilar membrane with at least two maxima of displacement: one near the apex for the lower resonance and one near the base of the cochlea for the higher resonance. If the speaker were

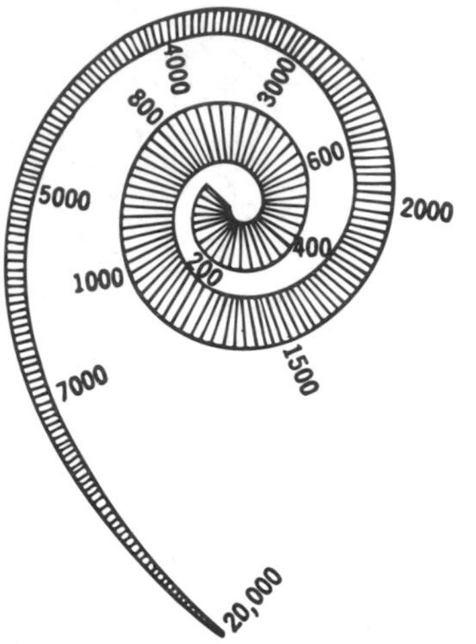

Figure 6.6. Schematic diagram showing the width of the basilar membrane (somewhat exaggerated) as it approaches the apex. The approximate positions of maximum amplitude of vibration in response to tones of different frequency are also indicated.

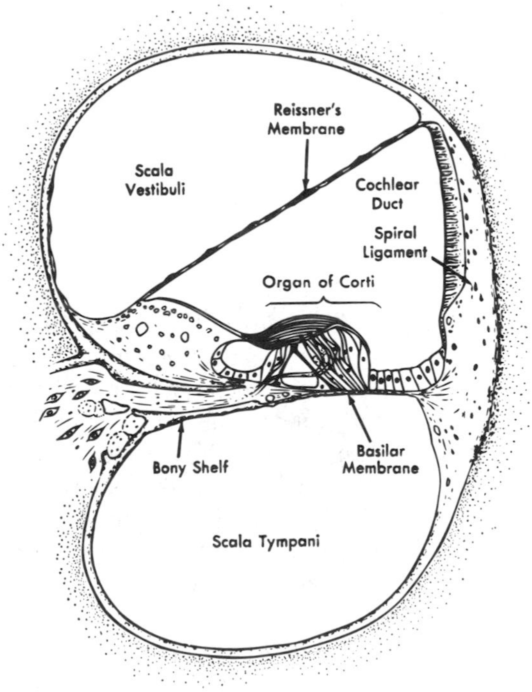

Figure 6.7. Cross section through the cochlea, showing the scala vestibuli, the scala tympani, and the cochlear duct. The Organ of Corti lies within the cochlear duct. (Reprinted with permission of Doubleday & Co., Inc. from P. B. Denes and E. N. Pinson: *The Speech Chain*, Doubleday © 1963.)

to say [si], "see," the membrane displacement would initially be maximum even closer to the base of the cochlea for the high frequency [s]. Also, the traveling waves would be aperiodic during [s] and become periodic during the phonated part of the word. Both the *traveling wave theory* and the description of the stiffness gradient of the basilar membrane are the result of the work of the late Georg von Békésy.

Frequency information is extracted from the signal by the combined factors of the place of stimulation (which activates the sensory nerve fibers at a particular location along the basilar membrane—the *place theory*) and also by timing of impulses along the nerve fibers. Ernest Glen Wever theorized that, at low frequencies, the displacement is not sharp enough to distinguish the frequencies by place; rather, they may be signaled by the number of cycles per second translated into a corresponding number of clusters of nerve impulses per second (Fig. 6.8). At high frequencies, place is

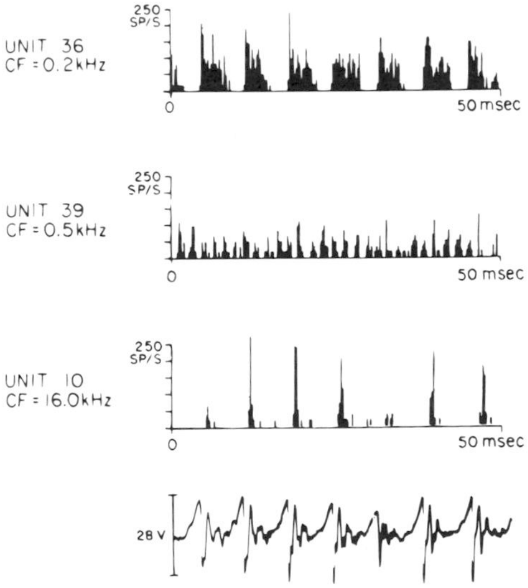

Figure 6.8. Responses of single neurons of the auditory nerve of a cat to a presentation of a segment of the vowel [æ]. The bottom display shows the acoustic signal. The three upper displays show the number of spikes per second for three different neural units. Notice that although different units have different firing frequencies, they maintain a fixed temporal relationship to the signal. (Reprinted with permission from N. Y. S. Kiang and E. C. Moxon: *Journal of the Acoustical Society of America*. 55, 1974.)

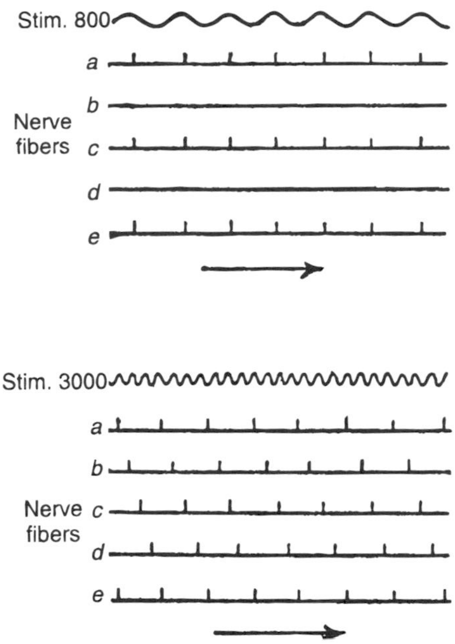

Figure 6.9. Diagram showing Wever's volley principle. Individual neurons can fire for each cycle of the stimulus, at low frequencies (800 Hz), but at high frequencies (3000 Hz), frequency is indicated by the organized firing of groups of neurons. (Reprinted with permission from C. E. Osgood: *Method and Theory in Experimental Psychology*, Oxford University Press, Inc., © 1953.)

probably important for indicating frequency because neurons cannot fire at high frequencies. Another possibility is Wever's *volley theory*, by which several neurons would cooperate in the neural transmission of high frequencies (Fig. 6.9). The coding of intensity may well be as complicated as frequency coding. It is thought, though, that it is primarily transmitted by relative rate of nerve impulse spikes, as it is throughout the body.

The Auditory Nerve

The 30,000 nerve fibers serving the cochlea, each fiber coming from a few hair cells and each hair cell exciting several nerve fibers, form a bundle known as the *auditory nerve or* VIIIth cranial nerve. Another branch of the VIIIth nerve relays information from the semicircular canals. When the nerve fibers are excited by the stimulation of the hair cells, the frequency analysis performed by the Organ of Corti is further refined because of *lateral inhibition*: when a certain place along the basilar membrane is maximally stimulated, surrounding cells and nerve fibers are inhibited in their response, to sharpen the effect.

The VIIIth cranial nerve does not have far to go between the cochlea and the temporal lobe of the brain. It exits the temporal bone by the *internal auditory meatus* and enters the brainstem where the medulla meets the pons. In the brainstem, most nerve fibers from each ear decussate (cross) to the contralateral pathway. At that point, comparisons can be made between signals from each ear to localize the sounds. It is thought that VIIIth nerve fibers in the brainstem may be specialized to detect certain auditory features. Such a specialization would be useful in detecting distinctions important to speech processing. From the brainstem, the VIIIth nerve courses to the midbrain and then to the temporal lobe. Along the way, fibers go off to the cerebellum and to a network of the brainstem that acts to focus attention. Motor fibers of the auditory nerve also descend to control the sensitivity of the cochlea.

When signals arrive at the auditory cortex of the temporal lobe, the impulses have preserved the place-frequency arrangement of the basilar membrane. In a three-dimensional display along the superior part of the temporal lobe, low frequency stimulation near the apex of the cochlea excites the layers of cortical cells along the lateral part of the primary auditory area, while high frequency stimulation of the base of the cochlea is registered in columns of cells within the lateral fissure. This topographical representation is present in both temporal lobes. Most of the contribution to each lobe comes from the contralateral ear. Thus, hearing is accomplished, but the signals must be processed further in order to "understand" what is heard. Cortical processing of speech sounds will be discussed further in this chapter when we consider the neurophysiology of speech perception.

PERCEPTION OF SPEECH

There is evidence that the auditory system is especially tuned for speech, or, to look at it in evolutionary terms, that our speaking mechanisms and auditory mechanisms have developed together, so that we are best at hearing speech sounds. Looking at it from the perspective of historical linguistics, we can consider that the languages of the Earth may have developed as they have by taking advantage of, and at the same time being constrained by, the speech production mechanisms and auditory mechanisms of the human being. As we shall discover later in the chapter, infants, according to their powers of auditory discrimination, categorize sounds of speech into groups similar to those used in many languages as distinctive categories or phonemes.

Given that we are especially endowed to perceive the same sounds of speech that we are especially endowed to produce, the processes involved in speech perception still remain far from clear. The evidence indicates that speech perception is a specialized aspect of a general human ability, the ability to seek and recognize patterns. In this case, the patterns are acoustic, and much of this chapter will describe acoustic patterns that listeners use as cues to the understanding of speech. The cues are often redundant, which permits speech perception to take place under difficult conditions. Speech sounds are rarely produced in isolation, as we have indicated in Chapters 4 and 5; they overlap and influence one another as a result of their production. For perception, this means that speech sounds often are not discrete and separable, as are the letters in a written word. The listener, therefore, must use context to decode the message. A speech sound is often perceived by simultaneously perceiving the acoustic information in neighboring segments. In addition, there is evidence that speech perception is a somewhat specialized and lateralized function in the brain, a subject we shall consider further. Finally, in this chapter, we shall consider some of the current theories of speech perception.

Acoustic Cues in Speech Perception

We know from the study of spectrograms that the acoustic patterns of speech are complex and constantly changing. Does the listener use all of the acoustic information available, or are some features of the acoustic patterns of speech more important for speech perception than others? By synthesizing and editing speech, speech scientists have altered various parameters of the acoustic signal and then tested listeners to discover the effects on perception.

In Chapter 5, we detailed the production of the general classes of speech sounds according to manner of articulation, starting with vowels, which are produced with the most open vocal tract, and concluding with the stops and fricatives, which are articulated with a more constricted vocal tract. We attempted to explain the production of each class of speech sound in terms of its articulatory features as well as its acoustic features. Following the same order, we shall consider the perception of the sounds of speech.

Vowels. Vowels are among the most perceptually salient sounds in language. They are usually voiced and thus relatively high in intensity; the vocal tract is relatively open for them, producing prominent resonances (formants) that are often held for a hundred milliseconds or so—a relatively long time for speech sounds. The most important acoustic cues to the perception of vowels lie in the frequencies and patterning of the speaker's formants. In the early 1950s, Delattre, Liberman, Cooper, and Gerstman, at Haskins Laboratories, produced vowels by synthesizing steady state formants on the Pattern Playback (as described in Chapter 2). They systematically varied the frequencies of the formants to determine which patterns elicited the highest level of listener identifications for each vowel (Fig. 6.10). Listeners usually required only the first and second formants to identify a vowel. The experimenters also found that although both F_1 and F_2 were required for the identification of front vowels, a single formant, intermediate in frequency to F_1 and F_2, was sufficient for the identification of the back vowels. In Gunnar Fant's laboratory in Sweden, experimenters found that the most highly identifiable two-formant synthetic vowels differ systematically from nat-

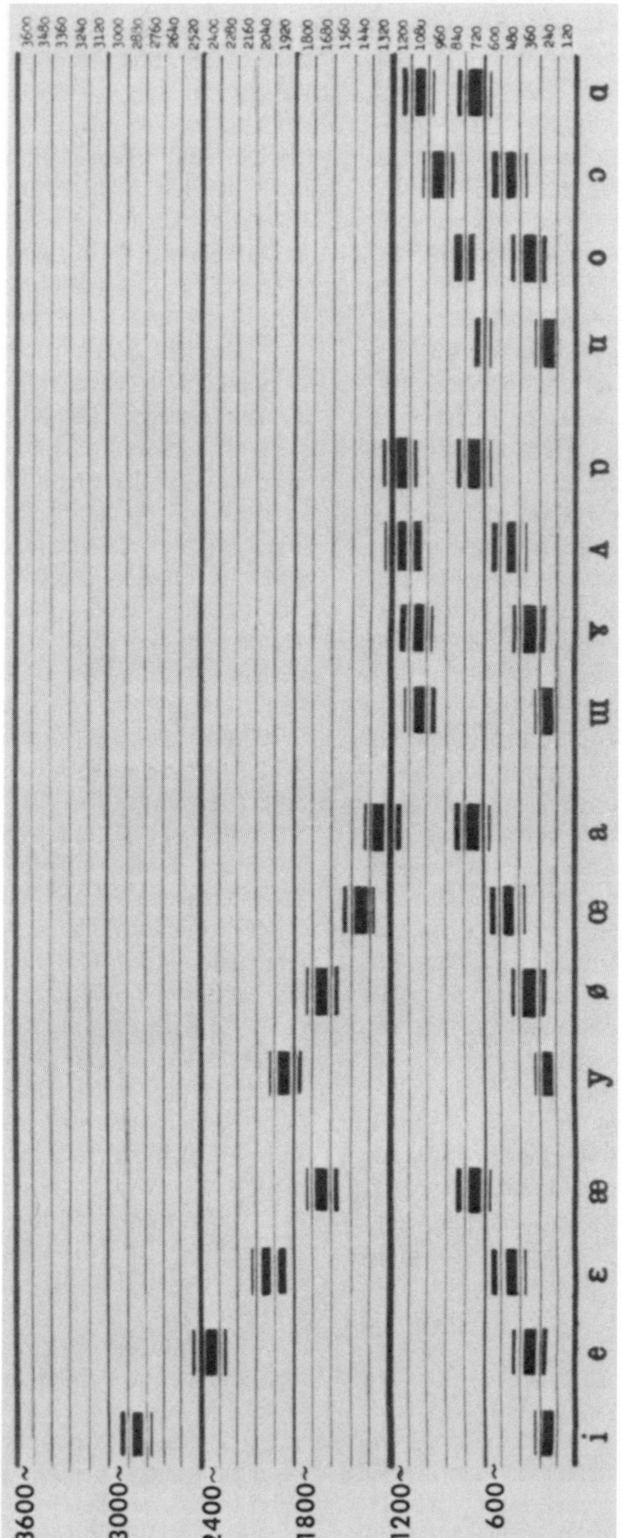

Figure 6.10. Two-formant synthetic vowels as patterns painted for the Haskins Pattern Playback. (Reprinted with permission from P. Delattre *et al*: *Word 8*, 1952.)

ural vowels. For /i/, the second formant must be very high, close to the natural third formant, while for the rest of the front vowels, the second formant was best placed between the frequencies of F_2 and F_3 in natural speech. Back vowels were best synthesized with the second formant close to a natural F_2. For speech perception, apparently, F_3 is more important for front vowels than for back vowels.

We must be careful not to assume that steady-state formant frequencies are the only cues that listeners use to identify vowels. We know that this can not be so for a number of reasons. The first is the variety of vocal tract sizes producing the formants. We know from the Peterson and Barney study cited in Chapter 5 that men, women, and children produce the same vowel with different formant frequencies. In addition, there is a good deal of formant frequency variability within each of their groups of subjects. A second reason that steady state formant frequencies cannot be the only cues to vowel identification is that they are affected by context and rate of articulation. Thus, a single speaker will, for example, produce somewhat different formant frequencies for the vowel /ɑ/ in the word "father" than in the word "clock." The same is true of the formant frequencies for /ɑ/ in the word "father" said at two different rates or with different degrees of linguistic stress. With increased rate of speaking, vowels are often neutralized to some extent. Lindblom has shown that, when vowels are not stressed, they become more similar to each other and to schwa /ə/. A third reason, and perhaps the most important one, is that one rarely finds steady state formants in speech articulated at normal conversational rates: Because the articulators are in virtually continual motion, the vocal tract shapes and therefore the peaks of resonance are continually changing.

If absolute formant frequency values are not reliable cues to vowel identification, how do listeners identify vowels? One possibility is that they use the patterns, rather than the actual values, of formant frequencies for the purpose of identification. No matter what the difference between the size of two speakers' vocal tracts, if each says the English vowel /i/, each will produce a sound with a very low frequency first formant and a very high frequency second formant. Even though those formant frequencies will be different from one speaker to the other, neither speaker will produce any other vowel sound displaying a greater frequency gap between F_1 and F_2. Analogous arguments can be constructed for the formant frequency patterns of the other point vowels, /ɑ/ and /u/.

But what of the vowels that lie between the point vowels? Given that the overall pattern of formant frequencies is quite similar across speakers, several researchers, including Liberman and Gerstman, have suggested that listeners use the point vowels as reference points to scale or normalize formant frequency values in order to identify vowels. Ladefoged and Broadbent demonstrated that some vowels of a given speaker could be used by listeners to normalize for different vocal tract lengths. In their study, a vowel in the context [b__t] was heard as [ɪ], or as [ɛ] depending on which of two different speakers uttered the accompanying carrier phrase.

This concept of normalization, however, presents a number of problems. In the first place, it appears that no simple scaling formula works to allow the listener to normalize the frequencies. This is partly explained by the fact that besides the difference in length between male and female vocal tracts, there is also a gender difference between the proportional areas of the pharyngeal and oral resonating cavities: a female vocal tract is shorter by about 2 cm in the pharynx, while only 1.25 cm shorter in the oral cavity. A second problem is that speakers may not need to normalize in order to identify vowels. Normalization presupposes familiarity with the point vowels so that they can be used as references for the scaling process. But studies by Verbrugge, Strange, Shankweiler, and Edman have shown that listeners can identify a vowel spoken by an unknown speaker without having previously heard him say any other vowels. They also found that vowel identification is more accurate for (1) vowels in context than for isolated formants, and (2) for vowels cued only by formant transitions (the formants of the vowel nucleus having been deleted) than for the formants of the nucleus heard in isolation.

Thus, although most researchers agree that formant frequencies, patterns, and transitions play roles in vowel identification, it is unclear exactly how the listener extracts the information needed for vowel identification from these acoustic cues. One suggestion is that the information about the articulation is somehow coded directly into the acoustic signal, and that since articulation across speakers is analogous, the listener can decode the articulatory information and recover the identity of the vowel. In fact, this type of theoretical construct will (as we shall see later) work for all classes of speech sounds, but the details of both the encoding and decoding processes it implies remain unclear at this time.

Diphthongs. In Chapter 5, we described diphthongs as vowel sounds of changing resonance, so it is not surprising to find that relatively rapid changes in the formants of synthetic vowels are sufficient cues to diphthong perception. Gay systematically varied the duration of the F_2 frequency change and found that the rate of change was a more important cue to the identification of a diphthong than the exact formant frequencies at the end of the diphthongs /ɔɪ/, /aɪ/, and /aʊ/. It appears, then, that the IPA renderings of these diphthongs are approximations to the actual sounds they contain, and that listeners depend more on the acoustic result of the tongue moving rapidly in the required direction rather than on the attainment of a particular target position.

Semivowels. The sounds /w/, /j/, /r/, and /l/, as in "wet," "yet," "red," and "led," like tense vowels and diphthongs, are voiced and are characterized by changing formant frequencies, called *transitions*. Formant transitions occur when a vowel precedes or follows a consonant, reflecting changes in resonance as the vocal tract moves to or from the more constricted consonant position. The formant transitions that characterize diphthongs and semivowels, however, are internal to the sounds themselves, and serve as critical acoustic cues to their identification. Especially important to the perception of semivowels are the frequency changes in F_2 and, in some cases, in F_3. Semivowels are distinguished from diphthongs by the greater rapidity of their formant transitions, which make them more consonant-like.

O'Connor, Gerstman, Liberman, Delattre, and Cooper found that they could synthesize perceptually acceptable, syllable- initial /w/ and /j/ with only two formants. This finding is not surprising when we recall that /w/ begins with a formant pattern similar to /u/, and /j/ with one similar to /i/. This means that it is the second formant that distinguishes /w/ from /j/, as the first formant for both these sounds is low, as it is for /u/ and /i/.

In contrast, three formants are usually required, for the perception of /r/ and /l/, and it is the third formant that distinguishes them from each other. For /r/, F_3 is lower than for /l/; therefore, in the context of a vowel, the F_3 must rise from the /r/ formant to that of the vowel. For /l/, F_3 is higher, and in most vowel contexts does not vary in frequency.

The best intervocalic semivowels, as synthesized on the Pattern Playback by Lisker are schematized in Figure 6.11. Note that the percent of identification of /l/ is generally somewhat lower than that for the other semivowels. Further cues must be needed for an unambiguous lateral sound. The F_2 by F_3 chart (Fig. 6.12) summarizes the formant relationships used by listeners to identify the semivowels.

Nasal Consonants. Perception of nasals may be considered to involve two decisions: whether a segment is nasal or non-nasal, and if nasal, whether it is labial /m/, alveolar /n/, or palatal-velar /ŋ/. Using a computer to segment natural speech, Mermelstein found that the formant transitions of the vowels preceding and following nasals were effective cues to the identity of the nasals as a class. The obvious change in the spectrum from an orally produced vowel to a nasal includes two important features. The first is a weakening of the intensity of the upper formants because of antiresonances. This general decrease in intensity is used by listeners as a cue to nasal manner. A second spectral feature is the addition of a resonance below 500

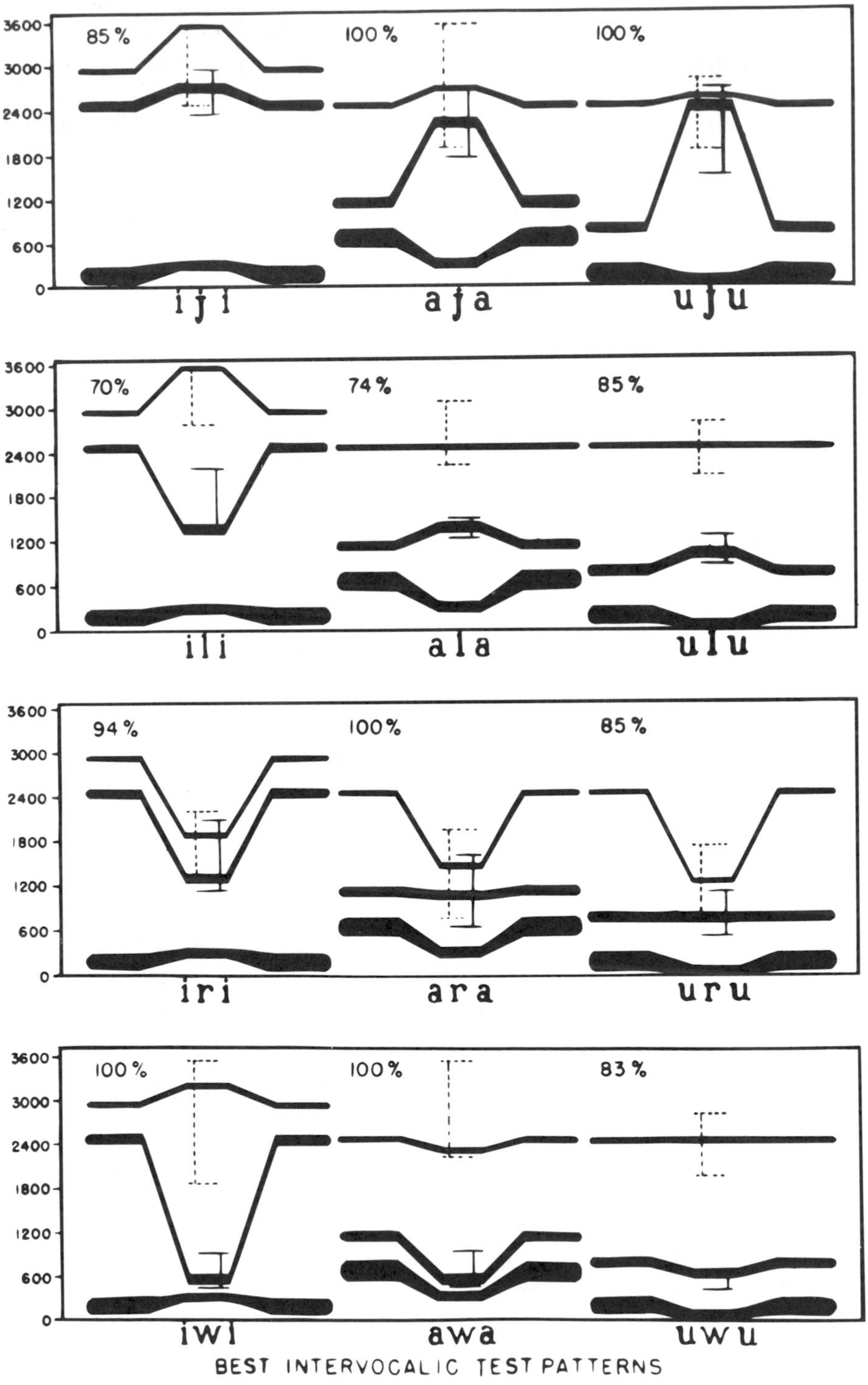

Figure 6.11. Three-formant synthetic patterns for intervocalic /j/, /l/, /r/, and /w/ with the vowels /i/, /a/, and /u/. Listeners were asked to identify each of a series of patterns as one of the four stimuli. The patterns shown here are those that were most consistently identified. (Reprinted with permission from L. Lisker: *Word, 13,* 1957.)

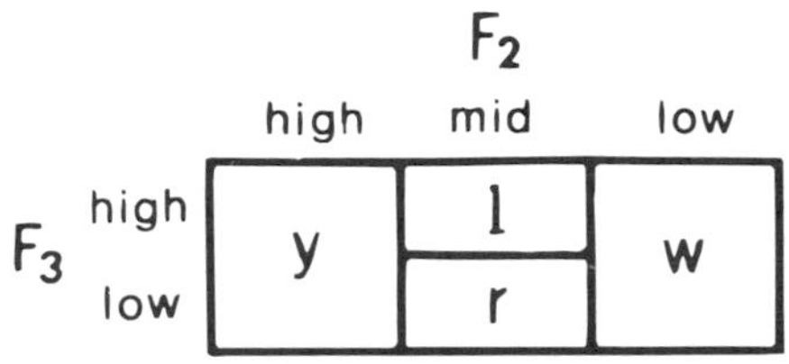

Figure 6.12. Schematic diagram describing the formant relationships for /y/, /w/, /r/, and /l/ sounds. (Adapted from L. Lisker: *Word, 13,* 1957.)

Hz (often around 250 Hz) that is called the *nasal murmur*. This low frequency nasal murmur has been shown to be a sufficient cue to nasal manner in synthetic speech stimuli from which upper formants were omitted.

Nasal manner can be cued in syllable-final nasals by the preceding vowel. In a tape-splicing study, Ali, Gallagher, Goldstein, and Daniloff found that listeners could perceive developing nasality during a vowel even when the VC transitions and the following nasal had been deleted from the acoustic signal. This, of course, is the acoustic effect of coarticulation in sequences of vowel + nasal that phoneticians refer to as vowel nasalization. It is especially easy for listeners to perceive open vowels as being nasal. This is because open vowels lack a low frequency resonance unless produced with nasality. High vowels, such as /i/ and /u/, normally have a low frequency resonance and, therefore, are acoustically more like nasals.

Perception of the place of nasal articulation is cued mainly by the direction of the transition (of F_2 particularly) to or from an adjacent vowel. Cooper, Delattre, Liberman, Borst, and Gerstman found that the nasals /m,n,ŋ/ could be synthesized on the Pattern Playback with the same formant transitions used to synthesize /p,b/, /t,d/, and /k,g/, respectively. Malécot found by tape-splicing natural speech, that although listeners used the frequency of the nasal murmur itself as a cue for place of articulation of the nasal, the VC transitions were a more powerful cue. After removing the transition between the vowel steady states and the nasal murmur, he found listeners much less able to report which nasal they were hearing. There are both frequency and durational cues in the transitions. The formant transitions from /m/ are the lowest in frequency and the shortest in duration; those for /n/ are higher in frequency and a bit longer in duration; and those for /ŋ/ are the highest and most variable in frequency and the longest in duration. The difference in transition duration between /n/ and /ŋ/ probably occurs because the back of the tongue is slower to move than the tongue tip. It is not known how well listeners are able to trade off transition and nasal murmur cues for one another. In analog studies of the nasals, House found that the resonance and antiresonance configurations were sufficient for listeners to identify /m/ and /n/, but that perception of the velar nasal /ŋ/ was less accurate; for /ŋ/, additional cues may be important. We shall find the same problem with the velar sounds /k/ and /g/ as we consider the perception of stop consonants.

Stops. The stop consonants /p,b,t,d,k,g/ have been studied more than have any other class of speech sounds. The stops are interesting because they clearly demonstrate the non-linearity of human perception when the stimuli are speech or speech-like synthesized sounds. This phenomenon of non-linear perception of speech will be discussed further in the section on categorical perception. Stops also demonstrate the redundancy of acoustic cues available to identify speech sounds. Finally, the nature of stop perception provides the best example of listener use of the acoustic overlapping of phonemes in the speech stream. The acoustic cues for the stops are to some degree overlaid upon the acoustic cues for neighboring vowels and consonants. Thus, the listener perceives a stop and the sounds adjacent to it according to their acoustic relationship to one another.

There are two obvious differences between stops and all the other classes of sounds (except the affricates). First, there is a complete occlusion of the vocal tract and thus a momentary cessation of airflow, which is heard either as silence, in the voiceless stops /p,t,k/, or as a brief attenuation of sound, in the voiced stops /b,d,g/. Second, the stopped air is often released in a burst, heard as a transient burst of noise.

Both the relative silence and the presence of a release burst are acoustic cues to stop manner.

The stops are also marked by a rapid change in the formant frequencies between the release of the occlusion and a following vowel and between a preceding vowel and the onset of the stop occlusion. These rapid formant transitions are caused by the sudden change in vocal tract shape as the articulators move from the position for a consonant to that for a vowel or vice-versa. They are found in many other classes of consonant sounds, but not in the semivowels, which display formant transitions of relatively long duration. The Haskins group found that they could synthesize /bɛ/ and /gɛ/ on the Pattern Playback (without including release bursts) simply by initiating the vowel with very brief formant transitions of less than 40 ms (Fig. 6.13). When they extended the duration of the transitions to 40 or 50 ms, listeners reported hearing the semivowel glides at the start of the syllables: /wɛ/ and /jɛ/. When the transitions were extended to 150 ms or more, listeners perceived a sequence of vowel sounds: /uɛ/ and /iɛ/.

These acoustic cues to the manner of articulation for stops—the relative silence, the burst, and the short transitions to the next vowel—are apparently more resistant to the masking effects of noise than are the acoustic cues to place of articulation, which distinguish the labials, /p,b/, from the alveolars, /t,d/, from the palatal-velars, /k,g/. Miller and Nicely analyzed perceptual confusions of English consonants in the presence of noise and found that listeners can identify the manner of production even when place cues are masked.

There are several cues that serve to indicate the place of articulation of a stop to listeners. Early tests, using Pattern Playback stimuli based upon real spectrograms, isolated two place cues as separate but sufficient: the frequency position of the burst in relation to a vowel and the F_2 transition. High frequency bursts preceding seven different two-formant synthetic vowels were all perceived as /t/. Low frequency bursts preceding the vowels were perceived as /p/. Bursts perceived as /k/ were slightly above the frequency of the F_2 of the following vowel (Fig. 6.14). Thus, /k/ percepts

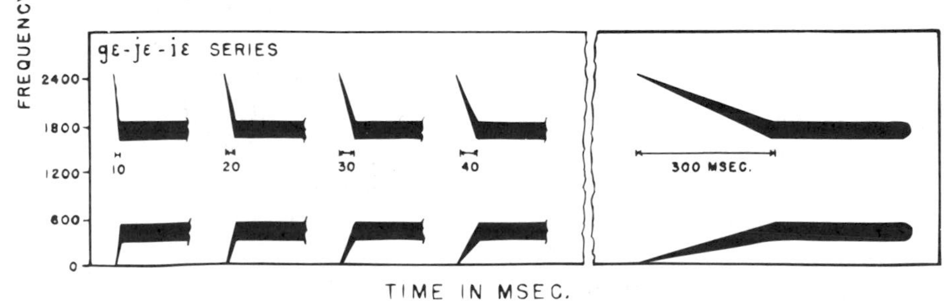

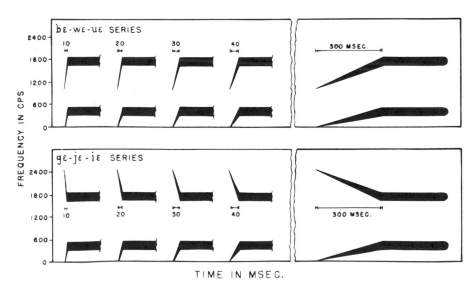

Figure 6.13. Spectrographic patterns with varying transition durations. The first four patterns in each row show how the tempo of the transitions was varied. At the *extreme right* of each row is a complete stimulus pattern, *i.e.*, transition plus steady-state vowel, for the longest duration of transition tested. The patterns at the *extreme left* and *right* of the *top row* are judged as /be/ and /ue/, respectively. The corresponding patterns in the *bottom row* as /ge/ and /ie/. (Reprinted with permission from A. M. Liberman *et al.*: *Journal of Experimental Psychology, 52,* © 1956, American Psychological Association.)

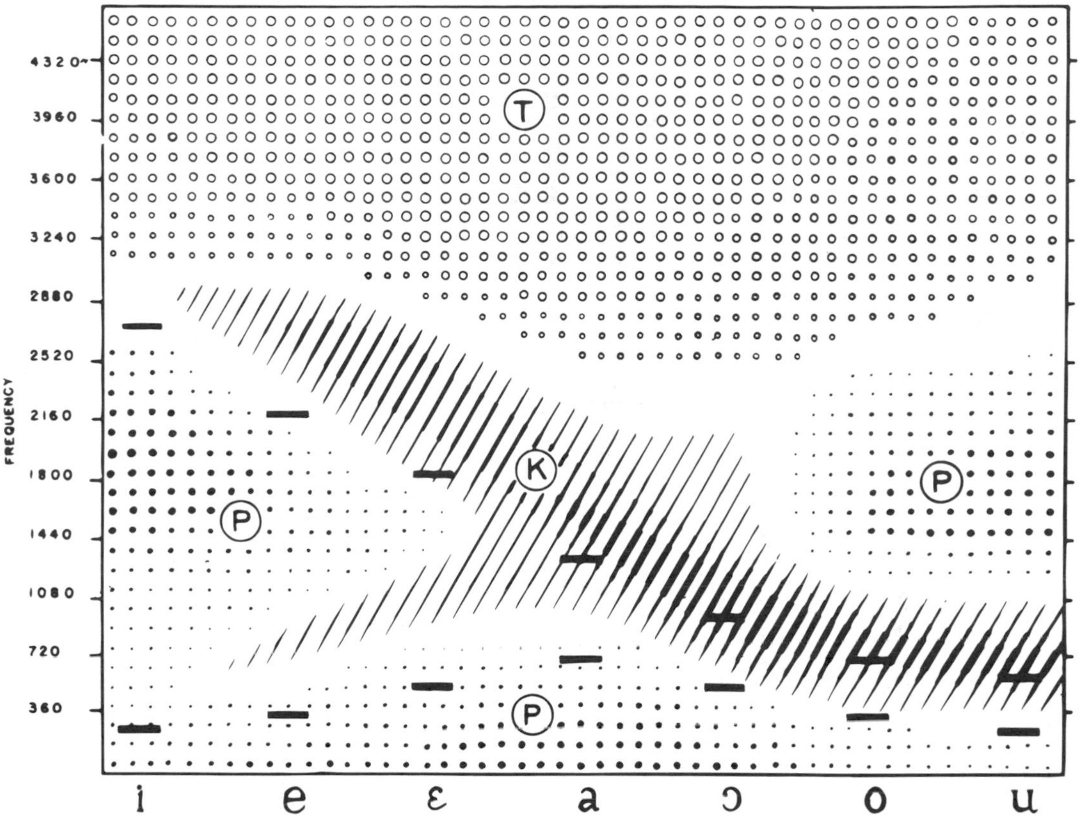

Figure 6.14. Center frequency of burst that will be perceived as a given voiceless stop, with various vowels. The filled dots indicate the frequency of bursts perceived as /p/, the open circles as /t/, and the slashes as /k/. The *bolder face symbols* in the grid indicate greater listener agreement. The two-formant pattern with which each burst was paired was appropriate for each of the indicated vowels. (Reprinted with permission from A. M. Liberman *et al.*: *American Journal of Psychology. LXV,* 1952.)

were reported for high frequency bursts before front vowels and for low frequency bursts before back vowels.

Further experiments indicated that stop place of articulation could also be cued by the rapid F_2 transitions between the stop consonants and the steady-state portions of the following vowels. The experimenters synthesized a series of two-formant C + /ɑ/ syllables (Fig. 6.15) initiated only by formant transitions (no release bursts were synthesized). The first formant transition and the steady state formant frequencies of the following /ɑ/ were held constant throughout the series. The independent variable was the slope of the F_2 transition, which varied systematically from sharply rising to sharply falling in 10 steps. Listeners identified all of the stops cued by the rising F_2 transitions as labial, /p,b/, but divided the stops cued by the falling F_2 transitions into two groups: Alveolar /t,d/ were reported when the slopes of the transitions were slightly falling, while the palatal-velar stops /k,g/ were reported when the slopes of the F_2 transitions fell sharply in frequency.

It is important to recognize that the patterns of F_2 transitions described above are limited to the context of the vowel /ɑ/, which has a low-to-mid range second formant frequency (around 1300 Hz). If the stops are synthesized before a vowel with a high second formant, such as /i/, the F_2 transitions leading from the

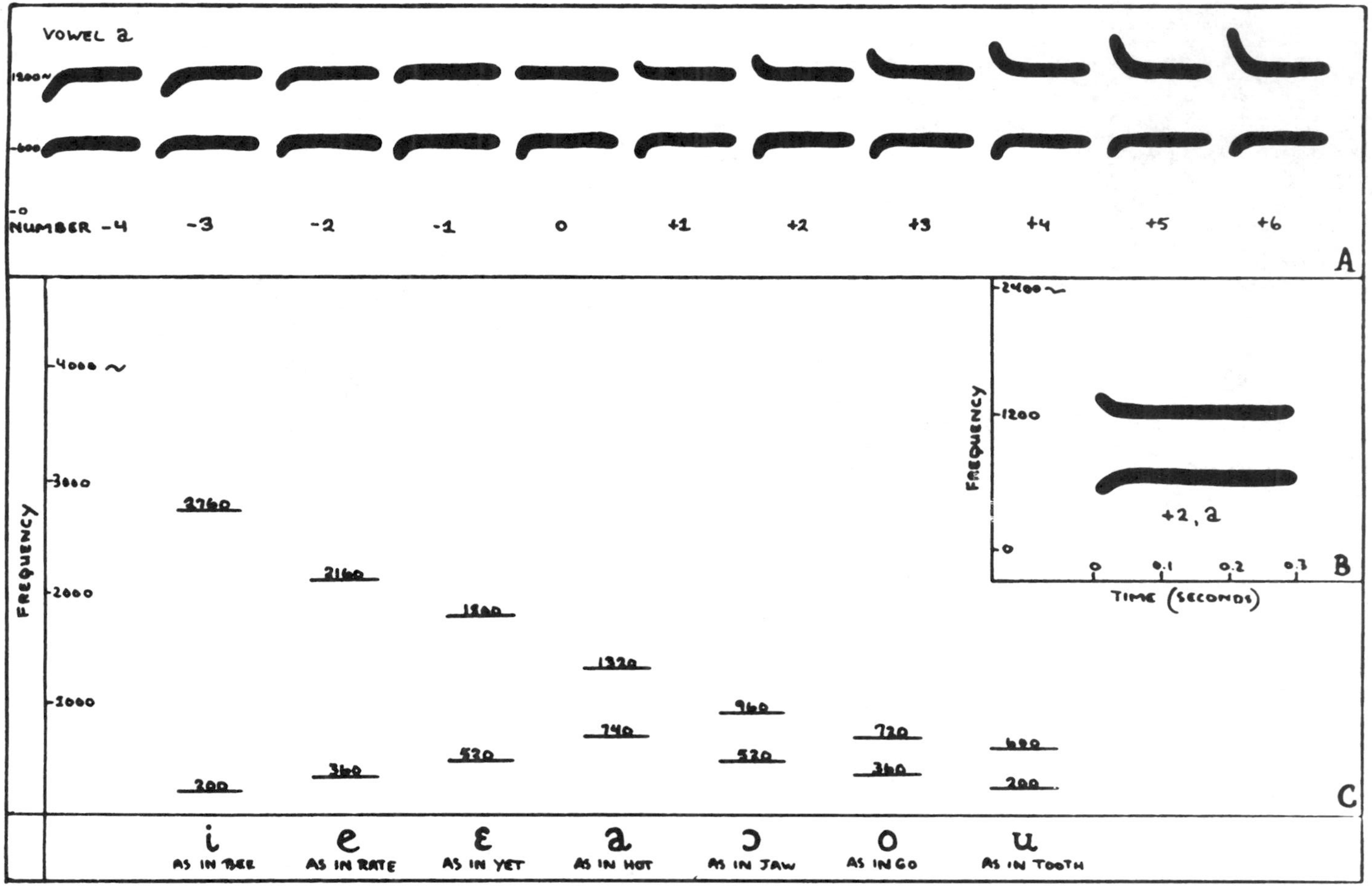

Figure 6.15. Two-formant synthetic pattern for the voiced stops. *Part A* shows the vowel /a/ with a full range of transitions. *Part B* shows a single pattern. *Part C* shows the two-formant synthetic patterns for various vowels, which were combined with the range of transitions shown in *Part A*. (Reprinted with permission from A. M. Liberman *et al.*: *Psychological Monographs: General and Applied. 68,* © 1954, American Psychological Association.)

labials will rise much more steeply than before /ɑ/, those leading from the alveolars will rise, rather than fall slightly, and the velar transitions will fall less sharply. Before a vowel with a low second formant, such as /u/, the transitions leading from both the alveolar and velar stops will fall in frequency (more sharply in the case of the velars), and the labial transitions will rise in frequency, but less sharply than before /ɑ/ or /i/. In short, each combination of the stops with a different vowel yields a pattern of frequency change in the F_2 transition that is more or less different from every other combination.

The disparity in the patterns of formant transitions led investigators to search for some unifying principle that could interrelate the differing transitions for each place of articulation. A study by Delattre, Liberman, and Cooper resulted in the theory that an acoustic locus exists for each place of articulation. In order to explain the concept, we must return to a consideration of stop consonant production. When a stop consonant occlusion is released, the vocal tract shape will be associated with particular formant resonances that change as the vocal tract shape changes toward the following vowel. Since the place of occlusion for a given stop in various vowel contexts is roughly the same, there should be a systematic relationship between consonant-vowel combinations and the starting frequency of the F_2 transition. It is this articulatory relationship that underlies the findings of the locus experiment.

Two-formant patterns were synthesized, with some stop-like characteristics and a steady-state F_2. The best /g/ sound was perceived when the flat F_2 was at 3000 Hz, the best /d/ at 1800 Hz, and the best /b/ at 720 Hz. When stimuli were synthesized with constant F_1 transitions, but with F_2 transitions graded from sharply rising to sharply falling, it was found that if the transitions all pointed to the loci (the best frequencies listed above) and if the first half of the transitions were removed or silent (Fig. 6.16B), listeners could distinguish the place of articulation on the basis of these acoustic loci. The locus was the place on the frequency scale to which the F_2 transitions pointed. This method worked particularly well for /d/, the alveolar stop. The difficulty in identifying a particular F_2 transition or locus with /g,k,ŋ/ results partly from the articulatory fact

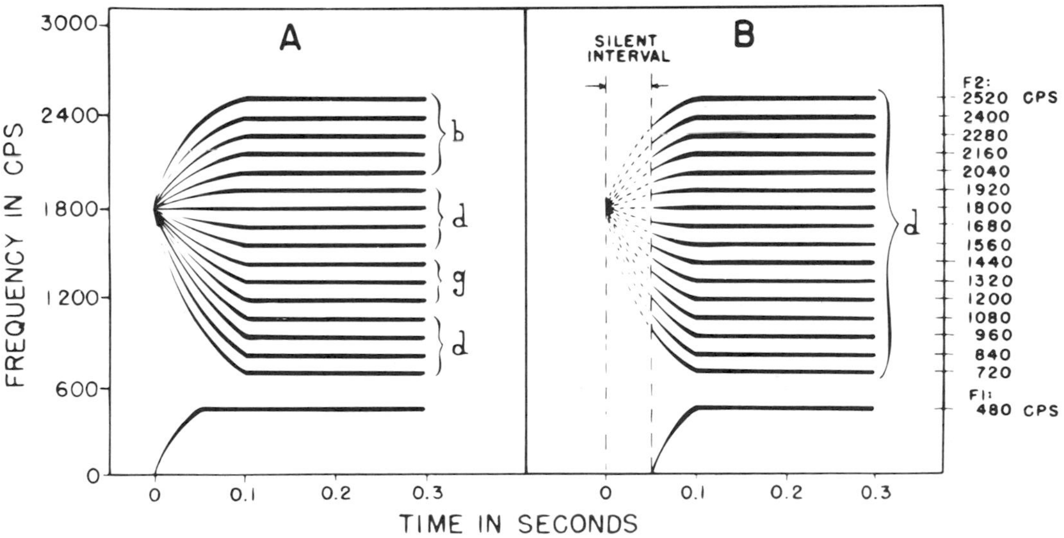

Figure 6.16. The locus principle. *Part A* shows the varying perceived identity of two-formant patterns with a rising first formant, and a second formant with the origin at 1800 Hz. If the first 50 msec of the pattern is erased, as in Part B, the patterns will all be heard as /d/, with a varying vowel. (Reprinted with permission from P. Delattre *et al.*: *Journal of the Acoustical Society of America., 27,* 1955.)

that these consonants are not restricted to one place of articulation and partly from the acoustic fact, pointed out by Kuhn, that as the place of constriction moves back in the oral cavity, the consonant resonance may change its allegiance from one formant to another. Thus, the transition of the third formant also plays a role in cuing the place of articulation of stops (as well as of other consonants).

Stops differ in voicing as well as place of articulation. For each place of articulation, there is a voiced and a voiceless stop. Cues to voicing class are the presence or absence of a fundamental frequency (phonation) during the period of stop closure (displayed as a low frequency voice bar on wideband spectrograms), the presence or absence of noise (aspiration) following stop release, and variation in onset time of phonation and F_1 following the release of prevocalic stops. The Haskins group studied the effects on perception of progressively "cutting back" the first formant transition in a series of stimuli. The first stimulus had a voice bar and transition rising from the baseline. In successive stimuli, 10 msec were removed from F_1 (Fig. 6.17). The resulting delay of F_1 relative to F_2 onset is referred to as F_1 cutback. Listeners reported hearing voiced stops for the first three stimuli in the series, and, in most instances, voiceless stops for the last three stimuli with F_1 cutbacks of 30 ms or more. Further research indicated that the voiced versus voiceless distinction depended more on the amount of delay than on the starting frequency of F_1, which increased as the amount of cutback increased (Fig. 6.17).

The presence of aspiration did not serve as a sufficient cue to voiceless stops by itself,

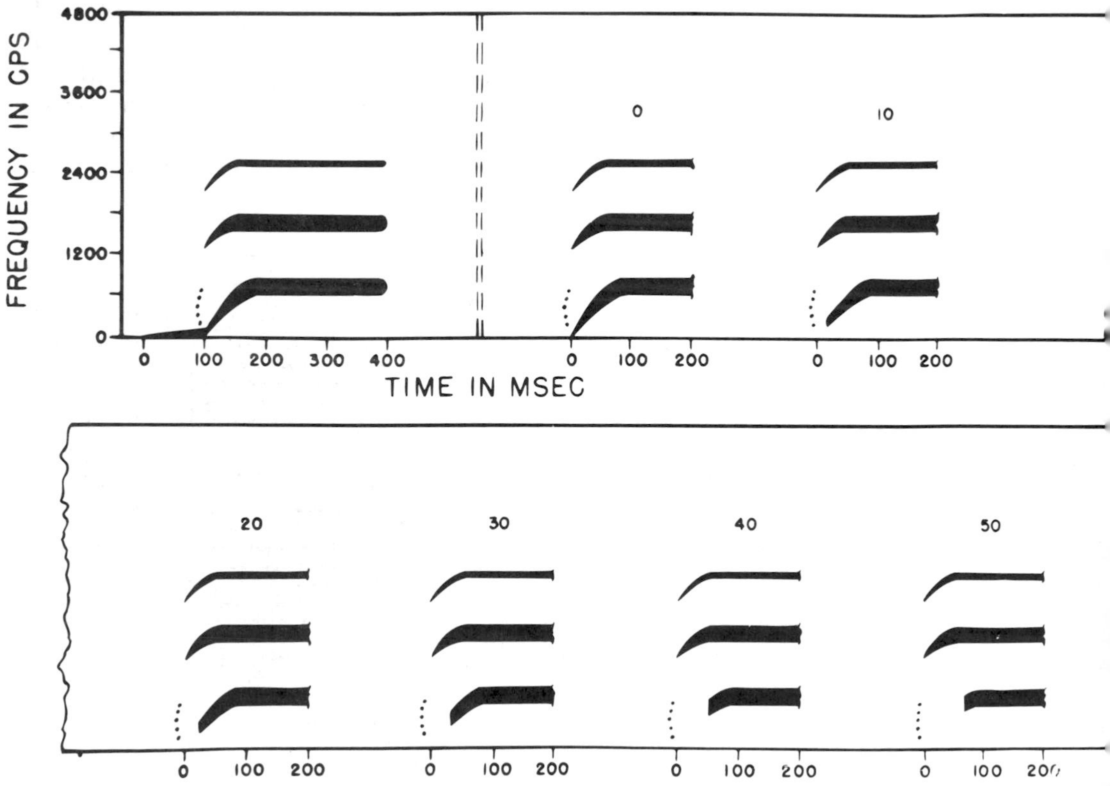

Figure 6.17. Synthetic patterns varying in F_1 cutback. The pattern at the *top left corner* has a voice bar. In the "0" pattern, F_1, F_2, and F_3 begin simultaneously. In successive patterns, F_1 onset is delayed, in milliseconds, by the time indicated above the pattern. After a certain degree of F, cutback, listeners reported hearing [pa] instead of [ba]. (Reprinted with permission from A. M. Liberman *et al.*: *Language and Speech. 1,* 1958.)

but when noise was added to the upper formants of stimuli with an F_1 cutback, listeners got a stronger impression of voicelessness than they did with the F_1 cutback alone.

The experiments on F_1 cutback prefigured the work on voice onset time by Lisker and Abramson. The timing of the F_1 onset in the synthetic stimuli corresponds to the timing of the onset of phonation in natural speech. Moreover, the differences between the amount of cutback required for listeners to report hearing a voiceless stop at the various places of articulation was, in general, mirrored in Lisker and Abramson's acoustic analysis of VOT in initial stops: Both F_1 cutback and VOT are greater for the velar stops than for the labials or alveolars. In VOT studies, this finding has held for the voiced stops as well.

The presence of silence has been mentioned as an acoustic cue for stops. Inserting silence between appropriate segments, such as the /s/ and /l/ of "slit," will cause the word to be heard as "split." Differences in the duration of silence sometimes contribute to the cuing of the voiced-voiceless distinction. For example, if the closure duration of the stop in the word "rabid" is increased to more than 70 ms, listeners report hearing "rapid," but only when the periodicity generated by phonation has been removed from the closure. The duration of vowels preceding syllable-final stops can also contribute to their classification as voiced or voiceless. Raphael, in experiments using both synthetic and natural speech stimuli, found that stops are perceived as voiceless more frequently when preceded by vowels of shorter duration, and as voiced when preceded by vowels of longer duration. Raphael points out that the normally redundant vowel duration cue helps disambiguate syllable-final stops when they are unreleased, as they frequently are in American English.

In summary, there are several acoustic cues that listeners use to determine the manner, place, and voicing classes of stop consonants. The presence of silence, a release-burst, and relatively rapid formant transitions can all serve as cues to the stop manner of articulation. The acoustic cues for the place of articulation of stops are the frequency of the burst relative to the vowel and the formant transitions, especially F_2. To recognize the voiced-voiceless contrast, listeners use several cues: the presence or absence of phonation and aspiration, F_1 delay, the duration of the silence marking the stop closure, and the duration of a preceding vowel. It is important to note that a single articulatory behavior can give rise to a number of different, redundant acoustic cues. For example, the timing of the initiation of phonation relative to stop release accounts for VOT, the presence or absence of aspiration, the degree of F_1 cutback, and other acoustic features that signal the voiced- voiceless opposition. This redundancy is useful for speech perception, which must be exact at rates of phoneme transmission that can, on occasion, exceed 20 phonemes per second.

Fricatives. The nature of fricative articulation gives rise to a relatively extended period of noise (frication) that is the principle acoustic cue to the perception of fricative manner. Al though there are other acoustic features that are associated with fricatives, none is as important as the presence of the noise generated by the turbulent airstream as it passes through the articulatory constriction required for the formation of this class of sounds.

Two of the acoustic cues to place of articulation are also a function of the noise generated by fricative articulation. These cues reside in the spectrum and intensity of the frication. Listeners are able to distinguish the fricatives with relatively steep, high frequency spectral peaks (the sibilants, /s,z,ʃ,ʒ/) from those with relatively flat spectra (the non-sibilants, /θ,ð,f,v/). This spectral distinction thus divides the fricatives into two general categories of place: posterior (sibilant) and anterior (non-sibilant). The posteriorly articulated sibilant fricatives can further be distinguished as being alveolar or post-alveolar on the basis of the location of their lowest spectral peaks: around 4 KHz for /s,z/ and 2.5 KHz for /ʃ,ʒ/. (Higher frequencies, of course, will be found for the smaller average vocal tract lengths of adult females and children.) The anteriorly articulated non-sibilant fricatives, labiodental /θ,ð/ and linguadental /f,v/, however, are not as reliably distinguished from each other because the dental constriction that characterizes them causes their spectra to be very similar. Miller and Nicely found /v/ and /ð/ to be among the most confusable of speech sounds to listeners when noise was added to the stimuli. Indeed, the dental fricatives are highly confusable in natural speech, and, in some dialects of English, one set (usually the labiodentals) is often substituted generally for the other (the linguadentals).

The intensity differences among the fricatives work in much the same way as the spectral differences to cue place of articulation. That is, the sibilant fricatives are marked by relatively high intensity levels, in contrast to the low intensity levels of the non-sibilant fricatives. The absence of an appreciable resonating cavity in front of the dental constrictions of /θ,ð,f,v/ accounts for their generally low level of intensity. Listeners do not seem to use intensity cues to distinguish further among the places of articulation of fricatives. This is of little importance with regard to the sibilant fricatives, which can be distinguished on the basis of spectral cues, but it adds another source of confusion to the identification of the place of articulation of the non-sibilants, /θ,ð,f,v/.

The place of articulation of fricatives is also cued by the second (and third) formant transitions of the resonant sounds preceding and following them. The transition cues appear to be less important for the identification of place of articulation for fricatives than for stops. This is not surprising, considering the salience of the spectral cues to fricative place of articulation, especially for the sibilants. Once again, however, the greater articulatory difference between the constriction locations of the sibilant fricatives provides a more salient formant transition cue than does the more similar constriction location of the non-sibilants, providing yet another potential source of confusion among the latter set.

To assess the relative importance of the spectral and transitional cues in fricative perception, Harris used recordings of fricative-vowel syllables in which each of the voiceless fricatives was combined with each of the vowels /i,e,o/ and /u/. The fricative noise in each syllable was separated from the vocalic portion. Each noise segment was then combined with each vocalic segment (which contained the formant transitions appropriate to the consonant that had originally preceded it). A similar test was constructed for the voiced fricatives. Regardless of the vowel in any stimulus, whenever the noise segment for /s,z/ or /ʃ,ʒ/ was paired with any vocalic portion, listeners reported that they heard /s,z/ or /ʃ,ʒ/, respectively. Listener judgments of /f,v/ or /θ,ð/, however, depended upon the formant transitions in the vocalic segments (much as in the case of the nasal murmurs, which are also minimally distinctive and of relatively low intensity).

To identify the voicing class of a fricative, the presence or absence of phonation, during the articulation of the sound, is a salient perceptual cue. Even without this cue, however, listeners can make reliable judgments about the voicing class of a syllable-final fricative based upon its duration relative to the duration of the vowel preceding it. Denes used tape-splicing techniques to interchange the final fricatives in the noun "use" /jus/ and the verb "use" /juz/. In making the exchange, he shortened the normally longer /s/ and lengthened the /z/. The /s/ from /jus/ was heard as /z/ when spliced on the end of the /ju/ of /juz/, because of the longer /u/ before voiced consonants than before voiceless consonants. Conversely, the /z/ from /juz/ was heard as /s/ when spliced after the shorter /u/. Denes showed that it is not the vowel duration alone that listeners take as their cue to final fricative voicing, but the relative durations of the vowel and the fricative. It is also possible that listeners use intensity differences between the frication of voiced and voiceless fricatives to distinguish between the members of such cognate pairs as /s/ and /z/: Because the pulsing of the vocal folds interrupts the airflow during the production of a voiced fricative, the volume of air forced through the oral constriction is less for voiced than for voiceless fricatives, resulting in a somewhat less intense acoustic signal.

The experimental data and the observations above suggest a possible perceptual strategy for fricative identification. First, listeners identify the presence of a fricative because they hear a noisy, aperiodic component of relatively long duration in the acoustic signal. They then seem to place the fricative into one of two groups, based on relative intensity: posteriorly articulated sibilants of higher intensity, /s,z,ʃ,ʒ/, or anteriorly articulated non-sibilant fricatives of low intensity, /θ,ð,f,v/. The sibilants are then further distinguished according to place of articulation on the basis of spectral cues, the alveolar fricatives /s/ and /z/ having a first spectral peak at about 4 KHz, and the alveolar-palatal fricatives /ʃ/ and /ʒ/ having a first spectral peak at about 2.5 KHz. The study by Harris indicates that listeners need to use both the spectral cues of the frication and those of the formant transitions into neighboring vowels to distinguish the linguadental from the labiodental fricatives. Decisions about voicing class are based on the presence versus absence of phonation during frication, the relative durations of vocalic and noise segments, and upon the relative intensity differences between voiced and voiceless fricatives (or some combination of these cues).

Affricates. Because affricates are stops with a fricative release, they contain the acoustic cues to perception that are found in both stops and fricatives. The silence, the release burst, the rapid rise time, the frication, and the formant transitions in adjacent sounds are all presumably used by listeners in identifying affricates. Raphael, Dorman, and Isenberg varied frication duration, closure duration, and rise time of the noise in utterances such as "ditch" /dItʃ/ and "dish" /dIʃ/, and found that a trading relationship among the cues. For example, inserting an appropriate duration of silence between the /I/ and /ʃ/ of "dish" will cause the stimulus to be heard as "ditch." Increasing the duration of the frication of /ʃ/, however, will cause the percept to revert to "dish." Listeners are, apparently, sensitive to the relative durational values of the acoustic cues in stimuli of this type.

Cues for Manner, Place, and Voicing. To summarize the wealth of information on acoustic cues important to the perception of speech segments, it may be helpful to recapitulate, by dividing the cues into those important to the perception of manner, place, and voicing distinctions. To identify the manner of a speech sound, listeners determine whether the sound is harmonically structured with no noise (which signals vowels, semivowels, or nasals) or whether the sound contains a nonperiodic component (which signals stops, fricatives, or affricates). The periodic, harmonically structured classes present acoustic cues in energy regions that are relatively low in frequency. In contrast, the aperiodic, noisy classes of speech sounds are cued by energy that is relatively high in frequency.

How do listeners further separate the harmonically structured vowels, nasals, and semivowels? The main manner cues available are relative intensity of formants and formant frequency changes. The nasal consonants have formants that contrast strongly in intensity with those of neighboring vowels. In addition, there is the distinctive low frequency resonance, the nasal murmur. Semivowels display formants that glide from one frequency to another compared to the relatively more steady state formants of the vowels and nasals. The formants for some diphthongs change in frequency as much as those of any semivowel, but the changes are generally more rapid for semivowels.

One manner cue for the classes of sounds having an aperiodic component, the stops, fricatives, and affricates, is the duration of the noise, which is transient for stops, but lasts longer for affricates and lasts the longest for fricatives. Our summary figure showing the acoustic cues for manner of articulation (Fig. 6.18) shows all of the parameters of sound to be important; manner contrasts rest on relative frequency, intensity, and timing.

The acoustic cues for place of articulation depend more upon a single parameter of sound frequency. For vowels and semivowels, the formant relationships, as we have seen, serve to indicate tongue placement, mouth opening, and vocal tract length. Vowel placement is reflected in the F_1–F_2 acoustic space, with F_1 frequency indicating tongue height or mouth

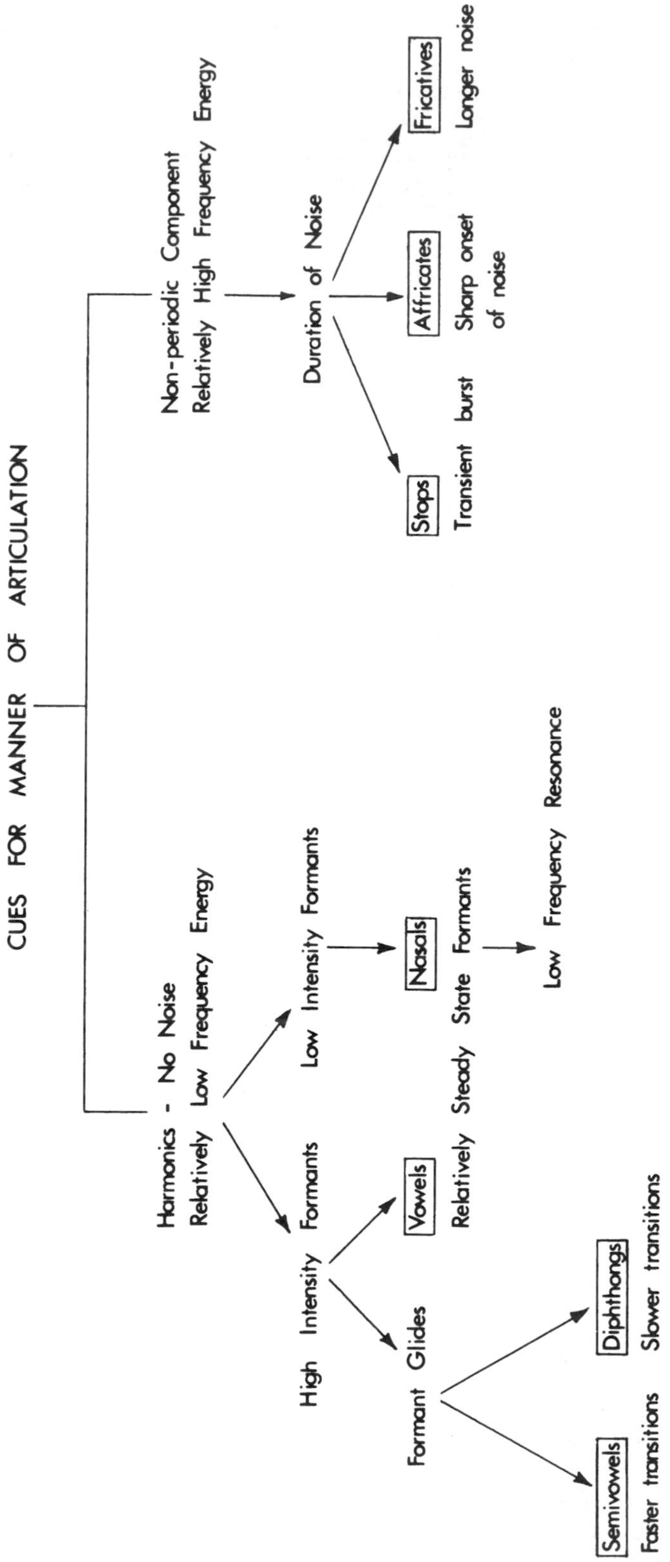

Figure 6.18. Summary of the cues for manner of articulation.

opening and F_2 frequency indicating place of maximum approximation of the tongue with the walls of the vocal tract. Semivowel production is mainly reflected in the frequency changes in F_2. The semivowel /j/ begins with the highest F_2, with /r/ and /l/ in the middle frequencies, and /w/ relatively low. F_3 serves to contrast the acoustic results of tongue tip placement for /r/ and /l/.

For stops, fricatives, and affricates, two prominent acoustic cues to place of articulation are the F_2 transitions into neighboring vowels and the frequency of the noise components (Fig. 6.19). In general, a second formant transition with a low frequency locus cues a labial percept, one with a higher locus cues an alveolar percept, and one with a varied, vowel-dependent locus cues a palatal or velar percept. The F_2 transition is also used to cue the difference between the labiodental and linguadental fricatives.

The frequency of the noise component of a consonant serves as a cue to place of articulation. The high frequency spectral peak for the noise in alveolar /s/ and /z/ is often at or above 4 KHz, while for the more retracted, alveolar-palatal /ʃ/ and /ʒ/, it is more often closer to 2.5 KHz. If the frication covers a wide band of frequencies, has no prominent spectral peak, and is of lower intensity than the neighboring vowel(s), it is more likely to be identified as /f,v/, or /θ,ð/. The spectrum of the noise component cues place of articulation even when the noise is extremely brief as in stop or affricate release bursts, with low frequency spectral peaks cuing labial percepts, high frequency peaks cuing alveolar percepts, and vowel-dependent, midfrequency range peaks cuing palatal and velar percepts.

Finally, the acoustic cues for consonant voicing depend more upon relative durations and timing of events than upon frequency or intensity differences. There is an exception, the cue of the presence or absence of phonation (glottal pulsing). The periodicity of voicing itself is important, but the fact that a speaker can whisper "The tie is blue" and "The dye is blue" and that a listener can perceive the "voicing" difference between "tie" and "dye" indicates that timing is an important cue to the perception of the "voiced-voiceless" distinction in consonants. The timing differences used to signal the voiced-voiceless contrast have been measured in different ways (see summary in Fig. 6.20). Longer voice onset times, periods of aspiration, and closure durations cue /p,t,k/, the voiceless stops, in contrast to the shorter voice onset times, periods of aspiration, and closure durations that cue the voiced stops, /b,d,g/. Other things being equal, cutting back the first formant in synthesized speech, to mimic the aspiration and voicing onset delays, results in the perception of voiceless stops. Thus, a stop-vowel syllable synthesized with F_1 rising from the baseline is perceived as voiced.

Fricatives and affricates are perceived as voiceless when the frication is of relatively long duration, and, in the case of affricates, when the closure duration is also relatively long. Finally, the duration of a vowel can cue the voicing class of a following consonant: A voiced consonant will be perceived when the preceding vowel is relatively long in duration, and a voiceless consonant will be perceived when the duration of the preceding vowel is relatively short.

Suprasegmentals. The suprasegmental, linguistic features of speech, including intonation, stress, and juncture, are perceived by listeners in terms of variations and contrasts in pitch, loudness, and length. As you know, the physical features of fundamental frequency, amplitude, and duration are, respectively, the principle determinants of the perceptual qualities. It is important to maintain the distinctions between the perceptual qualities and the physical/acoustic features that underlie them because linguistic percepts, such as stress and intonation do not have simple and direct representations in the acoustic signal. One cannot, for example, assume that because the second syllable in a word has a greater duration than the first that it will be perceived as bearing greater linguistic stress than the first. Similarly, a rise in fundamental frequency at the end of a sentence is not a certain indication that the listener will perceive that there was a rise in pitch or that a question had been ut-

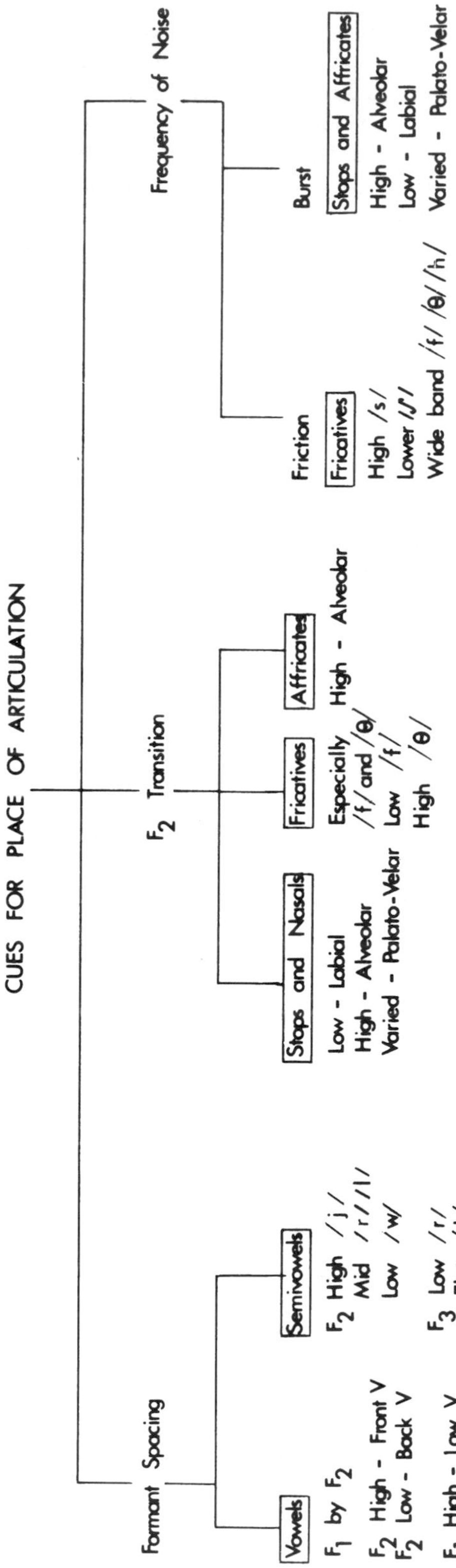

Figure 6.19. Summary of the cues for place of articulation.

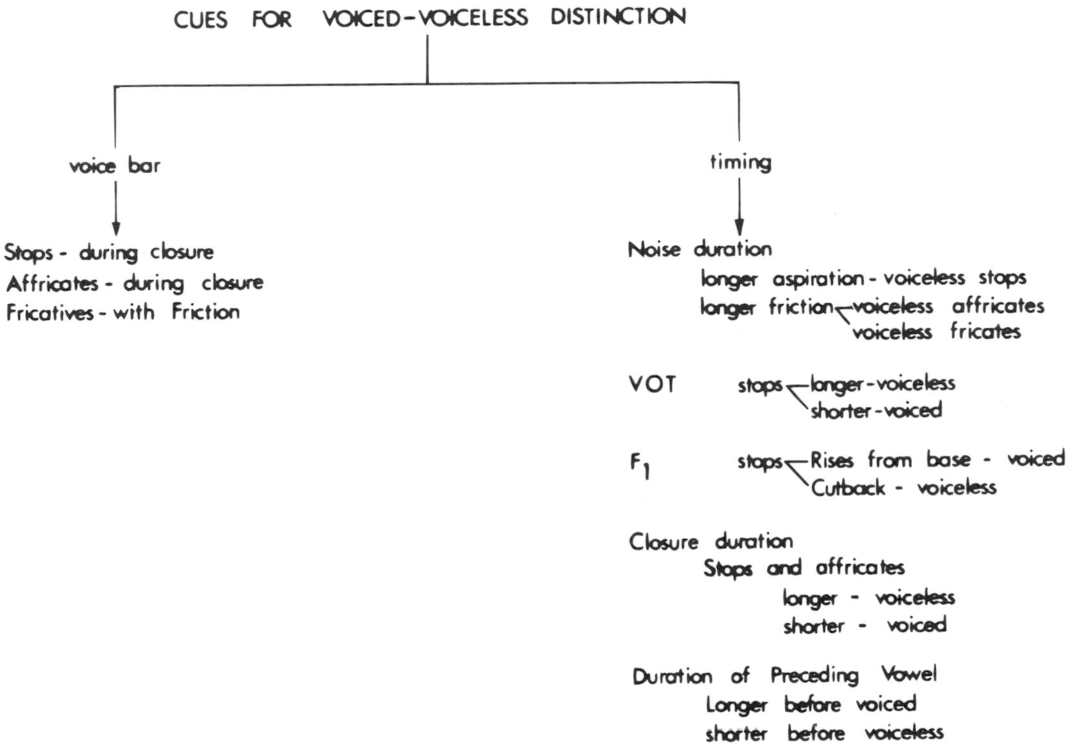

Figure 6.20. Summary of the cues for the voiced-voiceless distinction.

tered. Such percepts often depend on the extent of the physical changes, the covariation of a number of acoustic variables, and the degree of contrast between the values of the acoustic variables over a number of syllables.

The perception of intonation requires the ability to track pitch changes. This ability is one of the first skills acquired by infants. The tracking process is not, at this time, well understood. Clearly it allows listeners to detect changes in the direction of pitch and the extent of those changes. For instance, experiments by Hadding-Koch and Studdert-Kennedy have shown that, given ambiguous speech material, a rising intonation pattern is perceived by English (and Swedish) listeners as a question, and a falling intonation pattern as a statement. The process must also enable listeners to locate the peaks of pitch in the intonation pattern with some precision. This ability is important in the perception of stress.

Any syllable may be spoken with a greater or lesser degree of stress, depending on the meaning demanded by context. For example, the first syllable in the noun ˈPERmit will be perceived as carrying more stress than the first syllable of the verb perˈMIT if the speaker is following the usual convention. The reverse, of course, is true of the second syllables in these words. As we saw in the last chapter, certain acoustic features characterize a stressed syllable. Thus, the first syllable of the noun ˈPERmit is likely to have a higher fundamental frequency, and greater duration and amplitude than the "same" syllable when it appears in the verb perˈMIT. We would expect, therefore, that listeners perceive the more stressed version of the syllable as higher in pitch and greater in length and loudness. In fact, untrained listeners may be quite poor at making explicit judgements of pitch, length and loudness, or even at specifying the location of a stressed syl-

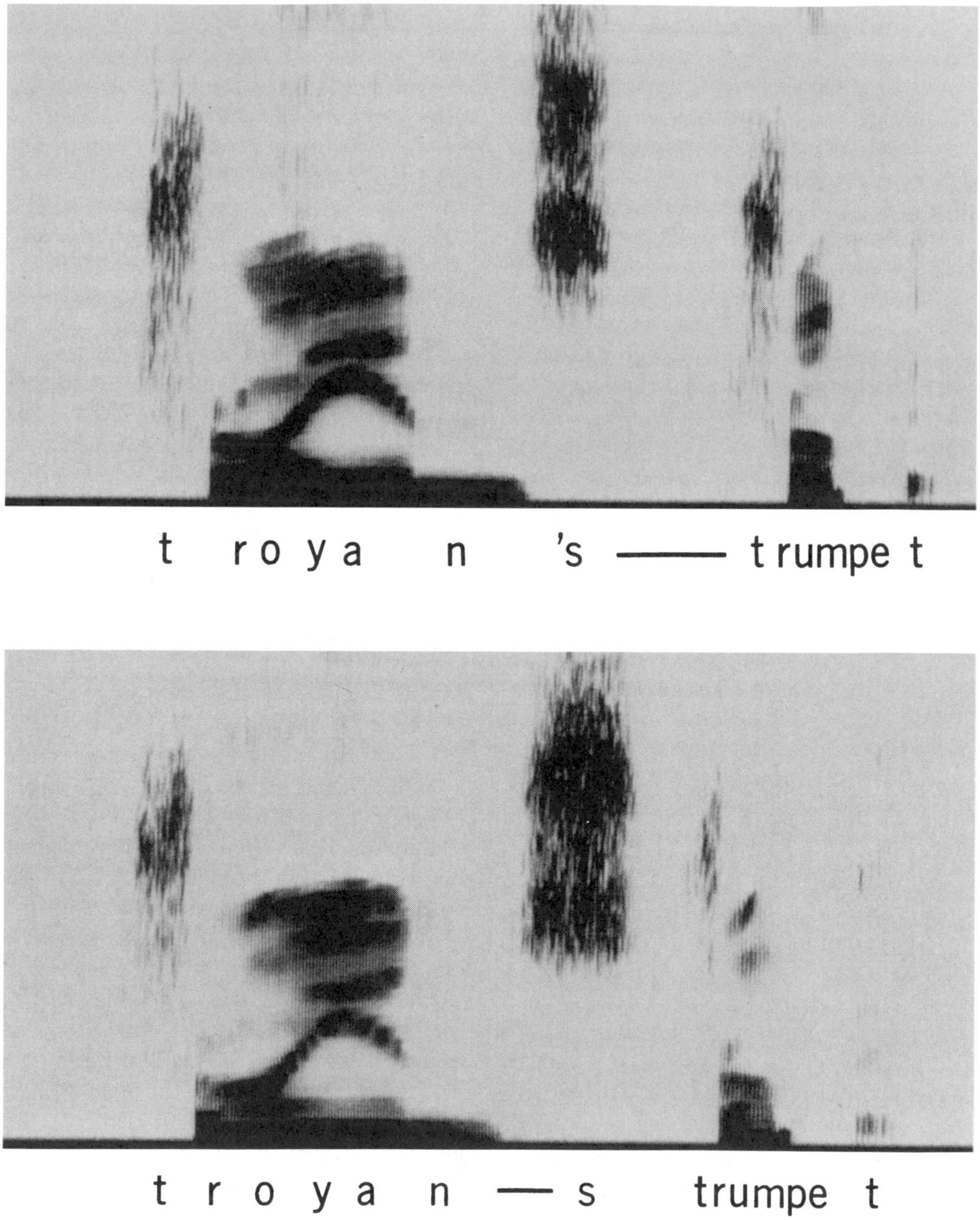

Figure 6.21. Spectrograms of "Troyans" trumpet!" and "Troyan strumpet!" Notice the acoustic results of the change in juncture. The fricative is lengthened when in word-initial position, as is the aspiration for the /t/ in "trumpet."

lable. Still, they must be capable of using the perceptual information if they understand speech in a normal manner. Listeners thus do far better at identifying 'PERmit as a noun than at identifying the syllable with the higher pitch or the greater length, loudness, or stress.

Although the acoustic features of fundamental frequency, duration, and amplitude all contribute to the perception of stress, they do not do so equally. Experiments by Fry, Bolinger, and others have shown that fundamental frequency is the most powerful cue to stress, followed by duration and amplitude.

The prosodic feature of internal juncture (marking the difference between "a name" and "an aim") can be cued by a number of acoustic features, such as silence, vowel-lengthening, and the presence of voicing or aspiration. We like an example that Darwin has cited from Shakespeare's *Troilus and Cressida*. The crowd shouts "the Troyans' trumpet!" which, if the juncture is misplaced by lengthening the frication of the /s/ in "Troyans" and decreasing the aspiration of the initial /t/ of "trumpet," would sound as if the crowd were announcing a prominent prostitute (Fig. 6.21).

The Context of Acoustic Cues. The importance of context to speech perception is apparent in the recovery of both segmental information and suprasegmental information. One word that we find ourselves writing repeatedly in this chapter is "relative." The importance of f_0 to the perception of stress is that it tends to be higher on the stressed syllable or word relative to surrounding syllables or words. Similarly, formants need not be of particular frequencies to be recognized as vowels, but they must bear a certain general relationship to one another, and further, to be identified with certainty, must sometimes be perceived in relation to the frequencies of some other bit of speech produced by the same vocal tract.

Machines can be made to read print much more easily than they can be made to recognize speech because the letters in printing or writing are discrete items that can be identified individually and then identified as a word. The letters, T, A, P, are segments and do not vary. T may appear as t or change size, but it is always a nearly vertical line with a nearly horizontal line crossing it near the top. It is difficult to make a machine that can recognize speech, because the acoustic signal for (tæp] changes so continuously that it cannot be segmented the way the written word TAP can. One of the important acoustic cues to the /t/ is in the initial second formant transition to the vowel /æ/. The second formant transition at the end of the /æ/ supplies the listener with information about the /p/ to follow. Thus, humans behave very differently in perceiving speech than the type of speech-recognizing machine designed to act on a segment-by-segment basis.

A question often asked by Liberman in connection with his work in speech perception is: why do people learn to understand speech so much more easily than they learn to read? People find speech easy and natural, yet it is easier to design a machine to read print than to recognize speech. It may be that when we learn to speak and understand speech, it is naturally coarticulated, producing a constantly changing pattern that is not easily segmentable, and we perceive it, too, as a dynamic assimilated event. The imposition of the idea of "phonemes" is a linguistic device, useful in constructing an alphabet or in describing a language, but artificial and one step removed from the flow of speech itself. The more abstract phoneme has to be learned as part of a system imposed on speech and is hence inherently more difficult.

Invariant segments are suited for machines, however. Computers deal with continuous information by digitizing it, segmenting, and assigning numbers to it. An alphabet is thus easier for such a machine to cope with than speech with its overlapping phones. The human brain is adept at seeing and hearing relationships, at finding patterns, at adapting to change, and at what we shall consider next, placing items into categories.

Categorical Perception

In searching for the acoustic features of speech that are particularly important to perception, investigators found that graded changes in the F_2 transitions of two-formant CV syllables resulted in the perception of three different phonemes: /b,d/ and /g/ (see Fig. 6.22). Subjects perceived /b/ for those stimuli having the most sharply rising transitions. Then, as the transitions rose less and then began to fall slightly in frequency, their percepts shifted abruptly to a different category: /d/. Stimuli near the end of the continuum, those with F_2 transitions that fell more steeply, evoked another abrupt change in perception to the category /g/. When listeners were asked to discriminate stimuli drawn from the continuum, they were able to do so only if they had labeled them differently. This phenomenon, the ability to discriminate only as well as one can identify, is called *categorical perception*. We shall present the details of one study of categorical perception as an example of how such studies were usually conducted.

The 1957 study by Liberman, Harris, Hoffman, and Griffith has served as the model for many studies of categorical perception conducted since then. The stimuli (Fig. 6.23) were synthesized on the Pattern Playback for precise control of frequency, intensity, and duration. The fourteen two-formant CV patterns differed only in the direction and extent of the F_2 transition. The rapidly and sharply rising F_2 transition necessary for perception of an exemplary /b/ formed the first of the stimuli, and the rapidly, sharply falling F_2 transition necessary for perception of an exemplary /g/ formed the last stimulus. The stimuli in between were constructed by raising the starting frequency of the F_2 transition in equal steps of 120 Hz. Each stimulus was then tape recorded several times. The recorded stimuli were then randomized and presented to listeners in an *identification test*. In this type of test listeners hear one stimulus at a time and are told to identify or label it, and to guess if they are not sure which sound they have heard. When the subjects are instructed to use a restricted set of responses (e.g., /b,d/ or /g/), the test is called a *forced choice test*. An *open response set* is used if the experimenters wish to allow the subjects to label the stimuli in any way they choose.

The stimuli were also arranged into a second type of perceptual test, a *discrimination test*. The task of a subject in a discrimination test is simply to indicate if two stimuli are the same or different, on any basis whatsoever, without overtly labeling them. There are a number of discrimination paradigms, but the one most frequently used is the *ABX format*. In each ABX set of the experiment being discussed, listeners heard one of the 14 stimuli (A), followed by a different one (B), followed by the third (X) which was the same as one of the

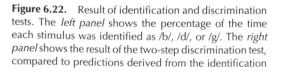

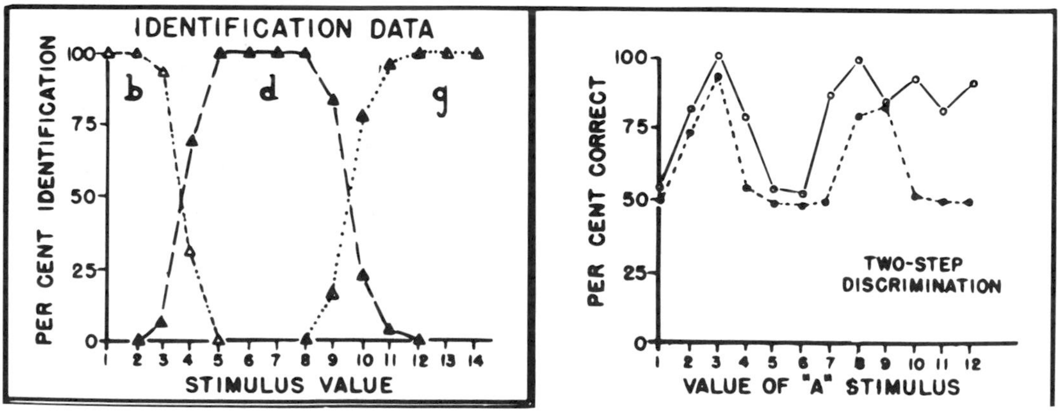

Figure 6.22. Result of identification and discrimination tests. The *left panel* shows the percentage of the time each stimulus was identified as /b/, /d/, or /g/. The *right panel* shows the result of the two-step discrimination test, compared to predictions derived from the identification test, using the technique described in the text of the article. (Reprinted with permission from A. M. Liberman *et al.*: *Journal of Experimental Psychology. 54,* © 1957, American Psychological Association.)

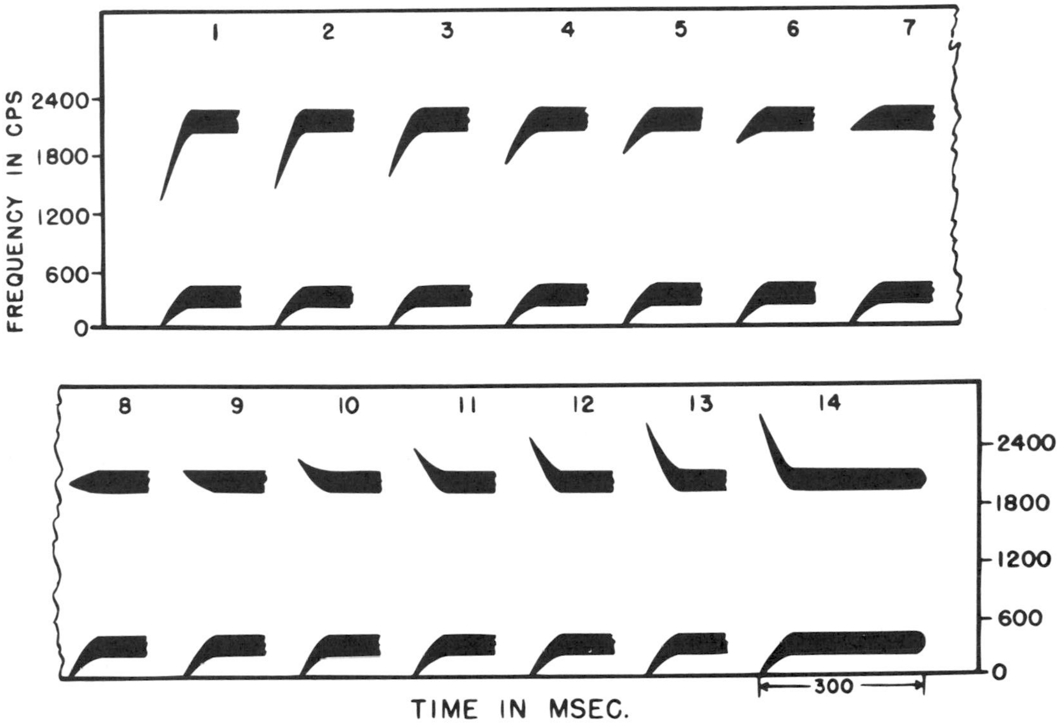

Figure 6.23. Two-formant synthetic CV pattern series: the stimuli for /ba/, /da/, and /ga/. (Reprinted with permission from A. M. Liberman *et al.*: *Journal of Experimental Psychology. 54,* © 1957, American Psychological Association.)

first two. The subjects were told that A and B were different (although they were not always able to detect the difference). The task of the subjects was to determine if X was identical to A or to B and to guess if they were uncertain. The percentage of correct matching of X with the identical member of the AB pair was the measure of discrimination in this test. If the subjects were guessing, because they could not discriminate A from B, their correct responses would be at chance level: 50%. The A and B were sometimes adjacent stimuli on the test continuum (a one-step test), sometimes separated from each other by one or two stimuli (two- and three-step tests).

The labeling and discrimination tests were presented in counterbalanced order to different subject groups. Results were equivalent regardless of the order of test presentation. Similarly, subjects responded in the same way (1) whether or not they were told at the outset that the stimuli were synthetic speech sounds and (2) when their response choices on the labeling test were forced or drawn from an open set. Labeling tests have most often been presented using a forced choice format since this early experiment.

Figure 6.23 shows the results of the identification test and a two-step discrimination test for one subject. The subject identified the first three stimuli as /b/ between 90 and 100% of the time. Stimulus 4 was identified more often as /d/ than as /b/, and stimuli 5 through 8 were always perceived as /d/. More than 80% of the presentations of stimulus 9 were labeled as /d/. A shift in perception, to /g/, occurred for stimulus 10, and the remaining stimuli, numbers 11 through 14 were reported to be /g/ almost all the time. There are two sharply defined perceptual shifts evident in this identification function. The first, the *phoneme boundary* separating /b/ from /d/, occurs between stimuli 3 and 4, and the other, separating /d/ from /g/, occurs between stimuli 9 and 10.

The discrimination function for the same subject, shown by the solid line at the right side of Figure 6.23, represents the percentage of correct responses to the 42 ABX triads in which the A and B were two steps apart in the stimulus series. Judgments at the 50% correct level indicate a failure to discriminate stimulus A from stimulus B: When a subject cannot hear a difference between the first two stimuli, he must guess which one of them is the same as X. Because he has two choices, there is a 50% chance of selecting the correct answer. Note the two 100% peaks in the discrimination function. The first peak, plotted at Point 3 on the abscissa, represents responses by this subject to ABX triads in which A and B were stimuli 3 and 5. Recall that the phoneme boundary between /b/ and /d/ for this subject was between stimuli 3 and 4, which is just the part of the stimulus series that this subject discriminates most accurately. The phoneme boundary between /d/ and /g/ was between 9 and 10 for this subject. Again, discrimination was perfect between stimuli 8 and 10. Thus, this subject discriminates best at phoneme boundaries, where the A and B stimuli belong to different phoneme categories, and less well between stimuli that belong to the same phoneme category.

The experimenters next tested the assumption that this subject (and each of the others) could discriminate the stimuli no better than he could label them as belonging to different phoneme categories—that is, that his perception was categorical. They used his labeling data as a basis to predict what his discrimination function ought to be, given the truth of the assumption. The predicted discrimination function is shown by the dashed line at the right side of Figure 6.23. The obtained discrimination function (the solid line) was higher than the predicted function, although the two were highly correlated. The fact that this (and the other) subject(s) could discriminate the stimuli somewhat better than if his perception was completely determined by his labeling ability, indicates that he might have been able to use some acoustic information to augment his phonemically based discrimination judgments.

It was surprising to find that people, listening to synthetic speech sounds that change in equal steps in some acoustic dimension, discriminate among them little better than they can identify them. It is a well-known fact of psychoacoustics that in judging the relative pitch of pure tones, people can discriminate as many as 3500 different frequency steps, but that they can only label a few pitches. Pitch perception is not linear with frequency change, because listeners can discriminate between low (50–500 Hz) frequency tones having only a fraction of a Hertz difference, while at 4000 Hz, about 4 Hz difference is needed for discrimination. Although pitch perception is not linear, it is a continuous function. There are no sudden changes in one's ability to detect pitch differences cued by frequency change as there are for differences between speech sounds cued by frequency change. One possible explanation for the discontinuities in the perception of speech stimuli has been provided by Stevens' *Quantal Theory*.

The thesis of the Quantal Theory is that certain, relatively large changes in articulator position will cause little change in the acoustic signal, while other, relatively small changes in articulator placement will cause large changes in the acoustic signal. The extent of the acoustic change that occurs appears to be related to the particular region of the vocal tract where the articulation is located. In certain critical regions, a slight adjustment of articulatory placement will cause a quantal change in sound. You can create an example of this sort of acoustic discontinuity by advancing the linguapalatal constriction for [ʃ] slowly forward until it becomes a lingua-alveolar [s]-constriction. You will hear very little change in the sound before the constriction reaches the alveolar ridge, but once it arrives at the ridge, there will be an immediate and substantial change in the frequency band of the frication. That is, there will be a quantal change from [ʃ] to [s]. Stevens has shown discontinuity for the acoustic effects of pharyngeal and velar consonant constrictions. He suggests that the various languages of the world have taken advantage of these regions of little acoustic change for locating distinctive places of constriction in developing consonant places of articulation.

We must keep in mind that the discontinuities that Stevens describes are acoustic and not perceptual. In the speech perception study discussed above, the synthesizer produced a continuum of stimuli that changed in equal acoustic steps (something that a human speaker could never do because of the acoustic discontinuities generated by the architecture of the vocal tract), yet the listeners perceived them according to the inherently quantal nature of articulatory place. This fact has led some investigators to view quantal theory as supporting evidence for theories of speech perception that relate perception to articulation, on the grounds that the human auditory system is especially sensitive to those quantal acoustic changes that the human articulatory system produces.

In light of the differences between the way listeners perceive nonspeech stimuli (such as tones), and speech stimuli, and in light of the quantal nature of place of articulation, the categorical discontinuities of the labeling and discrimination functions found in speech perception are extremely interesting and have given rise to several questions that have been addressed in speech perception research.

Do people perceive speech quite differently from the way they perceive nonspeech? Does the learning of a language sharpen some perceptions and dull others? Is categorical perception innate or learned? The first study reporting the categorical perception of speech did not answer these questions. It did, however, make the phenomenon explicit and sparked interest in looking further for the relative auditory and linguistic contributions to the effect.

Within-Language and Cross-Language Studies of Categorical Perception in Adults. As we have just seen, the phenomenon of categorical perception was first demonstrated for place of articulation contrasts among stop consonants that were cued by formant transitions. We shall look at another such contrast, this time for liquids, and then go on to review some of the experimentation that has demonstrated categorical perception for manner of articulation and voicing contrasts.

In Chapter 5 we saw that the differences in F_3 characterized the contrast between /r/ and /l/. It is, in fact, possible to construct a continuum of synthetic speech stimuli, beginning with /r/ and ending with /l/ by varying the transitions of F_2 and F_3. At Haskins Laboratories, one of us (Borden) synthesized a /ra/ to /la/ continuum similar to the series that Mochizuki prepared on an OVE synthesizer. (The use of an OVE synthesizer insured that the stimuli would be very similar to natural speech.) The third formant transition was graded from a relatively low to a relatively high starting frequency and the second formant transition was similarly varied, but to a lesser extent (Fig. 6.24). A group of students in an undergraduate speech science class was asked to identify two randomized lists of 50 items. In this identification test, each stimulus followed a precursor phrase in natural speech: "Does this sound more like rock or lock?" Typical identification functions are presented in Figure 6.25. The consonants of the first five stimuli were perceived almost unanimously as /r/. Stimulus 7 was ambiguous for the listeners and the consonants in the remaining stimuli, 8 through 10 were heard as /l/. The phoneme boundary between /r/ and /l/ for these listeners occurred, then, between stimuli 6 and 7.

Stimuli from the same continuum were paired in an AX discrimination test, using one-step, two-step, and three-step differences. Paired in every order, the test consisted of 48 pairs of stimuli randomized four times. Once again a precursor sentence was used: each pair of items followed the question "Do these sound the same or not the same?" Subjects responded by checking either the column marked SAME or the column marked NOT THE SAME. The one-step discrimination function plotted in Figure 6.26 shows a peak in discrimination between stimuli 6 and 7, exactly where the phoneme boundary was located in the identification test. Thus, the subjects discriminated the members of a pair of stimuli better when each was drawn from a different phoneme category

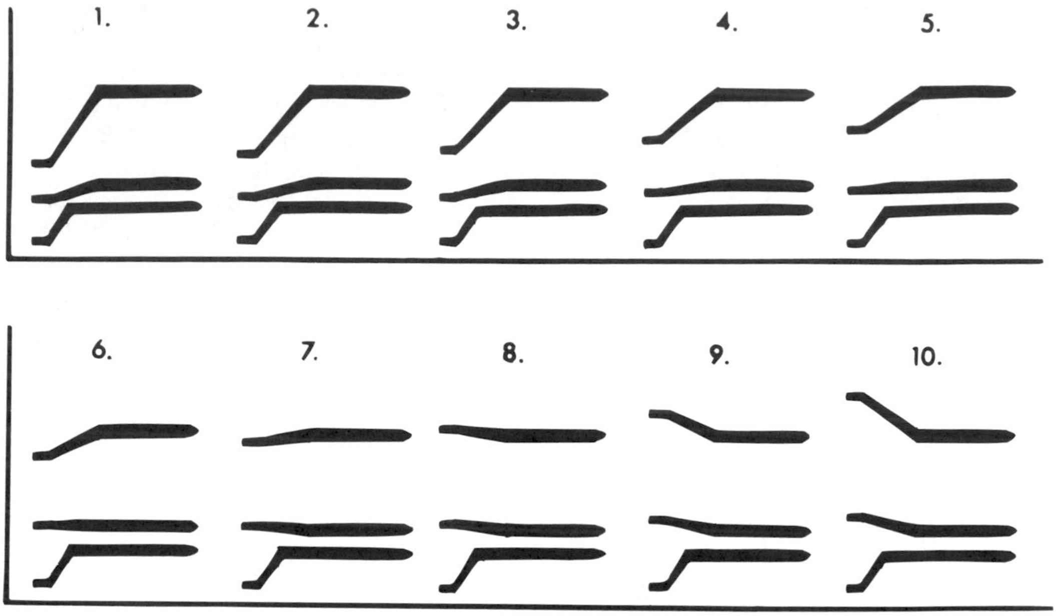

Figure 6.24. A continuum of synthetic stimuli perceived as /ra/ or /la/. Frequency is represented on the ordinate and time on the abscissa.

than when they were drawn from the same phoneme category. In other words, subjects were much better at discriminating stimuli if they had labeled them as different phonemes than if they had given them the same phonemic label.

Perception of the acoustic cues to manner of articulation has also been found to be categorical. For instance, increasing the duration of the transitions in such CV syllables as /ba/ and /ga/ will cause listeners' perceptions to shift categorically, first from stop to semivowel (/wa,ja/) and then to sequences of vowels (/ua,ia/). Similarly, variations in the rise time of the intensity of frication from slow to rapid causes listeners to change their perception of /ʃ/ (as in "shop") to /tʃ/ (as in "chop") in a categorical manner.

Voicing contrasts may also be perceived categorically. Abramson and Lisker varied voice onset time in equal steps from −150 ms to +150 ms and found that listeners' percepts shifted from the voiced to the voiceless categories. Having grouped the stimuli into voiced and voiceless categories, they were able to discriminate differences between stimuli on either side of the voiced-voiceless boundary. For pairs of stimuli within the same voicing category, however, listeners discriminated VOT differences relatively poorly.

The results of tests of vowel perception contrast somewhat with those of consonant perception. Fry, Abramson, Eimas, and Liberman synthesized a continuum of isolated, steady-state vowels ranging from /ɪ/ to /ɛ/ to /æ/ by varying formant frequencies. The slopes of subjects' labeling functions were much less steep than those found for stop consonants. More importantly, the peaks in the discrimination functions at the phoneme boundaries were lower and the discrimination of stimuli within each phoneme category were higher than for stop consonants. It would appear, then, that the perception of isolated vowels of relatively great duration is less categorical than the perception of stop (and some other) consonants. Stevens reports, however, that when the vowels are shorter in duration and embedded in CVC contexts (with appropriately rapid formant transitions), the discrimination-identification relationship is more like that for consonants.

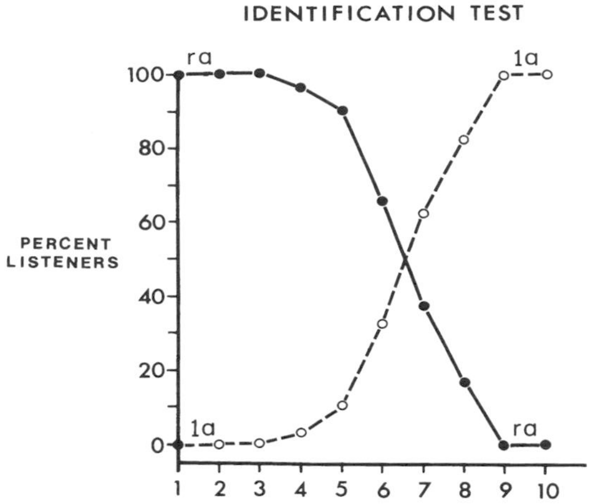

Figure 6.25. Identification functions for /ra/ and /la/. The 10 stimuli are represented along the abscissa and the percentage of listener judgments is represented along the ordinate. The boundary between /r/ and /l/ judgments lies between Stimuli 6 and 7.

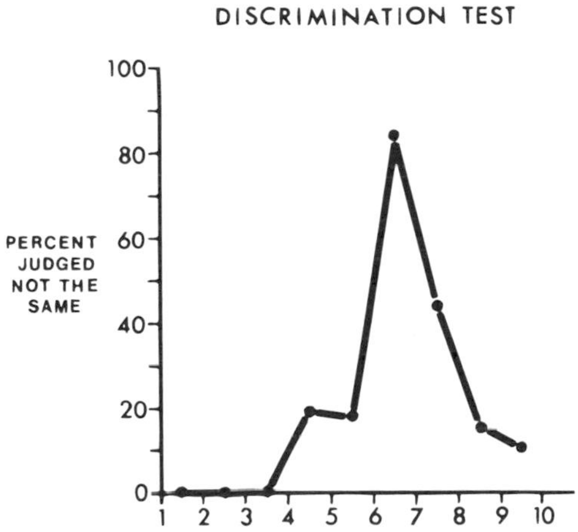

Figure 6.26. Discrimination function for pairs of stimuli separated by one step shown in Figure 6.24.

That is, perception is more categorical than for the isolated vowels.

Because steady-state vowels of long duration and nonspeech tones are perceived less categorically, while shorter vowels in CVC contexts and consonants are perceived more categorically, it seems that listeners perceive stimuli containing rapidly changing frequencies differently than they do stimuli that are more steady-state in nature.

An important aspect of categorical perception is the influence that linguistic knowledge can have on the categories perceived. The reason the /ra/–/la/ stimuli were prefaced with questions spoken in English is that Elman, Diehl and Buchwald found the language "set" that listeners have when making decisions about speech sound identity may change the boundary between categories. Bilingual subjects divide such stimuli according to the phonemic contrasts of the particular language they are using immediately before each stimulus.

Strange and Jenkins have reviewed many studies of both monolingual and bilingual speakers. These studies offer evidence that the language experience of adults can influence their perception. For example, Spanish, French, and Thai speakers use different VOT criteria for voicing contrasts than do English speakers. Japanese speakers, who do not contrast /r/ and /l/, perceive equal changes in F_3 in a /ra/ to /la/ continuum differently from the two-category manner in which it is perceived by speakers of English.

Because the location of phoneme boundaries along test continua seems to be language-specific and thus closely related to the phonemic contrasts used by the listener in his native language, investigators were surprised to find that creatures with little or no language ability (animals and infants) discriminate speech-like stimuli in a way that seemed to be related to the categorical perception of adults.

Studies of Infant Speech Perception. The classic report on infant perception of speech-like stimuli was published in *Science* in 1971, by Eimas, Siqueland, Jusczyk, and Vigorito of Brown University. They monitored infants sucking a pacifier wired to a transducer that recorded infant sucking responses. A continuum of synthetic stop-plus vowel syllables differing by 20-msec increments of VOT was synthesized. Infants as young as 1 month of age react to any new stimulus with a change in sucking rate. The investigators recorded the baseline rate of sucks per minute for each baby and then presented each auditory stimulus at an intensity that depended upon the rate of sucking. As long as the baby maintained a high

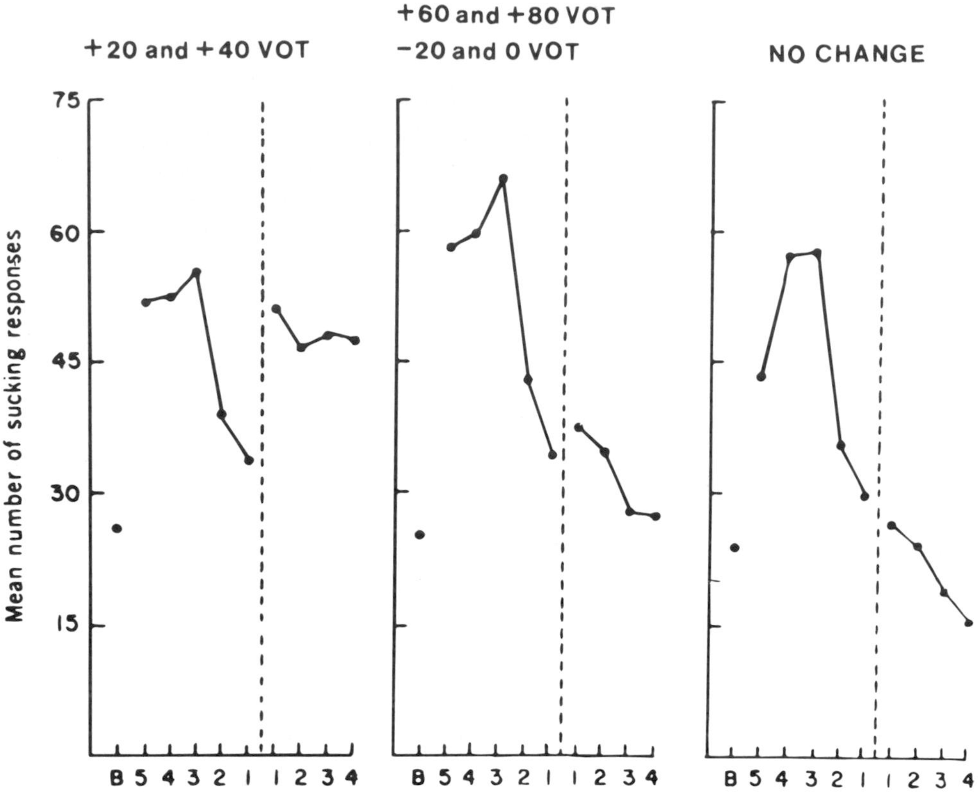

Figure 6.27. Mean number of sucking responses for 4-month-old infants in three experimental conditions. *B* represents the baseline before presentation of a stimulus. Each panel shows sucking as a function of time with a change of stimulus at the point shown by the *dotted line,* or, in the *right-most panel,* at the time the change would have occurred. In the *left-most panel,* the stimuli straddle the /b/–/p/ category boundary for adults, while in the *middle panel,* contrasting stimuli are within one category. (Adapted with permission from P. Eimas *et al.*: *Science. 171,* 304, © 1971, American Association for the Advancement of Science.)

rate of sucking responses, the sound continued at high intensity. As the rate of sucking decreased so did the loudness of the sound. Typically, the babies responded by increasing their rate of sucking. After a few minutes, as the novelty of the stimulus wore off, the sucking rate gradually decreased. This decrease in response rate, known as habituation, was allowed to proceed for 2 minutes and then a different VOT stimulus was presented for several minutes.

Figure 6.27 schematizes the mean responses of the 4-month-old infant group. The *dots* at the far *left* of the three graphs represent the baseline rate of sucking. With auditory reinforcement for sucking, the rate of responses increased, as can be seen by the sucking rates plotted to the *left* of the *dashed vertical line,* those representing 5, 4, and 3 minutes before the shift in stimulus. Then, the infants started to habituate to the stimulus, and sucking rate decreased. The graph at the *left* represents what happened when the first stimulus, a /ba/-like stimulus with a VOT of +20, was changed to a /pa/-like stimulus with a VOT of +40. The sucking rate increased dramatically, indicating that the infants heard this shift as something new. The middle graph reveals no such increase in sucking responses, even though the stimuli also differed by 20 msec VOT. In this condition, the VOT of the first stimulus was +60 VOT and that of the second was +80 (both perceived by adults as /pa/) or the VOT of the first stimulus was −20 and that of the second was zero (both perceived by adults as /ba/). The infants did not respond to these changes with a significant increase in sucking rate. The authors infer from these two functions that the infants perceive the +20 and +40 VOT stimuli as different, but do not perceive the +60 and +80 or the −20 and 0 VOT stimuli as different.

The data for the control condition are shown in the graph on the right of the figure. When there is no change in the stimulus, habituation continues and the sucking rate continues to decrease. Eimas and his colleagues concluded that infants as young as 1 month old seem to discriminate acoustic changes in this speech continuum in the same way as do adults. That is, the infants' discrimination is best at about the same location where adults locate a phoneme boundary. We should point out that this is not an instance of categorical perception on the part of the infants because there are, of necessity, no labeling data to which the discrimination data can be related. This and other infant studies, however, do present the possibility that the ability to categorize speech sounds is innate. We will return to this issue later.

There have been scores of studies in infant perception since this original study. Techniques for assessing infants' discrimination of speech sounds have changed. Researchers find they may get more reliable results by conditioning infants, those who are old enough, to turn and look at a dancing bear or a moving toy as a reinforcer. (Infants younger than 6 months, however, are generally too immature motorically for head-turning.) The infant is conditioned to look at the toy only in response to a certain sound. Sounds that are acoustically similar or different can be delivered to see if the infant perceives them as the same or different from the conditioned stimulus. Kuhl has reported that 6-month-old babies tested with this technique discriminate vowels and consonants even when stimuli vary in pitch, talker, and phonetic context. Jusczyk finds that infants can perceive consonant contrasts in word-initial, -medial, or -final position, and in multisyllabic stimuli as well as in monosyllables. There are some preliminary indications that infants can discriminate stress contrasts, although more research is needed to determine the validity of this finding.

The question that results from the increasing evidence of infant perceptual abilities is whether infants are innately equipped to detect linguistically significant contrasts, or whether the distinctions they perceive are a result of characteristics of the auditory system without reference to language. The infants are obviously making auditory distinctions, and at this point, we do not know at what age they begin to make phonetic distinctions. In a recent series of experiments using 6-month-old children in the United States and in Sweden, Kuhl and others found that the subjects showed demonstrable effects of exposure to their native language. The experimenters employed two synthetic vowels belonging to a single phonemic category in each language: /i/ (English), and /y/, a front, lip-rounded Swedish vowel. One vowel was judged by listeners to be the best exemplar of the /i/ or /y/ category in their language; the other was rated as a poor exemplar. The infants in each country performed two discrimination tasks for the vowels in their ambient language. In one task they discriminated the best exemplar from vowels that were more or less similar to it. They also performed the same task for the poor exemplar. Both the Swedish and the American children did less well in discriminating the best exemplar from similar stimuli. When each group was tested with the prototype from the other language, they were better able to discriminate it from other vowels than the prototype from their ambient language.

Kuhl has termed the discrimination results for the best exemplar the "magnet effect." She posits that the prototypical vowel has attracted similar vowels to it, perceptually. Thus, by at least 6 months of age, exposure to what will be their native language has rendered the children less able to make intraphonemic distinctions among sounds that are near the core of a phonemic category. It is as though the more prototypical allophones of the phoneme coalesce around the best exemplar, while the less prototypical allophones remain discriminable from each other. This change in the ability to discriminate is presumably overlaid on the innate ability to discriminate between different phonemic categories. How early on in development does the change occur? Continued experimentation should provide us with the information to answer this question, along with more information about the distinctions that infants make regardless of language environment.

Studies of Animal Speech Perception. Is the ability of infants to discriminate speech sounds based on purely auditory ability or on innate mechanisms of phonetic processing?

Some light is shed on this question by the finding that nonhumans discriminate acoustic differences in speech-like continua in what may be described as a categorical manner. Morse and Snowden monitored heart rate of rhesus monkeys in response to changes in F_2 and F_3 that mark place of articulation distinctions for humans. Waters and Wilson trained rhesus monkeys to avoid shock associated with a particular synthetic speech sound and thus measured the monkeys' perception of VOT changes. Kuhl and Miller used shock avoidance to study VOT contrast in the chinchilla. Results show that these nonhuman listeners display enhanced discrimination at adult category boundaries. The responses of chinchillas resemble those of people more than those of rhesus monkeys, perhaps because the auditory systems of humans and chinchillas are very similar.

It may be that the categorical perception of speech continua that we find for adult speakers, and that we know to be highly influenced by linguistic experience, is based upon specific sensitivities of the auditory system to acoustic features, sensitivities that are found in the auditory systems of human infants and some other mammals. That is, the location of some phoneme boundaries in a language may be determined, in part, by innate auditory sensitivities that render certain acoustic differences maximally discriminable. Deviations from the category boundaries predicated on auditory sensitivity could be accounted for by the historical development of the sound systems of particular languages and could require the type of phonetic processing that adults seem to display when they identify speech sounds. We shall consider next some theories about how these auditory and phonetic levels of processing interact in speech perception.

Auditory and Phonetic Analysis. We know that a specified complex acoustic event can result in a listener reporting that she heard the syllable /ba/. Furthermore, the listener can report that the initial consonant was /b/. Since we know that the acoustic cues for /b/ are overlaid on those for /a/, the listener must be analyzing the event on an auditory level to identify the /ba/ (they have to hear it) and on a phonetic level to extract the /b/ (they have to segment it). The question that remains is how the transformation from auditory to phonetic percept is made. How are phonemes individually recovered? Are features detected, and if so, are the features acoustic or phonetic? Is the syllable (or some larger unit) processed as a whole and then segmented, or is it first segmented and then recombined in a sort of perceptual synthesis?

We have seen that categorical perception can be influenced by phonetic processing, in that boundaries between phonemes are different for different languages. On the other hand, the results with infants and animals seem more likely to be determined by auditory than by phonetic factors. Another approach to the attempt to separate auditory and phonetic factors in speech perception is to examine acoustic signals that can be perceived as speech or as nonspeech, depending on the "set" of the listener.

Several researchers have experimented with sine-wave analogs of the speech signal. In the stimuli they synthesized, three sine waves replaced the first three formants. This is equivalent to synthesizing formants with bandwidths of 1 Hz. The acoustic signal thus generated contains almost none of the usual acoustic cues for speech. One aspect of the sine-wave stimuli that especially interested the researchers was that some listeners recognized them as speech, while other listeners did not, hearing them as nonspeech electronic beeps, chimes, and tones. The results of experiments indicated that listeners perceived the acoustic signal differently, depending on whether they heard it as speech or as nonspeech. Evidently, hearing the sine-wave stimuli as speech allowed (or perhaps forced) the listeners to process the signal phonetically; hearing them as nonspeech allowed them to access auditory information that was unavailable to the "phonetic" listeners. For example, the sort of trading relationships between durations of silence and spectral characteristics reported by Raphael, Dorman, and Isenberg (see Acoustic Cues to Affricates) were found for listeners hearing the stimuli as speech, but not for listeners hearing the stimuli as nonspeech.

Pisoni has proposed that the procedures used in testing listeners can themselves favor either phonetic or auditory processing of the stimuli because some methods put a greater load on memory than others. The usual method used to test discrimination in these studies is the ABX paradigm, which we have already described. Another discrimination paradigm is the "oddity" or "oddball" method, in which subjects hear a triad of stimuli in which one stimulus differs from the other two. The task is to pick out the "different" stimulus. Pisoni and Lazarus questioned whether these discrimination paradigms placed an undue load on short-term memory for acoustic information. They used a 4IAX (four-interval forced choice) paradigm in which listeners hear two pairs of stimuli. The members of one pair are identical (AA); the members of the other pair are different (AB). The listeners are asked which pair is composed of different stimuli. The point is that as each pair is heard, the listener labels it as "same" or "different." The linguistic label is then stored, relieving the listener of the need to store the acoustic information for later comparison. The experimenters found the 4IAX discrimination format resulted in better discrimination—that is, auditory processing of the speech stimuli.

Another group of experiments that bears upon the distinction between auditory and phonetic levels of speech processing is based upon *adaptation*.

Adaptation Studies. If a listener hears the stimulus at one end of a synthetic speech continuum repeatedly, /da/ for example, and is then presented with the usual randomized /da/ to /ta/ continuum for identification, the boundary between phonemes that would normally result is shifted toward the /da/ end of the continuum. That is, after exposure to so many prototypical /da/-like sounds, the listener identifies more of the stimuli as /ta/. Thus, VOT perception is adapted; the listener, having heard many tokens of the "voiced" end of the continuum, will perceive a smaller increase in VOT as a change to the "voiceless" category.

These results were originally explained by a theory positing the existence of phonetic feature detectors. If, in the nervous system, there are neurons especially tuned to detect contrastive linguistic features, then the particular detectors responsive to small VOT values corresponding to "voiced" stops, for example, might be fatigued by multiple presentations of /da/. With the detector for "voicing" fatigued, subjects would identify more "voiceless" items in the continuum.

Many studies on adaptation followed the original report by Eimas and Corbit in 1973. The studies are reviewed in detail by Darwin. As the data accumulate, it is becoming clear that interpretations other than a feature detector interpretation are plausible. Adaptation studies do show, however, that auditory factors can have a measurable effect upon categorical perception, just as cross-language studies show the importance of phonetic factors.

Categorical Perception and Learning. We have described cross-language studies that show the influence of a particular language upon perception of phoneme boundaries. We can infer from these studies that learning contributes to categorical perception. In addition, there are several more direct ways in which researchers have studied the effects of learning upon categorical perception: by direct training in the laboratory, by studying perception in children receiving speech therapy for an articulation disorder, and by testing second language learners. Reports are few, however, and conclusions are tentative.

Strange succeeded in training English speakers to improve intraphonemic discrimination in a VOT continuum of labial stops, but found that the training did not generalize to apical VOT stimuli. Carney and Widin found considerable improvement in subjects' discrimination ability after training. Several different labial VOT stimuli were used as standards. Subjects were trained to hear differences between each standard and the other stimuli in AX pairs, with immediate feedback. Listeners can be trained, then, to become more sensitive to differences among stimuli within a phonemic category.

Developmental studies are difficult to compare because few have used synthetic stimuli that could have been precisely described, and few have tested intraphonemic discrimination. The research on infants' speech perception shows that they discriminate stimuli in a similar fashion, regardless of the speech or language community into which they have been born. For example, they can discriminate stimuli of +20 VOT and +60 VOT and stimuli of −20 VOT and −60 VOT. They do not, however, discriminate stimuli of −20 VOT and +20 VOT. The reason may be that ±20 VOT sounds like the same event, while a longer time gap between a burst and voicing onset sounds like two events. Perception of speech seems to begin with an innate ability to make certain auditory distinctions. Stevens and Klatt point to the fact that adults divide a nonspeech continuum that is analogous to the VOT series with a boundary at approximately +20 VOT as further indication that some distinctions may be natural to the auditory system.

By at least 2 years of age, children perceive speech sounds categorically, and their phoneme boundaries are similar to those of adults. Zlatin and Koenigsknecht used voicing continua varying from "bees" to "peas," and from "dime" to "time" as examples, and found that although 2-year-olds perceived the stimuli with the same boundaries between categories as those of 6-year-olds and adults, the younger children's boundary areas were wider, indicating that they needed larger acoustic differences to mark the voiced-voiceless distinction. The longitudinal development of this perceptual ability has not yet been thoroughly studied; the difficulties in testing the abilities of very young children to label and to discriminate stimuli are considerable. There are indications, however, that identification and discrimination abilities may not develop at the same rate.

Age	Crossover Values by Exposure One	Two	Three
14–16	+2.0	+5.7	+8.7
8–10	+4.7	+7.5	+12.0
Difference	2.7	1.8	3.3

Figure 6.28. Differences (VOT in milliseconds) in labeling crossover values for native Spanish-speaking children of two age groups. The children were also divided on the basis of exposure to English, as measured by time in the United States: Exposure one (0–6 months), Exposure two (1½–2 years), and Exposure three (3–3½ years). (From L. Williams: unpublished doctoral dissertation, Harvard, 1974.)

Although it is easier to study changes in perception in people learning a second language, because they are typically older and easier to test, we are not sure that the processes for learning to recognize the phonemes of a second language are the same as those for a first language. Williams found a slightly faster shift of phoneme boundaries toward the English boundary among younger (8–10 years) Spanish-speaking children learning English than among older children (14–16 years) (Fig. 6.28). Again, longitudinal studies are needed to determine the progression. It would be particularly interesting to see more research in which production and perception are analyzed simultaneously.

Production and Perception. Williams did analyze both production (by measuring spectrograms of the subjects' speech samples) and perception (by identification and discrimination tests) of the phoneme contrasts important in the second language being learned. Establishing the monolingual identification boundaries for /b/ and /p/ and the discrimination peaks for both English and Spanish adult speakers, she found that their production of /b/ and /p/ in word-initial position corresponded to their perception. English speakers separated the phonemes at about +25 VOT, while Spanish speakers put the boundary at about −4 VOT. Spanish speakers learning English varied more than monolinguals in the crossover points of their identification functions, and the discrimination peaks spanned both the monolingual English and Spanish boundaries. Thus, perception of the /b/–/p/ series for adult bilinguals represented a compromise. For production, spectrograms showed that the bilinguals prevoice /b/ in accordance with the Spanish system, even when uttering English words.

In a second study, Williams tracked changes in production and perception in young Puerto Rican Spanish-speaking children who were learning English. She found the labeling crossover point gradually shifting toward the English boundary as exposure to English increased. In production, the children were using VOT patterns closer to English, both in their English and Spanish words.

Turning again to adult learners, a study by Goto indicates that adult bilinguals are often quite insensitive to perceptual distinctions in their non-native language, even if they can produce them. Japanese speakers judged by Americans to be making the English /r/–/l/ distinction appropriately as they produced words such as "lead," "read," "pray," and "play," nevertheless found difficulty in perceiving the distinctions, in word-initial position, either in recordings of their own speech or of other speakers. Similar results were obtained by Mochizuki. A more detailed analysis of /r/–/l/ perception by Japanese speakers by MacKain, Best, and Strange showed that, while a group of Japanese with little experience of spoken English showed near-chance performance in discriminating stimuli straddling the English /r/–/l/ boundary, an experienced Japanese group performed like American controls. Thus we can be quite sure that experience modifies the perception of speech-like stimuli, but we have little information about what aspects of experience are important. More information is needed, but this brings us to the interesting question of how perception of one's own speech may relate to perception of the speech of others.

The anecdotal observation that some children may perceive distinctions in their own speech that adults fail to distinguish, rests on experiences such as the following: A child protests when others imitate his misarticulation, "I didn't say 'wabbit', I said 'wabbit.'" This phenomenon can be interpreted as evidence that perception is ahead of production. When the child hears the adult say "wabbit," he perceives the mistake but is unable to produce an /r/ and fails to detect the mistake in his own speech. An alternate explanation is that the child perceives distinctions in his own speech in a different way than do adults. The child may make a perceptual distinction between his two /w/ sounds, in the example above, that the adult cannot; that is, the phoneme category for the child's /r/ is wide enough to include some sounds that the adult would classify as /w/. A third interpretation might be that the child's perception is confused, because he does not yet make the distinction productively. Thus, perception not only aids production, but the mastery of the production of speech sounds is viewed as an aid to the child in his efforts to discriminate the sounds in the speech of others.

Aungst and Frick found there was a low correlation between children's self-judgments of the correctness of /r/ production and their ability to identify errors in the speech of others: Children with /r/ misarticulations had no problem perceiving the misarticulations of others but failed to detect their own errors. Kornfeld showed that children may produce /w/ sounds in [gwæs] for "glass" and [gwæs] for "grass" that seem the same to adult listeners. There are spectrographic differences, however, which may reflect the basis on which the children make distinctions. Goehl and Golden suggest that the child in this case has a phoneme representation differing from that of the adult /r/. The child's phoneme /r^w/ is directly represented phonetically as [r^w], while the adult phoneme /r/ does not include the [r^w] sound. They found that children tend to recognize their own [r^w] as /r/ and are better at detecting it than other people.

This phenomenon of children perceiving a difference between their misarticulation and the substitution as perceived by an adult may not be as common, however, as is supposed. Locke and Kutz found that of 75 children who said /wIŋ/ in response to a picture of a ring, only about 20% of them pointed to the picture of a ring when they later heard their own misarticulation, while 80% pointed to a picture of a wing upon hearing their misarticulation. McReynolds, Kohn, and Williams found that children with misarticulations are worse at recognizing the sounds they misarticulate than the sounds they produce correctly.

It may be that in learning phonemic contrasts, identification of phonemes in the speech of others develops before the ability to perceive one's own errors, with production and self-perception developing in parallel as motor maturity permits. The time course of perception-production interaction remains unclear, and children learning a first language or correcting misarticulations may evidence quite a different time course of perceptual and production interaction than do second language learners.

Neurophysiology of Speech Perception

Both sides of the brain are important for hearing. The auditory nerve reports to the temporal lobes of both cerebral hemispheres. Further analysis of the sound patterns, such as those involved in the perception of speech, however, are to some extent lateralized to one cerebral hemisphere.

Cerebral Lateralization. Evidence that one cerebral hemisphere, usually the left, is dominant over the other during perception of speech comes from anatomical analyses, split brain experiments, dichotic listening studies, and electroencephalographic (EEG) recordings. Wernicke (see Chapter 4) was the first to implicate the left temporoparietal area surrounding the posterior portion of the Rolandic fissure in speech recognition and in linguistic expression. Not only did Wernicke find damage in the temporal part of that area upon autopsy of aphasic individuals, but Penfield and Roberts found stimulation of that area to interfere most severely with speech output in their patients.

Wernicke's area, as this part of the left cerebral cortex has come to be called, is important for decoding speech messages of others and for eliciting the acoustic model of what one intends to say. People who suffer a cerebral vascular accident (CVA) to the left temporoparietal area articulate distinctly despite some substitution of phonemes, and they speak fluently. Their conversation often makes little sense, however. Goodglass and Geschwind describe the tendency of such patients to substitute a general pronoun, such as "it," for the elusive nouns, or a general verb, such as "do," for the missing verbs. These sorts of substitutions result in the following kind of response to a request to name something: "I know what it is, I use it to do my. . . . I have one right here. . . ." Here is another paragrammatical, fluent, but meaningless example from Goodglass and Geschwind: "The things I want to say . . . ah . . . the way I say things, but I understand mostly things, most of them and what the things are."

Along with the inability to recall the words necessary to convey an idea, there is often a decreased ability to recognize the meaning of something said aloud. A person with Wernicke's aphasia may recognize the class of a word but not its specific meaning. Thus, for the word "lamp," the person with such a comprehension disorder might point to a piece of furniture, but the wrong one.

If Wernicke's area itself is intact, but the connections between the auditory centers of the temporal lobes and Wernicke's area are damaged or poorly functioning, a form of auditory agnosia results. The person may hear a word repeatedly with no comprehension at all and then suddenly understand it completely. This link between the centers for audition and the centers for comprehension may be what is manipulated and fatigued in people with normal perception who experience *verbal transformation* or *semantic satiation*. When an utterance is repeated over and over, people report several changes in perception as they listen to the repetitions. For example, the non-word "flime" might be heard as "flying" for awhile, then "climb," then "flank." Although we know nothing of the neural underpinnings of this phenomenon, it simulates a dysfunction in the link between hearing and perception.

Dramatic evidence of the role of the left hemisphere in language production and perception is in the test responses of patients who have undergone surgical separation of the cerebral hemispheres by section of the corpus callosum, to control severe epilepsy. The patients do not seem impaired unless certain tests are conducted to present information to the hemispheres independently. Since the main connecting body between hemispheres is severed, the patient has functionally separated hemicerebrums. Sperry and Gazzaniga, by testing one cerebrum at a time, have demonstrated that in split brain patients, the left side does not know what the right side is doing and vice versa (Fig. 6.29). With a curtain in front of such a patient, visually masking objects such as a key, a fork, a letter, and a number, the patient can name an object touched with his right hand (the image being referred to the left hemisphere) or exposed to his left visual field, but cannot name it if the name of the object is relayed to his right visual hemisphere (via his right eye), although he can point to its picture or select it with his left hand. Research by Sperry and others have shown that the left hemisphere is dominant in most people for both spoken and written language expression. Despite the dominance of the left hemisphere, however, the right hemisphere displays some perceptual abilities.

Zaidel designed special contact lenses used with prisms and mirrors to separate the left and right visual fields in one eye. Visual images were thus directed to only one cerebral hemisphere in people who had their corpus cal-

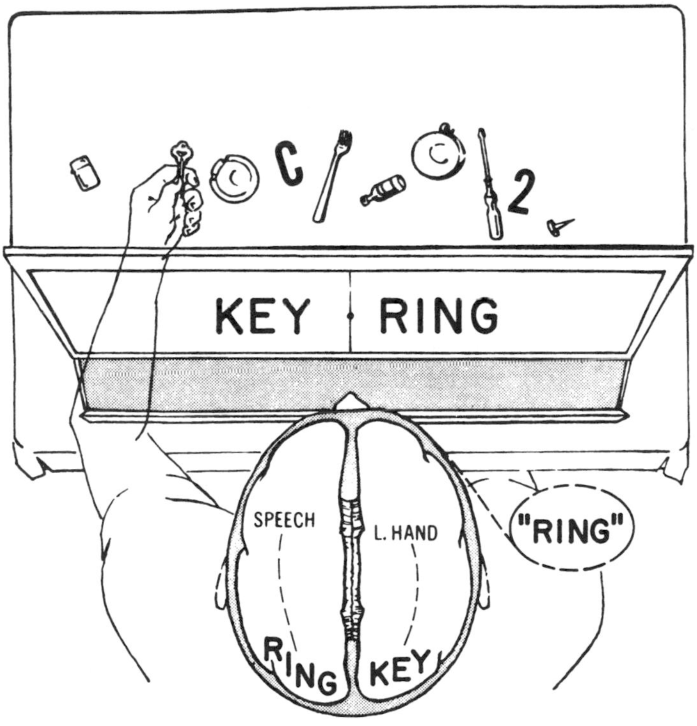

Figure 6.29. A Sperry experiment with a split-brain patient. A subject will report verbally on a visual stimulus ("ring" in this case) presented to the left hemisphere. At the same time, the left hand correctly retrieves objects presented to right hemisphere although the subject verbally denies knowledge of it. When asked to name an object selected by the left hand, the subject names the stimulus presented to the left hemisphere. (Reprinted with permission from R. W. Sperry: In *Hemispheric Specialization and Interaction*, B. Milner (Ed.), M. I. T. Press © 1975.)

losum severed and were wearing a patch over one eye. Written sentences and phrases of various complexity were presented to each side of the brain independently. The results indicated that the left hemisphere is clearly more linguistically sophisticated than the right. Whole sentences could be processed by the left hemisphere, while only single words could be processed by the right hemisphere.

Lateralization of speech perception has been studied in normal subjects as well. A classic study in the neurophysiology of speech perception was Kimura's study of cerebral dominance by use of dichotic stimuli. You recall that in dichotic listening, one sound goes to one ear and another sound to the opposite ear, both delivered simultaneously through earphones. Kimura used spoken digits as stimuli. When subjects were asked to report what they heard, they made mistakes because of the conflicting stimuli. Subjects made fewer mistakes in reporting stimuli delivered to the right ear than to the left ear. This effect is known as the *right ear advantage* (REA). Kimura's explanation of the REA was based upon anatomical evidence that more neurons of the auditory nerve cross to the contralateral temporal lobe than course directly to the ipsilateral lobe. Thus, information sent along VIIIth nerve fibers from the right cochlea would be strongly represented in the left cerebral hemisphere. Since the right ear demonstrates an advantage over the left in speech perception, she concluded that the left hemisphere is specialized for speech perception.

Shankweiler and Studdert-Kennedy, in a series of studies, found a small but consistent REA for CV nonsense syllables, such as /ba/, /ta/, or /ga/, presented dichotically to right-handed listeners. The REA was obtained for stop-vowel syllables in both synthetic and natural speech. Steady-state vowels, however, showed no consistent ear advantage.

Listeners appear to make fewer errors in identification when the competing syllables share a phonemic feature. For example, presenting /da/ to one ear and /ta/ to the other is likely to result in correct identification of both consonants because they share the same place of articulation. A similar presentation of the syllables /da/ and /ka/ might result in more identification errors. When the competing syllables share the same voicing classification, /da/ and /ba/ for example, accuracy of identification is better than when the syllables /da/ and /pa/ are competing. Shared place of articulation, however, yields greater accuracy than shared voicing class. There is no difference in ear advantage, however. Both ears are better when the dichotic pairs share features. Cutting, and Day and Vigorito have shown the right ear advantage to be greatest for contrastive stops, less extreme for liquids, and smallest, if found at all, for vowels.

If a dichotic test of vowel contrasts is made more difficult, however, by shortening the vowels or placing them in CVC context, the REA will be enhanced. The consonant-vowel differences and similarities found in categorical perception studies are thus mirrored in dichotic studies. Isolated vowels of relatively long duration and high intensity are more accessible to auditory analysis and so can be held longer in auditory memory, are less categorically perceived, and yield a weak (or no) right ear advantage. Stop consonants and brief low intensity vowels in CVC syllables, are less accessible to auditory analysis and so can be held only briefly in auditory memory, are categorized immediately, and yield a stronger right ear advantage. These results have been explained by positing a special speech processor in the left hemisphere or, alternatively, by suggestions that the left hemisphere is especially equipped to analyze stimuli that are brief, of low intensity, and/or marked by rapid spectral changes.

Experimenters have presented dichotic stimuli asynchronously. They found that listeners presented with a pair of dichotic stimuli having a *stimulus onset asynchrony (SOA)* estimated to be about 100 msec can identify the second stimulus with more accuracy than the first. This is called the *lag effect* because subjects are better at reporting the lagging syllable. The lag effect is an example of backward masking: the second syllable masks the first. If the syllables share voicing or other features, there is little backward masking or lag effect.

Yet, as one might expect, the more acoustically similar the vowels of the syllables are to one another, the more pronounced is the backward masking, as Pisoni and McNabb have demonstrated. Thus, vowel similarity seems to produce a backward masking effect that can be explained on an auditory level, while consonant feature sharing seems to facilitate perception and might be explained on either a phonetic or an auditory level.

The final bit of evidence for cerebral lateralization of speech perception comes from a study of electroencephalographic recordings made from the surface of the heads of subjects who are listening to speech. Wood, Goff, and Day recorded evoked auditory responses from 10 right-handed subjects as they performed two identification tasks on a series of synthesized speech stimuli differing in F_2 transition and in f_0. Task 1 was considered to be linguistic, as subjects identified syllables as either /ba/ or /da/ by pressing an appropriate response key. Task 2 was considered to be nonlinguistic, as subjects identified /ba/ syllables to be either low in pitch or high in pitch. Recordings were made from both hemispheres at central locations and over the temporal areas during each task. Evoked potentials from the right hemisphere were identical for both the linguistic and nonlinguistic tasks. The patterns from the left hemisphere for Task 1, however, were significantly different from those for Task 2. This result has been interpreted to mean that auditory processing occurs in both hemispheres but that phoneme identification is lateralized to the left hemisphere.

Something special is happening in the left hemisphere when we listen to speech, whether it is some kind of auditory analysis of transient, difficult stimuli, or whether it is some form of linguistic analysis, such as the extraction of features or phoneme categorization. Since any analysis presumes short-term memory, let us consider what is conjectured about the role of memory in speech perception.

Memory and Speech Perception. When one knows a particular language, it must mean that one has stored the rules and the lexicon of the language in long-term memory. The rules include the phonological rules and the articulatory rules for producing speech as well as the syntactic and semantic rules of the language. These rules are used as a reference not only for speech production but for speech perception. We hear speech patterns, analyze them, and refer to our stored knowledge of the speech patterns in that particular language for recognition of what was said.

It is assumed that there is also a short-term memory for auditory events. Some research has presented the possibility of two forms of short-term auditory memory. The first is a brief echo of an auditory event, lasting only a few milliseconds. This auditory image may present itself in the form of a neural spectrogram, and is continuously being replaced by new information.

The second, a longer lasting auditory memory, called *precategorical acoustic storage* (PAS) by Crowder and Morton, is evidenced by the *recency effect*. When a list of items (syllables, digits) is presented to subjects for recall, performance declines from the first item to the next-to-last item progressively, but the decline is reversed for the last item. Subjects tend to recall the most recent item in the list most accurately. The recency effect is stronger for lists in which the vowel changes than for lists in which the consonant changes. Lists differing only in voiced consonants produce little or no recency effect. One interpretation of the effect is that the last item suffers no interference from a following item, so phonetic analysis can take place uninterrupted. Darwin and Baddeley suggest that since acoustically similar items, like consonants, are auditorially confusable, they show little recency effect, fading quickly in precategorical acoustic storage. Items that are acoustically distinct, however, such as vowels, are posited to remain longer in PAS and are available for finer auditory analysis, resulting in a recency effect.

When hearing natural speech, a listener is likely to be perceiving a stream of sounds that are acoustically more dissimilar than the /ba/, /da/, /ga/ or /ba/–/pa/ continua often synthesized in the laboratory. If this is true, precategorical acoustic storage of speech material might operate on virtually all of the speech stream, allowing time for syllable and cross-syllable analysis. Studdert-Kennedy points out that another, longer term memory store of several seconds of auditory information is required for the recognition of prosodic patterns, intonation contours, and patterns of relative stress, since they may last for that period.

Neurophysiological Development and Perception. The auditory system of the human infant performs amazingly well, as we have only recently discovered from studies of infants' sound discrimination. Infant auditory sensitivity seems to be especially tuned to the sounds distinctive in human speech.

The occurrence of babbling, although considered to be nonlinguistic, does signify that sensory-motor neural associations are being formed. The infant, who has already demonstrated his auditory prowess, is slowly developing sound production abilities and so can make correlations between articulatory events and auditory results. During the babbling period, before speech has developed, the infant reveals his sensitivity to intonation patterns of other speakers by mimicking them.

Whitaker theorizes that the connections between Wernicke's area and Broca's area are activated during a time when babbling temporarily ceases. An auditory template of the language spoken in the infant's community may be registered at this stage. (See Chapter 8 for further discussion of auditory templates in connection with bird song.) Thus, as the child starts to speak at approximately 1 year, he has been sensitized to the particular language and the particular dialect of his community. If the connections between the child's perceptual and production centers for speech are not properly activated, a delay in language acquisition will result. The child hears sound but fails to associate sound with speech, and therefore, has difficulty in learning to speak himself.

Important in the neurophysiology of speech perception is the concept of a *critical period* for learning speech. The critical period applies to both perception and production and especially to the ability to relate perception to production. Lenneberg, and Penfield and Roberts have independently claimed that the critical period extends to puberty. It is easier to learn a language, and especially the sounds of a language, before puberty than after. Cerebral lateralization, too, is generally thought to be complete by puberty, but there are some indications that the left hemisphere may be dominant for speech at an early age, perhaps at birth. Kimura found the REA for dichotically presented speech to be established in 4-year-olds. The critical period for language learning relates to a flexibility and plasticity of brain function that diminishes in adulthood. Puberty is set as an outer limit; the younger the child, the more malleable the neural correlates of language learning. Thus, an acquired aphasia in a child is soon remedied by the other side of the brain assuming the functions of the damaged hemisphere. The neural flexibility during the youthful critical period allows children to compensate by establishing a linguistic center in an undamaged area of the brain, while the adult loses access to an already established linguistic store, and has little neural flexibility left to establish a new one.

Theories of Speech Perception

Someone says "We beat you in soccer." How does a listener begin to extract the information necessary to understand that message? Disregarding the semantic and syntactic operations that must occur, how do listeners identify individual speech sounds from the continuous stream of sound at rates of transmission that normally exceed the powers of resolution of the hearing mechanism? Do they process the speech signal on a purely auditory basis, or do they extract phonetic information from it that informs them about the way in which the sounds were produced? Or, do they do both? These are, perhaps the most important questions that a theory of speech perception must answer, and, as yet, no theory has provided a completely satisfying answer to any of them.

Any theory of speech perception must account for certain generally accepted facts about the acoustic speech signal. Among them is the high degree of intra- and inter-speaker variability among signals that convey information about equivalent phonetic events. This variability, as we have seen, is caused by differences between the sizes of speakers' vocal tracts, and the different phonetic contexts in which speech sounds occur. Theories must also account for the ability of speakers to resolve the stream of speech into linguistic units (phonemes), even when they are provided with an acoustic signal that contains no obvious discontinuities and that is delivered to them at rates as high as 20–25 speech sounds per second. The continuous nature of much of the acoustic signal for speech, as well as the high transmission rate of phonemes, derives from the ability of speakers to coarticulate sounds. Because of coarticulation, any given portion of the acoustic signal can contain information about two or more phonemes.

The theories that seek to explain these facts may divided into two general groups. One group views the process of speech perception as primarily auditory. Using the same hearing mechanism and perceptual processing employed for any other types of sound, the listener simply identifies acoustic patterns and/or features and matches them directly to the learned and stored acoustic-phonetic features of the language. The other group of theories posits a link between speech perception and speech production. The listener must, according to such theories, extract information about articulation from the acoustic signal in order to cope adequately with the problems posed by variability, segmentation, and transmission rate. Because of the reference to articulation in the perception process, this type of theory is often called a *motor theory*. We shall discuss some motor theories first and then conclude with a discussion of auditory theories.

Motor Theories. The first of the important motor theories that we shall consider is the *Analysis-by-Synthesis Theory*, which Stevens and Halle developed at the Massachusetts Institute of Technology in the 1960s. According to this theory the listener receives an auditory pattern and analyzes it by eliciting an auditory model of his own production of it. Assume, for example, that the listener hears [bitʃə] and hypothesizes that this represents "beat you." He rapidly generates a neural synthesis of the commands he would use to produce the utterance himself, and, if the patterns of his projected output match those of the signal that was input, he accepts his perception as correct. An advantage of a theory such as this is that the listener can apply his knowledge of phonological rules when performing the rudimentary synthesis and thereby can normalize variations caused by fast speaking rate and context. In this way, the speaker is able to control for the variability of phoneme representation in the acoustic signal.

As the authors of Analysis-by-Synthesis Theory, especially Stevens, came to support auditory theories of speech perception, they ceased to develop it. By some time in the 1970s it was more-or-less abandoned. Such was not the case for the Motor Theory of Speech Perception, proposed by Liberman and other researchers at Haskins Laboratories. Developed at about the same time as the Stevens and Halle theory, the Motor Theory of Speech Perception has been supported by ongoing research ever since, and has been revised, both implicitly and explicitly, many times.

Motor Theory starts with the premise that the sounds of speech are *encoded* in the acoustic signal, rather than *enciphered* in it. Codes and ciphers differ from each other in a number of ways. In the simpler forms of a cipher, the units to be enciphered, the *plaintext* units, are represented in an invariant, one-to-one relation by units of the *ciphertext*. For example, suppose we were to encipher the letters of the alphabet by giving each a number:

Plaintext Units	A	B	C	D	E	F	G .....
Ciphertext Units	1	2	3	4	5	6	7 .....

Using such a cipher, we could represent the word "BAD" as "214," the word "DAB" as "412," "DEAD" as "4514," "FADED" as "61454," and so on. The critical point about this type of representation is that it is invariant.

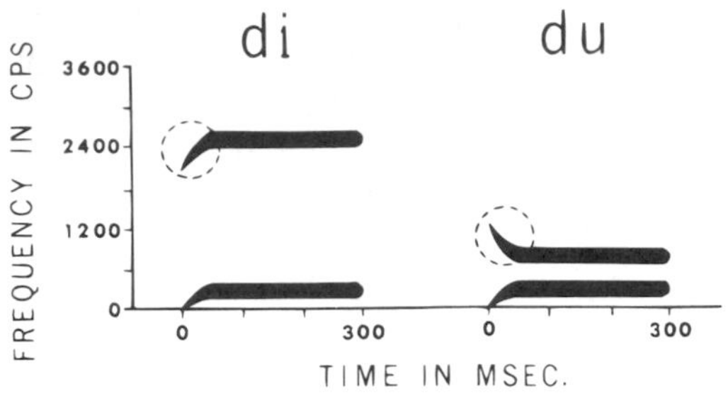

Figure 6.30. Synthetic patterns showing the syllables /di/ and /du/. Notice the difference in the direction of the F_2 transition. (Reprinted with permission from A. M. Liberman: *Cognitive Psychology. 1,* 1970.)

The number "4" always stands for the letter "D," which must always be represented in the enciphered message by "4." Notice that we do not need to use another number or a different form of the number "4" depending on the context of the letter "D" in the plaintext. "4" will always do the job of representing "D" no matter what its position in a word and no matter which letters precede and/or follow it. As we have seen, the representation of speech sounds in the acoustic signal is not of this nature. There is a *lack of invariance* in the way a particular phoneme is signaled acoustically. *Lack of invariance* is a characteristic of a code.

One often cited example of the lack of invariance in the acoustic signal is the representation of /d/ in the syllables /di/ and /du/ (Fig. 6.30): a rising second formant transition in /di/ and a falling one in /du/ both serve as acoustic cues for /d/. This would be akin to representing the letter "D" with one number when it occurred before the letter "A" and another number when it occurred before the letter "E." The acoustic signal for speech also contains examples of the sort of thing that would happen if it were possible to represent both "B" and "D" with the same number. In the study cited above on the frequency of stop bursts as cues to place of articulation, the experimenters found that the same burst, centered at 1440 Hz was heard as /p/ before /i/ and /u/, but as /k/ before /ɑ/. Schatz, cross-splicing stop bursts with vowels, obtained similar results. The lack of correspondence between discrete acoustic events and separate phonemes, then, works both ways: different acoustic events can be perceived as the same phoneme, while the same acoustic event can be perceived as different phonemes in different contexts.

A second difference between codes and ciphers is implicit in the examples of the enciphered words above: A ciphertext is segmentable into units that correspond to units of the plaintext. If we see the ciphertext "214," even if we don't have the key, we will know that the plaintext is a word of three letters, and that each number represents one of those letters. Moreover, the number "1" conveys no information about the letters that precede or follow the "A" that it represents. This, as we have seen, is in direct contrast with the *nonsegmentability* of the acoustic signal for speech. Nonsegmentability, another characteristic of a code, is accounted for in the speech signal by coarticulation, which distributes the acoustic features representing speech sounds to more than one place in the acoustic signal.

A final difference between codes and ciphers relates to the relative efficiency with which they are capable of conveying information. In the simple cipher we have been using as an example, a separate look-up operation is required to recover each unit of the plaintext: Four operations would thus be needed to decipher "6135" as "FACE." A code might convey the same information by representing the entire word with a single symbol. One look-up operation, for a code, therefore, will yield more information, faster. Listeners hearing a synthesized sentence such as "A bird in the hand is worth two in the bush," can accurately perceive more than 20 phonemes per second when pushed to the limits of their ability. This means when they hear such an utterance, and repeat it accurately or transcribe it in some fashion, they can correctly identify and order the 26 phonemes they have heard. But how well can they perform this task with enciphered, nonspeech stimuli? Listeners hearing a sequence of 26 tones, containing only three different tones, (far fewer than the number of phonemes in a language) can identify and order them accurately only when they are presented at about the rate of one per second. When the tones are presented at the rate of 20 per second, all the listeners report hearing is a blur of sound in which the individual tones are not even recognized as separate events.

A strong case, then, can be made that speech is encoded in the acoustic signal on the grounds of (1) lack of invariance between the acoustic signal and the speech sounds represented in it, (2) nonsegmentability of the acoustic signal, and (3) the relatively high efficiency of transmission of information by the acoustic signal. It then remains for motor theory to explain how the listener extracts speech sounds from the signal—that is, how decoding is effected.

It is, perhaps, a short step from acceptance of the fact that speech is an acoustic code generated by articulation to the incorporation of articulation into the process of perception. Early on, researchers noted that the discontinuities in labeling and discriminating speech sounds, revealed by studies of categorical perception, were coincidental with discontinuities in articulation. They argued, for instance, that just as there are no articulations intermediate to the labial and alveolar occlusions for stops, there are no percepts intermediate to, for example, /b/ and /d/: a listener will assign each stimulus of a smoothly varying acoustic continuum to one or the other category of stop sounds. Given the immense variability in absolute values of the acoustic cues that signal place of articulation, the listener must be able to relate those cues to the more-or-less invariant articulation that generated them. Further research, however, indicated that the articulations were, in fact, rather less than more invariant. Neither studies of muscle activity nor of articulator movement have revealed invariant gestures for particular speech sounds.

Motor theorists responded to this finding by positing more abstract representations of speech gestures, which they maintain are the actual objects of perception. The intended gesture for a particular sound is presumed to comprise a complex of movements that do not occur simultaneously because of the effects of context. Coarticulation, then, is responsible for the temporal distribution of the component movements and of the resulting acoustic cues. Because the production and perception processes are linked together, biologically, listeners are able to perceive the intended gestures and recover the encoded phonemes they represent from the acoustic signal.

What is the nature of the biological link between speech production and speech perception? According to motor theorists, humans possess a specialized perceptual *module* that has evolved for the processing of speech. This module is one of several, such as those for sound localization and visual depth perception, which exist in humans and other animals. It consists of specialized neural structures that respond specifically to the acoustic signal for speech and relate the features of that signal to the intended gestures that produced it. In this view, the listener, because he understands the dynamics of vocal tract behavior, perceives the gestures directly and immediately.

Motor theorists point to a substantial body of experimental work that supports their point of view. Among the experiments that purport to demonstrate that listeners rely on their knowledge of vocal tract behavior to decode the acoustic speech signal are several that explore the effect of silence on speech perception. If an appropriate duration of silence is inserted between the /s/ and the /ɑ/ of the utterance /sɑ/, listeners report hearing /stɑ/. Moreover, the duration of silence inserted must approximate the minimum needed for a speaker to articulate a stop consonant (about 50 ms). Listeners perceive stimuli containing less than about 50 ms of silence as /sɑ/. and cannot discriminate them from a /sɑ/ stimulus containing no silence whatsoever. Motor theory would argue that the speech module enables the listener to identify the silence as the stop gesture when its duration was appropriate to that gesture. Silent periods of lesser durations are not processed by the module because a vocal tract could not have produced them in the process of articulating speech. Motor theorists also point out that durations of silence well below 5 ms in duration can be perceived when they occur in noise or in portions of the speech signal where they could not be articulated by a speaker (e.g., in the middle of a relatively steady-state vowel). The assumption might be that an auditory processor or module, rather than a phonetic one is responsible for perceiving such silences.

In related experiments, Dorman, Raphael, and Liberman found that when listeners perceive a sequence of stops in a disyllable such as /ɛbdɛ/, they process the cues for the /b-d/ closure and the /d/ release in a normal fashion. If, however, the duration of the closure period for the two stops is reduced to zero ms, producing a stimulus than no single speaker could articulate, listeners do not perceive the first stop in the sequence. That is, they report hearing /ɛdɛ/. As the duration of the closure period is lengthened, again to about the minimum time required for a speaker to articulate two stops, then the /b/ is again heard, much as is the /t/ in the /sɑ - stɑ/ experiment reported above. But there are two conditions in which both stops can be perceived in stimuli with no closure interval: Listeners report hearing /ɛbdɛ/ if each syllable is spoken by a different speaker or if each syllable, spoken by the same speaker, is delivered to a different ear via a headset. A motor theory interpretation of these results is that the speech module recognizes that two vocal tracts could produce the sequence of stops without a closure interval. Thus both stops are perceived when the syllables are recognized as the outputs of two different vocal tracts, either because the voices sound different, or because the 180° separation of the voices in the headset causes the listener to believe that they could not have been produced by the same speaker. In all cases, the listener's knowledge of what vocal tracts can and cannot do conditions his perception.

Experimental support for the concept of modularity in general, and for existence of a speech module in particular, is, according to motor theorists, found in the work of Liberman and others on *duplex* perception. In duplex perception a two- or three-formant stop + vowel synthetic syllable is split into two portions. One portion, containing only the transition of the second formant, is presented to one ear, and the rest of the stimulus, called the "base," is presented to the other ear. Listeners report hearing both a complete stop + vowel syllable (in the ear to which the base is presented) and an isolated "chirp," a response to the F2 transition, in the other ear. Evidently, the two parts of the stimuli fuse at some level, and the phonetic module then evokes the perception of the CV syllable. At about the same time, another, auditory module, processes the "chirp," accounting for the other part of the duplex percept. Moreover, changes in the frequency of the F_2 transition (the "chirp") that are detected by the auditory module are not detected by the phonetic module unless they cue a difference in the place of articulation of the stop. The relative independence of the parts of the duplex percept suggest, then, that separate processors are at work and that one of them is phonetic in nature.

Evidence of a different sort pertaining to a link between speech perception and production was provided in an experiment performed by Bell-Berti, Raphael, Pisoni and Sawusch. Using electromyography, they found that each of their 10 subjects employed one of two discrete patterns of genioglossus activity to distinguish front tense vowels from front lax vowels. The subjects were then presented with two identification tests of a seven-step five-formant synthetic vowel continuum from /i/ to /I/. In the first test each stimulus was presented 10 times. A labeling function was plotted and the phoneme boundary between /i/ and /I/ was determined. In the second test, the first stimulus in the continuum, /i/, was heard 40 times, while each of the other 6 stimuli was again heard 10 times. The result of this type of test is much like that found in the selective adaptation experiments described above: there is a shift in the phoneme boundary toward the stimulus that is heard more than the others. Indeed, all of the subjects in the EMG experiment showed such a shift in their perceptual data, but, again, they fell into two discrete groups, based on the size of the boundary shift. The members of each group were same as the members of the groups using the different production strategies to differentiate the tense from the lax vowels. The experimenters concluded that the differences in the perception data reflected the differences in production strategies, establishing a production-perception link, at least for the vowels and the muscle they investigated.

Finally, work by Chistovich, Klass, and Kuzmin in Petrograd points to the importance of the knowledge of speech production in the perception of speech. They conducted "shadowing" experiments, in which a person repeats an unknown message as quickly as possible. The shadowers started to produce consonants before hearing all of the relevant acoustic cues. This finding indicates that cues at the beginning of the syllable signal what is to come, and that listeners refer the incoming patterns immediately to motor articulatory patterns, before they "understand" the message.

The general class of perceptual motor theory that we have been discussing has recently been extended to account for both production and perception. In Chapter 4 we mentioned *Action Theory* by referring to the work of Fowler, Turvey and Kelso. This explicitly ecological view of speech perception and production posits a direct connection between the coordinated actions of the speaker and the environment and a direct relationship between speech perception and the act of speaking. Although the similarity of Action Theory to the Motor Theory of Liberman and his colleagues is obvious, the two theories differ in several ways. Action Theory is as much a theory of speech production as of speech perception. It suggests that both processes are relatively simple and straightforward. The complex interactions, coarticulations, and acoustic signals that we study result from the natural properties of the production mechanism. Action Theory does not require that phonemes be extracted from the acoustic signal. The difficulties of segmentation are thus neutralized on the grounds that the listener perceives a larger, more abstract, more dynamic chunk of speech that is understood because of its direct relationship to the dynamic act of speaking. Since the person is both a producer and a perceiver of speech, no translation is necessary; according to this theory the listener is not extracting phonetic features or phonemes but rather information on how to produce the speech. For example, if you heard someone say [lɪdlæmzidaɪvi], you could repeat it exactly even if you failed to grasp the message "Little lambs eat ivy."

Michael Studdert-Kennedy points out that aspects of such an action theory are supported by research in speech perception and are in basic agreement with recent studies of speech and language acquisition: children can understand utterances such as /pinʌtbʌtɝndʒɛli/, long before they know "peanut" and "jelly" as separate words or that /dʒ/ is distinctive in the language. The biological foundation of such a theory of action has not been specified, but many, like Studdert-Kennedy, believe that we are getting closer to a biology of language.

We could cite other theoretical variants and many more experiments that support the several aspects of a motor theory. As is often the case, however, the interpretations of experimental results often differ depending on the theoretical orientation of the interpreters. Those who favor auditory theories of speech perception will interpret results differently from those who support a motor theory, and, of course, they will offer contrary evidence of their own. We will now turn to some of these alternative explanations and the data that support them.

Auditory Theories. Auditory theories of speech perception emphasize the sensory, filtering mechanisms of the listener, and relegate the role of speech production knowledge to a minor, secondary place, used only in difficult circumstances.

Fant has modeled speech perception as primarily sensory. He maintains that the perceptual and production mechanisms share a common pool of distinctive features (see Fig. 6.31), but that the listener need not refer to production in order to perceive speech. Linguistic centers in the brain are common to both incoming and outgoing messages, but the centers responsible for subphonemic, more peripheral aspects of production and perception are viewed as independent. According to this auditory model (Figure 6.31), speech perception proceeds along the route ABCDE, while

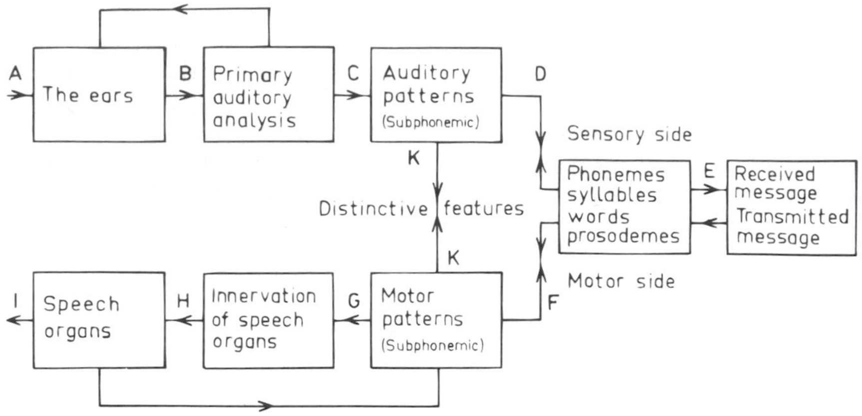

Figure 6.31. Fant's model of the brain mechanisms in speech perception and production. See text for explanation. (Reprinted with permission from G. Fant: *Models for the Perception of Speech and Visual Form,* W. Wathen-Dunn (Ed.), M. I. T. Press © 1967.)

for a motor model, the route would be ABCKFE. Fant's view is that listeners, having been exposed to language, are sensitive to the distinctive patterns of the speech wave and only need to refer to their own ability to speak when shadowing or listening under other unusual circumstances. A similar theory is held by Morton and Broadbent. They concur with Fant in the belief that listeners can decode directly, although reference to production may be made when the perceptual task is difficult, as in transcribing speech phonetically.

Inherent in most auditory approaches to speech perception, including Fant's, is the idea of sensitivity to acoustic patterns or to particular acoustic features. Some theorists, those who support the notion that speech perception can be explained by sensitivity to acoustic patters, have proposed a process of *template matching* as the basis for the recognition of speech sounds. The concept of an auditory template arises from experimental work on bird song. As we shall see in Chapter 8, some birds are born with a rudimentary version of the song characteristic of their species. This template is further refined as the young birds hear the song of mature birds in the environment. They later sing themselves, matching their efforts to their stored templates. Marler suggests that human infants may proceed somewhat similarly when learning speech. A similar process has been proposed to explain speech perception. Adult speakers are presumed to have stored abstract patterns of speech: templates of phonemes or syllables. When they listen to speech, they match the incoming auditory patterns to the stored templates in order to identify the sounds.

Theorists who believe that the auditory system is sensitive to particular acoustic features have proposed a process of *feature detection* as the basis for speech perception. The concept of feature detection was borrowed from research on vision that demonstrated that specific cortical nerve cells are sensitive to a particular aspect of an image. For example, there are special detectors for horizontal lines. By analogy, a feature detector for speech is thought to be sensitive to specific complex stimuli, such as F_2 transitions. Initially, adaptation studies were interpreted in terms of a feature detector theory. If repetition of a particular stimulus resulted in a shift in phoneme identification, it was theorized that the shift occurred because the detector for that particular feature had been fatigued by overstimulation (the multiple repetitions of a stimulus from one end of a continuum). Studies of infants' speech perception were also interpreted in terms of feature detection: The ability of the infants to discriminate stimuli belonging to different linguistic categories was explained by their sensitivity to certain acoustic features. The theory connotes a nativist approach; humans are viewed as possessing an innate linguistic capacity in the form of special neural receptors tuned to universal distinctive features of speech.

In the view of some theorists, the processes of template matching and feature detection are incapable of resolving the problem of variability in the acoustic signal. They point to the multiplicity of acoustic patterns that can represent a particular speech sound and conclude that storage of all the possible patterns would place an unacceptable load on memory. Similarly, the number of feature detectors required to process all of the acoustic features conveying a single phonological feature (e.g., voicing) often appears to inordinately large. One response to these objections has been to propose patterns or features that are more abstract than those found in the spectrographic representation of the speech signal.

Stevens and Blumstein, for example, have proposed that the place of articulation of stop consonants can be recognized from the shape of the spectrum averaged over the duration of the burst and the first few milliseconds following the burst. They describe what they call distinctive "spectral tilts" that characterize each place of stop articulation in an invariant fashion (Fig. 6.32): alveolar stops display an average short-term spectrum that is called "diffuse-rising," because there is an increase in the relative amplitude of successive spectral peaks; labial stops display a "diffuse-falling" pattern, as the spectral peaks decrease in amplitude as they increase in frequency; and velar stops display a compact pattern, with a single spectral peak at a mid-range frequency.

A somewhat different approach to the problem of acoustic variability within the framework of an essentially auditory theory has been proposed by Cole and Scott. They posit that perception of the syllable is accomplished by reference both to invariant and to context-conditioned cues. For example, they would view [s]-frication in the first syllable (/sɑ/ of "soccer" as an invariant cue, but would also

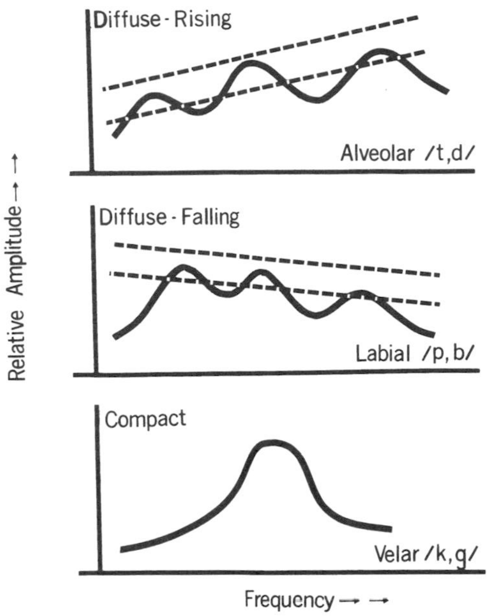

Figure 6.32. Steven's and Blumstein's averaged short-term spectra, displaying distinctive and invariant patterns that distinguish stop place of articulation.

recognize the existence of context-conditioned cues for both the [s] and the [k] in [sakɚ] inherent in the transitions to and from the relatively steady-state formants of [ɑ]. They agree with Liberman that transitions are important in providing the listener with the perception of the temporal order of sounds in a syllable. Cole and Scott suggest that the invariant and variable cues maintain their independence as cues, and that listeners make use of both for syllable recognition. Evidence of their independence is provided by studies of the repeated presentation of a stimulus that gives rise to an effect known as "streaming." If, for example, a listener hears the syllable [sɑ] repeatedly, the percept separates into two discrete streams: a hiss, conditioned by the [s]-frication and [dɑ], conditioned by the transition and steady state of the vocalic portion. In addition to the invariant cues and the context-conditioned cues, they propose a third cue, the waveform, which is processed over a longer time frame and gives rise to percepts of relative intensity, duration, and pitch.

Some theorists have attempted to com-

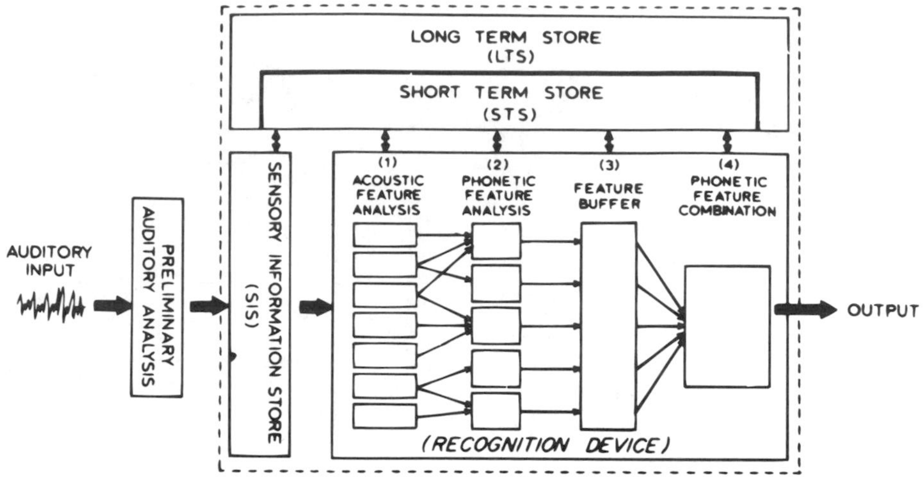

Figure 6.33. Pisoni and Sawusch's model of speech recognition. Phonetic and acoustic features are both analyzed, and short-term memory figures specifically in the model. (Reprinted with permission from D. B. Pisoni and J. R. Sawusch: In *Structure and Process in Speech Perception,* A. Cohen and S. G. Nooteboom (Eds.), Springer-Verlag © 1975.)

bine the notions of auditory and phonetic feature detectors in a single model of speech perception. Pisoni and Sawusch have proposed a model that provides for the short-term storage of information elicited from the long-term store during the period of recognition. The recognized speech is then referred simultaneously for phonological, syntactic, and semantic analysis (Fig. 6.33). According to this theory, features detected by auditory property detectors are mapped onto a system of phonetic features as detected within a whole syllable and then combined into a rough feature matrix for further analysis. We should make it clear that although this sort of theory encompasses the detection of both auditory and phonetic features, it does not address the relationship between production and perception. It is, rather, a theory about the sensory stage common to both motor and auditory theories.

The debate between the schools of thought supporting motor and auditory theories of speech perception will not soon end. A great deal of needed experimentation lies ahead, much of which will have to await the development of newer technologies. The outcome will reveal a great deal about the human ability to produce and perceive both speech and language: "If language is a window on the mind, speech is the thin end of an experimental wedge that will pry the window open."

REFERENCES

General Readings

Bartlett, F. C., *Remembering*. Cambridge, England: University Press, 1932. Reprinted in 1950.

Darwin, C. J. The Perception of Speech. In *Handbook of Perception, Vol. 7: Language and Speech*. E. C. Carterette and M. P. Friedman (Eds.) New York: Academic Press, 1976, pp. 175–226.

Denes, P., and Pinson, E. N., *The Speech Chain*. New York: Doubleday, 1963.

Fant, G., Descriptive Analysis of the Acoustic Aspects of Speech. *Logos. 5*, 1962, 3–17.

Kent, R. D., Atal, B. S., and Miller, J. L. (Eds.) *Papers in Speech Communication: Speech Production.* Woodbury, N. Y.: Acoustical Society of America, 1991.

Miller, J. L., Kent, R. D., and Atal, B. S. (Eds.) *Papers in Speech Communication: Speech Perception.* Woodbury, N. Y.: Acoustical Society of America, 1991.

Pickett, J. M., *The Sounds of Speech Communication*. Baltimore; University Park Press, 1980.

Studdert-Kennedy, M., Speech Perception. In *Contemporary Issues in Experimental Phonetics*. N. J. Lass (Ed.) Springfield, Ill.: Charles C. Thomas, 1975, pp. 243–293.

Hearing

Durrant, J. D., and Lovrinic, J. H., *Bases of Hearing Science; ed. 2*. Baltimore: Williams & Wilkins, 1984.

Fletcher, H., *Speech and Hearing in Communication*. Princeton, N. J.: van Nostrand, 1953. First published as *Speech and Hearing* in 1929.

Geldard, F. A., *The Human Senses*. New York: Wiley & Sons, 1953.

Helmholtz, H. L. F., *On the Sensations of Tone*. New York: Dover, 1961. Reprint of translation by A. J. Ellis, London: Longmans, Green and Co., 1875.

Kiang, N. Y. S., and Moxon, E. C., Tails of Tuning Curves of Auditory-Nerve Fibers. *J. Acoust. Soc. Am. 55*, 1974, 620–630.

Stevens, S. S. (Ed.), *Handbook of Experimental Psychology*. New York: Wiley & Sons, 1951.

Stevens, S. S., and Davis, H., *Hearing: Its Psychology and Physiology*. New York: Acoustical Society of America, 1983. (Originally published by Wiley & Sons, 1938.)

Van Bergeijk, W. A., Pierce, J. R., and David, E. E., Jr., *Waves and the Ear*. London: Heinemann, 1961.

Van Békésy, G., *Experiments in Hearing*. New York: McGraw-Hill, 1960.

Wever, E. G., and Lawrence, M., *Physiological Acoustics*. Princeton. N. J.: University Press, 1954.

Acoustic Cues

Vowels, Diphthongs, And Semivowels

Carlson, R., Fant, G., and Granstrom, B., Two-Formant Models, Pitch, and Vowel Perception. In *Auditory Analysis and Perception of Speech*. G. Fant and M. A. A. Tatham (Eds.) New York: Academic Press, 1975, pp. 55–82.

Delattre, P., Liberman, A. M., Cooper, F. S., and Gerstman, L. J. An Experimental Study of the Acoustic Determinants of Vowel Color: Observations on One- and Two-Formant Vowels Synthesized from Spectrographic Patterns. *Word. 8*, 1952, 195–210.

Fant, G., A Note on Vocal Tract Size Factors and Non-Uniform F-Pattern Scalings. *Q. Prog. Status Rep. Speech Transmission Lab. 4*, 1966, 22–30.

Fry, D. B., Abramson, A. S., Eimas, P. D., and Liberman, A. M., The Identification and Discrimination of Synthetic Vowels. *Lang. Speech. 5*, 1962, 171–189.

Gay, T., A Perceptual Study of American English Diphthongs. *Lang. Speech. 13*, 1970, 65–88.

Gerstman, L. J. Classification of Self-Normalized Vowels. *IEEE Trans. Aud. Electroacoust. AU. 16*, 1968, 78–80.

Joos, M. A., *Acoustic Phonetics*. *Language. Suppl. 24*, 1948, 1–136.

Ladefoged, P., and Broadbent, D. E., Information Conveyed by Vowels. *J. Acoust. Soc. Am. 39*, 1957, 98–104. Reprinted in Miller, J. L., *et al.* (q.v.), 493–499.

Lieberman, P., On the Evolution of Language: A Unified View. *Cognition 2*, 1973, 59–94.

Lindblom, B. E. F., and Studdert-Kennedy, M., On the Role of Formant Transitions in Vowel Recognition. *J. Acoust. Soc. Am. 42*, 1967, 830–843. Reprinted in Miller, J. L., *et al.* (q.v.), 501–514.

Lisker, L., Minimal Cues for Separating /w,r,l,y/ in Intervocalic Position. *Word. 13*, 1957, 256–267.

Nordstrom, P. E., and Lindblom, B., A Normalization Procedure for Vowel Formant Data. Paper Presented at 8th International Congress of Phonetic Sciences, Leeds, England, August, 1975.

O'Connor, J. D., Gerstman, L. J., Liberman, A. M., Delattre, P. C., and Cooper, F. S., Acoustic Cues for the Perception of Initial /w,j,r,l/ in English. *Word 13*, 1957, 22–43.

Strange, W., Verbrugge, R. R., Shankweiler, D. P., and Edman, T. R., Consonant Environment Specifies Vowel Identity. *J. Acoust. Soc. Am. 60*, 1976, 213–221.

Verbrugge, R. R., Strange, W., Shankweiler, D. P. and Edman, T. R., What Information Enables a Listener to Map a Talker's Vowel Space? *J. Acoust. Soc. Am. 60*, 1976, 198–212.

Nasals, Stops, Fricatives, And Affricates

Ali, L., Gallagher, T., Goldstein, J. and Daniloff, R. Perception of Coarticulated Nasality. *J. Acoust. Soc. Am.* 49, 1971, 538–540.

Cooper, F. S., Delattre, P. C., Liberman, A. M., Borst, J. M., and Gerstman, L. J. Some Experiments on the Perception of Synthetic Speech Sounds. *J. Acoust. Soc. Am. 24*, 1952, 597–606.

Delattre, P. C., Liberman, A. M., and Cooper, F. S., Acoustic Loci and Transitional Cues for Consonants. *J. Acoust. Soc. Am. 27*, 1955, 769–773.

Denes, P., Effect of Duration on the Perception of Voicing. *J. Acoust. Soc. Am. 27*, 1955, 761–764.

Harris, K. S., Cues for the Discrimination of American English Fricatives in Spoken Syllables. *Lang. Speech. 1*, 1958, 1–7.

House, A. S., Analog Studies of Nasal Consonants. *J. Speech Hear. Disord. 22*, 1957, 190–204.

Kuhn, G. M., On the Front Cavity Resonance and its Possible Role in Speech Perception. *J. Acoust. Soc. Am. 58*, 1975, 428–433.

Liberman, A. M., Delattre, P. C., and Cooper, F. S., The Role of Selected Stimulus-Variables in the Perception of the Unvoiced Stop Consonants. *Am. J. Psychol. LXV*, 1952, 497–516.

Liberman, A. M., Delattre, P. C., and Cooper, F. S., Some Rules for the Distinction between Voiced and Voiceless Stops in Initial Position. *Lang. Speech 1*, 1958, 153–167.

Liberman, A. M., Delattre, P. C., Cooper, F. S., and Gerstman, L. J. The Role of Consonant-Vowel Transitions in the Perception of the Stop and Nasal Consonants. *Psychol. Monagr. (Gen. Appl.) 68*, 1954, 1–13.

Liberman, A. M., Delattre, P. C., Gerstman, L. J., and Cooper, F. S., Tempo of Frequency Change as a Cue for Distinguishing Classes of Speech Sounds. *J. Exp. Psychol. 52*, 1956, 127–137.

Liberman, A. M., Harris, K. S., Eimas, P., Lisker, L., and Bastian, J., An Effect of Learning on Speech Perception: The Discrimination of Durations of Silence with and without Phonemic Significance. *Lang. Speech 4*, 1961, 175–195.

Lisker, L., and Abramson, A. S., A Cross-Language Study

of Voicing in Initial Stops: Acoustical Measurements. *Word 20,* 1964, 384–422.

Malécot, A., Acoustic Cues for Nasal Consonants. *Language 32,* 1956, 274–278.

Mermelstein, P., On Detecting Nasals in Continuous Speech. *J. Acoust. Soc. Am. 61,* 1977, 581-587.

Miller, G. A., and Nicely, P. E., An Analysis of Perceptual Confusions among Some English Consonants. *J. Acoust. Soc. Am. 27,* 1955, 338–352. Reprinted in Miller, J. L., *et al.* (q.v.), 623–637.

Raphael, L. J., Preceding Vowel Duration as a Cue to the Perception of the Voicing Characteristic of Word-Final Consonants in American English. *J. Acoust. Soc. Am. 51,* 1972, 1296–1303.

Raphael, L. J., and Dorman, M. F., Acoustic Cues for a Fricative-Affricate Contrast in Word-Final Position. *J. Phonetics 8,* 1980, 397–405.

Suprasegmentals

Bolinger, D. W., and Gerstman, L. J., Disjuncture as a Cue to Constructs. *Word 13,* 1957, 246–255.

Bolinger, D. L., A Theory of Pitch Accent in English. *Word 14,* 1958, 109–149.

Fry, D. B., Experiments in the Perception of Stress. *Lang. Speech 1,* 1958, 126–152.

Fry, D. B., Prosodic Phenomena. In *Manual of Phonetics*. B. Malmberg (Ed.) Amsterdam: North-Holland Publication Co., 1968, pp. 365–410.

Hadding-Koch, K., and Studdert-Kennedy, M., An Experimental Study of Some Intonation Contours. *Phonetica. 11,* 1964, 175–185.

Lehiste, I., *Suprasegmentals*. Cambridge, Mass: M. I. T. Press, 1970.

Categorical Perception

Adults

Abramson, A. S., and Lisker, L., Discriminability Along the Voicing Continuum: Cross-Language Tests. In *Proceedings of the Sixth International Congress of Phonetic Sciences.* Prague: Academia Publishing House of the Czechoslovak Academy of Sciences, 1970, pp. 569–573.

Abramson, A. S., and Lisker, L., Voice-Timing Perception in Spanish Word-Initial Stops. *J. Phonetics 1,* 1973, 1–8.

Elman, J. L., Diehl, R. L., and Buchwald, S. E., Perceptual Switching in Bilinguals. *J. Acoust. Soc. Am. 62,* 1977, 991–994.

Fry, D., Abramson, A., Eimas, P., and Liberman, A. M., The Identification and Discrimination of Synthetic Vowels. *Lang. Speech 5,* 1962, 171–189.

Fujisaki, H., and Kawashima, T., Some Experiments an Speech Perception and a Model for the Perceptual Mechanism. *Annu. Rep. Res. Inst. (Tokyo Univ.) 29,* 1970, 207–214.

Liberman, A. M., Harris, K. S., Hoffman, H. S., and Griffith, B. C., The Discrimination of Speech Sounds within and across Phoneme Boundaries. *J. Exp. Psychol. 54,* 1957, 358–368.

Lisker, L., and Abramson, A. S., A Cross-Language Study of Voicing in Initial Stops: Acoustical Measurements. *Word 20,* 1964, 384–422. Reprinted in Kent, R. D., *et al.* (q.v.), 527–565.

Miyawaki, K., Strange, W., Verbrugge, R. R., Liberman, A. M., Jenkins, J. J., and Fujimura, O., An Effect of Linguistic Experience: The Discrimination of [r] and [l] by Native Speakers of Japanese and English. *Percept. Psychophys. 18,* 1975, 331–340. Reprinted in Miller, J. L., *et al.* (q.v.), 405–414.

Repp, B. H., Categorical Perception: Issues, Methods, Findings. In *Speech and Language: Advances in Theory and Practice Vol 10.* N. J. Lass (Ed.) New York: Academic Press, pp. 243–335.

Stevens, K. N., Liberman, A. M., Studdert-Kennedy, M., and Öhman, S., Cross-language Study of Vowel Perception. *Lang. Speech. 12,* 1969, 1–23.

Stevens, K. N., On the Quantal Nature of Speech. *J. Phonetics 17,* 1989, 3–45.

Strange, W., and Jenkins, J. J., The Role of Linguistic Experience in the Perception of Speech. In *Perception and Experience*. R. D. Walk and H. L. Pick (Eds.) New York: Plenum Press, 1978, pp. 125–169.

Infants And Animals

Eimas, P. D., Speech Perception in Early Infancy. In *Infant Perception*. L. B. Cohen and P. Salapatek (Eds.) New York: Academic Press, 1975, pp. 193–231.

Eimas, P. D., Siqueland, E. R., Jusczyk, P., and Vigorito, J., Speech Perception in Infants. *Science 171,* 1971, 303–306. Reprinted in Miller, J. L., *et al.* (q.v.), 681–684.

Jusczyk, P. W., Perception of Syllable-Final Stop Consonants by Two-Month-Old Infants. *Percept. Psychophys. 21,* 1977, 450–454.

Kuhl, P. K., and Miller, J. D., Speech Perception by the Chinchilla: Voiced-Voiceless Distinction in Alveolar Plosive Consonants. *Science 190,* 1975, 69–72.

Kuhl, P. K., Infants' Perception and Representation of Speech: Development of a New Theory. *Proceedings, 1992 International Conference on Spoken Language Processing, Vol. 1,* 449–456.

Morse, P. A., Infant Speech Perception: A Preliminary Model and Review of the Literature. In *Language Perspectives: Acquisition, Retardation, and Intervention.* R. L. Schiefelbush and L. L. Lloyd (Eds.) Baltimore: University Park Press, 1974, pp. 19–53.

Morse, P.A., Speech Perception in the Human Infant and the Rhesus Monkey. Conference on Origins and Evolution of Language and Speech. *Ann. N. Y. Acad. Sci. 280,* 1976, 694–707.

Morse, P. A., and Snowdon, C. T., An Investigation of Categorical Speech Discrimination by Rhesus Monkeys. *Percept. Psychophys. 17,* 1975, 9–16.

Waters, R. S., and Wilson, W. A., Jr., Speech Perception by Rhesus Monkeys: The Voicing Distinction in Synthesized Labial and Velar Stop Consonants. *Percept. Psychophys. 19*, 1976, 285–289.

Auditory And Phonetic Analysis

Best, C. T., Morrongielllo, B., and Robson, R., Perceptual Equivalence of Acoustic Cues in Speech and Nonspeech Perception. *Percept. Psychophys. 29*, 1981, 191–211.

Carney, A. E., and Widin, G. P., Acoustic Discrimination within Phonetic Categories. *J. Acoust. Soc. Am. 59*, 1976, S25 (A).

Cutting, J., and Rosner, B. S., Categories and Boundaries in Speech and Music. *Percept. Psychophys. 16*, 1974, 564–570.

Eimas, P. D., and Corbit, J. D., Selective Adaptation of Linguistic Feature Detectors. *Cognitive Psychol. 4*, 1973, 99–109. Reprinted in Miller, J. L., *et al.* (q.v.), 3–13.

Pisoni, D. B., and Lazarus, J. H., Categorical and Noncategorical Modes of Speech Perception along the Voicing Continuum. *J. Acoust. Soc. Am. 55*, 1974, 328–333.

Remez, R. E., Rubin, P. E., Pisoni, D. B., and Carrell, T. D., Speech Perception Without Traditional Speech Cues. *Science 212*, 1981, 947–950.

Strange, W., The Effects of Training on the Perception of Synthetic Speech Sounds: Voice Onset Time. Unpublished doctoral dissertation, University of Minnesota, 1972.

Perception And Learning

Bremer, C. D., Discrimination and Identification of Synthetic Speech by a Child Exhibiting Voicing Confusions in Production. Paper presented at ASA meeting, Washington, D. C., 1976.

Stevens, K. N., and Klatt, D. H., Role of Formant Transitions in the Voiced-Voiceless Distinction for Stops. *J. Acoust. Soc. Am. 55*, 1974, 653–659.

Williams, L., Speech Perception and Production as a Function of Exposure to a Second Language. Unpublished doctoral dissertation, Harvard University, 1974.

Zlatin, M. A., and Koenigsknecht, R. A., Development of the Voicing Contrast: Perception of Stop Consonants. *J. Speech Hear. Res. 18*, 1975, 541–553.

Production And Perception

Aungst, L. F., and Frick, I. V., Auditory Discriminability and Consistency of Articulation of /r/. *J. Speech Hear. Disord. 29*, 1964, 76–85.

Borden, G. J., Use of Feedback in Established and Developing Speech. In *Speech and Language: Advances in Basic Research and Practice. Vol. 3*, N. J. Lass (Ed.) New York: Academic Press pp. 223–242.

Goehl, H., and Golden, S., A Psycholinguistic Account of Why Children Do Not Detect their own Errors. Paper presented at ASHA meeting, Detroit, 1972.

Goto, H., Auditory Perception by Normal Japanese Adults of the Sounds "L" and "R." *Neuropsychologia 9*, 1971, 317–323.

Kornfeld, I. R., What Initial Clusters Tell Us About the Child's Speech Code. *Q. Prog. Rep. Res. Lab. Electron. M. I. T. 101*, 1971, 218–221.

Locke, J. L., and Kutz, K. J., Memory for Speech and Speech for Memory. *J. Speech Hear. Res. 18*, 1975, 176–191.

MacKain, K. S., Best, C. T., and Strange, W., Categorical Perception of English /r/ and /l/ by Japanese Bilinguals. *Applied Psycholinguistics 2*, 1981, 369–390.

McReynolds, L. V., Kohn, J., and Williams, G. C., Articulatory-Defective Children's Discrimination of their Production Errors. *J. Speech Hear. Disord. 40*, 1975, 327–338.

Menyuk, P., and Anderson, S., Children's Identification and Reproduction of /w/, /r/ and /l/. *J. Speech Hear. Res. 12*, 1969, 39–52.

Mochizuki, M., The Identification of /r/ and /l/ in Natural and Synthesized Speech. *J. of Phonetics 9*, 1981, 293–303.

Neurophysiology of Speech Perception

Berlin, C., Hemispheric Asymmetry in Auditory Tasks. In *Contemporary Issues in Experimental Phonetics*. N. J. Lass (Ed.) New York: Academic Press, 1976.

Cole, R. A., Different Memory Functions for Consonants and Vowels. *Cognitive Psychol. 4*, 1973, 39–54.

Crowder, R. G., Visual and Auditory Memory. In *Language by Ear and Eye: The Relationships between Speech and Reading*. J. F. Kavanagh and I. G. Mattingly (Eds.) Cambridge, Mass.: M.I.T. Press, 1972, pp. 251–275.

Crowder, R. G., and Morton, J., Precategorical Acoustic Storage (PAS). *Percept. Psychophys. 5*, 1969, 365–373.

Cutting, J. E., A Parallel between Encodedness and the Ear Advantage: Evidence from an Ear-Monitoring Task. *J. Acoust. Soc. Am. 53*, 1973, 358 (A).

Darwin, C. J., Ear Differences in the Recall of Fricatives and Vowels. *Q. J. Exp. Psychol. 23*, 1971, 46–62.

Darwin, C. J., Dichotic Backward Masking of Complex Sounds. *Q. J. Exp. Psychol. 23*, 1971, 386–392.

Darwin, C. J., and Baddeley, A. D., Acoustic Memory and the Perception of Speech. *Cognitive Psychol. 6*, 1974, 41–60.

Day, R. S., and Vigorito, J. M., A Parallel between Encodedness and the Ear Advantage: Evidence from a Temporal-Order Judgment Task. *J. Acoust. Soc. Am. 53*, 1973, 358 (A).

Gardner, H., *The Shattered Mind*. Westminster, Md.: Knopf, 1975.

Gazzaniga, M. S., and Sperry, R. W., Language after Section of the Cerebral Commissures. *Brain. 90*, 1967, 131–148.

Godfrey, J. J., Perceptual Difficulty and the Right Ear Advantage for Vowels. *Brain Lang. 4*, 1974, 323–336.

Goodglass, H., and Geschwind, N., Language Disorders (Aphasia). In *Handbook of Perception, Vol. 7: Language and Speech*. E. C. Carterette and M. P. Friedman (Eds.) New York: Academic Press, 1976, pp. 389–428.

Kimura, D., Cerebral Dominance and the Perception of Verbal Stimuli. *Can. J. Psychol. 15*, 1961, 166–171.

Kimura, D., Functional Asymmetry of the Brain in Dichotic Listening. *Cortex 3*, 1967, 163–178.

Lenneberg, E. H., *Biological Foundations of Language*. New York: Wiley & Sons, 1967.

Massaro, D. W., Preperceptual Images, Processing Time, and Perceptual Units in Auditory Perception. *Psychol. Rev. 79,* 1972, 124–145.

Milner, B. (Ed.), *Hemisphere Specialization and Interaction*. Cambridge, Mass.: M. I. T. Press, 1975.

Norman, D. A., *Memory and Attention*. New York: Wiley & Sons, 1969.

Penfield, W. L., and Roberts, L., *Speech and Brain Mechanisms*. Princeton, N. J.: Princeton University Press, 1959.

Pisoni, D. B., and McNabb, S. D., Dichotic Interactions of Speech Sounds and Phonetic Feature Processing. *Brain Lang. 4,* 1974, 351–362.

Shankweiler, D. P., and Studdert-Kennedy, M., Identification of Consonants and Vowels Presented to Left and Right Ears. *Q. J. Exp. Psychol. 19,* 1967, 59–63.

Sperry, R. W., and Gazzaniga, M. S., Language Following Surgical Disconnection of the Hemispheres. In *Brain Mechanisms Underlying Speech and Language*. C. H. Millikan and F. L. Darley (Eds.) 1967, New York: Grune and Stratton, pp. 108–121.

Studdert–Kennedy, M., and Shankweiler. D. P., Hemispheric Specialization for Speech Perception. *J. Acoust. Soc. Am. 48,* 1970, 579–594. Reprinted in Miller, J. L., *et al.* (q.v.), 293–308.

Studdert–Kennedy, M., Shankweiler, D. P., and Schulman, S., Opposed Effects of a Delayed Channel on Perception of Dichotically and Monotically Presented CV Syllables. *J. Acoust. Soc. Am. 48,* 1970, 599–602.

Warren, R. M., Verbal Transformation Effect and Auditory Perceptual Mechanisms. *Psychol. Bull. 70,* 1968, 261–270.

Weiss, M., and House, A. S.. Perception of Dichotically Presented Vowels. *J. Acoust. Soc. Am. 53,* 1973, 51–58.

Wernicke, C. *Der aphasische Symptomencomplex*. Breslau: Franck and Weigert, 1874.

Whitaker, H. A., Neurobiology of Language. In *Handbook of Speech Perception, Vol. 7: Language and Speech*. E. C. Carterette and M. P. Friedman (Eds.) New York: Academic Press, 1976, pp. 389–428.

Wood, C. C., Auditory and Phonetic Levels of Processing in Speech Perception: Neurophysiological and Information-Processing Analysis. *J. Exp. Psychol. (Hum. Percept.) 104,* 1975, 3–20.

Wood, C. C., Goff, W. R., and Day, R. S., Auditory Evoked Potentials during Speech Perception. *Science 173,* 1971, 1248–1251.

Zaidel, E., Linguistic Competence and Related Functions in the Right Cerebral Hemisphere of Man. Unpublished doctoral dissertation, Calif. Institute of Technology, 1973.

Theories of Speech Perception

Abbs, J. H., and Sussman, H. M., Neurophysiological Feature Detectors and Speech Perception: A Discussion of Theoretical Implications. *J. Speech Hear. Res. 14,* 1971, 23–36.

Ades, A. E., How Phonetic is Selective Adaptation? Experiments on Syllable Position and Environment. *Percept. Psychophys. 16,* 1974, 61–66.

Bailey, P., Perceptual Adaptation for Acoustical Features in Speech. *Speech Perception Report on Speech Research in Progress*. Series 2, Belfast: Psychology Department, The Queens University, 1973, pp. 29–34.

Bell-Berti, F., Raphael, L. J., Pisoni, D. B., and Sawusch, J. R., Some Relationships Between Speech Production and Perception. *Phonetica 36,* 1979, 373–383.

Chistovich, L. A., Klass, V. A., and Kuzmin, Y. I., The Process of Speech Sound Discrimination. *Vopr. Psikhol. 8,* 1962, 26–39.

Cole, R. A., and Scott, B., Toward a Theory of Speech Perception. *Psychol. Rev. 81,* 1974, 348–374.

Cooper, W. E., Adaptation of Phonetic Feature Analyzers for Place of Articulation. *J. Acoust. Soc. Am. 56,* 1974, 617–627.

Cooper, W. E., and Blumstein, S., A "Labial" Feature Analyzer in Speech Perception. *Percept. Psychophys. 15,* 1974, 591–600.

Dorman, M. F., Raphael, L. J., and Liberman, A. M., Some Experiments on the Sound of Silence in Phonetic Perception. *J. Acoust. Soc. Am. 65,* 1979, 1518–1532.

Fant, G., Auditory Patterns of Speech. *Models for the Perception of Speech and Visual Form*. W. Wathen-Dunn (Ed.) Cambridge, Mass.: M. I. T. Press, 1967, pp. 111–125.

Lane, H. L., The Motor Theory of Speech Perception: A Critical Review. *Psychol. Rev. 72,* 1965, 275–309.

Liberman, A. M., The Grammars of Speech and Language. *Cognitive Psychol. 1,* 1970, 301–323.

Liberman, A. M., Cooper, F. S., Shankweiler, D. S., and Studdert-Kennedy, M., Perception of the Speech Code. *Psychol. Rev. 74,* 1967, 431–461. Reprinted in Miller, J. L., *et al.* (q.v.), 75–105.

Liberman, A. M., Isenberg, D., and Rakerd, B., Duplex Perception of Cues for Stop Consonants: Evidence for a Phonetic Mode. *Percept. & Psychophys. 30,* 1981, 133–143.

Liberman, A. M., and Mattingly, I. G., The Motor Theory of Speech Perception Revised. *Cognition 21,* 1985, 1–36. Reprinted in Miller, J. L. et al (q.v.), 107–142.

Marler, P., A Comparative Approach to Vocal Development: Song Learning in the White–crowned Sparrow. *J. Comp. Physiol. Psychol. 71,* 1970, 1–25.

Morton, J., and Broadbent, D. E., Passive versus Active Recognition Models or Is Your Homunculus Really Necessary? In *Models for the Perception of Speech and Visual Form*. W. Wathen-Dunn (Ed.) Cambridge, Mass.: M. I. T. Press, 1967, pp. 103–110.

Pisoni, D. B., and Sawusch, J. R. Some Stages of Processing in Speech Perception. In *Structure and Process in Speech Perception*. A. Cohen and S. G. Nooteboom (Eds.) Berlin: Springer–Verlag, 1975, pp. 16–34.

Schatz, C. D., The Role of Context in the Perception of Stops. *Language 30,* 1954, pp. 47–56.

Stevens, K. N., The Quantal Nature of Speech: Evidence from Articulatory–Acoustic Data. In *Human Communication: A Unified View*. E. E. David, Jr. and P. B. Denes (Eds.) New York: McGraw–Hill, 1972, pp. 51–66.

Stevens, K. N., Further Theoretical and Experimental Bases for Quantal Places of Articulation for Consonants. *Q. Prog. Rep. Res. Lab. Electron. M. I. T. 108,* 1973, 248–252.

Stevens, K. N., and Halle, M., Remarks on Analysis by Synthesis and Distinctive Features. In *Models for the Perception of Speech and Visual Form.* W. Wathen–Dunn (Ed.) Cambridge, Mass.: M. I. T. Press, 1967, pp. 88–102.

Stevens, K. N., and House, A. S., Speech Perception. In *Foundations of Modern Auditory Theory.* Vol. 2, J. Tobias (Ed.) New York: Academic Press, 1972, pp. 3–57.

Stevens, K. N., and Perkell, J. S., Speech Physiology and Phonetic Features. In *Dynamic Aspects of Speech Production.* M. Sawashima and F. S. Cooper (Eds.) Tokyo: University of Tokyo Press, 1977, pp. 323–341.

Stevens, K. N., and Blumstein, S. E., Invariant Cues for Place of Articulation in Stop Consonants. *J. Acoust. Soc. Amer. 64,* 1978, 1358–1368. Reprinted in Miller, J. L. et al (q.v.), 281–291.

Studdert–Kennedy, M., The Emergence of Structure. *Cognition 10,* 1981, 301–306.

Studdert-Kennedy, M., Liberman, A. M., Harris, K. S., and Cooper, F. S., Motor Theory of Speech Perception: A Reply to Lane's Critical Review. *Psychol. Rev. 77,* 1970, 234–249.

Whitfield, I. C., and Evans, E. F., Responses of Auditory Cortical Neurons to Stimuli of Changing Frequency. *J. Neurophysiol. 28,* 1965, 655–672.

7
Research Tools in Speech Science

To know that we know what we know, and that we do not know what we do not know, that is true knowledge.
—Thoreau, *Walden* (quoting Confucius)

The purpose of research is to find answers to questions about ourselves and the world about us. This goal may never be perfectly attained, however, because the results of research attain meaning only through the interpretations of researchers. Because the interpretive process includes, of necessity, a substantial subjective component, the significance of any single piece of research is often less clear-cut and more disputable than we would like. Nonetheless, the research process does, in the long run, allow us to analyze complex behavior into its components and, in turn, to better understand how those components are united to generate the behavior we are studying.

DESCRIPTIVE AND EXPERIMENTAL RESEARCH

When seeking the answers to research questions, the speech scientist usually proceeds in one of two ways: by carrying out a *descriptive* study or by carrying out an *experimental* study.

In a descriptive study the scientist simply observes and records behavioral events and then, in most instances, tries to systematize the relationships among them. In an experimental study, the scientist observes and records behavior under controlled conditions in which experimental *variables* are systematically changed by the experimenter. An example of a descriptive study that employs observation and the recording of data would be one in which the researcher seeks to describe the physiological factors controlling fundamental frequency in speech. To carry out such a study, the researcher would measure fundamental frequency, the output of a number of laryngeal muscles, and subglottal air pressure. The physiological parameters could then be correlated with the acoustic output. For instance, the researcher might determine the relationship between cricothyroid muscle activity and the fundamental frequency of phonation (Atkinson, 1978). Another example of a descriptive study is one in which the researcher examines sound spectrograms in order to relate formant and noise patterns to contrasting phonetic features, such as the difference between the high frequency ranges of /ʃ/ and /s/ frication in various vowel contexts (Stevens, 1960).

An example of an experimental study that employs observation and the recording of data both before and after the application of an experimental variable would be one in which the researcher seeks to discover the role of tactile feedback in speech production. In carrying out such an experiment, the researcher would have subjects produce a given sample of speech, first normally (the *control condition*), and then after the application of oral anesthesia (the *experimental condition*) in order to observe the effects of the desensitization (Borden, 1979). In this example, the *dependent variable* (the parameter observed for any changes) is the speech, and the *independent variable* (the parameter that the investigator manipulates) is the presence or absence of anesthetization.

Experimental studies are most common in studies of speech perception. The experimental variable might be the systematic change in some aspect of the formant pattern or the duration of synthetic speech stimuli (Raphael, 1972). The dependent variable is the effect of such changes on the perceptions of listeners. It is, of course, also possible to use natural speech stimuli in experimental studies of speech perception. The independent variable might be the insertion of clicks into a recording of natural speech, or the deletion of segments of the acoustic signal or the general distortion of some aspect of the acoustic signal (Fodor and Bever, 1965). As in an experiment using synthetic speech stimuli, the dependent variable is the effect of these modifications of the acoustic signal on listeners' perceptions of speech sounds.

Very often, when a research tool first becomes available to scientists, there is a period of time in which research tends to be mainly descriptive. The advent of the sound spectrograph, for example, fostered a large number of studies in which acoustic patterns were related to the features, phones, and syllables of speech. More recently, with the introduction of electromyography as a research technique, research focussed on describing the relationships between muscle activity patterns in EMG recordings and other, more clearly understood aspects of speech production. Usually, the period of description leads to the creation of theories or models that are later tested experimentally. As more information becomes available, the model or theory is modified and then retested in experiments. In this way, descriptive and experimental research complement one another.

In order to carry out descriptive or experimental studies, the speech scientist must employ a variety of research tools, both instruments and techniques. Some of these tools are used for the acoustic analysis of the speech signal, others are used for physiological measurements, and still others are employed to generate the stimuli used in the study of speech perception. We will consider each of these types of instruments and techniques in turn.

ACOUSTIC ANALYSIS

The recording and analysis devices used today vary widely in type and method of operation. One reason for the diversity of acoustic instrumentation is the rapid technological change of recent years. Not much more than a decade ago, most university laboratories used reel-to-reel tape recorders, oscilloscopes and sound spectrographs with analog circuitry and mechanically produced, hard-copy displays. Today, although many of these devices are still in use, we are more likely to find cassette tape recorders (or even digitizing devices for direct recording into a computer) and computer programs that perform all the analysis functions of oscilloscopes, sound spectrographs, and other devices as well. These programs, moreover, provide the means for automating acoustic measurement: Instead of ruling lines on a paper display and using a calculator to convert measurements of length into units of frequency, duration, and amplitude, the researcher simply moves cursors on the screen of a computer monitor and presses a key to obtain the data provided by the software.

The evolution of analysis and data extraction devices has affected acoustic phonetic research in two principal ways. First, the type of analyses previously performed on older equipment now takes much less time to complete, and, second, many more types of analyses and data are available to researchers.

Whatever the type of device a researcher may have at his disposal, it is likely to be one that generates a visual analog of some aspect(s) of the acoustic signal. The essence of acoustic analysis is, in fact, the conversion of sound waves to a visual representation that can then be inspected and measured in various ways. Certain types of analyses and their visual representations have proved more useful than others, and it is those types that we shall describe here. We shall not describe specific, commercially available devices because, as we have mentioned, they are numerous, various, and constantly undergoing change in response to technological innovations.

Recording Speech

Before discussing the types of acoustic analyses and visual displays available to the speech scientist, we must consider the nature of the input to the analysis devices. In most instances that input will be a tape recording of the speech sample(s) to be analyzed. The way the scientist makes a recording can be as important as the way that the acoustic analysis is carried out. A faulty recording may partially or completely invalidate an analysis, and so, appropriate care must be taken during recording sessions.

The goal in tape recording is to capture a clear speech signal with little or no distortion and a low level of background noise. The location for making the recording is an extremely important consideration. An acoustically shielded booth with sound absorbent walls (as pictured in Fig. 7.1) in which the speaker sits in front of the microphone with the door closed is ideal. If an acoustically shielded booth is not available, it is often sufficient to record speech in a quiet room, one with acoustic tiles, rugs, or other materials that absorb sound, and to record during the quietest time of day.

Microphones are responsive to pressure waves and convert the pressure variations into time-varying electrical signals. The signals are fed to the recording head of a tape recorder, where the signal alters the magnetic field and thus lays down a pattern on the metallic oxide coating of plastic audio tape. The choice of microphone is important. A unidirectional microphone placed several centimeters from the lips of the speaker transmits a higher signal-to-noise ratio than a multidirectional microphone that is responsive equally to the speaker and to sounds coming from other directions in the room.

The benefits of even the most optimal recording environment and microphone can be

Figure 7.1 Speaker making a recording in an acoustically shielded booth (Temple University).

overridden if the speech is not transferred to tape at an appropriate level of intensity. Most tape recorders, especially those of high quality, come equipped with some sort of intensity or VU (volume unit) meter. The VU meter on many tape recorders, however, is not ideal for monitoring running speech because it does not respond rapidly enough to the wide intensity variation in speech signals. Therefore, it is wise to keep the VU meter pointer a bit below the 0 dB mark during the recording of vowels. Too much amplification (overloading) will result in a distorted signal because the high amplitude peaks of the signal will be clipped.

The transition from reel-to-reel recorders to cassette recorders which we mentioned above has not been accomplished without the loss of some benefits. High quality reel-to-reel recorders provide the researcher with an option of tape speeds. This can be important because the faster the tape speed, the higher the signal-to- noise ratio and the better the quality of the recording. This is mainly because of the reduction in the amount of "tape hiss" at faster tape speeds. Tapes which are drawn over recording or playback heads at 7.5 or 15.0 inches per second (i.p.s.) (speeds found on many superior reel-to-reel recorders) contain less noise than those recorded at 1 7/8 i.p.s. (the speed of any standard cassette recorder). In addition, reel-to-reel recorders provide the researcher with easy access to the recording and playback heads which facilitates such tasks as marking and splicing the tape.

Although there is wisdom in Baken's admonition to clinicians to "have at least one high-quality reel-to-reel recorder, to be used when the best possible fidelity is needed, or when data recording demands recorder flexibility, such as high tape speeds that cassette units cannot deliver," we feel that most of the requirements of recording in the speech laboratory can be satisfied by a high quality cassette recorder. In such machines the problem of tape hiss has been satisfactorily solved by the addition of noise reduction systems in the circuitry of the recorder. Moreover, the frequency response of the better machines is more than adequate to record most of frequencies that a speech researcher might want to inspect. Finally, cassette recorders are often easier to use than reel-to-reel machines.

We ought to reinforce the point that we are recommending only high quality cassette units that run on line current. Under no circumstances should recordings be made on a unit of any sort that is powered by batteries. As batteries wear down the speed of the tape drive can be affected and measurements of frequency, duration, and amplitude will be rendered both invalid and unreliable.

Waveform Analysis

One way to make sound waves visible for analysis is to generate a waveform, an amplitude-by-time display of the acoustic signal. This can be done using devices such as the *oscilloscope* or the software of an acoustic analysis program. Some versions of the sound spectrograph (see below) can also produce waveforms.

The oscilloscope (Fig. 7.2), once the most frequently used instrument for generating waveforms, can display any time-varying signal which has been converted into current or voltage variations. A narrow beam of electrons from a cathode ray tube (CRT) strikes against a screen. For displaying speech, the beam can be made to sweep across the screen and the speech signal—input either from a microphone or tape recorder—deflects the beam, to form an amplitude-by-time display (Fig. 7.3).

A more efficient way of generating and making measurements from oscillographic displays is to use computer-controlled acoustic analysis. The software for such analysis permits the investigator to generate waveforms and to measure them very rapidly by positioning cursors on the screen of the monitor. In addition, the measurements at or between cursors are immediately converted to units of time or frequency by the computer, thus eliminating the time needed to photograph a CRT screen, to hand measure the points of interest and to convert the linear measurements to the appropriate units of Hz or ms.

Oscillographic displays are useful not

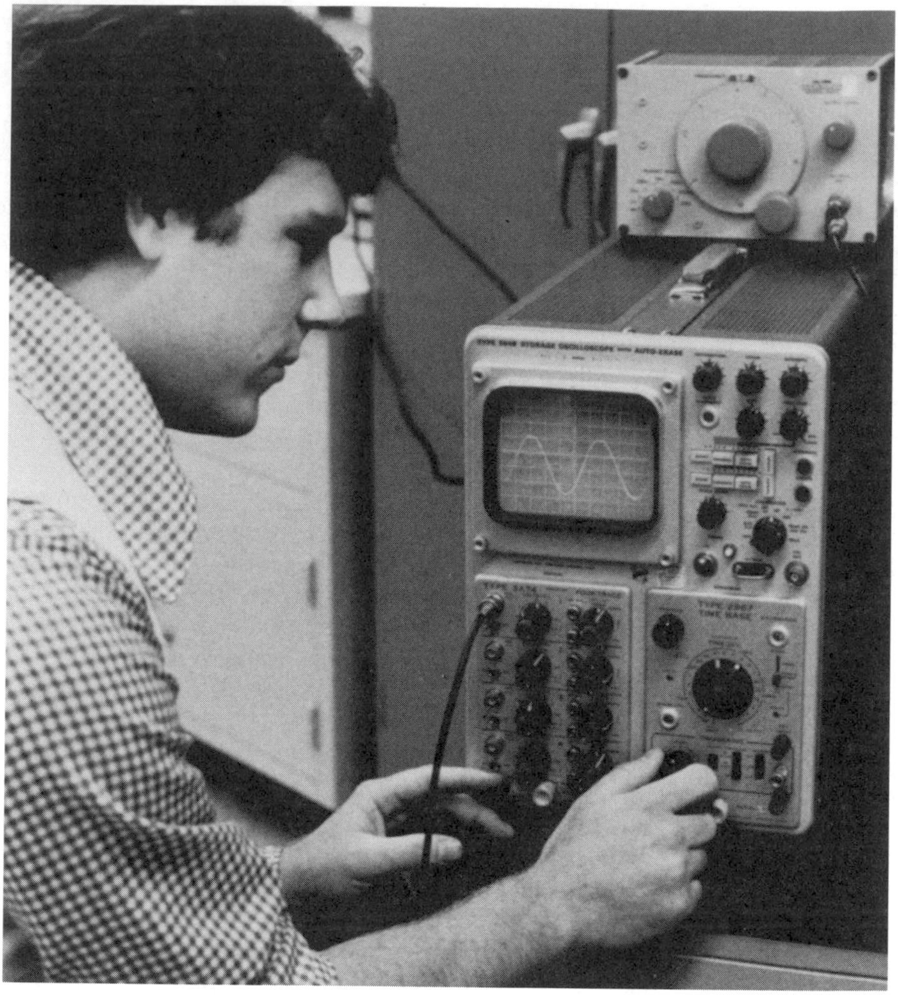

Figure 7.2 A storage oscilloscope (Temple University).

only for making acoustic measurements, but also for measuring variations in air pressure and flow (recorded within the oral and nasal cavities, or at the lips), transduced movement of articulators, electromyographic signals (EMG), brain waves (EEG), or any time-varying signal that has been transformed into voltage variation by microphones, transducers, or electrodes.

The frequency of periodic waveforms can be computed by measuring the period, the time in seconds taken for one cycle, and dividing 1 sec by the period. If, for example, the period of a signal is 5 ms (0.005 sec), its frequency would be 200 Hz.

$$f = \frac{1}{T} = \frac{1.000 \text{ sec}}{0.005 \text{ sec}} = 200 \text{ Hz}$$

Thus, the fundamental frequency of complex periodic waveforms typical of vowels can be established from an oscilloscographic display. However, the other frequency components in complex periodic waves and the many frequency components in aperiodic speech signals are not easily measured from oscillographic displays, because the waveform displayed is an *interference pattern*. An interference pattern is the sum of many different frequencies, having different amplitudes and phase relations. It would be difficult to quickly determine the

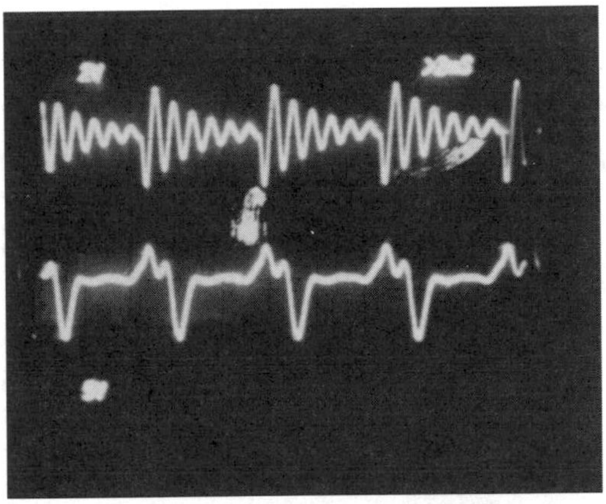

Figure 7.3 Hard copy of waveforms from a storage oscilloscope. Investigators can make measurements of signal duration, frequency, and amplitudes from displays of this type, whether generated by an oscilloscope or by other devices that digitize the waveform and display it on a computer monitor. (Haskins Laboratories).

component frequencies from this waveform alone. They can be determined however, by techniques to be described in the next section.

Spectral Analysis

We have already encountered brief discussions of some of the various forms of spectral analysis in Chapters 2, 4 and 5. Of these types of analysis, the one that has proved most interesting to speech scientists is the spectrogram. The value of the sound spectrogram rests in the fact that it can depict the rapid variations in the acoustic signal that characterize speech. Moreover, spectrograms provide an analysis of the frequency components of the acoustic signal, either in terms of the harmonics it comprises or of the peaks of resonance (formants) that it contains. Standard spectrograms also convey information about signal amplitude by rendering the more intense portions of the signal as darker than the less intense portions.

The instrumentation used to generate spectrograms, like that used to produce oscillographic displays, is undergoing change. The sound spectrograph, a free-standing machine largely dedicated to producing hard-copy versions of spectrographic displays, is being replaced by computer software that is available in several versions. Many laboratories, however, are still equipped with traditional sound spectrographs of various vintages that perform satisfactory analyses. It is reasonable to expect that these older machines will continue to provide acoustic data for many years to come. In any event, the types of displays they produce are the same as those that are generated by the newer technology.

A researcher who wishes to analyze the acoustic speech signal by making spectrograms must decide on the type(s) of information he wishes to see displayed. As we have seen, this is basically of two types: harmonic structure or resonance (formant) structure. Once the decision has been made, the researcher must make the appropriate filter bandwidth settings on the analysis device. In general, the choice is between a narrow bandwidth setting or a wide bandwidth setting. A narrow bandwidth setting will generate a spectrogram that displays harmonics on a *narrowband spectrogram*; a wide bandwidth setting will produce a spectrogram that displays formants on a *wideband spectrogram*. Figure 7.4 contains a narrowband and a wideband spectrogram of the utterance "speech and hearing science." Let us first consider the information in the narrowband spectrogram.

The Narrowband Spectrogram

The most noticeable features of narrowband spectrograms are the more or less narrow horizontal bands which represent the harmonics of the glottal source. The darker bands represent the harmonics that are closest to peaks of resonance in the vocal tract. The lighter bands represent harmonics whose frequencies are further away from the resonance peaks. If harmonics are far enough away from peaks of resonance, they may often not be too weak to be depicted on spectrograms; however, this depends to some extent on the settings used to generate the display. The relatively large horizontal blank spaces between the bands of harmonics in Figure 7.4 are at frequencies where these most weakly resonated harmonics are located. The complete absence

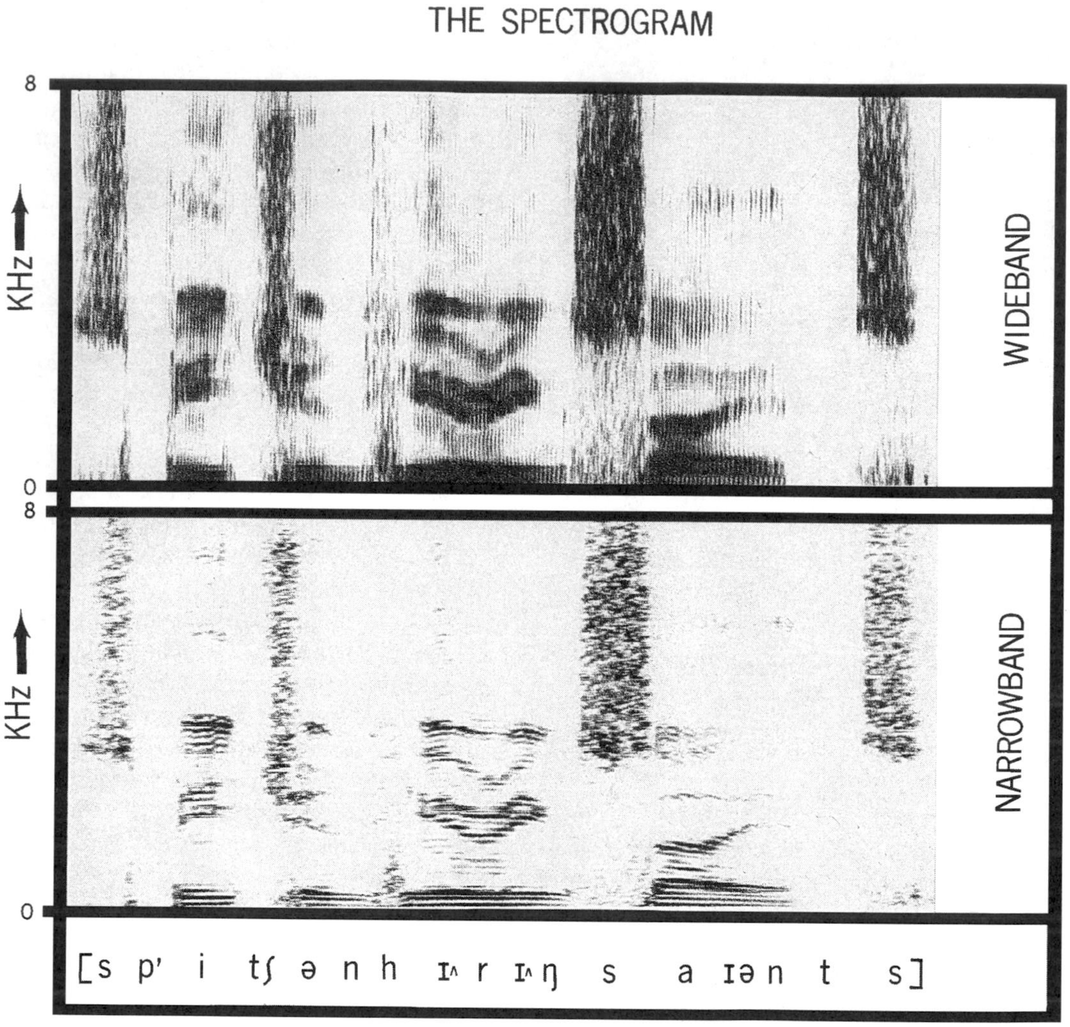

Figure 7.4 Narrowband and wideband spectrograms of the utterance "speech and hearing science."

of harmonics at any frequency at various temporal locations in the spectrogram indicates that there is no periodic (harmonic) source exciting the vocal tract. These areas, of course, occur when voiceless sounds such as [ʃ], [s] and [p] are being produced.

The bandwidth of the filter(s) used to generate narrowband spectrograms is usually somewhere between 30 and 50 Hz. To understand why the harmonics appear as they do on narrowband spectrograms we must recall that resonator/filters that are more narrowly tuned respond to a limited number of frequencies (See Fig. 5.6). Because it is unlikely that the fundamental frequency of phonation will be lower than 50 Hz, a filter with that bandwidth (or a smaller bandwidth) will respond to and capture each harmonic separately as it scans through the frequencies in the speech signal. In addition, if we also recall that resonator/filters with narrow bandwidths are lightly damped, then we will understand that each successive puff of air emitted during phonation will reach the analyzing filter before it has stopped resonating to the preceding puff of air. This means that the filter will respond continuously until some time after phonation has ceased. The continuous response of the filter is what underlies the unbroken band that represents each harmonic that falls at or near a peak of resonance. Finally, we should note that the light damping of the narrowband resonator/filter is complemented by a slow rise time. Taken together, these response characteristics explain why the harmonic display does not commence/cease until some time after the initiation/cessation of periodic vibration. Because of this, narrowband spectrograms are not used for making temporal measurements such as the durations of acoustic segments and voice onset time. As we shall see, it is the wideband spectrogram that is used for temporal measurements.

Narrowband spectrograms have traditionally been used for making measurements of fundamental frequency and intonation. Variations in the first harmonic are often difficult to detect on a narrowband spectrogram. Let us assume that you are interested in measuring the peak in the fundamental frequency in a syllable, and that the peak rises 10 Hz above the lowest value of the fundamental in that syllable. In a spectrogram with a frequency scale of 0–8 KHz or even 0–4 KHz, a 10 Hz change will not result in very obvious deflection of the trace representing the first harmonic. Such a change in fundamental frequency, however, is easily observable in a higher frequency harmonic. The peak in the 10th harmonic, for instance, would rise 100 Hz above its lowest value in the syllable. Thus, because changes in fundamental frequency are visually more salient in higher frequency harmonics than in the fundamental frequency itself, measurements are usually made from the 10th (or a higher) harmonic. The procedure is simply to measure the frequency of a harmonic at a particular point in time, and then to divide that frequency by the number of the harmonic.

It follows from what we have said that the shapes of intonation patterns (as well as the specific frequency values of intonation contours) are also easier to detect in the higher frequency harmonics than in the fundamental frequency itself. For instance, terminal rises or falls in intonation and the relative degrees of such changes are more apparent in the 10th harmonic than in the first.

Although narrowband spectrograms can be used for measuring harmonic frequencies, devices that isolate and depict variations in fundamental frequency as a function of time have become more available in recent years. Such devices scale the fundamental frequency appropriately for direct and automatic measurement, eliminating the need for counting harmonics, measuring them and arithmetically calculating the fundamental frequency.

The Wideband Spectrogram

As a practical matter, speech scientists are more often interested in the changing resonances of the vocal tract than in the harmonic structure of the speech signal. Although narrowband spectrograms do supply some information about formant frequencies, that information is not as useful or as relevant as that contained in wideband spectrograms. The precise (center) frequency of a formant is not easily measured in a narrowband spectrogram, especially when two formants lie close together on the frequency scale. Even the presence of particularly strong harmonics is not helpful, since they rarely coincide with the frequency of a peak of resonance. In addition, as we mentioned above, information about the timing of changes in vocal tract resonance is more reliably obtained from wideband spectrograms.

The most noticeable features of wideband spectrograms are the relatively broad bands of energy that depict the formants. The center of each of band of energy is taken to be the frequency of the formant (the actual peak of resonance at a particular moment), and the range of frequencies occupied by the band is taken to be the bandwidth of the formant. As in the narrowband spectrogram, the relative degree of darkness of a band of energy can be used as a rough estimate of the intensity of the signal, and the relatively large horizontal blank spaces, in this case, between the formants, represent troughs (zeroes, antiresonances) in the resonance curve of the vocal tract. Unlike a narrowband spectrogram, a wideband display will effectively represent an aperiodic source that is being resonated in the vocal tract. The blank spaces in the temporal dimension of a wideband spectrogram indicate silence, including pauses, and the sort of silent gaps that are generated by voiceless stop closures.

The bandwidth of a filter used to generate wideband spectrograms is generally between 300 and 500 Hz. A filter with such a relatively wide bandwidth will respond in the same way to one, two, three, or more harmonics that fall within its range. That is, the filter will not resolve the energy within its bandwidth into individual harmonics. The result is, as we have seen, the depiction of the resonance peaks in the acoustic signal. This lack of specificity, however, is precisely what an investigator wants, because the formants that characterize a particular sound for a particular speaker will be essentially the same, no matter what the frequencies of the fundamental or the harmonics—or, indeed, even if there are no fundamental/harmonic frequencies at all, as when sounds are whispered. There is a second important effect of the wideband filter in the generation of spectrograms. Because the wideband filter responds very quickly to the onset and termination of sound, it represents each glottal pulse separately. Each puff of air escaping from the glottis during phonation immediately excites the wideband filter, which then stops responding as soon the glottis closes and the air flow temporarily ceases. In other words, in contrast to the narrowband filter, the wideband filter responds intermittently, rather than continuously. If you look closely at Figure 7.4, you will notice that the horizontal bands of energy that represent the formants are actually composed of individual vertical striations. Each of these striations represents one glottal pulse. Each striation is darkest within the bandwidth of a formant, lighter or discontinuous in frequency regions that are removed from the peaks of resonance. The rapid response of the wideband filter thus generates a display from which accurate temporal measurements can be made. Speech scientists who want to measure the duration of an acoustic event or the time separating different acoustic events will employ wideband spectrograms.

Amplitude Spectra

It is often the case that an investigator might want a more quantified representation of the amplitudes of the component acoustic features of the acoustic signal than the one provided by the varying degrees of darkness in a spectrogram. Most analysis devices and computer programs permit the generation of an amplitude spectrum of the signal at any point in a wide or narrowband spectrogram. The bottom portions of Figures 7.5 and 7.6 show nar-

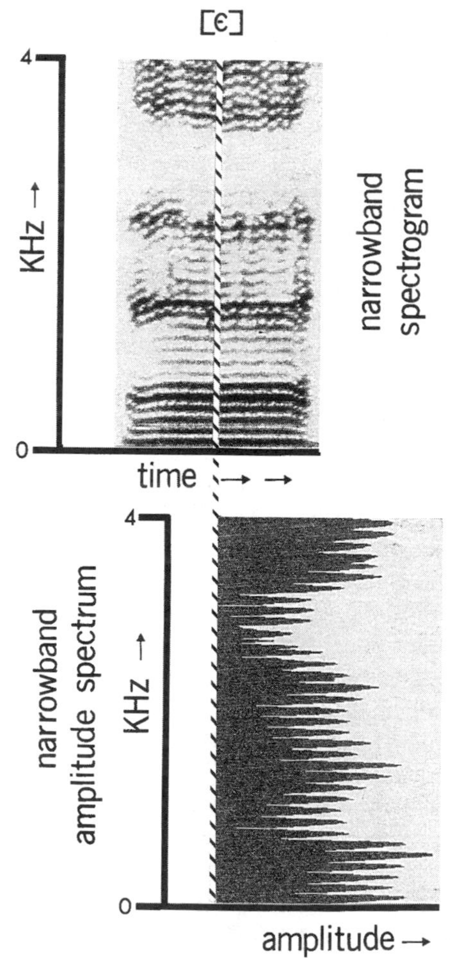

Figure 7.5 Narrowband spectrogram and corresponding narrowband amplitude spectrum of the vowel [ɛ].

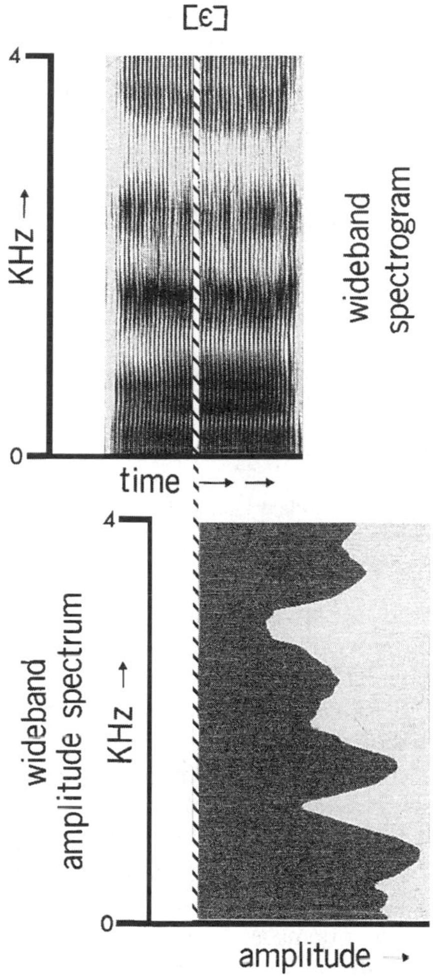

Figure 7.6 Wideband spectrogram and corresponding wideband amplitude spectrum of the vowel [ɛ].

rowband and wideband amplitude spectra of the spectrograms above them. Displays of this type are also called *amplitude sections*.

As you can see, the narrowband spectrum/section depicts the frequencies and relative amplitudes of each harmonic in the signal at the point in the vowel indicated on the spectrogram above. In the wideband spectrum/section we can see the frequencies and relative intensities of the peaks of resonance (formants). In most cases, the amplitudes of the harmonics or formants can be scaled in decibels. Many researchers use a wideband section to determine formant frequency at a particular point in time because the peak of resonance is more objectively depicted on the frequency scale than it is in a wideband spectrogram. Generating a series of spectra at various points in the duration of a sound can provide fairly accurate data specifying how the spectrum is changing over time.

The Amplitude Display

It is sometimes important to know how the overall amplitude of the acoustic speech signal varies over time (rather than looking at the amplitudes of component frequencies at a single point in time). Overall amplitude variation is depicted in an *amplitude display*, also called the *amplitude envelope*. This type of display is most often generated in the same display as a spectrogram, as in Figure 7.7. Many of the devices and programs that depict fundamental frequency variation directly (discussed above at the end of the section about the narrowband spectrogram) also allow the user to generate amplitude displays. If, however, it is important to relate amplitude variations to specific acoustic and articulatory events, it will be more useful to obtain the kind of combined display shown in Figure 7.7.

PHYSIOLOGICAL MEASUREMENTS

It is probably not unfair to say that the value of an acoustic analysis lies in our ability to infer articulatory and physiological events from it. It is, after all, these events that determine the acoustic signal. Such inferences, however, can not provide a complete picture of speech articulation and physiology, mainly because there is a great deal that is unknown about the behavior of the structures that generate speech. Moreover, there is no substitute for looking as directly as possible at the behaviors in which we are ultimately interested. A great many devices and techniques have been developed over the past few decades that allow us to specify speech articulation more or less closely. Some of them are indicated in Figure 7.8. We

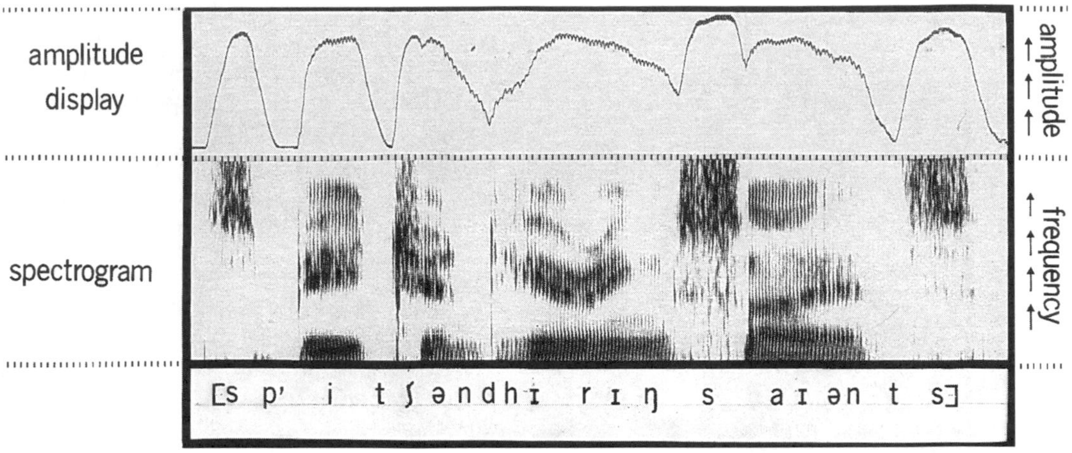

Figure 7.7 Wideband spectrogram with the corresponding amplitude display shown above it.

shall discuss several of them, concentrating on those that are most widely used or that provide important information that is not readily accessible without resort to invasive techniques.

Muscle Activity

Before going on to discuss instruments and techniques that are used in studying respiration, phonation, and articulation, let us first look at a technique that has been used to investigate all three of these aspects of speech production: *electromyography* (EMG).

Movements of the structures within the speech production mechanism usually result from the combined effects of muscular, aerodynamic, and biomechanical forces. Electromyography provides information about the muscular forces by allowing us to record *muscle action potentials*: the electrical activity accompanying muscle contraction. Recordings of action potentials are made by using bipolar electrodes in speech research. The two poles of these electrodes provide a measure of the difference in electrical energy at two points within a muscle as the electrical charge sweeps along the muscle fibers. Stronger muscle contractions result from the firing of more motor units and result in a greater difference in the electrical charge measured between the electrodes. Besides providing a measure of the strength of muscle contraction, electromyography provides temporal measures of muscle activity. By inspecting the onsets and offsets of activity we can specify the duration of muscle contractions, as well as the relative timing of the activity of different muscles contributing to the movements of structures.

The most commonly used type of bipolar electrode used in speech research today is the hooked-wire electrode (Fig. 7.9). Hooked-wire electrodes are made of two very fine platinum-iridium alloy wires. The two wires are inserted through the cannula of a hypodermic needle and the tips are bent back to form the hooks that give the electrode its name. The wires are then injected directly into the muscle to be studied, and the hypodermic needle is withdrawn (Fig. 7.10). The hooks anchor the wires in the muscle and prevent the electrode from moving while data are being gathered. At the end of the recording session, a sharp tug on the wires straightens out the hooks, and the electrode is easily removed.

Hooked-wire electrodes are most useful for muscles that are distant from the surface of an articulator (e.g., the genioglossus muscle). Another type of electrode, which can be used for muscles whose fibers are just below the skin (e.g., the orbicularis oris), is called a surface electrode. The most commonly used type of

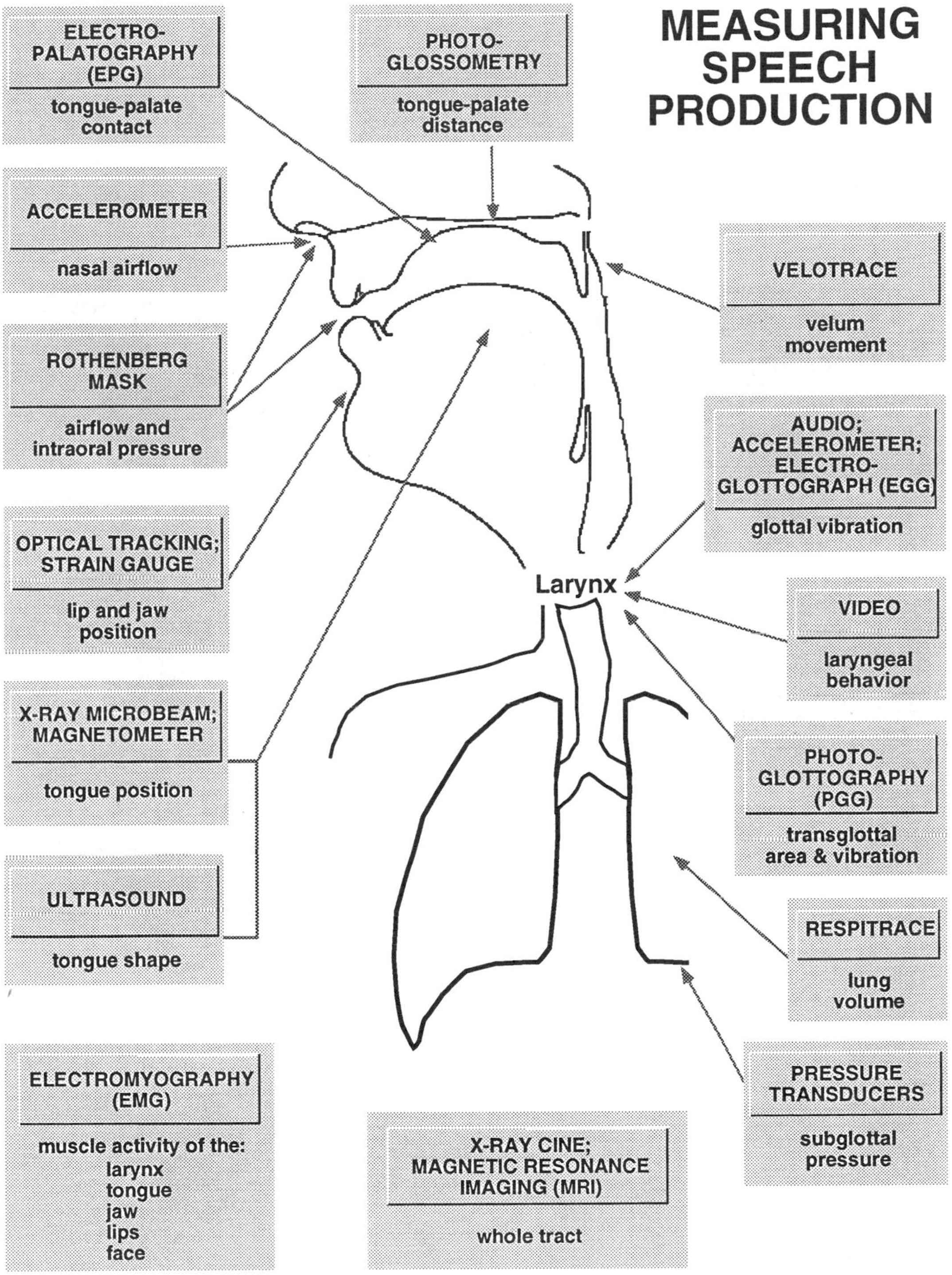

Figure 7.8 Types of physiological research techniques and instruments used in speech research. Courtesy of Philip Rubin and Erik Vatikiotis-Bateson © 1993.

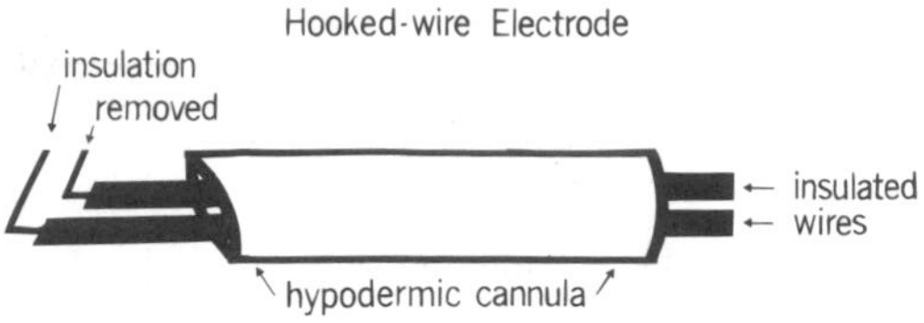

Figure 7.9 Schematic drawing of a hooked-wire electrode used in electromyographic research.

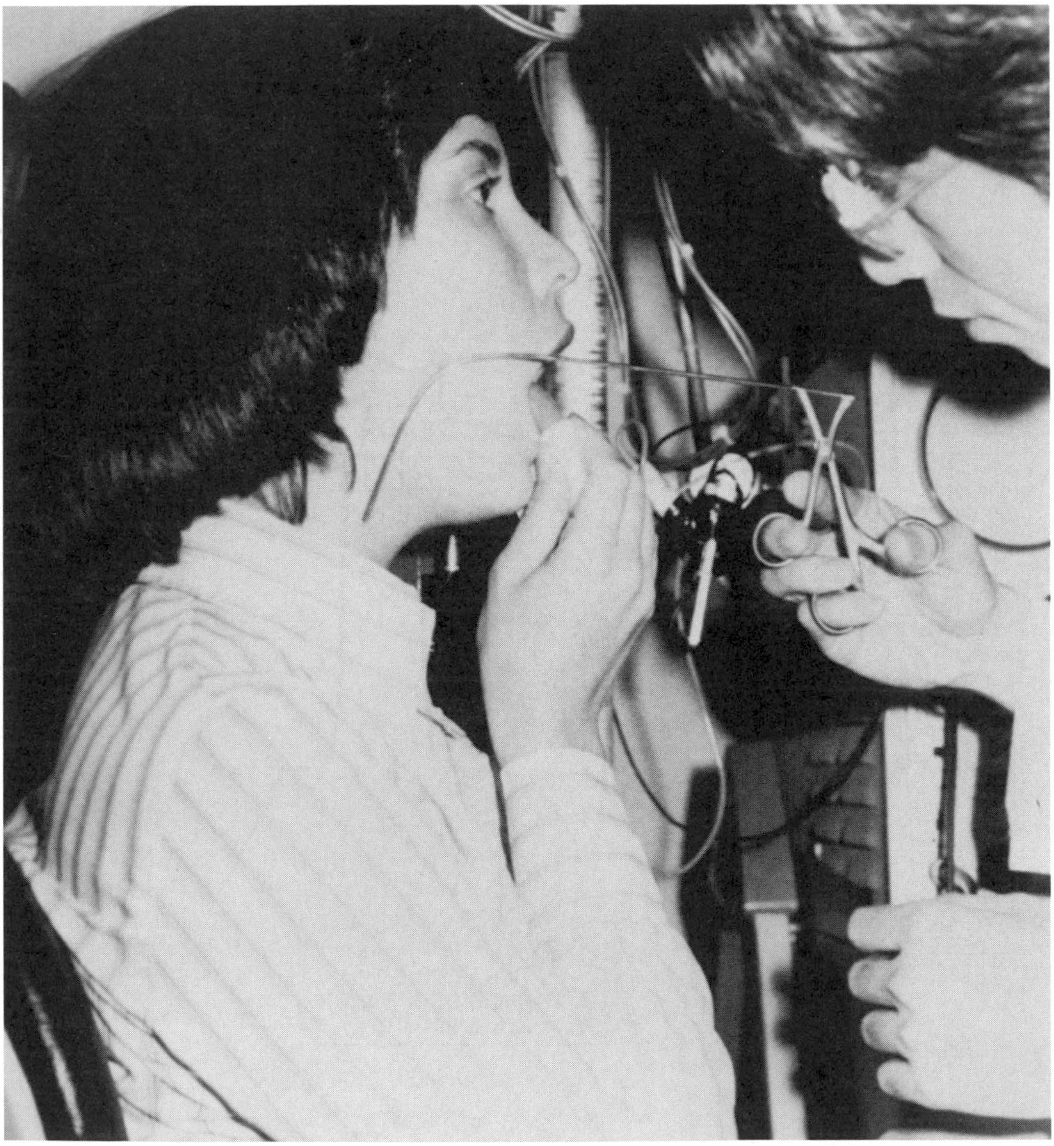

Figure 7.10 Insertion of hooked-wire electrodes into the posterior cricoarytenoid muscle. The curved needle holder, shown in the physician's hand, is inserted perorally. When the wires have been inserted into the muscle, the needle and needle holder are withdrawn (Haskins Laboratories).

surface electrode is created by painting some silver-based paint onto the skin, placing two fine wires, with the insulation removed from the end, onto the dab of paint, and then painting another silver dot on top to hold the wires. This is a hooked-wire electrode without the hook. Surface electrodes are often not as muscle-specific as hooked-wire electrodes because they may be recording from a relatively larger area. This causes them to transmit action potentials from more than one muscle, especially if several muscles lie in close proximity or at different depths beneath the same area of the skin surface.

As we mentioned in Chapter 4, the EMG signal is an interference pattern (Fig. 7.11), the sum of the action potentials of many motor units. A *motor unit* consists of the muscle fibers innervated by a single motoneuron. An electrode will record the electrical activity (action potential) of motor units lying near it. Thus, the EMG signal from a single electrode does not necessarily represent the activity of an entire muscle. This means that the absolute amplitude of the EMG signal recorded on one occasion cannot be compared to that from another occasion, because the exact locations of the electrodes and the firing motor units they are recording may vary substantially from one day to another. It is, however, possible to inspect the relative EMG signal amplitudes recorded from the same electrode placement for differences between the timing and patterns of activity, and to relate those differences to different phonetic events and to different conditions within the same experiment. For example, the activity of the orbicularis oris muscle for /p/ can be compared to that for /b/, or the action potentials for /p/, produced under different conditions of stress or speaking rate, can be compared.

In most EMG studies, the raw signal of the interference pattern (Fig. 7.11) is modified in at least two ways. First it is rectified, so that all the negative values become positive. Second, the signal is smoothed to some extent so that the more or less gradual increases and decreases in action potentials (and thus, muscular contraction) are more clearly depicted. In addition, the rectified and smoothed action potentials for many repetitions of the same utterance may be averaged together to reduce the variability in the data. The results of these processing techniques can be seen in Figure 7.12.

Respiratory Analysis

In the study of respiration for speech, many instruments are available, each with its specific purpose. Investigators have most often been interested in determining the air pressure, the rate of airflow, and the volume of airflow at various places in the vocal tract during speech production. EMG studies of respiratory muscle activity have also been carried out.

One of the obvious difficulties in making measurements of respiration (or, for that matter, of phonation and articulation) during speech is that the measurement devices may interfere with the normal behavior of the

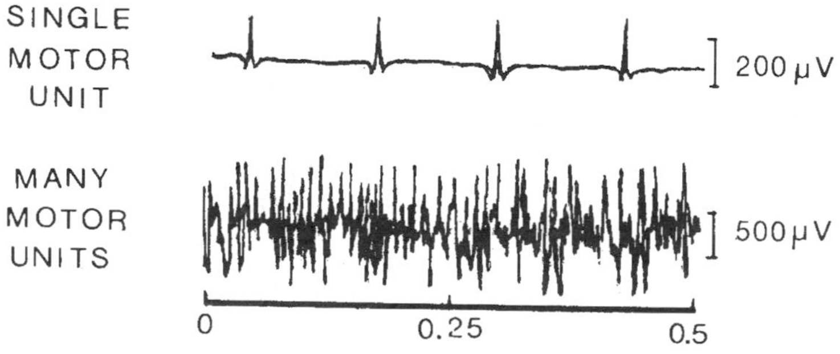

Figure 7.11 A raw (unprocessed) electromyographic signal. The lower part of the figure shows an interference pattern which reflects the summed activity of many motor units.

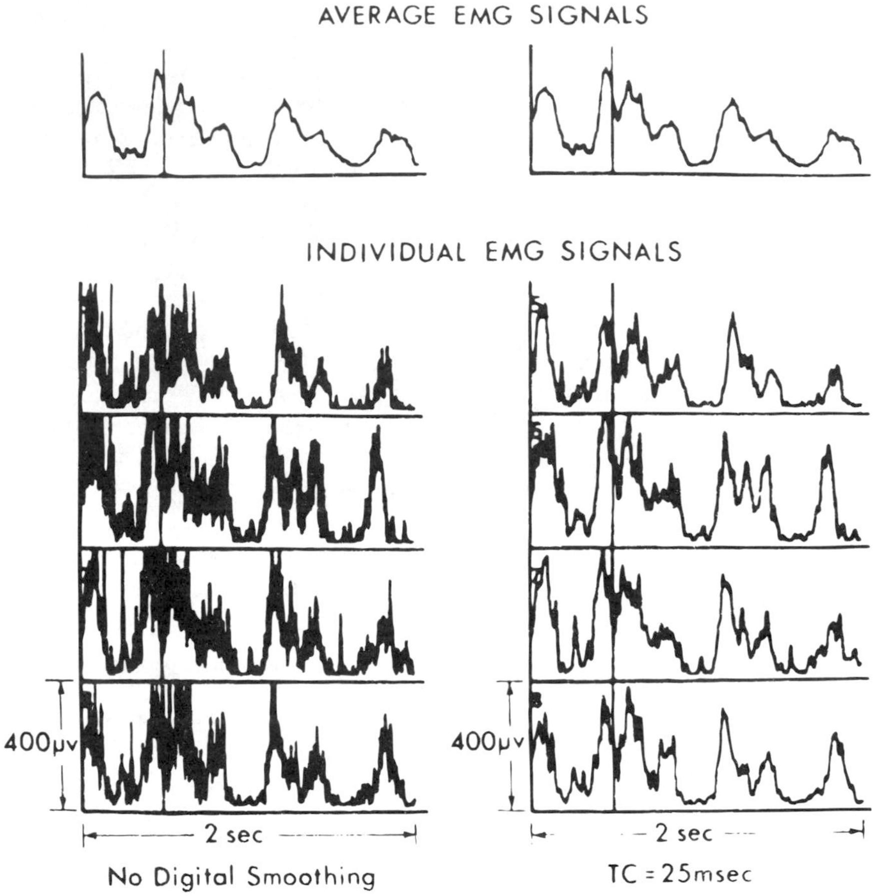

Figure 7.12 Rectified and integrated electromyographic signals from the levator palatini muscle for the utterance "Jean Teacup's nap is a snap." Averaged signals of both unsmoothed (at the left) and smoothed (at the right) individual EMG signals are shown at the top of the figure. A time constant of 25 ms was used in smoothing the signals in the righthand column. (Reprinted with permission of D. Kewley-Port: *Haskins Laboratories Status Report on Speech Research, SR-50, 140, 1971*).

speaker. For example, a simple device called a manometer can be used to measure air pressure (Fig. 7.13). While using it, the subject exhales into a tube, slightly wider in diameter than a typical straw, which is attached to the device. The air pressure can then be read (in units of centimeters of water—cm/H_2O) directly from the gauges on the face of the machine. The problem, of course, is that the subject cannot speak in anything close to a normal fashion while breathing through the manometer tube. There are, in fact, several other devices and techniques that, like the manometer, cannot provide useful data for the normal production of speech. The data they provide, however, may lead to a better understanding of some of the basic activities that underlie speech production, such as restful breathing, phonation, and swallowing.

Air pressure varies throughout the respiratory system/vocal tract during speech production. These pressure changes, whether subglottal, intra-oral or nasal, can be studied by introducing pressure sensing tubes or micro-

Figure 7.13 A manometer (Temple University).

phones to the area of interest. These sensing tubes, in turn, are attached to externally located pressure transducers. A pressure transducer converts air pressure measurements into an electrical signal that can be recorded and displayed in various ways.

Situating a pressure sensing device subglottally is obviously a difficult and intrusive procedure that may involve tracheal puncture or the situating, in the esophagus, of a small balloon attached by a tube to a transducer. Pressure readings taken directly from the subglottal area are more accurate than indirect measures obtained from the esophagus. Measurement of air pressure within the mouth is considerably easier and of great interest because intra-oral air pressure changes in response to a wide variety of influences throughout the speech mechanism, including the articulation of speech sounds. Sensing tubes used to measure intra-oral air pressure may be introduced nasally so that they hang over the velum in the area of the oropharynx. Alternatively, they may be bent around the back molars of a speaker with the tube exiting the oral cavity via the buccal cavity and the corner of the mouth. Pressure measurements may also be made from the nasal cavity by placing a version of a sensing tube called a nasal bulb at the nostril (Figure 7.14).

Measures of airflow, usually given in milliliters per second (ml/sec), can be made in a number of ways. Many of the devices used to measure airflow are appropriate for measuring air volume as well. This is so because airflow and volume are related: Air volume is the result of flow over a period of time. Most airflow measurements for speech are made using a device

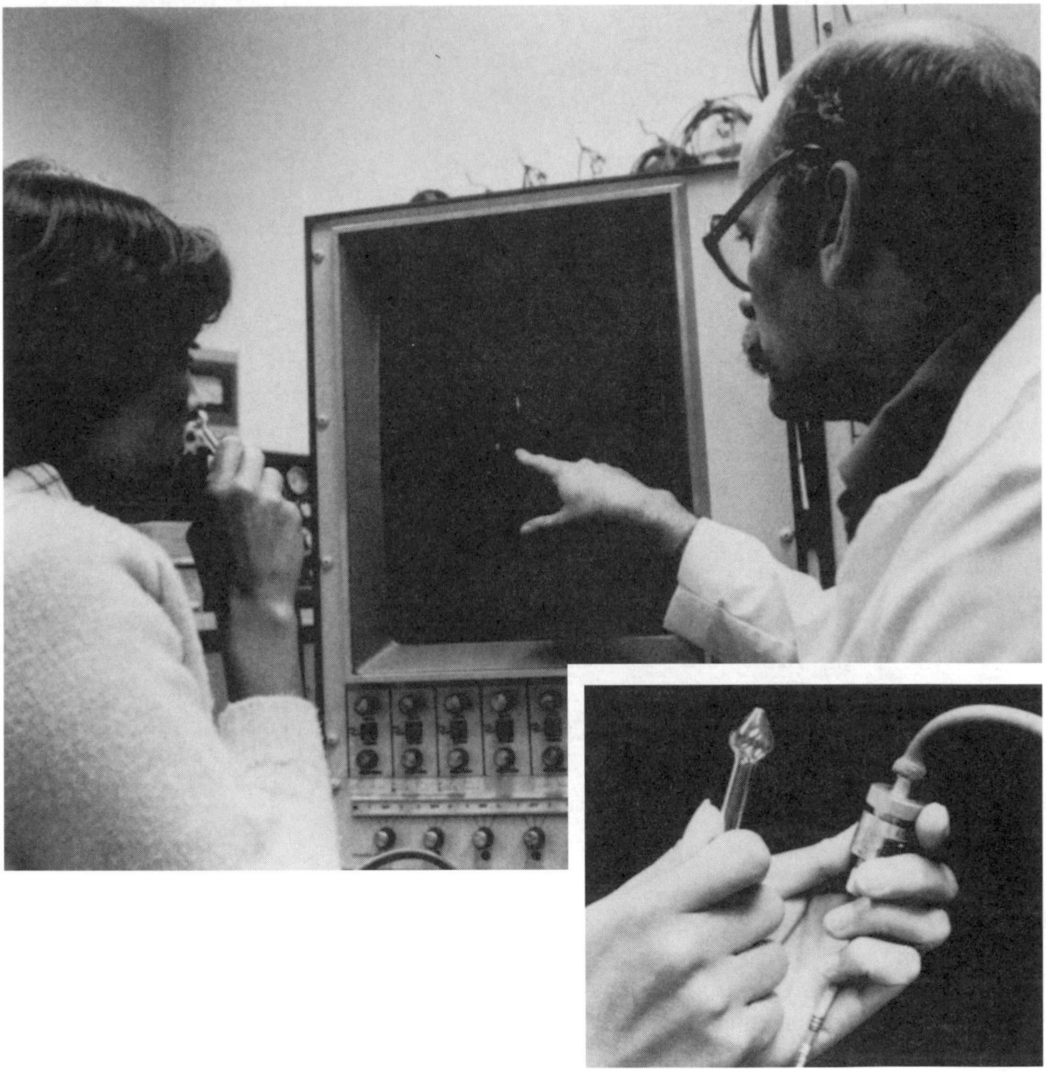

Figure 7.14 A nasal bulb and pressure transducer are shown in the *insert*. The bulb is placed at the nostril. Air pressure, from the bulb, is converted into a signal shown on the oscilloscope. Dr. Heuer uses visual feedback to decrease hypernasal production by the client (Temple University).

called a *pneumotachograph*, which is attached to an airtight face mask large enough to allow the subject to speak with minimal interference to articulation. The face mask may be divided into two chambers, permitting independent measurements of both oral and nasal airflow (Fig. 7.15). The pneumotachograph itself contains two pressure sensors separated by a resistor. The pressure drop across the resistor is fed to a transducer, which generates a signal that is proportional to the airflow. A speech sound produced with relatively high air pressure and flow, such as /s/, might show a value of 7 cm of H_2O oral air pressure and around 500 ml/sec airflow. The output of the pneumotachograph, as we indicated earlier, can also be converted to measurements of air volume.

It is also possible to measure the dynam-

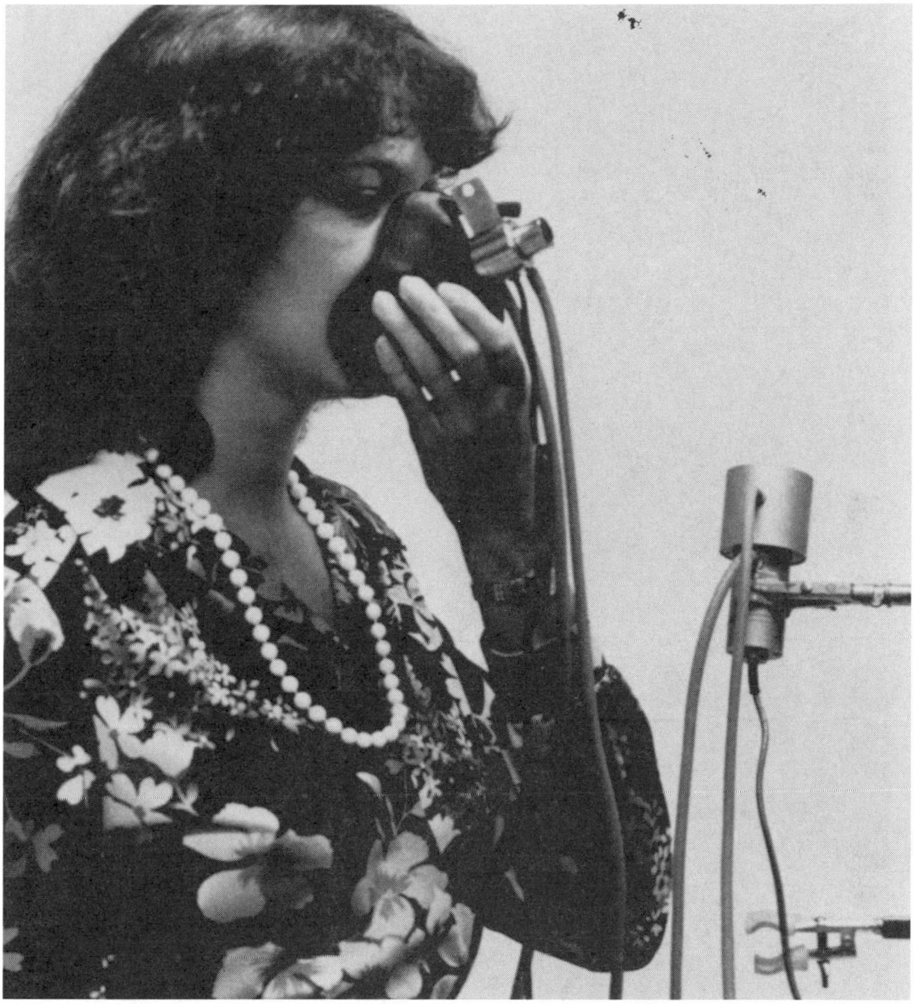

Figure 7.15 A pneumotachograph (Temple University).

ics of lung volume changes. The most commonly used instrument for recording from subglottal airways is the *spirometer*, which measures air volumes, such as the tidal volume or the vital capacity, and plots them on a revolving drum (Fig. 7.16). The response of the spirometer, however, even when attached to a face mask, is too slow to accurately track the rapid volume changes that occur during speech. To measure volume changes during speech, the air volume changes within a *body plethysmograph* can be recorded without the use of a face mask. The subject is seated in a sealed box so that any changes in thoracic or abdominal volume are reflected in the volume changes within the plethysmograph, which can be attached to a transducer for graphic output.

A device called a *pneumograph* may be used to record respiratory movements of the chest and abdomen during speech. This device consists of a series of thin elastic tubes or an elastic belt that is attached to the speaker. Changes in impedance or inductance of a signal across the tubes or wires in the belt are transduced for a record of inferred thoracic and abdominal movements. Figure 7.17 displays

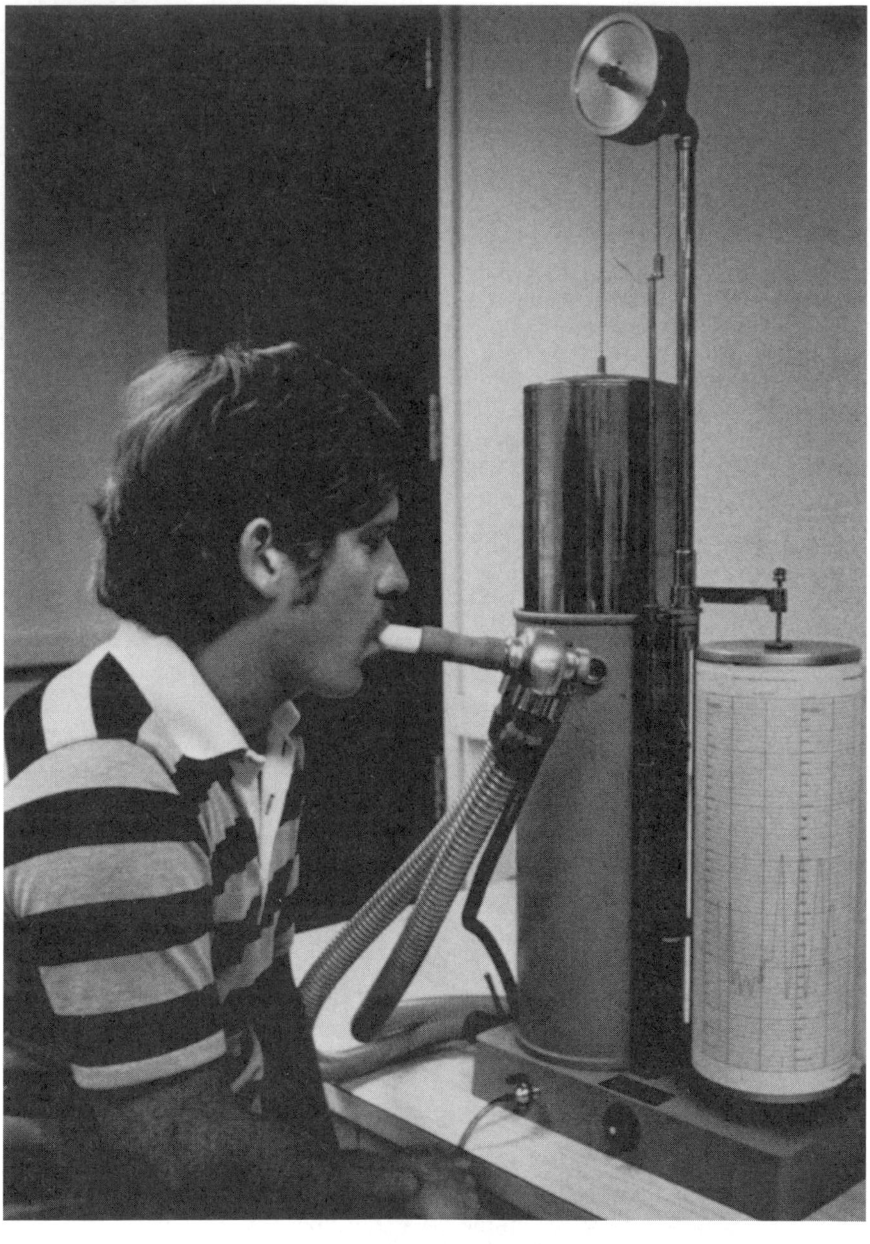

Figure 7.16 A spirometer (Temple University).

graphically the output obtained from a pneumograph.

Movements of the chest wall and abdomen can also be monitored and recorded by using a *magnetometer*. Magnetometers, essentially, comprise two coils of wire. An electric current passed through one of them generates an electromagnetic field that will induce an electric current in the other coil. The strength of the induced voltage depends on the distance separating the coils. If one coil is placed on a subject's back and another directly opposite on some point along his abdomen or thorax, the changes in the diameters of the rib cage or

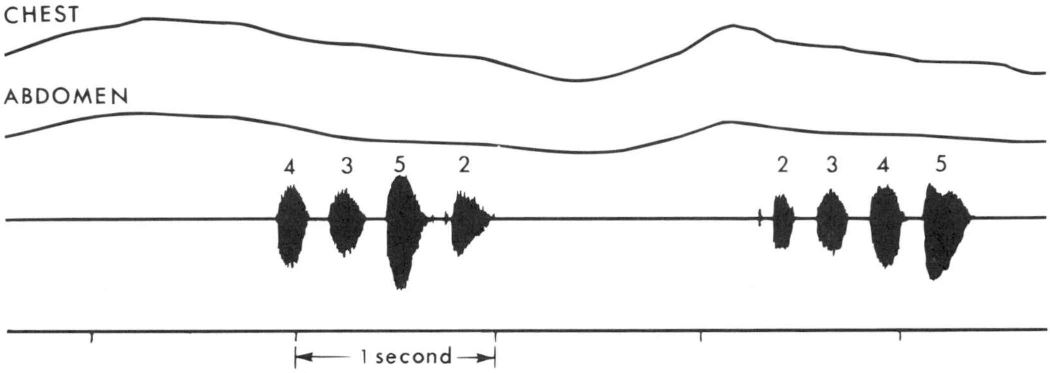

Figure 7.17 Above the time line along the abscissa is the acoustic signal derived from a speaker saying two four-digit number sequences. At the *top* of the figure are two pneumographic traces, the top one recorded from a semi-hemispheric mercury-filled elastic tube placed on the chest; the bottom trace from the abdomen. Upward deflection indicates inspiration.

abdomen can be calculated as a function of the variation in the strength of the induced current. On the assumption that such changes in diameter (caused by the movements of the chest wall and abdomen) are positively correlated with changes in lung volume, it is possible to gain information about patterns of respiratory behavior. The technique presents virtually no risk to the subject and does not interfere with normal respiration during speech. We will note other uses of the magnetometer below, in our discussion of articulatory analysis.

Laryngeal Function

Some of the instruments and techniques used to study the larynx and phonation allow us to look directly at the vocal folds; others provide indirect measures of laryngeal function. By using one or another of these instruments we can gather information about how the vocal folds behave during phonation, about how they alternate between phonatory and non-phonatory states (for the production of voiced and voiceless speech sounds) and about the area and shape of the glottis during speech.

The earliest device that permitted direct viewing of the vocal folds during phonation, the *laryngoscope*, was developed in 1854 by Manuel Patricio Rodriguez Garcia, a Spanish singing teacher who had taught in Paris and in London. He fashioned a mirror that could be inserted into the mouth and angled in such a way that sunlight shining on it reflected down upon the vocal folds, making them visible. Garcia's invention marked the beginning of modern laryngology, and his technique is still used today for laryngeal examinations. Garcia lived over 100 years (1805–1906), and on the occasion of his 100th birthday, he was honored by a dinner and received many accolades. It is said that his modest response to it all was, "It was only a mirror!"

Laryngeal activity can be recorded by making very high speed motion pictures from modern versions of the laryngoscope. The movies can then be replayed at speeds appropriate for frame-by-frame analysis. At most fundamental frequencies, however, it is not possible to introduce a cool light source that is sufficiently bright to resolve individual cycles of vibration. Alternatively, it is possible to observe the movements of the vocal folds by using a *stroboscope* (a light flashing at a fixed frequency). If the flash frequency is adjusted to be close to the frequency of vocal fold vibration, the movements of the folds will appear to be slowed, because the frames that appear to be from one cycle of vibration will have been "snapped" from successive cycles. This technique, however, is dependent on the speaker's ability to phonate at a constant fundamental frequency, so that the periods of successive cycles are identical.

As useful as the laryngoscope and the stroboscope may be for viewing the vocal folds, they so seriously obstruct the articulators that they cannot be used effectively for studying glottal behavior during speech. In contrast, the *fiberoptic endoscope* (often referred to as a *fiberscope*) can be used to view the folds directly during speech production (Fig. 7.18).

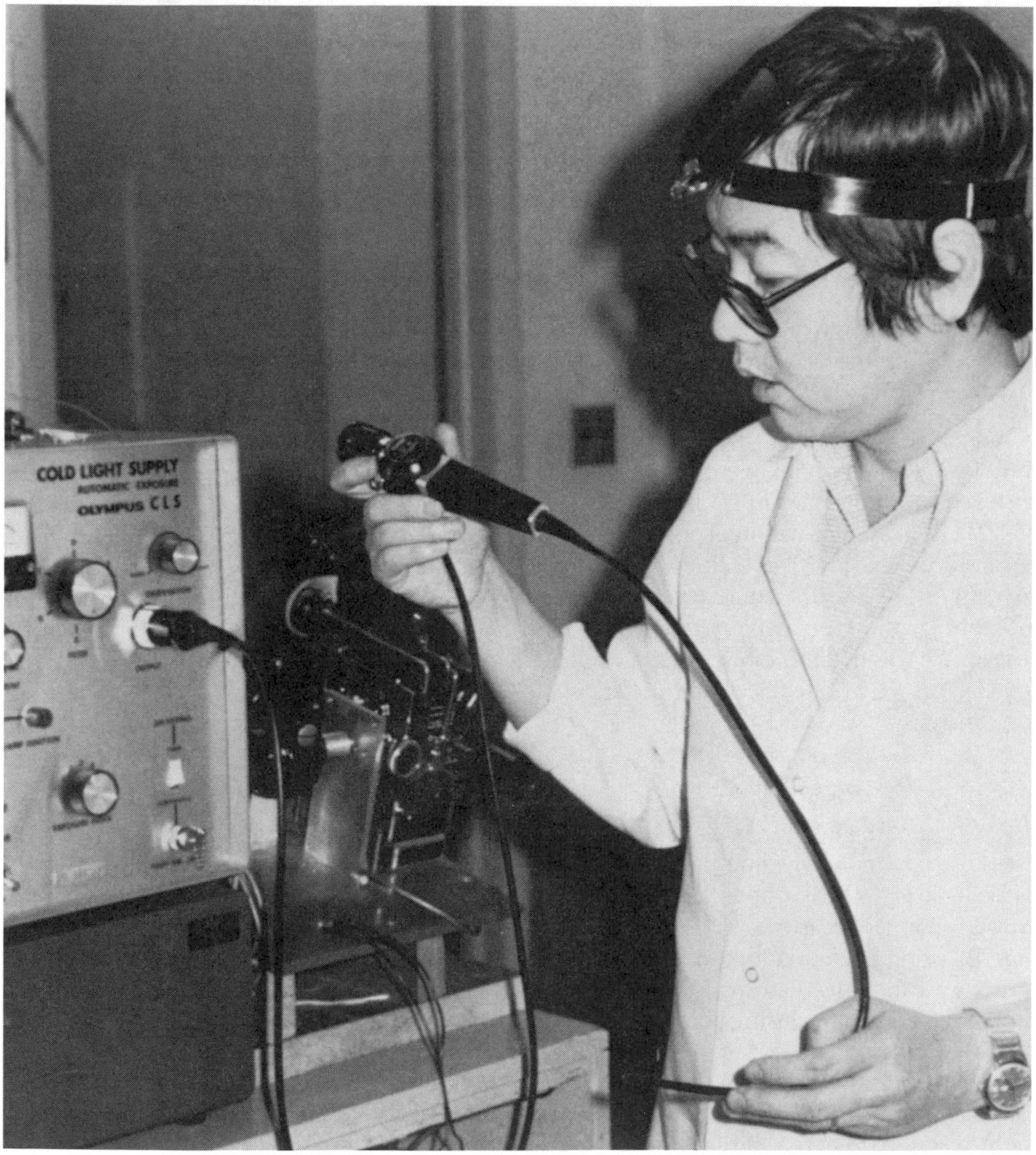

Figure 7.18 A fiberoptic endoscope. The flexible fiber bundle with its eyepiece, shown in the physician's left hand, is inserted into the nasal cavity. The larynx can be viewed with the eyepiece, shown in the physician's right hand (Haskins Laboratories).

The endoscope conveys an image of the glottis through a thin, coherent bundle of glass fibers. The bundle is called coherent because of the way in which it is constructed: The relative positions of the fibers at both ends of the bundle are exactly the same. This allows each fiber to pick up a small portion of the image and to deliver it to same place within the reconstructed image that is formed at the other end of the bundle. Light is conveyed into the larynx from an outside source through additional glass fibers surrounding the coherent bundle that conveys the image. The overall bundle is quite thin (as small as 4 mm in diameter) and flexible. The size and flexibility are what permit the direct viewing of the vocal folds during speech. The fiber bundle is inserted through the nasal cavity, over the top of the velum and down the pharynx where its objective lens is suspended above the glottis. The endoscope does not appear to hinder either oral articulation or velopharyngeal closure.

The image that is conveyed can be viewed directly through an eyepiece or can be recorded on videotape or film (See Fig. 4.36). It is possible, in the more advanced versions of the endoscope, to tape or film in color, using moderately high frame rates (which produce slow motion pictures). The disadvantage of this technique is that the folds cannot be lighted brightly enough for observation of individual vibratory excursions, as is possible with high speed motion pictures. The technique is, however, useful for direct observation of slower laryngeal adjustments, such as the phonatory repositioning of the vocal folds for voicing and devoicing gestures. It is also possible to obtain information about the shape and area of the glottis during speech production.

There are two other techniques for obtaining information about variations in glottal states as an indirect measure of vocal fold adjustment. The first of these is called *transillumination* or *photoglottography*, and is based on the straightforward notion that the amount of light shining through the glottis will be directly proportional to its area (the degree of separation of the vocal folds). The source of the light is, again, a fiberoptic bundle, nasally inserted and positioned just as the endoscope is (see above). A photocell is then positioned at the level of the "visor," the space between the thyroid and cricoid cartilages. The amount of light passing through the glottis at any moment is registered by the photocell. The changes in glottal area over time are mirrored by the changing output of the photocell (Fig. 7.19). Unlike endoscopic viewing, this technique gives no information on the shape of the glottis but only on the extent of the opening. It is, of course, also useful for providing information about the timing of the changes in glottal area. In addition, the technique allows resolution of individual vibratory cycles.

The *electroglottograph*, or *laryngograph*, is the second instrument that provides information about glottal states. In a sense, the output of the electroglottograph is the complement of the output of transillumination. Transillumination measures the degree of vocal fold separation, while electroglottography (*EGG*) measures the degree of vocal fold contact as a function of the relative conductance or impedance between two small electrodes placed on either side of the larynx. When the glottis is closed, and a small electric current is conducted across the folds (from one electrode to the other), the EGG signal peaks (Fig. 7.19). But, as the folds separate, the signal decreases because of the impedance created by the open glottis. The signal must be transmitted along vocal fold tissue, then across the glottal airspace to the opposite fold, a journey that it fails to make efficiently because of the mismatch of impedances of muscle tissue and air. Hence, the electroglottograph indicates the amount of vocal fold contact during each vibratory cycle. It does not, however, tell us anything about the width or shape of vocal fold opening. Once again, timing information, this time with regard to vocal fold contact, can be obtained from the EGG signal.

Figure 7.19 illustrates the complementary relationship between the measures of glottal width, obtained from endoscopy or transillumination, and those of vocal fold contact, obtained from the EGG signal. Because the EGG signal is free from the influence of the

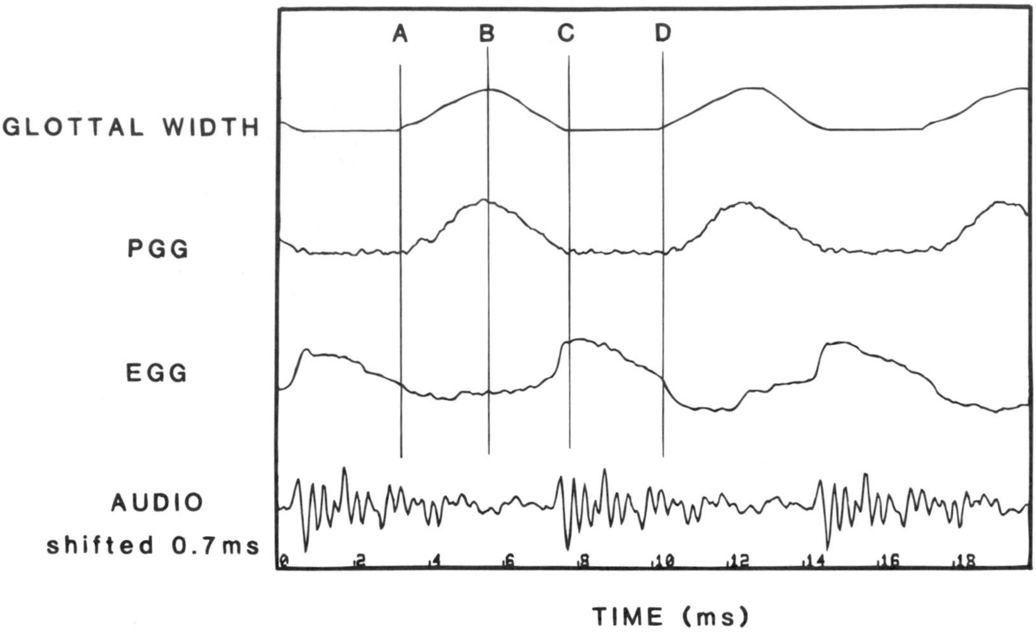

Figure 7.19 Three cycles of vocal fold vibration in a male speaker. The photoglottogram (PGG) was obtained by transillumination and corresponds closely to the glottal width measured from high speed films. Peak defections of the electroglottogram (EGG) correspond to maximum contact of the vocal folds. (Reprinted with permission from T. Baer *et al.*: *Journal of the Acoustical Society of America 73,* 1983, 1304–1308.)

resonant frequencies of the supraglottal vocal tract, the device can be used to record fundamental frequency, with the addition of an instrument that plots the frequency of the EGG peaks as a function of time (Fig. 7.20).

ARTICULATORY ANALYSIS

Studying the movements of the supralaryngeal articulators presents a difficult challenge for speech scientists. The crux of the problem is the fact that the movements of the most important articulator, the tongue, are very fast, very complex and, for the most part, not visible to an external sensor. Indeed, even the more slowly moving articulators, except for the lips and the mandible, cannot be observed externally during speech production. As a result, observation of the movements of various parts of the tongue, the velum, and the walls of the pharynx and the oral cavity often require instruments and techniques that are sophisticated, expensive, and, on occasion, potentially hazardous.

Perhaps the most obvious technique for studying articulatory movements, especially tongue shape and position, is x-ray photography. While this technique was used fairly often for research in the 1970s, more recently, concerns about the risks of radiation have led to its discontinuance. In order to reduce the risks of radiation and to avoid the concomitant limitations on the size of the speech sample that can be gathered by traditional lateral x-ray filming, scientists at the University of Tokyo developed the x-ray microbeam system. The subject in the experiment has a series of small lead pellets attached to his tongue with a cyanoacrylate adhesive. During speech, each pellet is tracked by an x-ray microbeam. The level of radiation from each beam is quite low, as is the sum of the radiation emitted by all the microbeams taken together. This allows the subject to produce substantial quantities of speech

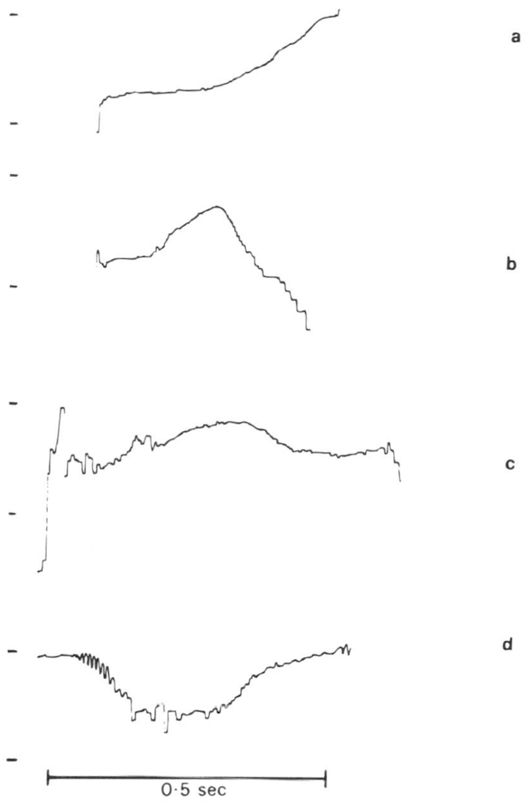

Figure 7.20 Waveforms of fundamental frequency as a function of time in a display derived from a laryngograph (electroglottograph). *Waveforms a* and *b* show rising and rise-fall intonations from a normal adult saying "Do you." *Part c* shows a rise-fall pattern from the same speaker when she had laryngitis. The restricted range and irregular voicing onset are typical features of this condition. *Part d* was produced by a man with chronic laryngitis. In *a, b,* and *c,* the *upper* and *lower marks to* the *left* of each graph correspond to 800 and 200 Hz, respectively. The marks by *d* correspond to 200 and 50 Hz. (Reprinted with permission from A. J. Fourcin: Laryngographic Examination of Vocal Fold Vibration. In *Ventilatory and Phonatory Control Systems: An International Symposium,* B. Wyke (Ed.), Oxford University Press © 1974.)

with relatively little risk. The tracking of the pellets is controlled by a computer, which predicts the location of each beam on the basis of its previous locations. Computer-controlled programs allow the investigator to measure the distances between the pellets and stable reference points in order to analyze both the vertical and horizontal movements of the pellets as the tongue changes shape and position during speech. The computer calculates and stores the x-y coordinates of each pellet and displays the distance between pellet positions.

Although the x-ray microbeam system can provide valuable data, it is a complex and expensive system to operate. Moreover, only one system (in Madison, Wisconsin) is currently being used to obtain data on articulation. The health risk from radiation, although lower than that in other x-ray techniques, is not completely eliminated. These considerations have led researchers to develop other, less costly, more risk-free techniques to study articulator movement.

Ultrasound is the sonar system of the vocal tract. As its name indicates, ultrasound is beyond the range of human hearing. The ultrasound wave used in imaging the vocal tract has a frequency of 1 MHz or more. The wave is emitted from a transducer that is in contact with the skin below the mandible. Sound waves of this sort will be reflected whenever they cross a border between media of two different densities. Thus, as the sound wave passes from the tissue of the tongue to the less dense air above the tongue, it is reflected back to a sensing device on the transducer. In effect, the sensing device detects an echo of the ultrasound wave. As in the case of the more familiar audible echoes of sound, the greater the time that has elapsed since the emission of the wave, the greater the distance between the transducer and the surface of the tongue.

A visual representation of the echoes can depict most of the oral surface of the tongue because the transducer rotates and so scans a given area with ultrasound waves. The current state of ultrasound technology allows speech scientists to videotape changes in the shape of the tongue surface at normal rates of speech production. In addition, the ultrasound wave can be directed in such a way that the shape of the tongue surface in the coronal plane can be observed (Fig. 7.21), a view that is essential for a complete picture of lingual behavior and one that has been essentially unavailable in the past. Finally, ultrasound imaging can be used to observe other areas and structures in the

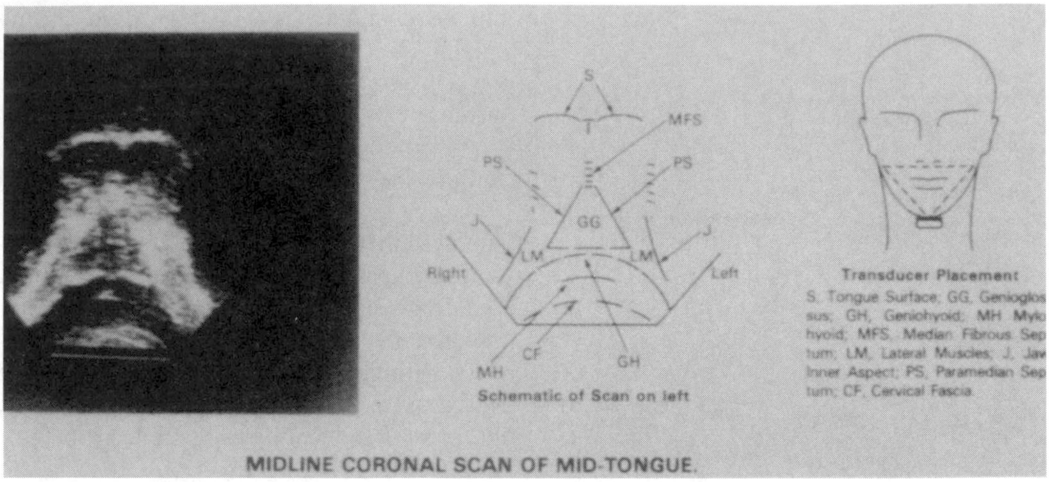

Figure 7.21 At the left, an ultrasound image of a coronal scan of the surface of the tongue during speech production. At the center, a schematic view of the ultrasound scan. At the right, a diagram of the transducer placement and the key for the labels in the schematic drawing in the center of the figure. (Reprinted with permission of M. Stone *et al.*: *J. Acoust. Soc. Amer., 83, 1587,* ©, 1988.)

vocal tract, such as the glottis and the walls of the pharynx, but only when the ultrasound wave can be directed to an interface between the tissue to be observed and a less dense medium, such as air.

In addition to tongue shapes, phoneticians have long been interested in the points of contact between the tongue and the roof of the mouth during the articulation of speech sounds. Indeed, traditional articulatory classifications of consonant production have always included "place of articulation" as a descriptor. A place of articulation can, in most instances, be understood as a point of contact between the tongue and the hard or soft palate. Tongue-palate contact can be investigated by using a technique called *palatography*.

Palatography, in one form or another, has been employed for more than a century by speech scientists. In its earliest form it could be used only to observe isolated, static articulations. A colored powder or paste was placed on the palate or on a prosthetic device fitted to the palate. The subject would then articulate a single sound (e.g., [s]) and then his palate or the prosthesis was photographed or drawn. The points where the powder had been removed by the tongue or the smooth surface of paste disturbed indicated the points of lingual contact.

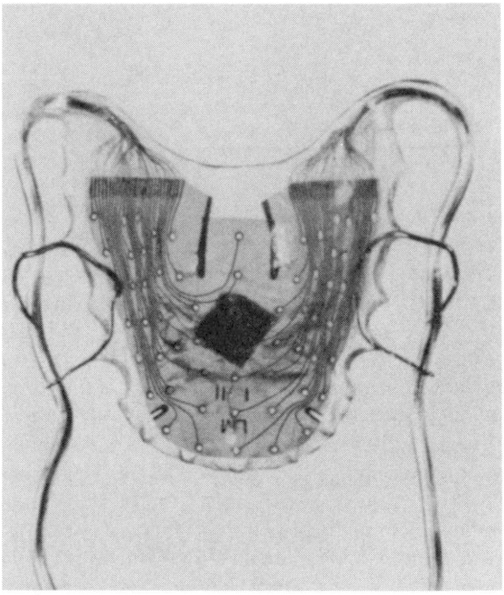

Figure 7.22 An electropalate. (Courtesy of Rion Trading Co., Tokyo, Japan.)

Contemporary palatography, often called *dynamic palatography*, or *electropalatography (EPG)*, allows investigators to monitor tongue-palate contact during running speech. This is accomplished by fitting the speaker with a palatal prosthesis in which transducers are embedded (Fig. 7.22). Each transducer generates a signal when the tongue touches it. The changing patterns of contact can be recorded on analog tape and displayed later on a computer screen. They can also be observed as the speaker articulates speech sounds, enabling clinicians and patients to use EPG for instant feedback during therapy.

The EPG prosthesis imposes some limitations on the usefulness of the technique. No transducers are located at the most anterior portion of the alveolar ridge, on the teeth, or on the velum, and so articulatory contact in these areas will not be recorded. Further, the amount of detail in the recorded data depends on the density of transducers in a particular region. A uniform distribution of the transducers on the surface of the prosthesis may thus provide less information than is desired from some areas and more than is needed from others, while an uneven distribution may provide a great amount of detail from the area where transducers are concentrated, but provide very little data about contact in other locations. Finally, each EPG prosthesis must either be fitted individually for each subject (they are hard cast from a dental mold) or must be selected from a set of flexible, re-useable prostheses held in place with a dental adhesive. The individually fitted prostheses are expensive and may have to be recast if the dental structures of a subject undergo change. The re-useable prostheses, on the other hand, present the problem of exact re-location for a given subject from one use to the next.

Articulatory movements of the lips and mandible can be transduced and measured by using *strain gauges* (Fig. 7.23). A strain gauge is constructed with two thin metal strips capable of conducting an electrical current. They are separated by a strip of insulation. When the strips are undisturbed, each will conduct an equal amount of current. But when the pressure of an articulator such as the mandible causes the strain gauge to bend into a slightly curved shape, the metal strip on the inside of the curve will conduct a different amount of current than the strip on the outside of the curve. The difference between the flow of current in the metal strips will be proportional to the movement of the articulator causing the gauge to bend. It is a relatively simple matter to record and plot the voltage difference as it changes over time during speech production.

Jaw and tongue movements have been investigated using magnetometers (see above, under respiratory analysis). With one coil of a magnetometer placed on the top of the head and the other under the symphysis of the mandible or on the surface of the tongue, it is possible to interpret the strength of the induced electrical current as a measure of articulator movement without fixing the position of the speaker's head or interfering with normal articulation.

Movements of the velum can be monitored by using the fiberoptic endoscope. The endoscope is inserted nasally with the objective

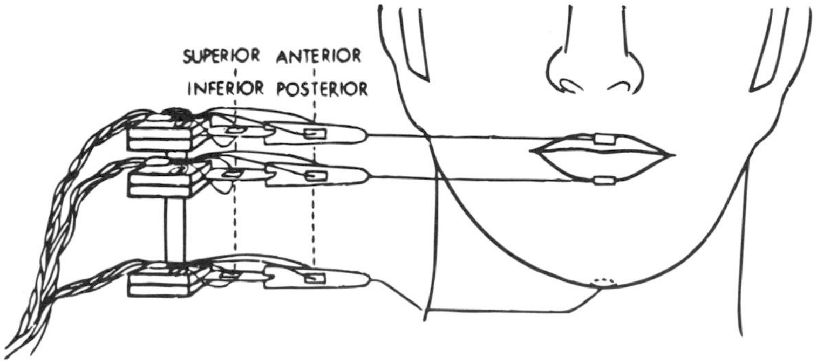

Figure 7.23 Two-dimensional lip and jaw strain gauge transducer. (Reprinted with permission from J. H. Abbs and B. N. Gilbert: *Journal of Speech and Hearing Research. 16,* 1973.)

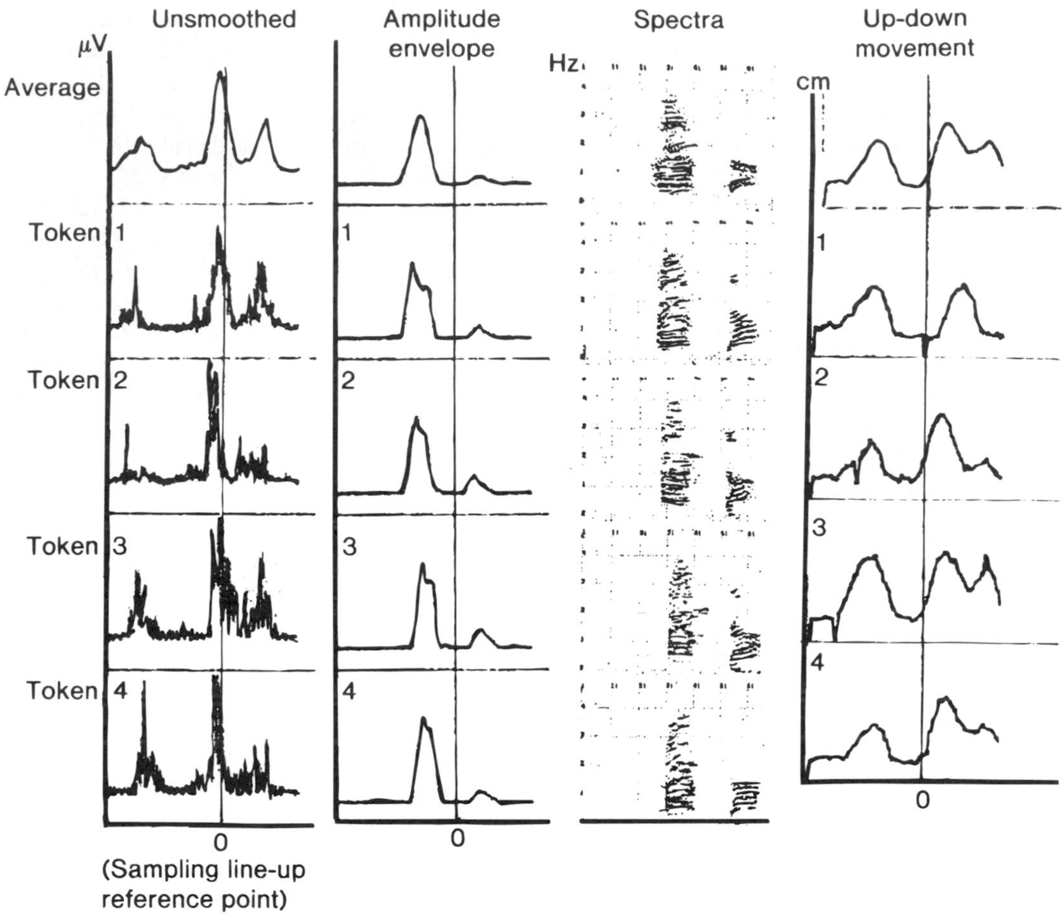

Figure 7.24 Results from an experiment on velopharyngeal closure. The movements of the velum, recorded by a fiberoptic endoscope, are shown in the *right-most* column. Spectrograms are also shown, as well as the audio envelope. The *left-most* column shows electromyographic signals from the levator palatini muscle, after rectification. Four individual samples of each token are shown. The *top* waveform shows an average of 16 tokens (Haskins Laboratories).

lens lying on the floor of the nasal cavity at a location appropriate for viewing the velum as it rises and falls during speech. Figure 7.24 displays endoscopic data along with other simultaneous physiological measures relating to velar elevation.

Finally, we should note that a complete three-dimensional image of the entire vocal tract can be obtained using *Magnetic Resonance Imaging (MRI)*. The limitation of this technique is that current MRI machines are capable of producing images only at rather slow rates (although this situation may change). Thus, the technique has been used primarily to produce images only for static shapes of the vocal tract, but is valuable because it can provide information in almost any plane of observation. It should be possible, for instance, to better understand the nature of the transfer function of the vocal tract by comparing the calculated output of a static shape with the actual output produced by the speaker whose vocal tract is being imaged.

The inventory of devices and techniques

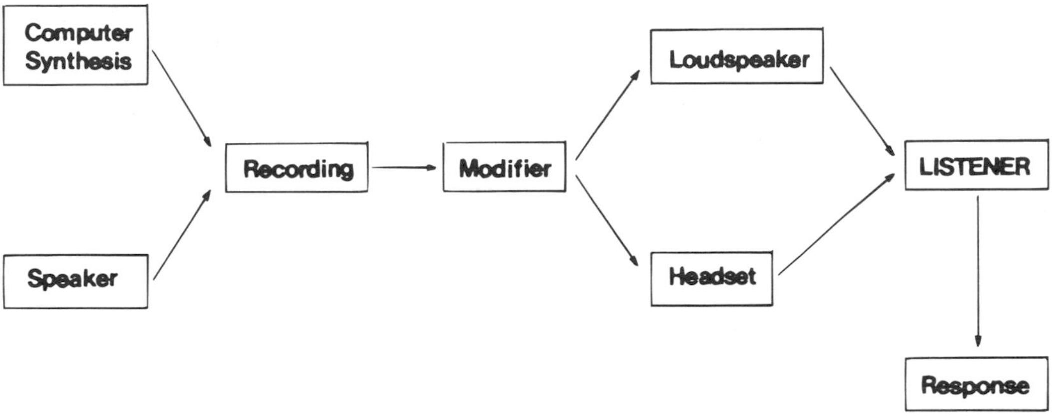

Figure 7.25 Instrumentation array used in speech perception studies.

we have discussed for observing and measuring aspects of speech production is far from exhaustive. More complete listings and explanations are available elsewhere. Moreover, the state of the art in instrumentation is changing rapidly. Existing devices are continually being improved and modified, and new instruments and techniques appear with great frequency. Staying abreast of developments requires constant and careful attention to the research literature.

Speech Perception

The instrumentation array required for studying the ways in which people perceive speech differs from that used in studying speech production (Fig. 7.25). Rather than analyze data produced by talkers, the investigator analyzes responses given by listeners to natural or synthetic speech.

CREATING STIMULI: WAVEFORM EDITING

The ability to digitize the speech signal and store it in computer memory has enabled speech scientists to perform complex editing tasks with speed and accuracy when preparing stimuli for perceptual testing. The stored speech is displayed as a waveform (or a spectrogram) on a computer monitor and cursors are used to select the portions to be edited. Portions of the signal can be simply excised (and the gap of silence created by their removal can be closed) or stored and reinserted one or more times at any place in the stream of speech. In this way the durations of naturally produced speech sounds may be decreased or increased in steps of any size.

One drawback of this sort of editing is that the experimenter is limited to making changes in the temporal domain (although adjustments of signal amplitude may also be made). Source frequencies and resonance frequencies cannot be manipulated directly by waveform editing. On the other hand, the experimenter has the advantage of using stimuli that approximate natural speech. (Synthetic speech stimuli, as we shall see, always contain simplifications and omissions of the features of natural speech.) Nonetheless, the experimenter using edited natural speech stimuli must always be aware of the acoustic structure of material being edited so that the effects of the editing on the stimuli can be specified and assessed when interpreting the perceptual judgements of listeners.

CREATING STIMULI: SPEECH SYNTHESIS

As we indicated in our discussion of waveform editing, the synthetic speech stimuli used in testing perception are never identical copies of natural speech. In spite of this, experimenters synthesize stimuli because they have the option of creating speech in which any or all of the acoustic features (frequency, amplitude, duration, source characteristics) can vary independently and can be specified exactly. Synthetic stimuli, for example, were essential in creating the experimental continua in which the frequencies of consonant-vowel formant transitions were systematically varied in order to discover the acoustic cues to place of articulation. The experimenters could be confident about their findings because all of the other potential variables in the stimuli were held at constant values. In theory, an experimenter knows everything about the acoustic structure of a synthesized stimulus because everything in it has been put there by him or her. Most of the perceptual experiments that we discussed in the last chapter employed synthetic speech stimuli, some generated by the Pattern Playback (see Chapter 2) as many as forty years ago, others produced by synthesizers of a more recent vintage.

There are, of course, substantial differences between the way the Pattern Playback operated and the way contemporary synthesizers generate speech. Most synthesizers in use today do not require a hand-made graphic input that is optically scanned by mechanical means and then converted to sound. Rather, the input is typed into a computer in the form of numbers that represent frequencies, durations, amplitudes, bandwidths, and any other acoustic features under the control of the experimenter. The computer then converts the input to digital instructions to the synthesizer which, in turn, generates the specified acoustic signal.

It is interesting to note that the computer programs controlling synthesis are virtually always capable of displaying the input as a schematic spectrogram. Experimenters, evidently, are so used to the visual representation of the acoustic signal that they rely on it as confirmation of the appropriateness of their numerical input to the synthesizer. It is important to remember, however, that such visual displays do not confirm that the output of the synthesizer matches the input: It is only a representation of the instructions that have been typed into the computer. If a synthesizer is not functioning properly, the experimenter will not find out by looking at a display of the intended input. The experienced and cautious user of a synthesizer will subject its acoustic output to acoustic analysis to verify the identity of input with output.

Acoustic speech synthesizers generally function in one of two ways. Parallel resonance synthesizers generate three (or, occasionally, four) formants (Fig. 7.26). The center frequencies and amplitudes of each formant are input by the experimenter, as are the choice of sound source (periodic/buzz, aperiodic/hiss, or both), the frequency range and amplitude of aperiodic resonances and the presence, frequency, and amplitude of nasal resonances. In parallel resonance synthesis the bandwidths of formants are fixed by the synthesizer.

Serial synthesizers generate five or more formants (Fig. 7.26). The frequencies of the lowest three formants are selected by the experimenter, but formants above the third have frequencies that are pre-determined. In serial synthesis the experimenter selects the bandwidths of all the resonances, but their relative amplitudes are determined by the serial connection of the synthesizer and by subsequent spectral shaping. As in parallel resonance synthesis, the experimenter has a choice of sound source: periodic (buzz), aperiodic (hiss), or both. When the aperiodic source is selected, the spectrum of the sound is determined by paired pole and zero in the synthesis program.

Serial synthesis can sometimes sound more natural than parallel resonance synthesis, but both, when carefully generated, are highly intelligible. It is interesting to note that intelligibility seems to be more important than naturalness in the preparation of synthetic speech stimuli. Using parallel resonance or serial synthesis to generate stimuli for replications of experiments that originally employed the highly unnatural (but intelligible) stimuli of the Pattern Playback has usually yielded equivalent results.

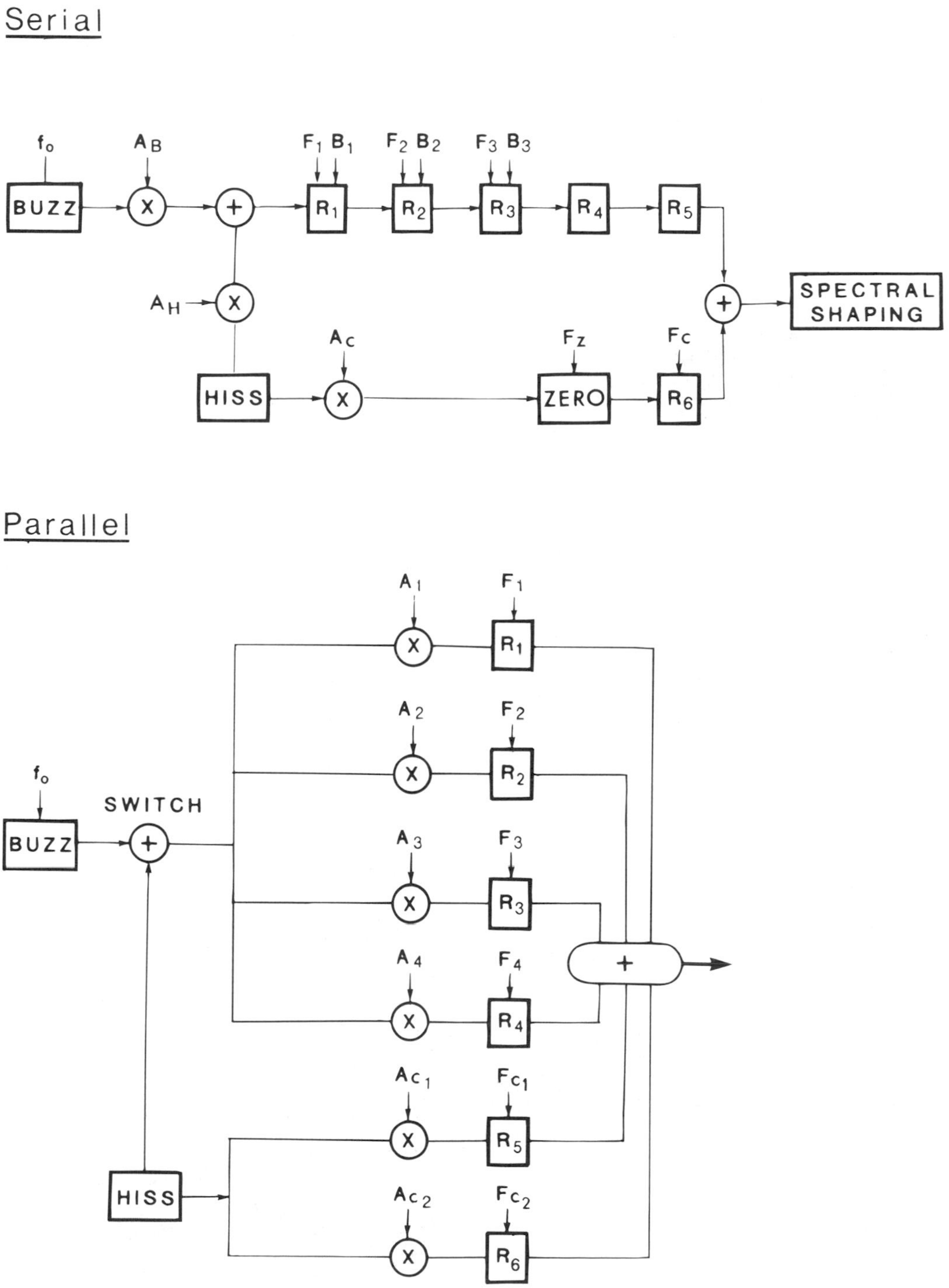

Figure 7.26 In a serial synthesizer, for the voiced sound, the bandwidths and frequencies of the resonances are set; the relative amplitude of the formants is fixed by the serial connection and the overall spectral shaping. When the hiss is connected, characteristics of the sound are a consequence of a spectral pole and zero pair.

In the parallel synthesizer, a switch controls the activation of a buzz or hiss source. The frequency and amplitude of each resonance is adjusted individually. The output of the separate formants is added together.

Recently, it has become possible to synthesize speech according to articulatory rather than acoustic rules. X-ray, ultrasound, magnetometer, EPG, and other types of data have provided us with information about the positions and movements of the articulators and the changing shapes of the vocal tract. Because we know the rules for making shape-to-acoustic-output conversions (see Chapter 4), we can program a computer-controlled synthesizer to use a schematic mid-sagittal drawing of a vocal tract as its input, and to generate the appropriate acoustic signal. If we produce a sequence of schematic vocal tract shapes, in effect, an animation, the computer will cause the synthesizer to generate the synthetic equivalent of articulated speech. Attainment of the predicted acoustic output can thus serve as a confirma-

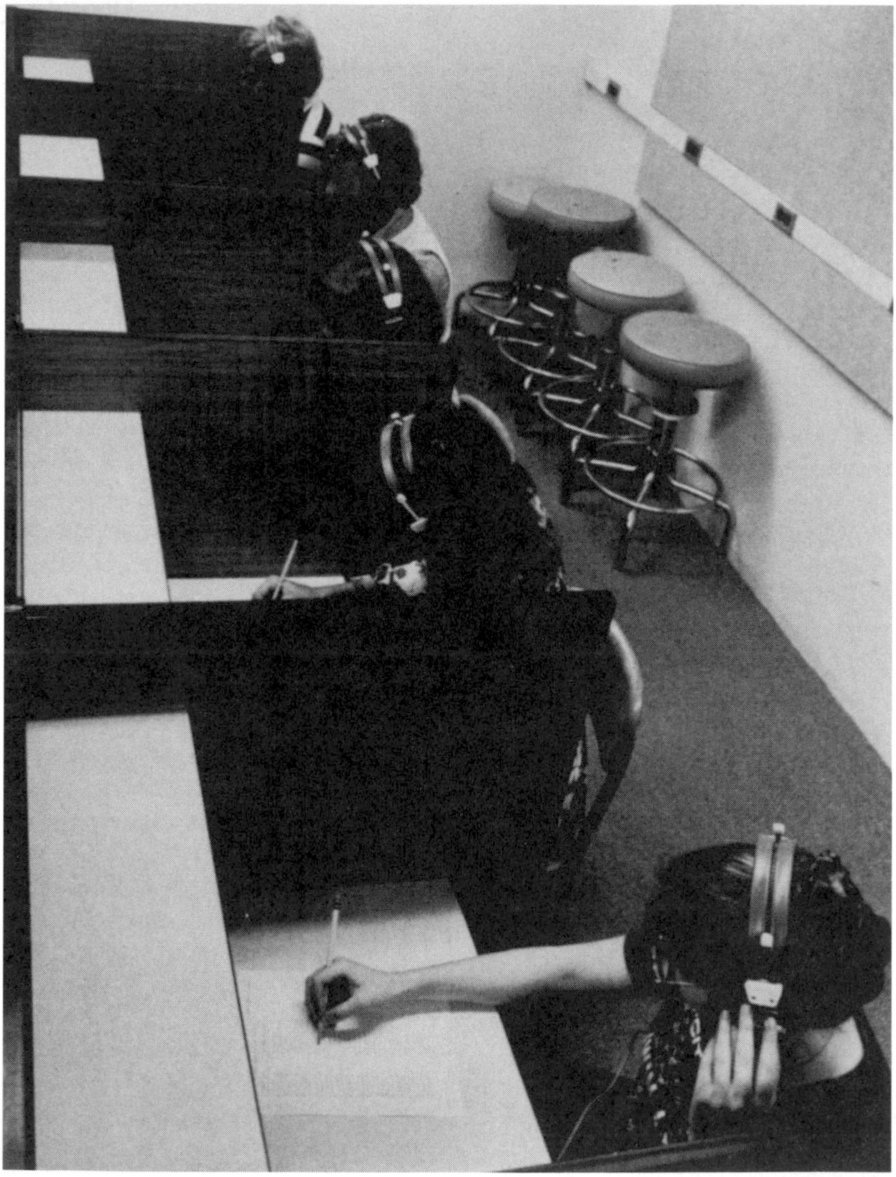

Figure 7.27 A listening station (Temple University).

tion of physiological research and so help us to better understand speech production as well as speech perception.

PERCEPTUAL TESTING

Once the stimuli have been prepared, the experimenter must present them to listeners in identification and/or discrimination tasks of various sorts (see Chapter 6). No special devices are actually required, but the arrangement of the equipment and the methods used to record responses must be carefully considered. It is convenient, for instance, to have a well-designed listening station available for the testing of subjects. Ideally, a listening station should be a sound-treated room equipped to permit the simultaneous testing of several subjects at the same time, whether over headsets or in an open field using a high quality loudspeaker equidistant from each subject (Fig. 7.27).

More sophisticated listening stations often have separate control rooms from which the experimenter administers the test, presenting stimuli generated directly from the synthesizer under computer control and allowing subjects to enter their responses directly into the computer for immediate processing. Aside from the speed, equivalent results can be obtained if the experimenter is in the room with the subjects and depresses a button to play the tape recording of the test stimuli while the subjects circle their responses on a prepared form.

Use of Computers in Experimental Phonetics

While you were reading this chapter, it should have become evident that computers are essential for conducting most descriptive and experimental studies in speech science, even though they are not, *per se*, instruments of speech science. The same, of course, can be said today of almost any field of scientific inquiry.

The only functions computers have not yet undertaken in speech research are envisioning an experiment, designing it, and interpreting it. Admittedly, these are probably the most important steps in any experiment, but, as we have seen, computers are used to do everything else. In studies of speech perception they control the production of stimuli and their presentation, record responses, reduce data and analyze their statistical significance, display and graph the results.

In the study of acoustic phonetics, computers digitize the waveform, display it as a waveform, spectrogram, or amplitude spectrum, expand the display for more precise editing or analysis, and, through the use of special software, perform accurate measurement of many acoustic features such as formant frequency, fundamental frequency, segment durations, and so on.

In the study of physiological phonetics, computers can transform any analog signal, for example, from devices that measure air pressure, articulator movement or EMG activity, into graphic displays. They are used to average data, measure reaction times and record frequencies of occurrence of observed events. And, of course, they provide a more or less permanent store of data and results that can be printed out or consulted on-line in the future.

Perhaps the most important facts about computers is that they continue to become less expensive, more compact, more powerful and easier to use. These facts suggest that the use of computers is bound to become even more widespread that it is today. This means that the ability to perform speech science research, for both normal and clinical purposes, will be within the reach of most students in the relatively near future.

REFERENCES

General Readings

Comprehensive

Baken, R. J., *Clinical Measurement of Speech and Voice*. Boston: College-Hill Press, 1987.

Flanagan, J. L., *Speech Analysis, Synthesis, and Perception*. New York: Springer-Verlag, 1965.

Holmes, J. N., *Speech Synthesis*. London: Mills & Boon Ltd., 1972.

Acoustic Phonetics

Fant, G., Sound Spectrography. *Proceedings of the Fourth International Congress of Phonetic Sciences*. Helsinki Conference. A. Sovijarvi and P. Aalto (Eds.) New York: Humanities Press, 1961, pp. 14–33.

Koenig, W., Dunn, H. K., and Lacy, L. Y., The Sound Spectrograph. *J. Acoust. Soc. Am. 17*, 1946, 19–49. Reprinted in *Readings in Clinical Spectrography of Speech*. R. J. Baken ansd R. G. Daniloff (Eds.) San Diego, CA and Pine Brook, NJ: Singular Publishing Group, Inc., and KAY Elemetrics Corp., 1991, pp. 3–34.

McDermott, J., The Solid-State Parrot. *Science 83, 4*, 1983, 58–65.

Strevens, P., Spectra of Fricative Noise in Human Speech. *Language and Speech 3,* 1960, 32–49.

Wakita, H., Instrumentation for the Study of Speech Acoustics. In *Contemporary Issues in Experimental Phonetics*. N. J. Lass (Ed.) New York: Academic Press, 1976, pp. 3–40.

Physiological Phonetics

Abbs, J. H., and Watkin, K. L., Instrumentation for the Study of Speech Physiology. In *Contemporary Issues in Experimental Phonetics*. N. J. Lass (Ed.) New York: Academic Press, 1976, 41–78.

Atkinson, J. E., Correlation Analysis of the Physiological Factors Controlling Fundamental Voice Frequency. *J. Acoust. Soc. Am. 63,* 1978, 211–222.

Borden, G. J., An Interpretation of Research on Feedback Interruption. *Brain Lang. 7,* 1979, 307–319,

Fujimura, O., Acoustics of Speech. In *Speech and Cortical Functioning*. J. H. Gilbert (Ed.) New York: Academic Press, 1972, pp. 107–165.

Harris, K. S., Physiological Aspects of Articulatory Behavior. In *Current Trends in Linguistics*. Vol. 12, No. 4, T. A. Sebeok (Ed.) The Hague: Mouton, 1974, pp. 2281–2302.

Perkell, J. S., *Physiology of Speech Production: Results and Implications of a Quantitative Cineradiographic Study*. Cambridge, MA: M. I. T. Press, 1969.

Sawashima, M., and Cooper, F. S. (Eds.), *Dynamic Aspects of Speech Production*. Tokyo: University of Tokyo Press, 1977.

Speech Perception

Cooper, F. S., Speech Synthesizers. *Proceedings of the Fourth International Congress of Phonetic Sciences*. Helsinki Conference. A. Sovijarvi and P. Aalto (Eds.) New York: Humanities Press, 1961, pp.3–13.

Denes, P., The Use of Computers for Research in Phonetics. *Proceedings of the Fourth International Congress of Phonetic Sciences*. Helsinki Conference. A. Sovijarvi and P. Aalto (Eds.) New York: Humanities Press, 1961, pp. 149–154.

Fodor, J. A., and Bever, T. G., The Psychological Reality of Linguistic Segments. *J. Verbal Learning and Verbal Behavior 4,* 1965, 414–420.

Raphael, L. J., Preceding Vowel Duration as a Cue to the Perception of the Voicing Characteristic of Word-Final Consonants in American English. *J. Acoust. Soc. Am. 51,* 1972, pp. 1296–1303.

A Sample of Papers on Instrumentation

Allen, G. D., Lubker, J. F. and Harrison, E., Jr., New Paint-On Electrodes for Surface Electromyography. *J. Acoust. Soc. Am. 52,* 1972, 124 (A).

Baer, T., Löfquist, A., and McGarr, N., Laryngeal Vibrations: A Comparison between High-Speed Filming and Glottographic Techniques. *J. Acoust. Soc. Am. 73,* 1983, 1304–1308.

Baer, T, Gore, J., Boyce., and Nye, P., Applications of MRI to the Analysis of Speech Production. *Magnetic Resonance Imaging, 5,* 1989, 1–7.

Baken, R. J., and Matz, B. J., A Portable Impedance Pneumograph. *Hum. Commun*. Autumn 1973, 28–35.

Bless, D. M., Assignment of Laryngeal Function. In *Phono-Surgery: Assessment and Surgical Management of Voice Disorders.* New York: Raven Press, 1991, Chapter 7.

Cooper, F. S., and Mattingly, I. G., Computer-controlled PCM System for Investigation of Dichotic Speech Perception. *Haskins Laboratories Status Reports SR–17/18,* 1969, 17–21.

Fletcher, S. G., McCutcheon, M. J., and Wolf, M. B., Dynamic Palatometry *J. Speech Hear. Res. 18,* 1975, 812–819.

Fourcin, A. J., Laryngographic Examination of Vocal Fold Vibration. In *Ventilatory and Phonatory Control Systems: An International Symposium*. B. Wyke (Ed.) London: Oxford University Press, 1974, pp. 315–326.

Fujimura, O., Kiritani, S., and Oshida, H., Computer-controlled Radiography for Observation of Movements of Articulatory and Other Human Organs. *Comput. Biol. Med. 3,* 1973, 371–384.

Gerratt, B. R., Haison, D. G., and Burke, G., Glottographic Measures of Laryngeal Function in Individuals with Abnormal Motor Control. In *Laryngeal Function in Phonation and Respiration*. T. Baer, C. Sasaki, and K. S. Harris (Eds.) Boston: College Hill Press, 1987, pp. 521–532.

Harris, K. S., Electromyography as a Technique for Laryngeal Investigation. In *Proceedings of The Conference on the Assessment of Vocal Pathology*. C. L. Ludlow and M.D. Hart (Eds.) ASHA Reports 11, 1981, pp. 116–124.

Hirano, M., and Ohala, J., Use of Hooked-wire Electrodes for Electromyography of the Intrinsic Laryngeal Muscles. *J. Speech Hear. Res. 12,* 1969, 362–373.

Hirose, H., Gay, T., and Strome, M., Electrode Insertion Techniques for Laryngeal Electromyography. *J. Acoust. Soc. Am. 50,* 1971, 1449–1450.

Huggins, A. W. F., A Facility for Studying Perception of Timing in Natural Speech. *Q. Prog. Rep. Res. Lab. Electron. M. I. T. 95,* 1969, 81–83.

Kent, R. D., Some Considerations in the Cineradiographic Analysis of Tongue Movements during Speech. *Phonetica 26,* 1972, 293–306.

Lisker, L., Abramson, A. S., Cooper, F. S., and Schvey, M.

H., Transillumination of the Larynx in Running Speech. *J. Acoust. Soc. Am. 45,* 1969, 1544–1546.

Moll, K. L., Cinefluorographic Techniques in Speech Research. *J. Speech Hear. Res. 3,* 1960, 227–241.

Moore, G. P., White, F. D., and von Leden, H., Ultra High Speech Photography in Laryngeal Physiology. *J. Speech Hear. Disord. 27,* 1962, 165–171.

Nakatani, L. H., Computer–aided Signal Handling for Speech Research. *J. Acoust. Soc. Am. 61,* 1977, 1056–1062.

Pollack, A. "Computers Mastering Speech Recognition" *New York Times (Science Times),* Sept. 6, 1983, C1–C7.

Rubin, P., Baer, T., and Mermelstein, P., An Articulatory Synthesizer for Perceptual Research. *J. Acoust. Soc. Am. 70,* 1981, 321–328.

Sawashima, M., Abramson, A. S., Cooper, F. S., and Lisker, L., Observing Laryngeal Adjustments during Running Speech by Use of a Fiberoptics System. *Phonetica 22,* 1970, 193–201.

Stone, M., Sonies, B., Shawker, T., Weiss, G., and Nadel, L., Analysis of Real-time Ultrasound Images of Tongue Configurations Using a Grid-digitizing System. *J. Phonet 13,* 1983, 189–203.

Subtelny, J.D., and Subtelny, J.D., Roentgenographic Techniques and Phonetic Research. *Proceedings of the Fourth International Congress of Phonetic Sciences.* Helsinki Conference. A. Sovijarvi and P. Aalto (Eds.) New York: Humanities Press, 1961, 129–146.

Unger, J., The Oral Cavity and Tongue: Magnetic Resonance Imaging. *Radiology 155,* 1985, pp. 151–153.

Watkin, K. L., and Zagzebski, J. A., On-line Ultrasonic Technique for Monitoring Tongue Displacements. *J. Acoust. Soc. Am. 54,* 1973, 544–547.

8
Evolution of Language and Speech

. . . and out of the ground the Lord God formed every beast of the field and every fowl of the air; and brought them unto Adam to see what he would call them: and whatsoever Adam called every living creature, that was the name thereof.

—King James Version, *The Bible*, Genesis 2:19

Homo sapiens is a group of creatures who name the world about them. They attach verbal tags to almost every person, place, thing, event, circumstance, thought, and feeling within their experience. They use these tags to order the world for themselves, to transmit information, and to ask questions. Curious as creatures, they seem to be the only animals who constantly ask the questions: Who am I? How did I develop? Within these larger questions are the queries: how does a person acquire speech and language and how did human language and speech originate and evolve?

In the 17th century, two philosophers wrote opposing theories of how human ideas develop, theories that continue to influence modern thought about language acquisition. Descartes (Fig. 8.1), the French philosopher and mathematician, was a *Rationalist*, holding that reason based on innate ideas was more important to human understanding than experiences with the physical world. He viewed the mind and the outside world as separate. A modern concept of human language that is consonant with Descartes' emphasis on innate ideas is Chomsky's, which maintains that although a person learns the language that is spoken in his particular community, competence to produce and comprehend language is an innate human characteristic that is fundamental to learning specific languages.

The 17th century philosopher Locke (Fig. 8.2) was an *Empiricist*, holding that human beings understand through their experiences, especially those gained via the senses. The human mind was viewed as a blank slate, a *tabula rasa*, upon which all sensory experiences are registered, thereby leading to learning and understanding. Condillac, following soon after Locke, theorized that language and speech are learned and not innate in humans. Modern behaviorists, such as Skinner, have maintained that learning is the key to language acquisition, and so perpetuate the empirical view of Locke and Condillac.

Theories about how human language and speech originated and evolved have been proposed for centuries, beginning, perhaps, with the Biblical account of the divine origin of language and continuing right up to the present day. The problem with theorizing about the origin and evolution of language and speech is that the evidence no longer exists. We have no knowledge of how language and speech originated nor are we likely to obtain any. It is a mystery of lost sounds and disintegrated soft tissue. Stones and bones remain, offering only fragmentary clues. In the past, speculation on the topic seemed so fruitless that in 1866, the Linguistic Society of Paris published an edict prohibiting discussion of the origin of language and speech in the papers of the society. The edict had little effect, however, and theories continued to proliferate. As recently as 1975, linguists, anthropologists, psychologists, neurologists, and speech scientists at a conference held at the New York Academy of Sciences presented a wide range of theories, from those that depicted human speech and language as having evolved from animal vocalizations to those that viewed them as having evolved from primate gestural communication to those that maintained that speech and language occurred *de novo* in man. Some theorists suggest that speech developed as recently as 40,000 years ago, during the 4th glacial period, while others propose that it developed between 2 and 3 million years ago.

There is no single field of inquiry that can supply sufficient evidence by itself, but if we gather together the evidence from studies of fossils, studies of vocal and gestural communication in living creatures, and studies of the brain and vocal tract, we can come closer to a likely theory of how the speech and language of man evolved and even a suggestion of how they originated.

Figure 8.1 René Descartes, French philosopher and mathematician (1596-1650).

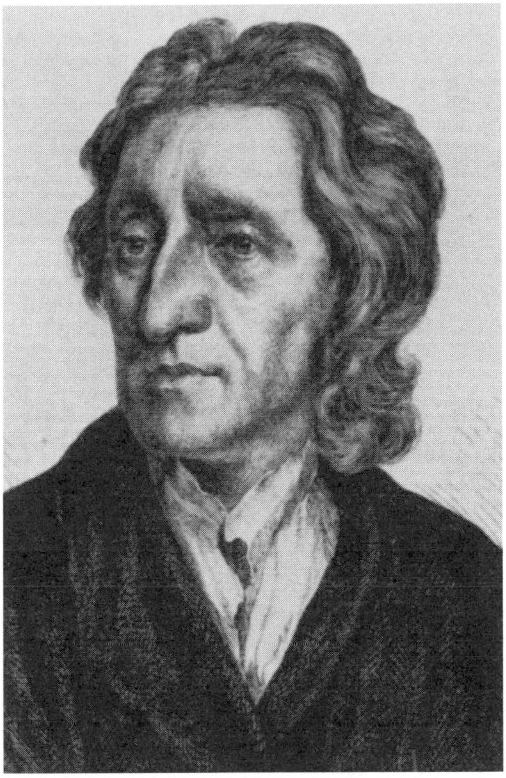

Figure 8.2 John Locke, English empirical philosopher (1632-1704).

SOCIAL FRAMEWORK

The Evidence from Hominid Fossils

If early *hominids* left the forest to wander in the savanna in search of food, it is conjectured by anthropologists that they needed to develop language to organize their kinship groups for survival. The line of hominid evolution to modern man is unclear, however. Most texts on the subject view Australopithecus africanus, a small ape-like creature who lived from more than 4 million to about 1 million years ago to be an ancestor of Homo erectus, a larger brained hominid who lived from about 1 to ½ million years ago, who was, in turn, the ancestor of Homo sapiens, or modern man. The size of the brain of Australopithecus africanus was only about 400 cm^3, while Homo erectus had a brain ranging from about 800 to 1300 cm^3 in volume, which overlaps the range of brain sizes of modern man. This represents a large change

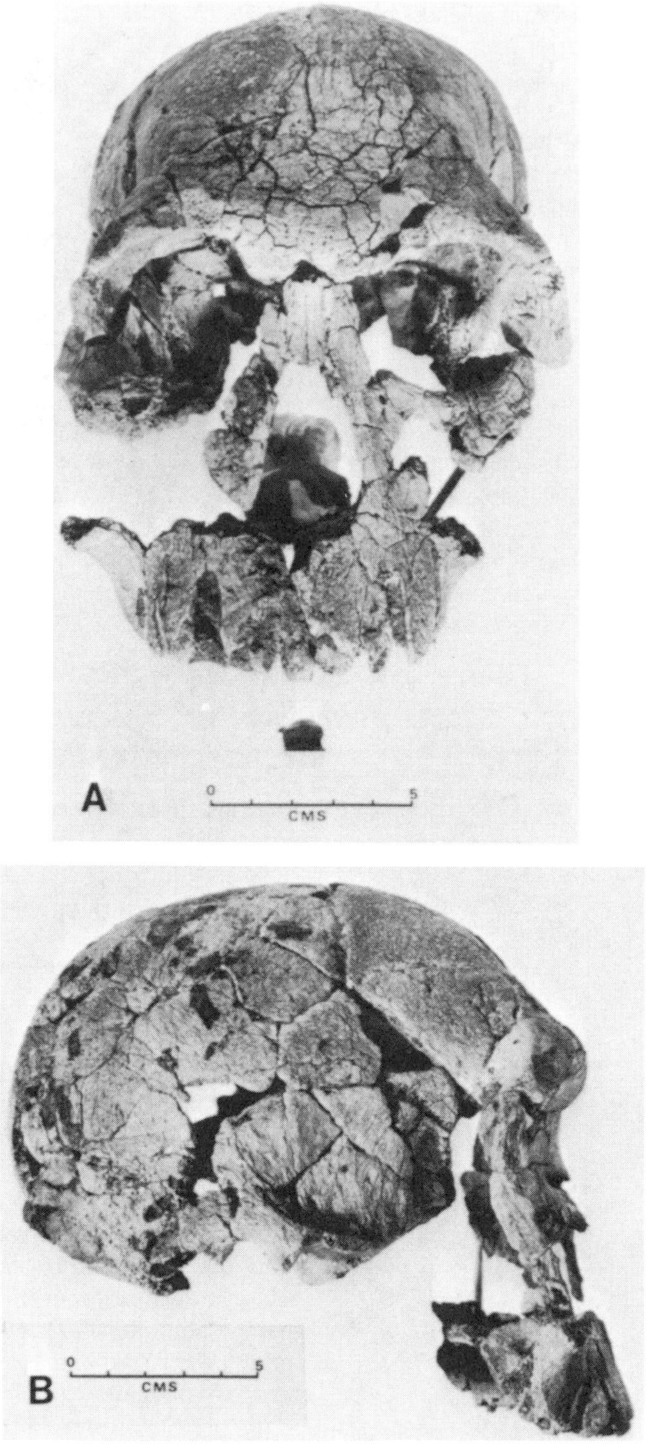

Figure 8.3 (*A* and *B*) Views of skull fragment KNM-ER 1470. (Reprinted with permission from M. H. Day, R. E. F. Leakey, A. C. Walker, and B. A. Wood: *American Journal of Physical Anthropology 42,* 1975. Courtesy of the National Museums of Kenya.)

in brain size, and the classical view was that during the almost 4 million years that elapsed between Australopithecus africanus and modern man, language, cognition, and brain size developed together.

Recent fossil finds in Kenya and Ethiopia, however, have raised questions about the lineage of modern man. There is a possibility that the genus Homo was living as a contemporary of Australopithecus africanus, 3 or 4 million years ago. At Lake Turkana (formerly Lake Rudolph) in Kenya, Richard Leakey found a Homo erectus fossil in 1975 dated at about 1 ½ million years ago. Earlier, in 1972, he found the skull fragment of a Homo fossil dated 2 to 3 million years ago. This skull, called by its catalog number KNM-ER 1470 (Fig. 8.3), is important for its Homo erectus-like cranial capacity and shape. Holloway has reported that the Broca's region on the ER 1470 is larger than that on Australopithecus skulls. It is possible, then, that modern man developed from the ER 1470 species of hominid and not from Australopithecus africanus or from the more recent Neanderthal Man, whose fossils, found in Europe, date from 100,000 to 35,000 years ago (Fig. 8.4). Further evidence of early man are the remains of a "family" of adults and children found in Ethiopia by Johanson (an American anthropologist) and Taieb (a French geologist). The skeletons have been assigned to the genus Homo and date from approximately 3 million years ago. Johanson and Leakey have suggested that the Homo skeletons are the remains of a food-sharing cooperative group and that, therefore, there is a strong possibility that they possessed some form of speech. It may be that the selective development of a problem-solving capacity to deal with the increasing complexity of life necessitated the parallel development of a complex and flexible communication code much earlier in history than has been assumed (Table 8.1).

The Interaction of Cognition and Language

In order for any language system to originate and be maintained, there must be a basic need for it by the species. The most obvious need for a system of communication arises when creatures need to cooperate and share in order to survive. As social dependencies increase and become more complex, the communication system must become sufficiently extensive and flexible to convey the necessary information. For example, language may be a convenience in conveying information about making tools for hunting or food-gathering. It is probably essential to convey information on how to fashion a tool to be used to make other tools. Cooperative planning to catch an animal or to design tools to make other tools requires the postponement of immediate gratification and forces the planners to think of the future. Normally, language presumes cognition and thus reflects its cognitive underpinnings. The more abstract the cognition (fashioning toolmaking tools), the more necessary is a complex language system.

Evidence of cognitive prerequisites to speech is scattered. The first known tool dates about 2 million years ago, and tools created as

Table 8.1. Reconstructed Timetable Based on Recent Finds of Homo Fossils

Years ago (approximate)		
4–5 million to 1 million	Australopithecus africanus	Became extinct
3 million	Homo finds in Ethiopia and Kenya	Ancestors of Homo sapiens?
2 million	First known tool	
1½ million to 500,000	Homo erectus	Ancestor of Homo sapiens
250,000	Homo sapiens	
100,000 to 70,000	Neanderthal finds in Europe	Became extinct
70,000 to 35,000	Evidence of religion and philosophy	
30,000	Evidence of art	
6,500	First known writing	

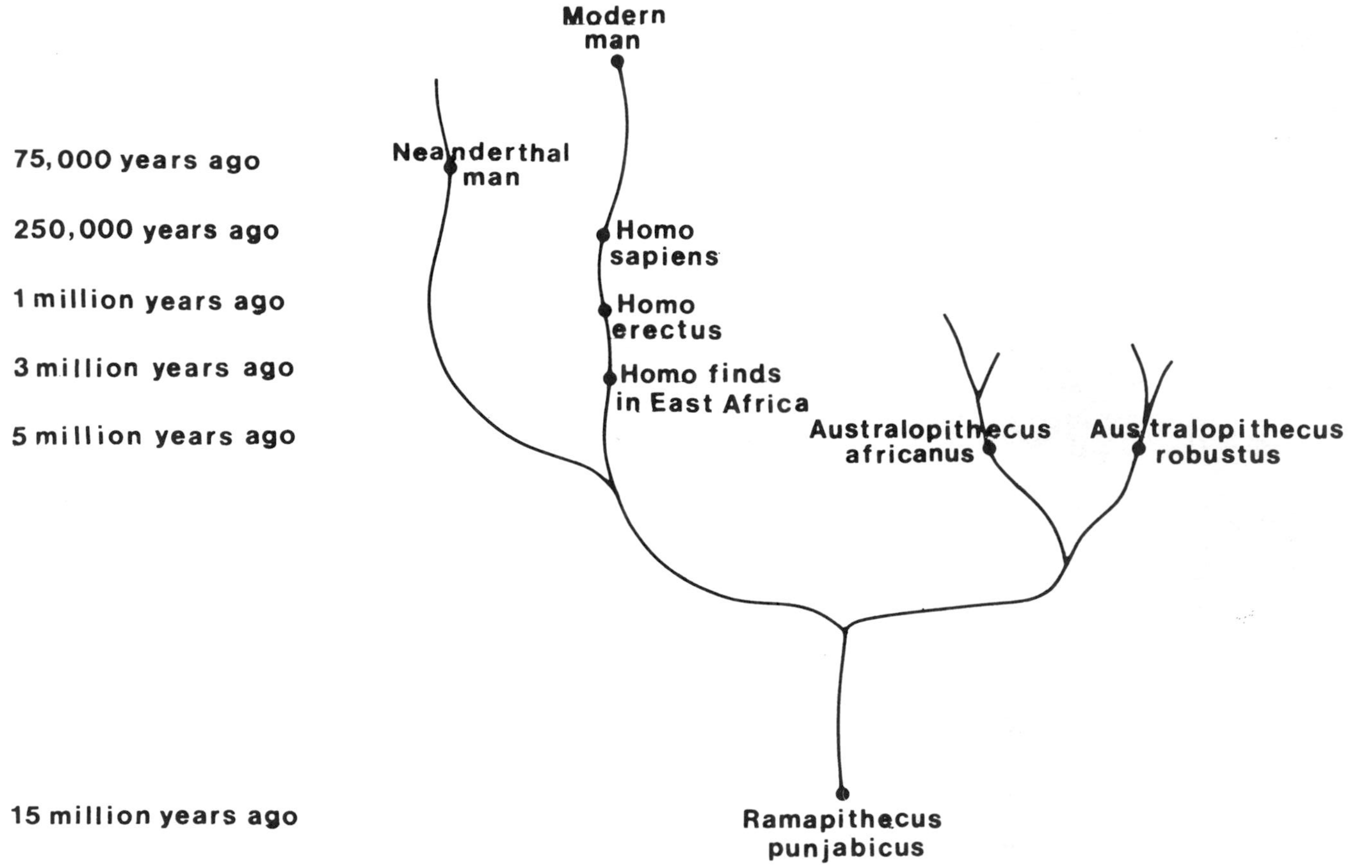

Figure 8.4 The evolution of man according to Leakey's view that 1470 and Australopithecus were contemporaries. Johanson would place the 1470 skull at 2 million years or less.

art objects date from 30,000 years ago. A skeleton found near La Chapelle-aux-Saints in southern France, dated to around 70,000 to 35,000 years ago, was found buried with tools, a tradition reported for many Neanderthal burials. This suggests the development of religion and philosophy, abstract concepts that presumably require language for their transmission from one generation to the next.

As we mentioned earlier, in the absence of direct evidence about the communication systems of hominids, scientists often study living creatures, especially those that are phylogenetically related to humans, such as chimpanzees. According to van Lawick-Goodall, chimps use tools to obtain food, and they communicate with gesture, facial expressions, and over 20 calls. They lack language of the kind used by humans, however, in which the signals are segmented to be recombined for infinite numbers of messages. In a simple communication system, one gesture or one call, as the case may be, signifies one thing and constitutes a complete message. A certain bird cry can serve to signal a danger warning, or a certain body posture in an animal can signify submission. In this kind of communication system, the numbers of distinct calls or gestures must be limited for at least two reasons. First, a large number of calls would overload the memory capacity of the animal. Second, if the calls or gestures were too numerous, they could lose their distinctiveness and become ambiguous. To avoid these problems, as communication systems evolve and become more complex, the calls or gestures become segmented and are used in combinations that generate multiple meanings without increasing the number of basic elements. The phonemic systems of human languages are, of course, advanced examples of this sort of segmentation and recombination process (in which, however, the segmental units, the phonemes, have no meaning of their own). Hockett and Ascher have suggested that animal warning calls might be modified to indicate the direction from which the danger is coming, and that unitary calls might be blended to yield new calls with combined meanings such as "food and danger." But, as we have mentioned, there are limitations imposed on these sorts of innovations: unless there is a change in cognitive ability, the increase or modification of the call inventory will eventually overload memory and/or diminish the distinctiveness of the calls. Can cognitive ability be enhanced by the use of a more complex communication system? Will the enhanced cognitive ability stimulate further changes in the structure of a communication system?

The research and theorizing of the last several decades indicates that it is quite likely that language and cognition interacted to stimulate their mutual development: Language evolved in response to the increasingly complex structures of early human society, and the elaborated linguistic code, in turn, stimulated the flow of information that led to the further evolution of social structure. As human tribal groups increased in size and the demand for food grew, there would be an advantage in being able to name the prey to be hunted and to assign specific hunting tasks to different individuals. If using language improved the efficiency of the hunt, the size of the tribe could increase further, freeing some members to take on more specialized roles in tribal society.

Why Speech?

If the social life of some hominids gave rise to the development of a complex communication system, why did speech become its mode of transmission? The reason appears to be that speech was selectively advantageous for a number of reasons. First, the vocal-auditory channel of speech facilitated communication under conditions in which a different channel, such as gestural-visual, would fail. Using speech, messages could be sent in the dark, around corners, or when visibility was limited for other reasons. Second, using speech allowed communication to occur at the same time as manual tasks, such as tool-making or food-gathering, were being performed. Third, as we saw in Chapter 6, because speech is encoded in the acoustic signal, it is a highly efficient means of communication. Coarticulation allows speakers to produce speech sounds in parallel, blend-

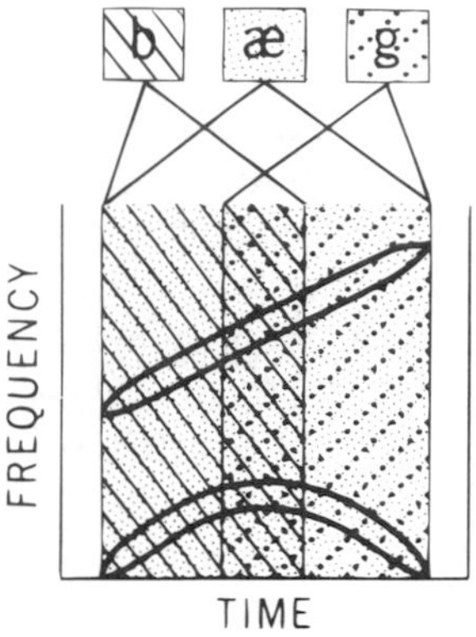

Figure 8.5 Schematic spectrogram showing the effects of coarticulation in the syllable [bæg]. (Reprinted with permission from A. M. Liberman: In *Coding Processes in Human Memory*. A. W. Melton and E. Martin (Eds.), Halsted Press © 1972.

ing the acoustic cues of one segment with those of another.

Liberman has used the word "bag" to exemplify this overlapping of acoustic cues. Note that in Figure 8.5 the acoustic cues for the /b/ overlap those for the /æ/, which, in turn, overlap those for the /g/. Thus, there is a shingling effect upon the acoustic output that the listener receives. Not only does speech allow for extremely rapid transmission of phonetic and linguistic information, much more rapid than if the sounds were produced sequentially, but the acoustic signal for speech is extremely robust because it is highly redundant. On the phonemic level, cues to the manner of articulation of the phoneme /b/, for example, may be given by the silence before the release burst, by the presence of the release burst, by the rising F_1 transition, and by the rapid rise time following the stop release. Multiple cues exist for the important features of virtually every phoneme. In addition, intonation patterns, stress, juncture, and other paralinguistic features such as vocal tone and gesture help to convey the syntactic, semantic, and phonological information conveyed, so that a message must be massively distorted before intelligibility fails.

Redundancy is not the only factor that accounts for the robust nature of the acoustic signal for speech. Mattingly has pointed out that certain acoustic cues to speech may function much as certain bird calls do, and for the same reason: The listener is genetically endowed to respond to them. The selection of speech, then, as means of conveying language, was not accidental or arbitrary.

PSYCHOLOGICAL FRAMEWORK

Some clues to the evolution of language and speech may be gleaned from observations of the communicative behavior of lower primates, birds, prelinguistic human infants, and the study of human and non-human auditory perception. Humans have long assumed that they alone had developed language, defined as a rule-governed symbolic communication system with which one can generate novel utterances. There had been a suspicion that dolphins might rival man in this ability, but the proof is lacking, because humans have thus far failed to understand the communication system used by dolphins. It was not until the last three decades that scientists began to suspect that our nearest living relatives, the greater apes, whose ability to learn human language was evidently poor, did, in fact, possess some measure of linguistic ability.

Communicating with Chimpanzees

Shortly after the Second World War, Hayes and Hayes raised a chimpanzee named Vicki in their home to see if she would acquire language and speech in the same manner as a human child. After six years, Vicki's only intelligible approximations to speech were the four words, "mama," "papa," "up," and "cup." Since the 1960s, however, humans have had to adjust their thinking about the linguistic abilities of chimps. The failure of the Hayes' experiment led some investigators to question whether the vocal-auditory mode of communication was optimal for chimpanzees to use. Studies of monkeys and apes suggested that visual signs outnumbered vocal signals in their natural communication systems. Later research, which we shall discuss below, revealed that the vocal tracts of primates were incapable of producing

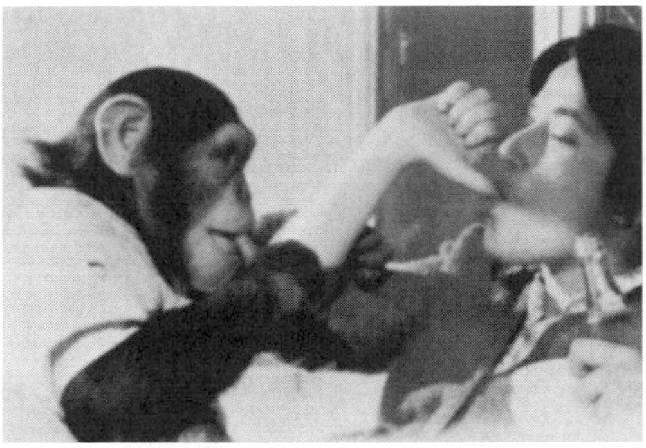

Figure 8.6 Washoe signing the word "drink" to Beatrice Gardner. (Photograph courtesy of R. Allen Gardner and Beatrice T. Gardner, University of Nevada.)

the full range of sounds required in human speech. Researchers thus turned to a visual gestural mode of signaling in their attempts to assess the linguistic abilities of chimpanzees and other primates.

The first successful attempt to teach a gestural mode of communication to a chimp was made by the Gardners at the University of Nevada. They taught a chimp named Washoe to use *American Sign Language* (*ASL*) to communicate (Fig. 8.6). Although Washoe was 10 months old when the Gardners began to work with her, by 15 months, she had learned her first word, by 2 years, she used her first sentence ("come-gimme sweet"), and by 5 years, had mastered over 130 signs. This was an significant improvement over Vicki's four words. More importantly, Washoe and the chimps subsequently trained using ASL appeared to be capable of learning some rules for sequencing signs and of creating sequences that they had not been taught. Most experimenters working with these chimps maintain that this symbolic behavior is evidence that the chimps have linguistic ability. The level of this ability has been estimated as being equivalent to that of a child between 2 and 3 years of age.

Among the ASL projects employing apes that succeeded the Gardners's experiment are those of Fouts (who inherited Washoe and trained several other chimps at the University of Kansas), Patterson (who trained a gorilla named Koko at Stanford University), and Terrace (who trained Nim Chimsky, a chimp named after Noam Chomsky, at Columbia University). Unlike the other experimenters, Terrace does not believe that chimpanzees have acquired language ability. Rather, he maintains that the chimps are simply demonstrating a sophisticated ability to mimic, aided by their trainers. In Terrace's view, the chimpanzee's "language" fails to develop like children's in sentence length and in variety of expression. Terrace's objections have been echoed by a considerable number of scholars in recent years, and the resolution of the question about chimps' linguistic ability will have to await further research.

Chimpanzee studies have not been limited to ASL as a mode of expression. Premack taught a chimp named Sarah to communicate using a different visual-manual mode. Sarah learned to use 125 plastic shapes to represent 125 different words and was able to produce sentences such as "Mary give apple." Premack reports that Sarah was capable of employing syntactic processes such as negation and conjunction, and that she was able to place the symbols (words) in a prescribed order.

A different visual-gestural mode was used by Rumbaugh at the Yerkes Regional Primate Research Center in Atlanta, Georgia. He trained a chimpanzee named Lana to use a computer-controlled teaching machine. Lana pressed coded buttons on her side of a computer console in order to demand action or food and to ask questions. Rumbaugh reported that Lana learned some basic syntactic rules of English and that she was able to use the rules to create novel sentences (Fig. 8.7).

The surprise in these experiments was that chimps have at least some of the cognitive prerequisites for a simple language. They clearly have the concepts for hundreds of things, and if given gestural or visual symbols to associate with these concepts, they can learn the rules for generating sentences with them. They lack the creativity with language shown by human children, but are capable of some novel utterances. Lana, lacking the word for an orange, but having learned the word for the color orange, pushed buttons indicating the "apple which-is orange," and Washoe, not knowing the sign for "ducks," signed "water

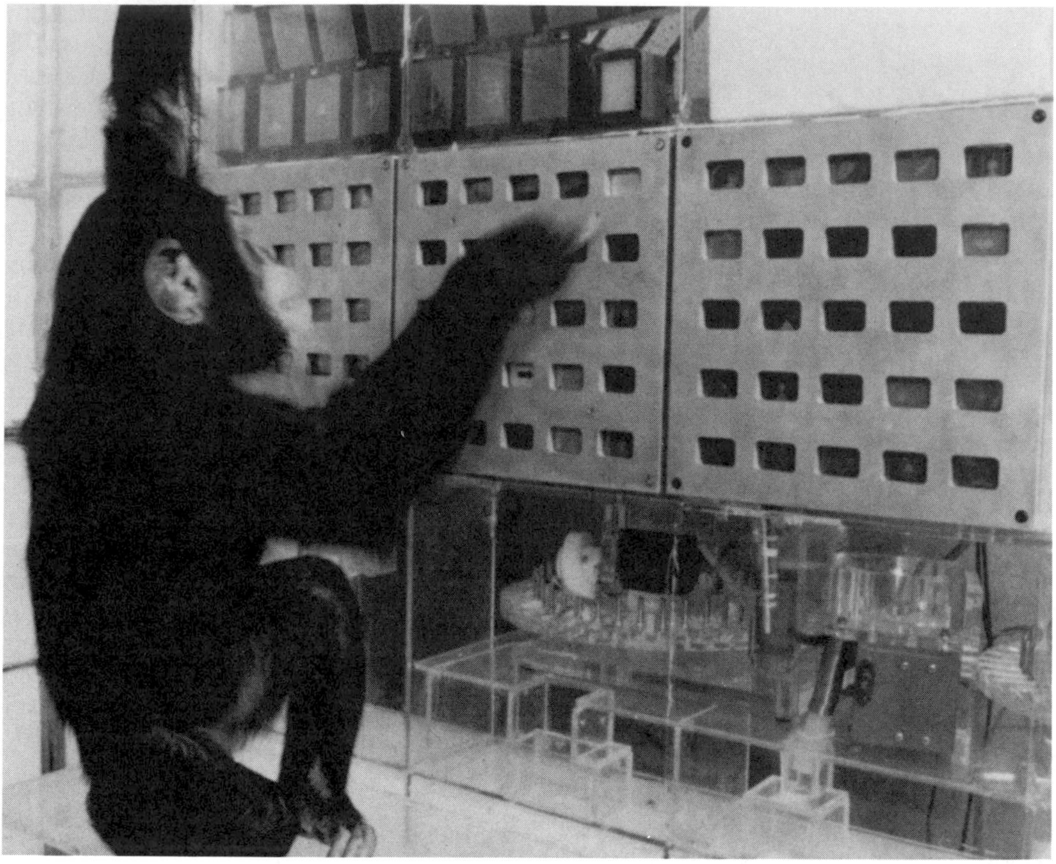

Figure 8.7 Lana at the keyboard of a computer. Each key has a distinctive symbol on its surface. (Photograph from Yerkes Regional Primate Research Center of Emory University, Atlanta, GA.)

birds." Important, then, to a consideration of the evolution of language and speech in humans, is the knowledge that the living greater apes show some linguistic ability. The volitional control evidenced by chimps over the use of their hands in the visual-gestural mode is impressive. In contrast to humans, they display obvious limitations in the auditory-vocal mode of communication. The differences between the speech-generating capacities of humans and chimpanzees can be accounted for by anatomical and physiological differences between the species with regard to vocal tract structure and neural control over motor activities.

Some theorists take the gestural competence of contemporary chimps as evidence that early hominids may have evolved language and speech from a purely gestural language accompanied by vocal emotive suprasegmentals (intonation, stress). The vocal sounds, according to this theory, gradually assumed more importance, as the use of gesture gradually diminished. Other theorists suggest that the evidence from chimp language shows that man developed along a completely separate line from chimps. In either case, a certain level of cognitive ability is presumed for symbolic behavior; language is one form of symbolic behavior, and speech is but one form of language. Chimps seem to be able to master a different form, gestural language, in the absence of a vocal mechanism adequate for producing the sounds of human speech.

Bird Song

Since humans evolved a vocal language, with non-verbal communication having assumed an important but secondary role, what cues to its development can be discerned from studying birds, which also use a vocal communicative system? Marler sees an analogy between much that linguists and psychologists have discovered about speech perception in humans and the studies that he and others have made on auditory perception and the development of bird song.

We have seen in the chapter on speech perception that humans perceive a continuum of speech-like sounds categorically, failing to discriminate subphonemic acoustic differences while successfully discriminating equal acoustic differences at phoneme boundaries. There has been some confusion about whether this perceptual categorization is done on a phonemic basis or whether it represents the discriminative function of the human auditory mechanism. The fact that rhesus monkeys and chinchillas demonstrate similar discriminative abilities despite their obvious lack of phonemic information upon which to base categories, indicates that humans may build their language, especially their phonemic distinctions, upon the contrasts that the auditory system finds to be more distinctive, and that this auditory tuning may have developed phylogenetically to include man and other mammals. There is, then, an innate tuning of auditory perception toward certain acoustic contrasts which can become linguistically useful. As we saw in Chapter 6, perceptual abilities evidently precede any corresponding production abilities. Eimas and others have demonstrated infants' ability to discriminate adult phoneme categories long before they can produce them. The discriminative abilities of rhesus monkeys and chinchillas may also be viewed as evidence that perception precedes production in phylogeny. Finally, there is the evidence of the critical period. Human beings are physiologically tuned to learning their first language during the first few years of life. When language learning is delayed, it becomes increasingly difficult. What seems to be learned almost effortlessly at 2 years of age is painfully difficult at 8, and at puberty, the plasticity of the brain for first language learning is almost lost. Hockett has pointed out that the longer period of childhood helplessness that evolved in man allows a longer time of plasticity for learning language.

The analogy between bird song and human speech is based on studies of the male white-crowned sparrow. As long as this sparrow hears the adult song during the critical period, when the bird is between 10 and 50 days old, and can hear himself singing, he will sing the full song, complete with local dialectal variations, when he is around 200 days old. If he is deafened during the critical period, however, the song will be abnormal (Fig. 8.8). If he is isolated so that he cannot hear the adult pattern but can hear himself, the song will be abnormal but will contain some normal characteristics. This indicates that a rudimentary trace of the song is innate. In order to be able to sing the full song, however, the sparrow must hear the model. When that happens, the model is imprinted in the bird's brain. Thus, some time later, when the bird begins to sing, its song will duplicate the imprinted model. Similarly, in human infants, innate perceptual and productive abilities are the foundation upon which the child learns a specific language to which he must be exposed during a critical period for language learning, and which he must hear himself use as he attempts to approximate the model in order to acquire normal speech.

Vocalization theories suggest that, however language and speech evolved, perceptual abilities probably preceded production abilities, in the sense that hominids may have chosen to contrast sounds, as they developed speech, which were already maximally differentiated by their auditory systems. Myers suggests that the species Homo erectus had greater cortical control over vocalizations and oral facial movements than other primates who used their hands for purposeful activities but had little cortical control over their calls. We know that the discriminatory ability necessary to perceive speech is widespread among animals, but there

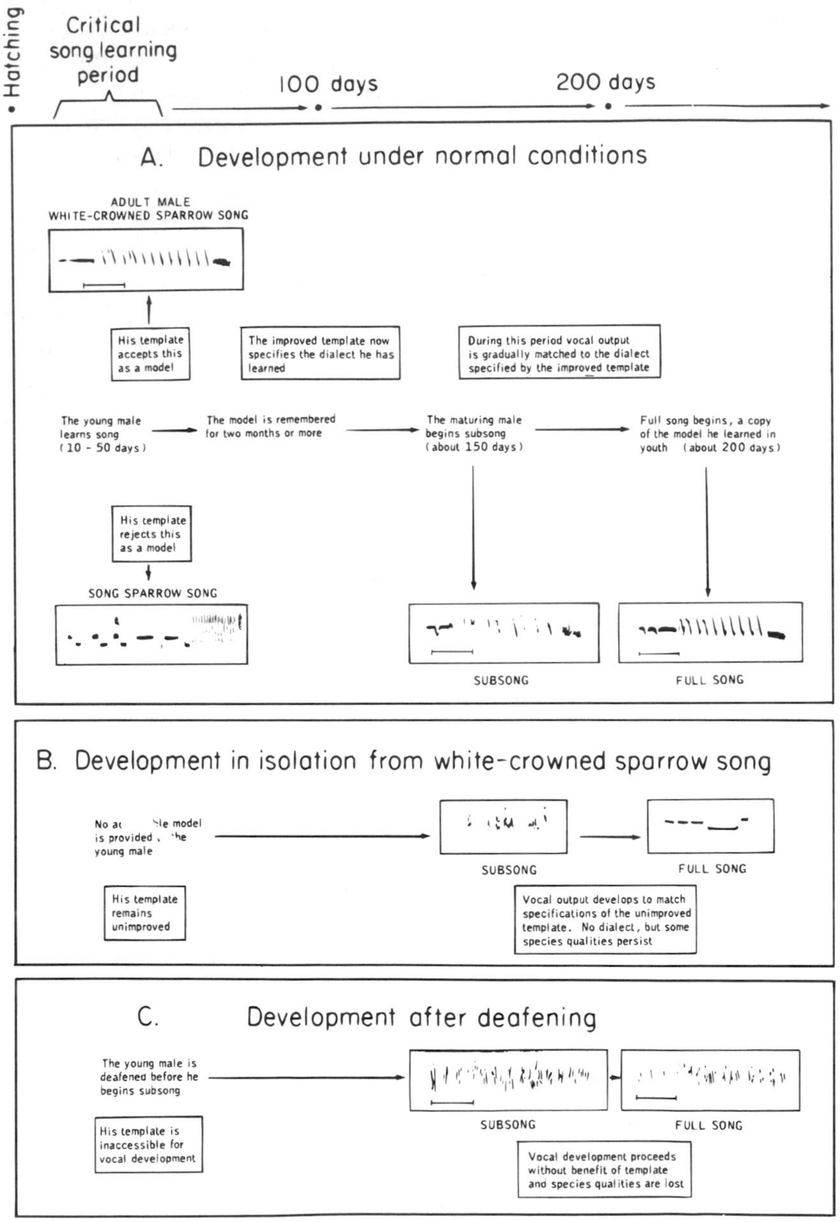

Figure 8.8 A representation of the "template" hypothesis for song learning in white-crowned sparrows, as applied to development (*A*) in a normal male, (*B*) in a social isolate, and (*C*) after early deafening. (Reprinted with permission from P. Marler: In *The Role of Speech in Language*, J. F. Kavanagh and J. E. Cutting (Eds.), M. I. T. Press, Cambridge, MA, © 1975.)

is no evidence of the existence of the complementary ability to produce speech. Chimpanzees seem able to use language productively, meaning they can create new utterances, but they possess vocal tracts that are incapable of producing speech. Birds use a vocal-auditory mode of communication, but possess a limited set of calls and lack a flexible production code with which to create new messages.

Child Language

It may be that the most persuasive clues to the evolution of speech may be found by studying the development of speech in human infants. The prelinguistic vocalizations of an infant are involuntary cries of distress, when they are hungry or uncomfortable, and comfort sounds, when they are nursing or content. The babbling stage may be similar to the innate rudiments of sparrow song evident in deafened song sparrows. Babbling seems to be innate; even deaf babies babble. The normal baby, however, starts to evidence voluntary vocal play as he babbles, while babbling in the deaf infant gradually dies out. After the infant discovers that a sound means something and that he, like Adam, can name things, language development proceeds quickly. The child produces his first words at about 1 year of age, and only 6 months later, he is usually producing sentences. An infant uses gesture with speech. As he is learning to name things, a child may point to something of interest, and through gesture and uninterpretable sounds, try to draw someone's attention to it. When gesture fails him, when it cannot signal all that he wants to express, he needs to name it. The development of syntax, too, is a direct reflection of the cognitive need underlying it. Relationships require the ordering of words into agent phrases and action phrases for full expression. Could it be that *ontogeny* in some sense recapitulates *phylogeny*? Lamendella suggests that we may see modifications of our phylogenetic history when we view the ontological development of a human being and that all of the seemingly disparate theories of speech evolution may be correct, as early man may have passed through successive stages similar to those experienced by a single infant. Figure 8.9 tracks the stages of communicative development during the first 2 years of a human child's life. Just as a child progresses from one type of communication system to another, man's ancestors may have gradually passed through similar stages.

BIOLOGICAL FRAMEWORK

Brain Organization

The final frame of reference for the development of language and speech in man is our knowledge of the structure and physiology of the brain and the vocal tract. We have already mentioned that there was a large increase in brain size from Australopithecus africanus to Homo erectus. However, if we interpret the recent finds of Homo skeletons that were contemporary with Australopithecus as ruling out Australopithecus africanus as a direct ancestor of modern man, then the difference in brain size becomes less significant. More important than size may be comparisons indicating brain reorganization. There is some evidence that the temporoparietal association cortex, critical to language, increased in size as hominids evolved to the Homo genus. Also, the earliest Homo skull fragments reflect a larger Broca's area, important to the motor control of speech, than that in primates outside the Homo genus. Holloway's study of hominid endocasts has led him to conclude that the human form of cortex emerged much earlier than is commonly thought. Fossil skulls are reconstructed from fragments, however, and it is hazardous to claim precision about the brains that once inhabited these skulls. Another way to approach the problem is to contrast and compare the intact brains of Homo sapiens and his nonspeaking relatives. Geschwind, at the Harvard Medical School, has demonstrated that the primary receptive areas in the brains of man and apes are similar; the difference between them lies in the development in man's brain of primary association areas, especially the temporoparietal area, which conveniently lies in the midst of the auditory, visual, and motor-sensory areas (Fig. 8.10). The development of this

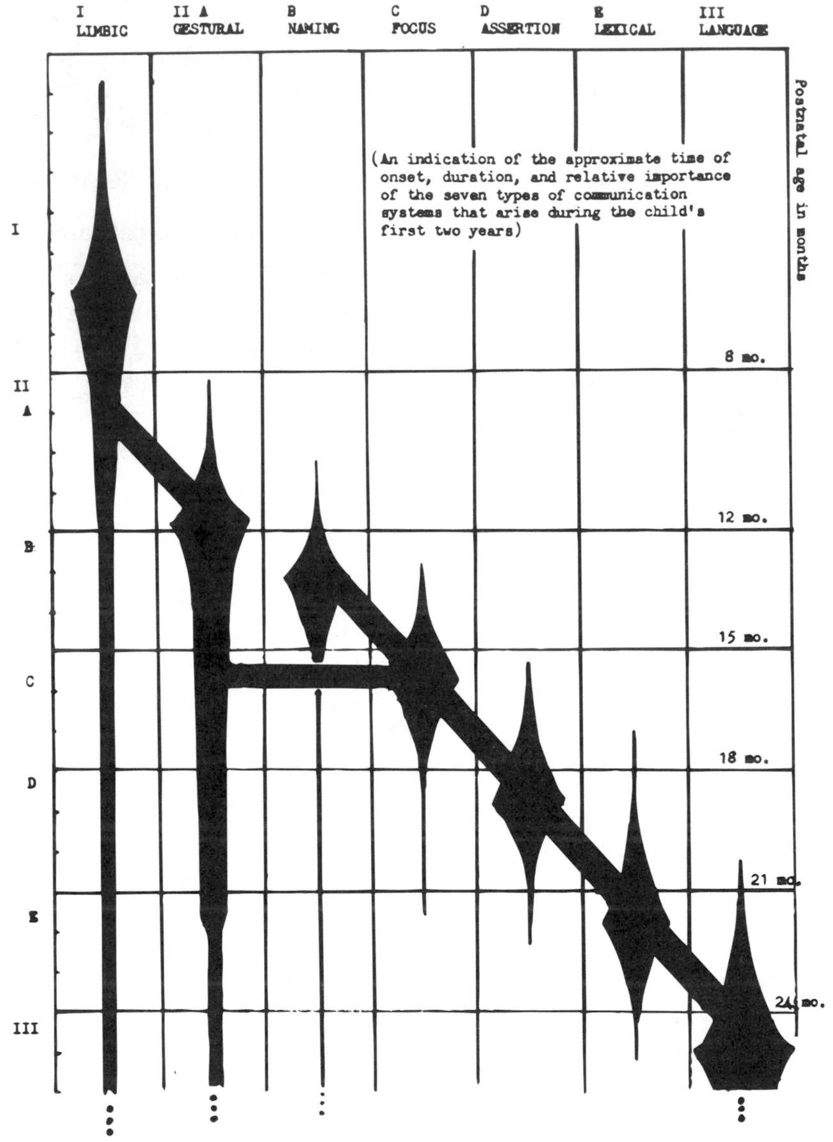

Figure 8.9 Outline of the maturational stages in the development of communication systems by the child. Starting with reflexive emotional messages governed by the limbic system, the child puts increasing emphasis upon conceptual messages through gesture, naming, focus of propositional messages into one-word sentences, two-word assertions, and lexical strings forming a telegraphic message. By 2 years, lateralized neocortical systems govern sentences that follow syntactic and morphophonological rules. (Reprinted with permission from J. T. Lamendella: *Annals of the New York Academy of Science*. 280, 1976, 408–409.)

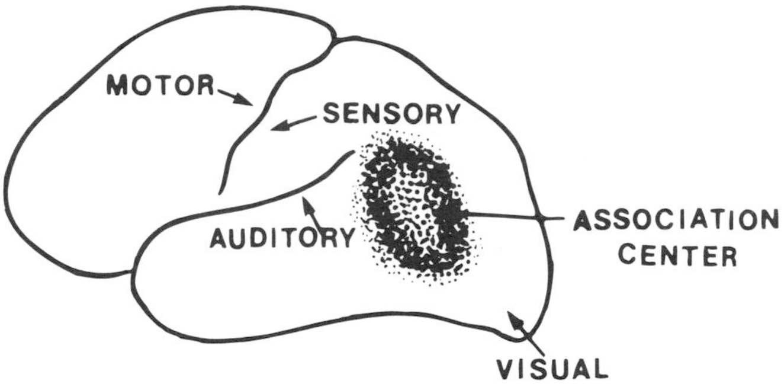

Figure 8.10 Illustration of the receptive and temporoparietal association areas in man. The latter area is well developed in Homo sapiens.

association area presumably accounts for the naming behavior in man. He sees and senses something, hears its name, and learns to produce the name himself, after connecting the visual, auditory, and motor-sensory correlates of the object to be named. Naming triggers further linguistic development, and damage to the association area in the temporoparietal juncture interferes with the ability to name and with other linguistic abilities.

Those who support the gestural origin of speech find support in the proximity of the hand and vocal representation of motor and sensory functions in the brain. As we have seen in the chapter on speech production, motor control of the hand and of the vocal tract are close together in the frontal lobe of the brain, and the same is true of the sensory representation in the parietal lobe.

Lateralization

It is interesting to consider the possible importance to language of the lateralization of brain function evident in man. Humans use one cerebral hemisphere of the brain for some functions and the other hemisphere for other functions. Language is typically dominant in the left hemisphere, although there are individual variations. There is little evidence of lateralization of brain function in mammals lower than primates. The greater apes have shown hand preferences. (It has been reported, for instance, that gorillas show a right hand preference in starting chest beating.) Most reports, however, indicate that hand preference is randomly distributed, rather than being predominantly to the right, and that it can be switched easily by training. Control of dominant hand function and of speech are not always housed in the same hemisphere in any case, since most left-handed people (right hemisphere dominance) use the left hemisphere to control speech and language processes.

Asymmetries presumed to be related to the lateralization of language have been observed in human brains. The Sylvian fissure in the left hemisphere is longer posteriorly and is lower than in the right hemisphere. Yet, this same difference in the Sylvian fissure has been observed in the orangutan brain. Thus, hemispheric specialization may be a prerequisite to language development both phylogenetically and ontologically. It has been shown by Kimura that children 3 or 4 years old indicate lateralization for speech perception when given dichotic listening tests. A dominant hemisphere for speech may be established earlier, but it is difficult to test younger children. The lateralization of speech processes, however, seems to be an adaptation that man's ancestors made to accommodate the increasingly complex linguistic code along with his other problem-solving abilities.

Vocal Tract Changes

The vocal tract has also changed during hominid evolution. The larynx has evolved from an organ adapted especially for respiration to one which, after other adaptations to such changes as erect posture, was finally uniquely suited for sound production in human speech. The supralaryngeal area has also evolved because of several factors: the improvement of vision to the extent that it surpassed olfaction as a means of gaining information about other animals, and the need to produce a wide variety of distinctive sounds. The final adaptation of the vocal tract for speech is unique to the Homo genus.

Negus, a British physiologist, was the first to systematically study the evolution of the larynx and the supra-laryngeal vocal tract. He illustrates how the simple sphincter of the lung fish, which was maximally efficient for respiration (it simply worked as a valve to open or close the access to the lungs), gradually changed during evolution to the complex arrangement of muscles and cartilage that we find in the human larynx (Fig. 8.11). The simple valve structure of the lung fish has, in contemporary humans, become elaborated and differentiated in order to control the opening, closing, and tension of the vocal folds and the shape of the glottis, creating the ability to vary fundamental frequency and other source characteristics. Researchers have noted that many of the structural characteristics of the evolved larynx have rendered it more efficient as a phonating mechanism, at the expense of efficiency for respiration. For example, the maximum glottal aperture in the human larynx is smaller in area than the trachea below it. The narrower glottis facilitates the initiation of vocal fold pulsing, but limits the volume of air that could be inspired if the glottal and tracheal areas were equal.

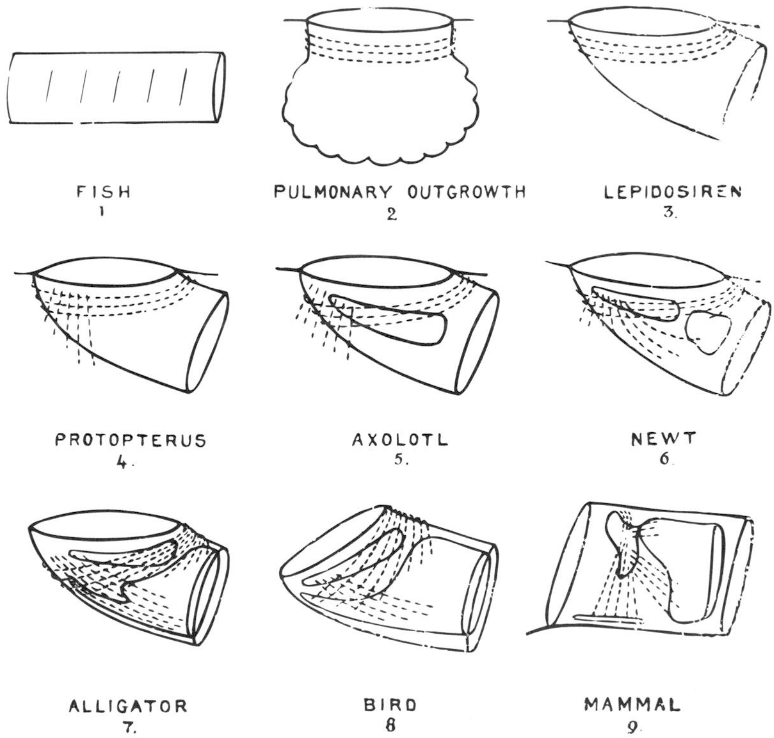

Figure 8.11 Evolution of the larynx. Starting with the gill slits in the first stage, the sphincter muscle in *Stages 2* and *3* is combined with a dilator muscle in *Stage 4,* with the appearance of cartilages in *Stages 5–8.* The mammalian larynx is characterized by a separation of cartilages and the division of the sphincteric muscle into components. (Reprinted with permission from V. E. Negus: *The Comparative Anatomy and Physiology of the Larynx,* Hafner Publishing Co. © 1962.)

In our discussion of the failure to teach chimpanzees to speak, we mentioned that the vocal tracts of primates are incapable of generating the full range of sounds found in human speech. This is because the structure of the primate vocal tract differs from that of humans in several ways. This fact is interesting in itself, but it takes on added significance when we note that many of the same structural differences also exist between adult human vocal tracts and those of human neonates, early hominids, and Neanderthal Man (according to reconstructions based on fossil evidence). Lieberman refers to the vocal tracts of apes, hominids, Neanderthals, human neonates and other mammals (e.g., dogs) as the *Standard-Plan Supralaryngeal Vocal Tract*, a practice we shall follow as we review some of the structural differences alluded to above.

First, in the Standard-Plan Supralaryngeal Vocal Tract, the tongue lies entirely within the oral cavity, with the larynx situated directly behind it. In effect, the supra-laryngeal vocal tract is an anterior-laryngeal vocal tract: There is virtually no pharyngeal cavity. Projected transfer functions of such a vocal tract indicate that it would be incapable of generating either the critical point vowels, /i/, /a/ and /u/, or the formant transitions for velar stops. Second, the high position of the larynx in the Standard-Plan vocal tract provides at least two adaptive benefits: During swallowing, the epiglottis comes into contact with the velum. This effectively separates the passageways for air and food and virtually eliminates the possibilities of asphyxiation caused by foreign objects lodging in the larynx or trachea and of aspiration of fluids into the lungs. The separation of the passageways in the Standard-Plan Supralaryngeal Vocal Tract also makes it possible for eating or drinking to occur simultaneously with respiration (Fig. 8.12). The adaptive advantage of this arrangement, especially for creatures in which olfaction rather than vision is a dominant sense, is that danger can be detected while feeding is taking place.

Adult humans, of course, do not possess this sort of Standard-Plan vocal tract (Fig. 8.13). During approximately the first year of

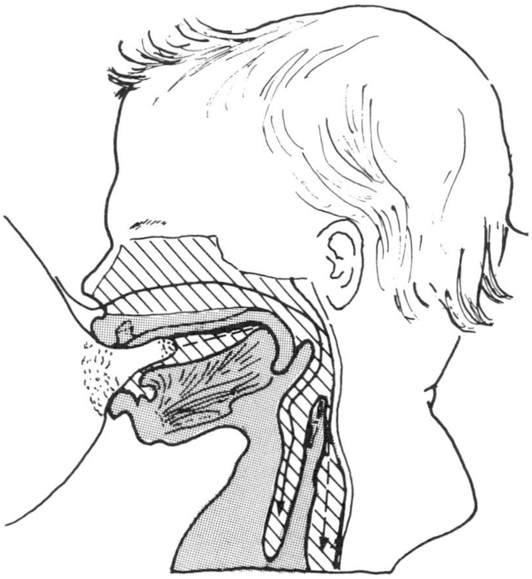

Figure 8.12 Respiratory and digestive tracts for a nursing baby. (Adapted from an original painting by F. H. Netter, M. D. in E. S. Crelin: *Clinical Symposia 28,* CIBA Pharmaceutical Co. © 1976.)

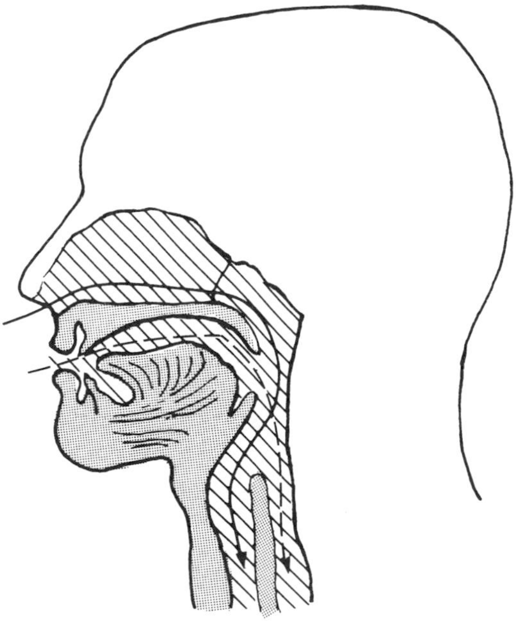

Figure 8.13 Respiratory and digestive tracts in an adult. (Adapted from an original painting by F. H. Netter, M. D. in E. S. Crelin: *Clinical Symposia. 28,* CIBA Pharmaceutical Co. © 1976.)

life, the larynx and tongue root of the neonate descend in the neck, creating a pharyngeal cavity, more or less at a right angle to the oral cavity, and permitting the generation of the point vowels and the velar formant transitions. These anatomical changes, like those within the larynx itself, enhance the ability to produce speech at the expense of other, more basic or evolutionarily primitive functions. Humans are in constant danger of choking to death on food (hence the signs explaining the Heimlich Maneuver that can be found in many restaurants) and can no longer simultaneously eat and breathe. The loss of this latter ability is of no great consequence, because vision is a more dominant sense than olfaction in humans. There is considerable debate, in fact, about whether vision came to dominate olfaction in response to the anatomical changes we have described, whether the cause and effect were just the reverse, or whether each change stimulated the other. It seems, then, that speech is not simply a function overlaid upon anatomical systems used for respiration and digestion, but that anatomical changes have taken place to tune the body especially for speech, even at some expense to the life-sustaining systems.

Let us take a closer look at some of the information we have alluded to concerning the evolutionary course of the changes in the vocal tract. Many of the data have been provided by the collaborative efforts of Crelin and Lieberman. Crelin, a specialist in neonatal anatomy and physiology, has made rubber silicone casts of the vocal tracts of human neonates, chimpanzees, and human adults and has reconstructed vocal tracts from casts of the fossil skulls of Neanderthal specimens. Vocal tract shapes were approximated by noting the angles of muscle facets in the skulls and comparing them to known vocal tracts, such as those of living apes and humans. Lieberman, a linguist with special training in the acoustics of speech, estimated the possible vocal tract configurations that each specimen might assume and computed the resulting range of formant frequencies (or resonances). Two comparisons were made. First, the actual resonant frequencies produced by chimpanzees and human neonates were compared to those that had been computed from the silicone casts of their vocal tracts. Second, the computed resonance frequencies of each of the types of vocal tracts studied (including the Neanderthal reconstruction) were compared to those actually produced by adult humans to determine how many of the acoustic patterns were held in common.

The computer simulations for human neonates and chimpanzees generated resonance patterns that corresponded well with the actual sounds made by such vocal tracts, although the calculations indicated that the chimp might be able to produce a larger variety of sounds than he actually does. Greater apes and human babies produce more neutral vocal sounds such as /e/ or /æ/, usually quite nasal, and are incapable, as we have mentioned, of the vocal tract adjustments necessary to produce the point vowels /i/, /a/, or /u/, or the formant transitions associated with velar sounds.

Figure 8.14 pictures the casts of a newborn baby, an adult chimpanzee, a reconstruction from a Neanderthal fossil (La Chapelle-aux-Saints), and an adult human. Figure 8.15 shows the vocal tract areas of the same specimens, with landmarks indicated. The casts are equated in size in these drawings. Notice how

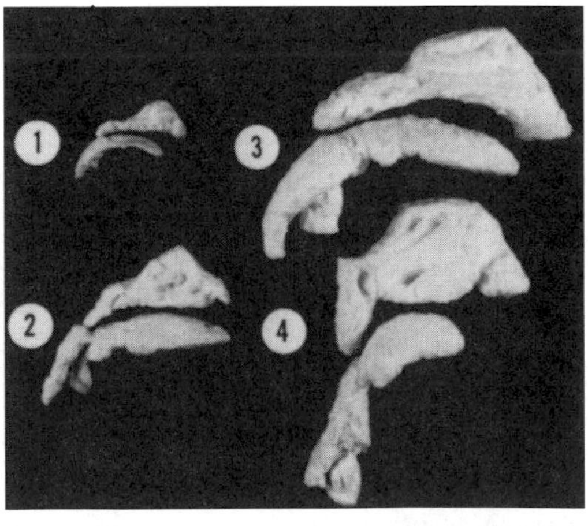

Figure 8.14 Casts of the nasal, oral, pharyngeal, and laryngeal cavities of (*1*) newborn modern man, (*2*) adult chimpanzee, (*3*) Neanderthal man, and (*4*) adult modern man. (Reprinted with permission from P. Lieberman, E. S. Crelin, and D. H. Klatt: *American Anthropologist.* 74, 1972.)

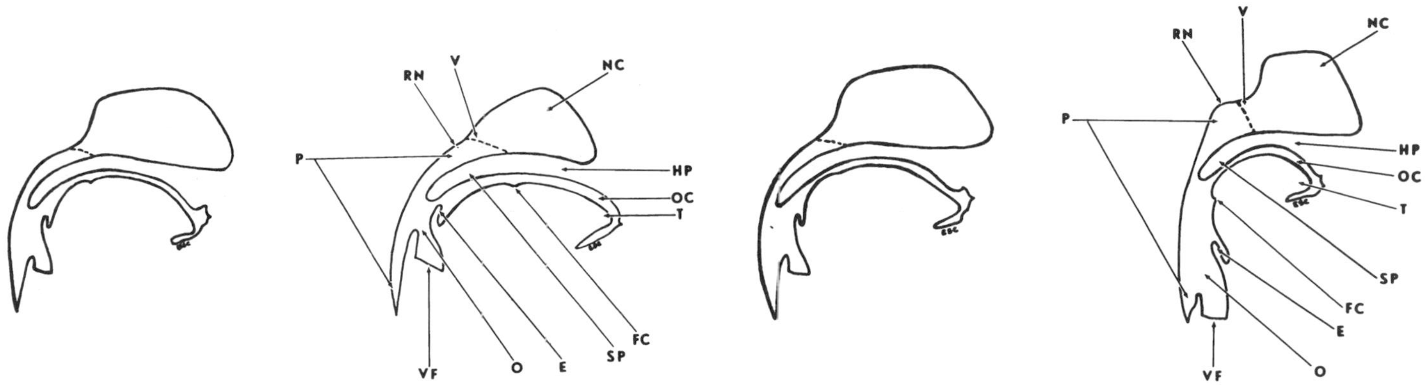

Figure 8.15 Diagrams of the air passages of a newborn human, adult chimpanzee, Neanderthal man, and adult human. Anatomical landmarks noted on the diagram of the chimpanzee and adult man are: *P*, pharynx; *RN*, roof of nasopharynx; *V*, vomer bone; *NC*, nasal cavity; *HP*, hard palate; *OC*, oral cavity; *T*, tongue; *FC*, foramen cecum; *SP*, soft palate; *E*, epiglottis; *O*, opening of larynx into pharynx; and *VF*, level of vocal folds. (Reprinted with permission from P. Lieberman, E. S. Crelin, and D. H. Klatt: *American Anthropologist* 74, 1972, 292.)

close the epiglottis is to the soft palate in the baby, the chimp, and the Neanderthal vocal tracts. Note, too, that the foramen cecum of the tongue (the point where the large papillae begin) has descended into the pharynx of the adult human, producing a humped tongue capable of three-directional movement, housed partly in the oral cavity, partly in the pharyngeal cavity, in contrast to the flat, relatively more massive tongue that occupies the oral cavity of the other specimens. Finally, notice the long pharynx in the adult human, which along with the oral cavity, produces the two-chamber resonator distinctive in human adults.

The results of the computer simulations indicate that the vocal tracts of some of the fossil forms, Australopithecus and the classic Neanderthal, like those of modern chimps and babies, could have produced only a limited repertoire of speech sounds. Other fossils, however, appear to have possessed vocal tracts quite similar to those of Homo sapiens. For example, Steinheim man, a fossil found in Germany, dating to about 250,000 years ago, had the necessary vocal tract size and shape and prerequisite brain capacity to generate a full inventory of speech sounds as the carrier for a fully developed linguistic code.

It is too bad that the very early Homo fossils discovered by Leakey and by Johanson and Taieb have been so fragmentary. More complete fossils might have provided evidence that the cranial vaults, teeth, and facial bones resembled those of humans more than those of contemporary hominids or the later Neanderthal. Such evidence would suggest that these fossils possessed vocal tracts adequate for producing speech more than 2 million years ago.

A LIKELY TALE

Is it possible to reconstruct the evolution of speech and language? We have enough evidence to attempt a general outline—though without any great degree of detail. Some of that evidence, as we have seen, concerns changes in social structure, some is drawn from comparative studies of the behavior of apes, birds, and humans, both neonates and adult, and some is based on studies of the anatomy and physiology of the brain and vocal tract. If we synthesize the available data, we can fashion a likely tale about how speech and language may have originated and evolved.

Stage I: Sound = Meaning

The tale begins millions of years ago, when families of apemen lived in the trees of the jungles of Africa, hunting for food in small groups or tribes. They communicated by using a limited number of visual signals (body stances, gestures, facial expressions) and an even smaller number of auditory signals (cries, grunts, comfort sounds). Like many animals living today, the apemen used sound and gesture in the same way. There was a simple relationship between a sound or a gesture and its meaning. A single sound or gesture was needed for each message that could be sent: one for "food here," another for "mating time," yet another to signify danger or hate or any other message in their inventory. Reliance on a partly gestural mode of communication kept members of hunting or food-gathering parties close together. Eventually, some of the groups left the forest to search for food in the more open lands of the savanna (Fig. 8.16). The change in habitat from a forest with dense vegetation to wide open terrain caused many changes in the social structure, individual habits, and even the morphology of the apemen. It certainly must have affected the communication system. Hunting and food gathering necessitated the spreading apart of the group members, to the point where gestural communication was not always practicable. Vocal signals became more functional than visual ones, and the repertoire of vocal signals probably expanded to meet the demands of the new habitat.

The need to see further in the open spaces of the savanna promoted the development of erect posture and binocular vision. Standing erect, in turn, freed the apemen's hands to perform tasks such as picking berries and making tools. As they became more manually adept,

Figure 8.16 A water hole; early man lived on such savannas. (Photograph courtesy of Stuart A. Altmann, University of Chicago.)

they found it efficient to use one hand to grasp and steady an object of interest and the other hand to manipulate it. As a result of the differentiation of manual function, one hand developed the large muscles needed to hold down a branch while the fingers of the other hand developed the more precise control over the smaller digital muscles needed to pick the berries. When later generations, who were hunters, began to fashion simple tools out of stone, they continued to use one hand to hold the stone and the other hand to chisel it. These tool-making apemen developed a hand use preference, unlike the tree-swinging apes who continued to use their hands interchangeably.

Because most apemen came to use their right hands for operations that required precise movements, the contralateral neural connections to the left cerebral hemisphere adapted to these delicate maneuvers. Since the activities demanded care, concentration, and problem-solving abilities, it was efficient for the left cerebral hemisphere to become dominant for the analytical processes associated with them. The right cerebral hemisphere, by contrast, became dominant for processes demanding synthesis, such as the ability to form gestalt perceptions, or indeed to perceive any spatial-visual stimuli. Once the brain function of the apemen had become lateralized to a certain degree, many of their abilities improved rapidly. As hand use was frequently accompanied by meaningful vocalizations and noises, the sounds were gradually incorporated into the established left hemisphere network of associations that interrelated thought, vision, motor behavior, and sound.

Stage II: Sound Combinations = Meaning

Thus it was, perhaps 3 million years ago, that early man stood fairly erect and became a tool user and an incipient speaker. He found that it would be useful to name things because doing so increased the potential for cooperation within the group, and increased cooperation meant increased productivity in obtaining and sharing food. Naming would have been a first step toward making plans and dividing labor efficiently among group members. His ability to use speech and language was restricted, however, by two factors: the anatomy of his vocal tract and his lack of a linguistic code. At first, all he could do was make a limited number of sounds that carried meaning to his listeners. Each sound always meant the same thing and was probably selected because it was highly contrastive with the other sounds in the group's inventory of auditory signals. Thus, confusion was minimized. The number of distinct sounds he could produce was limited because of the anatomical configuration of his vocal tract. He lacked a pharyngeal cavity because of the high position of his larynx directly behind his tongue. The tongue, in turn, lacked the mobility of modern man's because it could move only within the oral cavity. He could make a limited number of vowels, consonants and orally generated noises, including nasal sounds, transient noise bursts, grunts, hissing sounds, and clicks. But the number of different messages he could send was limited to the number of sounds he could produce.

Early man may have responded to the need to increase his inventory of messages by combining sounds. The discovery of combining different sounds to produce a large number of new messages was the first step in the development of a linguistic code. As the code developed, so did the cognitive mechanisms with which to use it.

As emerging man adopted an erect posture, his anatomy adapted to the pull of gravity upon the structures of his body. His larynx descended into his elongating neck, creating a pharyngeal cavity. The oral cavity, combined with the pharynx, created a longer resonating tube, capable of generating a larger number of distinct sounds. The greater number of possible tongue positions and movements in the enlarged vocal tract stimulated the development of fine motor controls over the lingual musculature. As speech emerged, early man became increasingly able to control the shape, position, and movement of his more mobile tongue with greater and greater precision.

Stage III: Structured Sound Combinations = Meaning

As man began to think more abstractly, he began to use language both to express and to refine thought. The evolution of speech and language production took another leap forward when man realized that not only would changing the order of sounds in sound combinations yield a larger number of possible utterances (/am/ and /ma/), but that changing the order of the combinations themselves could be used to signal even more differences in meaning. The development of a syntax, or set of rules for ordering morphemes, was a remarkable display of inventiveness in finding many ways to signal changes in meaning.

We can see the long-term results of this inventiveness in modern languages. Some, like German or Russian, use inflections (word endings) to indicate the function (e.g., subject versus object) of words in sentences. Inflected languages seem to be of greater antiquity than distributive languages, such as English and Spanish, where word order signals grammatical function. In the sentence "Sam hit Tom," we know that Sam did the hitting and that Tom got hit because of the order of the words. The study of the evolution of specific languages and language families suggests that inflected languages, such as Latin, often develop into distributive languages, such as Italian, French, and Spanish, but not the other way around.

We have no way of knowing, of course, what the syntax of the earliest languages might have been like. What seems clear, however, is that whatever form the syntax took, it was rule-governed. It is much more efficient to have rules for the placement of inflections or the ordering of words so that one need not learn each instance individually. Knowing that the inversion of subject and verb in English will change a statement into a question enables a speaker to create a virtually uncountable number of interrogatives. A child who has heard several pairs of sentences of the types "Tom is going." and "Is Tom going?" will discover the rule that converts statements into questions and will be able to create questions that he has never heard.

Humans discovered additional ways to change meaning by adding, deleting, or changing sounds that represent morphemes (run/ran, cat/cats), by adding syllables that represent morphemes (conTENT, disconTENT, disconTENTed, disconTENTedly), by varying stress placement (CONtract, "a document"/conTRACT, "agree"), or by varying intonation (She left?/She left.). Thus, the third stage in the development of speech and language was a structure for linguistic expression. Anyone who knew the structural rules of a given language along with its lexicon, or store of words, could, like the child who learns how to convert a statement to a question, create sentences he had never heard or learned. Because language is rule-governed behavior, and because of the recursive and conjunctive nature of some of the rules, the number of possible sentences in any particular language is infinite. It is more than likely that as the structure of language increased in complexity, so too did the cognitive mechanism supporting it.

As different tribes of early humans migrated in different directions, the sounds, sound combinations, words, and syntax of their language began to differ. Dialects emerged and, when the differences between dialects grew sufficiently large, separate, mutually unintelligible languages existed where once there had been a single language. A language might preserve a fair measure of the rules, sounds, lexicon, or vocabulary of its parent language (e.g., Old High German and modern German), or it might differ significantly from the parent language with regard to one feature or another, as modern English does from Anglo-Saxon with regard to syntax. The sound systems of related languages, however, often retain their similarities. Speakers appear to be far more resistant to adding items to, or deleting them from, phonemic inventories than to altering vocabulary or syntax. Indeed, there is a fair amount of similarity among the sound systems of unrelated languages, mainly because of the anatomical constraints and similarities of the human body.

Despite the obvious differences among the languages of the world, there are some abstract and highly significant underlying similarities. These include, at least, use of speech as the primary mode of communication in almost all languages, and the fact that all language behavior is rule-governed. The evolutionary path taken by speech and language, once it is more fully understood, may provide us with a more complete explanation for the existence of these similarities and may uncover others.

CONCLUSION

There are two questions that pervade any discussion of the evolution of human language: (1) How can we explain the brevity of the time span in which it is presumed to have occurred, and (2) to what extent did genetics and learning each contribute to its occurrence? An explanation for the "sudden" explosion of language evolution that is presumed to have taken place is that, like the child who moves quickly from simple naming at 12 months to using complex syntax by 24 months, early man's linguistic skills evolved rapidly as soon as the process was underway.

Another explanation may be that it was not an explosive development, but rather that it started much earlier than we have supposed, perhaps over 2 million years earlier, and that it occurred gradually. This idea is related to the question of whether man learns the language of his community entirely through his senses, as Locke suggested, or if, as Descartes maintained, the fundamental ability to use language is based on man's innate competence as a reasoning creature. Evolving man's ability to reason must have improved for him to have kept pace with the increasing complexity of the linguistic code, yet each new member of the language community had to learn the particulars of the code anew. Natural selection has favored our species, in part because of our ability to learn speech and language at an early stage of development. Thus, we might argue, what is innate is the ability to learn language and to speak, and what is learned is a particular language and the methods of conveying it by speaking. Descartes and Locke would probably agree with this distinction, as would Skinner and Chomsky; the disagreement would be about whether to place the primary emphasis on innate abilities or on learning.

And so we end this book on speech with a discussion of the beginnings of speech, and rightly so. The mind must move from the known to the unknown. Only through some knowledge of language systems, of the production of speech, and of speech perception can one hope to reconstruct the evolution of our language. As we discover more about the ways in which humans produce and perceive linguistic messages, we will be better able to flesh out our admittedly incomplete and overgeneralized theories.

The unanswered questions are numerous and provocative. How closely does the development of speech and language in a child mirror the evolutionary development of speech and language? To what degree are infants tuned to perceive the auditory distinctions important in speech? How do the processes of speech perception and speech production interact during language learning? How does the brain control the parallel and overlapping motor commands during speech production? Are feedback mechanisms necessary and under what circumstances? Answering these and other questions is the object of speech science, a discipline at one of the most important and challenging frontiers of human inquiry.

REFERENCES

General

Dimond, S. J, and Blizard, D. A. (Eds.), Evolution and Lateralization of the Brain. *Ann. N. Y. Acad, Sci. 299,* 1977.

Harnad, S. R., Steklis, H. D., and Lancaster, J. (Eds.), Origins and Evolution of Language and Speech. *Ann. N. Y. Acad. Sci. 280,* 1976.

Lenneberg, E. H., *The Biological Foundations of Language*. New York: John Wiley and & Sons, 1967.

Negus, V. E., *The Comparative Anatomy and Physiology of the Larynx*. New York: Hafner, 1962. This book is a rewritten version of *The Mechanism of the Larynx,* which was published in 1928 in London by Heineman Medical Books, Ltd.

Pfeiffer, J. E., *The Emergence of Man*, 2nd Ed., New York: Harper & Row, 1972.

Stam, J. H., *Inquiries into the Origin of Language: The Fate of a Question*. New York: Harper & Row, 1976.

A Sampling of Thoughts on the Origin and Evolution of Language and Speech

Geschwind, N., and Galaburda. A., Cerebral Localization, Biological Mechanisms, Associations and Pathology. I-III: A Hypothesis and Program for Research. *Archives of Neurology 42,* 1985, 428–459, 521–552, 634–654.

Hewes, G. W., Primate Communications and the Gestural Origin of Language. *Curr. Anthropol. 14,* 1973, 5–12.

Hockett, C. F., The Origin of Speech. *Sci. Am. 203,* 1960, 88–96.

Hockett, C. F., and Ascher, R., The Human Revolution. *Curr. Anthropol. 5,* 1964, 135–168.

Lamendella, J. T., Relations between the Ontogeny and Phylogeny of Language: A Neo-recapitulationist View. *Ann. N. Y. Acad. Sci. 280,* 1976, 396–412.

Lieberman, P., *The Biology and Evolution of Language*. Cambridge, MA: Harvard University Press, 1984.

Lieberman, P., *On the Origins of Language: An Introduction to The Evolution of Human Speech*. Series in Physical Anthropology. New York: Macmillan, 1975.

Lieberman, P., Crelin, E. S., and Klatt, D. H., Phonetic Ability and Related Anatomy of the Newborn and Adult Human, Neanderthal Man, and the Chimpanzee. *Am. Anthropol. 74,* 1972, 287–307.

Mattingly, I. G., Speech Cues and Sign Stimuli. *Am. Sci. 60,* 1972, 327–337.

Swadesh, M. *The Origin and Diversification of Language.* J. Sherzer (Ed.), Chicago: Aldine, Atherton, 1971.

Fossil Hominids

Day, M. H., Leakey, R. E. F., Walker, A. C., and Wood, B. A., New Hominids from East Rudolf, Kenya, I. *Am. J. Phys. Anthropol. 42,* 1975, 461–476.

Holloway, R. L., The Casts of Fossil Hominid Brains. *Sci. Am. 231,* 1974, 106–115.

Johanson, D. C., Ethiopia Yields First "Family" of Early Man. *Natl. Geogr. Mag. 150,* 1976, 791–811.

Leakey, R. E. F., Evidence for an Advanced Plio-Pleistocene Hominid from East Rudolf, Kenya. *Nature 242,* 1973, 447–450.

Living Primates and Birds

Fouts, R., Capacities for Language in Great Apes. In *Society and Psychology of Primates*. R. H. Tuttle (Ed.) Hillsdale, NJ: Erlbaum, 1975, pp. 371–390.

Gardner. R. A., and Gardner. B. T., Teaching Sign Language to a Chimpanzee. *Science 165,* 1969, 664–672.

Gardner, R. A., and Gardner, B. T., Comparative Psychology and Language Acquisition. In *Psychology: The State of the Art*. K. Salzinger and F. L. Denmark (Eds.) *Ann. N. Y. Acad. Sci. 309*, 1978, 37–76.

Hayes, K. J. and Hayes, C., The Intellectual Development of a Home-raised Chimpanzee. *Proceedings of the American Philosophical Society 95*, 1951, 105–109.

Marler. P., A Comparative Approach to Vocal Development: Song Learning in the White-crowned Sparrow. *J. Comp. Physiol. Psychol. 71*, 1970, 1–25.

Marler, P., On the Origin of Speech from Animal Sounds. In *The Role of Speech in Language*. J. F. Kavanagh, and J. E. Cutting, (Eds.) Cambridge, Mass.: M. I. T. Press, 1975. pp. 11–37.

Myers, R. E., Comparative Neurology of Vocalization and Speech: Proof of a Dichotomy. In *Ann. N. Y. Acad. Sci. 280*, 1976, pp. 745–757.

Patterson, F., and Linden, E., *The Education of Koko*. New York: Holt, Rinehart, and Winston, 1981.

Premack, D., Language in Chimpanzee? *Science 172*, 1971, 808–822.

Rumbaugh, D. M., Gill, T. V., and Van Glasersfeld, E. C., Reading and Sentence Completion by a Chimpanzee (Pan). *Science 182*, 1973, 731–733.

Sebeok, T. A., and Rosenthal, R. (Eds.) *The Clever Hans Phenomenon: Communication with Horses, Whales, Apes and People. Ann. N. Y. Acad. Sci, 364,* 1981.

Terrace, H., *Nim*. New York: Washington Square Press, 1979.

Terrace, H., Petitto, L. A., Sanders, R. J., and Bever, T. Can an Ape Create a Sentence? *Science 206*, 1979, 891–902.

Van Lawick-Goodall, J., *In the Shadow of Man*. Boston: Houghton Mifflin, 1971.

Appendix 1
The Phonetic Alphabet for American English

Based upon the International Phonetic Alphabet

The Sounds of American English*

Vowel sounds	Key words
i	each, free, keep
ɪ	it, bin
e	ate, made, they
ɛ	end, then, there
æ	act, man
a	ask, half, past
ɑ	alms, father
ɒ	hot, odd, dog, cross
ɔ	awl, torn
o	obey, note, go
U	good, foot
u	ooze, too
ə	alone, among
ɚ	father, singer
ʌ	up, come
ɜ, ɝ	urn, third
s	see, yes
z	zoo, as

Consonant combinations (affricates)	
tʃ	chew, each
dʒ	gem, hedge

Vowel combinations (diphthongs)	Key Words
eɪ	aid, may
aɪ	aisle, sigh
ɔɪ	oil, joy
au	owl, cow
ou	own, go

Consonant sounds	Key words
p	pie, ape
b	be, web
m	me, am
w	we, woe
ʍ	why, when
f	free, if
v	vine, have
θ	thin, faith
ð	then, clothe
t	ten, it
d	den, had
n	no, one
l	live, frill
r	red, arrow
ʃ	show, ash
ʒ	measure, azure
j	you, yes
ç	huge, human
k	key, ache
g	go, big
ŋ	sing, long
h	he, how

* Adapted from A. J. Bronstein: *The Pronunciation of American English*. New York: Appleton-Century-Crofts, Inc., 1960, pp. 28–30.

Appendix 2

Cranial Nerves Important for Speech and Hearing

I Olfactory	Nose	
II Optic	Eye	
III Oculomotor	Eye	
IV Trochlear	Eye	
*V Trigeminal	Face	Motor to jaw muscles and to tensor palatini muscle. Sensory from anterior ⅔ of tongue.
VI Abducent	Eye	
*VII Facial	Face	Motor to lip muscles.
*VIII Auditory	Ear	Sensory from cochlea with some motor fibers.
*IX Glossopharyngeal	Pharynx	Motor to pharynx. Sensory from back of tongue.
*X Vagus	Larynx	Motor to laryngeal muscles.
*XI Accessory	Soft palate	Motor to levator palatini.
*XII Hypoglossal	Tongue	Motor to tongue muscles.

* Only functions related to speech and hearing are listed.

Spinal Nerves Important for Speech

*C_1–C_8	Cervical	Neck	C_3–C_5 phrenic nerve to diaphragm.
*T_1–T_{12}	Thoracic	Chest	T_1–T_{11} to intercostal muscles. T_7–T_{12} to abdominal muscles.

* Only functions related to speech are listed. The dorsal roots (emerging from the back of the spine) are sensory. The ventral roots (emerging from the front of the spine) are motor.

Glossary

An informal reminder of the meaning of terms

Compiled by Jolie Bookspan

ABX Test–Procedure for testing discrimination by requiring the listener to indicate whether the third stimulus presented sounds more like the first or the second.

Abduct–[L. "ab"–away, off.] To move away from the mid-sagittal axis of the body or one of its parts.

Abscissa–The x coordinate of a point; its distance from the y axis measured parallel to the x axis (horizontal axis).

Absolute Threshold of Audibility–Magnitude of a sound detected by a listener 50% of the time.

Acceleration–The time rate of change of velocity.

Acoustic reflex–A bilateral reflex of the middle ear in response to loud sounds that alters middle ear impedance.

Acoustic Resonator–Air-filled structures designed to vibrate at particular frequencies.

Acoustics–[Gk. "akoustikos"–hearing.] The study of sound.

Action Potential–An electrical discharge produced by muscle activity.

Action Theory–A theory put forth by Fowler and Turvey that applies an ecological view of motor coordination to speech production and perception.

Adaptation Studies–Tests of speech identification and discrimination after the listener has been repeatedly exposed to a particular stimulus.

Adduct–[L. "ad"–toward, to.] To move toward the mid-sagittal plane of the body or one of its parts.

Afferent–[L. "ferre"–to bear.] Bringing to or into; in the nervous system, neurons conducting from the periphery toward the central nervous system (sensory nerves/neurons).

Affricate–A sound that combines a stop closure with a fricative release.

All-or-None Principle–When a single nerve is stimulated at or above threshold, it will fire at an amplitude independent of the intensity of the stimulus.

Allophone–One member of the family of sounds functioning as a phoneme; [p^h] is an allophone of the phoneme /p/.

Alpha (α) Motoneurons–Large efferent nerve fibers (9–16 μ in diameter) that innervate the skeletal muscles.

Alveolar Process–The inferior border of the maxillary bone or the superior border of the mandible, which contains sockets holding the teeth.

Amplitude–(Of a wave.) The absolute value of the maximum displacement from a zero value during one period of an oscillation.

Amplitude Spectrum–(Pl. spectra.) A graphic representation of a vibratory event in which the ordinate (the vertical axis) represents the amplitude of the signal while the abscissa (the horizontal axis) represents the component frequencies.

Analog-to-Digital Converter–Electronic device that transforms continuous signals into signals with discrete values.

Analysis-by-Synthesis Theory–A theory put forth by K. N. Stevens that speech analysis or perception involves some form of rudimentary reconstruction or synthesis of the acoustic signal.

Anterior Belly of the Digastric Muscle–Running from the mandible to the hyoid, this paired muscle acts to aid in jaw opening.

Anterior Faucial Pillars–(Also called the glossopalatine arch.) Arch-like downward continuations of the soft palate containing the glossopalatine muscles.

Antiresonance–A filtering effect of the vocal tract characterized by loss of acoustic energy in a particular frequency region.

Aperiodic–Pertaining to vibrations with irregular periods. A waveform with no repetitive pattern.

Aphasia–[Gk. "a"–not + "phanai"–to speak.] A partial or total loss of the ability to use or understand language following damage to the brain.

Apraxia–Difficulty in the voluntary coordination of muscles that function normally for less voluntary acts.

Articulation–Movements of the vocal tract to produce speech sounds.

Arytenoid–[Gk. ladle-shaped.] Triangular-shaped cartilages to which the vocal folds attach.

Aspirate–A sound with frication produced at the glottis, for example, /h/.

Assimilation–[L. "similis"–like, to become like.] A change in the articulation of a speech sound that makes it more similar to the articulation of a neighboring sound.

Athetosis–[Gk. "athetos"–without position or place.] A condition in which there is a constant succession of slow, writhing, involuntary motions of different parts of the body.

Audition–Hearing.

Auditory Agnosia–["a"–not + Gk. "gnosis"–knowledge.] Central auditory imperception of sound.

Auditory Nerve–VIIIth cranial nerve. A sensory nerve with two branches: the vestibular, which carries information about bodily position, and the cochlear, which carries auditory information; also called the vestibulocochlear nerve and the acoustic nerve, respectively.

Auricle–[L. "auris"–ear.] The visible cartilage of the outer ear; also called the pinna.

Autism–[Gk. "autos"–self.] A syndrome characterized by difficulty in forming interpersonal relationships and in developing language.

Autistic Theory–Mowrer's theory that children are internally rewarded for subvocal rehearsal of new words.

Axon–[Gk. "axon"–axis.] The part of a neuron that carries impulses away from the cell body.

Babbling Stage–The pre-linguistic period during which infants produce sounds with no semantic reference.

Basal Ganglia–[Gk. "ganglion"–knot.] A collection of several gray masses embedded in the white matter of each cerebral hemisphere (consisting of the corpus striatum, the claustrum, and the amygdaloid nucleus).

Basilar Membrane–Thin membrane forming the base of the Organ of Corti that vibrates in response to different frequencies of sound and stimulates individual sensory hair cells in the Organ of Corti.

Bernoulli Effect–The pressure drop caused by the increased velocity of a gas or liquid through a constricted passage.

Body Plethysmograph–An instrument in the form of a sealed box used to measure air displacement produced by respiratory movements.

Brainstem–The midbrain, pons, and medulla oblongata.

Buccal Cavity–[L. "bucca"–cheek, mouth.] The air space between the teeth and the cheeks.

CNS–See Central Nervous System.

CVA–See Cerebral Vascular Accident.

Carotid Artery–[Gk. "karro"–sleep or stupor.] Principle artery of the neck supplying blood to the brain.

Categorical Perception–The ability to discriminate (speech) stimuli only as well as one can label them.

Catheter–A slender tube inserted into a body passage or cavity.

Central Nervous System–(CNS) The portion of the nervous system consisting of the brain and spinal cord.

Central Tendency–A value chosen as typical of a collection of measures.

Cerebellum–[L. diminutive of cerebrum.] A main division of the brain situated behind the cerebrum and above the pons; its function is to coordinate movement.

Cerebral Hemispheres–The two halves of the cerebrum; the main portion of the brain.

Cerebral Palsy–A name given to a group of disorders characterized by paralysis or muscular incoordination caused by intracranial lesion at or near the time of birth.

Cerebral Vascular Accident–(CVA; stroke.) A clot or rupture of the blood vessels of the brain resulting in damage to the nervous system.

Cerumen–[L. "cere"–wax.] Ear wax.

Cervical Nerve–[L. "cervix"–neck.] One of eight pairs of spinal nerves that arise from the segments of the spinal cord in the neck region.

Cilia–Hair-like processes (found in the external auditory meatus and in the cochlea, as well as in other parts of the body).

Cinefluorography–Motion pictures of X-ray images.

Clavicle(s)–[L. "clavicula"–bolt.] The collar bone(s).

Cleft Palate–Congenital fissure in the roof of the mouth (the palate).

Closed Loop System–A system operating under feedback control.

Coarticulation–A temporal overlap of articulatory movements for different phones.

Cochlea–The snail-shaped cavity of the inner ear that contains the sense organs for hearing.

Cochlear Duct–The membranous labyrinth of the cochlea that contains the Organ of Corti; also called cochlear partition and scala media.

Cognate–(Voice.) A pair of sounds, identical in place and manner of articulation, which differ only in the presence or absence of phonation.

Collective Monologue–Several people speaking monologues as if alone, but taking turns, as if in conversation.

Communication–A giving, or giving and receiving of information.

Complex Tone–Sound having more than one sine wave component.

Compression–The reduction in volume and increase of pressure of a medium.

Conditioned Response–(CR) In classical conditioning, a response that comes to be elicited by a previously neutral stimulus; in Pavlov's experiment, the salivation that came to be elicited by the bell.

Conditioned Stimulus–(CS) In classical conditioning, a previously neutral stimulus that comes to elicit a response; in Pavlov's experiment, the bell that came to elicit salivation.

Contact Ulcers–Points of erosion occurring in the cartilaginous portions of the vocal folds apparently caused by forceful adduction.

Continuant–A speech sound that can be sustained while retaining its acoustic characteristics.

Control–A group in an experiment that is the standard of comparison to other groups in the experiment; often the control group is not subjected to the independent variable (e.g., the clinical treatment) that the experimental group receives.

Conus Elasticus–Membrane that continues the respiratory passageway upward from the cricoid cartilage to the vocal ligament that bounds the glottis.

Cortex–[L. "cortex"–bark.] The outer or superficial part of an organ, as the outer layer of gray matter of the cerebrum.

Costal Pleura–(Also called Parietal Pleura.) The membrane lining the walls of the thoracic cavity.

Cranial Nerves–The 12 pairs of nerves that emerge from the base of the brain. (See Appendix 2 for listing.)

Creaky Voice–See Vocal Fry.

Cricoid–[Gk. "krikos"–ring + "oid"–like.] The cartilage of the larynx that resembles a seal ring.

Cricothyroid Muscle–Intrinsic muscle of the larynx that tenses the vocal folds.

Critical Period–(For learning speech.) The period of life during which perception and production of a first language normally develop. It is believed that after this period certain aspects of language learning are difficult or impossible.

Cybernetics–[Gk. "kybernetikos"–a pilot, to steer.] The study of self-regulatory systems.

DAF–See Delayed Auditory Feedback.

Damping–The decrease in the amplitude of vibration over time.

Decibel–Unit of intensity; a ratio between the measured sound and a reference sound.

Declination–The decrease in fundamental frequency across a breath group or phrase.

Delayed Auditory Feedback–(DAF) A delay in hearing one's own speech, produced artificially.

Dendrite–[Gk. "dendron"–a tree.] The branching process that conducts a nerve impulse to the cell body.

Dependent Variable–The variable in an experiment that is observed and that changes as a result of manipulating the independent variable.

Developmental Aphasia–Abnormal acquisition of speech and language in children caused by central nervous system impairment.

Diaphragm–The muscular and tendinous partition that separates the abdominal and thoracic cavities; a respiratory muscle.

Digastric Muscle–See Anterior Belly of the Digastric Muscle.

Diphthong–Phonetically, a vowel of changing quality; linguistically, a combination of two vowel sounds within a single syllable, interpreted as a single speech sound (phoneme).

Discrimination Test–Type of test where stimuli are presented in ordered groups. The listener determines similarities and differences among the stimuli. (See ABX Test).

Dyne–A unit of force; the force required to accelerate during 1 second a 1-gram mass to a velocity of 1 cm per second.

Dysarthria–A disorder of articulation caused by the impairment of parts of the nervous system that control the muscles of articulation.

Dyslexia–Difficulty in learning to read.

Echolalia–Automatic repetition of what is said by another.

Efferent–[L. "ex"–out + "ferre"–to bear.] Conducting from a central region to a peripheral region; refers to neurons and nerves that convey impulses from the central nervous system to the periphery (motor neurons/nerves).

Egocentric Speech–Talking aloud to oneself. (See monologue and collective monologue.)

Elaborated Code–Bernstein's term for the speech of those who do not assume that the listener shares the socio-semantic context of the message; explicit. (See Restricted Code.)

Elasticity–The force that causes a deformed structure to resume its original shape.

Elastic Recoil–Return of a medium to its resting state because of its structural properties.

Electroglottograph–An instrument used to measure impedance across the vocal folds. (See Laryngograph.)

Electromyography (EMG)–Recording the electrical potential accompanying muscle contraction by inserting an electrode into the fibers of a muscle or by applying an electrode to the surface of the skin.

Empiricist–One who bases conclusions on experiment or observation rather than on reason alone; one who believes that experience is the primary source of human knowledge.

Encoded–(V., to encode.) Transformed in such a way that the original elements are no longer discrete or recognizable.

Endolymph–The fluid in the membranous labyrinth of the inner ear.

Epiglottis–[Gk. "epi"–on + "glottis"–tongue.] A leaf-shaped flap of cartilage that closes the opening to the trachea preventing food and liquids from entering.

Esophagus–[Gk. "eso"–within + "phagus"–food.] The hollow muscular tube extending from the pharynx to the stomach.

Eustachian Tube–[From Bartolommeo Eustachio, 16th century anatomist.] Narrow channel connecting the middle ear and the nasopharynx. The open tube allows the pressure on opposite sides of the eardrum to be equalized.

Experimental–(Condition.) The application of an independent variable in order to observe its effects on behavior.

External Auditory Meatus–Canal leading from the eardrum to the auricle; part of the outer ear.

External Feedback–A system's information about the consequences of its own performance; tactile and auditory feedback of speech. (See Internal Feedback and Response Feedback.)

External Intercostal Muscles–Muscles connecting the ribs and elevating them during inspiration.

External Obliques–Muscles of the abdomen coursing downward and forward in the lateral walls.

Feature Detector–A neural mechanism specialized to respond to a particular acoustic feature in the speech signal.

Features–Aspects of speech sounds that distinguish one from another.

Feedback–Information about performance that is returned to control a system; negative feedback conveys error information, while positive feedback conveys the information that performance is as programmed.

Fiberoptic Endoscope–A flexible and coherent bundle of optical fibers used for direct visual examination of interior of body cavities. Sometimes called a fiberscope.

Fissure of Rolando–A groove that separates the frontal from the parietal lobes of the cerebral hemispheres.

Fissure of Sylvius–A groove that separates the temporal lobes from the upper lobes of the cerebral hemispheres.

Fluoroscope–An instrument for direct visual observation of deep body structures by means of x-ray.

Forced Choice Test–A perceptual test in which the number of permitted responses is limited.

Forced Vibration–Vibration caused by an external force.

Fourier Analysis–The analysis of a complex wave into its sine wave components.

Formant–A peak of resonance in the vocal tract; formants are displayed in a wideband spectrogram as broad bands of energy.

Free Vibration–Vibration caused by the single application of an external force.

Frequency–The number of complete cycles of vibration occurring in a second.

Fricative–[L. "fricare"–to rub.] A sound produced by forcing the airstream through a narrow articulatory constriction.

Frontal Lobe–That part of either hemisphere of the cerebrum that is above the Sylvian fissure and in front of the Rolandic fissure.

Fundamental Frequency–The lowest frequency component of a complex periodic wave. The repetition rate of a complex periodic wave.

Gamma (γ) *Motoneurons*–Small motoneurons that transmit impulses to the intrafusal fibers of the muscle spindle.

Genioglossus Muscle–An extrinsic tongue muscle that acts to bring the tongue body upward and forward.

Glide–Sound whose production requires the tongue to move quickly from one relatively open position to another in the vocal tract; for example, /w/ and /j/ in English.

Glottal Attack–A mode of initiation of voicing in which the vocal folds are tightly adducted at onset.

Glottis–The space between the true vocal folds.

Glottograph–An instrument used to measure the relative amount of light transmitted through the glottis. (See Transillumination).

Gray Matter–Unmyelinated areas in the nervous system; such areas consist largely of cell bodies that contrast in color with the whitish nerve fibers.

Hard palate–The bony partition between the mouth and the nose; the roof of the mouth.

Harmonic–An oscillation whose frequency is an integral multiple of the fundamental frequency.

Harmonic Series–The fundamental frequency and harmonics of a complex periodic wave.

Hominids–Members of the family of modern and fossil man; does not include the apes.

Hyoglossus Muscle–An extrinsic tongue muscle that can lower the tongue.

Hyoid Bone–[Gk. "hyoeides"–U-shaped.] A horseshoe-shaped bone situated at the base of the tongue and above the thyroid cartilage.

Hypernasality–A voice quality characterized by excessive nasal resonance.

Hyponasality–Voice quality characterized by inadequate nasal resonance.

Identification Test–Perceptual test in which stimuli are presented separately to be labeled.

Impedance–Opposition to motion as a product of the density of the medium and the velocity of sound in it; the complex sum of reactances and resistances.

In phase–Two signals with pressure waves that crest and trough at the same time.

Incisors–The front teeth of the upper and lower jaw; eight teeth in normal dentition.

Incus–[L. "incus"–anvil.] The middle of the three ear ossicles; also called the anvil.

Independent Variable–The variable controlled by the experimenter in an experiment.

Inertia–The property of matter as a consequence of its mass by which it retains its state of rest or its velocity along a straight line so long as it is not acted upon by an external force.

Inferior Constrictor Muscle–One of the three pharyngeal constrictor muscles. Its fibers act as a valve separating the laryngopharynx from the esophagus.

Inferior Longitudinal Muscles–Intrinsic tongue muscles that act to depress the tongue tip.

Intensity–Magnitude of sound expressed in power or pressure.

Intensity level–The power of the signal; decibels derived from a power ratio; the usual reference is 10^{16} watts/cm^2.

Interarytenoid–Between the arytenoid cartilages; the transverse and oblique arytenoid muscles together compose the interarytenoid muscles. They function to adduct the vocal folds.

Interchondral–Between cartilages; used to refer to the parts of the intercostal muscles running between the cartilaginous portions of the ribs.

Intercostal Muscles–Muscles connecting the ribs; they act in respiration.

Interference Pattern–Display of a complex wave.

Internal Auditory Meatus–The canal from the base of the cochlea that opens into the cranial cavity; a conduit for the VIIIth cranial nerve, auditory veins and arteries, and the facial (VII cranial) nerve.

Internal Feedback–A system's information about its planned performance within the control center; the loops among the cerebrum, basal ganglia, and cerebellum during speech. (See Response Feedback and External Feedback.)

Internal Intercostal Muscles–Muscles connecting the ribs. Most act to lower the ribs during expiration.

Internal Obliques–Muscles of the abdomen coursing downward and posteriorly along the lateral walls.

Internal Pterygoid Muscle–See Medial Pterygoid Muscle.

Intonation–Changes in fundamental frequency during the course of an utterance.

Intraoral Pressure–Air pressure within the oral cavity.

Inverse Square Law–Intensity of a sound varies indirectly as the square of the distance from the source.

Isochrony–Equal intervals between stressed syllables (See Stress-timed).

Juncture–The affiliation of sounds within and between words. Changing the location of a juncture can change meaning; "a+name" and "an+aim" differ in juncture placement.

Kinesthesis–[Gk. "kinein"–move + "aisthesis"–feeling.] Perception of one's own movement based upon information from proprioceptors.

Lag Effect–More accurate identification of the stimulus presented later in a dichotic listening test.

Laminographic Technique–A radiographic method in which x-rays from several sources are focused in a plane yielding better definition of soft tissues; same as tomographic technique.

Language–[L. "lingua"–tongue.] The words, and rules for combining them, common to a particular group of people.

Laryngeal Ventricle–The space between the true and false vocal folds; also called the Ventricle of Morgagni.

Laryngograph–An instrument used to measure impedance across the vocal folds. (Term used by Fourcin for the Electroglottograph, q.v.)

Laryngoscope–A mirror and source of illumination for viewing the larynx.

Larynx–The cartilaginous structure, including the associated muscles and membranes, which houses the vocal folds. Commonly referred to as the "voice box" or "Adam's apple."

Lateral–A sound in which the phonated breath stream is emitted around the sides of the tongue; /l/ is an English lateral.

Lateral Cricoarytenoid Muscles–Muscles that act to compress the medial portion of the glottis by rotating the arytenoid cartilages.

Lateral Inhibition–The isolation of a stimulus on the basilar membrane because of the inhibition of response in the nerve cells surrounding the point of maximal stimulation.

Lateral Pterygoid Muscle–A paired jaw muscle; the superior portion acts to elevate the jaw, and the inferior portion acts to lower the jaw.

Latissimus Dorsi Muscle–Large broad muscle located on the back of the body on either side of the spine. It functions in forced respiration.

Lax–(Vowels.) Phonetic property of vowels that are produced with lower relative tongue height than tense vowels and with shorter durations.

Levator Palatini Muscle–Muscle running to and comprising most of the soft palate; its contraction elevates and backs the soft palate toward the pharyngeal wall.

Levatores Costarum Muscles–Twelve small triangular-shaped pairs of muscles which act in inspiration to raise the ribs.

Linear Scale–A scale in which each unit is equal to the next, permitting units to be summed by addition.

Linguistic Competence–What one knows unconsciously about one's own language; the ability to understand and produce the language.

Linguistic Performance–How the knowledge of a language is used in expressive behavior such as speech or writing.

Liquids–In English, /l/ and /r/, two of the semivowels produced with relatively prominent sonority and with some degree of lateral emission of air.

Logarithmic Scale–[Gk. "logos"–proportion + "arithmos"–number.] A scale based on multiples of a given number (base).

Lombard Effect–The increased vocal intensity of a speaker who cannot hear himself.

Longitudinal Wave–[L. "longitudo"–length.] A wave in which particle motion is in the same (or opposite) direction as wave movement.

Loudness–The subjective, psychological sensation of sound intensity.

Malleus–[L. "malleus"–hammer.] The outermost and largest of the three middle ear ossicles; also called the hammer. (See Manubrium.)

Mandible: [L. "madere"–chew.]–The lower jaw bone.

Manner–(Of articulation.) Classification of consonant sounds based on the method used to obstruct the airstream. For example, fricatives, which are produced by forcing the airstream through a narrow constriction formed by the articulators; stops, which are produced by a complete blockage of the airstream by the articulators.

Manometer–An instrument for measuring the pressure of liquids or gases.

Maxillary Bone–One of a pair of bones that form the upper jaw; the two together are often considered as one bone.

Maximum Expiratory Pressure–Combined active and passive forces available for expiration at a given lung volume.

Maximum Inspiratory Pressure–Combined active and passive forces for inspiration at a given lung volume.

Medial Pterygoid Muscle–A muscle on the inner side of the mandible that acts in speech to close the jaw. (Also called the internal pterygoid.)

Medulla Oblongata–The portion of the brain that is continuous with the spinal cord below and the pons above; it lies ventral to the cerebellum.

Mel–Unit of pitch; value of $\frac{1}{1000}$ of the pitch of a 1000-Hz tone.

Mental Retardation–Condition in which inadequate brain development slows or prevents learning and adaptation.

Metathesis–A reversal in the order of two sounds or letters in a word: [æsk] ⟶ [æks].

Middle Constrictor Muscle–The middle of three pharyngeal constrictor muscles that act to narrow the pharynx.

Middle Ear–Small cavity containing three ossicles: the malleus, incus, and stapes; functions as an impedance matching transformer between air and cochlear fluid.

Monologue–[Gk. "monos"–single + "logos"–speech.] Speech by a lone person. (See Collective Monologue.)

Monophthong–A vowel of unchanging quality.

Morpheme–The smallest meaningful linguistic segment. The word "books" contains two morphemes, "book" and "-s" which means "more than one."

Morphological–(Adj.) (Noun: morphology.) [Gk. "morphe"–form + "ology"–study.] Study of the form of words as affected by inflection or derivation.

Motor–Pertaining to movement. For example, a motor nerve or motor center of the brain that controls movement.

Motor Theory–A theory put forth by A. M. Liberman that speech perception makes reference to speech production.

Motor Unit–An efferent nerve fiber and the muscle fibers that it innervates.

Muscle Spindles–Specialized muscle fibers with sensory innervation that signal muscle length and changes in length.

Myelin–White fatty substance that sheaths many cranial and spinal nerves.

Mylohyoid Muscle–A thin sheet-like muscle that forms the floor of the mouth; acts to raise the tongue.

Myoelastic Aerodynamic Theory of Phonation–Theory that holds that vocal fold vibration is primarily caused by air pressure acting on the elastic mass of the folds.

Nasal Sounds–Those that are produced with an open velopharyngeal port (and, thus, nasal emission of the airstream).

Natural Resonant Frequency–That frequency at which a system oscillates with greatest amplitude when driven by an external vibrating source.

Negative Feedback–See Feedback.

Nerve–A bundle of neuron fibers that convey impulses from one part of the body to another.

Neuron–One of the cells of which the brain, spinal cord, and nerves are composed.

Oblique Arytenoid Muscle–Muscle that closes the glottis by approximating the arytenoid cartilages. Together with the transverse arytenoids, composes the interarytenoids.

Occipital Lobe–The most posterior lobe of the brain, lying behind the temporal and parietal lobes.

Oddball or Oddity Test–Procedure for testing discrimination by requiring the listener to indicate which of three presented stimuli differs from the other two.

Ontogeny–[Gk. "ontos"–being + "geneia"–origin.] The entire developmental history of an individual organism.

Open Loop System–A feedforward system that operates without benefit of feedback about performance.

Open Response Set–Used in perceptual testing. Subjects have a free choice of response to any stimulus with which they are presented.

Operant Conditioning–A process by which the frequency of response is increased depending on when, how, and how much it is reinforced.

Oral Cavity–[L. "oris"–mouth; L. "cavus" - hollow.] The space inside the mouth.

Oral Sounds–Sounds that are articulated and resonated in the mouth.

Oral Stereognosis–The tactile discrimination or recognition of the shapes of objects placed in the mouth.

Orbicularis Oris Muscle–The sphincter muscle of the mouth that contracts to purse, protrude, or close the lips.

Ordinate–The y coordinate of a point; its distance from the x axis measured parallel to the y axis (vertical axis).

Organ of Corti–The sensory organ of hearing that rests on the basilar membrane and contains sensory hair cells that are stimulated by movements within the cochlear duct.

Oscilloscope–An instrument that displays the magnitude of an electrical signal as a function of time; a cathode ray tube used to display waveforms.

Osseous–[L. "os"–bone.] Bony, or containing bones.

Ossicles–Small bones; especially the small bones of the middle ear: the malleus, incus, and stapes.

Ossicular Chain–Composite of the three middle ear bones: the malleus, incus, and stapes.

Oval Window–Membrane between the middle and inner ear connecting and passing vibrations from the stapes to the cochlear fluids; also called the vestibular window and fenestra vestibuli.

PNS–See Peripheral Nervous System.

Palatoglossus Muscle–Extrinsic tongue muscle that raises the back of the tongue and can lower the soft palate; also called the glossopalatine muscle; the palatoglossus muscles form most of the anterior faucial pillars.

Palatography–A method of measuring points of contact between the tongue and palate.

Parallel Processing–The coarticulation and assimilation of neighboring phones in speech production and the simultaneous decoding of neighboring phones in speech perception.

Parietal Lobe–A lobe in the upper center of the cerebrum behind the Fissure of Rolando and above the Fissure of Sylvius.

Parietal Pleura–See Costal Pleura.

Pectoralis Major Muscle–The most superficial muscle of the chest wall. It functions in forced inspiration by elevating the ribs.

Pectoralis Minor Muscle–A thin, flat, triangular muscle that lies under the cover of the pectoralis major. With the scapula fixed, it may elevate the ribs for inspiration.

Perilymph–The fluid in the space between the membranous and osseous labyrinths of the ear.

Period–The time taken for one cycle of vibration of a wave.

Periodic–Recurring at equal intervals of time.

Peripheral Nervous System–(PNS) Consists of the ganglia and nerves outside the brain and spinal cord.

Pharyngeal Plexus–[L. "plexus"–a tangle.] A network of nerves through which the glossopharyngeal nerve supplies the mucous membranes of the pharynx with sensory branches and the accessory nerve supplies the levator palatini muscle with motor fibers.

Pharynx–[Gk. "pharynx"–throat.] The throat cavity made up of the nasopharynx, oropharynx, and laryngopharynx.

Phon–A unit of equal loudness.

Phonation–Production of sound in the larynx caused by the periodic vibrations of the vocal folds.

Phone–A particular speech sound; an allophone, or variant of a phoneme; the aspirated [t^h] and [t] are allophones of the phoneme /t/.

Phoneme–[Gk. "phone"–sound.] A family of sounds that functions in a language to signal a difference in meaning.

Phonetic–Relating to the production and perception of speech sounds.

Phonology–Study of the sound system of a language.

Photoelectric–Electricity or electrical changes produced by light.

Phrenic Nerve–Motor nerve to the diaphragm composed of several cervical nerves.

Phylogeny–[Gk. "phylon"–race + "geneia"–origin.] The entire developmental history of a race or group of organisms.

Pinna–See Auricle.

Pitch–The subjective, psychological sensation of sound frequency; a low frequency sound produces a perception of low pitch.

Place of Articulation–Classification of speech sounds based on the location of articulatory contact or constriction and the articulators used. For example, the bilabial /p/ and lingua-alveolar /t/ differ in place of articulation.

Place Theory–Different frequencies activate the sensory nerve fibers at different places on the basilar membrane; higher frequencies closer to the base of the cochlea, lower frequencies toward the apical end.

Plethysmograph–Recorder of body volumes from which respiratory movements can be inferred.

Plosive–[L. "plaudere"–to clap.] A manner of consonant articulation made by sudden release of air impounded behind an occlusion in the vocal tract. Used synonymously with "stop."

Pneumograph–An instrument that records respiratory movements as changes in chest and abdomen circumference.

Pneumotachograph–Instrument for measuring respiration.

Poles–An engineering term for resonances.

Pons–[L. "pons"–bridge.] A large transverse band of nerve fibers in the hindbrain that forms the cerebellar stem and encircles the medulla oblongata.

Positive Feedback–See Feedback.

Posterior Cricoarytenoid Muscles–(PCA) Muscles that abduct the vocal folds by rotating and tilting the arytenoids, opening the glottis.

Precategorical Acoustic Storage–(PAS) Short-term auditory memory presumed to hold information during phonetic analysis.

Pressure–Force per unit area.

Pressure Transducer–A device that transforms relative pressure into an electrical signal.

Primary Stress–The heaviest stress or greatest emphasis placed on a syllable in a word. The second syllable of the word "because" bears primary stress.

Proprioception–The sense of one's own body position and movement.

Prosody–(Adj., prosodic) [Gk. "pros"–in addition to + "oide"–song.] The description of the rhythm and tonal patterns of speech.

Pulmonary Pleura–(Also called visceral pleura.) The membrane covering the lungs.

Pure Tone–A sound with a single sine wave component.

Pyramidal Tract–(Corticospinal.) A major relatively direct pathway for transmitting motor signals from the motor cortex.

Quantal Theory–A theory put forth by K. N. Stevens that there are quantal discontinuities in the acoustic output of the vocal tract.

REA–See Right Ear Advantage.

Rarefaction–Area in a wave between compressions where the conducting medium is reduced in pressure.

Rationalist–One who bases conclusions primarily on reason or intellect rather than on experience; often, one who believes that the structure of knowledge is caused by the properties of the mind.

Recency Effect–Subjects tend to remember the last item (most recent) on a list more readily than others on the same list.

Rectify–To reverse the direction of alternating impulses; transform an alternating current into a direct current.

Rectus Abdominis Muscle–Major muscle of the abdomen running vertically along the midline of the anterior wall.

Recurrent Nerve–The branch of the vagus (Xth cranial) nerve that innervates all intrinsic muscles of the larynx except the cricothyroid muscle; also called inferior laryngeal nerve.

Relaxation Volume–Amount of air in the lungs at the end of an exhalation during normal breathing; volume at which pressure inside the lungs is equal to atmospheric pressure, at about 40% vital capacity.

Resonance–Vibratory response to an applied force.

Resonator–Something that is set into vibration by the action of another vibration.

Response Feedback–Direct feedback from muscles. Part of the sense of movement and position called proprioception.

Restricted Code–Bernstein's term for the speech of those who assume that the listener knows the socio-semantic context of the message. (See Elaborated Code.)

Retroflex–Raising and retraction of the tongue tip; typical of the production of some allophones of /r/ in American English.

Reverberate–To be reflected many times, as sound waves from the walls of a confined space.

Ribs–Twelve pairs of bones extending ventrally from the 12 thoracic vertebrae and enclosing the thorax.

Right Ear Advantage–(REA) In dichotic listening tests, subjects usually more correctly identify stimuli delivered to the right ear than to the left.

Rise time–The time an acoustic signal takes to attain maximum amplitude.

Risorius Muscle–A paired muscle radiating from the corners of the mouth; used in spreading the lips.

Rugae–The irregular ridges behind the upper incisors.

Scalenus Medius Muscle–One of three pairs of muscles on each side of the neck which, acting from above, may elevate the first rib for inspiration.

Scapula–Flat triangular bone on the back of the shoulder. Also called the shoulder blade.

Secondary Stress–The degree of stress intermediate to primary and weak stress. In the word "underneath," the first syllable bears secondary stress, the second syllable bears weak stress, and the last syllable bears primary stress.

Section–A special form of spectrogram that shows the amplitude spectrum of a brief time segment of the signal.

Semantics–[Gk. "sema"–sign.] The study of meanings and the development of meanings of words.

Semicircular Canals–See Vestibular System.

Sensory–(Nerve.) A peripheral nerve conducting impulses from a sensory organ toward the central nervous system; also called afferent nerve.

Serratus Posterior Superior Muscle–Muscle extending obliquely downward and laterally from the upper portion of the thoracic region of the vertebral column to the superior borders of the upper ribs. The muscles serve to elevate the ribs during inspiration.

Servomechanism–An automatic device that corrects its own performance.

Sibilants–[L. "sibilare"–to hiss.] The high frequency fricative speech sounds of /s/ or /ʃ/ and their voiced cognates.

Simple Harmonic Motion–Periodic vibratory movement where the amount of displacement from the position of equilibrium is proportional to the force that tends to restore it to equilibrium.

Sine Wave–A periodic oscillation having the same geometric representation as a sine function.

Sodium Amytal Test–See Wada Test.

Software–Term for computer programs.

Sone–A unit of loudness equal to that of a tone of 1 kHz at 40 dB above absolute threshold.

Sound–The sensation produced by stimulation of the organs of hearing by vibrations transmitted through the air or another medium.

Sound Pressure Level–(SPL) With reference to sound, the pressure of a signal; decibels derived from a pressure ratio; the usual reference is 0.0002 dynes/cm^2.

Sound Spectrogram–A display of the components (harmonics or formants) of a sound as they vary in frequency and intensity over time. Frequency is shown on the ordinate, time on the abscissa, and intensity as relative darkness of the image.

Sound Spectrograph–An instrument that produces a sound spectrogram (q.v.).

Sound Wave–A longitudinal wave in an elastic medium; a wave producing an audible sensation.

Source Function–The origin of acoustic energy for speech; for vowels at the vocal folds, for voiceless consonants in the vocal tract, and for voiced consonants both at the folds and in the tract.

Spasticity–Involuntary contraction of a muscle or group of muscles resulting in a state of rigidity.

Spectrum–See Amplitude Spectrum.

Speech Perception–Understanding speech.

Spinal Nerves–The 31 paired nerves arising from the spinal cord that innervate body structures. (See Appendix 2 for listing.)

Spirometer–An instrument for measuring volumes of air taken in and expelled from the lungs.

Spoonerism–A transposition of the initial sounds of two (or more) words in a phrase; named for William A. Spooner.

Stapedius Muscle–Muscle of the middle ear that alters movement of the stapes in the oval window.

Stapes–[L. "stapes"–stirrup.] The innermost of the three ear ossicles; also called the stirrup.

Sternocleidomastoid Muscle–A paired muscle running diagonally across the neck that assists in forced inspiration by elevating the sternum.

Sternohyoid Muscle–An extrinsic laryngeal

muscle that depresses the hyoid bone and may act to lower the larynx; one of the strap muscles.

Sternothyroid Muscle–A extrinsic laryngeal muscle that can act to lower the larynx; one of the strap muscles.

Sternum–The breastbone.

Stimulus Onset Asynchrony–(SOA) A time difference between the onsets of two dichotically presented stimuli.

Stop–A manner of consonant articulation characterized by a complete blockage of the air stream for a brief period of time. Synonymous with "plosive" in those cases where the impounded air stream is suddenly released by the relaxation of the constriction causing the blockage of the airstream.

Storage Oscilloscope–A cathode ray tube instrument that can maintain a display for a period of time.

Strain Gauge–A transducer that converts movement patterns into patterns of electrical voltage.

Stress-timed–Languages that are stress-timed are said to be produced with equal intervals between stressed syllables. Used synonymously with isochrony.

Stroboscope–A device that emits brief flashes of light at a controlled frequency.

Styloglossus Muscle–One of the extrinsic tongue muscles; lifts the tongue upward and backward.

Subclavius Muscle–A relatively small flattened muscle that lies beneath the clavicle and assists in inspiration by elevating the first rib.

Subglottal Air Pressure–Air pressure beneath the vocal folds.

Superior Constrictor Muscle–Uppermost of three pharyngeal constrictor muscles that acts to narrow the pharynx in swallowing. May aid in velopharyngeal closure during speech.

Superior Longitudinal Muscle–Intrinsic tongue muscle that acts to turn the tip of the tongue upward.

Suprasegmental–Term for functions overlaid upon the segments of speech, including stress, juncture, and intonation.

Syllabic Consonant–A consonant that functions as a syllabic nucleus.

Syllabic Nuclei–(Sing., syllabic nucleus.) The relatively steady-state vocalic portions of syllables.

Syllable–A unit of speech consisting of a single vowel or a vowel and one or more consonants.

Synapse–The region of juncture between one nerve cell and another.

Syntagma–The uninterrupted speech phrase; the term figures in the theory of speech organization of Kozhevnikov and Chistovich.

Syntax–(Adj., syntactic) [Gk. "syn"–together + "tassein"–arrange.] Arrangement of the words of a sentence in their proper forms and relations.

Tabula Rasa–Blank slate; referring to the theory that the mind is initially a blank slate upon which experiences imprint themselves.

Taction–The sense of touch.

Tectorial Membrane–Gelatinous membrane overlying the Organ of Corti.

Template–A pattern.

Temporal Lobe–The lower, lateral portion of the cerebral hemisphere, lying below the Fissure of Sylvius.

Tense–(Vowels.) Property of vowels that are produced with more extreme relative tongue position than lax vowels and with longer durations.

Tensor Palatini Muscles–Muscles that open the eustachian tube and that may act to tense the soft palate.

Tensor Tympani–Muscle that tenses the eardrum.

Thalamus–[Gr. "thalmos"–inner chamber.] A mass of gray matter situated at the base of the cerebrum; thought to be important to speech.

Thoracic Nerves–Twelve pairs of spinal nerves that arise from the segments of the spinal cord in the chest region. (See Appendix 2.)

Thorax–The part of the body between the neck and the abdomen separated from the abdomen by the diaphragm; the chest.

Thyroarytenoid Muscle–An intrinsic laryngeal muscle that can shorten and tense the vocal folds; consisting of external and internal parts (see vocalis); forms part of the vocal folds.

Thyroid Cartilage–[Gr. "thyreos"–shield.] The large shield-shaped cartilage of the larynx.

Thyrohyoid Muscle–A muscle running between the thyroid cartilage and the hyoid bone; it may act to lower the hyoid or to change the position of the larynx; one of the strap muscles.

Tidal Volume–The amount of air normally inspired and expired in a respiratory cycle.

Tomographic Methods–See Laminographic.

Torque–A rotatory force; used to refer to the untwisting of the cartilaginous portions of the ribs.

Trachea–The windpipe, a tube composed of horseshoe-shaped cartilages leading to the lungs.

Tragus–Small cartilaginous flap that shields the opening to the external auditory meatus.

Transfer Function–The contribution of vocal tract resonance of the source function to the resulting speech sound. (See Source Function.)

Transient–Not lasting; an acoustic event of brief duration.

Transillumination–A method of indirectly measuring glottal opening by measuring the amount of light transmitted through the glottis. (See Glottograph.)

Transition–A change in formant frequency.

Transverse Arytenoid Muscle–See Interarytenoid.

Transverse Muscles of the Tongue–Intrinsic tongue muscles that act to narrow the tongue body.

Transverse Waves–A type of wave where particle motion is perpendicular to the direction of wave movement.

Transversus Abdominis Muscles–Muscles of the abdomen coursing horizontally across the walls and potentially active in respiration for speech.

Traveling Wave Theory–Theory that the cochlea analyzes incoming auditory signals into component "traveling waves."

Two-point Discrimination–The ability to perceive two discrete points in close proximity as such and not as a single point.

Tympanic Membrane–The eardrum, a fibrous membrane at the end of the external auditory meatus; its response is transmitted to the middle ear ossicles.

Ultrasound–Ultrasonic waves (those above audible frequencies); a method of measuring movement by bombarding an articulator with ultrasonic waves and displaying their reflections.

Unconditioned Stimulus–(UCS) In classical conditioning a stimulus that naturally elicits a response; in Pavlov's experiment, the meat powder that elicits salivation.

Uvula–[L. "uvula"–little grape.] Small fleshy mass that hangs from the back of the soft palate.

Uvular Muscle–The muscle within the uvula that can be active in velar raising.

Velocity–Change of position over time; speed in a certain direction.

Velopharyngeal Closure–The closing off of the nasal passages from the oral cavity by raising the velum against the pharynx.

Velopharyngeal Port–The passageway connecting oral and nasal cavities.

Velum–The soft palate.

Ventricular Folds–The "false vocal folds"; the folds above the true vocal folds.

Verbal Transformation–Changes in the auditory perception of a repeated utterance.

Vertebrae–(Sing., vertebra.) The segments of the bony spinal column.

Vertical Muscles–Intrinsic tongue muscle fibers that act to flatten the tongue.

Vestibular System–Three canals in the inner ear containing the sense organs for equilibrium.

Vestibule–The cavity at the entrance to the cochlea that houses the utricle and saccule, sense organs responsive to linear acceleration.

Visceral Pleura–See Pulmonary Pleura.

Vital Capacity–The total volume of air that can be expelled from the lungs after maximum inspiration.

Vocal Fry–(Creaky voice.) A vocal mode in which the vocal folds vibrate at such low frequency that the individual vibrations can be heard.

Vocal Tract–All the cavities superior to the larynx used as a variable resonator; includes the buccal, oral, nasal, and pharyngeal cavities.

Vocalis Muscle–The internal portion of the thyroarytenoid muscle; the vibrating part of the vocal folds.

Voiced/Voiceless–The linguistic classification of a speech sound related to the presence or absence of phonation and/or to other articulatory-acoustic features.

Voice Onset Time–(VOT) The interval of time between the release of a stop consonant and the onset of voicing of the following vowel. This duration is conventionally given positive values if release precedes voice onset and negative values if release follows voice onset.

Volley Theory–Frequency information conveyed directly by the firing of neurons. At frequencies higher than the firing capacity of individual neurons, groups of neurons cooperate.

Voltmeter–An instrument for measuring electromotive force in volts.

WADA Test–(Sodium Amytal Test.) A procedure to establish which side of the cerebrum is dominant for language.

Watt–A unit of electric power equivalent to 1 joule per second.

Waveform–A graphic representation of a vibratory event showing amplitude *versus* time.

Wavelength–(λ) The distance in space occupied by one cycle.

White Matter–Myelinated areas in the central nervous system.

Whorfian Hypothesis–The theory that language determines thought concepts to some extent.

Zeros–An engineering term for antiresonances.

Index

Page numbers in italics denote figures; those followed by "t" denote tables.